The Cambridge History of the English Language is the first multi-volume work to provide a full account of the history of English. Its authoritative coverage extends from areas of central linguistic interest and concern to more specialised topics such as personal and place names. The volumes dealing with earlier periods are chronologically based, whilst those dealing with more recent periods are geographically based, thus reflecting the spread of English over the last 300 years.

Volume I deals with the history of English up to the Norman Conquest, and contains chapters on Indo-European and Germanic, phonology and morphology, syntax, semantics and vocabulary, dialectology, onomastics and literary language. Each chapter, as well as giving a chronologically-oriented presentation of the data, surveys scholarship in the area and takes full account of the impact of developing and current linguistic theory on the interpretation of the data. The chapters have been written with both specialists and non-specialists in mind; they will be essential reading for all those interested in the history of English.

THE CAMBRIDGE HISTORY
OF THE ENGLISH LANGUAGE

GENERAL EDITOR Richard M. Hogg

VOLUME I The Beginnings to 1066

Facsimile page from the Exeter Book of Anglo-Saxon poetry
(Exeter D. & C. MS 3501, s. x): *The Wanderer*, 76v, lines 1–33.
Reproduced by kind permission of the Dean and Chapter
of Exeter Cathedral.

THE CAMBRIDGE HISTORY OF THE ENGLISH LANGUAGE

VOLUME I *The Beginnings to 1066*

EDITED BY

RICHARD M. HOGG

Smith Professor of English Language and
Medieval Literature, University of Manchester

CAMBRIDGE
UNIVERSITY PRESS

Published by the Press Syndicate of the University of Cambridge
The Pitt Building, Trumpington Street, Cambridge CB2 1RP
40 West 20th Street, New York, NY 1011-4211, USA
10 Stamford Road, Oakleigh, Victoria 3166, Australia

© Cambridge University Press 1992

First published 1992

Printed in Great Britain at the University Press, Cambridge

A catalogue record for this book is available from the British Library

Library of Congress cataloguing in publication data

The Cambridge history of the English language/edited by Richard M.
Hogg.
   p. cm.
Includes bibliographical references and index.
Contents: v. 1. The beginnings to 1066
ISBN 0-521-26474-X (v. 1)
1. English language–History. I. Hogg, Richard M.
PE1072.C36   1992   91-13881
420′.9-dc20   CIP

ISBN 0 521 26474 X hardback

UP

CONTENTS

Contents

Contents

ILLUSTRATIONS

Facsimile page from the Exeter Book of Anglo-Saxon poetry (Exeter D. & C. MS 3501, s. x): *The Wanderer*, fo. 76v, lines 1–33. Reproduced by kind permission of the Dean and Chapter of Exeter Cathedral *frontispiece*

Map of Anglo-Saxon England. Drawn by Dr David Hill of the Department of Extra-Mural Studies at Manchester University *page* xxi

CONTRIBUTORS

ALFRED BAMMESBERGER *Professor of English Linguistics, Katholische Universität Eichstätt*

CECILY CLARK *Cambridge*

MALCOLM GODDEN *Rawlinson and Bosworth Professor of Anglo-Saxon, University of Oxford*

RICHARD M. HOGG *Smith Professor of English Language and Medieval Literature, University of Manchester*

DIETER KASTOVSKY *Professor of English Linguistics, Institut für Anglistik und Amerikanistik, Universität Wien*

THOMAS E. TOON *Professor of Linguistics, Program in Linguistics, University of Michigan, Ann Arbor*

ELIZABETH CLOSS TRAUGOTT *Professor of Linguistics, Department of Linguistics, Stanford University*

GENERAL EDITOR'S PREFACE

Although it is a topic of continuing debate, there can be little doubt that English is the most widely-spoken language in the world, with significant numbers of native speakers in almost every major region – only South America falling largely outside the net. In such a situation an understanding of the nature of English can be claimed unambiguously to be of world-wide importance.

Growing consciousness of such a role for English is one of the motivations behind this History. There are other motivations too. Specialist students have many major and detailed works of scholarship to which they can refer, for example Bruce Mitchell's *Old English Syntax*, or, from an earlier age, Karl Luick's *Historische Grammatik der englischen Sprache*. Similarly, those who come new to the subject have both one-volume histories such as Barbara Strang's *History of English* and introductory textbooks to a single period, for example Bruce Mitchell and Fred Robinson's *A Guide to Old English*. But what is lacking is the intermediate work which can provide a solid discussion of the full range of the history of English both to the anglicist who does not specialise in the particular area to hand and to the general linguist who has no specialised knowledge of the history of English. This work attempts to remedy that lack. We hope that it will be of use to others too, whether they are interested in the history of English for its own sake, or for some specific purpose such as local history or the effects of colonisation.

Under the influence of the Swiss linguist, Ferdinand de Saussure, there has been, during this century, a persistent tendency to view the study of language as having two discrete parts: (i) synchronic, where a language is studied from the point of view of one moment in time; (ii) diachronic, where a language is studied from a historical perspective. It might therefore be supposed that this present work is purely diachronic.

But this is not so. One crucial principle which guides The Cambridge History of the English Language is that synchrony and diachrony are intertwined, and that a satisfactory understanding of English (or any other language) cannot be achieved on the basis of one of these alone.

Consider, for example, the (synchronic) fact that English, when compared with other languages, has some rather infrequent or unusual characteristics. Thus, in the area of vocabulary, English has an exceptionally high number of words borrowed from other languages (French, the Scandinavian languages, American Indian languages, Italian, the languages of northern India and so on); in syntax a common construction is the use of *do* in forming questions (e.g. *Do you like cheese?*), a type of construction not often found in other languages; in morphology English has relatively few inflexions, at least compared with the majority of other European languages; in phonology the number of diphthongs as against the number of vowels in English English is notably high. In other words, synchronically, English can be seen to be in some respects rather unusual. But in order to understand such facts we need to look at the history of the language; it is often only there that an explanation can be found. And that is what this work attempts to do.

This raises another issue. A quasi-Darwinian approach to English might attempt to account for its widespread use by claiming that somehow English is more suited, better adapted, to use as an international language than others. But that is nonsense. English is no more fit than, say, Spanish or Chinese. The reasons for the spread of English are political, cultural and economic rather than linguistic. So too are the reasons for such linguistic elements within English as the high number of borrowed words. This History, therefore, is based as much upon political, cultural and economic factors as linguistic ones, and it will be noted that the major historical divisions between volumes are based upon the former type of events (the Norman Conquest, the spread of printing, the declaration of independence by the U.S.A., rather than the latter type.

As a rough generalisation, one can say that up to about the seventeenth century the development of English tended to be centrifugal, whereas since then the development has tended to be centripetal. The settlement by the Anglo-Saxons resulted in a spread of dialect variation over the country, but by the tenth century a variety of forces were combining to promote the emergence of a standard form of the language. Such an evolution was disrupted by the Norman

Conquest, but with the development of printing together with other more centralising tendencies, the emergence of a standard form became once more, from the fifteenth century on, a major characteristic of the language. But processes of emigration and colonisation then gave rise to new regional varieties overseas, many of which have now achieved a high degree of linguistic independence, and some of which, especially American English, may even have a dominating influence on British English. The structure of this work is designed to reflect these different types of development. Whilst the first four volumes offer a reasonably straightforward chronological account, the later volumes are geographically based. This arrangement, we hope, allows scope for the proper treatment of diverse types of evolution and development. Even within the chronologically oriented volumes there are variations of structure, which are designed to reflect the changing relative importance of various linguistic features. Although all the chronological volumes have substantial chapters devoted to the central topics of semantics and vocabulary, syntax, and phonology and morphology, for other topics the space allotted in a particular volume is one which is appropriate to the importance of that topic during the relevant period, rather than some pre-defined calculation of relative importance. And within the geographically based volumes all these topics are potentially included within each geographical section, even if sometimes in a less formal way. Such a flexible and changing structure seems essential for any full treatment of the history of English.

One question that came up as this project began was the extent to which it might be possible or desirable to work within a single theoretical linguistic framework. It could well be argued that only a consensus within the linguistic community about preferred linguistic theories would enable a work such as this to be written. Certainly, it was immediately obvious when work for this History began, that it would be impossible to lay down a 'party line' on linguistic theory, and indeed, that such an approach would be undesirably restrictive. The solution reached was, I believe, more fruitful. Contributors have been chosen purely on the grounds of expertise and knowledge, and have been encouraged to write their contributions in the way they see most fitting, whilst at the same time taking full account of developments in linguistic theory. This has, of course, led to problems, notably with contrasting views of the same topic (and also because of the need to distinguish the ephemeral flight of theoretical fancy from genuine new insights into linguistic theory), but even in a work which is concerned to provide a unified approach (so that, for example, in most cases every contributor to a volume has read all the other contributions to that volume), such contrasts, and even contradictions, are stimulating and fruitful. Whilst this work aims to be authoritative, it is not prescriptive, and the final goal must be to stimulate interest in a subject in which much work remains to be done, both theoretically and empirically.

The task of editing this History has been, and still remains, a long and complex one. As General Editor I owe a great debt to many friends and colleagues who have devoted much time and thought to how best this work might be approached and completed. Firstly, I should thank my fellow-editors: John Algeo, Norman Blake, Bob Burchfield, Roger Lass and Suzanne Romaine. They have been concerned as much with the History as a whole as with their individual volumes. Secondly, there are those fellow linguists, some contributors, some not, who have so generously given of their time and made many valuable suggestions: John Anderson, Cecily Clark, Frans van Coetsem, Fran Colman, David Denison, Ed Finegan, Olga Fischer, Jacek Fisiak, Malcolm Godden, Angus McIntosh, Lesley Milroy, Donka Minkova, Matti Rissanen, Michael Samuels, Bob Stockwell, Tom Toon, Elizabeth Traugott, Peter Trudgill, Nigel Vincent, Anthony Warner, Simone Wyss. One occasion stands out especially: the organisers of the Fourth International Conference on English Historical Linguistics, held at Amsterdam in 1985, kindly allowed us to hold a seminar on the project as it was just beginning. For their generosity, which allowed us to hear a great many views and exchange opinions with colleagues one rarely meets face-to-face, I must thank Roger Eaton, Olga Fischer, Willem Koopman and Frederike van der Leek.

With a work so complex as this, an editor is faced with a wide variety of problems and difficulties. It has been, therefore, a continual comfort and solace to know that Penny Carter of Cambridge University Press has always been there to provide advice and solutions on every occasion. Without her knowledge and experience, encouragment and good humour, this work would have been both poorer and later. After the work for Volume I was virtually complete, Marion Smith took over as publishing editor, and I am grateful to her too, not merely for ensuring such a smooth change-over, but for her bravery when faced with the mountain of paper from which this series has emerged.

Richard M. Hogg

ACKNOWLEDGEMENTS

The contributors to this volume are grateful for the help and advice they have received from friends and colleagues, as well as from their fellow contributors and the editors of and contributors to other volumes. We wish especially to thank the following: John Anderson, Norman Blake, Bob Burchfield, David Burnley, Fran Colman, Catherine Coutts, David Denison, Heiner Eichner, Olga Fischer, Margaret Gelling, John Hamshere, Suzanne Kemmer, Roger Lass, Chris McCully, Oliver Padel, Matti Rissanen, Don Scragg, Ann Harleman Stewart, Patrick Stiles, Mary Syner, Linda Thornburg, Nigel Vincent, Anthony Warner and Nancy Wiegand.

ABBREVIATIONS

(a) General

Angl.	Anglian
Arm.	Armenian
Av.	Avestan
CWGmc	Common West Germanic
DB	Domesday Book
DEPN	see Ekwall (1960) in References
EPNS	English Place-Name Society
EWS	Early West Saxon
G	German
Gk	Greek
Gmc	Germanic
Go.	Gothic
Hebr.	Hebrew
Hitt.	Hittite
IE	Indo-European
IPA	International Phonetic Alphabet
Lat./L	Latin
Lith.	Lithuanian
LWS	Late West Saxon
ME	Middle English
ms(s).	manuscript(s)
OBrit.	Old British
OCS	Old Church Slavonic
OE	Old English
OED	Oxford English Dictionary (= Murray et al., 1888–1933)
OFr.	Old Frisian
OHG	Old High German
OIc.	Old Icelandic
OIr.	Old Irish
ON	Old Norse
OPers.	Old Persian
OSax.	Old Saxon
Osc.	Oscan
PDE	Present-Day English
PN	County Volume of English Place-Name Society survey (see References)
PrGmc	Primitive Germanic
RB	Romano-British
RP	Received Pronunciation
Scand.	Scandinavian
Skt	Sanskrit
VL	Vulgar Latin
W	Welsh
WS	West Saxon

(b) Grammatical

acc.	accusative
abl.	ablative

adj.	adjective	O	object
advb.	adverb	pa.	past
auxil	auxiliary verb	part.	participle
C	consonant	pl.	plural
compar	comparative	poss.	possessive
dat.	dative	post	postposition
dem.	demonstrative	pr.	present
dm	determinandum	prep.	preposition
dt	determinant	pret.	preterite
exhort	exhortative	pron.	pronoun
fem./f.	feminine	PT	particle
gen.	genitive	reflx.	reflexive
imp.	imperative	S	subject
ind(ic).	indicative	sg.	singular
inf.	infinitive	subj.	(i) subject (of nouns);
infl.	inflected		(ii) subjunctive (of
instr.	instrumental		verbs)
loc.	locative	uninfl.	uninflected
masc./m.	masculine	V	(i) verb (syntax); (ii)
N	noun		vowel (phonology)
neg.	negative	voc.	vocative
neut./n.	neuter	1sg, 2sg.,	first person singular, etc.
NP	noun phrase	3sg. etc.	
Num	numeral		

Map of Anglo-Saxon England

I INTRODUCTION

Richard M. Hogg

1.1 Political history and language history

Bede begins his story of the Anglo-Saxon invasions and settlements of Britain as follows (it seems more appropriate here to quote from the Old English translation than from the original Latin text):

> Ða wæs ymb feower hund wintra and nigon and feowertig fram ures Drihtnes menniscnysse þæt Martianus casere rice onfeng ond VII gear hæfde. Se wæs syxta eac feowertigum fram Agusto þam casere. Ða Angelþeod and Seaxna was gelaðod fram þam foresprecenan cyninge [Wyrtgeorn wæs gehaten], and on Breotone com on þrim miclum scypum, and on eastdæle þyses ealondes eardungstowe onfeng þurh þæs ylcan cyninges bebod, þe hi hider gelaðode, þæt hi sceoldan for heora eðle compian and feohtan. And hi sona compedon wið heora gewinnan, þe hi oft ær norðan onhergedon; and Seaxan þa sige geslogan. Þa sendan hi ham ærenddracan and heton secgan þysses landes wæstmbærnysse and Brytta yrgþo. And hi þa sona hider sendon maran sciphere strengran wigena; and wæs unoferswiðendlic weorud, þa hi togædere geþeodde wæron. And him Bryttas sealdan and geafan eardungstowe betwih him, þæt hi for sybbe and for hælo heora eðles campodon and wunnon wið heora feondum, and hi him andlyfne and are forgeafen for heora gewinne.
>
> *(Bede* 1.12)

It was four hundred and forty-nine years after the birth of our Lord that the Emperor Martian came to the throne, and reigned for seven years. He was the forty-sixth Emperor since Augustus. The Angles and the Saxons were invited by the aforesaid king [he was called Vortigern] and they came to Britain in three large ships and received dwelling places in the eastern part of this island by order of that same king who had invited them here, so that they would battle and fight for their land. And at once they fought against their enemies who had often come down on raids from the north, and the Saxons won the battles. Then they sent messengers home, ordering them to tell of the fertility of this land and the cowardice of the Britons. And then they immediately sent here a larger fleet with stronger warriors; and, when they were gathered together, they formed an invincible army. And the Britons gave them dwelling places to share between them, on condition that they fought for peace and for prosperity in their land and defeated their enemies, and the Britons would give them provisions and estates on account of their victory.

Bede was writing in the eighth century, although he uses as a source the writings of Gildas which date from the middle of the sixth. Even so, approximately 100 years stands between Gildas and the arrival of those two famous brothers Hengist and Horsa, the traditional founders of the English nation.

It is therefore reasonable to suggest that the truth of Bede's account is sanctified more by tradition than by a correspondence with actual events. There is, for example, a growing body of archaeological evidence of Germanic peoples being in Britain during the fourth century (note, for example the fourth-century rune at Caistor-by-Norwich mentioned in §3.2.2 of chapter 3 and see the careful discussion in Hills 1979). But a clue to the most important event relating to the Germanic settlements comes at the very beginning of the Bede extract, with the reference to the Roman Emperor. Until 410 the Romans had occupied and governed Britain, but in that year they left Britain, and there can be no doubt that a major consequence of their departure was that the organisational structures which the Romans had erected for the governance of the country began to decay. In essence a vacuum of authority and power was created by their departure, and the Germanic tribes on the other side of the North Sea, who would already have been aware of the country's attractions, perhaps by their fathers or forefathers being mercenaries in the Roman army in Britain, were eager and willing to step into the breach.

The first two hundred years of Anglo-Saxon occupation of Britain are almost wholly unsupported by contemporary documentary evidence, the evidence being primarily archaeological and also, although more speculatively, toponymical (see chapter 7), or to be deduced from later writers such as Bede. But it is safe to conclude that the earliest settlements were in East Anglia and the south-east, with a gradual spread along the Thames valley, into the Midlands, and northwards through Yorkshire and into southern Scotland. From the linguistic point of view the most remarkable feature of the Anglo-Saxon settlement must be the virtually complete elimination of the Celtic languages, principally Welsh and Cornish. In the whole of Old English it is doubtful whether there are more than twenty Celtic borrowings into literary vocabulary (of which the most widespread now, but not in Old English, is perhaps *cross*). On the other hand, outside the literary vocabulary a very large number of place-, especially river-, names were retained by the invaders, hence *Thames*, *Severn*, and settlement-names such as *Manchester* (with the second element OE *ceaster* 'former Roman settlement'). It would seem that, although relations were sometimes friendly, the fifth- and sixth-century Anglo-Saxons were in this respect as resolutely monolingual as their twentieth-century descendants.

It is linguistically improbable that the first Anglo-Saxons all spoke the same form of language. Indeed Bede states that the Anglo-Saxon invaders came from three Germanic tribes, the Angles, the Saxons and the Jutes, and such a division, if accurate, would as much reflect linguistic as geographical or social differentiation. Since Bede's account directly equates the Angles with Anglian, the Saxons with Saxon (for our purposes, West Saxon), and the Jutes with Kentish, it is clearly tempting to assume that the Old English dialects to which we most usually refer (see here chapter 6) have their origins directly in pre-settlement Germanic. Such a view was certainly widely accepted in the first half of this century and earlier, but it has been strongly challenged since then (see especially DeCamp 1958 and, for a contrary view, Samuels 1971).

Without attempting to draw any firm conclusions, it may be worth formulating a number of general principles relevant not only to this question but to other similar questions concerning the Anglo-Saxon period. On the one hand, the reports of Bede, the Anglo-Saxon Chronicles and other early records must be privileged by virtue of their closeness in time to the events. In addition, that closeness in time may be further enhanced by the reliance of, say, Bede, writing ca AD 700, on even earlier writers such as Gildas. On the other hand, we can be certain of one thing, namely that the transmission of historical information in the earliest period of the Anglo-Saxon settlement must have been considerably more unreliable than it is today, and hence subject to much (not necessarily deliberate) distortion. In general, too, we must beware of forcing anachronistic meanings on ancient terms. As, for example, Strang (1970:377–9) points out, terms such as Angles, Saxons and Jutes need not have been mutually exclusive nor need they have referred to the same kind of entity: thus Angle may have referred to a tribe, whilst Saxon referred to a tribal confederacy. Jute remains yet more mysterious.

These considerations seem to force us into a compromise position, namely that the Anglo-Saxon invaders, coming from northern Germany and Denmark, already bore with them dialectal variations which in part contributed to the differentiation of the Old English dialects, but that nevertheless the major factors in that differentiation developed on the soil of Anglo-Saxon England. Certainly the remarks of Bede and other early writers are perhaps best viewed as iconic representations of the truth, rather than as simply interpreted historical verities.

The expansion of the Anglo-Saxon settlements in the centuries immediately following the initial invasions cannot be traced in any detail. Broadly, the first settlements were in East Anglia and south-east England, and there was a fairly quick spread so that by the end of the sixth century Anglo-Saxon rule of whatever kind, but one presupposing the dominance of Old English as the language of the people, had been extended over most of what is now England and was quickly encroaching on southern and south-eastern Scotland. Areas where Celtic remained dominant certainly included Cornwall and Wales, where in the eighth century Offa's Dyke was to become an important divide. Of the further parts of north-west England little is known, but the best estimate is that in such a sparsely-populated and remote area Anglo-Saxon and Celtic settlements existed side by side.

In strictly political and secular terms the seventh century probably witnessed the consolidation of Anglo-Saxon authority over their newly won territory, best symbolized by what we now know as the Heptarchy or rule of the seven kingdoms. These were the kingdoms of Wessex, Essex, Sussex, Kent, East Anglia, Mercia and Northumbria. Linguistically the concept of the Heptarchy is extremely important for it is from that concept that we obtain the traditional Old English dialect names: West Saxon, Kentish, Mercian and Northumbrian (the term Anglian as a cover term for Mercian and Northumbrian is taken from Bede's tripartite division of the Germanic settlers discussed above). But several words of warning are needed here. Firstly, it would be misleading to think of these 'kingdoms' in modern terms: their boundaries must have been vague and subject to change, not susceptible to the precise delineation of the kind that we are accustomed to today. Secondly, kingdoms of the Heptarchy and dialects areas are not necessarily isomorphic, even when they share the same name. For example, although texts originating from the kingdom of Mercia are commonly held to be Mercian one and all, it is clear that they have widely varying dialectal features, to the extent that two 'Mercian' texts may show as many distinctions as a 'Mercian' text and a 'Northumbrian' text. Thirdly, the absence of a dialect corresponding to one or other of the kingdoms of the Heptarchy does not imply the non-existence of such a dialect. Thus the absence of an East Anglian dialect cannot sensibly be taken to imply that there were no dialect variations particular to that area during the Old English period. Rather, all that is implied is the quite prosaic claim that we know of no texts certainly originating from the East Anglian area during the period, although place-name evidence, when collected and assembled, should allow us to ascertain some of the phonological and lexical characteristics of the dialect.

Whatever the merits of the concept of the Heptarchy, from the linguistic point of view the most important fact is that the political centres of power fluctuated considerably from the seventh to the ninth centuries. At first, Kent was probably of major importance (so, too, at the time must have been East Anglia, but without major linguistic consequence). It was to Kent that the first Roman Christian missionaries came, notably St Augustine in 597. With the conversion of Anglo-Saxon England (but not necessarily the Anglo-Saxon inhabitants!) to Christianity, although not by virtue of St Augustine's mission (see below), came that crucial cultural artefact, the Roman alphabetic system of writing. The consequences of this are more fully spelt out both below and in chapter 5, §5.2, but it needs to be said here that the Roman alphabet was essential in the remarkably early development of a vernacular manuscript tradition in Britain compared with what obtained elsewhere in the Germanic areas. The Germanic runic alphabet was either not fully used for normal communicative purposes or was written on objects not likely to be preserved intact, or, most probably, a combination of both pertained.

By about the middle of the seventh century the major centres of political (and hence cultural) power had shifted northwards, to the Anglian kingdoms of Mercia and Northumbria, especially the latter. Indeed for several decades around 700 Northumbria could claim, at Jarrow, Durham and Lindisfarne, and in the persons of men such as Bede and Alcuin, to be one of the major cultural centres of Western Europe. Since it was also at this time that texts began to be written in English rather than Latin, it is not surprising that most of the earliest

English texts are of Northumbrian origin, as in the case of *Cædmon's Hymn, Bede's Death Song* and the runic inscription on the Ruthwell Cross. Other texts which survive in an early eighth-century form, such as the *Epinal Glossary*, are predominantly Mercian, although they seem to bear traces of an earlier southern origin. Even at a later time this early northern predominance leaves its traces in poetry. Although the point is now highly controversial (see Chase 1981 and especially the essay by Stanley 1981 therein), the composition of *Beowulf* may be attributable to the latter part of the eighth century, when the Mercian kingdom, especially under Offa, dominated much of England.

Accelerated by events which we shall discuss shortly, by the end of the ninth century political power had been transferred, irrevocably, to southern England, more particularly the kingdom of Wessex centred at Winchester. But even under Alfred, who ruled from 871 to 899, although we witness the first real flourishing of Anglo-Saxon literature, with the Anglo-Saxon Chronicles and various translations of Latin originals, the West Saxon dialect is markedly influenced by Mercian. This is because Alfred, in order to establish a firm cultural, educational and literary foundation, had to seek the help of Mercians such as Bishop Wærferth, and the Welshman Bishop Asser, for it was only in Mercia that the scholarly tradition of the North had been able to survive, and there is precious little evidence to support any such tradition in the South.

One of the Anglo-Saxon Chronicles reports for 793 that 'the harrying of the heathen miserably destroyed God's church in Lindisfarne by rapine and slaughter' (Garmonsway, 1954:56). Tall oaks from little acorns grow. This note of righteous indignation, no doubt a reaction to Alfred's later battles, indicates the first known intrusion of the Vikings onto Anglo-Saxon soil. Sporadic raids continued thereafter, but from 835 onwards, when the Vikings plundered Sheppey, raids became more and more frequent along the southern and, presumably, eastern coasts, until in 865 a Viking army over-wintered in East Anglia. By 870 these Danes had overrun not merely East Anglia but all the eastern and central parts of Mercia and Northumbria, whilst mainly Norwegian Vikings occupied the north-western parts of Britain, the Isle of Man and the area around Dublin. Indeed the Danes were clearly threatening Wessex.

If Alfred had not come to the throne of Wessex in 871 the course of England and of its language would no doubt have been immeasurably different. For Alfred's strategy and tactics in both war and diplomacy enabled him first to regroup his forces and then, in 878, by the Treaty of Wedmore, establish a truce with the Danish leader Guthrum which in only a few years was to lead to Anglo-Saxon dominance in the country, albeit heavily tinged in many areas by Danish influence. Viking raids and battles continued on and off for several years, but by about 895 the many Vikings who remained, rather than going off to fresh pastures and fertile plunder in northern France, posed no threat.

Although it is certainly an understatement of Alfred's strategy, from our point of view the most important feature of the Treaty of Wedmore was that it recognized the Danish settlement of northern and eastern England, roughly north-east of a line from London to Chester, in which areas Danish law was to hold. This area – the Danelaw – must have been occupied by many Danish speakers living alongside English speakers (see Ekwall 1930, Page 1971). The marks of the Danelaw are easily observable today, most obviously in the pattern of place-names ending in -*by*, the Danish word for 'settlement' (see further the discussion in chapter 7). But reminders of the Danelaw survive elsewhere in the language. In order to understand the situation it is necessary to remember that the Danes and the Anglo-Saxons were both Germanic peoples with the same Germanic traditions (see here the approving references to Danes in *Beowulf*) and that their languages, stemming from a common source not many centuries before, must have been to some extent mutually comprehensible, albeit with some difficulty. Furthermore, in national terms there was no relation of conqueror to vanquished, (although in one area Danes might be dominant rulers, in another Anglo-Saxons would be) and thus the groups met more or less as equals and certainly with much in common. In these circumstances Danish and English communities could not remain entirely separate and always hostile (although they were undoubtedly both often). It is not surprising, therefore, that Scandinavian linguistic features entered the English language quite extensively, even, in time, giving such basic words as *they* and *are*. This borrowing of function words is not a feature of the later borrowings from French, and is a significant indicator of the closeness of linguistic form between Scandinavian and English at the time. However, the majority of Scandinavian borrowing into English belongs to the post-rather than the pre-Conquest history, and there are few Scandinavian loan words in Old English, for example. Those there are, such as *lagu* 'law' and *wicing* 'pirate', belong primarily to the eleventh century. The reasons for the time-lag between Scandinavian settlement and loan-word borrowing are difficult to ascertain, but such a time-lag is also typical of the later borrowings from French, and it may be that no important conclusions should be drawn from it. Of course it is quite possible that some Scandinavian loans, typically of the Scand. *kirk* type vs. the English *church* type, are unrecognizable because of the failure of the Anglo-Saxon orthographic practice to distinguish between the relevant sounds (for further discussion, see chapters 3 and 5).

In political terms the tenth century saw the consolidation of Alfred's gains and the unification of Anglo-Saxon England under a single ruler. It was this as much as ecclesiastical history (see below), which contributed to the rise of a literary standard language or *Schriftsprache* based upon West Saxon norms. It is notable that from the tenth century onwards distinctively non-West Saxon texts only appear in any quantity from Northumbria, the area most heavily influenced by the Vikings and furthest from the West Saxon centre of authority. Kentish texts become more and more heavily influenced by West Saxon, and the production of unambiguously Mercian texts is more notable by its absence than its presence.

At the beginning of the eleventh century, when Ethelred the Unready (OE *unræd* 'the ill-advised one') was on the throne, the Danes again became of major importance, with the ultimate consequence that in 1016 Canute (Cnut) came to the throne, a Danish King of England for the first time. Since this achievement was more diplomatic than military, and since Cnut had at least as many opponents in Denmark as in England, the pattern of relations was somewhat different from that of the earlier Viking invasions. Essentially, Cnut's court was an Anglo-Danish one, and alongside Cnut's Danish followers there co-existed a considerable number of English advisers, of whom, perhaps, the best known is Wulfstan, archbishop of York. Under these circumstances it might be expected that over the next twenty-six years of Danish rule there would have been a considerable degree of Danish–English bilingualism and that much Danish vocabulary would have entered the language. But although this did happen to some extent with a writer such as Wulfstan, mainly because of his relations with Cnut and his archbishopric of York, elsewhere Danish influence remained by and large a property of what had been the earlier Danelaw. Occasional Scandinavian words are found in other writers, even including Ælfric, but their number is low.

When, in 1042, an English king regained the throne, namely Edward the Confessor, he turned out to be a harbinger of French influence rather than a restorer of the English tongue. A king perhaps wiser in the ways of heaven than the ways of earth (unlike Cnut, who seems to have been equally wise in both), and, what is more to the point, one who had spent a long period in exile, Edward cultivated close relations with the dukes of Normandy and even, in 1050, appointed a Frenchman as bishop of London. When Edward died in January 1066 he had managed, with the help of the rival claimants, to muddy the succession to the throne sufficiently to ensure that both Harold and William of Normandy could lay reasonable claim to the throne, and neither was reluctant to do so. The conclusion of that rivalry is well-known.

It is most reasonable to suggest that the most important immediate effect of the Norman Conquest was political and that the most important long-term effects were cultural. This is to imply that the Norman Conquest itself had rather less immediate effect on the linguistic structures of English than is often supposed. However it does not imply that the eventual influence of French upon English was not considerable, which would obviously be counter-factual. The point is rather more subtle. The eventual influence of French upon English was a long-term one, and can be ascribed to the cultural patterns which the consequences of the Norman Conquest imposed upon England. But if we concentrate solely on the eleventh and early twelfth century, virtually no French loans are found, and of the few that do occur, they are often ambiguously French or Latin, e.g. *castel* 'castle'. The reasons for this may be similar to the time-lag concerning Scandinavian influence, but it seems more likely that the lack of French influence was a result of the manner of the Norman assumption of rule, which involved relatively few people and had an immediate effect only on the upper echelons of English society.

This topic, however, is one more proper to Volume II of this History than to Volume I. There are clear linguistic indications that by about 1100 the structure of our language was beginning to be modified to such a considerable degree that it is reasonable to make that the dividing line between Old English and Middle English: in phonology the characteristic Old English diphthongal system was disappearing, and the variety of vowels in unstressed syllables was meagre; in morphology more and more inflexions were falling together, and morphosyntactic categories such as case and gender were no longer unambiguously expressed except in a minority of instances; in syntax the old word-order type SOV was clearly in decline. The important point to note, however, is that such shifts were not caused by the Norman Conquest, rather they were the product of a long-term trend in the history of the language. It is doubtful whether the Norman Conquest, in the first instance at least, contributed significantly to the acceleration of these trends.

1.2   Ecclesiastical history and language history

It is entirely fitting that the first major history of English-speaking Britain, although written in Latin, should be called *An Ecclesiastical History of the English People*. Throughout the Anglo-Saxon period the church existed in virtual equality as a centre of power and culture alongside the political structures. And this could give rise to considerable complication. One obvious point here is that the centre of the church quickly became Canterbury, in the heart of Kent. But politically Kent was one of the weakest kingdoms, squabbled over for centuries by the Mercians and the West Saxons. Thus, in the first half of the ninth century Mercian linguistic influence on Kentish texts was considerable, whilst towards the end of the period West Saxon texts can sometimes be seen to have Kentish influence, either because they were written in Kent or because the ecclesiastical influence of Kent was so much stronger than its political influence.

But this is to anticipate. Firstly, we should recall that Christianity did not come to Britain only with the mission of St Augustine in 597. During the Roman occupation of Britain the Romans had brought Christianity to the country and the native Celts had been converted. As long as the Romans remained, this form of Christianity did not diverge significantly from that on the Continent, but after the departure of the Romans and the arrival of the non-Christian Anglo-Saxons, the church became isolated from developments elsewhere, and although not wilfully persecuted, suffered depredation at the hands of the uninterested, albeit not actively hostile, invaders.

St Augustine's achievement, therefore, was not the conversion of Britain but rather the conversion of the Anglo-Saxons. And this conversion took place in a country where Christianity already existed. Indeed Augustine's mission gave a new impetus to British Christianity. From its stronghold at Iona off the west coast of Scotland British Christianity spread to Northumbria under the leadership of Aidan, who both founded the monastery at Lindisfarne and converted King Oswald of Northumbria to Christianity. The consequences of the differences which had arisen between Roman and British Christianity through the isolation of the latter were most strongly to be felt there in Northumbria, so that in the middle of the seventh century whilst the Northumbrian king, Oswy, was a British Christian, his Kentish wife followed the practices of the Roman Church. Although many of the differences between the two churches were trifling, one point above all was of major practical and symbolic importance, namely the date of Easter, which the two churches calculated differently. In order to resolve this, a synod was held at Whitby in 663, when Oswy settled the matter decisively in favour of the Roman Church. Henceforth, therefore, the Roman form of Christianity held sway over the whole of Anglo-Saxon England.

Yet the British Church left a considerable imprint on the cultural and linguistic history of the country. We have already noted, for example, that one of the few Celtic loan-words in the language is *cross*, and this borrowing from Irish in preference to the Latin *crux* is a revealing and permanent symbol of the earlier strength of British Christianity. Of rather more significance is the fact that the first use of the Roman alphabet was due to the influence of Irish missionaries, that is to say, Aidan and others who came from Columba's monastery at Iona. The type of writing used was the insular half-uncial, and although it was modified early in the Anglo-Saxon period, a continental-based script did not start to appear until the eleventh century, when, as we have seen, French influence became important. Thus although it is undoubtedly the case that we would not have the wealth of Anglo-Saxon material that we do have without the coming of Christianity, the credit belongs at least as much to British as to Roman Christianity.

Perhaps the wealth of literature has the same source, for Bede's account of Cædmon, the first Anglo-Saxon poet of whom we know anything at all, places him at the monastery of Whitby, governed by the Abbess Hild. Certainly, the majority of the earliest Old English literary material seems to have originated in Anglia, rather than further south, no doubt a combination of the political structures mentioned in §1.2 and the impact of Christianity. One revealing example here is the Ruthwell Cross, with its Celtic-inspired designs, a Latin text, and an Old English runic inscription which corresponds to part of the poem known as *The Dream of The Rood*. A heady combination of cultures and ideas for the beginning of the eighth century, even more remarkable for its situation in what is now south-western Scotland.

These earliest moments of Christianity amongst the Anglo-Saxons, therefore, were of the highest importance for the history of the language. From the death of Bede in 735 to the reign of Alfred in the last quarter of the ninth century, the impact of the church was relatively insignificant. Alfred, however, was as interested in cultural and educational reform as in warding off the Danes, and for these reforms he necessarily employed men such as the Mercian Bishop Asser. In Alfred's reign we see not only the production of the Anglo-Saxon Chronicles, designed to set the political and historical record straight, or at least, if not straight, nicely curved in Alfred's favour, but also the translation of Pope Gregory's *Cura pastoralis*, best known now for the accompanying letter from Alfred to various bishops (of which only the copy to Wærferth survives), in which Alfred set out his plans for educational reform. Under Alfred's influence other texts were also translated from Latin into English, notably Orosius's *Historia adversum paganos* and Bede's *Historia ecclesiastica*. It is difficult to tell whether these translations were made because of the general ignorance of Latin or pride in the vernacular language – Alfred explicitly refers to the first of these reasons, but implicitly refers to the second. Whatever the case, such translations placed English prose on a much firmer foundation than had existed up till then.

In §1.1 the impression may well have been given that the tenth century was a century of peace. This was hardly the case, but the political fighting and infighting was generally amongst those of the house of Wessex and had little linguistic consequence. Nevertheless, the significant and enduring rise in ecclesiastical power which the century witnessed was linguistically important. This rise took place especially during the reigns of Edgar (959–975), and then, after a short anti-monastic interregnum, Ethelred the Unready (978–1016). When Edgar came to the throne he was only 16 years old, and Ethelred was some five years younger at the same stage. Even by Anglo-Saxon standards they were both young for the throne, and naturally enough had to rely on their advisers.

Fortunately, both kings had (although in the case of Ethelred, only at first) excellent advisers. In 910 at Cluny in Burgundy a Benedictine house was established and with its strict asceticism revived the tarnished image of monasticism. The existing house at Fleury, on the Loire, was reformed on Benedictine lines, and by the 940's close links had been established between Fleury and England, mostly by the activities of

Æthelflæd at Glastonbury. Three English Benedictine monks were of particular importance: Æthelwold, abbot of Abingdon and late bishop of Winchester; Dunstan, abbot of Glastonbury, then bishop of Worcester and later archbishop of Canterbury; and Oswald, who succeeded Dunstan as bishop of Worcester. These episcopal and archiepiscopal appointments were all made at the beginning of Edgar's reign and are as clear an indication as could be desired of the dawn of a new area of monastic rule, secular as well as religious.

The consequences of the new monasticism were considerable linguistically. Yet perhaps we should note first of all that, at least during Edgar's reign, the power and authority of men such as Dunstan ensured that there was sufficient political stability and a clear source of political authority to allow the flowering of culture and education which Alfred had hoped for sixty years earlier. Whilst Dunstan was possibly the prime mover in the monastic movement, from the linguistic point of view the key figure was Æthelwold. At the monastery in Winchester he created a school devoted to the spread of learning and religion, and associated with that school we have, as Gneuss (1972) shows, a series of manuscripts which can lay claim, by their regularity and consistency, to be the first evidence in English of a written standard language or *Schriftsprache*. The consequences of this are more fully spelt out in chapter 5, but we should note here that although this standard language is of immense importance for the history of late Old English, it did not long survive the Norman Conquest and has no connexions with the standard language that was to develop from the fifteenth century onwards.

There is little point in having a written standard language unless there is something worthwhile to write in it. Æthelwold himself both translated Latin works and wrote original pieces in Old English, but the main figure we must mention here is Ælfric, a pupil of Æthelwold, then master of novices at Cerne and finally abbot of Eynsham. Ælfric was primarily a theological scholar (unlike many monks, whose interests were as often secular as religious), and a prolific writer. Best known for his series of *Catholic Homilies* and his *Lives of the Saints*, he also wrote a *Grammar* for his pupils studying Latin and translating into Old English. Whatever the literary merits of his work (see §1.3 below and chapter 8 for fuller relevant discussion), from the narrow linguistic point of view Ælfric's writings are remarkable for the consistency of language and the careful orthography, both key aspects of a standard language. Furthermore, the type of language which Ælfric used came, in the eleventh century, to be used throughout the country, in places as diverse as Canterbury, Worcester and York. Of course, these, like Winchester itself, were important ecclesiastical centres, and it might be better to think of this *Schriftsprache* as an ecclesiastical rather than literary standard. The principal prose texts were ecclesiastical rather than literary, and, as was inevitable at the time, almost all the centres of writing were in religious scriptoria.

Monasticism continued to be of prime importance in the later years of Ethelred's reign (although rarely to good effect) and beyond. At the same time the *Schiftsprache* continued to spread, though it was sometimes modified to local tastes and needs, as in the case of Wulfstan, bishop of Worcester, archbishop of York and a prominent figure both in the latter part of Ethelred's reign and in the first part of Cnut's.

Although the general linguistic situation changed only slowly in response to Norman influences, the Norman Conquest created a much more drastic change in ecclesiastical life. William very swiftly replaced English bishops by Norman ones, and this had a marked effect on the standard language. Monasteries could no longer act as the upholders of the *Schriftsprache*, for the Normans brought their own (Latin-based) orthography and spelling conventions, nor, in Anglo-Norman communities, was there the same perceived need for English texts. Latin was adopted as the language for all serious writing, including administrative records, and consequently the norms of the standard language created by Æthelwold, Ælfric and others, quickly faded, and by the mid-twelfth century texts written in English were becoming confused and inconsistent in their orthography, as scribes tried vainly to remember how they should write and to reconcile that with how their local dialect sounded. This, of course, gives texts of that time a distinctly un-Old English air, but the conclusion must be that this is the result of rapid orthographic rather than of rapid linguistic change.

1.3   Literary history and language history

The very earliest scraps of English which we have today are runic inscriptions. Of these, the earliest is an astragalus (ankle-bone) from Caistor-by-Norwich, the inscription on which is usually transcribed as 'ræʒhæn'. The shape of the letters suggests a Scandinavian rather than North Sea Germanic origin, and the meaning of the form is obscure, although it could be a reference to the fact that this astragalus seems to have been the ankle-bone of a roe-deer (see Page 1973). But these very early materials are so scanty as to have only the most limited value for linguistic history. With one runic inscription however, namely the Ruthwell Cross, we can get much further, at least in our investigation of poetry, and we shall return to the topic below.

Generally speaking, even the start of a manuscript tradition using the Roman alphabet, which must have begun in earnest in the second half of the seventh century, does not in the first instance provide much more evidence. Most prose was then written in Latin rather than English, and even the most extensive early pieces of English, such as the Epinal Glossary, are types of Latin–English dictionary for use in conjunction with the Bible. As such, although they provide invaluable information about vocabulary and phonology, they tell us very little about syntax and, of course, their literary value is small. Lists of names attached to the end of Latin charters, another frequent early source, are primarily of historical value, although they also provide some phonological evidence.

The most extensive pre-Alfredian text is the interlinear gloss to the psalter and canticles commonly known as the Vespasian Psalter gloss. This text is invaluable as a guide to phonology, morphology and vocabulary, especially since many other interlinear glosses of the psalter appeared in the Old English period and shortly after. But, since the text is essentially a word-by-word glossing of the Latin original, it too provides little information about syntax. Furthermore, its Mercian–Kentish origin (it may have been the work of a Mercian scribe at Canterbury), although it fits well with the political situation of the time, has caused considerable confusion ever since Old English dialects became the object of serious study.

It is only with the advent of Alfred to the throne, and his consequent pursuit of cultural and educational reform, that we begin to find a substantial corpus of Old English prose. Amongst the important texts of the Alfredian era are the Anglo-Saxon Chronicles (or, rather, the Parker Chronicle), the translation of the *Cura pastoralis*, Alfred's translation of Boethius, and, although not directly attributable to Alfred, the translations of Orosius' *Historia adversum paganos* and Bede's *Historia ecclesiastica*. For the first time we have long continuous passages of Old English prose, which enables us to paint a reasonable picture of Old English syntax and prose style. However, it can be seen that the majority of these texts (the same goes for later periods too) are translations from Latin, and a common argument amongst syntacticians concerns the degree to which certain constructions may be Latinisms stemming from the nature of translations. Such issues are discussed at several places in chapter 4.

The Alfredian texts, on phonological and morphological grounds commonly called Early West Saxon texts, are of immense importance in the history of the language. Above all this is because they represent the first attempts at a written literary prose style. To what extent these attempts are to be linked to later developments in style within the Old English period is scarcely a matter for discussion here (see the discussion in chapter 8). Nevertheless, the confusion which the reader must have when first seeing, say, the entry for 755 in the Parker Chronicle (the story of Cynewulf and Cyneheard), or Alfred's Preface to the *Cura pastoralis* (where he outlines his plans for educational reform) must surely receive adequate compensation through the knowledge that here, for the first time, someone is trying to tell a story, to express his ideas, in ordinary written English. Another important text probably stemming from the Alfredian era is *Bald's Leechbook*, a collection of medical recipes, which both provides information about the transmission of scientific ideas and is, like the glossaries, a valuable source of Old English vocabulary.

The central part of the tenth century seems to have been a time for the copying of Alfredian texts (several of the texts referred to above are extant only in manuscripts of the mid-tenth century), rather than for the production of new material. For a substantial body of new material we have to wait until the establishment of Æthelwold's school at Winchester and, more particularly, the work of Ælfric who wrote in the decades preceding and following the year 1000. Fortunately, since Ælfric was one of the most prolific prose writers of the Old English period, he is generally recognized as one of its most elegant practitioners. His best-known works include the *Catholic Homilies* and the *Lives of the Saints*, extracts from which are widely available in introductory textbooks. Those who wish to become acquainted with Old English prose might well be best advised to start by reading Ælfric rather than Alfred, since his style combines elegance with clarity in a way which makes the material more accessible to the beginner. Of particular relevance to the linguist, however, is the fact that Ælfric wrote a *Grammar*, the only treatise on syntax and morphology which we have for the period, although a Latin grammar tradition is evident (see Law 1982). Ælfric's *Grammar* is of Latin and Ælfric says of it:

Ic þohte, þæt ðeos boc mihte fremian jungum cildum to anginne þæs cræftes, oððæt hi to maran andgite becumon.

I thought that this book might help young children at the start of their study [of grammar], until they could achieve greater understanding.

In other words, he saw the *Grammar* as no more than an elementary textbook. As such, unsurprisingly, there is no noticeable contribution to medieval linguistic theory in the text. Rather, its interest lies in the manner in which Ælfric chooses particular Old English constructions as the most appropriate equivalents of Latin constructions.

Amongst Ælfric's contemporaries or near-contemporaries, the best-known prose writer was certainly Wulfstan, archbishop of York. Of his work the piece *Sermo Lupi ad Anglos* is an outstanding example of his striking literary style, which clearly owes a certain amount to the poetic tradition. But his rhetorical devices, like those of Ælfric, are also based on a knowledge of Latin rhetorical usage, a knowledge of which must have been reasonably widespread in Anglo-Saxon times (see the further discussion in chapter 8).

Another contemporary of Ælfric, but one who reminds us of an earlier age, was a priest called Aldred, who, based at Chester-le-Street near Durham in Northumbria, compiled an interlinear English gloss to the Latin text of the Lindisfarne Gospels, and also to other Latin religious texts. The interest of these texts lies in the fact that they were produced in an area which had been under Danish domination for over a century, and thus they are not merely unusually lengthy specimens of a non-West Saxon dialect, they also serve as indicators of what had happened to English in an area of Danish–English bilingualism. Already in Aldred's texts we see forms of the type *he lufes* 'he loves', alongside *he lufaþ* 'he loveth', a change which was not firmly established in southern dialects of English until about the time of Shakespeare.

For the end of the Old English period, including the time just after the Norman Conquest, little needs to be said. The Chronicles, it is true, continued, and provide us now with invaluable if not unprejudiced accounts of those turbulent times, but otherwise the main activity seems once more to have been copying rather than the production of original work. Naturally such copying is of intrinsic interest, since it is revealing to consider what, for example, a new scribe or copier, writing towards the end of the eleventh century, can make of a text first produced a hundred years earlier. But it would seem as if the Old English prose tradition was a somewhat fragile one, which withered without the presence of an Alfred or an Ælfric.

The history of Old English poetry is rather different from that of Old English prose, and also much more difficult to discern. The major reason for this is that the vast majority of Old English poetry is to be found in only four manuscripts, all compiled in the late tenth to early eleventh century. These manuscripts are: the Vercelli Book, the Exeter Book, the *Beowulf* Manuscript and the Junius or Cædmon Manuscript. There can be scarcely any doubt that these manuscripts were, by and large, compilations of poetry written at different times during the Old English period (although of the manuscripts only the Exeter is recognizably a literary anthology of a type with which we are familiar).

That these four manuscripts can all be dated around 1000 and are a product of the cultural renaissance associated with the Benedictine monastic revival, is certain. We can be equally certain, however, that the poetic tradition was of much longer standing. Firstly, there are enough significant parallels with other Germanic poetry, especially Icelandic, to suggest a common, if distant, literary inheritance. Secondly, the Ruthwell Cross inscription of *The Dream of Rood* implies that that poem existed in some form in the early eighth century. Thirdly, Bede's account of the poet Cædmon living at the abbey at Whitby when Hild was abbess (i.e. in the middle to late seventh century), is proof that poetry was being composed at that early date. Furthermore, it is now generally agreed that Old English poetry stems from an older, oral tradition of poetry.

Oddly enough, the consequences of all this for linguistic study are generally quite other than might be expected, even though it is true that the older oral tradition left its mark on the structure and style of poetry long after the poetry began to assume a written form as normal. Such matters are further discussed in chapter 8. But here the most significant feature is that these manuscripts, despite their origin and inspiration, are not normally written in the form of language associated with the monastic revival, i.e. the form of language found in, say, Ælfrician manuscripts. Rather, they tend (although this varies from manuscript to manuscript, with the Exeter Book being more predominantly West Saxon than the others) to share a common poetic dialect, which combines both West Saxon and Anglian forms to an extent which is unusual elsewhere, and of which, especially in terms of vocabulary, has forms which are unattested outside the poetry. Furthermore, there is often a fair number of apparently archaic forms, e.g. inflexional forms which are known to have disappeared from the language by about the eighth century.

This leads to two conclusions. Firstly, it is clear that there must have already existed at an early period and in vaguely Anglian territory (which would be implied by the political history, see §1.1 above) a considerable poetic tradition which continued to have a strong influence even at a much later date. Hence the otherwise odd mixture of dialect forms. Secondly, despite considerable investigation, it seems impossible to give an accurate chronological account of the poetry on the basis of the linguistic forms in the poems. Hence although apparent archaicisms may be identified, they do not ultimately help to clarify for us the linguistic history of poetry.

1.4   The nature of the evidence

Most people who study the language of the Old English period will, for most of the time, restrict their study to printed editions of texts, with only the occasional glance at a manuscript. This can lead unwittingly to two distortions. And there is a third distortion which is possible, however one looks at the evidence. This final section of the Introduction is intended to make readers aware of what kinds of distortion can occur.

Let us start with a distortion which is inevitable whenever one looks at a language of the distant past. When we study a present-day language the nature of the evidence we have is wide and varied. If we wish, we can always ask native informants for their reactions to certain constructions or pronunciations or elicit further material in the language. Indeed, if we are studying our own language we can, to a considerable degree at least, rely on our intuitions about it. There is considerable controversy in current linguistics over the validity of elicitation techniques and, especially, introspection, but, however limited their value, it remains true that there is always a much wider range and greater number of spoken and written texts for living languages than we can ever hope to attain for historical work. When we are studying a language of the past we are faced with a limited and unexpandable (except by chance discovery) body of data. The only native informants we have are manuscripts, and (therefore) the only evidence we have is written.

All these restrictions inevitably lead to problems which do not arise with a present-day language. For example, today we might reasonably suspect that a word such as *gallus* 'impish, wild', despite the OED entry under *gallows*, was restricted to Scottish dialects. To check our suspicions we need only ask a selection of speakers. But what about the Old English word *spyrd* 'course, measure of distance', which occurs only in Northumbrian (West Saxon uses *furlang*, cf. PDE *furlong*)? Is this like PDE *gallus* in being dialectally restricted? Or what about the possibility of some syntactic construction which happens not to occur in the extant data? Does that mean that construction was impossible in Old English? In morphology one would like to know a great deal more about the use of grammatical gender, especially with regard to words which apparently had variable gender in the period. In phonology even such simple questions as 'How was *eorþe* "earth" pronounced?' can receive no more than approximate answers. None of this means that the linguist has to give up. But it does mean that the process of linguistic investigation must proceed by deductive inference to a much greater degree than is necessary with a present-day language and, of course, that the results achieved must necessarily be that much less certain.

Now let us consider a distortion which in part, at least, is due to the easy accessibility of printed editions. Written material in Present Day English is, unlike spoken material, fairly homogeneous in character. But since language varies not only chronologically and dialectally, but also socially, it is to spoken material that we look for dialectal and social variation. For the Old English period not only do we not (obviously) possess spoken material, but the written material does not reflect the same dialectal homogeneity. Texts can usually be identified, on purely linguistic grounds, as originating from, say, Wessex or Northumbria. On the other hand, there is almost complete social homogeneity between texts. Virtually every linguistic item we possess must have come from a very narrow social band indeed. The consequence of this, of course, is that we have very little idea of how the 'ordinary' Anglo-Saxon spoke. As is discussed in chapter 6, modern linguistic theory can get us a little further along that path, but we still have to remember that sociolinguistically our investigations remain more limited than for any other period of the language.

The most important distortion of all concerns the data itself, for in considering a printed edition we are considering a text which inevitably departs from the original, and not merely in letter-shapes. Rather than elaborate at length on the differences, I wish to exemplify some of the issues by comparing one extract with the original. Extract (a) is an attempt at a faithful reproduction of the manuscript and then four reputable editions follow. The extract comes from the beginning of the poem known as *The Wanderer* from the Exeter Book (see the frontispiece

of this volume for a facsimile). The selected editions are: (b) Grein &
Wulcker 1883, (c) Krapp & Dobbie 1936, (d) Leslie 1966 and (e)
Dunning & Bliss 1969.

(a) OFT him anhaӡa are ӡebideð metudes miltse þeahþe
he mod ceariӡ ӡeond laӡu lade lonӡe sceolde hreran
mid hondum hrim cealde sæ padan præc lastas pyrd
bið ful aræd · Spa cpæð eard stapa earfeþa ӡemyndiӡ
praþra pæl sleahta pine mæӡa hryre · Oft ic sceolde
ana uhtna ӡehpylce mine ceare cpiþan nisnu cpic
ra nán þeic him mod sefan minne durre speotule
asecgan ic to soþe wat þ biþ ineorle indryhten þeap
þæt he his ferð locan fæste binde healdne his hord
cofan hycӡe spahe pille ·

(b) OFT him anhaӡa are ӡebideð
metudes miltse, þeah þe he modceariӡ
ӡeond laӡulade lonӡe sceolde
hreran mid hondum hrimcealde sæ,
wadan wræclastas: wyrd bið ful aræd!
Swa cwæð eardstapa earfeþa ӡemyndiӡ,
wraþra wælsleahta, winemæӡa hryre:
'Oft ic sceolde ana uhtna ӡehwylce
mine ceare cwiþan! nis nu cwicra nan,
þe ic him modsefan minne durre
sweotule asecӡan. Ic to soþe wat,
þæt biþ in eorle indryhten þeaw,
þæt he his ferðlocan fæste binde,
healde his hordcofan, hycӡe swa he wille;

(c)   Oft him anhaga   are gebideð,
metudes miltse,   þeah þe he modcearig
geond lagulade   longe sceolde
hreran mid hondum   hrimcealde sæ,
wadan wræclastas.   Wyrd bið ful aræd!
  Swa cwæð eardstapa,   earfeþa gemyndig,
wraþra wælsleahta,   winemæga hryre:
'Oft ic sceolde ana   uhtna gehwylce
mine ceare cwiþan.   Nis nu cwicra nan
þe ic him modsefan   minne durre
sweotule asecgan.   Ic to soþe wat
þæt biþ in eorle   indryhten þeaw,
þæt he his ferðlocan   fæste binde,
healde his hordcofan,   hycge swa he wille.

(d)   'Oft him ānhaga   āre gebīdeð,
        Metudes miltse,   þēahþe hē mōdcearig
        geond lagulāde   longe sceolde
        hrēran mid hondum   hrīmcealde sǣ,
        wadan wrǣclāstas;   wyrd bið ful ārǣd.'
         Swā cwæð eardstapa   earfeþa gemyndig,
        wrāþra wælsleahta,   winemǣga hryre.
        'Oft ic sceolde āna   ūhtna gehwylce
        mīne ceare cwīþan;   nis nū cwicra nān
        þe ic him mōdsefan   mīnne durre
        sweotule āsecgan.   Ic tō sōþe wāt
        þæt biþ in eorle   indryhten þēaw
        þæt hē his ferðlocan   fæste binde,
        healde his hordcofan,   hycge swā hē wille.

(e)   OFT him anhaga   are gebideð,
        Metudes miltse,   þeah þe he modcearig
        geond lagulade   longe sceolde
        hreran mid hondum   hrimcealde sæ,
        wadan wræclastas: wyrd bið ful aræd!
         Swa cwæð eardstapa,   earfeþa gemyndig,
        wraþra wælsleahta   winemæga hryre.
        Oft ic sceolde ana   uhtna gehwylce
        mine ceare cwiþan –   nis nu cwicra nán
        þe ic him modsefan   minne durre
        sweotule asecgan.   Ic to soþe wat
        þæt biþ in eorle   indryhten þeaw
        þæt he his ferðlocan   fæste binde,
        healde his hordcofan,   hycge swa he wille.

The Wanderer: a translation

Often the solitary dweller waits for favour.
the mercy of the creator, although he, troubled in heart,
has for a long time, across the sea-ways, had
to stir with his hands the ice-cold sea,
travel the paths of an exile; fate is fully determined.

Thus spoke the wanderer, mindful of troubles,
of cruel battles, of the fall of kinsmen.

Often, alone at each dawn, I have had
to lament my sorrow; now there is no one alive
to whom I dare openly reveal my thoughts. I know it to be true
that it is an aristocratic practice for a warrior

that he should bind fast his heart,
hold his heart firm, whatever he may wish to think.

It is immediately clear that considerable editorial intervention has taken place. But what may not be quite so clear is that much of this intervention is based on linguistic interpretation of great sophistication and that as such it crucially affects our ideas about the form and structure of the Old English language. For example, and most obviously of all, the editors have had to take a view of the structure of Old English poetry, since the manuscript version of this poem, like other Old English poems, is not easily distinguishable from prose. Thus the editors have had to determine the most probable metrical structures for Old English poetry and hence propose the most plausible line divisions. That the editors all agree on these divisions testifies only to the amount of research that has been done on this subject, and should not mislead anyone into thinking that what we are dealing with here is a given rather than a hypothetical deduction.

Even at a very minor level editorial intervention can be recognized. This is true even of text (a) where some letter shapes reasonably reflect manuscript forms, e.g. $<3>$, which in (c)–(e) is represented as $<g>$, but others do not, e.g. instead of $<s>$ it might have been preferable to use $<\int>$. The weight of editorial tradition may be considerable and influence even apparently faithful reproductions. If we remain with spelling, one might note that (d) has length marks or macrons over long vowels, a feature especially common in introductory texts. But these length marks normally represent etymological length, and hence there is no reason to suppose that, for instance, *hē* in the last line would have been recited with a long vowel, for if it were unstressed the etymological length would have been lost. The same would go for *tō* three lines earlier.

One of the best-known characteristics of Old English poetry (see chapters 5 and 8) is the frequent use of compounds, often nonce-formations unique to the poetry. The scribe of the Exeter Book was more precise than many other scribes in showing word-division. But, remarkably, he normally writes the elements of a compound, e.g. *lagulade*, as two separate words (here it is best to look at the facsimile itself, rather than (a), for the printed text fails quite significantly to reproduce the spacing of the original). Conversely, it is probable, but not absolutely certain that, say, three lines from the end the scribe is writing as a single word the prepositional phrase *in eorle*. Therefore, the identification of compounds is not an easy or certain matter, and, equally, modern conventions of word-division may hide from us illuminating information about processes such as cliticisation.

Punctuation, too, in modern editions is usually far removed from the punctuation of the original. At the purely syntactic level this means that modern printed editions often disguise completely quite tricky questions about the structure of Old English sentences, implicitly asserting or denying the grammaticality or, more frequently, the acceptability of particular structures. In the present extract, however, the questions which arise from punctuation are more often stylistic than syntactic, and different editors, by using variously such punctuations as the semi-colon, colon and period, take different views of possible paratactic and appositional constructions. Compare, for example the punctuations before *wyrd bið ful aræd*, where no punctuation exists in the original.

A striking case where lack of punctuation in the original (not an error, simply the Old English norm) creates major cruces of literary interpretation concerns the various methods of indicating different speakers at the beginning of the poem. The editors of (b) and (c) view the first seven lines as an introduction by the poet, which is then followed by the Wanderer's own story; the editor of (d), however, sees all except lines 6–7 as the words of the Wanderer, with those two lines an interpolated comment by the poet; and the editors of (e) take the first five lines as a general proposition, followed by two lines of introduction to the Wanderer's story by the poet, and then the Wanderer's story itself. Whatever the merits of each, it has to be said that on the one hand the manuscript provides no certain clues (note only the dots, indicating some kind of pause, after *aræd* and *hryre*) to the structure, yet on the other hand present-day conventions oblige the editors to commit themselves to one interpretation or another (to which the reader, in turn, must accord no particular priority).

Literary, and hence semantic, interpretation can be concealed even in the most minor matters. For example, both of the most recent editions capitalise the initial letter of *metudes* 'god'. This, of course, makes a strictly Christian interpretation of the poem inescapable, but semantically it might imply a clear shift from a pagan to a Christian epithet. The fact of a shift is clear enough, but that the shift was so clear-cut is far from indisputable and may not be an accurate portrait of the effect of Christianity on the structure of Old English vocabulary.

Most of our knowledge of the Old English period comes from two major contemporary sources, namely Bede's *Historia ecclesiastica* and the group of texts collectively known as The Anglo-Saxon Chronicles. The original Latin text of the former is edited with an excellent introduction and facing-page translation by Colgrave & Mynors 1969. For the latter, most of the Old English material is edited by Plummer & Earle 1899. Whitelock *et al.* 1961 is the most complete guide to the Chronicles, whilst Garmonsway 1954 remains a good 'crib' for the beginner. See also Whitelock 1955 for an excellent introduction to the documents of the period, but Robertson 1939, Whitelock 1930 and Harmer 1952 provide selections of the original material. There are numerous good introductions to the history of the period, amongst which might be mentioned Hunter Blair 1956 and Loyn 1984. For an authoritative full-length study, Stenton 1971 remains unrivalled. An interesting work which offers new perspectives on Anglo-Saxon history, as well as being lavishly and beautifully illustrated, is Campbell *et al.* 1982. Whitelock 1952 deals more specifically with the social structure of Anglo-Saxon society as, more recently, does Finsberg 1976. Hill 1981 provides many useful maps which illuminate helpfully the history of the period in all its aspects.

Amongst linguistic histories the beginner is likely to start with Baugh & Cable 1978, but for others a more profitable work, despite its rather odd reverse chronology (it starts at 1970 and works backwards), would be Strang 1970. Brunner 1950 is the standard short history of English in German. Another important work is Lass 1987, not a 'history of the language' but full of important historical insights. Introductions to Old English language are numerous, but the two which are most often used are Quirk & Wrenn 1957 and, more recently, Mitchell & Robinson 1986. The standard reference works in English are Campbell 1959 for phonology and morphology and Mitchell 1985 for syntax. Luick 1914 is equally essential for phonology. Other texts of relevance are mentioned in the Further Reading sections of individual chapters.

2 THE PLACE OF ENGLISH IN GERMANIC AND INDO-EUROPEAN

Alfred Bammesberger

2.1   Language change and historical linguistics

Greek philosophers were aware of the fact that human language is subject to change in the course of time. But only from the nineteenth century onwards did scholars develop a truly scientific approach to language change and its description. During the Middle Ages various suggestions had been put forward with regard to language development, but religious prejudices frequently stood in the way of a correct understanding of historical processes; thus one widespread view was that all languages somehow descended from Hebrew. Then in his justly famous Anniversary Discourse of 2 February 1786 (published in *Asiatick Researches* 1.415–431 (1788)) Sir William Jones brought basic features of Sanskrit to the attention of western scholars. He contended that Sanskrit, Greek and Latin stem from a 'common source, which, perhaps, no longer exists' and surmised that Germanic and Celtic derive from the same source 'though blended with a very different idiom'. The first quarter of the nineteenth century then saw the development of a reliable methodology in genetic linquistics. The main point concerning language relationship can be phrased as follows: two or more languages are genetically related if they stem from a common ancestor; the fact and the degree of the relationship are established on the basis of deep-cutting structural agreements which cannot be due to chance. Sanskrit, Greek, Latin, Germanic, Celtic and a few other languages stem from a common proto-language, which is usually termed 'Indo-European' (in German *indogermanisch*). The aim of historical linguistics consists in following up the development of a given language through its history. This involves the study of texts in as far as records are available.

A good deal of what will be said in the following paragraphs is speculation. Linguistic reconstruction can hardly ever be 'proved'; only very rarely do further discoveries confirm the reconstructions at which scholars arrived on theoretical grounds. The variety of reconstructions and reconstruction systems available and currently used in Indo-European linguistics is quite baffling. It must nevertheless be stressed that the surface differences mainly result from differing interpretations of the material, whereas the underlying methodology of reconstruction is basically agreed upon. It is the purpose of the following pages to explain this common methodology.

The main concepts which underlie historical linguistics are the regularity of sound change and the systematic character of diachronic change in general. Once the genetic relationship obtaining between certain languages has been clarified, the common underlying language, which we term a proto-language, can be reconstructed. It is perhaps best to illustrate the methodology here with reference to one concrete example. A noun meaning 'father' is found in surprisingly similar shape in a number of languages: Old English *fæder*, Old Frisian *feder*, Old Saxon *fadar*, Old High German *fater*, Gothic *fadar*, Old Icelandic *faþir*. If we omit further details for the moment it should be quite clear that the similarity of these forms can hardly be due to chance. Rather the similarity is the result of the words stemming from one common ancestor. The ancestral form was used in a language not attested but reconstructed on the basis of such correspondences. This ancestral language is termed 'Germanic', also 'Proto-Germanic'. The Germanic form for 'father' can be assumed to have exhibited initial *f-*; further details of the word's form will be dealt with below. We can then confront this form with correspondences in other languages: Latin *pater*, Greek πατήρ, Sanskrit *pitár-*. These cognate forms show that the Germanic languages exhibit initial *f-* where other related languages have initial *p-*. We can assume that there is a sound rule according to which initial *p-* of the ancestral language of Germanic, Latin, Greek and Sanskrit became *f-* in Germanic.

The systematic investigation of cognate forms and the reconstruction of common ancestral forms culminated in the work of the 'first' generation of Indo-Europeanists, the outstanding scholars being Rasmus Rask (1787–1832), Franz Bopp (1791–1867) and Jacob Grimm (1785–1863). A major revolution in Indo-European studies occurred in the 1870s. One of the principles of the 'Neogrammarians' was the *Ausnahmslosigkeit der Lautgesetze* (sound laws do not suffer exceptions). Modern Indo-European studies still largely build on the foundations laid by scholars like Karl Brugmann (1849–1919), Hermann Osthoff (1847–1909), Eduard Sievers (1850–1932), Hermann Hirt (1865–1936) and Wilhelm Streitberg (1864–1925). As a result of the work of such towering figures as Jerzy Kuryłowicz (1895–1978) and Emile Benveniste (1902–77) the reconstruction of Indo-European has undergone major changes in this century. Yet no general reconstruction system is accepted by all specialists. It is the purpose of the following sections to point out what may be considered as reasonably safe and at least widely agreed upon.

2.2   The Germanic languages

The term 'Germanic' is used to describe a group of closely related languages which were spoken in southern Scandinavia and northern Germany in the first millennium before Christ. Major migrations in the course of the first centuries of our era brought about a considerable spread of these languages. This section will first give some information about the documentation available for the various Germanic languages; then an attempt at characterising the linguistic structure of Germanic will be made.

Our earliest Germanic material is available in the writings of classical authors. It goes without saying that stray onomastic elements and terms for special weapons or other tools found in Greek or, mainly, Latin authors are generally difficult to interpret and do not reveal much about the linguistic structure of Germanic. A second and very important source of information about early Germanic is provided by borrowings into Finnish, a non-Indo-European language. Apparently Finnish has changed little phonetically since that time, so that a form like *rengas* 'ring' is nowadays quite close to the Proto-Germanic form, from which it was borrowed; we reconstruct the form as Gmc *$xrengaz$ > *$xringaz$ (cf. OE *hring* 'ring'). But by far the most important source for reconstructing Proto-Germanic is available in the textual attestations of the individual Germanic languages, among which the early documentation claims our major attention. The individual Germanic languages will be enumerated here in a roughly chronological sequence according to their earliest attestations (see Figure 2.1).

It is likely that at the time of our earliest runic inscriptions all the Scandinavian languages, which in historical times clearly fall into two groups (West Norse and East Norse), were rather similar. The oldest runic inscriptions may date back to somewhere round the year AD 200,

	2 3 4 5 6 7 8 9 10 11 12 13 14 15 16 17 18 19 20
Gothic	———
Runic (Scand.)	———————
O Ic.	———————————————
O E	—————————————————————
O Fr.	———————————
O Sax.	———————————————
O H G	—————————————————

(the Arabic numerals refer to the centuries AD, 2=200, 3=300, etc.)

Figure 2.1 The Germanic languages and their documentation

but the texts are short and in many cases unclear. Extensive documentation in the separate Scandinavian languages is available from the eleventh century onwards, especially in Old Icelandic; 'Old Norse' is often, but incorrectly, used to refer to material from Old Icelandic. The most comprehensive corpus of material from the first half of the first millennium is the Gothic translation of parts of the Old and New Testaments. The translation was carried out in the second half of the fourth century under Bishop Wulfila (bishop of the Visigoths from 341–381/382/383). Gothic will mostly be quoted below as being reasonably close to Proto-Germanic. Crimean Gothic is attested in a vocabulary of eighty-six words written down by the Flemish diplomat Ogier Gislain of Busbecq in 1560–2.

The remaining Germanic languages, which are amply attested from the period before or around 1000, are usually grouped together as West Germanic. West Germanic is put into contrast with East Germanic (= Gothic) and North Germanic (= Scandinavian). In the early centuries of our era the differences between East Germanic, North Germanic and West Germanic were certainly quite clear. It is, however, a highly disputed question whether the threefold distinction among the Germanic languages is genetically justified, since both East Germanic and North Germanic and North Germanic and West Germanic show some agreements which render it likely that originally Germanic fell into just two groups, and one of these two groups underwent further splitting.

The main members of West Germanic are the following:

German divides up into a number of dialects; the earliest texts of Old High German are available from the eighth century.

Low German is available in texts from the ninth century (*Heliand* and *Genesis*) and somewhat earlier.

Old Frisian is available from the twelfth century onwards only and is thus contemporaneous with Middle English; Frisian is the closest cognate of English.

English is often grouped together with Frisian as Ingvaeonic on the assumption that both represent a special linguistic group within West Germanic. The earliest Old English texts date from around the year 700; runic inscriptions are somewhat earlier.

Since linguistic subgrouping can be carried out only on the basis of shared innovations, some of the traits which are peculiarly characteristic of Germanic and set Germanic off from all the related languages must be listed here. It is probably true to say that none of these characteristics is limited to Germanic; but the sum total of the traits to be mentioned is peculiar to Germanic. In the absence of any clear geographic or ethnic definition of what 'Germanic' means we must use linguistic means in this context. The aim of the following lines is to provide a general idea of what 'Proto-Germanic' was like.

Within the sound system it can be pointed out that the Germanic obstruants and spirants differ considerably from those of the closely related languages. Thus we find /f-/ in the initial position of the word for 'father', where Latin and Greek exhibit /p-/: Gmc *fader- (> OE fæder, Go. fadar, OHG fater), Lat. pater, Gk πατήρ. It will be shown below that the opposition of Gmc *f- to *p- in the majority of the Indo-European languages is not an isolated phenomenon. By the side of Gmc *f-:IE *p- we also find Gmc *þ-:IE *t- and Gmc *x-: IE *k-, so that the Germanic consonantism can be said to represent a structurally coherent development of voiceless stops > voiceless spirants. A structural peculiarity of this type clearly sets Germanic off from the remaining Indo-European languages with regard to the consonantism. A further feature typical of the Germanic sound system is presented by the accent, which was generally on the first syllable of words, whilst in Indo-European the accent could theoretically occur on any syllable of a given word. This retraction of the accent onto the first syllable had considerable further consequences. The vowels of non-initial syllables, which were unstressed henceforth, were weakened and could be lost; the first syllable of a word was given special prominence.

Whereas the system of the Germanic noun can be said to exhibit the same basic categories as the Indo-European noun, the adjective developed a twofold inflexional pattern in Proto-Germanic, which is usually called the 'strong' and the 'weak' adjective. The morphological difference between 'strong' and 'weak' adjectives carried a semantic distinction. A number of striking innovations occurred in the verbal system. The Indo-European verb had a three-way formal contrast of present – aorist – perfect, whose precise functions are hard to define. The Germanic verb, however, above all indicates 'tense', and the German rendering of 'verb' as 'Zeitwort' is therefore quite meaningful. In the Germanic verbal system two tenses are expressed, which may be termed the 'present' and the 'preterite'. The verbs of Germanic are split up into two major groups, called 'strong' and 'weak' verbs, and the criterion for this arrangement is provided by the formation of the preterite. 'Strong' verbs form their preterite by a change in the root vocalism; this change in the vocalism is termed 'ablaut'. The process is found down to the present period in examples like *sing*:*sang*, *ride*:*rode*, *get*:*got*. The basis for the 'strong' preterite is the Indo-European perfect (with perhaps some forms from the aorist system blended in). 'Weak' verbs attach a dental suffix to the unchanged root or stem found in the present. This process remains vigorous today. Thus the preterite of *knock* is *knocked*, by the side of *love* we find *loved*, and for *greet* we use *greeted*. The weak preterite is certainly an innovation of Germanic, whose precise origin is hardly clear.

Proto-Germanic also has a number of special lexical items. But the lexicon is usually less reliable in establishing linguistic relationship than phonology and morphology.

2.3 The Indo-European languages

That Latin was somehow related to Greek was a common assumption already in antiquity. But the usual view then was that Latin 'descended' from Greek. Only in the course of the nineteenth century was the correct relationship established: Latin and Greek are genetically related because they both descend from a common ancestor, namely Indo-European. There is no reason whatsoever for positing any particularly close relationship between Latin and Greek. Since Latin and Greek are the two Indo-European languages most widely known in European tradition, the examples in the following presentation will often be drawn from them. Nineteenth century scholarship was based on material from the following Indo-European languages: Indic (Sanskrit), Iranian, Armenian, Greek, Italic (Latin and the remaining Italic dialects, of which Oscan and Umbrian are the best known), Celtic, Germanic, Baltic, Slavic and Albanian. The authoritative account of Indo-European comparative grammar as developed in the nineteenth century is Brugmann's *Grundriss* (Brugmann 1897–1916).

At the beginning of the twentieth century two further languages (or language groups) became available to Indo-Europeanists, namely Anatolian and Tocharian. Of these two, Anatolian, whose most important member in this context is Hittite, had a particularly deep influence on Indo-European studies. Whereas nineteenth century Indo-Europeanists drew on material that did not stem from a period earlier than 1000 BC (at the utmost), Anatolian documents can be dated back to somewhere around 1800 BC. Surprisingly, Anatolian did not confirm many of the reconstructions that had been established on the basis of the Indo-Iranian and Greek material; on the contrary, Anatolian presented strong deviations in various respects. This gave rise to a new theory concerning the split-up of the proto-language. A number of scholars favoured the view that Anatolian (Hittite) was not a daughter language of Indo-European, but rather a sister in the sense that both Anatolian and Indo-European descended from one common language, which was termed Indo-Hittite. The debate is still going on. Subgrouping in general is a controversial subject in Indo-European studies. Whereas most authorities agree that Indic and Iranian go back to a special subgroup called 'Aryan', none of the other assumed proto-languages between Indo-European and the individual Indo-European languages has been widely agreed upon; Figure 2.2 gives a schematic representation of some of the possible arrangements of the Indo-European languages within the system of genetic trees.

Since the present chapter cannot deal with any of these controversies it was deemed best to explain the linguistic system of Old English within what has come to be called the Greco-Aryan model. This reconstruction model, although by no means uniformly accepted by all scholars, had gained a certain amount of adherence around the turn of the century, and it still remains the background for much creative work in Indo-European reconstruction. It is mainly based on the systematic agreements of the two oldest branches of Indo-European then available to scholars. Since a number of individual reconstructions of Indo-European forms will be given in the subsequent sections (above all in the section on historical phonology), it may be best to illustrate the various concepts scholars have had of Indo-European by quoting a piece of reconstructed text. The famous piece called 'eine Fabel in indogermanischer Ursprache' ('a fable in Indo-European') was published more than a century ago by August Schleicher and showed the main ideas scholars had concerning Indo-European around the middle of the nineteenth century. The fable was then 'up-dated' by Hirt in the

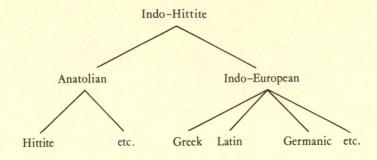

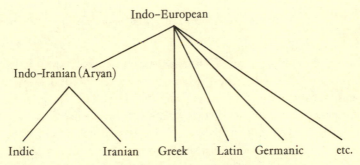

Figure 2.2 Schematic representation of the linguistic family tree

first half of our century, and a 'new version' was published by Lehmann
and Zgusta in 1979. The title '(das) Schaf und (die) Rosse' (the sheep
and the horses) and the concluding phrase 'Dies gehört-habend bog
(entwich) [das] schaf [auf das] feld (es machte sich aus dem staube)'
('having heard this, the sheep took flight into the plain') appear as
follows:

Schleicher (1868)	Hirt	Lehmann and Zgusta
avis akvāsas ka	*owis ek'wōses-kʷe*	*owis ekwōskʷe*
tat kukruvants avis	*tod k'ek'ruvos*	*tod kekluwōs*
agram ā bhugat	*owis ag'rom ebhuget*	*owis agrom ebhuget*

2.4   Historical phonology

The reconstruction of the Indo-European phonemic system is perhaps
the most controversial area in Indo-European studies at present. In
Figure 2.3 a listing is offered of the phonemes of Indo-European that
can be reached on the basis of equations of the type mentioned above:
The agreement between Skt *pitár-*, Gk πατερ-, Lat. *pater-* leads us

p	t	$\acute{k}$	k	k^w
ph	th	$\acute{k}$h	kh	k^wh
b	d	$\acute{g}$	g	g^w
bh	dh	$\acute{g}$h	gh	g^wh
w	s	y		
m	n, r,	l		
m̥	n̥, r̥,	l̥		

$$\breve{\bar{\imath}} \qquad\qquad\qquad\qquad \breve{\bar{u}}$$

$$\breve{\bar{e}} \qquad \partial \qquad \breve{\bar{o}}$$

$$\breve{\bar{a}}$$

Figure 2.3 The consonantal and vocalic phonemes of Indo-European

towards assuming that IE had a voiceless labial stop in the initial position of the word for 'father', a voiceless dental stop in medial position, and the stem ended in -r-. The main points of dispute concerning this system of consonants can be outlined as follows. The system is structurally 'unbalanced', because it has a very high number of stop consonants and only a single spirant (s). Within the system of the stop consonants it has been objected that the fourfold distinction of t – th – d – dh is actually found in Sanskrit only; we have thus no immediate evidence for ascribing the four series of stop consonants (voiceless: t, voiceless aspirate: th, voiced: d, voiced aspirate: dh) to the proto-language. But the reduction to t – dh – d, advocated by some scholars, is found objectionable on typological grounds, since a language that has the opposition t:d is likely to have a voiceless aspirate and not a voiced aspirate; typologically we would assume t:th:d rather than t:dh:d.

Perhaps the most deep-cutting innovations in twentieth century Indo-European studies centre around the concept of the 'laryngeal theory'. In its most widely accepted form the laryngeal theory states that Indo-European had three consonants, which may be represented as ∂_1, ∂_2 and ∂_3. The phoneme represented by ∂ in Figure 2.3 would then have to disappear from the sound system of Indo-European. These consonants, ∂_1, ∂_2 and ∂_3, should not be counted among the vowels. Since the laryngeals are assumed to have been consonants, a fairly widely adopted usage is to write h_1, h_2, h_3. It seems, however, that the consonantal value of h had no direct effect in Germanic. The most important development of the laryngeal(s) occurred in interconsonantal position, where vocalisation took place. In Germanic the result of vocalic ∂ is uniformly a.

Apart from these major points of dispute, many minor issues are controversial. For the present purposes it seems best to stick to a rather traditional account, however. The sound system of Indo-European as presented in Figure 2.3 results from systematic comparison of cognate lexical items in the individual languages. Only a fraction of the material (with emphasis on Sanskrit, Greek and Latin) can be presented here; the main purpose of the following sections consists in establishing the relationship between Germanic phonemes and their Indo-European starting-points.

2.4.1   Consonants

Indo-European had five voiceless stops:

/p/: IE *pətér- 'father' (Skt pitár-, Av. pitar-, Arm. hayr (IE p- > h- in Armenian), Gk πατήρ, OIr. athir (initial p- was lost in Celtic), Gmc *fader- (> Go. fadar, OE fæder, OSax. fadar, OHG fater))

/t/: IE *treyes 'three' (Skt tráyas, Gk τρεῖς, Lat. trēs (< *treyes with loss of intervocalic -y-), OIr. tri, Gmc *þrijiz̦ (> Go. þreis, OE þrīe))

/k̑/: IE *k̑m̥tóm 'hundred' (Skt śatám (IE k̑ > Skt ś), Av. satəm (IE k̑ > Av. s), Gk ἑκατόν (ἑ- is due to a secondary innovation), Lat. centum, OIr. cét, Welsh kant, Lith. šim̃tas (IE k̑ > Balt. š), OCS sŭto (IE k̑ > Slavic s, but the origin of -ŭ- is unclear), Gmc *hund- (> Go. hund, OE hund))

/k/: IE *krewə- 'raw flesh' (Skt kravís, Skt krūrá- 'bloody' = Av. xrūra- (from IE *kruə- > *krū-), Gk κρέας, Lat. cruor, Lith. kraũjas 'blood' (< *krewə-yo- or *krowə-yo-), Gmc *hraw-a- (> OHG hrō, OS hrā, OE hrēaw, ON hrár) < IE *krowə-o-). Note: Some of the forms quoted here show an alternation in the root vocalism termed 'ablaut', which will be dealt with further on; it should be noted that the root consonantism is stable in ablauting forms.

/kʷ/: IE *kʷis/*kʷey 'who?', also *kʷo- (Skt ki- (interrogative stem), Skt kas 'who?', Lat. quis, Osc. pís, píd, OIr. cia 'who?', cid 'what?', W pwy (IE *kʷ became p in Oscan and British, but in Irish k resulted from *kʷ with loss of the labial part), Lith. kàs, OCS kŭto 'who?', Gmc *hwaz̦ (> Go. hwas, OHG hwer, OE hwā))

The evidence for five voiceless aspirated stops is uneven; the following examples may be offered:

/ph/: IE *phol- 'fall' (It must be stressed that this root is quite uncertain, but the following points should be mentioned. Arm. p'lanim 'I fall' cannot have had p- because IE *p- > Arm. h- (cf. hayr 'father').

The remaining cognates, besides not being absolutely certain, may have had initial *p*-: Lith. *pùlti* 'fall' and Gmc **falla-* (> Go. *fallan*, OE *feallan*). Gmc **fall-* may also be connected with IE **pet-* 'fall', the immediate preform would be **pot-lo-* > Gmc **fadla-* > (assimilation) **falla-*. Other possible examples for IE *ph* have initial *s-* (*s* mobile), e.g. Skt *sphū́rjati* 'rumbles', Gk σφαραγέομαι 'rattle'.)

/th/: IE **ponthēs-* 'way' (Skt *panthās* (gen. *pathas*), Av. *pantā* (gen. **paθō* < *pṇthas*), Gk πόντος 'sea', Arm. *hown* 'ford', Lat. *pons* 'bridge', OCS *pǫtĭ* 'way'. The word is not directly inherited in Germanic, but Gmc **paþa-* (> OE *pæþ* 'path') may represent a borrowing from Iranian.)

/ḱh/: IE **skhid-* 'cut up' (Gk σχίζω 'I cut up', Skt *chinatti* (< **ḱhi-ne-d-ti*) 'he cuts'; the other languages show forms that may go back to *sk-*, e.g. Lat. *scindere* 'tear', Lith. *skíesti* 'separate', Gmc **skīt-a-* 'cacare' (> OE *scītan*).)

/kh/: IE *ḱā́khā* 'plough' (The reconstructed form **ḱākhā* is perhaps indicated by Skt *śā́khā* 'branch' and Go. *hoha* 'plough'.)

Most of the voiced stops of Indo-European are attested by a number of excellent equations. On structural grounds we posit five voiced stops, but it must be pointed out that the material allowing the reconstruction of /b/ is extremely weak.

/b/: no clear evidence (A reasonably good case for the occurrence of /b/ can be seen in the present formation of the root for 'drink'. The root is to be posited as IE **pō-* (Skt [aorist] *á-pā-t*). The thematic present was formed by reduplication: **pi-b-e-ti* (reduplication (consisting of root-initial consonant *p*- + reduplicating vowel *-i-*) + root initial consonant *p*, which was voiced to *-b-*, + thematic vowel *-e-* + person marker for 3 sg.) is found in Skt *pibati*, OIr. *ibid* (*p*- was lost in Celtic) and Lat. *bibit* (initial *p*- was assimilated in voice to *-b-*). No matter how the intervocalic *-b-* in IE **pibeti* is ultimately explained, it must be secondary, since it is identical with the root-initial *p*-. In Germanic, the phoneme /p/, which would be the regular continuation of /b/ is quite frequent. A root **dheub-* (meaning 'deep, hollow') has been assumed to underlie the following words: Gaulish *dubno-* 'world' (cf. OIr. *domain* 'world') in *Dubno-rix* 'world-king', Lith. *dubùs* 'deep', Gmc *deupa-* (> OE *dēop* 'deep').)

/d/: IE **déḱm̥(t)* 'ten' (Skt *dáśa*, Av. *dasa*, Gk δέκα, Lat. *decem*, OIr. *deich*, W *deg*, Gmc **tehun* (> Go. *taihun*))

/ǵ/: IE **ǵeus-* 'taste' (Skt *juṣáte* 'enjoys' (< IE **ǵus-e-toi*), Av. *zaoš-*, OPers. *daus-* (IE *ǵ-* > Skt *j-*, Av. *z-*, OPers. *d-*), Gk γεύομαι 'I enjoy', Lat.

gustus 'tasting', Gmc **keus-a-* (> Go. *kiusan* 'examine', OE *cēosan* 'choose'))

/g/ : IE **yugóm* 'yoke' (Skt *yugá-*, Gk ζυγόν, Lat. *iugum*, Gmc **juk-a-* (> Go. *juk*, OE *geoc*))

/g^w/ : IE **g^{w}em-* 'go, come' (Skt (aorist) *agan* 'he went' (< IE **e- g^{w}em-t*), Gk βάσκε 'go' (imperative of present **g^{w}m̥-ske-*), Lat. *venīre* 'come' (IE **g^w-* > Lat. *v-*), Gmc **kwem-* (> Go. *qiman*, OE *cuman* 'come'))

Indo-European had five voiced aspirated stops. They are unitary phonemes, just as the voiceless aspirated stops /ph/, /th/ etc. are unitary phonemes. The transliteration as *b^h*, *d^h*, etc. widely used nowadays has therefore a good deal to recommend itself, above all since it allows the distinction between the sequence **-d- + -h-* (= consonant + laryngeal) and the unitary phonemes **d^h*, etc. But the traditional representation as *bh*, *dh*, *ǵh*, *gh* and *g^{w}h* is kept here.

/bh/ : IE **bher-* 'carry' (Skt *bhárati* 'he carries', Av. *baraiti*, Gk φέρω, Lat. *ferō*, OIr. *biru*, Gmc **ber-a-* (> Go. *bairan*, OE *beran*))

/dh/ : IE **dhē-* 'place' (Skt *dádhāti* 'he places', Av. *dadāitī* < IE **dhe-dhē-ti* (reduplicating present; in words with two succeeding aspirates in syllable initial position the first loses aspiration by dissimilation: **dh-dh-* > *d-dh-* (Grassmann's law)), Gk τίθημι (both Aryan and Greek have a reduplicating present, but in Greek the reduplicating vowel is *-i-*; in **dhi-dhē-mi* a breath dissimilation similar to the one found in Skt *dádhāti* occurred, but it took place after the peculiarly Greek change of *dh* > *th*), Lat. *faciō*, *fēcī* (IE *dh* > Lat. *f-*; both present *faciō* < **dhə-k-* and perfect *fēcī* exhibit an extension in *-k-*), Lith. *déti* 'put', OCS *děti*, Gmc **dē-* (in nominal formations, e.g. **dē-di* (> OE *dæd* 'deed', OHG *tāt*)), **dō-* (in the verb OE *dōn* 'do', OHG *tuon*))

/ǵh/ : IE *weǵh-* 'move' (Skt *vahati*, Av. *vazaiti*, Gk (Pamphylian) Fεχέτω 'let him bring', Lat. *vehō*, OIr. *fēn* 'cart' (< **weǵh-no-*), Gmc **weg-a-* (> Go. *ga-wigan*, ON *vega* 'move', OE *wegan*))

/gh/ : IE **steigh-* 'go' (Skt *stighnóti* 'goes', Gk στείχω, OIr. *tíagu* 'I go', Gmc **stīg-a-* (> Go. *steigan*, OE, OHG *stīgan*))

/g^{w}h/ : IE **g^{w}hen-* 'beat' (Hitt. *kuenzi* 'he kills' (root present **g^{w}hen-ti*), Skt *hánti*, Av. *jainti*, Gk θείνω (< **g^{w}hen-yō*), OIr. *gonim* 'I kill', Lith. *genù giñti* 'drive cattle', OCS *ženǫ gunati*, Gmc **gw(e)n-* (reflexes of this root can be found in Go. **gunþ-* 'battle' > OE *gūþ*, but perhaps also in **ban-an-* 'murderer' > OE *bana*; the reflexes of **g^{w}h* in Germanic pose problems))

If the consonantal phonemes reconstructed in the preceding para-

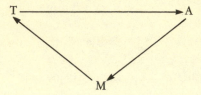

Figure 2.4 Schematic representation of the consonant shift in Pre-Germanic

graphs had the phonetic values of the corresponding Sanskrit phonemes, then the consonantal system of Indo-European underwent considerable change in the course of its development into Germanic. If the phonetic properties of the Indo-European phonemes differed, then the description of the development from Indo-European to Germanic would have to be revised. The traditional account assumes a shift in the consonantism, often termed Grimm's Law. The mechanism of this consonant shift can be described as follows. The voiceless stop consonants become voiceless spirants: $p > f$, $t > þ$, $k > h$, $k^w > hw$. The voiceless aspirated stop consonants fell together with the voiceless stops and became voiceless spirants; from the point of view of Germanic, the two series cannot be distinguished. The voiced stop consonants became voiceless: $b > p$, $d > t$, $g > k$, $g^w > kw$. The voiced aspirated consonants first became voiced spirants. At least in some positions they became the corresponding voiced stop consonants. The following rules can tentatively be set up: $bh > \beta > b$, $dh > \delta > d$, $gh > \gamma > g$, $g^wh > \gamma w > g$, w (b?). In Figure 2.4 a simplified picture is drawn up to show the mechanism of the Germanic consonant shift.

T stands for tenuis (= voiceless stops, but these include also the voiceless aspirated stops), **A** stands for aspirated (the assumption is that the tenues were first aspirated and then became spirants, but **A** also means aspirated stops of the type IE *bh*, and these are the precursors of the Germanic voiced stops at least in some cases), **M** stands for media (and means in this context voiced stops). The complicated process of the Germanic consonant shift can be visualized as follows:

> IE **T** (e.g. *t*) > Gmc **A** (*þ*)
> IE **A** (e.g. *dh*) > Gmc **M** (*d*)
> IE **M** (e.g. *d*) > Gmc **T** (*t*)

The basic correspondences of Germanic consonants as outlined above were known to scholars throughout the nineteenth century. But a surprisingly high number of exceptions caused considerable difficulties. Thus the word for 'brother' can be assumed to have had -*t*- in intervocalic position on the basis of clear correspondences like Lat. *frāter*, Skt *bhrā́tar*-, and Gk φράτηρ; the voiceless spirant found in Go. *broþar* (voicing of intervocalic *þ* in OE *brōþor* is secondary) is consequently quite regular. But the words for 'father' and 'mother' clearly also exhibited -*t*- (cf. Skt *pitár*-, Gk πατήρ, Lat. *pater*, Skt *mātár*-, Gk μήτηρ, Lat. *māter*), and yet the Germanic cognates have -*d*- in medial position (OE *faeder*, *mōdor* (-*t*- in OHG *fater*, *muoter* is due to a secondary development of -*d*- > -*t*-)). This baffling discrepancy was explained by Karl Verner in a famous paper published in 1877. The regulation has ever since been referred to as Verner's Law. According to Verner's Law voiceless stops of Indo-European, which regularly yielded voiceless spirants in Germanic, became voiced if the accent in Indo-European was not on the immediately preceding syllable. Thus -*t*- in IE *pətér- appeared as δ in Germanic in contrast to -*t*- in IE **bhrā́ter*-, which led to -*þ*-.

The only spirant which is assumed for the consonantal system of Indo-European is /s/. The spirant /s/ is basically kept unchanged in Proto-Germanic. But it took part in the voicing process ruled by Verner's Law. Thus we find an alternation of /s/:/z/ in Germanic, which reflects the original position of the accent. Gmc /z/ yielded /r/ in intervocalic position in Old English (rhotacism, for the process compare Lat. *flōs*/*flōris* 'flower'), but in final position it is generally lost. The paradigm of the verb for 'choose' has the following stem forms in Old English: *cēosan*, *cēas*, *curon*, *coren*, which go back to Gmc *keus-:*kaus-: *kuz-. The underlying root is IE *géus-, which is reflected in Gmc *keus-, whereas Gmc *kaus- goes back to the ablauting form IE *góus- (with *o*-grade), and Gmc *kuz- represents yet another ablaut grade, namely the zero-grade IE *gus-' (with unstressed root).

The sound correspondences described so far provide an excellent example for the regularity of sound change. One major set of apparent exceptions was eliminated by the discovery of Verner's Law, and a few minor details may also be mentioned. The voiceless stop consonants (together with the voiceless aspirated stop consonants) undergo no change in the course of their development into Germanic when they are preceded by *s*-, thus *sp*-, *st*-, and *sk*- remain unchanged: *standan-, the Germanic verb for 'stand' (OE *standan*), exhibits the initial group *st*- found in Lat. *stāre*. Furthermore it must be noted that in a sequence of two stop consonants only the first is shifted and the second remains. This phenomenon can mostly be observed in medial position: a form corresponding to Lat. *captus* (formation in -*to*- from root *kap*-) is found in Gmc **hafta*- (> OE *hæft* 'captive'). Clearly only the first consonant in the group -*p*-*t*- is shifted. Finally it has to be pointed out that a group of two dentals always yields -*ss*- in Germanic; thus the *to*-formation belonging to the root **sed*- 'sit' can be posited as IE **sed-to*- > **setto*- and led to Gmc **sessa*- > OE *sess* 'seat, bench'. Loanwords, which entered the language only after the respective sound change was over, do not show the effects. Thus Gmc **paþa*- 'path' is probably ultimately due to borrowing from Iranian *paþ*-, and the initial consonant is not shifted.

2.4.2   Resonants and semivowels

In addition to the stop consonants and the spirant /s/, Indo-European had six further consonants, which have closely related vocalic correspondences. They are termed resonants and semivowels: *m, n, r, l, j, w* function as consonants, whereas *m̥, n̥, r̥, l̥, i, u* function as vowels. Furthermore there was at least one sound which was similar to the spirants and tended to vocalisation; this sound will be termed 'laryngeal'. This section will illustrate the consonantal value of these phonemes, their vocalic realisation will be dealt with subsequently.

The six consonants *m, n, r, l, j* and *w* can be exemplified as follows:

/m/: IE **māter*- 'mother' (Skt *mātár*- 'mother', Av. *mātar*-, Arm. *mayr*, Gk μήτηρ, Lat. *māter*, OIr. *máthair*, Gmc **mōder*- (> OE *mōdor*, OHG *muoter*))

/n/: IE **nomn̥* 'name' (Skt *nāma* 'name', Av. *nāma*, Arm. *anun*, Gk ὄνομα, Lat. *nōmen*, OIr. *ainm*, Gmc **naman*- (> Go. *namo*, OE *nama*))

/r/: IE **rḗǵ-s* 'king' (Skt *rāj*- 'king' (*rāj-an*- is extended by -*an*-), Lat. *rēx* (< **rēg-s*), OIr. *rí* (< **rēg-s* (IE *ē* yielded *ī* in Celtic); the Germanic stem **rīk*- in Go. *reiks* 'ruler', OE *rīce* 'kingdom' has often been explained as due to borrowing from Celtic **rīg*- with substitution of Gmc -*k*- for -*g*-))

/l/: IE **leudh*- 'grow' (Skt *ródhati* 'grows, rises' (Skt *r* continues IE *l*), Av. *raoδaiti*, Gk ἐλεύθερος 'free' (adjectival formation in -*ero*- from root **leudh*-, the prothetic vowel *e*- is due to a specially Greek development), Lat. *līberī* 'children', Gmc **leud-a*- (> Go. *liudan*, OHG *liotan* 'grow'))

/j/: IE **jugóm* 'yoke' (cf. above under /g/)

/w/: IE **wīró*- 'man' (Skt *vīrá*- 'man', Av. *vīra*-, and Lith. *výras* point back to a proto-form **wīró*-, whereas Lat. *vir*, OIr. *fer*, and Gmc **wer-a*- (> Go. *wair*, OE *wer*) indicate a starting-point **wiro*- with short

-*i*-. The noun *wiro*- is probably to be analysed as a *ro*-formation from a root (zero-grade) *wī*-.)

The most controversial phoneme in the Indo-European sound system as offered in Figure 2.3, is ə; this phoneme was formerly assumed to be a vowel. The underlying reasoning can be briefly summed up as follows. If we confront Skt *pitár*- with Lat. *pater*, it is immediately clear that the vowel following upon /p-/ cannot have been /-i-/ in Indo-European since /i/ was kept unchanged in Latin, nor can it have been /-a-/, because /a/ was kept unchanged in Sanskrit. Consequently it was assumed that the phoneme following /p-/ in the Indo-European word for 'father' was yet another vowel, which was represented by ə and referred to as 'schwa' (the term 'schwa' is taken from Hebrew grammar). In the course of the twentieth century the position and interpretation of 'ə' has stood in the centre of prolonged research and discussion. The main points of dispute can be outlined as follows. There are strong indications that 'ə' originally had consonantal value(s). For historical reasons the term 'laryngeal(s)' is used to describe these sounds. It was furthermore argued that the comparative material points to the existence of more than one 'ə', although no agreement as to the precise number of these phonemes was reached. The most influential scholars in Indo-European, however, tend towards positing three laryngeals. As a result of the prolonged dispute, different transcription systems are now in use. Thus the laryngeal(s) can be represented as φ_1, φ_2, φ_3, or h_1, h_2, h_3 or $\hbar_1$, $\hbar_2$, $\hbar_3$. For the present purposes some simplification may be justified in view of the complexity of the question. Furthermore Germanic does not offer any strong evidence in favour of the view that the distinction between three (or more) laryngeals was phonemically relevant in its prehistory. There is no support for the view that the consonantal value of the laryngeal(s) was kept in Germanic. Therefore it is reasonable to use the traditional sign 'ə' in our reconstructions. In as far as ə was kept during the development into Germanic it became vocalised and fell together with the reflexes of IE /a/ and /o/.

2.4.3   Vowels

In the early period of Indo-European studies it was thought that the vocalic system of Sanskrit was particularly close to that of the proto-language. Consequently the system of short vowels was reconstructed as having exhibited *i*, *a* and *u*. But by the second half of the nineteenth century the Sanskrit system was shown to be due to secondary innovations in that IE *e*, *a* and *o* had merged in one phoneme /a/. The most direct testimony for the Indo-European vocalism can be found in Greek, where ε, α and ο frequently reflect the vowels *e*, *a* and *o* of the proto-language undisturbed. Apart from the equations to be given below, the fact that *e* and *o* were phonemically distinct in the proto-language can be deduced from ablaut relations. Thus the reduplicating perfect of the root *g^wem-* had the *o*-grade *g^wom-* preceded by the reduplicating syllable *g^we-* in the singular: *g^w-* of the basic form IE *g^we-g^wom-e* 'he has gone' is reflected as -*g*- before -*ā*- from IE -*o*-, but as *j*- before -*a*- from IE -*e*- in Skt (perf.) *jagā́ma*, so that the difference of the vowels *e/o* can indirectly be inferred from the difference of the consonantal development. The following sections will present material for the short vowels, the long vowels, vocalic nasals and liquids, and diphthongs. Finally ablaut phenomena will be briefly dealt with.

The equations between the related lexical items evidence the following five short vowels for the proto-language: *i*, *e*, *a*, *o*, *u*. A sixth vowel is indicated for pre-Germanic; it arose from vocalisation of ə.

/i/: IE *wid-* 'know, see' (Skt *vid-má* (1 pl. perf., without reduplication) 'we know', Gk ἴδμεν, (infinitive aorist) ἰδεῖν 'see', Lat. *videō* 'I see', OIr. (*ro*)*finnadar* 'gets to know, finds out' (< *wi-n-d-n-*), Gmc *wit-* (> Go., OE *witan*, OHG *wizzan*)).

/e/: IE *és-ti* '(he) is' (Skt *ásti*, Gk ἐστί, Lat. *est*, Gmc *ist(i)* (> Go. *ist*, OE *is*))

/a/: IE *áǵ-e-ti* '(he) leads, drives' (3 sg. of thematic present of root *aǵ-*; *áǵ-e-ti* consists of root *aǵ-* + thematic vowel -*e*- + person marker -*ti* for 3 sg. present indicative) Skt *ájati* 'he drives', Av. *azaiti*, Gk ἄγει, Lat. *agit*, OIr. (*ad-*)*aig*, Gmc *ak-a-* (> ON *aka*))

/o/: IE *ówis* 'sheep' (Skt *avis*, Gk ὄϊς, Lat. *ovis*, Lith. *avìs*, OCS *ovica*, Gmc *awi-* (> OE *eowu*, OSax. *ewi*, OHG *ouwi*, cf. Go. *awistr* 'sheep pen')). Note: OE *eowu* has secondarily switched its declension class; the regularly expected form would be OE *ewe*. For the proto-form Luvian *hawi-* indicates an initial laryngeal: IE *howi-*.

/u/: IE *médhu* 'honey' (Skt *mádhu* 'sweet drink, honey', Gk μέθυ, OIr. *mid*, Lith. *medùs*, Gmc *medu-* (> ON *mjǫþr*, OE *me(o)du*, OHG *metu*)).

IE/ə/: IE *pətér-* (see above under /p/).

2.4.4   Vocalic resonants

The resonants which were enumerated above function as consonants in word-initial position. They also function as consonants in the sequence *TeRC*, where *e* is the vocalic kernel, *T* and *C* are any two stop consonants, and *R* stands for *m, n, r, l*. If by the process of ablaut -*e*- is absent in a root of the structure *TeRC*, then -*R*- in the sequence *TRC*- assumes vocalic function. R̥ (R̥ = *m, n, r, l*) represents the resonants in vocalic function. In the development to Germanic, R̥ yielded *u*R, as can be seen from the following equations.

/m̥/ : IE **km̥tóm* 'hundred' (material above under *ḱ*)

/n̥/ : IE **tn̥*- (zero-grade of *ten- 'stretch') (Skt *tatá*- 'extended' (*to*-formation IE **tn̥-tó*-), Gk τατός, Lat. *tentus* (IE **n̥* > Lat. *en*), OIr. *tét* 'string' (< IE **tn̥-tā*), Gmc *þun-n-i (> ON *þunnr* 'thin', OE *þynne*, OSax., OHG *thunni*))

/r̥/ : IE **wr̥t*- (zero-grade of *wert- 'turn') (Skt *vr̥ttá*-, Lat. *vorsus*, *versus* (< IE **wr̥t-to*- (IE *-*t-t*- > Lat. -*ss*-)), Gmc *wurd- (weak alternant in perfect, e.g. OE *wurdon* 'we became'))

/l̥/ : IE **wl̥kʷos* 'wolf' (Skt *vr̥kas*, Gk λύκος, Lat. *lupus*, Gmc *wulfaz (> Go. *wulfs*, ON *ulfr*, OE *wulf*, OHG *wolf*))

The phonemes traditionally posited as m̥̄, n̥̄, r̥̄, l̥̄ can be viewed as m̥ə, n̥ə, r̥ə, l̥ə (= m̥h₁,₂,₃, etc.) within the framework of the laryngeal theory. The reflexes of IE m̥h₁,₂,₃, etc. are identical with those of IE m̥, etc. in Germanic.

2.4.5   Long vowels and diphthongs

The equations given below allow us to set up the following long vowels for the proto-language: *ī, ē, ā, ō, ū*. But the status of the individual long vowels within the morphonological system of Indo-European differs a good deal.

/ī/ : IE *-*īno*- is a suffixal element found in Lat. *su-īna* (*caro*) 'pork' (derived from *sūs* 'swine') and recurs in Gmc *swīna- (> Go. *swein*, OSax., OHG, OE *swīn*)

/ē/ : IE *rēǵ-s 'king' (the comparative material was given above, see 'resonants and semi-vowels')

/ā/ : IE *māter- 'mother' (Skt *mātar*-, Gk μήτηρ, Lat. *māter*, OIr. *máthair*, Lith. *mótė* 'wife', OCS *mati* (stem *mater*-), Gmc *mōder- (> OE *mōdor*, OHG *muoter*))

/ō/ : IE *dō- 'give' (Skt *dádāmi* (reduplicating present), Gk δίδωμι (<

di-dō-mi, also reduplicating present, but -*i*- in reduplication), Lat. *dōnum* 'gift', Lith. *dúoti* 'give', OCS *dati* 'give', *darŭ* 'gift')

/ū/: IE *mūs* 'mouse' (Skt *mūs-*, Gk μῦς, Lat. *mūs*, Gmc *mūs-* (> OE, OHG, ON *mūs*))

The diphthongs of Indo-European can be interpreted as sequences of *e*, *a*, or *o* + *i* or *u*. Furthermore the sequences of *e*, *a*, *o* + R can also function as diphthongs. The following equations can be offered for the basic diphthongs *ei*, *ai*, *oi*, *eu*, *au*, *ou*.

/ei/: IE *bheid-* 'split' (Skt *bhedāmi* (aorist subjunctive < *bheid-o-*, the archaic present is formed by a nasal infix, Skt *bhinádmi* 'I split'), Gk φείδομαι 'I spare', Gmc *bīt-a-* (> Go. *beitan* 'bite', OE *bītan*, OHG *bīʒʒan*))

/ai/: IE *kaikos* 'one-eyed, squinting' (Skt *kekara-* squinting' (not certainly connected), Lat. *caecus* 'blind', OIr. *caech*, Gmc *haih-a-* (> Go. *haihs* 'one-eyed'))

/oi/: IE *le-loik^w-e* 'he has left' (perfect of root *leik^w-*) (Skt *rireca* (*i* in reduplication is due to an innovation), Gk λέλοιπε, Gmc (with loss of reduplication) *laihw* (> Go. *laihw*))

/eu/: IE *bheudh-* 'be aware' (Skt *bodhati* 'is aware', Av. *baoδaite*, Gk πεύθομαι 'notice', Gmc *beud-a-* (> Go. *ana-biudan* 'order', OE *bēodan*, OHG *biotan*))

/au/: IE *aug-* 'increase' (Skt (comparative) *ójīyas-* 'stronger', Lat. *augēo* 'increase', Gk αὐξάνω, Lith. *áugti* 'grow', Gmc *auk-a-* (> Go. *aukan* 'increase', OE (past participle) *ēacen* 'pregnant'))

/ou/: IE *louk-o-* 'clearing' (*louk-o-* is a nominal formation from the root *leuk-* 'shine'; in this nominal formation the root appears in *o*-grade; Skt *loká-* 'free space, world', Lat. *lūcus* 'grove', Lith. *laûkas* 'field', Gmc *lauh-a-* (> OHG *lōh*)).

Although at a given point, the sequences *ei*, etc. probably consisted of *e* + consonantal *j*, the 'diphthongs' *ei*, *eu*, *ai*, *au*, *oi*, *ou* certainly had phonemic status in the period preceding the emergence of Germanic.

It will have been noticed that in Indo-European 'roots' the consonantal skeleton is stable, whereas alternation in the vocalism is found within certain morphologically describable limits. This alternation in the root vocalism is usually referred to as 'ablaut' (sometimes translated as 'apophony'). The precise reasons for the rise of ablaut are unknown, but at least partly ablaut is connected with the movement of the accent. Indo-European was a language with so-called 'free' accent, in other words the accent is not predictable in a given word. Thus the accent was on the second syllable in the word for 'father' (IE *pətér-* >

Gk πατήρ, etc.), whereas the word for 'brother' had initial stress (IE *bhráter- > Skt bhrátar-). In Germanic accent was uniformly retracted to the initial syllable of words, but Verner's Law still shows the effect of the original accent position. Of the two types of ablaut to be described in this subsection, quantitative ablaut may be connected with accent, but we still lack a reasonable explanation for the rise of qualitative ablaut.

The basic type of qualitative ablaut can be described as an alternation of *e* and *o*. The *e*-alternation is called the normal grade (also *e*-grade); *o* represents the qualitative ablaut in the sense that the vowel quality is changed. This is the type of ablaut most frequently encountered. Lat. *tegō* 'I cover' contains the verbal root *teg-* in the *e*-grade. The noun *toga* (a garment) exhibits the *o*-grade of the root *teg-* followed by a suffixal element *-ā*. The stem *tog-ā* (final *-ā* was shortened in Lat. *toga*) originally had abstract meaning ('a covering') but was then used in concrete sense referring to a garment. Apart from the *e/o*-ablaut, all other types of qualitative ablaut are less clear and of minor importance.

The most frequently encountered type of quantitative ablaut consists of the absence of the vowel *e* found in *e*-grade. A root of the type IE *leikʷ-* appears in zero-grade *likʷ-*, and it is quite reasonable that the incidence of zero-grade is intimately linked to the absence of accent on the root. The *to*-formation IE *likʷ-tó-* (> Skt *rik-tá-*), which had a function comparable to the past participle, had the accent on *-ó-* and may thus have 'caused' the reduction of the diphthong *-ei-* in *e*-grade *leikʷ-*. In roots exhibiting the structure *TeiC-*, the zero-grade regularly appears as *TiC-*. Roots of the structure *TeRC-* exhibit vocalization of *-R-* in the zero-grade *TR̥C-*. Theoretically zero-grade would be expected to occur with all roots under corresponding morphological conditions. But in roots of the structure *TeC-* (*e*-grade vowel followed by a consonant which cannot assume vocalic function, i.e. a stop consonant or *s*), the regularly expected zero-grade *TC-* is found only rarely. A relevant example is the word for 'nest', which is to be reconstructed as IE *ni-sd-ó-* and contains the zero-grade of the root *sed-* 'sit' (a 'nest' is the place where a bird 'sits down'): IE *ni-sd-ó-* was phonetically realized as [nizdo-] and is found in Skt *nīḍa-* 'resting place' and Lat. *nīdus*; Gmc *nesta-* (> OE, OHG *nest*) is the regular continuation of IE *ni-sd-o-* [*nizdo-*]. But apart from such isolated items, in which the zero-grade root occurred in word-medial position, the zero-grade of *TeC*-roots was generally replaced by *e*-grade through analogy. Thus the past participle of Gmc *set-ja-* 'sit' might be expected to exhibit zero-grade of the root (cf. past participle Gmc *rid-ana- > OE ge-riden, infinitive rīdan), but in fact we find Gmc *set-ana- > OE seten (with e-grade). In a number of forms we find a lengthening of the basic vowel or of the qualitative ablaut of the basic vowel. Both ē and ō are found in certain categories of Indo-European nominal (and perhaps verbal) formations. The precise origin of this 'lengthened' grade is unclear in most cases. The root noun for 'foot' (root *ped-) appears with -ē- in Lat. pēs (< *pēd-s), but Germanic *fōt- in all probability indicates a nominative IE *pṓd-s (cf. Skt pā́t), which must also have occurred in this paradigm.

The Germanic innovations in the vocalic system were hardly less deep-cutting than those concerning the consonantism. Some of the most important changes will be briefly enumerated here with, as far as possible, reference to the material as given above.

The accent was uniformly retracted to the first syllable of words. As a consequence of the then general initial stress unstressed syllables tended towards weakening. By the time of Old English, medial and final syllables had already undergone considerable reduction, in Modern English they are widely lost.

The vowels /a/ and /o/ fell together as /a/ in Germanic; IE /ə/, when vocalised, also yielded /a/ (IE *aǵ- > Gmc *ak-, IE *howis > Gmc *awiz, IE *pətér- > Gmc *fader-).

The vowels /ā/ and /ō/ fell together as /ō/ in Germanic (IE *māter- > Gmc *mōder-, IE *dhō- (o-grade of *dhē-) > Gmc *dō-).

A new long monophthong usually termed ē² arose in the early history of Germanic. This phoneme is found in some isolated lexical items like the adverb Gmc *hē²r 'here' and in the preterite of a number of verbs of class VII. It is most likely that ē² is due to an innovation, but the precise origin of this phoneme is unclear.

The diphthong ei was monophthongized to ī, the other diphthongs remained unchanged (IE *bheid- > Gmc *bīt-).

The short monophthongs /e/ and /i/ remained basically unchanged, but a good deal of overlapping occurred because /e/ merged with /i/ if i/j followed in the next syllable, and /i/ was lowered to /e/ before /a/ of the following syllable (IE *ni-sd-o- > Gmc *nesta-); but /i/ and /e/ clearly had phonemic status in Germanic.

The inherited patterns of ablaut were kept and even elaborated in the verbal system; the preterite and past participle of strong verbs regularly exhibit ablaut.

2.5 Historical morphology

Morphology deals with the changes a given word undergoes when used in a concrete chain of speech. Morphology is subdivided into inflexion and derivation. Inflexion is subdivided into declension and conjugation. Conjugation deals with the changes verbal forms undergo in certain syntactic contexts, whereas declension analyses the changes exhibited by nouns, pronouns, numerals and adjectives. Derivation, also referred to as word-formation, describes the patterns according to which new lexical units can be created in a language on the basis of the existing lexical stock. In view of the enormous complexity found in the pronominal forms, the brief overview of historical morphology presented in the following lines will be concerned with the noun, the adjective and the verb only.

2.5.1 The noun

An Indo-European noun can be analysed as consisting of three constituent parts: the root element is followed by one or more stem-forming elements ($\emptyset$ is also a possible stem-forming element), and the stem precedes the marker(s) for case and number. In theory we would expect the markers for case and number to be analysable into an element which indicates the number and another which indicates the case; in practice this distinction is carried through only rarely. The Germanic and hence the Old English nominal system is the regular continuation of the underlying Indo-European morphological patterns. For Indo-European we can postulate a noun $*w\underline{l}k^w$-o-s 'wolf', which consists of a root element $w\underline{l}k^w$-, a stem-forming suffix $*$-o-, and a marker $*$-s for nominative singular. Lat. *lupus* is the continuation of the o-stem $*w\underline{l}k^w$-o-s, but by classical times final $*$-os had developed into Latin -us. Since IE $*o$ became $*a$ in Germanic, the reflex of IE $*w\underline{l}k^w$-o-s is $*wulf$-a-$ʒ$ (the reflex of IE $*k^w$- is regularly Gmc $*hw$-, but apparently -hw- in Gmc $*wulhw$-a- became $*$-f-); hence we speak of a-stems in Germanic.

The Indo-European nominal system may be reconstructed as having had three genders, three numbers and eight cases. The Modern English noun system with no grammatical gender, two cases (general case and possessive) and two numbers (singular and plural) exhibits extreme reduction of the original patterns. But the reduction was slow and gradual. The three genders of Indo-European were masculine, feminine and neuter. How this system arose is a controversial question. By no means all individual noun forms are marked for gender. But a demonstrative pronoun (or an adjective) referring to a given noun takes special forms according to the gender of the noun. To put it the other way round: the gender of a noun is recognisable from the form of the pronoun or adjective which is in 'congruence' with it. Lat. *dominus* 'lord' and *agricola* 'farmer' are masculine, because an adjective referring to the nouns will take the 'masculine' form (*dominus, agricola bonus* 'good farmer'), whereas *domina* 'lady' and *fagus* 'beech tree' are feminine (*domina, fagus alta*). The three gender system of Indo-European was kept basically unchanged in Germanic. The three numbers of Indo-European were singular, dual and plural. As far as we can reconstruct backwards, the dual paradigm showed fewer distinctions than the plural, and the number of distinctions in the plural was lower than in the singular. The dual has been lost in many Indo-European daughter languages, and in Proto-Germanic it was on the verge of dying out. In Old English we find dual forms in the personal pronoun, and some nominal forms may perhaps be traced to fossilised duals. But in historical times, English has only two numbers, singular and plural, which remain fully alive to the present day. The system of eight cases is found in Indo-Iranian, and the case patterns of the remaining languages can generally be explained on the basis of eight cases.

The table on p. 49 is intended to illustrate the inflectional system of Indo-European. The word chosen for this purpose is the noun for 'wolf', which can be reconstructed as IE (nom. sg.) $*w\underset{\circ}{l}k^{w}os$ on the basis of the forms from the individual languages. The reconstruction methodology will be illustrated with regard to a few case forms. Above all, the reconstruction of the Proto-Germanic paradigm has been simplified a good deal.

For the paradigm of the Indo-European *o*-stems (Germanic *a*-stems), which are also referred to as 'thematic stems', the following case forms can be reconstructed:

Nominative singular:

The marker -*s* occurred with so-called 'animate' nouns (masculine or feminine), e.g. $*w\underset{\circ}{l}k^{w}$-*o*-*s* 'wolf'; in the neuters the nominative was identical with the accusative, e.g. IE $*jug$-*ó*-*m* 'yoke' (> Skt *yugám*, Gk ζυγόν, Lat. *iugum*, Gmc $*juka^{n}$ (> Go. *juk*, OE *geoc*)). Since final $*$-*s* became voiced in Germanic, the Indo-European thematic stems ended in $*$-*az* (cf. Runic -*aR* and, with syncope of the thematic vowel and unvoicing of $*$-*z*, Go. -*s* in *wulfs*) in Proto-Germanic, and $*$-*az* was

The system of Indo-European nominal declension (*o*-stems)

		Sanskrit	Greek	Latin	Lithuanian	Gothic	Germanic	Indo-European
sg.	nom.	vŕkas	λύκος	lupus	vilkas	wulfs	*wulfaz	*wĺkʷos
	voc.	vŕka	λύκε	lupe	vilkè	wulf	*wulfe	*wĺkʷe
	acc.	vŕkam	λύκον	lupum	vilką	wulf	*wulfa^n	*wĺkʷom
	gen.	vŕkasya	λύκοιο	lupī		wulfis	*wulfas(a)	*wĺkʷosyo
	abl.	vŕkād		lupō(d)	vilko			*wĺkʷōd
	dat.	vŕkāya	λύκῳ	lupō(i)	vilkui		*wulfai	*wĺkʷōi
	loc.	vŕke			vilkè			*wĺkʷei
	inst.	vŕkā, -ena			vilkù	wulfa	*wulfē	*wĺkʷō, -ē
pl.	nom.	vŕkās	λύκοι	lupī	vilkaĩ	wulfos	*wulfōs(iz)	*wĺkʷōs
	acc.	vŕkāns	λύκους	lupōs	vilkùs	wulfans	*wulfanz	*wĺkʷons
	gen.	vŕkāṇām	λύκων	lupōrum	vilkũ	wulfe	*wulfō̄^{n}	*wĺkʷom
	dat.	vŕkebhyas			vilkáms	wulfam	*wulfamiz	*wĺkʷobhyos
	abl.	vŕkebhyas						*wĺkʷobhyos
	loc.	vŕkeṣu	λύκοισι	lupīs	vilkuosè			*wĺkʷoisu
	inst.	vŕkais	λύκοις	lupīs	vilkaĩs		*wulfamiz	*wĺkʷois

dropped in the course of the development to Old English, so that the nominative is endingless there (OE *wulf*).

Vocative singular:

The vocative singular lacked the distinctive marker *-s* for the nominative. In thematic stems, the vowel *-e* is found in the vocative. The vocative has a form distinct from the nominative in Gothic, but in West Germanic nominative and vocative became identical when both *-az* (nominative) and *-e* (vocative) were lost.

Genitive singular:

The reconstruction of the genitive singular of thematic stems is problematic. The form *godagas* found in Runic Norse would seem to indicate an ending *-as(a)* for the genitive singular, and early Old English forms like *domæs*, which led to *domes* by weakening of -æ- in unstressed position, confirm this reconstruction. But Go. *dagis* cannot directly be derived from Gmc *dagas(a)*. The prehistory of Gmc *-as(a)* is also somewhat unclear. In the individual Indo-European languages we find a variety of forms for gen. sg. of thematic stems. By the side of *-osyo*, clearly indicated by Skt *-asya* and Gk -οιο (in Homer), which later became -ου (intervocalic -s- became -h- > -ø- in Greek), we may assume the existence of a form *-oso*, which could explain the Germanic ending

-as. We would have to assume that the accent fell on the thematic vowel, so that Verner's Law did not affect *-s-* in *-óso,* and the final *o* was dropped in Germanic.

Dative singular:

The Gothic form *daga,* which functions as dative singular, is generally assumed to continue an instrumental. The dative singular would have ended in *-ai* in Germanic, and the regular reflex of this form may occur in OE *-æ,* which later became *-e.* The regular continuation of IE *-ōi* is *Gmc *-ai,* which may be due to contraction of the thematic vowel *o-* with the marker *-ei* for dative singular.

Accusative singular:

In the accusative singular the marker *-m* was attached to the stem. In the neuter paradigm the accusative functioned also as nominative.

Nominative plural:

The form for nominative plural ended in *-ōs* in Indo-European. Since the marker *-es* for nom. pl. is immediately recognisable in the class of the root nouns (IE *pód-es* (> Gk πόδες 'feet') consists of the root *pod-* + the marker *-es* for nom. pl.), it is indeed most likely that *-ōs* represents a contraction of the thematic vowel *o-* and the marker *-es* for nom. pl. The same form functioned also as vocative plural. The reflex of *-ōs* is expected as *-ōȝ* in Germanic, and Go. *wulfos* and ON *ulfar* can be interpreted as the regular continuations of the inherited nominative plural. In West Germanic, *-ȝ* would have been lost. Hence the final *-as* of OE *wulfas* cannot be explained on the basis of IE *-ōs* > Gmc *-ōȝ.* It has been suggested that OE *-as* represents a preform IE *-ōs-es,* in which the plural marker *-es* was attached to *-ōs* (itself already a plural form). In ancient Aryan we find the nom. pl. of *a*-stems (Indo-European *o*-stems) ending in *-āsas,* and the ending *-āsas* can also be projected back to IE *-ōs-es.* In the neuter paradigm we find Gmc *-ō* going back to IE *-ā:* Lat. *iuga* 'yokes' corresponds to Gmc *juk-ō* (> Go. *juka,* OE *geocu*).

Genitive plural:

The genitive plural originally had the marker *-om* or *-ōm,* which was attached to the stem. But numerous innovations occurred in this case form. In Gothic we find *-e* mostly (but not exclusively) in the genitive plural of masculine and neuter nouns, which must be due to an innovation, although the precise origin of *-e* remains obscure. The Old English ending for gen. pl. is *-a* in all declension classes.

Dative plural:

Whereas the majority of Indo-European languages exhibit forms characterised by suffix initial -*bh*- in the dative, instrumental, ablative plural (e.g. Skt -*bhis* (*padbhis*, instr. of *pad*- 'foot'), -*bhyas* (*padbhyás*, dat. abl. of *pad*-), Lat. *pedibus* (the dat./abl. of *o*-stems continues the historical locative and instrumental, therefore *lupīs* is entered for 'loc.' and 'inst.' in the table on p. 49), Germanic deviates considerably in that forms with suffix initial *m*- are used, and the closest correspondences of this case marker are found in Baltic and Slavic. Gmc *-*miz*, possibly also *-*maz* can be compared to Lith. -*ams* ((dat. abl. pl.) *vilkáms*) and OCS -*omŭ* ((dat. abl. pl.) *vlikomŭ*). The dative plural for Gmc *wulf-a*- can be posited as *wulf-a-miz* or *wulf-a-maz*.

Accusative plural:

The accusative plural of *a*-stems ends in -*ans* in Gothic, and the underlying Gmc *-*anz* can be interpreted as the regular continuation of IE *-*ons* (= thematic vowel + marker *-*ns* for accusative plural). It has been suggested that the marker *-*ns* for accusative plural consists ultimately of the marker *-*m* for accusative followed by the sign -*s* for plural: *-*m-s* > *-*ns*. In Old English the accusative plural adopted the form of the nominative plural.

The usual grammatical analysis distinguishes between vocalic and consonantal stems in Germanic. As one example for vocalic stems the *a*-stems (IE *o*-stems) have briefly been dealt with. The remaining stem classes will simply be enumerated here, since they will be dealt with in full in chapter 3. Beside the stems in Gmc *-*a*- the vocalic stem classes include the following types: *ō*-stems (Gmc *geb-ō*- 'gift' (> Go. *giba*, OE *giefu*)), *i*-stems (Gmc *gasti* 'guest' (> Go. *gasts*, OE *giest*)), and *u*-stems (Gmc *sunu*- 'son' (> Go. *sunus*, OE *sunu*)). All Germanic *ō*-stems were feminine, the *i*- and *u*-stems were both masculine and feminine; a few neuters occurred in the *i*- and *u*-stems. Apart from the stems in Gmc *-*ō*-, *-*i*- and *-*u*-, which continue Indo-European stems in *-*ā*-, *-*i*- and *-*u*-, Germanic had also inherited a number of consonantal stems. The term 'consonantal' refers to the fact that in this class of noun stems the respective marker(s) for case and number followed upon a consonant, whereas in the vocalic stems the respective marker(s) followed upon a vowel. Since in the vocalic stems a number of contractions occurred, which tended to blur the boundary between the stem forming element and the respective case markers, consonantal stems usually are more transparent in this respect. Thus nom. pl. IE *pód-es* clearly has the marker *-es, whereas in *$w\!l\!k^w$-ōs the long vowel *-ō- is due to a contraction of the thematic vowel with the initial vowel of the plural marker.

The basic type of consonantal stems consists just of a 'root' to which the respective markers for case and number are directly attached. The noun for 'foot' is a case in point. The root here is IE *ped-/pod-, and the various forms found in the individual languages clearly show that the noun originally had ablaut in the root: e-grade is found in Lat. (genitive) ped-is, whereas Gk (accusative) πόδ-α exhibits o-grade; in Germanic the lengthened grade, which originally occurred in the nom. sg. was carried through in the whole paradigm, but OE fēt, the plural of fōt, still shows clearly the effect of the plural marker IE *-es > Gmc *-iz, which caused i-umlaut of the root vowel. In Indo-European a number of suffixes were in use which ended in a consonant. But only one category of the consonantal stems with a clearly demarcable suffix became productive in Germanic, namely the stems in *-n- of the type OE guma m. 'man', tunge f. 'tongue', ēage n. 'eye'. This class corresponds to nouns of the type homo, hominis 'man' in Latin, and it is worth noting that Lat. homo, hominis ultimately represents the same stem as Gmc *guman- (> OE guma); the basic element for the n-stem IE *ghm-en- is the word for 'earth' (cf. Lat. hūmus), and the derivative in *-en- showed a full system of ablaut, the o-grade appearing in OE (accusative) guman (< Gmc *-an- + case marker < IE *-on- + case marker), whereas the e-grade is found in Go. (genitive) gumins (< Gmc *-en- + case marker < IE *-en- + case marker), and the zero-grade of the suffix *-en-, namely IE *-n̥, may occur in OE (dat. pl.) gumum (< Gmc *-um(m) < *-un-m(iz) < IE *n̥- + case marker).

2.5.2 *The adjective*

A given 'adjectival' form of Indo-European probably lacked special morphological characteristics which would have set it off from a noun. In Latin, bonus has basically the same declension pattern as dominus, bonum follows the paradigm of iugum, and bona can be put in parallel with toga. But this example also shows one peculiarity of the adjective. A given adjective may take special forms in accordance with the noun to which it refers. The adjective and the demonstrative pronouns are the prime carriers of 'grammatical' gender. The development of the adjective is perhaps one of the most conspicuous innovations in Germanic morphology. In Germanic the adjective is not only semantically delimited by generally expressing some 'quality' (cf. the German term 'Eigenschaftswort'), but it is also morphologically clearly definable. Also most of the Germanic adjectival forms differ from comparable substantival forms. For the following discussion the paradigms of Go. *blinds* 'blind', for both 'strong' and 'weak', will serve as a starting point.

Go. *blinds* 'blind' (strong paradigm)

		masculine	feminine	neutral
Sg.	nom	*blinds*	*blinda*	*blind*, -ata
	acc.	**blindana**	*blinda*	*blind*, -ata
	gen.	*blindis*	**blindaizos**	*blindis*
	dat.	**blindamma**	*blindai*	**blindamma**
Pl.	nom.	**blindai**	*blindos*	*blinda*
	acc.	*blindans*	*blindos*	*blinda*
	gen.	**blindaize**	**blindaizo**	**blindaize**
	dat.	**blindaim**	**blindaim**	**blindaim**

Go. *blinds* 'blind' (weak paradigm)

		masculine	feminine	neutral
Sg.	nom.	*blinda*	*blindo*	*blindo*
	acc.	*blindan*	*blindon*	*blindo*
	gen.	*blindins*	*blindons*	*blindins*
	dat.	*blindin*	*blindon*	*blindin*
Pl.	nom.	*blindans*	*blindons*	*blindona*
	acc.	*blindans*	*blindons*	*blindona*
	gen.	*blindane*	*blindono*	*blindane*
	dat.	*blindam*	*blindom*	*blindam*

The major innovation in the Germanic adjectival system concerns the rise of a twofold declension, which is usually referred to as the strong and the weak adjective declension. The rise of the 'weak' adjective has been discussed extensively, but it must be pointed out that the paradigm of the 'strong' adjective is by no means without problems of its own.

The strong adjective can be projected back to the Indo-European stems in *o* (masculine and neuter) and *ā* (feminine); the *u*-stems also provided a considerable number of adjectives; there were probably fewer *i*-stems. In Germanic, the *u*-stems were still available in great number, but the *blinda*- type (*a/ō*-stem) was the most productive category. There were also stems in -(*i*)*ja-*/-(*i*)*jō*, which partly stem from the feminine formation corresponding to *u*-stem adjectives, partly they represent extensions of *i*-stems, and partly they continue genuine formations in IE *-*yo*-. Some forms of the strong adjectival inflexion are clearly influenced by the paradigm of the demonstrative pronoun. Thus dat. sg. Go. *blindamma* exhibits the same ending as the dat. sg. *þamma* of the demonstrative pronoun *sa* 'this'. Similarly the acc. sg. *blindana* was formed on the pattern of *þana*. Corresponding innovations can be found in the remaining Germanic languages. In the paradigms of Germanic adjectives it is customary to mark out those forms that are influenced by the pronominal inflexion; in the 'strong' paradigm given above, the so-called 'pronominal' forms of the adjective are in bold face.

The 'weak' adjective is a Germanic innovation. Morphologically **blindan-/blindōn-* clearly follows the pattern of **guman-/tungōn-*, but it is anything but obvious how the duality of adjectival inflexions could have come about. The 'weak' adjective generally carries a nuance of 'definiteness'. This semantic shade can secondarily be observed in the fact that in German (as well as in Old English) the weak adjective is generally used when the noun is accompanied by the article (= demonstrative pronoun); cf. (strong adjective) *guter Mann* (OE *gōd mann*): (weak adjective) *der gute Mann* (OE *se gōda mann*).

The Germanic adjective can exhibit comparison. There are two degrees of comparison, the comparative and the superlative. The comparative has two suffixes, namely *-izan-* and -*ōzan-*; the comparative always follows the paradigm of the 'weak' adjective. The suffix *-izan-* represents an extension in -*an-* (< IE *-*on*-) of the zero-grade -*is-* of the marker *-yos-*. The origin of *-ōzan-* is somewhat unclear, but it seems likely that *ō* may be identified with the lengthened grade -*yōs* of the suffix -*yos*. The superlative is formed by -*ista-*. It may follow the strong or the weak declension. The suffix -*ista-* can be projected back to IE *-*isto*-. IE *-*isto*- represents a *to*-formation from the zero-grade -*is-* of the suffix -*yos-*.

2.5.3 The verb

While clearly containing a number of features inherited from Indo-European, the Germanic verb at the same time exhibits considerable innovations. Germanic verbs have traditionally been classified according to the formation of their preterite. Every Germanic verb opposes a specifically marked preterital form to the morphological system functioning in the present. Therefore the principle for describing the rise of the Germanic verbal system within the categories inherited from Indo-European must be the explanation of the present – preterite dichotomy. The Germanic verbal system distinguishes three moods in the present and two moods in the preterite: present indicative, present subjunctive, present imperative, preterite indicative and preterite subjunctive. Periphrastic forms were probably extremely rare in Germanic, if they occurred at all. The following account will be concerned with simple forms only.

The reconstruction of the Indo-European verbal system is controversial in more than one way. For the purposes of the following account, the Graeco-Aryan model will be adopted. This means that the agreements between Greek and Aryan in the verbal system will be assumed to be direct continuations of the Indo-European verbal system. Such difficult questions as to how the aberrant system of Anatolian can be explained will not be touched. The Indo-European verbal system is assumed to have exhibited the following categories:

1   aspect (it is quite doubtful whether this term may be used here): present, aorist, perfect
2   mood: indicative, subjunctive, optative, imperative, injunctive
3   voice: active and middle
4   person: three
5   number: three

A few brief indications will be provided towards defining these categories. It should be noted, however, that the definitions are as far as possible based on morphology, since functional definitions are extremely difficult.

The three 'aspects' (1) can be defined as follows:

A perfect form like IE *le-loik^w-a > Gk λέλοιπα consists of a reduplication, the root, and a person marker: *-loik^w- is the o-grade of the root *leik^w-, the reduplication consists of the root initial consonant l- followed by the vowel -e-, and -a is the marker for first singular. Gk λέλοιπα means 'I am left over'. The perfect has stative meaning. The o-grade root was used in the singular, the dual and plural exhibited the root in zero-grade.

The aorist can appear in more than one form. The most archaic (perhaps, originally, the only) form of aorist was the athematic root aorist of the type Gk ἔστην 'I stood' = Skt *ásthām* < IE *$é$-$stā$-m*. This form consists of the root IE *$stā$-*, to which the person marker -m for 1 sg. was attached. *$é$-* is termed the 'augment', but it is found only in a limited number of Indo-European languages. The root aorist probably had ablaut originally in that the singular exhibited the respective root in full grade, whereas the root appeared in zero-grade in the dual and plural, but the full-grade of the root was largely levelled throughout the paradigm. The aorist had punctual value: *$é$-$stā$-m* probably meant something like 'I stood' (without any emphasis on duration).

The present has polymorphism, i.e. a number of different formations can be encountered. A form like IE *es-mi* 'I am' (> Gmc *$izm(i)$* > Go. *im* 'I am') is structurally comparable to *$(e-)stā$-m* dealt with above. IE *es-mi* consists of the root *es-* 'be', to which the primary marker *-mi* for 1 sg. is attached. A present form may be preceded by the augment in those languages that use the augment; but in that case the 'secondary' set of person markers is used: IE *e-es-m* (the secondary marker for 1 sg. is -m, which becomes vocalic -$m̥$) > Skt *ā́sam* 'I was'. A form consisting of the root + the secondary person marker for 1 sg., *es-$m̥$*, would be termed 'injunctive'. The augmentless aorist *$stā$-m* is also to be classified as an injunctive. From the morphological point of view the only difference between a present injunctive and an aorist injunctive consists in the fact that the present injunctive can be turned into an indicative by the use of the primary ending (*es-mi* 'I am'), whereas the primary set of endings is excluded from the aorist system. The present usually expresses some durative action.

The formation and the function of the moods (2) in Indo-European can be described as follows:

The injunctive of present and aorist is augmentless and exhibits the secondary set of person markers: injunctive forms, which only can be distinguished in languages that regularly use the augment, serve to just 'mention' an action.

The indicative is characterised by the primary endings in the present. Those languages that lack the augment lack a difference between injunctive and indicative in the aorist. The indicative is the mood regularly used for statements.

The imperative expresses an order. Apart from a few special person markers, the imperative lacks formal characteristics that would set it off from other verbal categories.

The subjunctive is characterised by the presence of the 'thematic' vowel. Verbal stems that were 'athematic' became so to speak 'thematic' in the subjunctive, whereas thematic stems added another thematic vowel, so that the thematic vowel became long. The subjunctive allows the use of the primary and secondary set of person markers. The subjunctive of the athematic present *es-ti 'he is' appears as *es-e-t(i), whereas the thematic present *bher-e-ti 'he carries' forms *bher-e-e-t(i) > *bherēt(i) in the subjunctive. The subjunctive expresses the 'will' of the speaker. It consequently often has reference to the 'future'.

The optative is marked by the ablauting suffix -yē-/-ī-, which can be projected back to *yeə-/-yə (e-grade/zero-grade). Athematic verbal stems attached the suffix to the weak stem, the e-grade of the suffix appeared in the singular, the zero-grade in the dual and plural. The optative exhibits the secondary set of person markers. The optative of *es-ti 'he is' can be posited as IE *s-yē-/s-ī- (cf. Skt syām, Lat. sim, sīs, sit, in Old Latin siet). Thematic stems attach the zero-grade of the optative marker to the stem in -o-. The optative of *bher-e-ti 'he carries' is to be posited as IE *bher-o-ī-t, -ī- could be shortened to -i- and contract with -o- to form the diphthong -oi-: Gk φέροι is the immediate continuation of *bher-oi-(t). The optative expresses the wish of the speaker. Whereas the subjunctive often expresses a probability, the optative renders the nuance of the possibility.

In the present and aorist two diatheses (voices) were formally expressed, which are usually referred to as active and middle. The active and the middle were formally distinguished by special shapes of the person markers, as can be seen from the contrast of active *bher-e-ti 'he carries' against middle *sekʷ-e-toi 'he follows' (> Gk ἕπεται, Lat. sequitur (-r is a special feature of the middle paradigm found in some languages)). The perfect had only one set of person markers; a middle of the perfect was secondarily shaped in some languages.

The following subsections will provide some information on how the Germanic verbal system can be accounted for on the basis of the inherited structure of the Indo-European verb. Since from the point of view of Old English the dual is no longer relevant, only two numbers will be listed, namely the singular and the plural. The Indo-European verb distinguished three persons (speaker, person spoken to and person or thing spoken about), and these categories have remained alive down to the present.

The main categories of the Germanic verb can be exemplified with the following Gothic paradigm of the verb niman 'take', which will be quoted for the active. The middle paradigm Go. *nimada* 'I am taken' occurs in Old English only with the verb *hātan* 'call', OE *hātte* means 'I am called'; therefore the middle paradigm will not be quoted here. The dual forms will also be omitted.

Present

		Indicative	Subjunctive	Imperative
Sg.	1	*nima*	*nimau*	
	2	*nimis*	*nimais*	*nim*
	3	*nimiþ*	*nimai*	*nimadau*
Pl.	1	*nimam*	*nimaima*	*nimam*
	2	*nimiþ*	*nimaiþ*	*nimiþ*
	3	*nimand*	*nimaina*	*nimandau*

Preterite

		Indicative	Subjunctive
Sg.	1	*nam*	*nemjau*
	2	*namt*	*nemeis*
	3	*nam*	*nemei*
Pl.	1	*nemum*	*nemeima*
	2	*nemuþ*	*nemeiþ*
	3	*nemun*	*nemeina*

The following remarks can be offered on the comparative aspect of the above paradigm.

The indicative of the present basically goes back to the Indo-European present indicative. The verb chosen as an example is Gmc *nem-a-*, which consists of a root *nem-* and an alternating vowel Gmc *-e-/-a-*, which goes back to IE *-e-/-o-* and is termed the thematic vowel; the stem Gmc *nem-a-* precedes the respective markers for person and number. The thematic present formations of the type Gmc *nem-a-* correspond to the class found in Gk φέρω 'I carry', φέρετε 'you carry' (2 pl.). The thematic vowel is *-e-* in the second and third person singular and in the second person plural; the other persons use IE *-o-* > Gmc *-a-* as the thematic vowel. The subjunctive of Germanic continues the Indo-European optative, which in thematic verbs attached the marker *-ī-* to the thematic vowel *-o-*; thus 2 sg. Gmc *nem-ai-z corresponds exactly to Gk -οις in φέροις. The imperative used the bare verbal stem in 2 sg.

The Germanic preterite of strong verbs basically goes back to the perfect of Indo-European. This derivation is particularly clear in the singular, since Gmc *nam-a > Go. nam corresponds morphologically exactly to the type found in Gk λέλοιπα, but in Germanic preterites of this type reduplication has generally been lost. The plural of some strong verbs can readily be projected back to the Indo-European reduplicationless perfect. But the origin of preterites with long -ē- in the plural (Gmc *nēm- > Go. nem-) is hardly clear. The weak preterite is an innovation of Germanic, whose origin is very controversial.

With regard to the person markers the following observations may be noted: in the first singular we find *-mi in athematic present formations of the type IE *es-mi 'I am' (> Gk εἰμί), but in thematic verbs *-ō occurs. In 2 sg. and 3 sg. the markers *-si and *-ti respectively were used following the thematic vowel (cf. Skt bhár-a-si 'you carry' [2 sg.], bhár-a-ti 'he carries'), on the basis of which Gmc *-ezi and *-edi are the regular phonological continuations. The marker for 1 pl. may have been of the shape IE *-mes, whereas *-te occurred in 2 pl. In 3 pl. the marker *-nti followed upon the thematic vowel -o-. In the preterital system the singular endings clearly go back to the markers found in the Indo-European perfect: 1 sg. *-a (cf. Gk λέλοιπα), 2 sg. *-tha, 3 sg. *-e. The endings *-a and *-e for 1 sg. and 3 sg. were lost in all Germanic languages. The ending *-t(a) for 2 sg. is regularly found in Gothic and Norse; but in West Germanic only the preterite present verbs which go back to the Indo-European perfect preserve this marker (cf. OE scealt 'thou shalt', þearft 'thou mayest', etc.), whereas the strong preterite introduced a new ending *-i (OHG buti 'you ordered', OE bude), which may have originated from the aorist system or from the optative.

2.6   Syntax

In theory the morphological system of a language can be described without having recourse to 'meaning', which in this case means rather the 'function' of the forms concerned. Dealing with the meaning of morphological elements is the domain of syntax. In contrast to the forms of a language which, after all, can be described rather objectively, an analysis of the function of these forms encounters considerable difficulties because a certain subjective element is hardly avoidable in this context. What one might call 'word-syntax' has occasionally already been referred to. 'Word-syntax' is concerned with the function of precise forms; thus we would have to describe in detail the various functions covered by the accusative, we would have to explain the choice of tenses and moods, we would have to analyse the use of the 'strong' adjective in contrast to the 'weak' adjective, etc. In the absence of native speakers who could be asked whether a certain sequence of free and bound morphemes is 'meaningful', the discussion of prehistoric syntactic features must of necessity be rather incomplete. The following sections illustrate prehistoric syntax with regard to larger groups than the word. We will here be concerned with the arrangement of word groups.

The basic criterion for grouping languages from the point of view of syntax is the position of the verb. Although the distinction is rarely absolutely clear-cut, it can be stated that languages have a so-called 'regular' word-order pattern. If we take the predicate as the centre of reference, it becomes possible to classify languages according to whether the object precedes or follows the finite verb. If we represent the object with O and the finite verb with V, the following two basic patterns can be set up:

VO/OV

Whereas Modern English is clearly a VO-language, Old English was an OV language, and this characteristic was inherited from Germanic and Indo-European. In an OV-language like Indo-European it is by no means excluded that on occasion the finite verb may appear preceding the object, but the sequence OV is the so-called 'unmarked' order; a deviation from this basic arrangement serves to render some special emphasis. As illustration of the Germanic word-order sequence the runic inscription on the Gallehus horn may be quoted:

ek hlewagastiR holtijaR horna tawido

The object *horna* 'the horn' is found preceding the finite verb *tawido* 'I made'. The subject of the clause consists of three parts: *ek* 'I' is the personal pronoun for first singular, *hlewagastiR* is the person's name, and *holtijaR* (probably meaning 'from *Holt*') is used attributively with regard to the name. The text of the inscription can be translated as 'I HlewagastiR from Holt made the horn.'

The position of the finite verb after the object can be found in a high number of examples from the most varied Indo-European languages. Thus the beginning of the Aeneid may be quoted: *arma virumque cano*...'the weapons and the man I sing...', and the following more complex Hittite phrase exhibits the same word-order pattern: *man LUG[A]Lwas piran seskanzi kuis hazzizzi nusse GESTIN-an akuwanna pianzi*, which means 'if someone shoots in front of the king [in a contest] then the one who hits the mark is given wine'. The following Vedic passage shows that the finite verb regularly appears in final position both in main and in subordinate clauses: *yébhyo mádhu pradhávati, tāṁś cid eva ápi gacchatāt* 'those for whom the honey flows, those too it (the honey) shall join' (*Rig Veda* 10.154.1).

Languages with complex morphological systems certainly allow a greater freedom with regard to word-order than languages like English, where, because of the poverty of the morphological system, word-order is an essential constituent of the 'meaning' of a phrase. Whereas in German both *Der Vater sieht den Sohn* and *Den Sohn sieht der Vater* are acceptable and carry basically the same meaning (although with a difference in emphasis), in English *The father sees the son* is the only possible way of rendering the underlying notion, since *The son sees the father* would have a totally different meaning. It must be stressed, however, that, in spite of some surface variations, even in a language like German word-order follows closely knit patterns. Word-order is by no means free.

The word-order rules for prehistoric stages of Old English can to a certain extent be deduced from the consideration of Latin syntactic patterns. At first sight a passage from Horace like the following might indicate absolute freedom in word-order: *aequam memento rebus in arduis servare mentem* 'remember to keep an even mind in adverse conditions' (*Odes* II 3.1–2). Apart from poetic licence, which accounts for the 'corner' position of adjective *aequam* and noun *mentem*, it should be noted that the preposition *in* follows the noun *rebus* it governs and precedes the adjective *arduis* (in congruence with *rebus*). In Vedic we find adherence to rather strict word-order rules, and occasional deviations may have a number of different reasons. The following two passages are nearly identical, but in the second the finite verb *vocam* has shifted from the final position to the second position in the clause:

prá te pūrvāṇi káranāni vocam
prá nūtanā maghavan yā cakártha

(5.31.6)

let me proclaim thy deeds of yore, and, too, the present deeds, which thou Maghavan (Indra) hast performed.

> *préndrasya vocam prathamā́ kṛtā́ni*
> *prá nū́tanā maghávā yā́ cakā́ra*

(7.98.5)

Let me proclaim Indra's deeds which he, Maghavan, hath performed.

Word-order definitely allowed some freedom in prehistoric stages of Old English, but there were certainly constraints. Some of these will be briefly analysed in the following sections.

Since verb final position was 'unmarked', a verb in initial position expressed a special nuance. The verb is usually in initial position in commands, and it is easy to imagine sentences in which only an imperative (without an object) is used; e.g. Gk ἴθι 'go' (< IE *i-dhi*). It should be noted, however, that in a sequence of two imperatives we find the first in initial position whereas the second imperative tends toward clause final position. This rule can be illustrated with the following passage from the Iliad:

> χαίρετε, κήρυκες ... ἄσσον ἴτε

(*Iliad* I 334–5)

rejoice, o heralds, come closer (literally '...closer come').

A comparable case can be quoted from Beowulf:

> *Bruc þisses beages,*   *Beowulf leofa,*
> *hyse, mid hæle,*   *ond þisses hrægles neot*

(*Beo* 1216–17)

enjoy this necklace, dear Beowulf, man, with prosperity, and make use of this mantle (literally '...and of this mantle make use').

A particularly difficult problem concerns the distinction between main and subordinate clauses. Although the view formerly widely held according to which originally only parataxis (i.e. sequential arrangement of main clauses) was in use cannot be upheld, it is nevertheless clear that the distinction between parataxis and hypotaxis (subordination of subclause to mainclause) is by no means clear-cut. This is particularly true of relative clauses. Whatever the Indo-European way of producing relative clauses may have been, Germanic evidently did not continue that formation pattern; in the Germanic languages new ways were found for shaping relative clauses. Whereas Gothic has a particle *-ei* attached to the demonstrative pronoun so that we find *saei* 'he who', etc., in Old English (apart from more elaborate ways of rendering the relative) an unchangeable particle *þe* may be used to introduce a relative clause. The following passage from The Wanderer may illustrate the relative clause introduced by *þe*:

> *Nis nu cwicra nan*
> *þe ic him modsefan   minne durre*
> *sweotule asecgan*

(*Wan* 9–11)

there is now no one to whom I dare openly tell my thoughts.

2.7   The lexicon

Old English clearly inherited a basic stock of lexical items which ultimately go back to Indo-European. Some of these lexical items have already been mentioned because they are the basis for setting up the sound correspondences and hence for deducing the sound changes which led from Indo-European to Proto-Germanic and ultimately Old English. But delimiting precisely the Indo-European vocabulary is very difficult indeed, because new lexical items could at any time be created on the existing patterns. Down to the present day, English preserves a number of words which may well go back to very old stages of Indo-European. Among these items we should certainly include the basic terms for family relationship such as *father* (cf. Lat. *pater*, Gk πατήρ, etc.), *mother* (cf. Lat. *māter*, Gk μήτηρ, etc.), *brother* (cf. Lat. *frāter*, Skt *bhrātar-*, etc.), *sister* (cf. Lat. *soror*, Lith. *sesuõ*, etc.), *son* (cf. Lith. *sūnùs*, Skt *sūnús*, etc.), *daughter* (cf. Gk θυγάτηρ, Lith. *duktḗ*, etc.). Among the clearly inherited items which certainly have a long prehistory belong also the basic numerals such as *one* (cf. Lat. *ūnus*, Lith. *víenas*, etc.), *two* (cf. Lat. *duo*, Gk δύο, Lith. *dù*, *dvì*, etc.), *three* (cf. Lat. *trēs*, Gk τρεῖς, Skt *tráyas*, etc.), *four* (cf. Lat. *quattuor*, Gk τέσσαρες, Skt *catvāras*, Lith. *keturì*, etc.), *five* (cf. Lat. *quinque*, Gk πέντε, Skt *páñca*, etc.).

Some lexical items which can, with high probability, be attributed to Indo-European allow us some glimpses into the set-up of the culture and social set-up, although we are still far from agreement on where the original homeland (*Urheimat*) may have been. In a recent and authoritative work on Indo-European Cowgill (see Mayrhofer 1986) tended towards accepting the views of Maria Gimbutas according to whom the speakers of Indo-European may have settled in the North Caucasus and Lower Volga area in the fourth millennium BC. From the lexical agreements among the most ancient Indo-European languages we can deduce that those speakers of Indo-European engaged in warfare, had a fairly well-developed agricultural system and were familiar with cattle, horses, sheep and swine. They probably knew how to build vehicles with wheels. The use of some metals may also have been available to them.

But details of the vocabulary beyond the most basic items are not readily retrievable. It must be borne in mind that even in the cases where we find perfectly agreeing forms in more than one Indo-European language we cannot be certain that the underlying common form was really used in the proto-language, because innovations could occur at any time on the pattern of existing forms. Thus Indo-European had a productive category of neuter stems with *e*-grade of the verbal root preceding an alternating suffix which ended in -*s*. One member of this formation class is probably found in the noun for 'ore', IE **ay-es*. This word is regularly continued in OE *ār*. Other *s*-stems could be easily created secondarily, however. Thus the agreement of Skt *janas*-, Gk γένος and Lat. *genus* would certainly seem to indicate the existence of a proto-form IE **gén(ə)-os*; and in spite of the fact that this may well be a 'correct' reconstruction in the sense that the word may actually have been in use, it should not be forgotten that **gén(ə)-os* could also have been shaped at any given time in the prehistory of the languages in which it is found.

Perhaps the most productive way of forming new words is by juxtaposing two items and gradually coalescing them into a new unit. The process is termed 'composition'. For Indo-European compounds can be defined morphologically as exhibiting an unchangeable first part, whereas the syntactically required changes occur in the second part only. In Indo-European only nouns could be compounded. It is usually assumed that the rise of composition dates from a period when the regular inflexion was not yet fully developed. Germanic certainly inherited the ability to form compounds, but compounding was definitely not as frequent as it is in Modern English. The types of compounds which can be assumed for Germanic can be briefly described as follows.

Determinative compounds originally consist of two nominal stems the first of which qualifies (= 'determines') the second. For Proto-Germanic we may assume a formation **brūdi-fadi-* (< IE **bhrūtípoti-*) on the basis of Go. *bruþfaþs* 'bridegroom'. The nominal stem Gmc **faþi-* (< IE **póti-*) apparently fell out of use early, and the compound gradually lost its transparency. In Old English *brȳdguma* another term for 'man', namely *guma*, was substituted. But OE *guma* was obsolete, and so the compound became again opaque. It was rendered transparent by introducing the term *groom* as second element of the compound. *Bridegroom* is due to a popular etymology: *-guma* having dropped out of use was replaced by the similarly sounding but originally quite different noun *groom*.

Copulative compounds, which apparently were not numerous in Germanic, consist of two elements where the sum total of the two makes up the meaning of the compound. This type of compounding is found in numerals like *thirteen* (= 'three and ten'), *fourteen* (= 'four and ten'), etc. Old English had a compound *suhtergefæderan* (found in *Beo* 1164), which means 'nephew (= brother's son) and (paternal) uncle'. But otherwise copulative compounds were rare.

A type of compounds that was clearly inherited usually consisted of adjective + noun, but the compound did not have the same reference as the noun (as was basically the case with determinative compounds); in this special type the whole compound basically functioned as an adjective and referred to somebody or something endowed with what the sequence adjective + noun expressed. These compounds are usually termed possessive compounds or, using an Indic example of the type, bahuvrihi-compounds. *Barefoot* is an example in point, since it means 'having bare feet'. The possessive compounds were above all frequently used in naming. The anonymous author of the Old English poem *Widsiþ* refers to himself as 'having (made) a wide journey'.

In many cases we can be reasonably certain that the second element of a compound was weakened, thereby lost its transparency and ultimately came to function as a suffix. In Modern English the suffix *-dom* can be attached to a number of nominal stems in order to form abstract nouns of the type *kingdom*. The suffix *-dom* is in origin identical with the noun *doom*, which may have meant something like 'judgement'. In Old English, nominal compounds of the type *cyne-dom* could regularly be formed. In a similar way *-ship* in *friendship* and *-hood* in *maidenhood*, *boyhood*, etc. were originally nominal stems that could occur both in isolation and as second elements of compounds: OE *hād*, the precursor of *-hood*, did in fact occur on its own, whereas the noun serving as second member of the compounds of the type *friendship* was also in Old English used in composition only.

But apart from the clearly inherited items and those formed from inherited material on existing patterns, we find a considerable group of lexical items in Germanic which so far defy satisfactory etymological analysis. In some cases we may be concerned with borrowings (e.g. *path*). But in a number of cases we must also reckon with the possibility that the right cognates have simply not been found so far.

FURTHER READING

The subject matter dealt with in the preceding chapter is covered by an enormous number of publications. A good introductory account into the main concerns of Indo-European and Indo-European comparative grammar is provided by Baldi (1983). The best modern compendium of Indo-European grammar is Szemerényi (1980/1989). A very specialised account of Indo-European phonology (together with a general introduction to the various Indo-European languages) is available in Mayrhofer (1986); the book also offers up-to-date bibliography. The hotly debated issue as to how the system of stop consonants in Indo-European should be reconstructed is also dealt with in Mayrhofer's book. The views of Gamkrelidze are so far accessible through a number of specialised articles as well as in the Russian publication Gamkrelidze and Ivanov (1984); an English translation of that work is in preparation. The current work on Indo-European is listed in 'Indogermanische Chronik' published twice a year in the journal *Die Sprache*.

For comparative grammar of the Germanic languages the most widely used book is Prokosch (1939), which is stimulating but not always reliable. The 'state of the art' around the turn of the century is found in Streitberg 1896. Seebold 1970 gives an etymological account of the primary verbs of Germanic. The standard grammars of Old English (Campbell 1959 and Brunner 1965) also offer excellent material on the subject as well as rich bibliography. Questions of Germanic syntax have been dealt with by Hopper 1975. On a rather modest scale my textbooks (Bammesberger 1984a, 1984b, 1984c and 1989) may be mentioned.

With regard to the early period of comparative linguistics, there is a good account available in Robins 1987.

3 PHONOLOGY AND MORPHOLOGY

Richard M. Hogg

3.1 Introduction

Whatever their other achievements, the Anglo-Saxons could not lay claim to being outstanding grammarians. Indeed, to judge by the paucity of grammatical writing during the Old English period, where Ælfric's Latin Grammar (ca 1000) stands out because it is the exception that proves the rule, the Anglo-Saxons would not have wished to make such a claim, their intellectual interests lying in entirely different areas. This, of course, makes the task of reconstructing the nature of the Old English language that much more difficult. Thus, in the areas which are the concern of this chapter, we have no equivalent of the Icelandic First Grammarian, who, writing in the thirteenth century, gives a wealth of detail about the sound system of Old Icelandic (see Benediktsson 1972, Haugen 1950). At much the same time as the First Grammarian was writing, an East Midlands monk of Scandinavian origin, Orm, composed a lengthy verse work entitled *Orrmulum*, in which he employed a writing system of his own devising from which we can glean a considerable amount of information about his pronunciation (see Burchfield 1956, Sisam 1953b : 188–95 and vol. II, ch. 2 of this History). However, Orm's spelling system, valuable as it is, is not only ambiguous in its aims and effects, but also relates to a period when the English language had considerably altered in structure and system. For Old English itself we have no direct testamentary evidence from any contemporary or near-contemporary source.

Two questions arise from this. Firstly, how can we go about reconstructing the linguistic system of Old English? Secondly, how precisely can we hope to reconstruct that system? The methods of linguistic reconstruction have been dealt with in chapter 2 of this volume, and therefore need be repeated only briefly here. In phonology they comprise the following components. Firstly, there are, unlike for the pre-Old English period, written documents. For the vast majority of their writing, see §3.2 below, the Anglo-Saxons used a form of the Roman alphabet. At the very least (and the same would apply if they had used some other alphabet in current use today, for example, but improbably, the Cyrillic alphabet), we can assume that the spelling conventions in use during the Old English period would not have been completely at odds with those in later periods. Thus, given the Old English word *bedd* it is reasonable to assume that the first letter represents some kind of consonant, the second some kind of vowel, the third some consonant different from the first. On the other hand the fourth letter causes us problems, since it could well represent a departure from present-day orthographical conventions. When we then consider that this word is likely to be the same word as present-day *bed*, this takes us one step further forward. It is surely legitimate to assume, at least for the moment, that the Old English pronunciation of the word must have been quite close to /bed/ or the like. This example is, of course, almost misleading in its simplicity. Consider another word, namely *werc*, which we can assume is the Old English predecessor of present-day *work*. Only <w> seems readily interpretable. What might the significance of the change of <e> to <o> be? In Received Pronunciation /r/ is not pronounced before a consonant – was there an /r/ present in that position in Old English? If so, what kind of an /r/ was it: an approximant as in Received Pronunciation or General American English, a trill as in stage Scots; retroflex as in West Country dialects, or uvular as in the Newcastle dialect? Can we claim that <c> is an equivalent spelling for <k>?

The spelling evidence of the Old English texts, although helpful, is clearly not enough. We have to look for additional evidence, which might either add to the spelling evidence or negate it. Already, in fact, we have mentioned another source of evidence, the present-day dialects. The evidence of these dialects helps in two ways. Firstly, the dialects provide us with a range of information much greater than that found in the standard language. Amongst this may be forms which are direct descendants of Old English forms now ousted from the standard language. For example, in the West and North-West Midlands of England it is still possible to hear forms of the 3rd person feminine pronoun which begin with /h/ – *hoo* and the like rather than *she*. This serves as confirming evidence about the pronunciation of OE *hēo* 'she'.

Secondly, because one general principle of linguistic reconstruction (cf. Lass 1980:53–7) is that we should not hypothesise for older stages of the language forms which do not appear in later stages, the dialects define limits of reconstruction. One classic case here centres on the so-called 'short diphthongs' in Old English, as, for example, in *eald* 'old', which some linguists would transcribe as /æɑɫd/. Other linguists have objected to such an analysis on the grounds that such diphthongs are not to be found in any later stage of the language. But even if it is the case that no present-day dialect has such diphthongs, we may still have to suppose that Old English did, because of the weight of the spelling evidence and the difficulty of postulating a plausible series of sound changes to produce the Middle English forms if the short diphthongs are assumed, after all, to be simple vowels.

A further crucial type of evidence comes from linguistic plausibility. If we reconstruct a linguistic system for one stage of the language, then it must be possible to account for the differences between that system and some later system by a plausible series of linguistic changes. So, if we reconstruct the 3rd person neuter pronoun in Old English *hit* as /hit/, on the grounds of spelling evidence and morphological parallelisms (here, the supposed structure of the other 3rd person personal pronouns), then it follows that a sound change which causes loss of initial /h-/ must be postulated. Now such a sound change is indeed plausible, for it is evidenced not only in English (consider 'Cockney *h*') but in a wide range of languages. On the other hand, if we reconstruct (quite properly, as it turns out) OE *geat* 'gate' as having initial /j-/, then it is difficult to link that Old English word up directly with PDE *gate*, for we would have to suppose a sound change of the form /j/ > /g/, a change which otherwise does not occur and is therefore implausible. The problem here is that PDE *gate* is probably from Old Norse, not Old English, the OE form surviving in place- and personal names such as *Yeats*.

There are other sources of evidence. As chapter 2 shows, Old English was closely related to the other contemporary Germanic languages. Thus, whatever structures we suppose for Old English should not be drastically out of line with the structures supposed for those languages. Similarly, although the Anglo-Saxons borrowed relatively few words from other languages, they did borrow some, especially from Latin. So when the Anglo-Saxons borrowed the Latin word *candēla* 'candle' and spelled it *candel*, provided that we are reasonably sure about the pronunciation of Latin we can make reasonable inferences about the spelling/pronunciation relationship in Old English. But both these types of evidence have to be treated with caution. After all, the reconstruction of the linguistic systems of any older languages has always to be based upon the same general principles. Therefore there is no guarantee that we are more secure in our assumptions about the pronunciation of one rather than another, although see Allen (1978) for evidence concerning the pronunciation of Latin. Indeed, a comparison with the other older Germanic languages is particularly difficult, since the evidence for Old English before the tenth century is more extensive than for any of these.

Finally, it has to be made clear that none of these types of evidence can be used to the exclusion of others. In reconstructing an older language we are, as it were, trying to complete a jigsaw without a picture, or only a few scattered bits of the picture, to help us, and we may not even know how many pieces there are. Sometimes one kind of solution is suggested, sometimes another, and it is our job to reconcile what can often be contradictory suggestions.

It should be clear from the above that the process of reconstructing the linguistic system of an older stage of the language is an uncertain one. The important word to remember here is <u>system</u>. What we cannot hope to do, indeed should not even think of doing, is to reconstruct how individual Anglo-Saxons spoke. Our aim, rather, must be to see how the different elements of the language are distributed and how they interact with one another, so that, for example, we may wish to claim that the sound represented by < t > is different from the sound represented by < d >, without giving any detailed specification of what these sounds might be. In phonology this has meant to some linguists that we can do no more than reconstruct the phonemes or contrastive sounds of the language. Thus we could claim that < t > represented the phoneme /t/ which contrasted in voicing with the phoneme /d/. This would be established by the presence of minimal pairs such as *tǣlan* 'blame' vs. *dǣlan* 'distribute'. Similarly, other minimal pairs will show that /t/ contrasts with /p/ and /k/.

This, it can be argued, is unduly pessimistic. Certainly, it would seem foolish to try and determine whether Old English /t/ was a dental or alveolar stop. The present-day language does indeed show that the two possibilities (and more) are available, both according to dialect and to position in the word (see Gimson 1980:164–5), but there is no systematic evidence one way or the other for Old English. On the other hand, if there is systematic evidence there seems no reason not to go beyond the phoneme. Thus, as we shall see later, there is considerable evidence from sound change that Old English /l/ had two allophones, namely 'clear' [l] and velarised or 'dark' [ɫ] (like many dialects of the present-day language). Here we can surely go beyond the phoneme to some kind of phonetic detail, although we must continue to ensure that our speculation is firmly embedded in a rock of substantial systematic evidence. Each such case must be treated on its own merits.

In morphology the questions posed by reconstruction are usually of a rather different kind. Of course problems related to phonology do occur. Consider PDE *foot – feet*, where the alternation in vowel between singular and plural is clearly irregular. This is a relic of a sound change in the history of Old English called *i*-mutation. We can for proto-Old English reconstruct singular */foːt/, plural */foːtiz/. The /i/ in the second syllable of the plural then caused the vowel of the first syllable to become a front vowel, eventually emerging as /eː/, so that we find singular *fōt*, plural *fēt*, and hence the present-day forms. Thus, whilst at a very early stage the stem morpheme of the word had the unchanged form /foːt/ throughout its paradigm, at a later stage there were two allomorphs of that morpheme, namely /foːt/ and /feːt/. This might appear to parallel the situation in present-day English. But whereas the alternation *foot – feet* is simply irregular, it could be that in Old English the alternation *fōt – fēt* was felt by speakers of the language to be a regular alternation typical of the declension to which *fōt* belonged.

Another kind of problem associated with morphology can be illustrated as follows. There can be no doubt that OE *swimman* 'swim', with pret. sg. *swamm*, and *drincan* 'drink', with pret. sg. *dranc*, belonged to the same morphological group or class of verbs, just as today *swim* and *drink* both follow the same pattern in forming their tenses. But in Old English we have other verbs such as *helpan – healp* 'help', *weorþan – wearþ* 'become' and *berstan – bærst* 'burst', which, although their patterns are similar to that of *swimman – swamm*, nevertheless show clear differences in the quality of their stem vowel. Should these verbs all be treated as members of the one class? Traditional grammar books, e.g. Campbell (1959), do so, because these verbs all belonged to the same class in pre-Old English times. Diachronically, therefore, this analysis is correct. Except for one point. A verb such as *berstan* was not historically a member of this group but of a different group, and it only transferred to this group in the Germanic period. What we mean by saying this is that it adopted the form and structure of this group from a synchronic point of view, having, as it were, been detached from its historical roots.

Linguists have decided in this case, and in the case of a few other verbs like it, that the synchronic analysis is preferable to the diachronic analysis. Once this small breach in the dyke is made, it is of course conceivable that other larger breaches could form. Given the actual forms in Old English, it is possible to claim that the other verbs cited above did not all belong to the same group synchronically, even if they do when viewed diachronically. If we were to look forward to later stages of the language, then the case for treating each of these types of verbs differently would become stronger and stronger.

Whatever the actual solutions to the two morphological problems cited above, they make it clear that the principal difficulty in morphological reconstruction, as opposed to phonological reconstruction, is to decide which type of analysis should be preferred, rather than to decide how detailed one particular analysis ought to be. This is not to claim that phonological and morphological problems are either completely separate or completely different in kind. That would be nonsense. There is considerable overlap as well as difference.

3.2   Orthography

The most common method of writing during the Old English period was on parchment or vellum and using a form of the Roman alphabet. In addition, the runic alphabet which the Anglo-Saxons had brought with them across the North Sea has a linguistic importance far in excess of its usage, since that alphabet was used for inscriptions and dedicatory formulae rather than for purposes of communication. Old English manuscripts have a form and shape far removed from that presented in the usual modern editions. Present-day conventions of word-division, paragraphing, etc. are precisely that, and were unknown to the Anglo-Saxons. Their own conventions, also, differed from scribe to scribe or from scriptorium to scriptorium, and can look strange to the modern reader. For details of such conventions see Ker (1957: xxxiii–xxxvi), Sisam (1953b: 186ff.), an edition such as Godden (1979) which adheres to the punctuation of the original, and the Introduction to this volume. For phonology and morphology, however, these different and differing conventions are by and large not crucial. Nevertheless it is always worth recalling that the editions we use today are substantially different from the manuscripts they report. In particular one should note that the use of a macron to indicate a long vowel, as in $\bar{e}$ against e, and the common practice of distinguishing palatal and velar examples of < c > and < g > by dotting the palatal examples of both, i.e. *ċ*, *ġ*, is a modern editorial practice not found in the Anglo-Saxon manuscripts.

3.2.1 The Roman alphabet

For the period between the time of the first arrival of the Anglo-Saxons in Britain and the coming of Augustine in 597, no manuscripts survive. As we shall see in §3.2.2, this does not imply that before 597 the Anglo-Saxons were wholly illiterate. Yet it is only during the reign of Æthelberht, the Kentish king of the time, that the first manuscript writings in the Roman alphabet appeared (even if they now survive only in much later copies) and this is clear evidence that the usage of the Roman alphabet in Anglo-Saxon England owed its origins to Christianity. Further evidence for this is the fact that manuscripts were first written in a version of the half-uncial script brought to England by Irish missionaries. This minuscule script, with clear, simple, rounded letter shapes, can be seen at its best in the Latin text of *The Lindisfarne Gospels* of the early eighth century. Very soon, however, this script was to be developed into what is known as the insular script, a pointed and cursive version of the half-uncial, and this was to remain the predominant style of handwriting until the eleventh century when a few letter-forms from the continental caroline minuscule began to appear. The insular form was to disappear by the end of the twelfth century (see Ker 1957:xxv–xxxiii, Keller 1906).

That the letters of the alphabet and even the very style in which they were written should be so dependent upon the arrival and spread of Christianity is far from surprising. Throughout the Anglo-Saxon period the teaching, and to a considerable extent the practice, of writing was predominantly a property of the church. It was in monasteries and their scriptoria that instruction in reading and writing was carried out, and scribes were normally clerics. Even when the structure of government became seriously developed, from the time of Alfred onwards, the scribes in the king's secretariat were clerics, not laymen. It is a matter of guesswork how many lay people were literate, but, even if, as we must assume, the proportion gradually increased with the passage of time and especially in the second half of the tenth century, that proportion could never have been more than tiny. Recall here the words of Alfred himself, talking of the situation when he came to the throne:

Swǽ clǽne hīo wæs oðfeallenu on Angelcynne ðæt swīðe fēawa wǽron behionan Humbre ðe hiora ðēninga cūðen understondan on Englisc oððe furðum ān ǽrendgewrit of Lǽdene on Englisc areccean; ond ic wēne ðæt[te] nōht monige begiondan Humbre nǽren. Swǽ fēawa hiora wǽron ðæt ic furðum ānne ānlēpne ne mæg geðencean be sūðan Temese ðā ðā ic tō rīce fēng.

(*CP* 3.13)

So completely had it [learning] declined in England, that there were very few on this side of the Humber who could understand their services or even translate a letter from Latin into English; and I guess that there were not many beyond the Humber. There were so few of them that I cannot even think of a single one south of the Thames when I came to the throne.

Alfred is talking about clerics; amongst laymen the situation would doubtless have been far worse. Brooks (1984:172) describes a situation at Canterbury at this time when it would appear that the principal scribe was a very old man who by then could scarcely read or write. It is certainly true that the situation at Winchester by the end of the tenth century was very different, for the Benedictine monastic revival, under the leadership of men such as Æthelwold, had produced a massive flourishing of literacy, but still that literacy must have been the property of a privileged few.

The alphabet used by the Anglo-Saxons was much the same as that used today. Some letter shapes, however, were rather different from those of later scripts notably the shapes for < e, f, g, r, s > (for details see Ker 1957). For example, < s > most usually appeared in a long form, rather like < ſ >. Confusion is only likely to occur with the shape of the letter < g >, which in insular script has the shape < ჳ >. In later periods of the language the insular < ჳ > and caroline < g > were often distinguished so that they represented different sounds, but in Old English only the one symbol, the insular one, which we write here as < ჳ > only when a contrast with < g > is relevant, was used. The naming of < ჳ > as 'yogh' is best kept for the Middle English period when the contrast between the two shapes first became linguistically significant.

But there are differences between the Old English and present-day alphabets. Firstly, the letters < j,v > were not used, the phoneme /j/ usually being represented by < g >, and [v] normally being spelled with < f >. Nor was the letter < w > used, for instead the Anglo-Saxons borrowed the runic letter 'wynn' (ƿ) (see §3.2.2). Some older editions print wynn, but this is not usual today, and here we follow the unambiguous practice of using <w> instead. Three other letters were rarely used in Old English manuscripts although they had their normal usage in Anglo-Saxon Latin manuscripts: <q,x,z>. The letter <x> was rare except for the sequence /ks/, as in *æx* 'axe' and <z> was similarly, but less frequently, used for /ts/, e.g. *milze* for *miltse* 'mercy'. The letter <q> was mainly restricted to very early texts, where, followed by <u>, it represented the sequence /kw/ as in present-day English, e.g. *EpGl quiða* 'womb' rather than usual *cwiða*. Secondly, the Anglo-Saxons had, as well as runic wynn, three further letters of their own: <æ,þ,ð>. Like the other Anglo-Saxon letters, the first two of these had individual names originating in runic practice (see §3.2.2): <æ> was called 'ash', <þ> 'thorn'. <ð> is nowadays called 'eth' or 'edh' and the name appears to be a nineteenth-century coinage; in the Old English period its name was 'ðæt' (see Robinson, 1973:450–1). Ash was an Anglo-Saxon adaptation of Latin <ae>, whereas thorn, like wynn, is an example of borrowing from the runic alphabet. The origin of eth, like its name, is more obscure, and although it is sometimes said to be a borrowing from Irish scribal tradition, this is not certain. The usual Anglo-Saxon alphabet contained, therefore, the following letters: a, æ, b, c, d, e, f, g, h, i, k, l, m, n, o, p, r, s, t, þ, ð, u, w, y. In addition to these single letters or graphs, there were several digraphs, that is to say, combinations of two letters to represent a single sound, like the PDE digraph <th> in *thin* (for the use of such digraphs see §3.3).

Orthographic usage was reasonably stable during the Old English period. Nevertheless the above alphabet, which represents the usage of the late tenth century, underwent modifications of two different kinds with the passage of time. Firstly, and especially with regard to the particularly Anglo-Saxon letters, some orthographic usages were replaced by others. Secondly, sound changes occasionally interfered with graphic conventions. In this section we shall deal only with the first type of change (the second type of change is discussed in §3.3).

Anglo-Saxon manuscripts of Latin normally kept to the Latin spelling conventions and alphabet, and in the earliest vernacular manuscripts the spelling system remained close to that of Latin texts, usually of Irish origin. Thus, at first we do not find spellings with <æ>, <w>, <þ> or <ð>. As we have said, <æ> was a development of Latin <ae> and before 800 the digraph was freely found. However, during the eighth century ligatured <æ> became more and more frequent and after 800 it was the standard form. There was one exception to this, for in many Kentish texts of the ninth century and later a ligatured form without the hook of the $<$a$>$, i.e. $<$æ$>$, was often used – this is often transcribed as $<$ę$>$. It is not easy to determine whether this particular graph was intended to equate with $<$æ$>$ or $<$e$>$, because of the particular developments which Kentish had undergone (see chapter 6). Similarly, in the earliest manuscripts, and especially in manuscripts written by continental scribes, $<$w$>$ is not often found, for instead either $<$u$>$ or $<$uu$>$ was written. The earliest examples of $<$w$>$, nevertheless, appear in a late seventh-century charter *Ch* 1171, where we find the place-name *writolaburna* and *triow* 'tree'. After the earliest period $<$w$>$ predominated, and it is only in the north that $<$u$>$ and $<$uu$>$ remained as frequent spellings for the sounds otherwise represented by $<$w$>$.

The histories of $<$þ$>$ and $<$ð$>$ are more complex, for there are three factors to consider: (i) the chronology of their introduction; (ii) the letters they take over from; (iii) their interaction with one another. But one basic point is clear: they were in principle interchangeable with one another, whatever the generality of their usage or the habits of individual scribes. Thus in *Beowulf* we can find the following spellings of the Old English word for 'since': *syððan* (line 6), *syðþan* (line 132), *syþðan* (line 283), *syþþan* (line 604), and the variation must be purely orthographic, for it is produced by one scribe of one manuscript. The first certainly dated instances of $<$ð$>$ and $<$þ$>$ are at the beginning of the seventh and eighth centuries respectively, but the Mercian *Epinal Glossary* which was most probably written early in the eighth century (see Pheifer 1974:§88) has many instances of $<$þ$>$ and several of $<$ð$>$. The evidence of that and related texts suggests that both letters must have been used by the last quarter of the seventh century. Although these graphs represented the same sounds interchangeably, there were differences in their usage. Up to about the time of Alfred $<$ð$>$ was the more frequent choice. Thenceforth $<$þ$>$ was more and more used, but it was mainly restricted to initial position, with only a minority of *þ*-spellings in medial position and very few finally.

The symbols which these two graphs replaced are found only in the very earliest manuscripts, mainly from the north of the country. They are the digraph $<$th$>$ or the simple graph $<$d$>$. Thus in the Moore manuscript of *Cædmon's Hymn*, written about 737, we find the word *mōdgidanc* 'thought' where the Leningrad version, written about ten years later, has *mōdgithanc*, whilst the West Saxon version of the first half of the tenth century has *mōdgeþanc*. As will be seen in §3.3, all these graphs represented variously the voiceless and voiced dental fricatives [θ] and [ð]. <th> appears to have been borrowed from Irish; the use of <d> represented an older and more widespread practice which we shall discuss below. At present we need only note that both these forms were quickly replaced by the Anglo-Saxon innovations <þ> and <ð>. The use of <d> to represent a fricative as well as a stop was paralleled in early texts by the use of <b> to represent a voiced labial fricative and <g> to represent a voiced velar fricative. An example of the use of <b> is in *EpGl scēabas* 'sheaves' against later and more usual *scēafas*. This, rather like the use of <d>, was most common in the North and Midlands. It is probable that the usage, although part of a more general convention allowing all three letters to represent fricatives, was reinforced by the character of the earliest Old English phonemic system (see §3.3.3.1). Like <d>, <b> in this usage disappeared by about 800, except that it is found alongside <f> in several ninth-century Kentish charters, where it is likely to have been an archaising convention on the part of the scribes at Canterbury. On the other hand, the use of <g> to represent a voiced fricative as well as a voiced stop was one which persisted right through the Old English period. Therefore a word such as *dagas* 'days', which undoubtedly contained a voiced velar fricative, was always spelled with <g>, just like *singan* 'sing', where <g> equally certainly represented a voiced velar stop. As we have seen, for velars it was only the introduction of the caroline letter-shape which allowed an orthographic distinction between stop and fricative to be made, when generally insular <ʒ> was used for the fricative, caroline <g> for the stop. This post-Conquest innovation was to persist right through the Middle English period.

After about 800 the Old English alphabet settled down into a pattern which remained unchanged until the time of the Conquest, when Norman French influence and the conventions of the caroline script, of which the Anglo-Saxons were aware from their Latin manuscripts, started to make their appearance felt. Yet even if the alphabet was fixed, spellings varied to a much greater extent than they do today, albeit to a lesser extent than in Middle English. One major reason for this was that the cultural and educational infrastructure for a standardisation of spelling simply did not exist for much of the time. We must also remember that scribes were making individual copies of manuscripts for a tiny and generally locally restricted audience. This meant that each scriptorium at any one time would have its own spelling conventions, which would differ from the conventions both of other scriptoria and of the same scriptorium at some other time. In part this would be a matter of dialect, for at least in the earlier period scribes probably attempted to represent in a recognisable form the speech of those around them. But it has also to be remembered that the concept of 'correct' spelling is a modern one. For the Anglo-Saxon scribe it would not necessarily have been 'incorrect' to spell a word one way in one line and another way in the next.

In the second half of the tenth century much of what has just been said began no longer to apply. One of the leading figures of the Benedictine monastic revival, Æthelwold, became abbot of Abingdon around 954 and then, in 963, after Edgar had come to the throne, he became bishop of Winchester. As Gneuss (1972) has demonstrated, Æthelwold, with the encouragement and help of the king and his fellow church leaders Dunstan and Oswald, then set upon a vigorous programme of teaching and instruction and a regularisation of the language so that we find, for the first time in England, a standard written language or *Schriftsprache*. One of Æthelwold's pupils was Ælfric, who became abbot of Eynsham and who is one of the outstanding figures in Old English literature. If we look at the manuscripts of his works, we find a highly regular spelling system and orthography, and there can be no doubt that this was the result of Æthelwold's teaching. Æthelwold, Ælfric and most of the other leading figures in this movement were West Saxons born and bred, and the *Schriftsprache* which they established (and which was a matter not only of spelling but also, for example, of vocabulary) was founded upon the speech of Winchester and the surrounding areas. Yet in the late Old English period we can find documents from many other parts of England written in a form which is recognisably part of the *Schriftsprache*.

At the end of the Anglo-Saxon period and in the fifty or so years after the Conquest when we are still dealing with manuscripts which are demonstrably Old English, spelling conventions did start to change. These initial changes were minor, as can be seen from a comparison of the following two versions of the Lord's Prayer. The first is taken from a copy of Ælfric's *Catholic Homilies* made about 1000, whereas the second is taken from the interlinear gloss to *The Salisbury Psalter* of ca 1100 (Sisam & Sisam 1959: §§ 24, 29). The changes in spelling convention in the later text are indicated in bold:

þu ure fæder þe eart on heofonum sy þin nama ʒehalʒod. cume ðin rice. sy ðin wylla on eorðan swa swa on heofonum. syle us todæʒ urne dæʒhwamlican hlaf. and forʒyf us ure ʒyltas swaswa we forʒyfað ðam þe wið us aʒyltað. and ne læd ðu us on costnunʒe. ac alys us fram yfele. sy hit swa.

(ÆCHom I.19.258)*

fæder ure þu ðe eart on heouenum si gehalgod nama þin. to becume rice þin. gewyrpe willa þin swa on heouenum and on eorþan. ... urne dæihwamlice syle us todæi. and forgif us gyltas ure easwa and we forgiuan gyltendrum urum. and na us ingelæd on costninge. ac alys us fra yuele. þæt si.

(PsCa(K) 13)*

As can be seen, there are only two types of change. Firstly caroline <g> is used instead of insular <ʒ> (in fact the scribe used both indiscriminately). Secondly, <i> replaced <g> where the sound represented is /i/ as the second element of a diphthong and <u> replaces <f> as the representation of [v]. It is doubtful if either of these signal a change in phonological structure – they are more likely to be the result of the influence of the caroline script in Latin texts (see Scragg 1974:13–14).

3.2.2   The runic alphabet

The runic alphabet is a peculiarly Germanic property. Its ancient origins are obscure and the source of considerable speculation. Whatever these origins, it was to flourish in later centuries in Scandinavia and Anglo-Saxon England. The Anglo-Saxon knowledge of runes probably stemmed from Scandinavia, but the tradition seems to have travelled south-west through Frisia and thence with the Anglo-Saxon settlements into England. This judgement, based on the shapes of the runic letters and the known distribution of runes (see Page 1973:18–21) is reinforced by what we know and presume about the origins of the Anglo-Saxons themselves. Runes can be found from every part of the Old English period, the earliest inscription, at Caistor-by-Norwich, being, remarkably, of the fourth or early fifth century, and runes continued to be written up until the eleventh century. Their geographical distribution is more limited, as can be seen from Figure 3.1. The earliest runes are to be found in East Anglia, then comes a group in Kent, but after about 650 almost all the runic inscriptions we have are from north of a line from Anglesey to the Wash. Northumbria, indeed, seems to have been

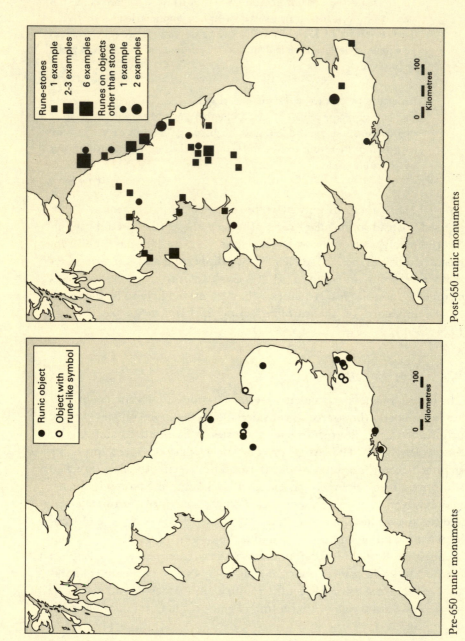

Pre-650 runic monuments

Post-650 runic monuments

Figure 3.1 Maps of pre-650 and post-650 runic monuments (Page 1973)

ᚠᚢᚦᚨᚱᚲᚷᚹᚺᚾᛁᛃᛈᛇᛉᛊᛏᛒᛖᛗᛚᛜᛞᛟ

f u p a r k g w h n i j p ī R s t b e m l ŋ d o

1 2 3 4 5 6 7 8   9 10 11 12 13 14 15 16 17 18 19 20 21 22 23 24

Figure 3.2 Futhark from Kylver, Gotland, ca 400 (Page 1973)

1	2	3	4	5	6	7	8:		9	10	11	12	13	14	15	16:
ᚠ	ᚢ	ᚦ	ᚨ	ᚱ	ᚺ	ᚷ			ᚺ	ᛏ	ᛁ	ᛉ	ᛊ	ᛲ	ᛃ	ᛡ
f	u	p	o	r	c	g w:			h	n	i	j	ȝ	p	(x)	s:

17	18	19	20	21	22	23	24:		25	26	27	28	29	30	31:
ᛏ	ᛒ	ᛖ	ᛗ	ᛚ	ᛟ	ᛞ			ᚨ	ᚠ	ᛗ	ᛠ	ᛣ	ᚸ	
t	b	e	m	l	ŋ	œ	d:		a	n	y	êa	k	k̄	g̱

Figure 3.3 Old English futhorc (Dickins 1932)

the principal centre of rune-making in the country. The main source of Anglo-Saxon runes is carvings on stone, although some occur on coins and in manuscripts we have, for example, the *Rune Poem* (ed. Dobbie 1942), and the poet Cynewulf signed his name acrostically in runes in four of his poems: *The Fates of the Apostles, Elene, Christ II* and *Juliana*. The best-known and most important of runic inscriptions are the extract from *The Dream of the Rood* carved on the Ruthwell Cross in Dumfriesshire and the beautiful runic carving on the ivory Auzon Casket. The latter can be dated to ca 700 and the former is of roughly the same date.

The overwhelming majority of runic inscriptions that remain from the Old English period (and Page 1973:15 estimates the total number of extant reliable texts at under thirty, some containing no more than a single name) are monumental or decorative in purpose, and it is probable that this was their main usage once the Roman alphabet had been introduced into this country. But, to judge from the evidence of Scandinavia and common-sense, it is likely that before then they could also have been used for everyday purposes of communication (see Page 1973:ch. 8). There is also a strong tradition that runes had a magical signification (see Elliott 1959, but cf. Page 1973 for a more sceptical view).

A good example of the Germanic runic alphabet is the Gotlandish alphabet of ca 400 shown in Figure 3.2, which may be compared with the Anglo-Saxon runic alphabet in Figure 3.3. The letter shapes are sometimes similar to those of the Roman alphabet (e.g. the rune for 'r' is close to Roman R) and others may be related to the Greek alphabet – this has been argued for the Germanic *o*-rune in relation to Greek omega. There are, however, others whose origin is obscure but most likely internal to Germanic, e.g. the rune for 'g'. Furthermore, the elaboration of the original alphabet which is to be seen in Old English is a demonstration that the runic alphabet was well capable of continual modification and adjustment, that it had an active life of its own whatever its origin.

The Germanic runic alphabet is called the fuþark (or futhark) after the first six characters. The Old English one is called the fuþorc. This change of name points to the major significance of runes for the student of Old English phonology. As mentioned in §3.2.1, each Old English letter had its own name, and this was a practice inherited from the runic tradition, where it was originally established. A good guide to the naming practice is to be found in the *Rune Poem*. Thus, the fourth letter of the alphabet had, apparently, the Germanic name **ansuz* 'god'. And in the development of the alphabet it was the name which determined the sound, rather than the sound which determined the name (the initial sound of the name was identical to the sound represented by the letter). In the Germanic dialects bordering the North Sea (the so-called Inguaeonic dialects), **a* before a nasal plus fricative became /o:/ due to rounding, loss of the nasal and compensatory lengthening of the vowel. Thus **ansuz* changed to **ōsuz* (later **ōs*). With the change in pronunciation of the name, the rune came to represent the new sound rather than the old. At least, that is more or less the position. In fact, however, the common shape of the fourth rune appears to have been ᚠ, and this was preserved as a rune representing /æ(:)/, the usual Old English development of **ã̄*. The rune was then altered in shape and the altered shape turns up as the rune representing /o(:)/. But as can be seen from Figure 3.2, it is the altered rune which keeps the fourth position in the alphabet, the original rune now being tacked on at the end, a good demonstration of the power of the name. The position was more complex yet, for sometimes Gmc **a* remained as /a/ and another rune, no. 25, had to be formed from the one original shape to cover yet another pronunciation of the original sound in Old English.

From that one could go on to note that rune 24 has changed its value from /o(:)/ to /ø(:)/, partly because its rune name **ōþil* had changed, as the result of *i*-mutation, to *ōēþel* 'land' (the Northumbrian form, = WS *ēþel*), but also because of the new symbol for /o(:)/. As we can see, these changes in the runic alphabet interlock on a considerable scale, and both the changes themselves and the nature of their interaction with one another can help us to a better understanding of various sound changes in the development of the language. It would, however, be dangerous to take the changes at their face value. For example, what Page (1973:152) calls 'a skilled use of the various characters available for the guttural stops' may, in the light of recent research (see Ball 1988) be rather less skilled and more accidental than has usually been supposed. As we shall see in §3.3, the Old English scribal tradition paid rather less attention to the sound system of the language than linguists would have liked. There is little reason to suppose that the rune-makers were any more sensitive in such matters, although the different conventions of rune-making can certainly cast a different, and therefore revealing, light on pronunciation.

3.3 Phonology

Just as the sound system of English has changed drastically between the time of the Norman Conquest and today, so too it changed drastically between the time of the first Anglo-Saxon settlements and the Conquest. Similarly, just as today we find different sound systems in different dialects, so in Old English there was considerable dialect variation. On both counts, therefore, it is improper to speak of the phoneme system of Old English. We should, rather, speak of the phoneme system of one particular dialect at one particular point in time. In what follows we have attempted to solve these two problems in different ways. The discussion of chronological or diachronic variation is facilitated by establishing as a reference point, the phoneme system of classical Old English, that is to say the phoneme system of West Saxon at the time of Ælfric, ca 1000. Having established that point of reference (§3.3.1) we trace, in §3.3.3, the evolution and development of that system from the time of the earliest settlements both up to and then beyond that point. These sections do not merely attempt an historical account of the evolution of that system, but also attempt an explanation of it.

The consideration of dialect variation is rather different. As has just been said, the sections below concentrate on the emergence of classical Old English, i.e. Late West Saxon. If that were all, then there would be no difficulty. But the concentration on West Saxon creates two further problems which are of considerable importance both for Old English and for the further history of the language. Firstly, as we shall see, there is no direct chronological line of descent between Early West Saxon and Late West Saxon (hence the use of capitals for 'Early' and 'Late'). The former might better be described as Alfredian Saxon, since it is best characterised by the texts produced in the court of King Alfred. The latter might better be described as Æthelwoldian Saxon, since it is a product of the standardisation introduced by Æthelwold (see §3.2.1). This, at least, would avoid the misleadingly chronological impression given by the traditional terminology (see Hogg 1988). However, with this caveat in mind the traditional terminology is retained here. Secondly, it is well known that the core antecedent of what is later to become Standard English was not West Saxon at all – which is the antecedent of the dialects of the Thames Valley and the area to its south-west. The antecedent of Standard English was, rather, a variety of the Old English Mercian dialect (see in this respect the discussion in vol. II, ch. 2). Even worse, that variety would be East or South-East Mercian, for which our knowledge is scanty and uncertain. West Saxon had only a marginal influence on the later standard (even Kentish had more). It is unavoidably true that what was to be the standard language of Old English is far removed from the central developments in the later Middle English period and beyond. What must have looked so broad and clear a trail 1000 years ago was soon to fizzle out into an overgrown and indistinct woodland path.

3.3.1   *Phonemic/graphemic correspondences*

Let us now consider the phoneme system of classical Old English and the relationship between that and the orthographic system. In what follows we deal firstly with stressed vowels and diphthongs, then with unstressed vowels, and finally with consonants. It must be emphasized that the system postulated here is one which is still a subject of much controversy amongst Old English scholars, not merely on points of detail but also on questions of general principles. Usually these matters of controversy will not be discussed immediately (although they may be referred to), but later in §3.3.3.

3.3.1.1   Vowels

Three of the principal parameters for phonological contrasts in Old English were similar to those today: backness, height and lip-rounding. But in addition vowel length formed a significant contrast. Let us take these in turn. For backness there was a two-way contrast, i.e. [front] vs. [back]. For height there was probably a three-way contrast, so that vowels were either [high], [mid] or [low]. The situation regarding lip-rounding was different from that in Received Pronunciation, for in the latter only non-low back vowels, e.g. /u,o/, are normally found with lip-rounding. In Old English, however, lip-rounding could be phonemically significant for all non-low vowels, whether front or back, so that, for example, there was a high front rounded vowel /y/ (compare French *tu* or the Scottish pronunciation of *book*). The most obvious difference between Old English and present-day English, however, concerns the question of vowel length. In the present-day language the phonological contrast of vowel length seems not to be primary. If we contrast the pair *bead* and *bid*, although it is true that the vowel of the first is longer than the vowel of the second, this correlates directly with a shift of quality, so that the second vowel is both lower and more centralised (see Gimson 1980:96–8, 101–6). In contrast, in Old English, although there was clearly a quantitative contrast, so that we find *riden* 'ride' pa.part. vs. *rīden* 'ride' pr.subj.pl., cf. PDE *ridden, ride*, there is no consistent evidence of any corresponding qualitative shift. This does not mean to say there was none, but if there was, as might be suggested by later developments, it seems to be one of those phonetic details which are immune to our techniques of reconstruction.

In classical Old English there were seven long vowels and seven corresponding short vowels which contrasted along the parameters just outlined. We can identify them by means of a (schematic) vowel chart.

$$i(:) \quad y(:) \qquad u(:)$$
$$e(:) \qquad\quad o(:)$$
$$æ(:) \qquad ɑ(:)$$

There is no major difficulty in identifying these phonemes with their graphic equivalents, although it should be recalled that the Anglo-Saxons rarely distinguished between long and short vowels. If we move anti-clockwise round the chart, starting with /i(:)/, the following are typical spellings of these phonemes: *riden* 'ride' pa.part., *rīden* 'ride' pr.subj.pl.; *metan* 'measure', *mētan* 'meet'; *mæst* 'mast', *mǣst* 'most'; *hara* 'hare', *hāra* 'hoary' wk.; *god* 'god', *gōd* 'good'; *dun* 'dun', *dūn* 'hill'; *syl(l)* 'sill', *sȳl* 'pillar'.

There is thus a fairly direct correlation between grapheme and phoneme. Yet despite the excellent parallelisms, it is worth saying a few words about two troublesome cases, the front and back low vowels. Although it is true that the normal transcriptions of, say, *mæst* and *mǣst* are, respectively /mæst/ and /mæ:st/, these transcriptions are more conventional than accurate. In both cases, certainly, we are dealing with a low front vowel, but we cannot be precise about the phonetic values.

And this is one case where a quantitative difference may have correlated with a qualitative difference. The evidence of later stages especially indicates that the long vowel must have been higher and further front than the short vowel, for in Middle English /æː/ turns up as /ɛː/ whereas /æ/ turns up as /a/, hence OE *sǣ* > ME *sea/see* (= /sɛː/ > PDE *sea* against OE *sæt* > ME *sat* > PDE *sat*. Although the situation is obscure (for discussion of the short vowel see Lass 1976:132–4), in part at least because of the conservatism of the late Old English spelling system, we can reasonably claim that before the end of the Old English period the long and short low front vowels had begun to diverge qualitatively. It may even have been a process extending further back in time, but that is pure speculation. The other troublesome case is the short low back vowel /ɑ/. The relevant cases are where this vowel appears before a nasal, as in *mann* 'person', which, and this is the crux, could also be spelled *monn*. This variation in spelling suggests that we might be dealing with instances of the phoneme /o/ rather than /ɑ/, or even an extra phoneme /ɔ/. In Late West Saxon, however, *a*-spellings predominate, and it is pretty certain that such cases are in fact instances of /ɑ/. Whether or not the situation might have been different in other dialects or at other times remains debatable (see Kuhn 1961 and Hogg 1982b for discussion and different views).

3.3.1.2 Diphthongs

Despite these last two points, it is safe to claim that the classical Old English vowel system is relatively uncontroversial. When we come to the diphthongs the situation is radically different. Almost every aspect of the diphthongal system is uncertain and subject to fierce debate and the most controversial of these are discussed in §3.3.3 in the context of the development of the language.

The situation is as follows. In classical Old English diphthongs were always 'falling', that is to say, the first element of the diphthong was the more prominent. There were only two principal diphthongs (other possibilities are considered further below, see especially the account of *i*-mutation in §3.3.3.1 for discussion of the Early West Saxon spelling <ie>), which were spelled <eo> and <ea>. But, and this is the major point of controversy, each of these diphthongs contrasted in length. Thus the four diphthongs can be characterised graphically as <ēo, eo, ēa, ea>. Occasionally *eo*-spellings were substituted for by *io*-spellings, but such cases are no more than relics of a previous stage without synchronic relevance. Examples of the usual spellings are *cnēowe* 'know' pa.subj.sg., *cneowe* 'knee' dat.sg.; *nēah* 'near', *seah* 'he saw'. If we assume a diphthongal interpretation of these digraphs, it is incontestable that the principal difference between the sound represented by, say, <eo> and that represented by <ea> lies in the height of the first, more prominent element of the diphthong and that whatever differences there may have been between the second elements of the diphthongs were secondary, not primary. The reasons for this are overwhelmingly a matter of the chronological development of the language (see further § 3.3.3). From a synchronic point of view however, we can note that, for example, <eo> occurs in positions where we would expect <e> (representing /e/) and that <ea> occurs where we would expect <æ> (representing /æ/). Thus a strong verb of class III, cf. 3.4.2.1, such as *weorpan* 'throw' has <eo> for expected <e>, compare *berstan* 'burst', and in the preterite singular it has <ea>, i.e. *wearp*, where <æ> would be predicted, compare *bærst*. Since the second element of the diphthong was less prominent, its behaviour and status was probably more akin to that of unstressed vowels than that of stressed vowels. The precise value of these elements is impossible to ascertain, cf. § 3.3.1.3 below. If we are dealing with diphthongs, the second elements must have been back rather than front, and if they were like unstressed vowels, then they would have been either mid or low in height. This variation was dependent upon the height of the more prominent first element. Thus we can suggest the four phonemic diphthongs: /eːo, eo, æːɑ, æɑ/. One important point to note is that although this description implies that the major difference between the two pairs of diphthongs was between the height of the first elements, the Old English orthographic system showed this contrast only by a difference in the spelling of the second element of the digraphs, i.e. <eo> vs. <ea>. One plausible explanation for this is that advocated by Stockwell & Barritt (1951:16), namely that scribes generally avoided trigraphs of the type <aea> and hence <æa>. Thus the digraph <ea> was used *faute de mieux*.

The question of whether or not there were other diphthongs in Old English apart from the above remains a matter of dispute. The only possible cases concern front vowels plus /j/, as in *weġ* 'way', *wrēġ* 'accuse' imp., *dæġ* 'day', *grāēġ* 'grey'. To take the example *weġ*, there can be no doubt, see § 3.3.3, that at one time this was phonologically /wej/. The point at issue is whether during the Old English period the post-vocalic and word-final /j/ was vocalised to give /wei/. It is clear that this did not happen if /j/ was not word-final, as in *weġes*, etc., but occasional spellings such as *wei* have suggested to traditional scholars that vocalisation did take place (see, for example Campbell 1959: §266). However this position has been attacked on theoretical grounds (see Stockwell 1962, Colman 1983b). There is no doubt that such diphthongs did appear after the end of the Old English period, but to posit an earlier date for their development does seem dubious.

3.3.1.3 Unstressed vowels

The Old English period showed a steady decline in the number and variety of unstressed vowels, so that by the end of the period it may be doubted whether there was phonemically more than one unstressed vowel, namely the reduced schwa vowel /ə/. However, in classical Old English the distinction between front and back unstressed vowels is generally well maintained, the former normally being written <e> and the latter <o> or <a>, thus *stānes* 'stone' gen.sg. vs. *stānas* 'stones'. Since in the eleventh century even these sounds were confused, so suggesting /ə/, it may be that they were already in the classical period quite centralised vowels and that the distinction between them was as much a matter of lip rounding as of tongue position (see §3.3.3.2 and Bately 1980: xliv). Phonemically, nevertheless, the front and back vowels can be represented as /e/ and /ɔ/ (to indicate the merger of earlier /o/ and /a/) respectively. This, of course, has implications for the transcription of diphthongs. Should they, perhaps, be transcribed as, say, /eɔ, æɔ/ or, as many scholars do, /eə, æə/?

One exception to the above concerns the spelling <i> before palatal or palatalised consonants, as in *mihtiġ* 'strong', *Denisċ* 'Danish', *dyseliċ* 'foolish', where it would appear that an earlier contrast between unstressed /i/ and /e/ had been retained. However, there are other examples where earlier unstressed /e/ became written with <i>, for example *hāliġ* 'holy' < *hāleġ* < *hālæġ*, and this occurred only before palatal /j/. The conclusion to be drawn from this is that there was an [i] allophone of unstressed /e/ occurring only before palatal consonants.

A further exception concerns the back high vowel /u/. As indicated above, the spelling evidence suggests that unstressed /u/ was normally lowered and centralised. However, word-finally after another /u/, as in *sunu* 'son', or before /m/, as in the dative plural inflexion -*um*, and also in the suffix -*uc*, -*ung*, e.g. *munuc* 'monk', *costung* 'temptation', the <u> was normally preserved. The circumstances which combined to thus protect the high vowel and the phonemic status of unstressed [u] are equally obscure, see §3.3.3.2 for further discussion.

3.3.1.4 Consonants

In many respects the Old English consonant system was not unlike the system in the present-day language. Thus there were the following principal classes of consonants: stops, fricatives, sibilants, affricates, nasals, liquids and approximants. On the other hand, there were several general features which contrast with those in the present-day language. For example, the feature of [voice] was contrastive only for stops and affricates, so that in Old English there were no minimal pairs of the type *ferry – very* as found today. Also, even if the principal classes of consonants were the same as today, there were distributional gaps, so that, for example, in Old English the velar nasal [ŋ] was not phonemic as it is today – contrast OE *sang* = /sɑng/ and PDE *sang* = /sæŋ/.

Perhaps the most obvious difference between Old English and present-day English is the existence in the former of geminate consonants. In Old English we find a contrast between, say, *sete* 'set' imp.sg. and *sette* 'set' 1sg.pr.ind. This serves to indicate a difference not unlike that in present-day English between *black it* (*out*) and *black kit*, transcribed as /blæk ɪt/ and /blæk kɪt/ respectively. The two Old English examples can be transcribed as /sete/ and /sette/. One important question is whether the consonants in *sette* are best described as geminate or long (the latter implying the transcription /set:e/). In order to answer this we have to consider the distribution of these consonants. Now although it is clear that they occur relatively freely between vowels, as in the example above, it is doubtful whether they can occur anywhere else. Word-final spellings such as in *mann* 'man' and *bedd* 'bed', although normal, are found alongside spellings such as *man*, *bed*, and it seems certain that in classical Old English the 'double' consonants were restricted to medial positions (see §3.3.3.1). It is therefore preferable to analyse these consonants as geminate rather than long. As for which Old English consonants could be geminate, and which could not, it is probable, despite some partially defective cases, notably [ff] and [gg], that all the consonants except /ʃ/ and the approximants /j,w/ could be doubled.

Let us now consider in more detail the consonant phonemes of classical Old English. We shall discuss these in the following order: (i) voiceless stops; (ii) voiced stops; (iii) fricatives; (iv) affricates; (v) nasals; (vi) liquids; (vii) approximants. In the English of ca 1000 the voiceless stops were very similar to those of the present-day language. Thus there was only a three-way distinction in place of articulation: bilabial – dental(-alveolar) – velar, phonemically /p,t,k/. It is impossible to be more precise about the articulation of the dental consonants (see §3.1), and similarly there is no way of telling whether these stops would have aspiration in initial position in the syllable, a characteristic feature of present-day English which distinguishes it from, say, Dutch. As regards the distribution of these phonemes, /p/ was relatively rare in Old English, since, except in loan-words, it was derived from the rare Indo-European sound */b/, but the other two phonemes /t/ and /k/ were found with a frequency and distribution similar to that in present-day English. In the cases of /p/ and /t/ the relationship to spellings is straightforward, so that typical instances of these phonemes are: *pōl* 'pool', *grīpan* 'grip', *sċip* 'ship', *hoppian* 'hop'; *tōð* 'tooth', *metan* 'measure', *ġeat* 'gate', *hātte* 'is called'. For the velar stop /k/, however, the situation was more complex. As we have noted, both <c> and <k> were available graphs. In §3.3.4.1 we shall see that a sound change called <u>palatalisation</u> had affected all the velar consonants, so that some original velars remained but others had become palatals or affricates. In this case the change gave a /k/ − /tʃ/ contrast. Old English scribes normally made no systematic attempt to distinguish these even though they became different phonemes. Most particularly, it is important to note that, for instance, it was not the case that <c> was used for the affricate, <k> for the stop. Instead, in both cases the usual graph was <c>, with <k> only used as an occasional spelling. In order to disambiguate the use of <c>, editors frequently place a superscript dot over <c> when it represents an affricate, as in, say, *ċȳse* 'cheese', but other instances of <c> are left undotted. Normal examples of /k/, therefore, are: *cyning* 'king', *lōcian* 'look', *bōc* 'book', *locca* 'curl'. Occasional spellings with <k> would be of the form *kyning*, etc. A minor exception to the above is that <x> was often used to represent the sequence /ks/, as in *fox* 'fox'.

The voiced stops are more problematic than the voiceless ones, from both the phonological and the orthographical points of view. It is probably best to start by assuming that the voiced stops paralleled their voiceless counterparts, thus giving the series /b,d,g/. Let us take /d/ firstly, since its distribution and frequency was exactly parallel to that of /t/, and hence similar to that in present-day English. Moreover, /d/ was represented by <d>, typical examples being: *dæġ* 'day', *rīdan* 'ride', *tīd* 'time', *ġebedda* 'bedfellow'. Bilabial /b/, on the other hand, was more restricted, following from the situation in West Germanic. It occurred freely initially, but medially and finally it occurred only after a nasal or in gemination (the geminate being simplified finally). Although in early Old English (see §3.3.4.1) the phonemic status of the geminate was complex, there can be no doubt that in classical Old English the geminate was simply /bb/. In all cases /b/ was represented orthographically by <b>, and therefore typical examples are: *bindan* 'bind', *climban* 'climb', *lamb* 'lamb', *sib(b)* 'relationship', *habban* 'have'.

The voiced velar stop is one of the most controversial and complex of Old English phonemes. From the phonological point of view, it is to be derived from Gmc */ɣ/, a voiced velar fricative. Before the time of the earliest texts that fricative had become a stop after nasals and in gemination, as in the case of /b/, which is from earlier */β/. Initially /ɣ/ remained a fricative until a fairly late, but unspecifiable, date. Only once the caroline and insular forms of <g> became used to distinguish the velar stop and velar fricative does the orthography tell us that initially the sound had developed into a stop. Even so, it is probably best to assume that this had occurred by the time of classical Old English. Finally the fricative had become devoiced by the time of classical Old English. In gemination, because of other changes, the velar stop occurred only in a very small number of forms, often pet or zoological names, e.g. *dogga* 'dog'. All this implies that, whatever the situation earlier, the voiced velar fricative is only to be found medially in classical Old English. Thus it is best analysed as an allophone of a velar stop phoneme /g/, i.e. [ɣ]. So we can state that the voiced velar stop occurred freely in initial position, medially after nasals, in gemination and singly in the allophonic variation [ɣ], and finally after nasals. Not only is the position phonologically complex, it was also complex orthographically, for the Old English scribes used the letter <g> to represent three sounds: (i) the voiced velar stop; (ii) the voiced velar fricative; (iii) the palatal approximant /j/, (derived from Gmc */ɣ/ by palatalisation and also directly from Germanic initial */j/). As with <c>, modern editors frequently dot <g> when it represents a palatal sound, and we follow this practice here, hence *ġēar* 'year'. In gemination, two digraphs were available: <cg> and <gg>, and no distinction was made between the representation of velar /gg/ and the affricate /ʤ/. Again, modern practice is to dot examples representing an affricate, hence *seċġan*, *seġġan* 'say' against *docga*, *dogga* 'dog'. Given the above difficulties, we can suggest as typical examples of the voiced velar stop: *gōd* 'good', *singan* 'sing', *dagas* 'days' (= [ɣ]), *sang* 'he sang', *docga* 'dog'.

Moving to the fricatives, we come to a major difference between Old English and present-day English, for, as we have said, there was no phonemic contrast of voice amongst the Old English fricatives. Thus we find only labio-dental /f/, dental /θ/, velar /x/, the alveolar sibilant /s/ and the palato-alveolar /ʃ/. That does not mean there were no voiced fricative sounds in Old English other than [ɣ] mentioned above. There were, but they were allophones of the above phonemes and occurred only between voiced sounds, so that, for example, *fisċ* 'fish' and *wulf* 'wolf' had [f], but *wulfas* 'wolves' (note the present-day alternation /f/ – /v/) and *drīfan* 'drive' had [v], all four cases being representatives of the phoneme /f/. In southern dialects from the tenth century onwards these fricatives appear to have been voiced in initial positions also (see Bennett 1955), and although this does not have any phonemic consequences it is a feature which remains characteristic of present-day south-western English dialects.

The only complication in a discussion of /f/ concerns its voiced allophone, for it could derive from two sources, namely Gmc */f/ and Gmc */β/. In earliest Old English the former should have been [v], the latter [β], but by the classical period the two sounds must have merged. Given our comments above about geminate /ff/, we can therefore assume a fairly straightforward distribution of /f/, which was regularly represented by <f> as in *fisċ* 'fish', *drīfan* 'drive', *wulf* 'wolf', *pyffan* 'breathe out'. The dental fricative /θ/ poses no phonological problems, and the only point of interest orthographically is the interchange between <þ> and <ð> discussed in §3.2.1. Typical examples of this fricative are: *þing* 'thing, *baðian* 'bathe', *bæð* 'bath', *syððan* 'since'. The velar fricative had a slightly more complex distribution. At first sight it would appear that it was found only in medial position if geminate and in final position, earlier instances of single medial /x/ having been lost and in final position /x/ being the result of both earlier */x/ and earlier */ɣ/. This fricative was regularly spelled <h>, as in *hliehhan* 'laugh' *seah* 'he saw'. It is certain, however, that, as with the other velars, there had developed a palatal as well as a velar sound. But, in contrast to the others, there was no phonemic split here, so that we only have two allophones, namely [ç] and [x], whose distribution and pronunciation must have been similar to the 'ich' and 'ach' sounds in Modern German. We can further distinguish a third allophone of /x/, for initially <h> represented the glottal fricative [h], as in *hand* 'hand', and this is best treated phonemically as /x/.

Next come the sibilants /s/ and /ʃ/. The former paralleled the voiceless fricatives (thus becoming voiced [z] medially) and is represented by <s>, examples being *sittan* 'sit', *rīsan* 'rise', *hūs* 'house', *cyssan* 'kiss'. On the other hand /ʃ/ had developed from earlier */sk/, once again by palatalisation, and because of this it had a slightly defective distribution, occurring freely in initial and medial positions, but finally only after a front vowel and never as a geminate. The usual spelling, namely <sc>, was used both for /ʃ/ and the sequence /sk/ without distinction, but we follow the normal practice of dotting the <c> in cases where /ʃ/ is represented. Thus we find examples such as: *sċip* 'ship', *fisċes* 'fish' gen.sg., *disċ* 'dish', contrasting with *ascaδ* 'he asks', *tusc* 'tusk'. Note that in this case not only are there no geminate examples but also there are no instances of the voiced allophone [ʒ]: in *fisċes* the medial consonant was simply [ʃ].

There were two affricate phonemes, one voiceless, one voiced, and these were the result of palatalisation of earlier /k(k)/ and [g(g)]. As in present-day English, these affricates were the combination of a dental stop and palatal sibilant, hence /tʃ/ and /dʒ/. We have already noted that the former was spelled <c>, the latter <g>. When they occur as geminates, as the result of development from geminate velar stops, the stop was lengthened to give /ttʃ, /ddʒ/, the former being spelled <cc>, the latter as <cg> or <gg>. The voiceless affricate occurred freely, as in *ċild* 'child', *rīċe* 'kingdom', *diċ* 'ditch', *streċċan* 'stretch'. But the voiced affricate could occur only where [g(g)] had originally occurred, i.e. medially and finally after nasals and in gemination. Hence we only find the following types: *senġan* 'singe', *ecġ* 'edge', *secġan* 'say'.

We have already noted that there was no velar nasal phoneme /ŋ/ in Old English. This was because [ŋ] only occurred when followed by a velar consonant, as in *sang* 'he sang', and therefore it can be analysed as a velar allophone of /n/, i.e. /sɑng/, with only a two-way phonemic contrast between labial /m/ and dental /n/; this remains a feature of many West Midlands and North-West PDE dialects. The major patterns of distribution and spelling are straightforward, and so we find typical examples such as: *meltan* 'melt', *niman* 'take', *bēam* 'tree', *fremme* 'I perform'; *nama* 'name', *mōna* 'moon', *stān* 'stone'. The dental nasal no doubt not only assimilated to a following velar consonant to give the velar allophone [ŋ], but also to a following palatal, as in *benċ* 'bench', giving the palatal allophone [ɲ]. See the discussion below of the spelling sequence <hn> as in *hnutu* 'nut'.

There were two liquids in Old English, namely /l/ and /r/, spelled <l> and <r> respectively. It is probable that /l/ had two allophones, a 'clear' [l] and a dark [ɫ], as in many present-day dialects, the latter occurring between back vowels and before consonants, see §3.3.3.1 for discussion. Otherwise its distribution presents few problems, typical examples being: *lamb* 'lamb', *talu* 'tale', *smæl* 'narrow', *tellan* 'tell'. The phonetic value of /r/ is much more uncertain, opinions having ranged from an alveolar trill to a retroflex to a uvular fricative (see Lass 1983 for an up-to-date survey). Its distribution is, however, straightforward: *rīdan* 'ride', *beran* 'bear', *fȳr* 'fire', *steorra* 'star'. For both liquids we find spellings with preceding <h>, i.e. <hl>, <hr>, compare <hn> and see the discussion of <hw> below.

There were two approximants, one palatal, the other labial-velar, i.e. /j/ and /w/. Both these sounds were the reflexes of equivalent Germanic sounds, but /j/ could also arise by palatalisation of *[ɣ], see above, and this would have produced a voiced palatal fricative. In fact it seems fruitless to attempt to determine whether /j/ was pronounced with friction, (see Hogg 1979b). The distribution of /j/ is difficult. It must have occurred initially and medially before vowels, where, as elsewhere, it was represented by <g> (see above), thus: *gēar* 'year', *hergas* 'armies'. It probably also occurred finally after a liquid, as in *byrġ* 'cities'. The real problem is whether or not it occurred after vowels, as in *weġ* 'way', see §3.3.1.2. On the other hand the distribution of /w/ is clearly restricted to initial position and medially before vowels. It was in classical Old English represented by <w>, e.g. *wind* 'wind', *snāwas* 'snows'.

The final point to which we must turn is the question of <hw> spellings, paralleling the <hn, hl, hr> spellings mentioned above. These spellings only occurred initially, typical examples being: *hnutu* 'nut', *hlāf* 'loaf', *hrēod* 'reed', *hwæt* 'what'. In present-day English these words usually show initial /n, l, r, w/ respectively, except that in the last case some dialects, especially Scots and Irish, show /ʍ/ or /hw/, giving minimal pairs such as *whether* (/ʍ/) and *weather* (/w/). The evidence especially of later periods, e.g. the development of *who* < OE *hwā*, Middle English spellings such as <quh>, suggest that we are dealing with a sequence of sounds here, consisting of [h] followed by the appropriate nasal, liquid or approximant (which may have been phonetically voiceless). This gives the four phoneme sequences /xn, xl, xr, xw/.

The above discussion allows us to present the following phoneme table for the consonants of classical Old English (excluding geminates):

The consonant phonemes of classical Old English

	Labial	Dental	Palatal	Velar
Voiceless stops	/p/	/t/	—	/k/
Voiced stops	/b/	/d/	—	/g/
Fricatives	/f/	/θ/	—	/x/
Sibilants	—	/s/	/ʃ/	—
Affricates	—	/ʧ,ʤ/	—	—
Nasals	/m/	/n/	—	—
Liquids, approximants	—	/l,r/	/j/	/w/

3.3.2   Suprasegmental phonology

From what we can tell about the syllable structure and the stress patterns of Old English, it seems unlikely that they changed much during the period, even although the stress patterns of Old English were often unlike those of present-day English and the structure of syllables differed in several details from that found today. There are, of course suprasegmental phenomena other than syllable structure and stress, for example, intonation. Phenomena such as this are not discussed below, since it seems impossible to reconstruct any useful systematic information about them. In the absence of information to the contrary we might suggest that the situation would not have been radically different from that pertaining today, but perhaps even to say that would be misleadingly rash.

3.3.2.1   Syllable structure

Most linguists today accept the syllable as a linguistic unit containing two or three components, namely onset and rhyme, the latter being divisible into nucleus and coda. The onset consists of the consonantal segments preceding the vowel or (in unstressed syllables) liquid or nasal which forms the sonority peak of a syllable. The nucleus consists of the vowel (etc.) which forms the sonority peak and any associated vocalic element. The coda contains the remaining consonantal elements in the syllable. Thus in present-day English *grind* = /graind/ would have as its onset /gr/, as its nucleus /ai/ and as its coda /nd/. These same principles apply in Old English. The length or 'weight' of a syllable is determined by considering the structure of the rhyme (i.e. nucleus

+ coda), where length is specified in terms of a unit called the mora. A short vowel (= V) contains one mora, as does a short consonant (= C), whilst a long vowel (= VV) contains two morae, as does a long or geminate consonant (= CC). A major problem in Old English concerns the diphthongs, where (cf. §3.3.1.2) there is a length contrast between short and long diphthongs. In present-day English, where there is no such contrast, diphthongs pattern with long vowels and are therefore always bimoric. But in Old English short diphthongs patterned with short vowels and long diphthongs patterned with long vowels. Hence short diphthongs, even although they have phonemically two different segments, must be analysed as monomoric, i.e. V. Long diphthongs were bimoric, like the present-day diphthongs.

In Old English stressed monosyllables there were always at least two morae. Thus the minimal length for an Old English stressed syllable is either -VV or -VC, as in *hwā* 'who', *scip* 'ship'. This means that monosyllabic words with a rhyme structure -V, e.g. *se* 'this', were either unstressed or, if stressed, subject to vowel lengthening, e.g. *sē*. An unstressed syllable need only contain one mora. The maximum length of a syllable in Old English was probably similar to that in present-day English, that is to say, there could be no more than four morae in the rhyme, and in these cases the final consonant had to be a dental. Thus we find examples such as *fyrst* 'first' with -VCCC and *hēold* 'he held' with -VVCC. Very rarely there were extra-long syllables of the type -VVCCC as in *ēhst* 'thou persecutest', but these examples necessarily involve an inflexion where the vowel of the inflexion has been lost. In unstressed syllables it is possible to find examples possibly containing a syllabic nasal or liquid, e.g. *bōsm* 'bosom', *hræfn* 'raven', *spātl* 'saliva', *nǣdl* 'needle'. But these forms are often also spelled with an epenthetic vowel, e.g. *hamor* 'hammer', *æppel* 'apple'. Exactly how this variation should be analysed is difficult to determine.

Probably, as in present-day English, consonants in polysyllabic words were assigned to the following syllable wherever this was consistent with the constraints on possible syllable structures outlined above. Thus, for example, *stānas* 'stones' would have had the basic syllable division of [staa][nas] (where [aa] represents a long (bimoric) vowel, rather than [staan][as], and *wordum* 'word' dat.sg. would have had the division [wor][dum], not [word][um] or [wo][rdum] the latter being excluded both because syllables could not begin /rd-/ and because short stressed syllables had to be closed by a consonant. In the case of geminate consonants, it is presumably best to analyse them with one mora in the first syllable and one in the second, so that, say, *fremman* 'perform' would have the structure [frem][man]. It is likely, notwithstanding the above, that the initial consonants of onsets would become ambisyllabic, that is to say, members of the preceding as well as the following syllable, provided that the preceding syllable was stressed. Thus, a more accurate representation of *stānas* would be [staa[n]as], with /n/ ambisyllabic, and of *wordum* [wor[d]um], with /d/ ambisyllabic. Some evidence for this comes from back formations such as *ræfnan* 'perform' < *aræfnan* 'perform', where in fact the original verb was derived from *or + aβnjan*.

The other major issue concerning syllable structure is the matter of collocational restrictions. These are primarily a matter of which consonant clusters can occur initially in onsets and finally in codas. For onsets many of the facts which hold for present-day English hold equally for Old English, and the only points which need be noted are cases where Old English allowed a wider range of onset clusters than allowed today. The most important set to note contains a stop + nasal, although even in Old English this was restricted to velar stop + nasal. Thus we find examples such as *cniht* 'boy' (> PDE *knight*) with /kn-/ and *gnæt* 'gnat' with /gn-/. Perhaps we could also include the combination /fn-/ found in a few words such as *fnǣsan* 'sneeze', although that may have been a phonaesthetic cluster, see Hogg (1984). Quite similar to the above are cases of initial /w/ + liquid, i.e. /wl-, wr-/, found in words such as *wlispian* 'lisp' and *wrītan* 'write'. In all the cases discussed so far, these clusters persisted well beyond the Old English period, but we can assume that their disappearance in late Middle English or early Modern English brought about, or was brought about by, a reorganisation of possible syllable structures. On the other hand, a further group of clusters no longer found in English, namely /x/ + liquid, /n/ or /w/ (see §3.3.1.4), seem to have been lost purely as the result of the loss of /x/, and their loss can scarcely be seen as a reorganisation of collocational restrictions.

In codas the permissible range of final consonant clusters was very similar to that of initial consonant clusters. Again, there are strong similarities to the present-day language, but it is noticeable that whereas today nasal + stop clusters are found only where the stop is either voiceless, e.g. *clamp*, *drink* or a dental, e.g. *ground*, in Old English the full range of such clusters could be found, e.g. *clamb* 'he climbed' with final

/-mb/ and *sang* 'he sang' with final /-ng/. Also, it was probably possible to find final sequences of liquid plus velar (or palatal) fricative, as is suggested by spellings such as *byrġ* 'cities', see the discussion of epenthesis above. The above types would seem to constitute the principal structural differences in syllables between Old English and the present-day, but it has to be remembered that other differences would arise because of the different phonemic inventories of the two stages of the language. Thus in *cniht* 'boy', as we have seen, the initial cluster /kn-/ signals a change in possible syllable structure types, but the final cluster /-xt/ only points to the later loss of the phoneme /x/.

3.3.2.2 Stress

Old English, like present-day English, seems to have been a stress-based language. The evidence that we have for stress patterns derives essentially from four sources: (i) certain sound changes, especially involving diphthongisation, seem to have been restricted to stressed syllables, for Old English did not permit diphthongs (or long vowels) to occur in unstressed syllables, see point (ii) immediately following; (ii) weakly-stressed elements had a tendency to reduce or be lost altogether; (iii) metrical practice was usually based on a two-stressed half-line where stressed syllables might alliterate; (iv) the assumption, where the evidence permits, of an unchanging stress system throughout the history of the language. None of these sources is wholly satisfactory. For example, however close the rhythms of Old English poetry may have been to normal speech, they could hardly have been identical. Furthermore, the stress system of English has changed over the centuries. What we have to say about the stress system of Old English must therefore be seen as even more hypothetical than our remarks about other aspects of Old English phonology. This is especially so for sentence accent, where, in any case, factors such as rhetorical emphasis could quite easily distort 'normal' stress patterns. Virtually no work has been carried out recently on sentence accent in Old English, and what we know about the topic is largely confined to the question of which word classes could carry primary stress. Here it is probable that only nouns, adjectives, adverbs and verbs could carry primary stress, with the first two always carrying primary stress, the last two often showing only secondary stress. But the investigation of phrasal and sentence stress patterns has not yet progressed beyond this simple stage.

We know rather more about word stress. We can suggest that the following morphemes were capable of bearing primary stress in Old English: (i) the root morphemes of all nouns, adjectives, adverbs and verbs; (ii) prefixes of nouns and adjectives; (iii) derivational suffixes which were historically free morphemes; (iv) second elements of compounds including proper names. The principles by which one syllable was assigned stress rather than another and for determining the relative strengths of stressed syllables in words with more than one stressed syllable were different in Old English from those in present-day English, and indeed generally simpler. For only one basic principle was at work. This was that Old English words were 'left-strong', that is to say, in words with only one stress it was the left-most syllable which was stressed and in words with more than one stress it was the left-most stress which was the strongest. Thus, if we take monomorphemic words such as *yfel* 'evil' and *fǽtels* 'tub', they were stressed as *ýfel*, *fǽtels*, regardless of the syllable structure. It follows from the above that if only one of the morphemes of a polymorphemic word carried stress, then the stress pattern remained unaltered. This is most obviously the case when an inflectional syllable is added. Hence we find *frémþ* 'he does', *frémme* 'I do', *frémedon* 'they did'. It is probable that in sequences of unstressed syllables, for example *frémedon*, that there would be some kind of rhythmic alternation so that every other unstressed syllable received an element of rhythmic protection, but yet again this is a matter which has not been extensively explored. If a word contained two or more stressable syllables, for example a prefixed noun such as *angin* 'beginning', then the first stress would be the strongest (i.e. primary-stressed) and the remaining stressed syllables would be secondary-stressed, hence *ángìn*. Typical examples involving a derivational suffix are *gódcùnd* 'sacred' and *éorlscìpe* 'courage'. But often the diachronic status of these suffixes as free morphemes became obscured with the passage of time and thus we find examples such as *hláford* 'lord' against older *hláfwèarde*. Compounds would have had the same pattern as words with a derivational suffix derived from a free morpheme, so that we find *stǽfcrèft* 'grammar', *gúþgelàc* 'battle', etc.

One important consequence of the above system is that the stress pattern of prefixed nouns and adjectives was different from that of prefixed verbs, since, as we mentioned above, it was only the prefixes of nouns and adjectives which could be stressed. Thus we find numerous contrasting pairs such as *ángìn* 'beginning' and *angínnan* 'begin', *ǽlǽte* 'divorced woman' and *alǽtan* 'let go'. Not unexpectedly, when nouns and verbs were closely related this could give rise to confusion so that, for example, nouns such as *forġífness* 'forgiveness', to be derived from a verb, apparently showed a verbal rather than nominal stress pattern. One prefix which systematically violated the above patterns is *ġe-*, which was never stressed, and therefore a word such as *ġescéaft* 'creation', always had stress on the first syllable of its root morpheme, despite being a noun.

3.3.3 The Old English sound changes

In attempting to determine and explain the changes in the Old English sound system from about the time of the earliest invasions up to classical Old English and beyond, it must always be borne in mind that where changes took place before the time of our earliest texts we are engaged in a process of hypothetical reconstruction, and this means that we can do no more than establish, at best, a helpful relative chronology. That is to say, we can only say that some sound change occurred before another, or later than another, or at much the same time as another. We cannot say that some sound change, if prehistoric (before the time of our earliest texts), took place at some defined point in time, e.g. the fifth century. Even when we come to changes which only make their appearance felt at the time of our recorded texts, the absolute chronology may still be somewhat uncertain, since it is not always the case that date of first appearance can be safely equated with date of first occurrence.

In §3.3.3.1 below we discuss the sound changes occurring in stressed syllables in their presumed chronological order, and then in §3.3.3.2 we discuss the sound changes in unstressed syllables. Each syllable type had its own sound changes, even if the two could sometimes overlap.

3.3.3.1 Sound changes in stressed syllables

At the time of the invasions we can assume (see chapter 2) the following stressed vowel and consonant systems:

Stressed vowels and diphthongs of proto-Old English

i(:)	iu		u(:)
e(:)	eu		o(:)
	ai	au	
æ:	a		

Consonants of proto-Old English

	Labial	Dental	Palatal	Velar
Voiceless stops	/p/	/t/	—	/k/
Voiced stops	/b/	/d/	—	—
Voiceless fricatives	/f/	/θ/	—	/x/
Voiced fricatives	—	—	—	/ɣ/
Sibilants	—	/s/	—	—
Nasals	/m/	/n/	—	—
Liquids, approximants	—	/l,r/	/j/	/w/

The following points should be noted. Firstly, amongst the low vowels the only long vowel was /æ:/ and this occurred only in the antecedent form of West Saxon, for in other dialects it had already become /e:/ at a very early stage. Also, there was only one short low vowel, which may be best analysed as central, since it had no front or back contrasts at this stage. All the consonants except the approximants could occur as geminates. Further, at this stage the voiced fricative */ɣ/ had not yet become a stop in initial position, and hence the language lacked a voiced velar stop phoneme but had instead a voiced velar fricative phoneme. Another voiced fricative did occur, bilabial [β], but at this time, in contrast to later periods, it was an allophone of the corresponding voiced stop rather than the voiceless fricative. One problem is the status of the voiced fricative [v] derived from */f/ by Verner's Law (see chapter 2). This is discussed in detail below.

The first stage in the evolution of the Old English sound system involved a complex series of relations between the low vowels and the diphthongs. Taking the latter firstly, the /ai/ diphthong became a long low back vowel /ɑ:/. For the other diphthongs the first change to note is that /au/ became /æu/. The consequence of this was that Old English now had three diphthongs all consisting of a front vowel plus the back vowel /u/, a radical change in system. During the Old English period these diphthongs were affected by two further factors: (i) the second element, being less prominent than the first, acted rather like an unstressed vowel, so that eventually the /u/ should have become /o/; (ii) this change was modified by the fact that the second element adjusted its vowel height to the height of the first vowel, so that we find /iu, eo, æɑ/. Further, at about the time of the earliest texts in West Saxon the diphthongs /iu/ and /eo/ merged together as /eo/. These changes mean that where Germanic had the series: *biun, *deur, *dauþ, *stain, Old

English eventually developed *bēon* 'be', *dēor* 'animal', *dēaþ* (= /æ:ɑ/) 'death', *stān* 'stone'.

It can be seen that a further result of these changes is that Old English very early gained a contrast between front and back long low vowels, because of the monophthongisation of /ai/. This was paralleled by a change affecting the low short vowel /a/. This vowel normally fronted to /æ/ by the sound change of Anglo-Frisian Brightening (or First Fronting). Thus we find in OE *dæġ* 'day' against, say, G *Tag*. If the change had occurred in all circumstances, it would, of course, have been purely phonetic and without phonemic consequences. But it is known that the change did not occur in at least one circumstance. When */a/ was followed by a nasal, as in *man 'person', the */a/ was nasalised, and this seems to have been enough to prevent fronting. Indeed, during the Old English period, nasalised */a/ was certainly a back vowel, i.e. [ã], and seems to have been subject to some degree of rounding, at least to [ɒ̃]. Furthermore, as we shall see, later sound changes created new examples of a low short back vowel, and it is probable that these new examples, together with the examples before a nasal, were members of a phoneme /ɑ/. These developments all signal a feature of Old English not found in the immediately preceding, or, for that matter, following, stages, which is that both long and short low vowels showed a phonemic contrast between front and back. This type of contrast is one that has been unstable throughout the history of English (compare the present-day dialectal variation in the pronunciation of words such as *bath*). It is not surprising, therefore, that the contrast was new in Old English and was not to last, and that even in Old English it was a relatively marginal phenomenon (see Colman 1983a). From the above it follows that the vowel system of Old English in the early fifth century, must have already become:

```
i(:)   iu          u(:)
 e(:)   eu          o(:)
  æ(:)    æu         ɑ(:)
```

Another radical shift in the Old English vowel system then took place, the result of a sound change called <u>breaking</u>. By this, the front vowels, both short and long, appear to have been diphthongised whenever followed by either *l* or *r* plus a consonant or *h*. In spelling terms the change could be outlined as *ĭ > *ĭo*, *ĕ > *ĕo*, *ắ > *ắa* before *l*+C, *r*+C, *h*. Typical examples of this change are: *betwīh > *betwīoh* 'between', *tihhian > *tiohhian* 'consider', nWS *nēhwest* > *nēohwest

(> *nēowest*) 'nearest', **fehtan* > *feohtan* 'fight', **nǣh* > *nēah* 'near', **sæh* > *seah* 'he saw'. Though this much is clear, the phonological interpretation of breaking is a central area of controversy for Old English studies. There are two phonological issues to be discussed: (i) the phonological environment in which the change takes place; (ii) the nature of the change itself. We deal with these in turn.

It is certain that *h* represented /x/, the voiceless velar fricative. We can also tell that *r* only caused breaking when it was followed by another consonant, so that we find *eorþe* 'earth' < **erþe*, cf. *here* 'army'. The situation with *l* is similar, thus we find *eald* 'old' < **æld*, cf. *fela* 'many'. Why should this be? A clue to the answer comes from comparing forms such as *nearwe* 'narrow' nom.pl. and *nerian* 'save'. The first comes from earlier **nærwe* and undergoes breaking, but the latter, which comes from **nærjan* by *i*-mutation (of **æ* > *e*), does not show breaking. What this suggests is that the *r* or *l* which caused breaking must have been velarised or acquired some equivalent back articulation and that this happened when the liquid was followed by another consonant. In the case of *nearwe* this is straightforward. In the case of *nerian* we can suppose that breaking was inhibited precisely because of the palatal nature of the following consonant (as the table of proto-Old English consonants on p. 101 shows, /j/ was the only palatal consonant at the time). Similar support comes from the forms *sealde* 'he gave' < **sælde* and *sellan* 'give' < **sælljan*, the latter having *i*-mutation but not breaking. Here again, to cut a long story short, in the latter case palatal /j/ appears to have inhibited breaking, perhaps by palatalising the /ll/ cluster, whereas in the former case we have velarised [ɫ]. We can therefore claim that front vowels were broken when followed by a velar fricative or a velarised liquid.

The above points also help us to see what breaking entailed. The process is remarkably similar to a process in Received Pronunciation which Wells (1982:258–9) calls 'L Vocalisation'. In this process /l/ is velarised (> [ɫ]) in roughly the environments we stated for Old English and then may become vowel-like, so that *milk*, for instance, is pronounced [mɪɤk] rather than [mɪlk]. Furthermore, in Received Pronunciation long vowels are diphthongised before /r/ (Wells 1982:213 calls the historical process 'Pre-R Breaking'), so that we find forms such as [bɪə] rather than [bi:r] for *beer*. Wells says of this process (1982:214): 'This is a very natural kind of phonetic development. To pass from a "tense" close or half-close vowel to the post-alveolar or retroflex posture associated with /r/ requires considerable movement of the tongue. If this is somewhat slowed, an epenthetic glide readily develops...'

The explanation of breaking, therefore, which fits best with both the spelling evidence and the range of phonetic possibilities is that it involved the introduction of an epenthetic glide between a front vowel and a following velar or velarised consonant. If we take an example such as *nǣh > nēah, there is no reason to doubt that the end-product of breaking was identical to the original Germanic diphthong in hēah 'high'. This prompts us to suppose that the epenthetic glide introduced by breaking behaved in exactly the same way as the second elements of Germanic diphthongs in Old English discussed above. It might be asked why we have made such a fuss about a sound change which, in terms of the whole history of the language, is of only minor consequence (for the effects of breaking are largely eliminated at the end of the period). The reason is as follows. Let us accept that breaking of long front vowels resulted in diphthongs which were phonologically identical to the diphthongs developed from Germanic. If we also accept that the breaking of short front vowels was phonetically parallel, so that *sǣh > seah involved epenthesis of a back glide just as in hēah then, given that length contrasts were maintained, breaking will have introduced the contrast between long and short diphthongs referred to in §§3.1 and 3.3.1.2, see also §3.3.2.1. Many linguists have argued that such a contrast is typologically improbable and that the short diphthongs (at least) should be analysed as centralised monophthongal allophones of the front vowels. In recent times this point of view has been most forcely argued by Daunt (1939), Stockwell & Barritt (1951) (and later papers) and Hockett (1959). Traditional grammarians have largely been unpersuaded by this view and maintained that a length contrast did exist between Old English diphthongs (see, for example, Campbell 1959:§§248–50). From the discussion above it should be clear that the interpretation of breaking as an epenthesis is not only plausible but also has significant analogies with developments in the recent history of the language. The only criticism which carries any weight, therefore, must be one relating to the alleged improbability of a length contrast between diphthongs. Even if we were to assume that such an argument could be convincing, it has to be recognised that the present-day language does show such contrasts, albeit in a modified form. For example, in Scots there is a contrast between *tied* = [taʋed] and *tide* = [tʌid], and it may well be best to treat the two diphthongs as separate phonemes (see Wells 1982:405–6). Therefore it is reasonable to conclude that breaking had in Old English at least one significant phonological effect, namely the introduction of a phonological contrast of length in diphthongs.

At this point it is worth introducing a footnote about transcriptions. In this chapter we have indicated long diphthongs by a macron in orthography, e.g. *ēo*, and a length marker in phonemic transcription, e.g. /e:o/, whereas short diphthongs have been left unmarked. But this is somewhat misleading, both historically and phonologically. Historically it is the short diphthongs which are odd, for they occur regularly only in Old English and not in earlier or later stages of the language. Phonologically our transcriptions suggest that the long diphthongs contained three morae (see §3.3.2.1), and the short diphthongs contained two morae, that is to say, /e:o/ = /eeo/, etc. But the long diphthongs behaved like long vowels and the short diphthongs behaved like short vowels, and therefore the former must have been bimoric, the latter monomoric. Transcriptions which would demonstrate this would be of the type *eo*, /eo/ for the long diphthongs, *ĕo*, /ĕo/ for the short diphthongs. Indeed, this method of transcription is used in vol. II, chapter 2 for the Old English diphthongs. However, it is not used here, for the purely pragmatic reason that the traditional transcriptions are so widely used and known that this type of amendment might create more confusion than clarity.

For the period of Old English being discussed at present one further sound change, known as <u>Restoration of *a*</u>, must be noted. This is best seen as a final adjustment to the low vowel system in the light of the modifications just discussed. We saw above that the earliest developments of Gmc **a* resulted in a phoneme contrast /æ(:)/ ~ /ɑ/. But by the sound change we are now concerned with /æ/, and to a lesser extent /æ:/, were retracted to /ɑ, ɑ:/ when a back vowel was present in the following syllable. This sound change had widespread morphological consequences, for example nouns such as *fæt* 'vessel' would have the plural form *fatu*. The effect of the change would be to harmonise low vowels to a following vowel, so that any low vowel followed by a back vowel would be back itself, and all other low vowels (except nasalised ones) would be front. This would imply that the vowel system had reverted to an earlier stage, with, ignoring length, only one low vowel phoneme, namely /a(:)/, with front and back allophones, the phonemic contrast having been lost. However, largely because of later morphologically motivated changes, affecting alternations of the type *fæt* ~ *fatu*, we do find in Old English minimal pairs such as *fære* 'journey' dat.sg.masc. vs. *fare* 'journey' dat.sg.fem. It has to be said that the case for therefore assuming a phonemic contrast between /æ/ and /ɑ/ is not unassailable, cf. Colman (1983a), although the contrast between /æ/ and /ɑ:/, where the sound change was in any case rather sporadic, was much secure. It seems likely that once again the Old English sound system developed features which were to be characteristic of the whole history of the language and that here we have an early demonstration of the enduring instability of the contrast between front and back low vowels.

So far we have been concerned only with sound changes affecting vowels and diphthongs, but we must now look at a number of sound changes which affected consonants. We shall be dealing with three different changes here: (i) palatalisation; (ii) voicing; (iii) metathesis. The first two types are important for the structure of both Old English and later periods, whilst the latter, although without any great structural implications, reflects a phenomenon which is persistent throughout the history of the language and in the present-day language as well.

Consider the pronunciation of PDE *keel* and *cool*. Although both have initial /k/, there is a difference between the two instances of the phoneme, for in the first the /k/ tends to assimilate to the following front vowel, and therefore be slightly fronted, whereas in the second the /k/ is produced slightly further back in the mouth. The process by which the velar consonant is fronted is called palatalisation, and this process is found in several Germanic languages. For example, note the Swedish contrasts *gata* 'road' with [g], *genast* 'instantly' with [j], and *kal* 'bald' with [k], *kyrka* 'church' with [ç]. In prehistoric Old English this phonetic process affected all the Germanic velar consonants, both the stops /k/ and [g], the stop allophone of /ɣ/ which occurred after nasals and in gemination, and the fricatives /x/ and /ɣ/. The change took place whenever the velar consonant was adjacent to and in the same syllable as a front vowel or a palatal consonant (this could only be /j/, see the table above, p. 101). At first the change was purely allophonic and produced palatal allophones of the velar phonemes, giving *[k] > [c], *[g] > [ɟ], *[x] > [ç], *[ɣ] > [j]. By the ninth century, however, the new palatal stops had developed into the palato-alveolar affricates /tʃ/ and /dʒ/, as is demonstrated by other forms such as *feċċan* 'fetch' < *fetjan*, where /tj/ became /tʃ/. The affricate development is usually called assibilation. As Penzl (1947) demonstrated conclusively for *[k] > [c], the change would at first have done no more than create a new allophone of /k/, but after the change of *i*-umlaut discussed below there would have been a phonemic split with a new phoneme /c/, later to become /ʧ/. The status of palatalised *[g] is more complex, but it too was eventually to become a new phoneme. The fricatives could not, of course, undergo assibilation, since that was a process by which stops became affricates. Instead, palatalised *[ɣ] was to merge with the already existing /j/, while [ç] was to remain an allophone of /x/. Typical examples of these developments are: *kīdan > čīdan 'chide', *bōki > *bōči (> bēč) 'books', *dīk > dīč 'ditch', *þankjan > *þančjan (> þenčan) 'think', and similarly for the other sounds, where forms such as senġan 'singe', riht 'right' and ġeard 'yard' result (note that in the case of palatalisation of *[x] traditional grammars do not normally distinguish the palatal fricative by a superscript dot).

The cluster */sk/ underwent a parallel, change to /ʃ/. The change here, however, was much more widespread, probably because /s/ was phonetically alveolar (see Gimson 1980:186–7) and this reinforced the movement of the /k/ towards a palatal articulation. The eventual development to /ʃ/ need have involved no more than complete assimilation of the two sounds. This change occurs everywhere except between vowels, where it must be supposed that the two segments were always quite separate segments. Medially the palatalisation of */sk/ took place only if the conditions for palatalisation of */k/ were present, so we find forms such as wasče 'I wash' < *waske, but ascað 'he asks' < *askað with /k/ before a back vowel. The separate nature of the two segments in medial position is made clear by examples of metathesis where the /sk/ is reversed to /ks/, so that we find both ascian 'ask' and metathesised axian, cf. PDE dialects with axe instead of standard ask. Amongst many examples of palatalisation of */sk/ are: sčip 'ship', sčrincan 'shrink', disč 'dish', æsč 'ash'. This also is a widespread feature of the Germanic languages, as in, e.g. G Schiff 'ship'.

Palatalisation (and the associated assibilation) is one of the most important sound changes in Old English, not only for the period itself but also for the later history of the language. In terms of Old English, the new phonemes /ʃ,ʧ,ʤ/ were introduced, as well as [ç] as an allophone of /x/. The incidence and distribution of /j/ was also extended drastically. It has to be emphasised how unusual such a major change in the phoneme system is. One of the consequences of this is that there must then have been a considerable rise in the extent of allomorphic variation in the language. Consider a word such as disč: the plural of this would be discas with medial /sk/, compare ascað above. Another type of example is the strong verb čēosan 'choose', which would have /tʃ/ in the present and preterite singular, but /k/ elsewhere, e.g. *coren* 'chosen'. Because of the ambiguities of the Old English spelling system (see §3.3.1.4), we usually cannot tell whether this kind of variation was preserved or eliminated in Old English without resorting to the evidence of later periods, when spelling evidence becomes more helpful. We are probably correct to suspect that levelling of /sk/ to /ʃ/ did take place at an early point in the history of, say, *discas*, but in the case of *ċēosan* it was clearly a much later phenomenon (see here the OED entry for *choose*).

PDE *disk* shows how the existence of sound change can permit the reborrowing of a foreign word (the first citation in OED is for 1664) with both a different meaning and pronunciation, but it also points the way to another feature. It is well known that the earliest Scandinavian forms of Germanic did not show palatalisation. Consequently, after the establishment of Scandinavian settlements in the north and east of England, there could easily arise doublets, where a single Germanic word turns up both in its native palatalised form, e.g. *sċyrte* glossing Lat. *praetexta* of obscure meaning, and in its Scandinavian unpalatalised form, e.g. *skirt* 'skirt' (only recorded from ME) giving PDE *shirt* and *skirt* respectively. Thus we have a means of increasing the vocabulary of the language (for further discussion, see chapter 5 of this volume). The change is also well reflected in place-names, consider the variation between *-chester* and *-caster* and see chapter 7 of this volume.

Let us now move on to voicing, where our particular concern is with fricatives. As the table above shows (p. 101), in pre-Old English there was only a contrast between voiceless and voiced velar fricatives; there was no dental voiced fricative and the labial voiced fricative *[β] was an allophone of /b/. By the time of classical Old English, however, there were voiced fricative allophones of /f,θ,x/ and /s/. How did this come about? The situation at the time of the first settlements was not as simple as we have suggested, especially with regard to the labials. If we take, first of all, the phoneme /b/, what we find then is that /b/ was realised as a stop initially, after nasals and in gemination. Elsewhere it was realised as the bilabial fricative [β]. Thus we would find *[habban] 'have' but *[haβaθ] 'he has'. The phoneme /b/ normally contrasted with /f/, but (see chapter 2 and above) /f/ was voiced by Verner's Law, so that there were two allophones of /f/, namely *[f] and *[v]. When the Germanic stress system stabilised (see again chapter 2), we would find a contrast between [f] in *drīfan* 'drive' and [v] in *drifon* 'they drove' which would not be predictable from stress and the operation of

Verner's Law. Therefore [v] could hardly have been an allophone of /f/, but rather must have been an allophone of /b/. Now it is extremely unlikely that the unstable contrast between [β] and [v] could have been preserved, and it seems most probable that those two merged. At this stage the resulting sound, which we could write as either [β] or [v] must have represented the neutralistion of the two phonemes /b/ and /f/ between vowels (see Anderson 1985). For velars the situation was much clearer, since /x/ and /ɣ/ contrasted initially, medially and finally, even if initially /x/ was already realised as *[h] as in *helpan* 'help'. In Germanic *[ð] had already become *[d] in words such as *fæder* 'father' < *faðar* and hence no problems arose there.

After these beginnings the first important development to take place is that between vowels /x/ was weakened, as it had already been in Germanic in initial positions, to the glottal fricative [h], and this [h] was then lost. Thus we find sequences such as *sehan* > *seohan* (by breaking before /x/) > *sēo-an* (for the loss of [h] involves lengthening of the preceding vowel in compensation) > *sēon* 'see'. This change, with morphological consequences such as the formation of 'contracted verbs' (see §3.4.2.1), means that there was no longer any contrast between voiceless and voiced fricatives medially, but the contrast remained elsewhere.

Next voiceless fricatives become voiced when surrounded by voiced segments (typically vowels). The results of this process of assimilation can still be seen today. For example, *wulf* 'wolf' came to have the plural *wulfas* with medial [v], a shift reflected in usual PDE *wolf*, *wolves*. This change, which only fails to take place if the fricative is initial in a stressed syllable (thus *befæstan* 'apply' keeps [f]), gives the following series of changes: [f] > [v], [θ] > [ð], [s] > [z]. Because [x] had already become [h] or been lost medially, it was never affected by the voicing. Old English spelling never shows these changes, so that we find in strong verbs alternations such as *drīfan*, *drāf*, *drifon*, *drifen* 'drive'; *rīsan*, *rās*, *rison*, *risen* 'rise'; and *snīþan*, *snāþ*, *snidon*, *sniden*. In the first two verbs the first form has [v,z] due to this voicing, the second form has [f,s] unchanged and the third and fourth have [v,z] due to Verner's Law. In *snīþan* the first form has [ð], the second [θ] and the third and fourth have [d] < Gmc *[ð] by Verner's Law. Phonemically, voicing only introduces new allophones of the voiceless fricatives, except in the case of the labials. If we assume that previously [β/v] represented the neutralisation of /b/ and /f/ medially, this new change meant that the number of instances of [β/v] from /f/ noticeably increased, and this would probably have meant that the first stage in the reanalysis of [β/v] as [v], an allophone of /f/, had taken place.

There are two further changes to be discussed here, the precise dating of which is somewhat uncertain. Firstly, voiced fricatives in final positions became unvoiced, e.g. *burg 'city' became burh, and *stæb (= [stæβ]) > stæf 'letter'. This could only affect [v] and [ɤ], since neither [ð] nor [z] could appear finally. The change is a partial implementation of the more general Germanic phenomenon by which voiced sounds become voiceless in final position, cf. G Hund 'dog' with [t]). The more general phenomenon is rare in Old English, although occasionally forms such as ðrēt 'thread' < ðrēd can be found. Secondly, the voiced velar fricative became the stop [g] initially as in gōd 'good'. These changes had definite effects on the system. The devoicing of final [v] gave rise to a paradigm such as hebban, hōf, hōfon, hafen 'heave', which now had the alternation [bb] ~ [f] ~ [v] ~ [v] as opposed to earlier *[bb] ~ [β] ~ [β] ~ [β]. If we were to ignore the infinitive the alternation would be the same as in drīfan, despite the fact that the original post-vocalic consonant was in the case of the former *[b], in the case of the latter *[f]. This devoicing which we have just discussed aligns [β/v] more firmly than ever with /f/ (and hence it should always be represented as [v], since, as a form such as hōf shows, [β] when devoiced became [f]. In the case of the velars, final devoicing together with the stopping of [ɤ] > [g] initially, meant that the voiced velar fricative only occurred medially between voiced segments, and thus must be an allophone of [x], with a new phoneme /g/ appearing.

The consonant shifts we have been discussing are undoubtedly complex. Therefore they are presented in schematic form in Figure 3.4 (where the geminate phonemes and some special cases, e.g. after nasals, are ignored).

Let us now consider metathesis. This sound change involved the inversion in order of two (usually adjacent) segments, cf. the pair ascian/axian noted above. Metathesis of two adjacent consonants was quite common in Old English, especially if one of the consonants is /s/, so that we find both wæsp and wæps 'wasp', wlips and wlisp 'lisping', bæstere and bæȝere (ȝ = ts) 'baptist, clænsian and clæsnian 'cleanse' and several others. The change was of no great structural importance, but it is worth mentioning because metathesis is something that persists throughout the history of the language; note, for example, the children's form wopse for PDE wasp. There is, however, another form of metathesis in Old English which was more frequent and perhaps more structurally

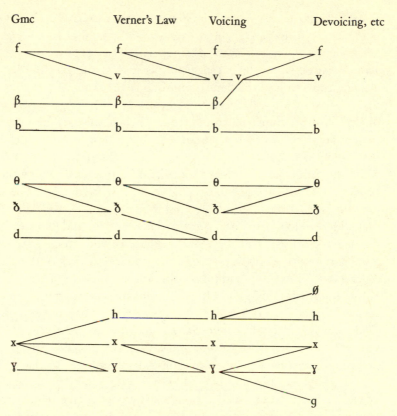

Figure 3.4 The development of consonants (especially voiced stops and fricatives) from Germanic to Old English

organised. This involves the metathesis of /r/ + short vowel, usually where the short vowel was originally followed by /s/ or /n/. Thus we find: *ræn* > *ærn* 'he ran', *brinnan* > *birnan* 'burn', *frost* > *forst* 'frost', *cresse* > *cerse* 'cress', and many other examples, usually showing both metathesised and unmetathesised forms. This variation is again one that continues (note that *cress* reverts to the unmetathesised form whereas *burn* has not reverted), and even today there are dialects, such as Ulster Irish, where we can find *r*-metathesis in words such as *northern* = /nɔːrðrən/. Although *r*-metathesis cannot be chronologically pinned down to one period (see Stanley 1952, Hogg 1976), it most usually happened after the time of breaking, compare *ærn* < *ræn* without breaking and *earn* 'eagle' < *ærn* with breaking, and indeed probably after palatalisation, for otherwise *cerse* would have become **ċerse.

We can now return to the development of the vowel system. After palatalisation the new palatal consonants appear to have had an effect on immediately following front stressed vowels, so that *ġēt > ġīet 'yet', ġefan > ġiefan 'give', *sċǣp > sċēap 'sheep', and ċæf > ċeaf 'chaff'. This sound change is puzzling, especially because in the case of *[æ(:)] the change seems to give the same diphthong as breaking of *[æ(:)] did, and that is phonetically odd. Further, in the case of *[e(:)] the result was a digraph not previously encountered and whose history is obscure. We shall discuss the latter when we come to *i*-mutation, so let us concentrate here solely on the so-called <u>palatal diphthongisation</u> of *[æ(:)]. How could the influence of a preceding palatal on that vowel have the same result as the influence of a following velar (as in breaking)? The answer can only be that the influence was not the same, but that the diphthongs that did develop were not greatly different and did not result in a phonemic contrast, and therefore, because of the paucity of available graphs, the same digraph was used for both regardless of the phonetic differences. This fairly traditional opinion, espoused quite explicitly in Kuhn & Quirk (1953) and Hogg (1979b), has been attacked by other scholars, notably Stockwell & Barritt (1951), more recently Lass & Anderson (1975:279-82), who claim that, for example, the < e > in ċeaf was no more than a diacritic indicating the palatal nature of the preceding consonant. This solution is very attractive. We have already seen that Old English scribes could not distinguish between palatal and velar consonants, even when phonemically contrastive. Here, it would appear, was a way of doing so, which does not involve rather vague speculation as to a possible phonetic interpretation of palatal diph-thongisation. The problem is that one word, *ċȳse 'cheese', seems to require diphthongisation to have occurred, for otherwise it cannot be derived from Lat. *caseus*. For discussion of this complex case see Kuhn & Quirk (1953:146–7) and the attempted rebuttal in Stockwell & Barritt (1955:382–3).

Even if one accepts (as this writer does) the reality of palatal diphthongisation of front vowels, there is no need to accept that a parallel change affecting back vowels, represented by examples such as sċ(e)op 'poet' and sċ(e)acan 'shake', was ever anything more than an orthographic variation. The change was inconsistently carried out, and the arguments of, for example, Campbell (1959:§176) to demonstrate that the change had phonetic consequences are insubstantial. Notably, we find forms such as sēċean 'seek' alongside sēċan where the same phenomenon appears to be happening in unstressed syllables, but this cannot be so since diphthongs did not occur in Old English unstressed syllables.

After considering a change which is almost as unimportant as it is controversial, we come now to a change which is almost as uncontroversial as it is important. When we discussed restoration of *a*, we noted that the change was a type of vowel harmony, whereby one vowel becomes more like another following vowel in the same word. We now have to look at another more thoroughgoing change of the same type, called *i*-mutation or i-umlaut, whereby Old English vowels harmonised to an /i/ or /j/ following them in the same word. This caused all back vowels to front and all short front vowels (except, naturally, /i/) and diphthongs to raise when an /i/ or /j/ followed in the next syllable. We can tabulate this as follows:

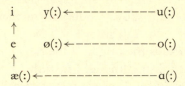

Before we give examples it is worth pointing out that this simple statement is muddied by several factors. Firstly, although the *i*-mutation of back vowels was to the corresponding front vowels, hence in the case of the non-low vowels to front rounded vowels, not unrounded vowels, /ø(:)/, in West Saxon at least was regularly unrounded to /e(:)/ before the time of our written texts. Secondly, if the short back vowel /ɑ/ which was mutated comes from Gmc *a + nasal, as in words of the *man*-type discussed earlier, then, although the mutation was originally to /æ/, this developed to /e/. This may be because the sound before a nasal was originally slightly raised. Thirdly, there were, because of the position in Germanic (cf. chapter 2), no cases where /e/ could be subject to *i*-mutation, which is therefore purely hypothetical. Typical examples of the sound change are: *brūdi* > *brȳd* 'bride, *trummjan* > *trymman* 'strengthen'; *fōtiz* > *fēt* 'feet', *oli* > *ele* 'oil'; *hāljan*; *hǣlan* 'heal', *ladin* > *læden* 'Latin', *sandjan* > *sendan* 'send'; *bæddj-* > *bedd* 'bed'.

From the examples just given, two points are immediately clear. Firstly, *i*-mutation had an effect throughout the language – note that we have given examples of both nouns and verbs, of various different declensional types, and of Latin loan words (*ele* and *læden*) as well as native vocabulary. Secondly, later sound changes in unstressed syllables mean that the conditioning environment for the change was not usually discernible in classical Old English, since either the /i/ had changed to /e/ (*ele*) or it had been lost (*brȳd*), and the /j/ was almost always lost (*trymman*). There are a few cases, such as *cyning* 'king' < **kuning*, where the /i/ remained, and whilst /i/ usually went to /e/ if it remained after a light syllable, /j/ in a similar position remains (spelled as < i >, as in *nerian* 'save' < **nærjan*. But these together form no more than a minority of cases. Further scope for confusion arises from words which in classical Old English showed an /i/ in a mutation environment which was not there at the time of *i*-mutation, for example, *huniġ* 'honey' < **hunæġ*.

Probably the most obvious influence of *i*-mutation was on nouns of the athematic declension (see §3.4.1.1) such as *fōt* 'foot', *man* 'person', and *mūs* 'mouse', for all such nouns show *i*-mutation in the dative singular and nominative-accusative plural. Thus we find the nominative plurals *fēt*, *men*, *mȳs*. This, of course, is the origin of the same group of irregular plurals in present-day English, although, as with *bōc* 'book', pl. *bēċ*, the irregularity has often been levelled out. A parallel case concerns certain irregular adjectives whose comparative and superlative are formed with *i*-mutation, e.g. *eald* 'old', *yldra*, *yldest*. In Old English weak verbs of class 1 normally show *i*-mutation throughout their paradigm (as opposed to weak verbs of class 2, where the stem vowel was never *i*-mutated), but there is a sub-group of such verbs which show *i*-mutation only in the infinitive and present, so that we find *sellan* ~ *sealde* 'give', relating to PDE *sell* ~ *sold*. Finally, in derivational morphology it is frequent to find an original form without *i*-mutation, e.g. *feallan* 'fall', and a derived form with *i*-mutation, e.g. *fyllan* 'fell'.

So far we have avoided discussion of the *i*-mutation of diphthongs. Orthographically the situation in West Saxon is straightforward: all diphthongs, both short and long and of whatever origin, were *i*-mutated to a sound represented in the first instance by the digraph < ie >. Thus we find: **ċīosið* > *ċīest* 'he chooses', **wiorsira* > *wiersa* 'worse'; **hēarjan* > *hīeran* 'hear', **ealdira* > *ieldra* 'older'. Examples with /e(:)o/ are generally lacking for the same reason as examples with *i*-mutation of /e/ are lacking, but if they did occur then they behaved like the other diphthongs, pace Sievers (1900:44–5), hence eWS *elðīediġ* 'foreign' with *i*-mutation of either /i:o/ or /e:o/. This situation is both different from and less simple than that in the other dialects, where the *i*-mutation of /æ(:)a/ was to /e(:)/ and of /e(:)o/ to /i(:)o/, with /i(:)o/ itself being unaffected. Two questions arise. Firstly, why should (in all dialects) the long diphthongs have been mutated when long front vowels are not? Secondly, what value(s) might be represented by the digraph <ie> and why did that occur only in West Saxon? To the first question no satisfactory answer has ever been given, partly, one suspects, because the wrong question has always been asked: we should ask not why the long diphthongs have been mutated but why the long front vowels have not been mutated. To the second question a variety of answers have been given. Let us assume that <ie> represented a diphthong, which would be in line with our assumptions about the other digraphs. Under those circumstances the first element must surely be /i(:)/, but what might the second element be? Luick (1914:§§ 191–3) suggests something within the range of a slightly rounded [ə] to [y], and it is this area that more recent scholars have explored. Kuhn (1961:530) suggests [ɛ], Stockwell (1958) and Lass & Anderson (1975:127) [u], McLaughlin (1979) and Colman (1985) [y]. Given later developments to be discussed below, it seems improbable that the second element was completely unrounded, thus arguing against Kuhn (1961). Otherwise it is difficult to choose between the competing proposals, especially because, as we shall see, the diphthong was a very temporary phenomenon indeed.

It should be clear from the above that *i*-mutation radically reorganised the vowel and diphthong phonemes of Old English, both by the introduction of new phonemes such as /y(:)/ and by the increased incidence of front vowel phonemes and the corresponding decrease in the incidence of back vowel phonemes. Bearing in mind the gradual development of diphthongs, so that by the time of *i*-mutation a diphthong such as /æu/ would have probably become /æɑ/, we can suggest the following position after the operation of *i*-mutation, where /i(:)y/ is provisionally the diphthong represented by <ie> and /i(:)o/ that represented by <io>:

$$
\begin{array}{llll}
\text{i(:)} & \text{y(:)} & \text{i(:)y} & \text{u(:)} \\
 & & \text{i(:)o} & \\
\text{e(:)} & \text{e(:)o} & & \text{o(:)} \\
 & \text{æ(:)} & \text{æ(:)ɑ} & \text{ɑ(:)}
\end{array}
$$

The changes discussed so far are usually described as 'prehistoric', i.e. they occurred before the time of our earliest texts. From now on the changes were either contemporary with or later than these texts. Thus we can set a date of ca 700 for the earliest of these, which is called back mutation. This change has many parallels with the much earlier one of breaking. It involved exactly the same diphthongisation process, except that in the later change only short vowels are diphthongised, i.e., /i/ > /io/, /e/ > /eo/, /æ/ > /æɑ/. The other principal difference between the two is that the environment for back mutation was a following back vowel not a back (velar) consonant. Nevertheless we must recognise that breaking and back mutation comprise an instance of the repetitive character over time of many sound change types. Furthermore, back mutation bears similarities to restoration of *a*. Just as that earlier change retracted /æ/ before a back vowel, this change should diphthongise /æ/ to /æɑ/ before a back vowel. One consequence of this is that in all except one dialect of Old English the two changes are incompatible, for restoration of *a* would remove all instances of /æ/ before a back vowel and thus one could not get back mutation of /æ/.

In West Saxon back mutation was even more restricted, for it occurred only if there was a single intervening consonant which was either a labial or a liquid (see Davidsen-Nielsen & Ørum 1978 for a possible acoustic explanation). By the time of the change, at least in West Saxon, there were only two unstressed back vowels, /o/ and /ɑ/, and it is often helpful to distinguish between *o*-mutation and *a*-mutation. Although *o*-mutation was regular, in West Saxon *a*-mutation occurred only if the preceding vowel was /i/ (see chapter 6 for other dialects). Typical examples are: **sifon* > *siofon* 'seven', **hefon* > *heofon* 'heaven', **lefað* > *leofað* 'he lives', but a word such as *fela* 'many', since it had /e/ before /ɑ/ rather than /o/, was unmutated. Examples such as *leofað* show that morphological alternations could be caused by this sound change, but in West Saxon the alternations were normally levelled out in favour of unmutated forms, and many words such as *clifu* 'cliffs' never show back mutation on the analogy of unmutated singular forms such as *clif*. The only change in the phoneme system caused by back mutation is an increase in the incidence of short diphthongs.

One point stands out from the diagram above, namely that there occurred a clustering of diphthongs in the left-hand top corner of the vowel chart with, ignoring length, three diphthongs there: /iy/, /io/ and /eo/. The two developments we are about to discuss can be seen as providing a solution to this problem. The first is quite simple, for what happened was that the diphthongs /io/ and /eo/ merged together as /eo/. In Early West Saxon this gave rise to considerable confusion with either original diphthong being spelled as either <io> or <eo>, so that, for example, original *līoht* 'light' is also spelled as *lēoht* in the *Cura pastoralis*, whilst original *ċeorl* 'churl' can be spelled *ċiorl* in the same manuscript. By Late West Saxon, however, the <io> spelling had practically disappeared. It seems probable, therefore, that this was essentially a ninth-century merger which only gradually became recognised orthographically.

The second change concerns the diphthong /iy/, the sound represented by the digraph <ie>. In Early West Saxon the <ie> digraph was partially replaced by <i>, so that we find *fird* 'army' alongside *fierd*, *hīran* 'hear' alongside *hīeran*, and so on. Also, words which had original /i/ sometimes turned up with <ie>, as in *rīeċe* for *rīċe* 'kingdom'. This is overwhelming evidence that /iy/ and /i/ must have merged together as /i/ by a process of monophthongisation. The only exception was if /iy/ was between a labial consonant and /r/, where we find *wyrsa* 'worse' for *wiersa*. Again this is clearly a monophthongisation, and the differential development must have been caused in part by the rounding environment of labial + /r/, in part by the presence of a rounded element in the original diphthong.

In Late West Saxon the situation was quite different, although the driving force remained monophthongisation. Here the normal shift of /iy/ was to /y/, so we find *fyrd* rather than *fird*, *hȳran* rather than *hīran*, etc. Of course, a word such as *wyrsa* would have /y/ as in Early West Saxon. But if /iy/ was before a palatal, then the monophthongisation was to /i/, presumably because the palatal consonant had an unrounding effect, so that *miht* 'might' was a form common to Early and Late West Saxon. But *fyrd* could not have undergone the sequence of changes: *fierd* > EWS *fird* > LWS *fyrd*, since forms with original /i/ such as *biterness*, which it merged with in Early West Saxon, cf. above, remained with /i/ in Late West Saxon and did not turn up as, for example, **byterness*. The change of /iy/ > /i/ before palatals was paralleled by unrounding of /y/ > /i/ before palatals, as in *drihten* 'lord' < *dryhten* where /y/ was due to *i*-mutation, so perhaps for a word such as *miht* we should suppose the sequence *mieht* > *miht*. These developments are of considerable interest to the Old English scholar, largely because of the mismatch between Early and Late West Saxon which comes to light. It follows from what we have just said that <ie> as a digraph representing /iy/ or some later development of that was a usage which, although very frequent in Early West Saxon, was confined to that dialect. Its very obviousness has led to its importance being overestimated, for in the long run it contributes virtually nothing to the later history of either Old English or the language after the Conquest.

In contrast, the changes we are about to discuss are immensely important for the post-Conquest periods. Originally, as we have seen, vowel length was entirely phonemic and unpredictable in English. But by about the end of the ninth century, a series of changes had begun which were to continue well into the Middle English period and which all had the effect of tending to make vowel length predictable (for a full discussion of this see vol. II, chapter 2 of this History). The earliest examples involved the shortening of a long vowel when followed by either three consonants, as in *gōdspell > gŏdspell 'gospel', *nǣddre > nǎddre 'adder', or by two consonants and two syllables, as in *ǣndlufon > ĕndlufon 'eleven'. These changes must already have begun to take effect before the time of the earliest texts. In themselves they scarcely form a tendency, but their importance can be seen in the fact that short vowels later became lengthened when followed by a liquid or nasal plus homorganic voiced consonant, e.g. before /mb, ld, rd, rl, rn, nd, ng/. This is a change which can scarcely be other than ninth century, since it was later than back mutation but earlier than a set of minor changes affecting Late West Saxon (see Luick 1914:§268, Anm.3, Campbell 1959:§284). The lengthening is not normally marked by grammarians of Old English, but below, for the sake of clarity alone, we mark it by a circumflex rather than a macron. Examples, therefore, include: *camb > câmb* 'comb', *ċild > ĉîld* 'child', *bindan > bîndan* 'bind'. PDE *child, children* and other examples show that the change did not take place when a third consonant followed, and even in OE there were exceptions to the above lengthening, for example LWS *swurd* 'sword' must come from *sweord*, not **swêord*, as the minor Late West Saxon change of /eo/ > /u/ (cf. Campbell 1959:§§320–4) did not affect long vowels. By about the time of the Conquest the tendency to make vowel length predictable had gone even further, for long vowels appear to have by then shortened before all other types of consonant clusters. Hence we find *brōhte > brŏhte* 'he brought' and many other examples (for further discussion, see vol. II, chapter 2 of this History).

The final change we have to consider concerns geminate consonants. So far we have outlined a system in which geminate consonants can occur either medially, as in *sittan* 'sit', or finally, as in *bedd* 'bed'. At the beginning of the period geminates could only occur medially, but when final unstressed syllables were lost (see §3.3.3.2) examples such as *bedd* < Gmc *baddjaz showed final geminates. This position was not to last, for by the classical period variant spellings with single final consonants appeared, e.g. *bed*, and, as Kurath (1956:435) argues, these are best explained as due to degemination of final consonants. Thus the language reverted to a system in which geminate consonants could only appear medially.

The developments we have discussed above, together with some minor undiscussed developments, bring us up to classical Old English. During the first half of the eleventh century there were further developments which are usually regarded as being proper to the study of post-Conquest rather than pre-Conquest English, but it is worth mentioning them briefly, if only as a signal of events to come. The two most important changes are: (i) the contrast between front and back short low vowels was lost and /æ/ and /ɑ/ merge as /a/; (ii) the Old English diphthongs became monophthongs. Most examples of these are to be found on coins (for which Colman 1984:120–3 provides a good introduction), but *Ch* 1489 of 1035–40 (perhaps a slightly later copy, see Whitelock 1930:181–2) is also a useful source. Thus the latter has *maġe* 'may' for *mæġe*, *ǣstan* 'east' for *ēastan* and *marc* 'mark, coin' for *mearc*. The first of these changes is as much a reflection of the continual instability of the /æ/ ~ /ɑ/ contrast as anything else, although it does point forward to a reorganisation of the vowel system which was to become fully apparent in the post-Conquest period. The second shows that the Old English diphthongs, about which there has been so much controversy, were not to outlive the period by any significant length of time.

3.3.3.2 Sound changes in unstressed syllables

During our period there were a great many changes in unstressed syllables, but we shall not go into these in any detail; anyone interested should instead read the relevant sections in Luick (1914) or Campbell (1959). All that is attempted now is a general sketch of the major trends. In fact there was one single and obvious trend which applies not only to the Old English period but to the history of English as a whole. This is that sounds tended to be reduced, so that, for example, long vowels became short, short vowels lost their distinctive phonetic characteristics and merged, eventually as the reduced vowel schwa, and reduced vowels were lost. Similarly, final consonants were often lost. Thus if we take the Germanic word *namanin* 'name' nom.pl., this developed in Old English through the stage *namani to naman*. If we move to Middle English and to the accusative singular form we then see the development *naman* > *nama* > *name* (= [naːmə]) > *name* (= [naːm]). So by the time of Chaucer the Germanic ending had completely disappeared. In what follows we shall consider the exemplification of these trends in two specific areas, namely the reduction in variety of unstressed vowels and the loss of unstressed vowels, and then look briefly at some of the consequential changes.

At the time of the invasions the unstressed vowel system (see chapter 2) must have been something like the following diagram:

$$i \qquad\qquad u$$
$$o$$
$$a$$

By First Fronting (see §3.3.4.1) /a/ became /æ/ as in stressed syllables and, perhaps by a chain shift unstressed /o/ then became /ɑ/, so that we then find the following system:

$$i \qquad\qquad u$$
$$æ \qquad\qquad ɑ$$

By the time of the earliest texts it would appear that the front vowels had merged together as /e/, for in those texts, although inflectional *-i* and *-æ* were often preserved, even the best of scribes make enough errors, e.g. RuthCr *rōdi* 'cross' dat.(?) sg., to make one suppose that they were attempting with only a limited degree of success to represent a stage which was fast becoming a hazy memory. We are thus entitled to claim that by about 700 all unstressed front vowels had become /e/. The only exception is that [i] was preserved in derivational suffixes such as *-iġ*, *-ing*, *-isċ*, e.g. *mihtiġ* 'mighty', *cyning* 'king', *Englisċ* 'English'. This could be because the syllable was secondary-stressed. However we have already noted (in §3.3.1.3) forms such as *hāliġ* 'holy' < *hāleġ* < *hālæg* < *hailag*, where unstressed [e] was raised to [i] before a palatal consonant. All the relevant cases with <i> probably had an immediately following palatal consonant, and this was the probable source of the variation.

This merger of /i/ and /æ/ as /e/ gave a three-way contrast between front /e/, back /u/ and low /ɑ/. /e/ and /ɑ/ remained relatively well preserved, but /u/ had a strong tendency to lower, especially when a consonant followed, so we find, for example, *heofon* 'heaven' in Early West Saxon rather than *heofun*, although if /u/ is in absolute finality, as in the nominative plural inflexion of *a*-declension neuter nouns, e.g. *sċipu* 'ships', it more usually remained. The general rule when /u/ was followed by a consonant is that the later the text the more likely it is that *o*-spellings would prevail. In Late West Saxon the back vowel and the low vowel were well on the way to merger, probably as /ɔ/ (see §3.3.1.3), and by the time of the Conquest <u>, <o> and <a> were becoming interchangeable spellings. But the above account may place too much reliance on texts which are the product of the Æthelwoldian school, such as the best Ælfric manuscripts, where fairly careful distinctions may be the result of good training rather than actual speech habits. If we take other texts, e.g. the Lauderdale manuscript of *Orosius* (ed. Bately 1980) written at the beginning of the tenth century, then we seem to have already a much more advanced stage. Bately (1980: xliv) writes: 'The evidence of the spellings … is that by the time the manuscript was written the unstressed back vowels *u, o, a* had largely coalesced in a single unaccented back vowel and that this was becoming – or had become – confused with unaccented *e*.' Whatever the precise chronology, we can clearly see the gradual reduction in number of unstressed from four to three to two to one.

The loss of unstressed vowels was generally earlier than the reduction in variety and was due either to apocope or the loss of vowels in absolute finality or to syncope or the loss of medial vowels. Apocope affected the high vowels /i/ and /u/ and occurred most regularly when they were preceded by a single heavy syllable, so that, for example, **fēti* 'feet' became *fēt*, and, in neuter plurals of the *a*-declension we find *word* 'words' alongside *scipu* 'ships'. But apocope also occurred in trisyllabic words if the first syllable was light, and therefore we find *weorod* 'troops' from **weorodu*, compare *hēafodu* 'heads' without apocope because the first syllable is heavy!

The high vowels were also subject to syncope in medial positions after a heavy syllable, thus **yldira* became *yldra* 'older'. This gave rise to further complications, as can be seen if we take the example of **hēafudu*. From the above we could postulate the following development: firstly, by syncope we would get *hēafdu*, then apocope would give ***hēafd*. In fact the following forms are found: *hēafodu, hēafod, hēafdu*. Parallel to these we find both *weorod* and *weorodu*. It seems likely that apocope and syncope were two quite different types of change operating at the same time, the first dependent upon syllable structure, the second more dependent upon principles of rhythmic alternation (as the name implies). The two changes often gave contradictory results and much irregularity ensued, which could be levelled out through analogy. It is clear that the above changes must have taken place later than the time of *i*-mutation, since otherwise the mutated vowel in a word such as *fēt* 'feet' could not be explained. There was, in addition to the above, syncope of /a/ at a much earlier stage, and this proceeded quite regularly (for examples see Campbell 1959: § 341).

One of the peculiarities of West Saxon is that syncope of /i/ occurred even after short syllables in the second and third person singular of both strong verbs and weak class 1 verbs. Therefore we find forms such as *cwist* 'thou speakest' < *cwiðest*. This process seems to have arisen because of inverted forms such as **cwiðest þu* 'speakest thou' (see Hedberg 1945: 280–3). This process highlights an important consequential change, namely assimilation and simplification in consonant groups. These changes are too complex to allow any detailed discussion here, but we should note at least that sequences of consonants tended to assimilate in voice, more particularly consonants devoiced when adjacent to a voiceless consonant, since this was like the voicing of fricatives between voiced segments discussed in § 3.3.3.1. Furthermore, if by syncope a group of three consonants arose (where a geminate consonant counts as two), this was often simplified by the loss of one of the three. Thus in the example quoted above the probable development is: *cwiðest* (medial [ð]) > **cwiðst* (with medial [θ] by assimilation) > *cwist* by simplification of the triple consonant cluster.

3.4 Morphology

Compared with the present-day language, Old English was highly inflected. Nouns had four cases and three genders; verbs inflected for person and number and for the indicative and subjunctive moods. Where inflexions for any of these categories exist today, they either do so in a greatly altered form, as with the modern possessive, or are little more than relics of an older stage, as with, for example, the subjunctive. Further, in the Old English noun phrase there was agreement between noun and modifying adjective rather as in present-day German, something lost from English at about the time of Chaucer. Like a language such as Latin, Old English also had noun (and adjective) declensions and verb conjugations. Similar categories could be proposed for present-day English (see below for further discussion), but might be of little relevance. Compared with Latin, however, Old English appears somewhat degenerate in its inflexional systems; there is not the same richness in inflexions – fewer cases, fewer distinctions of tense, no genuine inflexional passive. This state of affairs is by no means surprising. The Old English inflexional system derived directly from that in Germanic, which, although different from that in Latin, shares the same Indo-European origin (but, of course, Latin and Germanic each have their own characteristics, especially amongst verbs, since they proceeded along divergent paths of linguistic development). But Old English begins to show the loss and simplification of inflexions which characterises the later stages of English and which eventually creates a language with remarkably few inflexions compared with most other Indo-European languages.

The presentation below attempts to capture the changes in inflexional systems up to the time of the Conquest. The starting-point, therefore, must be the inherited Germanic systems. Then, however, the concentration is on the gradual collapse of those systems. This means that the eventual morphological classifications which are suggested for classical Old English differ in several respects from those in the standard handbooks such as Campbell (1959) and Brunner (1965), which are strictly historically based.

It was remarked in §3.1 that the major problem in morphological reconstruction is the decision as to the type of analysis which might most fruitfully be employed. As we shall see below it seems clear that in Old English the dominant feature of inflexional morphology was the paradigm, that is to say, a word is best conceived as consisting of a base together with a set of inflexions which correspond to morphosyntactic categories. A particular set of inflexions and the set of bases which associate with those inflexions form a declension (in the case of nouns and adjectives) or a conjugation (in the case of verbs). To take a (crudely simplified) example from present-day English, we might say that one set of nominal inflexions consists of the morpheme $\{s_1\}$, signifying the morphosyntactic category 'possessive' and the morpheme $\{s_2\}$, signifying the morphosyntactic category 'plural'. Nominal bases, such as *cat*, *dog*, *church*, which take these two inflexions could then be said to belong to the *s*-declension. On the other hand, *ox*, which has the possessive morpheme $\{s_1\}$ but the plural morpheme $\{n\}$, would belong to the *n*-declension. The paradigm of *cat*, then, would be $\{cat\} \sim \{cat\} + \{s_1\} \sim \{cat\} + \{s_2\}$, and similarly for *dog* and *church*, by virtue of their membership of the same paradigm. On the other hand, the paradigm of *ox* would be $\{ox\} \sim \{ox\} + \{s_1\} \sim \{ox\} + \{n\}$.

But there appears to be an obvious objection to the above, for the plurals, for instance, of *cat*, *dog*, *church* are all different: *cat* apparently has /s/ added, *dog* has /z/, and *church* has /ɪz/. One amongst several ways of accounting for this is to suppose a morphophonemic rule which states that the basic or underlying form of the plural morpheme $\{s_2\}$ is

/s/, but that where the base of a noun ends in a voiced consonant or vowel the /s/ is voiced to /z/ and where the base ends in a sibilant (/s, z, ʃ, ʒ/ the morpheme is realised as /ɪz/.

Essentially it is this type of analysis which we shall use in our description of Old English inflectional morphology. The central feature will be the word and its paradigm, and we shall suggest some morphophonemic rules which will be intended to account for allomorphic variations within and between members of the same paradigmatic class. The choice of this analysis is equivalent to the claim which we have already mentioned, namely that the paradigm is the central organisational feature of inflectional morphology in Old English. Two points need to be made here. Firstly, such a claim is not obviously true for other periods of the language, for instance, present-day English. Secondly, such a claim can only be substantiated by evidence that in Old English the paradigm was such a significant linguistic domain that it was able to control, cause or restrict particular instances of linguistic change during the period. Obviously this can only be substantiated by discussion of relevant examples later in this chapter.

3.4.1 *The noun phrase*

There are three major word classes to consider: nouns, adjectives and pronouns. For each, inflexions were determined by three systems of morphosyntactic categories: number, case and gender. The number system was basically as in present-day English, i.e. there was usually only a distinction between singular, referring to one, and plural, referring to more than one (see, however, §3.4.1.3 for dual number). In the immediately antecedent form of Germanic there were probably five cases: nominative, accusative, genitive, dative and instrumental. The last of these is obscure both syntactically and morphologically, but morphologically in nouns it seems to have completely merged with the dative case no later perhaps than the very earliest texts. However, adjectives and pronouns continued to have a separate instrumental singular inflexion available throughout the period. The question of the status of this inflexion is really syntactic, see therefore chapter 4 for discussion of the syntactic functions of this and the other cases.

Present-day English has only natural gender: *boy* is masculine because the word refers to a male, *girl* is similarly feminine, and *stone* is similarly neuter. Exceptions are most commonly for one of two reasons: (i) metaphor, as in the use of *she* to refer to a ship; (ii) avoidance of embarrassment as in the use of *it* to refer to a baby. The basis of gender assignment in Old English was quite diffrent, for what we find there is grammatical gender, see further the discussion of anaphora in chapter 4. Grammatical gender, as expressed not only in Old English but also in other languages, is not based on sex. Thus we find examples such as masculine *se wīfmann*, feminine *sēo hlǣfdiġe* and neuter *þæt wīf*, all with the core meaning of 'woman', although this is not to deny that gender was sometimes determined by sex, as, perhaps, with Old English proper names. What, then, does determine grammatical gender? To answer this we have to consider declensions. What do we mean when we say that a noun (or an adjective) belongs to some particular declension? We mean that that noun follows a particular paradigm, that it has attached to it a set of inflexions (and possibly other morphological changes) which are also attached to some other nouns. A group of nouns which all have the same set of inflexions attached to them are the members of a particular declension. It is perhaps best then to view gender as the means by which one grammatical category is related to another. Thus an Old English noun such as *scip* 'ship' takes a demonstrative article with the shape *þæt* by virtue of its neuter gender. The gender of a word is expressed through its membership of one declension rather than another (although nouns of different gender may sometimes belong to the same declension.

3.4.1.1 Nouns

Nouns in Indo-European had the characteristic structure of root + theme + inflexion. Let us take as an example the nominative singular of the word for *stone* in Primitive Germanic, i.e. **stainaz*. At first sight it looks as if its structure is stem **stain-* + inflexion **-az*. But this is not so. The *-a-* which we have analysed as part of the inflexion is an ending common to all nouns of the same declension, whereas the *-z* is the normal ending of the nominative singular, compare here PrGmc **wīniz* 'friend'. The crucial difference between the two words, therefore, is the vowel which occurs after the root (the lexical unit distinguishing one word from another) and before the inflexion, which the two words share. In these words this differentiating vowel is called the theme. The combination of root + theme gives us the morphological element which is called the stem.

Themes in Germanic were of three types: (i) a vowel; (ii) a consonant;

(iii) zero, and so we can talk of vocalic nouns, consonantal nouns and athematic nouns. In the development of the Germanic languages one type of consonantal nouns assumed an importance far in excess of all others; these are nouns with thematic -*n*-. Traditionally the vocalic stems (i.e. stems with a theme containing a vowel) are called strong nouns, the *n*-stems are called weak nouns, and the remaining consonantal and athematic stems are grouped together in the so-called minor declensions. As we shall see later, the terms 'strong' and 'weak' have been overworked and we shall, to avoid ambiguity, restrict their usage to adjectives and verbs. Let us instead use for nouns the three-way distinction: vocalic ∼ consonantal ∼ athematic. The following diagram gives the approximate proportion of nouns in each of the main types, namely vocalic and *n*-stems. One or two other types ignored here, notably the athematic and *r*-stems, although they contain very few nouns, do contain nouns of extremely high frequency.

masculine vocalic	35%
masculine *n*-stem	+10%
feminine vocalic	25%
feminine *n*-stem	5%
neuter vocalic	25%

Let us firstly consider the vocalic nouns. At the time of the invasions Old English had four major types of vocalic nouns, inherited from Germanic. These were the *a*-stems, the *ō*-stems, the *i*-stems and the *u*-stems. Of these, the first two were by far the most common. The *a*-stem nouns were all masculine or neuter, and the *ō*-stems all feminine (compare the Latin second and first declensions), whilst the *u*-stems contained no neuter nouns.

If we take a typical masculine *a*-stem at this time (ca 400), such as OE *stān* 'stone', we can suppose the following paradigm (for sound changes affecting the stem, usually ignored here, see §3.3.3.1):

	Singular	Plural
Nom.	stān	stānōs
Acc.	stān	stānōs
Gen.	stānas	stānōm
Dat.	stānai	stānum

By the time of the earliest texts (ca 700) the normal operation of sound change in unstressed syllables would give:

	Singular	Plural
Nom.	stān	stānas
Acc.	stān	stānas
Gen.	stānæs	stāna
Dat.	stānæ	stānum

As has been said (§3.3.3.2), it is doubtful whether any text reliably reports this sytem, and examples such as Cæd *metudæs* 'lord' gen.sg. have to be treated with, at least, a pinch of salt. Certainly by 800 the paradigm had reached the stage which is valid for the central period, namely:

	Singular	Plural
Nom.	stān	stānas
Acc.	stān	stānas
Gen.	stānes	stāna
Dat.	stāne	stānum

The above clearly shows that the inflexional system in classical Old English differed from that for the Germanic period. Most importantly, it is no longer sensible to analyse the noun into root + theme + inflexion: nominative and accusative singulars show no sign of a thematic vowel, and elsewhere sound changes have obscured any former consistency. When we come to other declensions we shall see further reasons for casting the earlier analysis aside, but even now it seems reasonable to suggest that there was no separate theme, and that the inflexional pattern for the declension was:

	Singular	Plural
Nom.	∅	-as
Acc.	∅	-as
Gen.	-es	-a
Dat.	-e	-um

The *a*-stems form the most important declension for the later history of the language. Thus, as PDE *stones* indicates, the plural inflexion -*as* is the antecedent of the modern standard plural marker. Even in Old English it was probably the most important declension, containing about one-third of the nouns in the language. As such it had the power to attract other nouns towards it, a process we shall look at very shortly. There were two variants of this declension in Germanic, one where the thematic vowel was preceded by /j/, the other where it was preceded by /w/, respectively *ja*-stems and *wa*-stems. The development of the *ja*-stems is difficult to determine (see Brunner 1965 :§ 246, Anm.1), but it is likely that the regular result was identical to that for *a*-stems except that nominative and accusative singulars had inflexional -*e*, e.g. *ende* 'end', pl. *endas*. At this stage, however, we have to introduce an important morphological contrast which not only existed in Germanic but also persisted throughout the Old English period. The contrast is between nouns (verbs, etc.) with a heavy base, such as *ende*, where the root contains either a short vowel plus two consonants or a long vowel, and words with a light base where the stem contains a short vowel plus only one consonant, a typical light *ja*-noun being **seġe* 'man'. In such nouns the West Germanic change of gemination (see chapter 2) would have applied in all cases except the nominative and accusative singulars, so that the paradigm of the word should be:

	Singular	Plural
Nom.	*seġe	seċġas
Acc.	*seġe	seċġas
Gen.	seċġes	seċġa
Dat.	seċġe	seċġum

However geminated forms were extended analogically to the nominative and accusative singulars to give *seċġ*. But since gemination did not affect */r/, short-stemmed nouns ending in /r/ had yet another paradigm, as in *here* 'army':

	Singular	Plural
Nom.	here	herġas
Acc.	here	herġas
Gen.	herġes	herġa
Dat.	herġe	herġum

If we take all these types together and consider solely their inflexions, what we discover is that the original division into *a*-stems and *ja*-stems was considerably altered, for there were now three types:

(a) original *a*-stems and light *ja*-stems

	Singular	Plural
Nom.	∅	-as
Acc.	∅	-as
Gen.	-es	-a
Dat.	-e	-um

(b) heavy *ja*-stems

	Singular	Plural
Nom.	-e	-as
Acc.	-e	-as
Gen.	-es	-a
Dat.	-e	-um

(c) light *ja*-stems in /r/

	Singular	Plura
Nom.	-e	-jas (= ġas)
Acc.	-e	-jas
Gen.	-jes	-jas
Dat.	-je	-jas

In both Early and Late West Saxon forms such as dat.sg. *here*, nom.pl. *heras* are found beside the expected forms; doubtless type (c) was gradually being lost, with *here* and the other nouns like it becoming type (b) stems. It is likely that by the end of the period *a*- and *ja*-stems had been reanalysed into two new groups, those, like *stān*, with zero inflexion in nominative and accusative singular, and those, like *ende*, with -*e* rather than zero.

The original *wa*-stems are much simpler, splitting into the two categories of heavy and light bases. If they were heavy, e.g. *þēow* 'servant', *snāw* 'snow', then they pattern exactly as *stān*, because of some early analogies which promote a reduction of declensional types. If they were light, then the final /w/ was preserved except in the nominative and accusative singulars where it turned up as (phonologically predictable) /u/. Thus *bearu* 'grove' had the paradigm:

	Singular	Plural
Nom.	bearu	bearwas
Acc.	bearu	bearwas
Gen.	bearwes	bearwa
Dat.	bearwe	bearwum

Neuter nouns belonging to these declensions showed only one major variation from the masculines: in the nominative and accusative plural the inflexion was either -*u* or zero, according to whether the base was light or heavy (/u/ was lost by apocope after long syllables, see §3.3.3.2). Thus the paradigms of *sċip* 'ship' and *word* 'word' were:

	Singular	Plural	Singular	Plural
Nom.	sċip	sċipu	word	word
Acc.	sċip	sċipu	word	word
Gen.	sċipes	sċipa	wordes	worda
Dat.	sċipe	sċipum	worde	wordum

Turning to *ja*-stems we find that original light bases which had undergone gemination, e.g. *cynn* 'race', behaved like *word* and the other heavy *a*-stems, whereas the original heavy bases behaved like *sċip* except that they had final *-e* in the nominative and accusative singulars, e.g. *wīte* 'punishment'. The *wa*-stem neuters had paradigms such as the following for *searu* 'device' and *cnēow* 'knee':

	Singular	Plural	Singular	Plural
Nom.	searu	searu	cnēow	cnēow
Acc.	searu	searu	cnēow	cnēow
Gen.	searwes	searwa	cnēowes	cnēowa
Dat.	searwe	searwum	cnēowe	cnēowum

This looks messy, and the reason is that we have been considering all these nouns from the diachronic viewpoint. But that was not an option open to Anglo-Saxon speakers. For them it must have been the case that all the masculine nouns had the basic inflexional pattern shown in (a) of the diagram on p. 128. and neuter nouns would have had exactly the same pattern except that the nominative and accusative singulars would have had either *-u* or zero on phonologically predictable grounds. If one takes the different types of noun we have examined, twelve in all, and considers the nominative singular of each then we have: *stān, seċġ, bearu, snāw* (all masculine); *sċip, word, cynn, searu, cnēow* (all neuter); *ende, wīte, here*. All except the last three fit into the following inflexional system:

	Singular	Plural
Nom.	∅	-as (masc.), -u (neut.)
Acc.	∅	-as (masc.), -u (neut.)
Gen.	-es	-a
Dat.	-e	-um

The assumption is that final *-u* was apocopated after long stems and that if /u/ remained it became /w/ before a vowel. If we also suppose that *ende* and *wīte* were bisyllabic nouns with zero inflexion in the nominative and accusative singular, then they can also be accommodated within the above schema provided that we allow for an allomorphic variation which caused stem-final -e to be lost before another vowel. The only form which will not fit into the above pattern is *here* with plural *hergas*, but once the plural form was replaced by *heras*, and we have seen that this happened from Early West Saxon on, it will behave exactly like *ende*.

If the above analysis is correct (see further below), what we are seeing in the development of the various *a*-stems from proto-Old English to classical Old English is a massive simplification of the system so that we have a single declension for all the above masculine nouns and a single declension for all the neuter nouns. In the later history of English (see vol. II, chapter 2) the key factor in the morphology of nouns is probably the nominative plural, so we can call these two declensions the *as*-plural declension (= masculine) and the *u*-plural declension (= neuter).

The importance of the above can be seen if we turn now to *i*-stem masculine nouns. At the time of the invasions such nouns would have had a paradigm not dissimilar to that of the *a*-stems, the only variations being due to differential effects of sound change on */i/ rather than */a/. Thus we can suppose for a word such as OE *wine* 'friend' the paradigm:

	Singular	Plural
Nom.	wini	wini
Acc.	wini	wini
Gen.	wini	winja
Dat.	wini	winim

This should have given a paradigm of hypothetical development something like:

	Singular	Plural
Nom.	wine	wine
Acc.	wine	wine
Gen.	wine	winiġa
Dat.	wine	winim

But the usual paradigm in both Early and Late West Saxon was:

	Singular	Plural
Nom.	wine	winas
Acc.	wine	winas
Gen.	wines	wina
Dat.	wine	winum

Wine is a light base; in the long-stemmed nouns the nominative and accusative singular had zero inflexion, e.g. *wyrm* 'worm', pl. *wyrmas*.

Clearly the *i*-stems lost their separate identity and transferred to the *a*-declension or, in later periods, the *as*-plural declension. This seems to have occurred gradually, with the genitive and dative singular and plural taking the *a*-declension form well before the time of the earliest texts. The expected nominative and accusative plural in -*e* can be found with light bases, e.g. *wine* 'friends', and was only slowly superseded by the -*as* plural, but the shift occurred earlier with heavy bases where **wyrm* rather than *wyrmas* is never found.

Since the light neuter *i*-stems all declined in the same way as *wīte* and the heavy bases all declined like *word*, they need not be discussed. The neuters, like the masculines, are further examples of the simplification of the declensional system. But the motivation for the shift was not merely to reduce the number of different declensions, as can be seen from the fact that names of nationalities and other nouns which were always plural retained the original nominative and accusative plural inflexion, e.g. *Engle* 'Englishmen'. If the original plural had been kept in the case of *wine*, singular and plural would have been identical. This happened elsewhere, e.g. *word*, pl. *word*, but it was presumably avoided where possible, and the class transfer involved in *winas* was an obvious solution. *Engle* could only be plural, the problem did not arise, and the solution was not taken.

Let us now turn to the *ō*-stems, which formed the principal vocalic declension of feminine nouns, parallel to the *a*-stem masculines and neuters, and also accounted for the vast majority of feminine nouns in the language (see the proportion of major noun declension types listed on p. 126). The paradigm of such nouns at the time of the invasions must have been like that for *lufu* 'love' (cf. the *a*-stem paradigm ca 400 on p. 126):

	Singular	Plural
Nom.	lufō	lufōz
Acc.	lufa	lufa
Gen.	lufōz	lufōm
Dat.	lufai	lufum

The predicted, but unattested development of this paradigm is to:

	Singular	Plural
Nom.	lufu	lufa
Acc.	lufe	lufe
Gen.	lufa	lufa
Dat.	lufe	lufum

What we find instead is:

	Singular	Plural
Nom.	lufu	lufa
Acc.	lufe	lufa
Gen.	lufe	lufa
Dat.	lufe	lufum

What we see here is a series of simplifications. In the singular the genitive appears to have been modelled on the other singular cases. In the plural the accusative at first remained as -*e*, but by the classical period it had disappeared. Looking back at the *a*-stems, we can see there that nominative and accusative cases were regularly identical, and the change in the accusative seems part of a more general falling together of nominative and accusative plurals everywhere (a phenomenon which perhaps started in late Indo-European, compare Latin forms such as *homines* 'men' nom.acc.pl.). The *ō*-stems were clearly in danger of losing all their inflexional information. With the gradual reduction of unstressed vowels it is probable that by the Conquest all the inflexions except the dative plural would have fallen together. This is one of the strongest grounds for claiming that by the end of the period English was only marginally a language inflecting for case. The syncretism of nominative and accusative forms makes one realise how dependent Old English was on factors other than inflexion of nouns for the determination of the syntactic roles of subject and object, for example, word order and prepositions, see chapter 4.

The above discussion relates to heavy as well as light *ō*-stems, for the only difference between the two was the predictable loss of inflexional /u/ in the nominative singular of the long stems, e.g. *lār* 'learning' < *lāru*. During the period, however, another difference began to emerge, for a new genitive plural inflexion -*ena*, borrowed from the *n*-declension, became common with the light bases, e.g. *lufena* 'of loves' vs. *sāula* 'of souls'. Since for classical Old English the significance of the term '*ō*-stem' had clearly been lost, it is perhaps best to classify these nouns as belonging to the *a*-plural declension.

As with the *a*-stems there were in Germanic two variant types, namely *jō*-stems and *wō*-stems. The development of these variants, however, was simpler than of the corresponding masculines and neuters. *Jō*-stems, e.g. *synn* 'sin', *wylf* 'she-wolf', followed the same pattern as *lār* and are best analysed as heavy base feminines. In the case of the *wō*-stems the final /w/ was retained, although, as in the *wa*-stems, the /w/ became

/u/ finally and that /u/ was apocopated after a long syllable. Typical examples are *sinu* 'sinew', pl. *sinwa*, *mǣd* 'meadow', pl. *mǣdwa*. Since in both types the nominative singular would have a form identical to that of the corresponding *ō*-stems (*lufu*, *lār*), it is no surprise that in classical Old English *w*-less forms such as acc.sg. *sine*, *mǣde*, etc. are found.

In the *i*-stem declension there were at first feminine nouns which corresponded to the masculine and neuter nouns discussed above. In Old English these feminines underwent an entirely expected development, for they took on the inflexions of the *a*-plural declension, so that *denu* 'valley' *dǣd* 'deed' declined like *lufu* and *lār* respectively. This seems to have happened even earlier than the other mergers, since they can only be recognised as original *i*-stems by the *i*-mutation of the stem vowel, and there are no relic forms with the original inflexions. This may give a clue to the pattern of merger. Although there were examples of individual inflexions, notably the dative plural, merging at a very early date, to give *-um* in all declensions, we might suggest that the merger of the *i*-stem feminines with the *ō*-stems was the first real class merger and that it happened after *i*-mutation but before the time of the earliest texts, say, in the seventh century. The other *i*-stems perhaps merged with their *a*-stem counterparts during the eighth century, since there are early eighth century texts with the phonologically expected forms. Although Early West Saxon texts show many of the other simplifications we have discussed, Late West Saxon texts show many more, and this makes one suppose that the reorganisation into *as*-plurals, etc. was a feature of the ninth and tenth centuries. After the classical period, what we witness is yet further confusion of the declensions, no doubt due as much to the merger of the various unstressed vowels as to morphological simplification.

There is one other vocalic declension, the *u*-stems. There were only a few such nouns in Old English, all either masculine or feminine, and not surprisingly they showed a strong tendency to transfer to the *as*-plural declension or the *a*-plural declension as appropriate. These nouns were, however, often of high frequency, e.g. *sunu* 'son', *feld* 'field', *nosu* 'nose', *hand* 'hand'. A typical light base paradigm is that of *sunu*, heavy bases apocopated final /u/:

	Singular	Plural
Nom.	sunu	suna
Acc.	sunu	suna
Gen.	suna	suna
Dat.	suna	sunum

When the nouns remained in this declension there was no distinction between masculine and feminine inflexion.

As we have said, the most important consonantal declension was that of the *n*-stems, the so-called 'weak' nouns. Originally these nouns contained a thematic element of vowel + /n/, cf. Latin *homo, hominis* 'man'. To this theme inflexions were added in the normal way. But by the Old English period the unstressed inflexions had been lost, and so what had originally been a thematic element became at least partly inflexional. The historical development of the forms was fairly simple, the basic pattern remaining throughout the period. Therefore all we need do is give the paradigm of a masculine noun such as *guma* 'man' (= Lat. *homo*):

	Singular	Plural
Nom.	guma	guman
Acc.	guman	guman
Gen.	guman	gumena
Dat.	guman	gumum

This was an important declension in Old English, since it contained a large number of masculine and feminine nouns (see proportions of major noun declension types on p. 126 above), the feminines only differing from the masculines in their nominative singular, which had inflexional *-e*, e.g. *hearpe* 'harp'. There were only two consistently neuter *n*-stems, *ēage* 'eye' and *ēare* 'ear', where the accusative singular also had inflexional *-e*. The traditional classification '*n*-stem' is somewhat backwards-looking, and it might be better to call these nouns *n*-plurals. Apart from anything else, this will serve as a reminder that this declension gave the later *-en* plural, fairly common in Early Middle English but now, in the standard language, existing only in *oxen* (< OE *oxan*) and the double plurals *children, brethren*.

Before we look briefly at the other original consonantal nouns, let us consider the athematic nouns, which were originally characterised by the fact that the inflexion was added directly to the stem, with no intervening theme, cf. Lat. *rex* 'king' = /reː k-s/ vs. *domus* 'house' = /dom-u-s/. These nouns were either masculine or feminine. The most obvious and important characteristic of these nouns is that they should have shown *i*-mutation in the genitive and dative singular and in the nominative plural, where in proto-Old English there was an inflexional *-i-*. Thus a word such as *fōt* 'foot' should have declined in this way:

	Singular	Plural
Nom.	fōt	fēt
Acc.	fōt	fōt
Gen.	fēt	fōta
Dat.	fēt	fōtum

This paradigm at one stage must have applied to both masculine and feminine nouns, but two competing tendencies of simplification changed matters. Firstly, as elsewhere the nominative and accusative plurals fall together (as *fēt*). Secondly, all these nouns tended to fall in with the dominant masculine and feminine declensions. Thus masculine nouns began to decline in the following way:

	Singular	Plural
Nom.	fōt	fēt
Acc.	fōt	fēt
Gen.	fōtes	fōta
Dat.	fēt	fōtum

The genitive singular clearly derives from the *as*-plural declension. In the same way *hnutu* 'nut' shows the usual system for the feminine nouns (square brackets indicate predicted but unattested forms):

	Singular	Plural
Nom.	hnutu	[hnyte]
Acc.	[hnutu]	hnyte
Gen.	hnyte	hnuta
Dat.	hnyte	hnutum

Note that final -*e* was usually preserved but cannot always be distinguished from the final -*e* of *a*-plurals, especially if *i*-mutation was lost, as in the equally common *hnute* gen.sg. *Hnutu* was a light base; heavy bases followed the same pattern except for the predictable loss of final -*e* and -*u*, e.g. *bōc*, *bēċ* 'book, books'.

The importance of this declension lies partly in the fact that to it belonged a number of very common nouns, e.g. *mann* 'person', partly in that it is the source of irregular plurals such as PDE *foot* ~ *feet, man* ~ *men, goose* ~ *geese*. But during the Old English period the most salient feature of these nouns, the vowel change due to *i*-mutation, was already beginning to be lost. In this respect English is unlike German, where *i*-mutation (Umlaut) remains an important morphological feature; indeed it spreads to forms where it did not originally occur, e.g. *Haus* 'house' vs. *Häuser* 'houses'.

There were, as we have said, several minor consonantal declensions, some containing important words; for instance the kinship terms *fæder* 'father', *mōdor* 'mother', *brōðor* 'brother', *dohtor* 'daughter', *sweostor* 'sister' constituted the *r*-declension, and *frēond*, *frȳnd* 'friend, friends' and *fēond*, *fȳnd* 'fiend, fiends' were members of the *nd*-declension. These are not discussed here, since they are complex both in origin and in history. Suffice it to say that they shared some features in common with the athematic nouns (with *i*-mutation in the dative singular and, for the *nd*-stems, the nominative and accusative plural also), but, like all nouns belonging to smaller declensions, there was a strong tendency to transfer to the *as*-plurals or (less probably) the *a*-plurals as appropriate, hence *fædras* 'fathers'.

In conclusion, it is worth emphasising how radical were the changes in Old English noun morphology. At first, nouns had a tripartite structure of root + theme + inflexion, and the shape of the theme determined the declensional class to which a noun belonged. Such a structure can easily be seen in the paradigms on pp. 126, 129, 131 and 132, but other declensional types had a similar structure also. But, as we have seen, due mostly to general phonological processes of reduction, the characteristics which enabled the thematic element to be determined were lost at a very early stage, and only a bipartite structure remained.

Now this is not a matter of interest merely to specialists, for the loss of the element which defined declensional class opened the way to a complete reorganisation of noun morphology, one which laid the foundations for the system of the present-day language. Naturally some parts of this reorganisation appear irrelevant to later stages of the language, but the irrelevancy is only apparent, for each development is part of a larger and long-lasting tendency. The most important feature, of course, is that declensional type was no longer marked by the thematic element but by the inflexional element. But, as the preceding pages should have shown, there was another feature, namely the growing domination of just three nominal declensions, which are best defined by the form of the nominative plural inflexion. These three declensions, which we have called the *as*-plurals, the *a*-plurals and the *n*-plurals, can be recognised as dominant not so much by their relative frequency as by the fact that other nouns could transfer to one or other of these declensions, but transfer in the opposite direction was extremely rare. Thus *i*-stem nouns usually transferred either to the *as*-plurals or the *a*-plurals, according to gender, but *a*- or *ō*-stems did not transfer to the *i*-stems. Furthermore, it can quite easily be observed that the most dominant of these declensions was that of the *as*-plurals, for this was the target of choice for those nouns which were transferring declension. Other factors confirm this, such as the generalisation of the dative plural inflexion *-um*, which was the regular phonological development of that inflexion for the old *a*-stems.

In Middle English (see vol. II, chapter 2), this tendency for the *as*-plurals to become dominant increased, and by the end of that period we find a system virtually identical to that in the present-day language. The point to emphasise here is that the developments are not solely post-Conquest. They are very easily observable in Old English, and the development of the present-day system is something which began at the very earliest stage of the emergence of English as a separate language.

3.4.1.2 Adjectives

Adjectives in Old English always agreed in case, number and gender with the nouns they modified. Of course, we would expect this of any inflected language, not just a Germanic one, cf. French or Italian. But in Germanic there was one peculiarity which still exists in most of the present-day languages with the exception of English. This is that adjectives normally belonged to two declensions. Which declension an adjective followed in any given context was syntactically determined (see chapter 4). Broadly, if the adjective was in a definite noun phrase (usually made definite by a demonstrative or possessive), then one declension was used, elsewhere the other was used. For morphological reasons most grammarians used the terms 'weak' for the first type and 'strong' for the second type, since adjectives in a definite NP patterned according to the *n*- or weak declension, and adjectives in an indefinite NP patterned according to the vocalic or strong declensions (see §3.4.1.1). It is important to note that an adjective was not weak or strong because the noun it modified was weak or strong; as has been said, the assignment of declension in adjectives was syntactically determined; in this respect, therefore, the adjective did not agree with the noun. Adjectival inflexions differed from nominal inflexions in two ways. Firstly, in a number of cases the inflexion was taken not from nouns but from pronouns: these are written in italics in the paradigms below. Secondly, as mentioned in the introduction to §3.4, the adjectives, unlike the nouns, can retain a separate instrumental case inflexion, but only in the singular. Finally, under the term 'adjective' we include both numerals and quantifiers (see chapter 4). These groups are not usually morphologically distinct from the adjectives, but on syntactic grounds, they may, for example, lack forms in the weak declension and in other ways not have the full pattern of the core set of adjectives.

Let us now consider the declensions in more detail, looking first at the strong declensions. Since strong adjectives declined like strong or vocalic nouns, it is no surprise to discover that they were (ignoring the pronominal inflexions), if masculine, *as*-plurals, if neuter, *u*-plurals and if feminine, *a*-plurals. That is to say, the adjectives followed the dominant vocalic declension in nouns for each gender. In fact, adjectives were even more prone to transfer to these declensions than nouns were, and in Old English no adjectives completely followed the *i*- or *u*-stems, and original *ja*-, *wa*-stems, etc. were assimilated to the major types in the way described in §3.4.1.1. The kinds of variations we noticed in §3.4.1.1, such as between heavy and light base nouns, naturally existed equally among the adjectives, and we shall not discuss these below.

Since the situation in the plural was slightly different from that in the singular, let us firstly consider only the singular forms of the adjective, starting with masculine and neuter forms, exemplified by *sum* 'some' (heavy bases behaved in the same way):

	Masculine	Neuter
Nom.	sum	sum
Acc.	sum*ne*	sum
Gen.	sumes	sumes
Dat.	sum*um*	sum*um*
Instr.	sume	sume

The accusative masculine inflexion has the distinctive -*ne* shape which we shall later see in pronouns, e.g. *hine* 'him', *þone* 'that' a.s.m., and the dative singular inflexion too was borrowed from the pronominal declensions. The paradigm outlined above is valid for both Early and Late West Saxon, except that there was an increasing tendency to replace the separate instrumental inflexion by the dative, with the instrumental being retained only in set phrases such as *sume dæġ* 'one day' (where the noun too has a fossilised locative ending).

Turning to the feminine forms we can trace a greater degree of simplification. In Early West Saxon the usual singular paradigm was:

Nom.	sumu
Acc.	sume
Gen.	sum*re*
Dat.	sum*re*

Given the presence of pronominal endings, this is what we would expect for light bases; heavy bases, predictably, lost the final -*u* in the nominative singular so that we find there forms such as *blind* 'blind'. Already for feminines there was no separate instrumental inflexion. In classical Old English there was a very strong tendency to lose final -*u* even in the short stems, to give nom.sg. *sum* rather than *sumu*, which, of course, made the nominative singular of indefinite adjectives identical for all genders.

The simplification is carried yet further in all genders of the plural. In Early West Saxon the patterns were:

	Masculine	Neuter	Feminine
Nom.	sum*e*	sumu	suma
Acc.	sum*e*	sumu	suma
Gen.	sum*ra*	sum*ra*	sum*ra*
Dat.	sumum	sumum	sumum

For heavy bases the same paradigm was followed except that final -*u* of the nominative and accusative of neuters was regularly apocopated. The most important point to note here is that even in Early West Saxon (due to normal sound change) the genitive and dative inflexions were identical for all three genders. During the classical period such merging of inflexion over all genders was carried over into the nominative and accusative forms also, with the masculine -*e* becoming standard (see Pope 1967:184). Thus we find the plural declension simplified to *sume* ~ *sume* ~ *sumra* ~ *sumum*. So by the eleventh century gender distinctions in the strong adjectives only persisted in the oblique cases of the singular.

Very little needs to be said about the weak adjective forms, for in essence they were identical to the forms of the *n*-declension nouns, and can be directly deduced from the paradigms given in §3.4.1.1. There are only two differences to note. Firstly, although the genitive plural of all forms ought to be -*ena*, this ending, frequent in Early West Saxon, was often found elsewhere as *blindra*, with the inflexion of the strong adjective. Secondly, from Early West Saxon on there was an increasing tendency to change the dative plural ending from -*um* to -*an*. This could well be the result of a sound change, for it was eventually found in all examples of the inflexion. However, it is in the indefinite adjectives that the change is first seen, and there it could easily be morphologically motivated (as a first stage towards the reduction of all the plural inflexions of that declension to a single -*an* form). By the classical period -*um* had become -*an* to a greater or lesser extent in other forms of the adjectives too, and also in the nouns.

As today, adjectives in Old English showed two degrees of comparison (but in Old English this was almost the only method of comparison; the periphrastic comparison with an equivalent of *more*, *most* was relatively rare and mostly restricted to late texts). The normal method of comparison was with the proto-Old English suffixes *-*ora*, *-*ost*, with the -*o*- of the comparative being lost through syncope (§3.3.3.2). These were simply added to the stem of the adjective, e.g. *earm*, *earmra*, *earmost* 'poor, poorer, poorest'. Sometimes the suffixes came from earlier *-*ira*, *-*ist*, and in those cases *i*-mutation is found in the comparative and superlative, e.g. *eald*, *yldra*, *yldest* 'old, older, oldest', *ġeong*, *ġingra*, *ġinġest* 'young, younger, youngest'. Other common words with such comparison were: *hēah* 'high', *lang* 'long', *sċeort* 'short', see Quirk & Wrenn (1957:§56) and Brunner (1965:§§307–11). A further type of formation is seen in the superlative of locational adjectives, e.g. the points of the compass, where a new ending -*mest* was used, e.g. *norðmest* 'northmost'. Such forms can be found in Ælfric's *Grammar*, e.g. ÆGr 240.2 *innemest* 'inmost', but in late texts the suffix became identified with *mǣst* 'most' and was so respelled.

Finally, as in present-day English there were a few very common adjectives which formed their comparison by suppletion, that is to say, by taking the compared form from another root. There are four examples: *gōd*, *betra*, *betst* or *sēlra*, *sēlest* 'good, better, best'; *lȳtel*, *lǣssa*, *lǣst* 'little, less, least'; *miċel*, *māra*, *mǣst* 'much, more, most; and *yfel*, *wyrsa*, *wyrst* 'bad, worse, worst'.

3.4.1.3 Pronouns

Morphologically as well as syntactically (see chapter 4) pronouns did not form a homogeneous class. To some extent the morphological variations were dependent upon the syntactic; on the other hand, some of the variation was due to historical events long before the Old English period: thus third person personal pronouns, although they have an inflexional system quite different from the other personal pronouns, behaved syntactically as if they were ordinary personal pronouns. From the point of view of historical morphology, and disregarding syntax, it is probably best to class the pronouns into two types: (i) <u>personal pronouns</u>, by which we mean the first and second person personal pronouns only; (ii) <u>impersonal pronouns</u>, by which we mean not only the demonstratives, possessives, interrogatives and indefinites, but also the third person personal pronouns. For reflexive pronouns see the discussion below. The indefinites, e.g. *man* 'one', are of no separate morphological interest, and we shall not discuss these.

Even if this classification is reasonably correct historically, it is inconvenient for the purposes of discussion. Below, therefore, we discuss the various pronouns in the following order: demonstratives; interrogatives; first and second person personal pronouns; possessives; third person personal pronouns. One other point has to be made now. Throughout the period all the pronouns appeared in a considerable variety of forms, even within one dialect. Probably this was largely because pronouns could occur both in stressed and in unstressed positions, and so there would exist alongside one another both stressed or 'strong' forms and unstressed or 'weak' forms. These could not only differ from one another, but could also interact with one another and so produce alternative strong and weak forms. This is not particularly different from the situation in present-day English, to which we are all unconsciously accustomed, but what we are not accustomed to, and yet exists in Old English, is the variety of spelling to reflect these variations. Below we only try to give the most common forms in Early and Late West Saxon and to give those only in their stressed form. Brunner (1965: §§ 332–49) gives a good overview of the full variety of forms available during the period.

There were two demonstrative pronouns in Old English: *sē* (from unstressed *se*) 'that' and *þes* 'this'. There is also a single example, at CP 443.24, of *ġeonre* 'yon' dat.sg.fem. Of the two demonstratives *sē* was by far the more common, and it was used as the neutral demonstrative equivalent to PDE *the*. Both demonstratives inflected fully for case, number and, in the singular, gender. Since amongst nouns the distinctions for nominative and accusative had often been lost, singular forms of *sē* often provide the only clue other than word order to the function of the noun phrase. But, as everywhere else, the nominative and accusative plurals were identical in the demonstratives.

In Early West Saxon the declension of *sē* was as follows:

	Masculine	Neuter	Feminine	Plural
Nom.	sē, se	þæt	sēo	þā
Acc.	þone	þæt	þā	þā
Gen.	þæs	þæs	þǣre, þāre	þāra, þǣra
Dat.	þǣm, þām	þǣm, þām	þǣre, þāre	þǣm, þām

The variations, as we have said, probably were due largely to alternation of strong and weak forms, although one might also suspect a tendency to reduce alternation of the root vowel. In the classical period the reduction of alternation is perhaps more obvious: there it was likely that the forms with -ā-, e.g. dat.sg., pl. þām would replace forms with -ǣ-, and in the masculine accusative singular the form þæne sometimes appears instead of þone, suggesting a generalisation of -æ-. Doubtless the situation was thoroughly confused by frequent shortening of the long vowel in unstressed forms, and it is difficult to know how much importance to attach to many of these changes. As with the adjectives, there was a masculine and neuter instrumental singular, appearing as þon or þȳ. For the classical period and later, however, it must be doubtful whether it should be thought of as a 'real' inflexional form, rather than a fossilised relic at least partially detachable from the normal paradigm.

In Early West Saxon the declension of þes 'this' was as follows:

	Masculine	Neuter	Feminine	Plural
Nom.	þes	þis	þēos	þās
Acc.	þisne	þis	þās	þās
Gen.	þisses	þisses	þisse	þissa
Dat.	þissum	þissum	þisse	þissum

All the forms with -i- also occurred with -y-, and in both Early and Late West Saxon there was degemination of medial /ss/ in the unstressed form. In Early West Saxon but not later, there was also an instrumental singular form þȳs. By the classical period the feminine genitive and dative singulars had changed to þissere and the genitive plural to þissera, where the -e- was due to epenthesis and the inflexion was taken over from feminine and plural adjectives. Thus in the genitive and dative of both numbers and all genders the inflexional system aligned with that for indefinite adjectives. If we turn back to se, we can see that the same process was at work there, giving an analysis of, say, þāra as þā + ra. Yet again, therefore, there was a simplification of inflexional systems.

The interrogative pronoun hwā 'who, what' had only singular forms and also only distinguished between non-neuter and neuter, the neuter nominative form being *hwæt*. In Germanic there had been distinct masculine and feminine forms, but in Old English all the feminine forms had been ousted by the masculine ones. It might not be too much to suppose that this process is the beginnings of a natural gender system (with an opposition in the first place between animate *hwā* and inanimate *hwæt*) but unfortunately there is precious little evidence in Old English to support this (see Mitchell 1985: §§ 349–51 for some typically sceptical remarks on the topic). Whatever the rights of the matter, the morphology of this pronoun followed, entirely predictably, the morphology of demonstrative *se*.

There are two striking differences between the Old English first and second person personal pronouns and those existing today. Firstly, in Old English there was in the second person both a singular form *þu* 'thou' and a plural form *ġe* 'you'. Furthermore, the difference between these was purely one of number: there was no sociolinguistic difference as there was in Middle English and as still exists in, for example, some Yorkshire dialects, between *tha'* and *you*. These differences only arose after the time of the Conquest. Secondly, as well as singular and plural forms, there also existed, albeit only occasionally, a dual form, used for referring to two persons, e.g. *wit* 'we two'. The dual form was essentially restricted to Old English, although some examples of it persisted into the fourteenth century.

At about the time of the earliest texts (ca 700) the forms of the first person pronoun were probably as follows:

	Singular	Dual	Plural
Nom.	iċ	wit	we
Acc.	meċ	uncit	ūsiċ
Gen.	mīn	uncer	ūser
Dat.	me	unc	ūs

By Early West Saxon, however, this system had changed in two respects. Firstly, probably because of variation between strong and weak forms, the accusative always lost its distinctive ending and became identical with the dative, thus paving the way for the three-way contrast which persists today. It is doubtful whether the morphological identity of accusative and dative meant that the distinction of case had been lost, since, as we have seen, it survived everywhere else, but no doubt the merger here helped the merger to be promoted elsewhere after the Conquest. Secondly, and more trivially, because of inflected forms of *ūser* as a possessive (see below), syncope and assimilation take place to give regular *ūre*.

The second person pronoun developed in parallel to the first person, and therefore only the normal Late West Saxon paradigm is given below, from which earlier forms can easily be deduced:

	Singular	Dual	Plural
Nom.	þu	ġit	ġe
Acc.	þe	inc	ēow
Gen.	þīn	incer	ēower
Dat.	þe	inc	ēow

The genitives of these personal pronouns also functioned as possessives – that was indeed their normal usage. When used as possessives they then behaved exactly like strong adjectives and agreed in number, case and gender with their modifying noun following the usual declensional pattern, see §3.4.1.2. In poetry, but hardly at all in prose, there was a third person possessive *sīn*, which comes from an old reflexive pronoun. This declined as a strong adjective too, and although it was almost always used reflexively, it sometimes was not, see Mitchell (1985: §§290–3).

We have already said that the third person pronouns, although syntactically like the personal pronouns, were morphologically like the demonstratives. This can be seen quite clearly if we consider the paradigm of these pronouns in Early West Saxon (the forms in *-i* existed alongside forms in *-ie*, see §3.3.3.1):

	Masculine	Neuter	Feminine	Plural
Nom.	he	hit	hēo	hī, hēo
Acc.	hine	hit	hī	hī, hēo
Gen.	his	his	hire	hira, heora
Dat.	him	him	hire	him

A close comparison of this with the paradigm of *se* 'that' (see above, p. 143), should be enough to show that the two declensions are inflexionally identical. To the modern reader this must seem surprising, since there no longer exists any inflexional system for the demonstratives except for the plural forms *these*, *those*, and the inflexional system of personal pronouns has become quite irregular (i.e. isolated from all other existing inflexional systems), but it would have required no great effort for the speaker of Old English to see the two declensions as one. The only odd forms above are the nominative and accusative plurals *hēo*, which come from an old neuter form, and gen.pl. *heora* by back mutation (§3.3.3.1). In Late West Saxon the principal forms were similar, but there was frequent substitution of *y* for *i*, as would be expected. Unlike the true personal pronouns, when the genitive forms are used as possessives, they remain uninflected.

One noticeable feature of these third pronouns is that they all begin with /h/, i.e. the <th> (=/ð/) forms of present-day English are completely absent. *They, their, them* are not to be traced back to Old English, but are due to Scandinavian influence after the time of the Conquest. In very late West Saxon texts there are about six examples of a form *þæge* instead of *þā* 'that' nom.pl. It might be tempting to see this as a precursor of PDE *they*, but the temptation should be resisted.

3.4.1.4 Other elements

There is little to say about other elements which can be inflected. Adverbs generally followed the same patterns as adjectives in comparison, so that, for instance, *lange* 'long' had *i*-mutated comparative and superlative forms, *wel* 'well' had suppletive forms just like *gōd* 'good'. The numerals for 1–3 declined similarly to strong adjectives, although the inflexions were different, e.g. masc. *twēġen*, neut. *twā, tū*, fem. *twā* 'two', and we can note oddities such as that the numeral *ān* 'one' could have a plural inflexion when followed by a collective plural.

3.4.2 The verb phrase

In all the Germanic languages there were two principal types of verb, traditionally called strong verbs and weak verbs. The difference between them lay in the formation of tenses: strong verbs formed their preterite or past tense forms (principally) by means of vowel variation, cf. PDE *sing, sang, sung*, whereas weak verbs formed their preterite by suffixation. In addition there were various irregular verbs, some of which grouped together as preterite-presents (see §3.4.2.4), some of which were, by the Old English period, simply irregular. The strong conjugation was the older, being Indo-European in origin, but the weak conjugation was the primary one in Old English. Its origins, although obscure, were strictly Germanic (see chapter 2) and it is this conjugation to which new verbs usually belonged, just as new verbs today join the regular conjugation exemplified by *love, loved*. The weak conjugation is indeed the source of today's regular conjugation. The irregular verbs were only a small minority, but, as would be expected, they contained some of the most frequent verbs, e.g. *bēon* 'be'. The strong conjugation, too, contained many verbs of fairly high frequency, and therefore the three types were roughly similar in frequency.

In Old English, verbs inflected for person, number, tense and mood. As in all the Germanic languages there were only two tenses, present and past, and there were also three moods, indicative, subjunctive and imperative. In Germanic there had been three numbers, but as with nouns and adjectives, the dual inflexions had been lost early on. Also, there was earlier a partial set of inflexions for passive voice, but only one survivor existed in Old English, *hātte*, pl. *hātton* 'was called'.

3.4.2.1 Verbal inflexions

The inflexional systems of strong and weak verbs were generally identical except for the preterite indicative singular and the past participle (the separate weak inflexions are discussed in §3.4.2.3). After the very earliest changes such as first fronting (see §3.3.3.1), the inflexions attached to strong verbs were probably as follows:

Present

	Indicative	Subjunctive	Imperative
1sg	-u	-æ	
2sg	-is	-æ	-ø
3sg	-ið	-æ	
Plural	-að	-æn	-að

Past

	Indicative	Subjunctive
1sg	-ø	-ī
2sg	-i	-ī
3sg	-ø	-ī
Plural	-un	-īn

Infinitive	-an
Present Participle	-andi
Past participle	-æn

Anyone with even a slight acquaintance with Latin should be able to spot correspondence between some of the inflexions shown above and the verbal inflexions of Latin. Thus pre-Old English *scrīfu* 'I decree', *scrīfis*, *scrīfið* corresponds closely to Latin *scribo* 'I write', *scribis*, *scribit*.

The loss of separate inflexions for the different persons of the plural compared not only with Latin but with the earliest stages of Germanic (as in Gothic) was characteristic not only of Old English but also of the other North Sea Germanic dialects, Old Frisian and Old Saxon. We can also see that the singular of the subjunctive did not show different forms for each person, but this was the result of normal sound change.

The above system should have developed, by, around 800, to the following:

Present

	Indicative	Subjunctive	Imperative
1sg	-u,-o	-e	
2sg	-es	-e	-∅
3sg	-eð	-e	
Plural	-að	-en	-að

Past

1sg	-∅	-e
2sg	-e	-e
3sg	-∅	-e
Plural	-on	-en
Infinitive	-an	
Present Participle	-end	
Past participle	-en	

In a regular strong verb such as *stelan* 'steal' these endings would be added to the appropriate part of the verb (where the vowel would vary, see §§ 3.4.2, 3.4.2.2) without modification. Thus to the form of the stem *stel-* would be added all the present tense forms, including the infinitive and present participle; to *stæl-* would be added the inflexions of the first and third persons past indicative only; to *stǣl-* would be added all the other inflexions except that of the past participle, where *-en* was added to *stol-*. The participles and the infinitive had other features also. Both participles could be inflected as strong adjectives (see § 3.4.1.2) and the infinitive had an inflected form *-enne*, only found after the preposition *tō*. In addition, the past participle, unless already prefixed, regularly had the prefix *ġe-*, at least in transitive verbs – the situation with respect to intransitive verbs was rather different. This prefix, still found in, say, German and Dutch, was lost from English in the Middle English period, after first becoming *y-*, as in ME *yclept* 'called'.

It is noteworthy that these inflexions regularly overrode normal sound change. For example, we would have expected the -*u* of the first person present indicative and the -*i* of the second person preterite indicative to be lost after long syllables, giving **iċ rīd, not *iċ rīdu* 'I ride' and **þu stǣl, not *þu stǣle* 'thou stolest', But in normal strong verbs the inflexion was always added to the stem, regardless of quantity. Further instances of analogical changes eliminating allomorphic variation occur in the preterite subjunctive and in the second person preterite indicative, where earlier -*i* or -*ī* would be expected to have caused *i*-mutation, but this did not occur. However, in the second and third person present indicatives *i*-mutation did occur regularly (in West Saxon at least). Such morphological conditioning of the operation of particular sound changes suggests that, even if, say, *i*-mutation were a part of the synchronic phonology of Old English at a later stage, it was not purely phonological but may have been restricted to particular grammatical categories, say to nouns but not to verbs. The theoretical consequences are certainly worth exploring further.

The inflexion of strong verbs, ca 800 (see above, p. 148), did not fully survive even in Early West Saxon, the most important changes occurring in the singular present indicative. In the first person the -*u* inflexion is hardly ever seen, and -*e* is found instead. The source of this inflexion has been much disputed, although most scholars have supposed that it came, quite remarkably, from the subjunctive (see Bazell (1939:63–4) for another view). Whatever the case may be, it was a particularly West Saxon feature extending only to Kentish under West Saxon influence. In the second person we would expect forms such as *þu rīdes* 'thou ridest'. The -*t* in our gloss is a West Saxon innovation, where we find, other things being equal, *þu rīdest*. But other dialects retain the -*es* form, cf. present-day Northern English *tha' loves* against biblical *thou lovest*. The source of the -*t* is rather odd, for it would appear to have come from inverted forms, e.g. *rīdes þu 'ridest thou', the /t/ being introduced to ease the transition from /s/ to /θ/, and then being reinterpreted as part of the inflexion even in normal order. That this is what happened is confirmed by a further development in the West Saxon second third person present indicatives. The forms we would expect, e.g. *rīdest, rīdeð*, were normally confined to the more northern dialects; in West Saxon we find *rītst, rīt(t)*. This can be explained if we take as our starting point the inverted *rīdest þu, and then suppose cliticisation to *rīdestu (occasional forms testify to this, and we have used it to explain the -*t* in any case). This would permit syncope after the long first syllable, and then simplification and assimilation of the consonants would give the normal West Saxon forms. It is important that the dialectal spread of these syncopated forms and of the -*est* inflexion in the second person virtually coincided, giving added weight to the theory. Syncopation also occurred in short-stemmed verbs, e.g. *cwist*, *cwið(ð)* 'speak' 2nd,3rd sg. pres.indic., where it was clearly an analogical process equating these verbs with their long-stemmed partners.

One other feature already apparent in Early West Saxon and extensive by the classical period concerns the inflexions of the subjunctive. The inflexions of strong verbs (see above, p. 148) suggest there were only two inflexions for the subjunctive: -*e* for the singular, -*en* for the plural, regardless of both person and tense. This, although largely due to normal sound change, is unsurprising, for it is normal for less frequent grammatical categories to simplify their inflexional system. But in the ninth and tenth centuries the inflexion of the preterite plural subjunctive changed to -*on*. This was not the complication it might appear to be, for what we are certainly witnessing is the falling together of the indicative and subjunctive inflexions under the indicative, that is to say, we are witnessing the beginnings of the demise of separate inflexions for the subjunctive, a process almost, but not quite, complete today (although it may be being reversed in American English).

Four paragraphs ago we noted that whereas the first and third singular preterite indicative inflexions were added to one form of a strong verb stem, so that, for example, one finds *ić stæl*, *he stæl* 'I,he stole', the second person singular inflexion was added to another form of the stem, so that one finds *þu stǣle* 'thou stolest'. This persisted throughout the period, and even today there is one, albeit archaic, such example, namely, *I was*, *thou wert*, *he was*, *they were*, where the old second person singular has the structure of the plural, not the singular stem.

From the above we can see that the paradigm of a regular strong verb such as *stelan* 'steal' would be as follows in classical Old English:

Present

—	Indicative	Subjunctive	Imperative
1sg	ić stele	ić stele	
2sg	þu stelst	þu stele	stel!
3sg	he stelð	he stele	
Plural	hī stelað	hī stelen	stelað!

		Past
1sg	iċ stæl	iċ stæle
2sg	þu stæle	þu stæle
3sg	he stæl	he stæle
Plural	hī stǣlon	hī stǣlon

Infinitive	stelan
Present Participle	stelend
Past participle	ġestolen

One important feature which during the Old English period was associated only with the Northumbrian dialect and is therefore absent from the above paradigm, was the development, probably through contact with Scandinavian settlers, of the third singular present indicative inflexion *-es*, i.e. *he steles*. This, of course, is the origin of PDE *he steals*, but although it is first seen in the late ninth century, it was not until Shakespearian times that it became the standard in the whole of the country.

3.4.2.2   Strong verbs

As we saw in chapter 2, strong verbs usually formed their tenses by variation of the root vowel, with one vowel for the present, another for the preterite singular, a third for other preterite forms, and a fourth for the past participle. This variation of the root vowel or ablaut followed six regular patterns, and strong verbs are assigned to one verb class or another depending upon the pattern they followed. In Germanic the ablaut system was at first very clear (see chapter 2), and, disregarding the few sound changes which disrupted the pattern, we can suppose the following six ablaut series:

	Present	Pret.sg.	Pret.	Past Part.
I	ī	ai	i	i
II	eu	au	u	o
III	e	a	u	o
IV	e	a	ǣ	o
V	e	a	ǣ	e
VI	a	ō	ō	a

The regular development of these series, excluding disrupting sound changes which only affect a sub-group of verbs within a particular class, would be to:

	Present	Pret.sg.	Pret.	Past Part.
I	ī	ā	i	i
II	ēo	ēa	u	o
III	e	æ	u	o
IV	e	æ	ǣ	e
V	e	æ	ǣ	o
VI	æ	ō	ō	æ

Thus, for example, a strong verb of class I such as Gmc *rīdan 'ride', would have the pattern in Old English of: rīdan ~ rād ~ ridon ~ (ġe-)riden. But the history of strong verbs in Old English was characterised above all by the progressive disruption of the relatively clear Germanic system. Even the 'normal' ablaut series (see diagram above) shows, for example, that the presence of an /i/ element in all parts of class I verbs was no longer de rigueur. What we shall do in the following paragraphs, therefore, is trace the extent of the collapse in the system during the period.

Strong class I verbs, e.g. rīdan above, remained strikingly homogeneous. Apart from the so-called <u>contracted verbs,</u> which we discuss separately below, the only feature to note concerns Verner's Law. As shown in chapter 2, we would expect Verner's Law to have caused voicing of voiceless fricatives in the preterite plural and past participle forms, as indeed is the case with, say, snīðan 'cut' ~ snāð ~ snidon ~ sniden, where /d/ is from earlier /ð/ (see §3.3.3.1). In some verbs, e.g. drīfan 'drive', it is impossible to tell whether the alternation was preserved or not because of the more general voicing of medial fricatives in Old English (see again §3.3.3.1), and the only unambiguous examples are those where some other sound change intervened. This happened in the case of [s] ~ [z], where Gmc *[z] developed to [r]; [θ] ~ [ð], where *[ð] > [d]; and [x] ~ [ɣ], where *[x] was lost intervocalically (giving contracted verbs, see below). Leaving aside the last group, we find in class I as much elimination of Verner's Law, e.g. hī rison 'they rose', not **hī riron, as preservation, cf. snīðan. This is to be expected, for levelling of Verner's Law reduced allomorphic variation and simplified the system. This verb class was not only well preserved in Old English, it forms the basis of a fairly stable group of irregular verbs in Present-Day English, e.g. ride, drive, rise, write.

The expected pattern of strong class II verbs is exemplified by bēodan ~ bēad ~ budon ~ boden 'command'. In this class Verner's Law was usually preserved, thus ċēosan 'choose' but coren 'chosen'. Class II remained fairly stable in Old English, although by the modern period it is much fragmented, with *cēosan* 'compare' *frēosan* giving PDE *freeze*. In Old English some verbs which must originally have patterned exactly like *bēodan* had instead a present tense with /u:/, e.g., *lūcan* 'lock'. This was probably a Germanic innovation based on the analogy of class I verbs, where the alternation /i:/ ~ /i/ existed. In verbs like *lūcan* the analogy gave the parallel alternation /u:/ ~ /u/.

Classes I and II give the impression of stability within strong verbs. Unfortunately, this is misleading, as we can see when we come to class III. As the diagram of the 'normal' ablaut series shows (p. 152), we should expect there the ablaut variation *e* ~ *æ* ~ *u* ~ *o*. Some verbs did follow this pattern, e.g. *berstan* ~ *bærst* ~ *burston* ~ *borsten* 'burst', other examples including *þerscan* 'thresh', and, less regularly, *feohtan* 'fight'. But the problem with these is that they were not originally strong class III verbs, as can be seen by the fact that the ablauting vowel is not followed by a liquid or nasal and another consonant (see chapter 2, also §1). Rather, they were once class V verbs which during the Germanic period adopted the ablaut variation of class III. In original class III verbs, the most stable pattern was that followed by verbs which had a nasal after the ablauting vowel, e.g. *bindan* ~ *band* ~ *bundon* ~ *bunden* 'bind', where the divergences from the predicted pattern are due to Germanic raising of */e/ and */o/ before a nasal, or the failure of Gmc */a/ plus nasal to undergo first fronting in proto-Old English. This group remains remarkably stable throughout the history of the language, cf. PDE *bind, drink, find, shrink, spring, swing, swim,* all of which come directly from Old English with little modification. One important form here is the preterite singular of *findan*, where *fand* 'I,he found' would be expected. But in West Saxon the normal form was *funde*. This was the result of the merger of the preterite singular and plural forms, so reducing the number of ablaut variants to three rather than four as was usual in Old English. This, therefore, is a precursor of the standard Middle English reduction in ablaut variation from four to three (which persists today).

The forms with following liquid plus consonant showed yet more divergences from the expected pattern. Before /l/ we find paradigms such as *helpan* ~ *healp* ~ *hulpon* ~ *holpen* 'help', where the preterite singular shows breaking of /æ/ (see §3.3.3.1). Before /r/ breaking was also found in the present, hence *weorpan* ~ *wearp* ~ *wurpon* ~ *worpen* 'throw', and in classical Old English *weorpan* normally further developed to *wurpan*. The variety of pattern exemplified by these different class III verbs can be illustrated thus:

	Present	Pret.sg.	Pret.	Past Part.
berstan	e	æ	u	o
bindan	i	a	u	u
helpan	e	ea	u	o
wurpan	u	ea	u	o

The most important point to note is that, although there were identities everywhere, the ablaut vowel varied greatly in the present tense and the preterite singular. But these two forms best define class membership for a strong verb. This leads one to suppose that class III was already breaking down in the Old English period, except for the *bindan*-type, yet we may be being misled by the situation in West Saxon, which showed a rather greater variation than did the other dialects.

Class IV had only a few verbs, and even amongst them we have to make a division between those with a following liquid and those with a following nasal. Those with the liquid were straightforward, as typified by *stelan* 'steal' (see above), other examples being *beran* 'bear', *cwelan* 'die', and *teran* 'tear'. Oddly, despite the relative infrequency of this group, two verbs appear to have been attracted to it, namely *brecan* 'break' and *hlecan* 'unite', as shown by the past particles *brocen, tohlocene*. Only two verbs in this class had a following nasal, but they were both of high frequency, even if only one survives today: *cuman ~ cōm ~ cōmon ~ cumen* 'come' and *niman ~ nam ~ nāmon ~ numen* 'take'. In *cuman* only the preterite plural and past participle are phonologically predictable (for *-ō-* is the equivalent of *-ǣ-* before nasals). The present tense showed an 'aorist' present, that is to say, it had a short vowel originally associated with Indo-European aorist or past tense, cf. *cumen*. Such aorist presents could occur elsewhere too, e.g. class I *ripan* 'reap', class III *spurnan* 'spurn'. The preterite singular had an unexpected long vowel, and it is likely that this vowel was transferred from the plural on the analogy of class VI (see below, but cf. also *funde* above). The forms of *niman* are more complex still. The infinitive had the expected form, so too had the past participle. The preterite plural would be expected to be *nōmon*, and this form can be found in Early West Saxon alongside *nāmon*, which was normal Late West Saxon. In Early West Saxon the preterite singular was often *nōm* and the explanation of this is parallel to that of *cōm*, at least if the long vowel is genuine. The example in *CorpGl fornoom* 'he seized' suggests so, but the West Saxon Lauderdale *Orosius* has both *nom* and *nam*, suggesting a short vowel from Gmc */a/ plus nasal, which would be regular. In later West Saxon we find only the alternation *nam*

~ *nāmon*. The spelling <a> is what we would expect for */a/ plus nasal, and the long vowel in the plural would be on the analogy of the short ~ long contrast in other class IV (and V) verbs. Clearly, both *cuman* and *niman* showed more analogical levelling than the other verbs. The reason for this may be that they were no longer perceived as regular strong verbs at all, and therefore were to some extent free from the constraining influences of the predicted ablaut pattern.

Class V verbs were very like class IV verbs, being distinguished only in the past participle, e.g. *sprecan* ~ *spræc* ~ *sprǣcon* ~ *sprecen* 'speak'. Since the consonant which followed the ablaut vowel could be any consonant other than a liquid or nasal (see chapter 2), Verner's Law could apply, and it usually did, e.g. *cweden* 'said' from *cweðan* 'say'. However it should be noted that originally these verbs only showed the operation of Verner's Law in the past participle, and therefore past plural forms such as *cwǣdon* 'they said' demonstrate, against the normal trend, analogical extension of Verner's law. The most reasonable conclusion is that the preterite plural and the past participle were felt to be closely related and therefore they came to show the same kind of Verner's Law alternation as in the verbs of the more salient classes I and II. Two members of this class, *etan* 'eat' and *fretan* 'devour' already had a long vowel in the preterite singular in Germanic; this remained and may even have extended into the present. Class VI verbs should, because of the sound change of restoration of *a* (see §3.3.3.1), have varied between /a/ and /æ/ in the present tense and the past participle, but in West Saxon at least /a/ was generalised throughout the present and was normal in the past participle. Hence we find *faran* ~ *fōr* ~ *fōron* ~ *faren* 'go'. Two verbs had from Germanic a nasal infix in the present tense: *standan* 'stand', *wæcnan* 'wake', cf. *stōd* 'stood', *wōc* 'woke'. In both classes V and VI some verbs formed their present tense according to the conjugation of weak class 1 verbs (see below), although otherwise they patterned normally. Typical examples are: *biddan* 'ask', *licġan* 'lie', *sittan* 'sit' (all class V) and *hebban* 'raise', *hlyhhan* 'laugh', *sċyppan* 'create' (all class VI).

These so-called 'weak presents' have to be distinguished from another phenomenon associated with strong verbs, which is that there was a slight tendency for strong verbs to become weak. This, of course, is much more common later in the history of the language, when numerous strong verbs become weak, compare OE *helpan* and PDE *help*. The Old English weak presents were a quite different phenomenon, as can be deduced from considering PDE *sit* alongside OE *sittan*. Relatively rare examples of strong verbs transferring to the weak conjugations include *rēohte* 'it smoked' from class II *rēocan*; *spurned* 'spurned' and *murnde* 'he mourned' from class III *spurnan* and *murnan*. In West Saxon *streġdan* 'strew', which should have paralleled *berstan* and similar class III verbs, went completely over to the weak conjugation. But these examples formed a tiny minority, and it would be too much to claim that the transfer to the weak conjugation was fully under way in the Old English period. There are signs that it was about to happen, but the overwhelming impression is that the strong verbs remained relatively stable. This, however, was not so true of Northumbrian, in this respect as in others more 'advanced' than the other dialects, where transfer to the weak conjugation was much more frequent.

In Germanic, verbs of classes I, II, V and VI could have had a single /x/ after the ablaut vowel. This /x/ would by Verner's Law have voiced to /ɣ/ in the preterite plural and past participle, giving alternations such as **wrīxon ~ *wrāx ~ *wrigon ~ *wrigen* 'cover' by about the fifth century. But then (see §3.3.3.1) the /x/ was lost between vowels, and the result was the class of 'contracted verbs'. By later changes class I contracted verbs appeared in Early West Saxon with a paradigm such as *wrēon ~ wrāh ~ wrigon ~ wrigen*, so too *tēon* 'accuse', *þēon* 'thrive' and a few others. For class II we find *flēon ~ flēah ~ flugon ~ flugen* 'flee' and *tēon* 'draw', and the similarity of the two series allowed the original class I contracted verbs to transfer to class II with increasing frequency, giving forms such as *wrēon ~ wrēah ~ wrugon ~ wrugen*. Contracted verbs of class V included *sēon* 'see' and of class VI *flēan* 'flay', *lēan* 'blame', *slēan* 'slay' and *þwēan* 'wash', but in these cases the non-present forms were more or less regular.

Class VII verbs had an entirely different origin from the other strong verbs. In Germanic they formed their preterite not merely by ablaut but also by reduplication. For example Go. *grētan* 'weep' had the preterite singular *gaígrōt*, where the initial /g/ of the stem is doubled and then linked to the stem by /ɛ/ = <aí>. This phenomenon was of Indo-European origin. But by the Old English period, or at least by the time of the earliest texts, almost all traces of reduplication had been lost, the most common examples being of *hēht* 'he commanded' alongside *hēt*, cf. inf. *hātan* and Go. *haíhait* 'he commanded'. For Old English we have to analyse these verbs quite differently, one type being like *hātan ~ hēt ~ hēton ~ hāten*, the other type being like *bēatan ~ bēot ~ bēoton ~ bēaten* 'beat'. These verbs all had one vowel in the present and past participle and another vowel in the preterite singular and plural, so that from the first two forms in each series we can predict the remainder, the difference between the two types being simply whether the preterite was formed with -$\bar{e}$- or -$\bar{e}o$-. There is no way of predicting what will occur (even in Gothic the situation is irregular). Note especially that the vowel of the present, which could vary considerably, is not a firm indicator of the vowel of the preterite. Verbs of this class were more likely to transfer to the weak conjugation than other strong verbs, doubtless because of their apparent irregularity.

3.4.2.3 Weak verbs

Weak verbs differed from strong verbs in three respects. Firstly, and most importantly, they formed their preterite by the purely Germanic innovation of a dental suffix (Gmc */ð/ > OE /d/, usually) being added to the stem. This is *the* sign of this conjugation, one of the major defining features of the Germanic branch of Indo-European, but nevertheless somewhat obscure in origin (see chapter 2). Secondly and more trivially, weak verbs had their own set of inflexions for the preterite indicative singular. In the very earliest period of Old English these were -$æ$, -$æs$, -$æ$, which become in West Saxon -e, -est, -e, see §3.4.2.1. Thirdly, these verbs were quite distinct in origin from strong verbs, for they were formed by a derivational suffix being added to the stem. Thus OE *trymman* 'strengthen' was formed from the nominal root **trum* plus suffix **j* plus inflexion. In Germanic this suffix could have four basic shapes: **j*, **ōj*, **aij*, and **nōj*, so giving four different classes. By the Old English period, however, only the first two fully remained, the third had a few relic forms, which we analyse in §3.4.2.4 as irregular verbs, and the fourth class had completely disappeared.

Let us start with the paradigm of class 1 verbs in about the fifth century (ignoring the special inflexional developments of the first and second person present indicatives, see §3.4.2.1). For *trymman*, the paradigm would have been rather like:

	Present		
	Indicative	Subjunctive	Imperative
1sg	trumm + j + u	trumm + j + æ	
2sg	trum + is	trumm + j + æ	trum + i
3sg	trum + ið	trumm + j + æ	
Plural	trumm + j + að	trumm + j + æn	trumm + j + að

		Past
1sg	trum + id + æ	trum + id + ī
2sg	trum + id + æs	trum + id + ī
3sg	trum + id + æ	trum + id + ī
Plural	trum + id + un	trum + id + īn
Infinitive		trumm + j + an
Present Participle		trumm + j + andi
Past Participle		trum + id

Clearly there was already allomorphic variation, for the stem varied between having a geminate consonant and a single consonant, and the suffix was sometimes /j/, sometimes /i/ and sometimes lost. These variations can be explained by postulating three sound changes which disrupted a previously regular pattern where the suffix */j/ was always present. Firstly, that */j/ was lost before */i/. This gives the forms of the second and third person present indicative. Secondly, that */j/ became */i/ except where it was followed by another vowel. This gives all the forms of the preterite and also the imperative singular. Thirdly, that */j/, where it remained after these two sound changes, doubled the preceding consonant in a short-stemmed syllable (West Germanic gemination, see chapter 2). As can be seen above, double consonants always occurred when /j/ followed.

Perhaps the most obvious feature of the above paradigm is that the stem vowel was always followed by either */i/ or */j/. This means that the stem vowel would always be *i*-mutated, and so at one time the presence of an *i*-mutated stem vowel must have been a striking characteristic of weak class 1 verbs. But even by Early West Saxon times it is doubtful that Old English speakers would have made much of this fact (despite Dresher 1981:193 and see the comments on *i*-mutation in verbs in §3.4.2.1 above). Apart from *i*-mutation, other sound changes intervene at an early stage. Most notably */j/ and */i/ were lost after long syllables (see §3.3.3.2), and so every */j/ was lost (since because of gemination it always followed in pre-Old English a long syllable). Otherwise one finds the normal reduction of unstressed vowels to /e/. Therefore the paradigm of *trymman* in Early West Saxon developed as:

	Present		
	Indicative	Subjunctive	Imperative
1sg	trymme	trymme	
2sg	trymest	trymme	tryme!
3sg	trymeð	trymme	
Plural	trymmað	trymmen	trymmað!

	Past	
1sg	trymede	trymede
2sg	trymedest	trymede
3sg	trymede	trymede
Plural	trymedon	trymeden

Infinitive	trymman
Present Participle	trymmende
Past Participle	trymed

In Early and then Late West Saxon the development of inflexional endings was similar to that of strong verbs, and so we find forms such as *trymð* 'he strengthens'. For long-stemmed class 1 verbs we can postulate essentially the same developments as for short-stemmed verbs, but it should be noted that gemination did not occur, and that */i/ was lost in the preterite and imperative singular, so that Gmc *dōmjan* 'judge' gives OE *dēman* (without gemination), *dēmde* 'he judged' (with syncope of */i/).

There was a considerable group of weak class 1 verbs which had a significantly different pattern from that given above. These verbs all had a root which in Germanic ended in either a velar consonant or */l/. Although the present tense forms of these verbs were normal, in Germanic the preterite came to be formed without connecting */i/. This process probably started in stems with a final velar and then spread to stems with final */l/ (see Prokosch 1927), which may itself have been velar (see Hogg 1971). Thus Gmc *sōkjan* 'seek', *talljan* 'tell' would have had preterites *sōktǣ*, *taldæ*, giving proto-Old English *sōhtǣ*, *tældæ*. Therefore in these verbs the preterite did not show *i*-Umlaut, and we find alternations in Old English such as *sēċan ~ sōhte*, *tellan ~ tealde* (here breaking intervenes as well, see §3.3.2.1). This failure of *i*-mutation in the preterite, often known as *Ruckumlaut*, is seen in many verbs of high frequency, e.g. *brenġan* 'bring', *byċġan* 'buy', *leċġan* 'lay', *tǣċan* 'teach', *þenċan* 'think', *þynċan* 'seem', *settan* 'set', *wyrċan* 'work', *cwellan* 'kill', *sellan* 'give', *stellan* 'place'. The phenomenon is important for later periods also, for it is from this type that we get PDE *seek* ~ *sought*, *buy* ~ *bought*, *tell* ~ *told*, *sell* ~ *sold*, etc., and even the French loan-word *catch* was eventually attracted into this irregular conjugation.

By the fifth century the verbs of class 2 had probably modelled themselves on the pattern of the class 1 verbs (see Cowgill 1959), so that wherever class 1 verbs had */j/ they would have */o:j/ (later /oj/), and wherever class 1 did not have */j/ class 2 would have */o:/ (later /o/). Thus for OE *lufian* 'love' we can postulate the following paradigm:

Present

	Indicative	Subjunctive	Imperative
1sg	lufoju	lufojæ	
2sg	lufos	lufojæ	lufo!
3sg	lufoð	lufojæ	
Plural	lufojað	lufojæn	lufojað!

Past

1sg	lufodæ	lufodī
2sg	lufodæs	lufodī
3sg	lufodæ	lufodī
Plural	lufodun	lufodīn

Infinitive	lufojan
Present Participle	lufojandi
Past Participle	lufod

In the development to Early West Saxon the most important point is that, as with class 1 verbs, */j/ caused *i*-mutation, but in this class the *i*-mutated vowel was the suffixal */o/, which *i*-mutated to */e/ and was then raised to /i/ before palatal /j/, cf. *hāliġ* 'holy' discussed in § 3.3.2.2. That /ij/ sequence was then simplified to /i/. Otherwise */o/ either remained or was lowered to /a/, so that we find the following paradigm in Early West Saxon:

Present

	Indicative	Subjunctive	Imperative
1sg	lufie	lufie	
2sg	lufast	lufie	lufa!
3sg	lufað	lufie	
Plural	lufiað	lufien	lufiað!

		Past
	Indicative	Subjunctive
1sg	lufode	lufode
2sg	lufodest	lufode
3sg	lufode	lufode
Plural	lufodon	lufoden
Infinitive		lufian
Present Participle		lufiende
Past Participle		lufod

This paradigm then underwent exactly the same kinds of changes as affected class 1 verbs and strong verbs except that since the second and third person present indicative forms had -a- rather than -e-, syncopated forms of these inflexions did not occur.

We now have to turn back and look at a small group of class 1 verbs not previously considered. These verbs were once exactly like *trymman*, except that their stem syllable ended in */r/. The problem here is that West Germanic gemination did not double */r/. Otherwise the development of these verbs paralleled the other class 1 verbs, except that they, because of the absence of gemination, were the only short-stemmed verbs in the class. Typical examples are: *herian* 'praise', *nerian* 'save', *werian* 'clothe'. The Early West Saxon paradigm of *nerian* is:

		Present	
	Indicative	Subjunctive	Imperative
1sg	nerie	nerie	
2sg	nerest	nerie	nere!
3sg	nereð	nerie	
Plural	neriað	nerien	neriað!

		Past
	Indicative	Subjunctive
1sg	nerede	nerede
2sg	neredest	nerede
3sg	nerede	nerede
Plural	neredon	nereden
Infinitive		nerian
Present Participle		neriende
Past Participle		nered

This paradigm was more different from the paradigm of class 2 verbs than it would seem to be, for *nerie* was disyllabic, i.e. /nerje/, whilst *lufie* was trisyllabic, i.e. /lufie/. This follows from their historical development. But by the tenth century the medial /j/ became vocalised, as shown by spellings such as *neriġe*. Furthermore, at about the same time unstressed vowels began to merge (see §3.3.2.2), and this affected preterite forms such as *lufode*, which became *lufede*. The consequence of these changes is that whilst the short-stemmed class 1 verbs differed from the class 2 verbs only in the second and third person present indicative, they differed more radically from the long-stemmed class 1 verbs, notably in the absence of geminate consonants. Therefore, by the time of classical Old English what we find is that the short-stemmed class 1 verbs had transferred to class 2, with forms such as *nerað* rather than *nereð*. This occurred despite the fact that *nerian*, etc. had *i*-mutated stem vowels, and demonstrates clearly that in classical Old English the *i*-mutation of stem vowels no longer defined a weak verb as a class 1 verb. Soon after the Conquest we can see further evidence of the collapse of the old division amongst weak verbs, when they reclassified into long-stemmed verbs and short-stemmed verbs, or the two classes merged completely, but this was essentially a post-Conquest move, of which the *nerian*-type was only a precursor.

3.4.2.4 Irregular verbs

There were three types of irregular verbs: (i) preterite-present verbs; (ii) weak class 3 verbs; (iii) 'anomalous' verbs. It is not proposed to consider their inflexions in any detail here, see instead Campbell (1959: §§762–8) and Brunner (1965: §§416–30). Rather, we shall merely consider the most interesting characteristics of each.

The preterite-present verbs were originally strong verbs but in Germanic, perhaps sometimes even earlier, the preterite came to acquire a present tense meaning. This then formed a new preterite with a dental suffix. For example, *wāt* 'he knows' can be seen by its form to be the preterite of a class I verb, but it had a present tense meaning, and the past tense has the form *wiste* 'he knew'. Other similar verbs were: *cann* 'he knows', *dearr* 'he dares', *sċeal* 'he shall', *mōt* 'he must', *mæġ* 'he may', *āh* 'he possesses', *þearf* 'he needs', *ann* 'he grants'. They are especially important for later periods, for it is from these verbs that we get the present-day core modal verbs, e.g. *can*, *shall*, *must*, *may* (*will* has a different origin, see below). But there is an important difference between Old English and present-day English, for whilst today modal verbs are syntactically defined, in Old English the parallel verbs were morphologically defined (see further chapter 4).

Four verbs in Old English preserve very clear signs of the Germanic weak class 3, namely *habban* 'have', *libban* 'live', *seċġan* 'say' and *hyċġan* 'think'. Such signs included: (i) variation between unmutated and mutated forms, e.g. *hæbbe* 'I have' but *habbað* 'we have'; (ii) similar variation between geminated and ungeminated forms, e.g. *libbe* 'I live' but *leofað* 'he lives'; (iii) syncopation of the medial vowel in all forms of the preterite, e.g. *hæfde* 'I had'. It is also certain that many other verbs showed very occasional traces of this class although they usually transferred to class 2. This massive movement away from class 3 clearly indicates that class 3 was a dying phenomenon in Old English, and even a well established verb like *libban* shows many class 2 forms in classical Old English, the normal preterite there, for example, being *leofode* instead of *lifde*. All these verbs were prone to analogical reformation and it seems best to treat them as the irregular residue of a once regular class.

We are now left with four verbs: *dōn* 'do', *gān* 'go', *willan* 'will' and *bēon* 'be'. All these verbs came from an Indo-European group of athematic verbs which were drastically reorganised in Germanic. *Dōn* and *gān* were relatively simple in the present tense, where both showed *i*-mutation in the second and third person present indicative but in other respects just had the appropriate inflexion directly attached to the stem. The preterite of *dōn* was already *dyde*, from which we get PDE *did*. As today *gān* had a suppletive preterite, but in Old English this was *ēode*, a form which survived into early Middle English only to be lost and replaced by *went*. The most notable feature of *willan* (with pret. *wolde*) was the unusual form of the third person present indicative, namely *wile*.

As with PDE *be*, OE *bēon* had no preterite forms, these being supplied by the strong class V verb *wesan* (which could also be used in the infinitive instead of *bēon*). But to make up for this lack, as it were, *bēon* had two sets of forms in the present tense: one made up from Gmc *es-/*s-* and *ar-*, the other from Gmc *beo-*. By classical Old English the principal forms of this verb (much subject to variation and irregularity) were:

Indicative

1st	eom	bēo
2sg	eart	bist
3sg	is	bið
Plural	synd(on), aron	bēoð

	Subjunctive	
Singular	sī	bēo
Plural	sȳn, syndon	bēon
Imperative	bēo (sg.) bēoð (pl.)	
Infinitive	bēon, wesan	

The Anglo-Saxons appear to have distinguished in meaning between the two sets of forms more often than not (but not, alas, always), see chapter 4. But in later periods, of course, the *es-/s-* forms are the normal forms of the first and third person present indicative, and the *ar-* forms are used for the second person and plural present indicative, with the *bēo-* forms reserved for the subjunctive, imperative and infinitive, and *wesan* restricted to the past tense. Occasionally dialects use the *bēo-* forms throughout the present, e.g. some south-western English dialects.

FURTHER READING

3.1 Lehmann (1962) is a clear elementary introduction to the problems of reconstructing older stages of the language. A more detailed and fuller account can be found in Anttila (1972) and a general overview of historical linguistics is presented in Bynon (1977). More advanced work on internal reconstruction is contained in Kuryłowicz (1973) and on comparative reconstruction in Hoenigswald (1973), see also the references therein, especially Hoenigswald (1960). Meillet (1922) remains an important work from an earlier generation. Not everyone is sanguine about the possibilities of reconstruction, see the critical remarks of Lass (1975). On the other hand Lass (1976:chs. 4–5) gives an enlightening example of the possibilities open to us, and the same writer elsewhere presents a challenging paper on the limits of reconstruction (Lass 1978). For generative grammarians reconstruction is a rather different task with rather different aims; a relatively early but then authoritative account can be found in King (1969:ch. 7).

3.2 A good general account of English orthography is Scragg (1974), see also Bourcier (1978).

3.2.1 There is no helpful introduction to Old English palaeography and orthography. The introduction to Ker (1957) is authoritative but not for the beginner. Of older works Keller (1906) remains useful. Campbell (1959:§§23–70) gives a full, if linguistically outdated, account of the variations in orthographic practice, especially for the older periods.

The suggestion that Anglo-Saxon scribes attempted to reproduce local pronunciation is controversial although it informs such works as Luick (1914). To suppose, *au contraire*, that scribes merely repeated a set of learned spelling conventions seems to me to suppose a degree of sophistication and organisation which was improbable for most of the period and most of the country. On the other hand the creation of a *Schriftsprache* at Winchester seems to be an exception to this. Stanley (1988) offers the most recent defence of the view that scribes were only repeating conventions, see also Bierbaumer (1988).

3.2.2 The best introduction to runes is Page (1973), but Elliott (1959) offers a useful and often contrasting supplement.

3.3 Despite its age the classic text for Old English phonology remains Luick (1914), although Campbell (1959) is an adequate substitute for those who cannot read German. See further the remarks under §3.3.3 below.

3.3.1 The traditional grammars do not often deal in terms of phonemes, as can all too easily be seen by a glance at Campbell (1959:§§30–53). For a structuralist phonemic account the best works are Kuhn (1961) and Moulton (1972) for vowels, and Kuhn (1970) for consonants. Good generative treatments using distinctive feature analysis are presented in Wagner (1969) and Lass & Anderson (1975).

3.3.1.1 The status of /æ:/ deserves more investigation. In this context it should be pointed out that the West Saxon dialects have an incidence of /æ:/ quite different from that of the other dialects, see chapter 6 of this volume.

3.3.1.2 For a phonemic analysis of diphthongs quite different from that presented here see Hockett (1959) and also the works mentioned under 3.3.3.1 below. Traditional accounts rarely offer a useful account of the second element of diphthongs, although Luick (1914:§§119–29) is a characteristic exception. See instead Lass & Anderson (1975:90ff.).

3.3.1.4 Luick (1914:§633) suggests that even initially */ɣ/ became a stop in prehistoric times before palatalisation and the same position is found in Lass & Anderson (1975:134). That position is simply untenable, see Hogg (1979b:92–4).

The best discussion of the /hw/-type sequences is in Kuhn (1970:9.12–16).

3.3.2 There is very little material on Old English suprasegmentals, and most of it stems from the early work of Sievers on metrics, especially Sievers (1893). For elaborations of Sievers' views and alternative approaches see chapter 8. The question of how closely connected were poetic metre and the rhythms of colloquial speech has often been debated, not always fruitfully, see Daunt (1946). Halle and Keyser (1971) offer a generative view of Old English stress. McCully (1989) offers a new synthesis of traditional and generative accounts.

3.3.2.1 Traditional grammars make use of the concept of syllable but only in an atheoretical way. Perhaps the most extensive treatment of syllable structure in the history of English is Anderson & Jones (1977:ch. 4), see also Lass (1984:248–70). Hogg & McCully (1986) give an overview of some recent trends in syllable theory.

3.3.2.2 Campbell (1959:§§71–99) is the most useful source for traditional descriptions of Old English stress patterns. For a generative treatment see Maling (1971) and now McCully & Hogg (1990).

3.3.3 For an introduction to this area Quirk & Wrenn (1957) is the best of the more elementary guides. Luick (1914) is the clearest and most authorative account, which can be supplemented by Campbell (1959). Brunner (1965) is a useful third reference work in this area. All these works are in broad agreement with one another, but a rather different view of the chronology is presented in Girvan (1931), a much underrated and underused text. All these handbooks make very little use of current linguistic theory, but one general work which does is Lass & Anderson (1975), although it does not aim to be comprehensive. Anderson & Jones (1977) also touches on many aspects covered here. On more particular issues brief references follow below, but these should be taken only as supplementing the above, which always have remarks of relevance. My own views are more fully developed in Hogg (1992).

3.3.3.1 For the development of Gmc */a/ + nasal see Toon (1983).

Some problems remain in the analysis of breaking, see Hogg (1979b:§2).

The controversy over short and long diphthongs has occupied many scholars. A short bibliography is included in Kuhn (1961), and Giffhorn (1974) offers an overview of the whole controversy together with an extensive bibliography. For a newcomer to the dispute the best starting point is probably Stockwell & Barritt (1951), followed by Kuhn & Quirk (1953), then followed by a sequence of papers in the periodical *Language* over the next decade. Many of the papers espousing the traditional point of view can be found in Quirk (1968) and many of those attempting revision in Lass (1969).

To other works cited under §3.3.1, e.g. Kuhn (1970), may be added Moulton (1954).

It is generally accepted that palatalisation preceded *i*-mutation, but the chronology is difficult to prove, see Hogg (1979b:§5) and also Colman (1986a).

Traditional grammarians have always recognised the similarities between breaking and back mutation, but have insisted on separating them on chronological grounds. The alternative approach is best seen in Anderson & Jones (1977:ch. 5).

3.3.2.2 Keyser & O'Neil (1985:ch. 1) suggest, albeit in an as yet untested and sketchy form, a method of representing the different causations of syncope and apocope.

3.4 Most introductions to Old English give a good overview of the principal features of Old English morphology, and of these Mitchell & Robinson (1986) and Quirk & Wrenn (1957) are the most widely used. The former is based on Early West Saxon, the latter on Late West Saxon. Luick (1914) does not deal directly with morphology, see instead Brunner (1965), which is extremely full, and Campbell (1959). Wagner (1969) gives an interesting account of Old English morphology from a generative point of view.

Matthews (1974) offers the best general introduction to morphology and morphophonemics. For the generative approach Kiparsky (1970) offers a brief guide and King (1969) offers a much fuller, yet easily readable, introduction. The collection of papers in Kiparsky (1982) gives an excellent impression of the gradual development of the generative approach to historical linguistics. Amongst early generative work on Old English Wagner (1969) stands out, especially because of its interest in the paradigm as a linguistic unit. Lass & Anderson (1975) is another full-length study which, perhaps, pushes the abstract generative approach to its limits. Criticisms of early generative approaches can be found in Hogg (1971, 1977, 1979a), but see Lass (1975) for a critique of both internal reconstruction and generative phonology. The most important recent works in generative phonology, which reintroduce at least some aspects of the word-and-paradigm model, are Dresher (1978) and Keyser & O'Neil (1985).

3.4.1 For early forms of the vocalic nouns Dahl (1938) is invaluable. The instrumental case survives in place-name elements, see chapter 7.

3.4.2 The standard reference works are the best source of other work on verb morphology. For the situation in Germanic see chapter 2, but also Wright (1954) gives a good view of the situation in Gothic, which could not have been far removed from the general position in Germanic.

3.4.2.2 Lass & Anderson (1975:ch. I) provides a reanalysis of strong verbs with an abstract generative framework.

4 SYNTAX

Elizabeth Closs Traugott

4.1 General background

The study of syntax is the study of the patterns by which morphemes and grammatical categories such as Noun, Adjective, Verb, Preposition and conjunctions are organised into sentences.

To understand the syntax of a language fully, one needs to have access to grammaticality judgements. For example, to understand how the perfect works in English one needs to know not only that *She has arrived* is possible, that is, that it is part of the system of English, but also that ***She has arrived yesterday* is not (** signals that the pattern is not part of the structure of the language, or at least of the variety in question; as is traditional in historical grammars, * is reserved for reconstructed, hypothetical forms). To understand the interaction of indefinite Noun Phrases and subject, one must know that ***A man is over there* is not part of the system, whereas *There is a man over there* is. We obviously have only partial access to the syntax of an earlier stage of a language. This is in part because we have only indirect access to any grammaticality judgements, usually through the negative evidence of absence of a pattern, sometimes through inferences that can be drawn from cross-linguistic generalisations about constraints on possible syntactic patterns given certain word orders, etc. In part, it is because we have access only to written, not to spoken language. Furthermore, in the case of Old English (OE), much of the prose is dependent on Latin (this is particularly true of the interlinear glosses). Where the OE is similar to Latin we do not always know whether this is a result of the Latin or of the OE; however, when the two are distinctly different, we may assume that we have fairly clear evidence of OE rather than of Latin structure. Where the poetry is concerned, there are clearly conventions that are peculiar to the genre. In all cases, it is difficult to know whether differences in texts are due to changes in the language, influence of other languages (especially Latin and, in the North, Scandinavian), dialect differences, stylistic preferences, effects of literacy, etc. (for fuller discussion, see chapters 6 and 8). Nevertheless, the materials for OE are very extensive, and evidence from later English as well as from other languages can give us substantial insight into many aspects of OE syntax.

No attempt is made here to provide complete coverage of OE syntax. For a far fuller study see Mitchell (1985). The focus in this chapter is on constructions that are of particular interest in the history of English, and which highlight differences between OE and later stages of the language. The data (cited from Venezky & Healey 1980) are taken primarily from prose, since prose is less likely to be influenced than poetry by literary conventions (see further chapter 8). The prose selected is largely that of the Alfredian era (late ninth century) and of Ælfric (early eleventh century), since this reflects the greatest body of prose relatively independent of Latin. However, some citations are earlier, and some date from the early twelfth century.

The focus on Alfredian and Ælfrician prose means that the present chapter presents a relatively static picture of OE syntax. There is no question that there were changes in the syntax during the OE period and they will be summarised at the end, but for the most part, the changes represent tendencies toward greater or lesser use of a particular pattern rather than innovations in OE. By contrast, the Middle English (ME) period was one of significant change. It is possible that the period of prehistoric OE was also characterised by extensive changes. However, whereas the ME changes are accessible through extensive textual evidence, those that occurred between PrGmc and OE are not, and so we cannot be certain that it was. We can hypothesise much about PrGmc phonology, because we are dealing with a relatively small inventory of phonemes, and with relatively arbitrary forms not dependent on meaning or meaning-change (see chapter 2). But in the case of syntax we are dealing with a highly complex system often subject to constraints of parsability (including semantic interpretation), planned (and unplanned) production, and so forth. It is therefore very difficult to reconstruct syntax without textual evidence, and any claims about changes between PrGmc and OE must be considered only tentative. On the other hand, the syntax of OE is in some of its details so much closer to Modern German than to present-day English (PDE), that it seems likely to be essentially an extension of PrGmc syntax, rather than substantially different from it.

In order to help the reader follow the examples, a few of the major differences between OE and PDE are mentioned here. They are discussed in greater detail in the relevant sections below.

(a) Word order in OE is organised according to two main principles. In main clauses the verb is typically in non-final position. In subordinate clauses, the verb is typically in final position. An example of a verb-final subordinate clause followed by a verb-non-final main clause is:

(1) Ða   ic ða ðis eall gemunde,   ða   gemunde
     When I then this all remembered, then remembered

     ic eac hu ic geseah...
     I also how I saw...

                                                        (*CPLetWærf* 26)

When I remembered all this, then I also remembered how I saw...

It should be noted, however, that these word orders are by no means consistently followed through (see §4.6).

(b) There is no auxiliary verb *do* in OE; this means that questions and negative sentences often appear to be very different from their PDE counterparts (see §4.5.9 and 4.5.10):

(2) Hwæt getacniaþ ðonne ða   twelf oxan...?
     What signify   then those twelf oxen...?

                                                        (*CP* 16.105.5)

What do the twelve oxen signify...?

(c) 'Negative-concord' (also called 'multiple negation') is frequent, indeed the norm, in OE (see §5.10):

(3) ne bið ðær nænig ealo gebrowen mid   Estum
     not is there no   ale brewed   among Ests

                                                        (*Or* 1.20.18)

no ale is brewed there among the Ests.[1]

(d) A grammatical subject is not obligatory in OE (see §4.4.2 and 4.4.3):

(4) ...and him (DAT) ðæs (GEN) sceamode
     ...and to-him   of-that   shamed

                                                        (*ÆCHom* I, i.18.10)

...and he was ashamed of that.

(e) There was a widely used subordinating particle *þe*; since it has no exact equivalent in PDE, and its structural properties are not fully agreed on (see §4.5), it is glossed here simply as PT (short for 'particle'):

(5) Ohthere sæde þæt sio scir hatte   Halgoland þe he on bude
     Ohthere said that that shire was-called Halogaland PT he in lived
                                                      (*Or* 1 1.19.9)

   Ohthere said that the shire he lived in was called Halogaland.

We turn now to a fuller account of OE syntax, starting with the Noun Phrase.

4.2   Noun Phrases

N(oun) P(hrases) are phrasal units consisting of a noun along with optional modifiers: demonstrative, quantifier and adjective phrase, itself a phrase consisting of an adjective along with an optional intensifier). NPs in OE, as in PDE, are definite or indefinite; unlike in PDE, noun modifiers agree in number, gender and case with the noun.

4.2.1   *Definite and indefinite NPs*

Definite NPs are personal or demonstrative pronouns, nouns with unique reference, such as proper nouns, and nouns with a possessive or demonstrative determiner. Adjectival modifiers in these constructions are weak (e.g. *se blinda man* 'that blind man', cf. chapter 3). It appears that in PrOE the weak adjective alone, that is, without demonstrative or possessive, could signal definiteness (cf. Funke 1949, cited in Mitchell 1985:137). However, this was no longer the case in OE, which requires a demonstrative to be present.

The chief demonstratives in OE are: *se* 'that' and *þes* 'this'. The latter is far less frequent than the former. Both have pronominal and adjectival (modifying) functions.

OE pronominal *se* had a rather wider distribution than in PDE. In main clauses it can refer to an animate subject, where PDE might prefer *he* or *she*. In this case it usually signals emphasis or change of subject:

(6) Hi   habbað mid him   awyriedne engel, mancynnes feond
     They have   with them corrupt   angel, mankind's enemy
     and se   hæfð andweald on...
     and that-one has   power   over...
                                            (*ÆCHom* II, 38 283.113)

   They have with them a corrupt angel, the enemy of mankind, and he has power over...

It is also used in the construction of relative, causal and other subordination types (see §4.5). As will be seen in §§4.5.3 and 4.5.5 on complementation and causal constructions, the *se* demonstrative is frequently used in cataphoric (forward-pointing) constructions where PDE might prefer *this*. For example, in PDE we would probably say *He said this: (that) the king had left*; whereas in OE the *se* pronoun is used in a construction of the type *He that said: that the king had left* (note that the demonstrative precedes the verb).

Modifying *se* (i.e. *se* functioning as a determiner) does not contrast in OE with a definite article. In many ways it covers the domains of both the demonstrative *that* and the definite article *the* in PDE. However, there are some differences. For example, *se* can be used with proper nouns where either no demonstrative or *this* would be preferred in PDE:

(7) Her Cynewulf benam Sigebryht his rices...
In-this-year Cynewulf deprived Sigebryht of-his kingdom...

& se Cynewulf oft miclum gefeohtum feaht uuiþ
and that Cynewulf often in big battles   fought against

Bretwalum
Brit-Welsh

(Chron A (Plummer) 755.1)

In this year Cynewulf deposed Sigebriht... and this Cynewulf often waged mighty battles against the Welsh.

On the other hand, *se* is often not present where an article or demonstrative might be expected in PDE. This is especially true of the early poetry. In the prose, absence of *se* is common in possessive constructions involving body parts of a possessor that is the subject of the clause:

(8) on sumre stowe hine man   mihte mid heafde geræcan
in certain place it one (SUBJ) could with head touch

(ÆCHom I, 34 508.18)

In one place one could touch it (the roof) with the head. (See §4.4.1 for further discussion of such constructions.)

Because there is no exact equivalent of the demonstrative *se* in PDE, it has been difficult to know exactly how to translate it in the literal glosses in this chapter; the form 'that' has been used, even though 'the' may at times appear more appropriate.

Demonstrative and possessive can both precede a noun in OE. When an adjective is present, both the order poss. + dem. + adj. + noun (as in (9)) and the order dem. + poss. + adj. + noun (as in (10)) may occur, though the first is more frequent, compare:

(9) and we sceolan gehyhtan on Godes þa   gehalgodan cyricean
     and we must   trust   in God's that hallowed   church
                                                    (*BlHom* X.111.8–9)

And we must trust in the hallowed church of God.

(10) þa   com þær gan   in to me heofoncund Wisdom,
      then came there going in to me heavenly   Wisdom,

      &   þæt min murnede mod mid his wordum gegrette
      and that my sad   spirit with his words   greeted
                                                    (*Bo* 3.8.15)

then heavenly Wisdom came to me there and greeted my sad spirit with his words.

When the adjective is not present, the order dem. + poss. + noun is preferred. However, some potential constructions of this type may actually involve not a demonstrative modifier but a pronoun. For example, in:

(11) Se   heora cyning ongan ða   singan
      That their king   began then to-sing
                                                    (*Or* 1 14.56.31)

He, their king, then began to sing.

se is probably a pronoun in a topicalised construction because the adverb *ða* follows the subject rather than being verb-initial (see §4.6.1). It is possible that other instances of demonstrative preceding possessive, as in (10), are also to be interpreted as pronominal.

Indefinite NPs are of three kinds: indefinite pronouns, a noun with a strong adjective, or with indefinite determiners and quantifiers, or a common noun which is unmodified. In PreOE the strong form of the adjective appears to have been neutral to definite vs. indefinite, by contrast to the weak form of the adjective, which signalled definiteness. In OE the strong form came to be associated with the indefinite only, cf. *blind man* '(a) blind man' vs. *se blinda man*.

There are several indefinite pronouns and determiners in OE, for example, *man* 'one', *hwa* 'whoever', *ænig* 'any'. The focus in this chapter will be on the absence of a determiner to express indefiniteness and on the question of whether there is evidence for an indefinite article in OE.

Absence of a determiner with a common singular noun does not necessarily signal indefiniteness, that is, new, non-anaphoric information, or generic information, or information not assumed to be shared with the addressee (see (8) for an example of a noun without determiner that must be interpreted as definite). However, there is a strong tendency for common singular nouns without a determiner to be indefinite, cf. the example in (6). The use of any kind of determiner in predicate nominal constructions is rare, and common nouns in such constructions are typically indefinite:

(12) He was swyðe spedig man on þæm æhtum   þe heora speda
      He was very rich   man in those possessions PT their wealth

      on beoð
      in is
                                                    (*Or* 1 1.18.8)

      He was a man very rich in those possessions which constitute their
      wealth.

(13) & on ælcere byrig   bið cynincg... & þær is mid   Estum
      and in each fortress is king...   and there is among Ests
      ðeaw... þæt...
      custom... that...
                                                    (*OR* 1 1.20.14)

      and in each fortress there is a king... and there is among the Ests a
      custom that...

Two indefinite determiners, *sum* and *an*, are widely used to introduce new information:

(14) In ðeosse abbudissan mynstre wæs sum broðor syndriglice...
      In this   abbess's   minster was a   brother specially...
      gemæred
      honoured
                                                    (*Bede* 4 25.342.3)

      In this abbess's minster there was a certain brother who was
      especially... honoured.

(15) Ualens wæs gelæred from anum Arrianiscan biscepe Eudoxius
      Valens was taught by an   Arian   bishop Eudoxius
      wæs haten
      was called
                                                    (*Or* 6 33.288.13)

      Valens was taught by an Arian bishop called Eudoxius.

Both serve a 'presentative' function, that is, both serve to introduce to the discourse an entity (usually human) to whom reference will subsequently be made on several occasions (cf. PDE 'a certain'). *Sum* is more strongly presentative than *an* in that the entity introduced by *sum* is more often the main protagonist in an episode in narrative, and almost always occurs at the beginning of that episode. Both serve an individualising, that is, specific indefinite, function (cf. *She wants to buy a dog* (and she has a specific one in mind)) and a nonspecific indefinite function (cf. *She wants to buy a dog* (and any dog will do)).

Sum continues to be used in PDE for the specific indefinite in the singular (cf. *Some boy came by this morning trying to sell binoculars*); in the plural it is a nonspecific indefinite (cf. *I want some apples*), or an approximative (cf. *Some twenty boys came by*). In OE the plural nonspecific indefinite is relatively rare. One example is:

> (16) Uton smeagan nu   georne þæt we sume wæstmas godra
>   Let-us wish   now eagerly that we some fruits   of-good
>
>   weorca Gode   agyfan
>   works to-God may-give
>
> (ÆlfHom 3.182)
>
> Let us sincerely hope that we may give some fruits of our good works to God.

The use of singular *sum* declined toward the end of the OE period, as *an* gradually encroached on its presentative use.

An is usually inflected strong, even when preceded by a demonstrative. It may occasionally be found inflected for the plural before cardinal numerals, perhaps indicating a collective (e.g. a set or batch of):

> (17) ...ane seofon menn ætgædere
>   ...one seven men   together
>
> (ÆLS (Edmund) 239)
>
> ...a group of seven men.

An derives from the numeral 'one', hence its association with specific indefinites. We may assume that in (18) (and in (44) below), *an* is being used as the numeral, since specific distances are being discussed:

> (18) Alecgað hit ðonne forhwæga on   anre mile þone mæstan
>   They-lay it then   at least within one mile that greatest
>   dæl fram þæm dwelling, þonne oþerne,   ðonne þæne þriddan,
>   part from that dwelling, then   the-second, then   that third,

oþ þe hyt eall aled   bið on þære anre   mila
until it   all laid-out is   within   that one mile

(*Or* 1 1.20.30)

Then they lay the largest amount within one mile of the dwelling, then the second largest, then the third largest amount, until it is all laid out within the one mile.

But we can assume it is being used more like an article in the next example, since the number of arrows does not seem to be of as much import as the nature of the missile (furthermore, the Latin original does not have a numeral):

(19)   Ðær   wearð Alexander þurhscoten mid anre flan
There was   Alexander pierced   with an   arrow

(*Or* 3 9.134.22)

Alexander was pierced with an arrow there.

(cf. also *on anne tune* 'into a fortress' in (84) below).

We may conclude that there was an incipient indefinite article function in OE, but that it was very restricted. Incipient too was the *there*-construction introducing an indefinite subject in existential sentences, cf. (13) above. This construction is further discussed in §4.4.3 on the status of subject in OE.

In PDE there are three roughly equivalent generic constructions with nominal (as opposed to pronominal) NPs: *The cat is a mammal*, *A cat is a mammal* and *Cats are mammals*. Generic NPs introduced by the incipient definite article clearly exist in OE:

(20)   Se   lareow sceal bion on his weorcum healic,
That teacher must be   in his works   excellent,
ðæt he on his life gecyðe   lifes weg his   hieremonnum
that he in his life may-teach life's way to-his followers   (*CP* 14.81.2)

The/A teacher must excel in his works so that he may be a model to his followers.

There is little evidence that generics occur in OE either with the incipient indefinite, *sum* or without a quantifier. However, there is a possible example with both *an* and no determiner in:

(21)   swa swa an mon   bið man   þa   hwile ðe sio saul
as   a person is person for-that time PT that soul
& se lichama ætsomne bioð
and that body   together are   (*Bo* 37.114.4)

As a person is an earthly person while their soul remains with the body.

4.4.2 Agreement within the NP

Modifiers of noun heads generally agree with the head in number, gender and case. The few exceptions are chiefly motivated by two tendencies, which become clear only when inflections begin to be lost, and then most notably in northern texts like the Lindisfarne and Durham Ritual glosses, possibly under Scandinavian influence, and in other Late Old English texts. One tendency is to focus on natural rather than grammatical gender in the case of humans: feminine demonstratives may be used with words like *wifman* 'woman' (masc.), and *wif* 'woman' (neut.) (see volume III of this History); there are also some instances of the use of neuter demonstratives with inanimate nouns, cf. *lofsong* 'hymn' (masc.). The other tendency is to generalise *þæt* (neut. dem.) to objects, and *-ne* (masc. acc.), and *-es* (masc. neut. gen.), without regard to gender, to indicate accusative or genitive endings respectively.

Appositional phrases such as occur in (22) agree in case, and usually in gender and number:

(22)   Cuthberhtus se   halga biscop, scinende on manegum
       Cuthbert   that holy bishop, shining in many
       geearnungum
       merits

(*ÆCHom* II, 10 81.1)

Cuthbert, the holy bishop, shining with many merits.

However, plural nouns treated as collectives may have a singular noun in apposition, or vice versa. Participles in apposition are usually uninflected, or inflected strong. An example of the uninflected appositive participle is:

(23)   ... & him sædon from burgum &   from tunum
       ... and them told about cities   and about villages
       on   eorþan besuncen (not *besuncenum*)
       into earth   sunk

(*Or* 2 6.88.11)

... and they told them about cities and villages submerged in the earth.

When concord is at a distance from the head, anaphoric demonstrative, personal and relative pronouns generally agree with their antecedents in gender and number, cf. (8) with *hine* (nom. acc.) referring back to *hrof* 'roof'. However, there is also a tendency for *he* 'he' or *heo* 'she' to be used anaphorically to refer to nouns with male or female human referents, whatever their grammatical gender, cf. *ÆCHom* I, 1 14.21 *ænne wifman* (masc.) ... *heo* (fem.) 'a woman ... she'. The reverse, where *hit* 'it' is used anaphorically to refer to nouns with inanimate referents, whatever their grammatical gender, is very rare, but does occur, cf. *ÆCHom* I, 1 22.4 *þonne arc* (masc.) ... *hit* (neut.) 'that ark ... it'. This suggests that human animacy was more important in OE than animacy in general. The preference for natural over grammatical gender in reference to humans may have contributed to the demise of the grammatical gender system.

Recapitulatory pronouns in topicalised constructions may be singular even if the topic is plural. In such cases the topic is presumably treated as a collective or singular entity for purposes of anaphora (although the verb itself may be plural):

> (24) Eorðe and eal hyre gefyllednyss, and eal imbhwyrft
> Earth and all her fullness,   and all inhabited-world
> and þa   ðincg þe on þam wuniað, ealle hit sindon
> and those things PT on that live,   all   it are
> Godes æhta
> God's possessions
>
> <div align="right">(<i>ÆCHom</i> I, 11 172.8)</div>
>
> Earth and all her fullness, and all the inhabited world and all those things that live in it, they are all God's possessions.

Predicative adjectives agree in number, gender and case with subject NPs. So do participial adjectives (as opposed to participles in periphrastic perfect and passive constructions; see §4.4.3.1). It should be noted, however, that it is impossible to distinguish masc. and neut. sg. participial adjectives from participles because the participial adjective ending in these instances is ∅. Furthermore, the fem. sg. and neut. pl. are somewhat unstable: fem. short-stemmed adjectives and (potential) participial adjectives in *-u* are often uninflected, and the masc. pl. ending *-e* is often generalised to all genders in nom. and acc. pl. (i.e. it may be used where fem. pl. *-a* and neut. pl. *-u* are expected).

Before concluding this section, it should be noted that there is a tendency in OE to use the singular of the thing possessed with a plural possessive if each of the individual possessors has only one item. The construction is most common when the thing possessed is the human mind, spirit or a body part (even when the body part occurs in pairs, as do eyes, or sets, as do fingers):

(25) heafud (sg.) maehtigra (pl.) bioð onstyred
      head   of-mighty   are moved

(PsCaA 1 (Kuhn) 6.24)

the heads of mighty people are moved

4.3   Verbal groups

By 'verbal group' is meant both the finite verb alone (verb plus subject-
verb agreement, tense or mood marker), and verbal phrases consisting
of a main verb and one or more auxiliary verbs. This section will begin
with discussion of the finite verb alone, with focus on subject-verb
agreement, tense and mood, and then move on to constructions with
auxiliary verbs.

4.3.1   *The finite verb*

4.3.1.1   Subject-Verb agreement

As regards subject-verb agreement, the verb usually agrees with the
subject in number. However, number agreement may be overriden
under certain conditions involving conjoined subjects and word order.

   If two or more singular subject NPs are conjoined by *and*, the verb
may be singular; the subject NPs are then interpretable as a unit:

(26) Se   frumsceapena man and eall his ofspring
      That first-created   man and all his offspring
      wearð adræfed
      was   driven-out

(ÆCHom I, 7 118.23)

The first-created man and all his offspring were driven out.

Also, when two or more subject NPs are conjoined, if the first is
singular and the verb separates them, the verb may be singular:

(27) God bebead   Abrahame   þæt he sceolde and his ofspring
      God commanded to-Abraham that he ought   and his offspring
      his wed   healdan
      his covenant keep   (ÆCHom I, 6 92.30)

God commanded Abraham, that he and his sons should keep his
covenant.

   In constructions in which the verb precedes the subject, the verb may
be singular if it precedes a conjoined plural, as in (28); the same is

occasionally true when the post-verbal NP is a plural that can be interpreted as a collective, as in (29):

(28) ða   wæs þæt wæter and ealle wyllspringas gehalgode
      then was that water and all   well-springs hallowed

(ÆCHom II 3 22.96)

then the water and all the wells were blessed.

(29) On þæm gefeohte wæs ærest anfunden Sciþþia   wanspeda
      In that battle   was first   found   Scythians' insufficiencies

(Or 3 7.116.33)

The Scythians' insufficiencies were first revealed in that battle.

When the verb precedes a subject involving a cardinal numeral higher than 'one', the verb is normally singular. This is especially true if the numeral denotes 'ten' or a multiple of ten, and can therefore be treated as a collectivity:

(30) ...in Egyptum wearð (SG) on anre niht fiftig manna ofslegen
      ...in Egypt   was   in one night fifty of-men slain

(Or 1 8.40.12)

In Egypt fifty men were slain in one night.

Occasionally, in the second of two conjoined clauses with the indefinite subject *mon* 'one', a plural verb may be used; in this case *mon* invites the interpretation of a group of individuals:

(31) &   ælce dæg mon com (SG) unarimedlice oft   to
      and every day one came   uncountably often to
      þæm senatum & him   sædon (PL)...
      those senators and to-them said...

(Or 2 6.88.11)

and every day people came innumerably often to the senators and said to them...

4.3.1.2 Tense

As in PDE, there are two morphological tense-markers in OE: past and non-past. Together with temporal adverbs and temporal conjunctions, they are the prime indicators of temporal relations. This is amply illustrated by Ælfric's *Grammar*, in which he uses adverbs but not periphrastic verbs to differentiate present from future on the one hand, imperfect past and past from perfect and pluperfect on the other:

(32) ...PRAESENS TEMPVS ys andwerd tid: *sto*, ic stande;
      ...PRAESENS TEMPVS is present   tense: *sto*, I stand;
      PRAETERITVM TEMPVS ys forðgewiten tid: *steti*, ic stod;
      PRAETERITUM TEMPVS is past   time: *steti*, I stood;
      FVTVRVM TEMPUS is towerd tid: *stabo*, ic stande nu
      FUTURUM TEMPVS is future time: *stabo*, I stand now
      rihte   oððe on sumne timan... PRAETERITVM
      straightaway or   at some time... PRAETERITVM
      IMPERFECTUM,   þæt is unfulfremed forðgewiten,
      IMPERFECTUM,   that is unfinished   past,

      swilce þæt ðing beo   ongunnen and ne beo
      such   that thing may-be begun   and not may-be

      fuldon: *stabam*, ic stod. PRAETERITUM
      completed: *stabam*, I stood. PRAETERITUM

      PERFECTVM ys forðgewiten fulfremed: *steti*, ic stod   fullice.
      PERFECTVM is past   completed: *steti*, I stood to-the-end.
      PRAETERITVM PLVSQVAMPERFECTVM is forðgewiten
      PRAETERITVM PLVSQVAMPERFECTVM is past
      mare, þonne fulfremed, forðan ðe hit was gefyrn   gedon:
      more, than   completed, for-that PT it   was long-ago done:
      steteram, ic stod   gefyrn.
      steteram, I stood long-ago.

                                                      (*ÆGram* 123.13)

The degree to which periphrastic perfect and progressive were present
in OE, or to which modal verbs like *willan* 'to will, wish, want' had
temporal meanings will be discussed below in §4.3.4 on periphrastic
verbal constructions.

   Non-past tense, whether indicative or subjunctive, primarily refers to
the present ('now'):

(33) Ic Beda...   sende gretan   ðone leofasten   cyning
      I Bede...   send to-greet that most-beloved king
      Ceolwulf, & ic ðe   sende þæt spell...
      Ceolwulf, and I to-thee send   that narrative...

                                                      (*BedePref* 2.1)

      I Bede... send this to greet the beloved king Ceolwulf; and I send you
      that story...

It also refers to timeless present and habitual action:

(34) He sæde þeah   þæt þat land sie (SUBJ) swiþe
He said   however that that land is   very
lange norþ þonan
far   north from-there

(Or 1 1.17.3)

He said, however, that the land runs very far north from there.

(35) Fela   wundra worhte   God, and dæghwamlice wyrhð
Many wonders performed God, and daily   performs

(ÆCHom I, 12 184.24)

God performed many wonders and does so daily.

It can also express the future:

(36) ... & ic arise   of   deaðe on þam þriddan dæge
... and I will-arise from death on that third   day

(ÆCHom I, 10 152.7)

... and I will arise from death on the third day.

The non-past can also be used when continuity up through the present or present relevance are of prime importance (PDE usually requires the periphrastic perfect here, cf. *I have lived here for six years*; it may be noted that Modern German and Dutch among other modern Germanic languages do not):

(37) Efne   min wif is for manegum wintrum untrum
Indeed my wife is for many   winters   sick

(ÆLS (Apollonius) 41)

Indeed my wife has been sick for many years.

There appear to be no convincing examples of the historical present in OE, i.e. of the 'narrative' present used to refer to the past, although it is common in Latin writings translated into OE. There are also no examples of 'free indirect style' (characterised by, among other things, past tense co-occurring with present tense adverbs such as *now*, as in *what would she be doing now?*).

There seems to be no absolute distinction between *beon* (present tense *ic beo, þu bist, he biþ, we/ge/hie beoþ*; there is no past tense of this verb), and *wesan* (*ic eom, þu eart, he is, hie sindon*, etc.). However, *beon* is preferred over *wesan* when time reference to the future is concerned. Indeed, if a contrast between present and future is made, it can be expressed precisely through this lexical distinction:

(38)   Eala, ðu halige ðrynnes... ðu ðe æfre   *wære*, and æfre
        Oh, thou Holy Trinity... thou PT always were, and ever
        bist,   and nu *eart*, an ælmihtig God, untodæledlic
        will-be, and now art, one almighty God, indivisible

(HomM 5 (Willard) 35 6)

Oh Holy Trinity... who always were, and ever will be, and now are,
one Almighty God indivisible.

Beon also seems to be preferred for reference to habitual, repetitive and
therefore pluralised, situations, cf. (3), (12), (13), (21), (25). By contrast,
wesan is favoured for singular situations, as in (12) or situations regarded
as eternal, and therefore singular, as in (13) and (24). The favouring of
wesan for eternity is characterised by Ælfric when he says of *sum*, the
Latin first person present tense form of the verb 'to be':

(39)   *Sum* ic eom is edwistlic   word and gebyrað   to gode
        Sum I am   is of-existence word and is-suitable to god
        anum synderlice forðan þe god is æfre unbegunnen and
        alone solely   for-that PT god is ever unbegun   and
        ungeendod
        unended

(ÆGram 201.8)

Sum, I am, is a word referring to existence, and is suitable for God
alone because God is forever without beginning and without end.

The past tense marker, as opposed to the non-past, is primarily used
to refer to past time, cf. *wære* in (38). It is also used where we might
expect the perfect in PDE, usually with verbs of motion or process, as
in:

(40)   Fæder min, se   tima com
        Father mine, that time came   (*ÆCHom* II, 25 206.6)

Father, the time has come.

(By contrast, the present tense is used where we might expect the perfect
with stative verbs, cf. (37) above.) The past tense can also be used to
express past of past ('pluperfect'):

(41)   On þam dagum wæron on Wihtlande   þreo wif,   þa
        In those days   were   in Isle-of-Wight three women, those
        twa wæron blinde geond   nigon geara fec
        two were   blind through nine   years' time

(ÆLS (Swithun) 156)

In those days there were three women in the Isle of Wight. Two of
them had been blind for nine years.

4.3.1.3 Mood

Beside two tenses, OE distinguished three moods morphologically: indicative, subjunctive and imperative. Details of differences between indicative and subjunctive are discussed throughout as they pertain to particular sentence structures, but some broad generalisations are given here. The focus in this section is on the use of subjunctive vs. imperative in simple sentences functioning as directives and exhortations.

In general, indicative is used to present a proposition as true, and subjunctive is used to cast some doubt on the truth of the proposition or to express obligation, desire and so forth. However, there are many counter-instances. The indicative may be used where some doubt is expressed, most notably, many *if*-clauses in conditional sentences are indicative (see §4.5.6). Furthermore, the subjunctive may be used where the proposition clearly expresses a fact, for example, in reported speech (see §4.5.3.1).

The imperative is restricted to second person singular and plural. Morphologically it is marked by -$\emptyset$ and -*aþ* respectively. The verb is usually clause-initial, although an adverb may precede. In affirmative clauses the subject is absent in reflexive constructions, see (42), and sometimes present in non-reflexive constructions, cf. (43) and (44):

(42) Far þe (ACC/REFLX) ham
      Go thyself   home

                                   (*ÆCHom* I, 8 126.21)

        Betake yourself home/Go home.

(43) beoð blowende and welige   hwilwendlice
      be   flourishing and prosperous while

                                   (*ÆCHom* I, 4 64.15)

        flourish and prosper a while.

(44) Ic ðe secge, forgang ðu anes   treowes wæstm
      I thee say,   forego thou of-one tree   fruit

                                   (*ÆCHom* I, 1 14.9)

        I say unto you, forego/do not eat the fruit of one tree.

In negative clauses the pronoun subject is usually present:

(45) Ne hera ðu nænne man on his life
      Not obey thou no   man in his life

                                (*ÆCHom* II, 43 325.217)

        Obey no man in his life-time.

The hortative subjunctive does not occur in the first person singular. However, it occurs in all other persons. Usually the verb is initial, but subject – verb order may occur in third person constructions in main clauses.

(46) Ne yldan   we na from dæge to dæge
      Not let-us-delay we not from day   to day

(HomU 37 (Nap 46))

Let us not delay from day to day.

(47) God us gerihtlæce
      God us correct

(ÆCHom II, 36.1 271.104)

May God correct us.

Because the imperative and subjunctive contrast morphologically, we must assume that there was a difference in meaning, at least in early OE times, between more and less directive, more and less wishful utterances. By the time of Alfredian OE this difference was losing ground in many registers; nevertheless, the subjunctive continued to be preferred in monastic and legal regulations; charms, medical prescriptions and similar generalised instructions are normally in the subjunctive.

Among alternatives to the affirmative imperative and imperative expressing a command or wish is *uton* (*we*) + V-infinitive 'let us', historically derived from a tense of *witan* 'to go':

(48) ...Ac uton we beon carfulle
      ...But let us be   careful

(ÆCHom I, 28 414.27)

...But let us be careful.

Among alternatives in negative constructions is *nelle þu/ge* + V-infinitive 'do not', derived from the subjunctive of *ne willan* 'to not-want', possibly under the influence of Latin *nolite* 'do not let' < *non volite* 'do not want':

(49) Nelle   ge eow adrædan
      Not-will you you dread

(Lk (WSCp) 2.10)

Don't fear.

4.3.2 Auxiliary verbs

We turn now to discussion of auxiliary verbs. Semantically they express temporal meanings such as duration or completion, modal meanings such as obligation and possibility, or voice relations such as passive. Syntactically they are constrained as to position. Phonologically, unlike main verbs they may have reduced stress. There is considerable debate whether or not OE had syntactic auxiliary verbs, and if so how many. One of the problems is the relative paucity in OE texts, which are largely narrative or exegetical, of opportunities to find evidence for one of the criterial properties of PDE auxiliaries – availability in tag-questions (cf. *She could dance, couldn't she?* with auxiliary *could*, vs. *She danced, didn't she?*, but not ***She danced, dancedn't she?*, with main verb, not auxiliary *dance*). Absent too are clear criteria for assessing the potential presence of non-stressed and reduced forms such as we find in PDE *She must've arrived by now, She'll arrive soon*, or of reduced negatives, as in *I won't go*.

It is unquestionable that there was a set of verbs in OE, either cognate with modern auxiliaries or subsequently lost, which for the most part behaved like main verbs, but which also had several characteristics of the PDE auxiliaries in certain contexts. Most notable among them were the BE-verbs (*beon, wesan, weorþan*), *habban, willan, *motan, *sculan, magan* and *cunnan*. As will be discussed below, these verbs could be used to express tense, aspect and modality as well as their full lexical meaning of existence, possession, desire, ability and so forth.

It should be noted in passing that there was an OE verb *don* 'do', used both as a main verb (cf. PDE *Do the washing*) and as a substitute for the main verb (cf. PDE *Jane laughed and so did Joan*) as in (235) and (236) below. It will not be discussed here as it did not have properties directly associable with its PDE reflex, including dummy auxiliary status in sentences like *Do you like linguistics?, I don't like sugar in my coffee*. The auxiliary *do* developed in late Middle English and especially Early Modern English.

In this section some of the semantic and syntactic evidence is given for the auxiliary status of the BE-verbs in V-*ende* constructions ('progressives'), for *habban* or BE-verbs with V-past participle ('perfect' and 'pluperfect'), for verbs like *willan, *motan, *sculan, magan* and *cunnan* as 'pre-modals', and for BE-verbs in passive constructions. The term 'pre-modals' is used for verbs like *willan* because they show the beginnings of behaviour like that of their PDE modal counterparts *will, must, shall, may* and *can*.

4.3.2.1   The 'expanded/progressive' construction

The BE-verbs *beon, wesan* and sometimes *weorþan* are used with V-*ende* in what is often called 'the expanded form' of the verb to indicate that an action is ongoing, or to provide the frame of reference for some other activity. Like the PDE progressive *be + ing* construction, the OE *BE + ende* construction is largely restricted to activity verbs, i.e. verbs of doing rather than verbs of being (e.g. PDE *She is running* but not **She is knowing the answer*). However, although some OE constructions can be translated by PDE *be + ing*, not all can, and the constructions are therefore clearly not exactly equivalent:

(50)   Europe hio onginð... of   Danai þære ie,   seo is
        Europe she begins... from Don   that river, that is
        irnende of   norþdæle...   &   seo ea   Danai irnð þonan
        running from northern-part... and that river Don   runs thence
        suðryhte on   westhealfe   Alexandres herga
        due-south into western-part Alexander's kingdom

        (Or 1 1.8.14)

Europe begins... at the river Don, which runs from the North... and the river Don runs thence due South into the Western part of Alexander's kingdom.

(Note the switch from *irnende* to *irnð*, which does not appear to be semantically or syntactically motivated.)

There are many variations depending on subject-matter and author, but OE *BE + ende* appears to be favoured by verbs denoting activities without inherent beginning or ending such as *wunian* 'live', *faran* 'go', *cweþan* 'speak', *feohtan* 'fight', *libban* 'live', and *growan* 'grow'. Many are intransitive, and they are often accompanied by temporal, local or modal adverbs. For the most part BE + *ende* occurs with past tense and can be construed as signalling action that continued through a limited period of time. It may occur with pre-modal verbs such as *willan* and *magan*, but not with passive or (plu)perfect auxiliary (phrasal) constructions. Some examples are:

(51)   ...þæt scip wæs ealne weg yrnende under segle
        ...that ship was all   way going   under sail

        (Or 1 1.19.32)

that ship was running under sail all the way.

(52)   Petrus wearð æfterweard þus cweðende
        Peter   was   afterward   thus saying

        (ÆCHom I, 26 374.5)

Peter afterward said this...

(53) ... gif his hreofla wyrsigende wære
      ... if   his leprosy worsening   were

(*ÆCHom* I, 8 124.24)

... if his leprosy was getting worse.

(54) þæt se   wisdom mage on him wunigende beon
      that that wisdom might in him living   be

(*ÆCHom* II, 21 186.195)

that this wisdom might be alive in him.

The development of the progressive, which is of considerable importance in later periods of English (contrast the situation in French and German), appears in OE to have been partially influenced by Latin, but also to have been part of the growth of phrasal constructions in general, most especially of the (plu)perfect with which it contrasted as a marker of temporal relations. Nickel (1966) attributes the origins of the progressive to three types of constructions:

(a) BE + predicative adjective, e.g. *hie wæron blissiende* beside *hie wæron bliþe* 'they were happy'; according to Nickel this predicative adjective in *-ende* was originally essentially identical to the plain adjectival form, but later it came to be reinterpreted as part of the verb paradigm, which included *blissodon* 'they rejoiced'

(b) appositive participles, e.g. *he wæs on temple lærende his discipulas* 'he was in the temple, teaching his disciples', versus *þa he on temple wæs lærende his discipulas* 'when he in the temple was, teaching his disciples'; the latter was open to reinterpretation as 'when he was teaching his disciples in the temple'

(c) BE + agentive predicate nominal, e.g. *hie wæron ehtende cristenra monna* 'they were persecutors of Christian men', reinterpreted as 'they were persecuting Christian men' (the noun ending is *-end* in the singular, but *-ende* in the plural).

In many instances it is impossible to tell whether the old or the new construction is being used.

Evidence of progressive (i.e. verbal) rather than adjectival structure is perhaps provided by the use of the substitute verb *don* 'do' in (55), since one would expect *wesan* 'be' as the substitute verb if the antecedent was an adjectival phrase, but *don* if the antecedent was a verb.

(55) þonne beo   we sittende be þæm wege,
      then   should-be we sitting   at that   way-side,
      swa se   blinda   dyde
      as   that blind-man did

(*HomS* 8 (*BlHom* 2) 147)

then we should be sitting at the way-side, as the blind man did. (Contrast: 'then we should be seated at the way-side as the blind man was'.)

Other evidence for the progressive rather than the participal adjective may be the presence of expressions for repetition or continuation:

(56)   ...hio ðyrstende wæs on symbel mannes blodes, ac
      ...she thirsting was in eternity of-man blood, but
      eac   swelce mid ungemetlicre wrænnesse manigfeald
      moreover also   with immense   wantonness much
      geligre   fremmende wæs
      fornication performing was

(Or 1 2.30.26)

she was continually thirsting for a man's blood but yet also was performing many acts of illicit intercourse with immense licentiousness.

In (56) although the first form with -*ende* could express a state ('always thirsty' rather than 'always thirsting'), the second can hardly do so (?'always in the state of doing' rather than 'always doing'). Less criterial, but nevertheless of some significance for verbal status, is the fact that the *BE + ende* construction is found in translation of a Latin verb in the simple perfect:

(57)   Æfter þam Scipia... wæs monega gefeoht donde
      After that Scipio... was many   fights   doing

(Or 4 8.188.18)

After that Scipio... was fighting many flights.

where the Latin is *Scipio...plurima bella gessit* 'Scipio...many wars waged'.

In view of the later history of the progressive in English, and the replacement of the *BE + ende* construction by *be + ing*, it is interesting to note that Dal (1952:101–2, referenced in Mitchell 1985:§984)) cites four contexts in which the present participle appears to be equivalent to a preposition plus a nominal derived from a verb and ending in -*ung/-ing*:

(a) the appositive: *spræc wepende/on wepinge* 'spoke weeping/in the act of weeping'

(b) with a verb of rest or movement: *com ridende/on ridinge* 'came riding/in the act of riding'

(c) with a verb of causation or perception: *geseah hine ridende/on ridinge* 'saw him riding/in the act of riding'

(d) and with *beon/wesan*: *wæs feohtende/on feohtinge* 'was fighting/in the act of fighting'.

This suggests that the origins of the *be + ing* construction may be traced back to OE; it was, however, in many instances, a nominal phrase rather than a verbal group construction in OE.

4.3.2.2 The perfect and pluperfect constructions

The semantic perfect (completed event with present relevance) and pluperfect (past of past) were often rendered in OE by the simple past, see (41) and the translation of the Latin perfect *peccavi* 'I have sinned' by the simple past in Lk(WSCp) 15.18 *fæder, ic syngode* 'father, I sinned/have sinned'. In his *Grammar*, Ælfric uses such terms as *fullice* 'fully, completely), and *fulfremed* 'fulfilled' to distinguish the Latin perfect from the imperfect, see (32) above. Adverbs such as *gefyrn* and *ær* appear to have been used for the pluperfect from earliest OE times on:

> (58) ...þær manna lic   lagon þe wæran ær   acwealde
> ...there of-men bodies lay   PT were   before killed
> on ðam cwearterne gefyrn
> in that prison   distant
>
> (*ÆLS* 4.210)
>
> ...the bodies lay there of the men who had been killed in that distant prison.

One of the phrasal constructions involved *habban* 'to have' with a main verb in past participial form. The past participle could be inflected for case, number and gender if it modified an accusative object, but was more frequently uninflected in this context. It was never inflected with genitive or dative objects, prepositional phrases, or sentential complements functioning as objects. Since past participles were uninflected in the accusative singular neuter, it was not possible to tell whether the construction was inflected or not in sg. neuter object contexts.

The number of inflected constructions became less frequent during the OE period, but they were never predominant. An example with the inflected participle is:

> (59) ...þa þa   ge hiene gebundenne hæfdon
> ...then when you him   bound   had
>
> (*Or* 6 37.296.21)
>
> ...then when you had bound him/had him in the state of being bound.

By contrast, we find, without inflection:

(60) Ic hæbbe gebunden þone feond (acc. masc. sg.)
      I   have   bound   that enemy
      þe hi   drehte
      PT them afflicted

(ÆCHom I, 31 458.18)

I have bound the enemy who afflicted them.

Throughout the period the *habban* construction occurred with in-transitive verbs, i.e. in non-possessive constructions:

(61) ...æfterðæmðe hie gesyngod habbað
      ...after-that   they sinned   have

(ÆCHom I, 39 578.24)

...after they have sinned.

However, many intransitive verbs favoured a BE rather than *habban* periphrasis (see below).

The fact that the *habban* construction could be used from the earliest times with intransitive verbs and with transitive verbs the objects of which are not accusative, suggests that it could be used as an auxiliary in OE. It is difficult to say whether the inflected forms were understood with truly adjectival (that is, stative) meanings, as the presence of inflection suggests, especially since the inflected forms are sometimes co-ordinated with non-inflected participles, as in:

(62) Fela Godes   wundra we habbað gehyred (UNINFL)
      Many of-God's wonders we have   heard
      and eac gesewene (INFL)
      and also seen

(ÆCHom I, 39 578.24)

We have heard and also seen many of God's wonders.

However, since the inflected forms occur only with accusative objects, it is reasonable to assume that they were adjectival in meaning as well as form. Presumably, the adjectival construction originally consisted of the main verb *habban* 'to have' (a verb of possession), the object possessed, and an adjectival (semantically passive) past participial predicating this object:

(63) ðonne hæbbe we begen fet gescode (acc. pl.)
      then   have we both feet in-a-state-of-having-been-shod
      suiðe untællice
      very blamelessly

(CP 5.45.10)

then let us have both our feet very well shod.

The restructuring of the main verb *habban* with accusative possessed objects to auxiliary *habban* with nonaccusative objects or no object at all involved the reinterpretation of the participial as part of the verb complex. It is likely to have occurred first in constructions with neuter accusative singular objects, since these had $\emptyset$ inflection, and thus did not have overt morphology marking them as adjectives. Thus a construction like *we habbaþ* [*geweorc geworht*] 'we have the stronghold in-a-state-of-builtness' was reanalysed as *we* [*habbaþ*] *geweorc* [*geworht*] 'we have built the stronghold'. Then the *habb-* + participial construction was free to be extended to formerly inflected transitive contexts and also to intransitive contexts.[2]

As indicated above, there was a second (plu)perfect construction. This consisted of a BE verb and a past participle construction, and was mainly restricted to intransitive verbs of the type involving change of place or state, cf. *faran* 'go', *cuman* 'come', *weaxan* 'grow', *oðfeallan* 'fall into decay'. A somewhat similar situation exists in e.g. present-day German and French. The complementary use of *habban* vs. *wesan* is illustrated in:

(64) Wæs Hæsten þa   þær cumen mid his
     Was Haesten then there come   with his
     herge... Hæfde Hæsten ær   geworht þæt geweorc   æt
     army... Had   Haesten earlier built   that stronghold at
     Beamfleote & wæs þa   utafaren on hergaþ
     Benfleet   and was then out-gone on pillage

(*Chron* A (Plummer) 894.43)

Haesten had arrived there with his army... Haesten had previously built the stronghold at Benfleet and had then gone out on a foraging expedition.

Like the *habban* (plu)perfect, the BE (plu)perfect could be inflected, but often was not:

(65) Craccuse   wæron monege cyningas (PL)... to fultume
     To-Gracchus were   many   kings...   as help
     cumene (PL)
     come

(*Or* 5 4.224.5)

Many kings had come to Gracchus... as support.

(66) Hie (pl.) wæron cumen (UNINFL) Leoniðan   to fultume
     They   were   come   to-Leonidas as help

(*Or* 2 5.82.13)

They had come to Leonidas to help him.

The inflected participial construction with BE was probably truly adjectival in PrOE. By OE, however, it appears to have been reanalysed as a verbal complex (as happened to *habban* during the OE period), or at least to have been partially reanalysed. The evidence for reanalysis is that the participle is typically uninflected in the feminine singular, whereas a truly adjectival participle would be inflected with *-u*, see chapter 3 (a few rare examples with the inflection do exist, e.g. CP LetWærf 13 *hio wæs oðfeallenu*). On the other hand, the *-e* plural inflection occurs quite frequently, suggesting that the construction was not fully verbal either. It should be noted that the participial with BE was always semantically active (as is to be expected from intransitive verbs). Mitchell (1985:§737) notes that in the following example the participial form would have been *besencte* had the construction been passive:

(67)   ... on þære ondrædinge hwonne hie   on þa
       ... in that fear   when   they in that
       eorþan besuncene wurden
       earth   sunk   might-be

                                                        (*Or* 2 6.88.14)

... in their fear of the time they might be sunk in the earth (due to an earthquake).

4.3.2.3   Pre-modals

The set of pre-modals includes *cunnan* 'know how to, have the power to, be able, can', **durran* 'dare', *magan* 'be strong, sufficient, in good health, be able to' (with more focus on physical ability [cf. PDE *might*] than *cunnan*), **motan* 'be allowed to, be obliged to', **sculan* 'owe, be necessary', *þurfan* 'need', *willan* 'will, wish, desire'. To these should be added some uses of *beon* and occasionally *wesan* (*þas þing sint to donne* 'these things are to do', i.e. 'to be done'), and *habban* expressing necessity and obligation. There are some possible readings of *agan* 'have, possess' from the late tenth century that suggest the modal meaning 'owe, be obliged to'.

All the verbs are used as main verbs. Most may be intransitive:

(68)   Eac neah þan ealle þa   ðing þe ðanon
       Also nearly then all   those things PT thence
       cumað, wið   ælcum attre   magon
       come, against every poison they-prevail

                                                        (*Bede* 1 1.30.3)

But nearly all those things that are extracted from it can be used as antidote to any poison.

In intransitive constructions they frequently occur with a directional expression:

(69)   ... þa   hi   to scipan woldon
       ... when they to ships   wanted

(Chron E (Plummer) 1009.38)

... when they wanted to go to their ships.

All the verbs also allow either NP objects (which are never passivised) as in:

(70)   ... þæt he   geornor wolde sibbe wið hiene þonne gewinn
       ... that they rather   wanted peace with him   than   conflict

(Or 3 1 96.17)

... that they wanted peace with him rather than conflict.

or infinitive complements. *Beon, wesan* and *habban* take *to* + the inflected infinitive, as in (71); the others all take the uninflected infinitive, as in (72), or both (for the distinction see §4.5.3).

(71)   ... hwæt is us   to donne
       ... what is for-us to do

(ÆCHom I, 22.314.32)

... what we must do.

(72)   ... swa þæt hi   næfre ne   mihton ne   noldon
       ... so   that they never not might   nor not-wanted
       syððan fram his willan gebugan; ne hi   ne   magon nu, ne
       since from his will   bend;   not they not may   now nor
       hi   nellað   nane   synne gewyrcan
       they not-want not-any sin   to-do

(ÆCHom I, 1 12.7)

so that they never were able or wanted after that to revolt from his will; nor are they able to do so now, nor do they want to sin.

In addition, *magan, willan* may introduce a *þæt*-complement, see (238) below.

One piece of syntactic evidence that the pre-modals may have been auxiliaries as well as main verbs is that, although **sculan* and **motan* are clearly main verbs in some contexts, they never appear in non-finite forms; if they were exclusively main verbs, one would expect them to appear at least occasionally as infinitival complements. Stronger evidence is provided by the fact that if they occur with a verb that demonstrates 'impersonal' syntax (see §4.4.2), the pre-modals share all the properties of that verb, rather than being 'personal', that is, they do not appear to have a subject of their own, see Denison (1990b):

(73)   þonne mæg hine (ACC) scamigan þære brædinge (GEN/DAT)
Then may to-him   shame   of-that spreading
his   hlisan
of-his fame

(Bo 46.5)

Then he may be ashamed of the extent of his fame.

The semantic evidence is strong that pre-modals had properties of auxiliaries (that is, expressed obligation, possibility, probability, temporal relations or even mood).

*Sculan in particular has distinct modal properties. It could express moral as well as financial obligation, as in (9). A particularly striking example of the use of a pre-modal to express mood is the use of *sculan in the meaning 'supposedly' (i.e. like a subjunctive, casting doubt on the truth of the proposition):

(74)   & to þam Pentecosten wæs gesewen... blod weallan of
and at that Pentecost was seen...   blood to-well-up from
eorþan. swa swa mænige sæden þe hit geseon sceoldan
earth. as as many said PT it see   should

(Chron E (Plummer) 1100.4)

and at the Pentecost... blood was seen welling up from the ground, as many said who supposedly saw it.

(See also (175) below.)

Magan, willan and **sculan* are occasionally used with what appear to be meanings expressing probability and possibility. *Magan* in (73), for example, seems to express possibility rather than ability or permission. Occasionally, particularly in the case of *willan* and **sculan*, probability seems to verge on temporal generality or futurity, as in Or 5 7.230.26 *elpendes hyd wile drincan wætan* 'elephant's hide will drink/absorb water' where *willan* does not have a volitional meaning, but rather expresses a general truth (or at least a typical one). Particularly interesting is (75), in which the first instance of *wolde* appears to be predictive of the future, while the second retains the older meaning of 'wish':

(75) Þa   Darius geseah þæt he oferwunnen beon wolde, þa
      When Darius saw   that he overcome   be   would, then
      wolde   he hiene selfne on þæm gefeohte forspillan
      wanted he him   self in that fight   to-destroy

(Or 3 9.128.5)

When Darius saw that he would be defeated, he wanted to destroy himself/die in the battle.

An example of the apparent predictive use of *sculan* is the translation of the Latin -*turus* as *sceal* in ÆGrm 246.9 ... *lecturus sum cras ic sceal rædan to merigen* '... I shall read tomorrow'. But it is important to note that -*turus* is not purely future; as a future active participle, it also expresses necessity, or at least inevitability in the normal course of events, cf. PDE *be going to*). One of the conditions for the extension of the *scul-* of obligation to prediction may have been its use in sentences such as (9) and the following where the modal adverb *niede* stresses the obligation:

(76) Ic sceal   eac niede   þara   monegena
      I must/shall also of-necessity of-those many
      gewinna geswigian
      battles   be-silent

(Or 5 2.218.20)

I must also necessarily be silent about those many battles.

Another context may have been the use of *sculan* in statements of divine or royal ordinance:

(77) ...Uton nu   brucan þisses undernmetes swa þa
      ...Let-us now enjoy   of-this breakfast   as   those
      sculon   þe hiora æfengifl on helle gefeccean sculon
      must/shall PT their supper in hell get   must

(Or 2 5.84.31)

Let us now enjoy this breakfast as befits those who must eat their supper in hell.

It may also have been influenced by similar shifts in meaning of the Late Latin verb *debere* 'be owing, necessary'.

All the same, there are very few instances of OE *magan, willan* or *sculan* where the meaning without question expresses the speaker's assessment of probability and nothing else. (73) may express feasibility. Even (75) may have had not the 'bleached' meaning of 'would be overcome' but rather the stronger meaning of modal necessity best translated by 'was destined to be overcome'. The generic construction typified by *elpendes hyd wille drincan wætan* certainly involves some sense of necessity. We may note that in PDE, it is only with inanimate subjects that prediction is the primary meaning of *will* (cf. *It will rain tonight*). There do not appear to be any such sentences with inanimate subjects in OE.

It is necessary for an understanding of modality in OE to note that there are some rather fundamental differences between OE and PDE with respect to the grammatical encoding of modal meaning. All the PDE modals (*can, may, must, shall* and *will*), can be used to express assessment of probability and possibility on a continuum between 'fully asserted' and 'fully negated', otherwise known as 'epistemic' modality, in addition to their 'root' meanings of ability, permission, volition, etc. There are also a large number of adverbs that express epistemic modality in PDE, such as *probably, possibly, obviously, evidently*. The situation is different in OE. The pre-modals *cunnan*, *motan and *agan* show no traces of epistemic meaning in OE, while *magan*, *sculan, *willan* and possibly *beon* show only marginal epistemic colouring in most instances. The only constructions in which epistemic colouring appears to be strong are 'impersonal' ones such as (73) and:

(78)   ...ic wat   þæt hine (ACC) wile tweogan
        ...I know that him   will doubt
        hwæder heo him soð   secge
        whether she him truth may-say

                                          (*HomU* 21 (Nap 1) 35)

I know that he will doubt whether she will tell him the truth.

(79)   Hu wolde þe   nu   lician gif...
        How would to-thee now please if

                                          (*Bo* 41.142.2)

How would it please you if...

Wolde, being past tense, seems to express remote possibility.

Further evidence for the relative absence in OE of epistemic meanings is that even the subjunctive mood does not express doubt (low probability) in main clauses; it does so only in subordinate clauses. In addition, there are very few epistemic adverbs in OE expressing probability and possibility. Of the few adverbs with this meaning, most are found in glosses, e.g. *gewene* 'possibly'. Probability and possibility are expressed in OE primarily by phrases such as *wen is þæt* 'hope is that'. There are, however, adverbs of certainty (i.e. expressing the extreme positive end of the scale), e.g. *æfæstla* 'certainly', *forsoþ* 'truly'. In other words, epistemic modality appears to have been only marginally grammaticalised in OE.

4.3.2.4   Passive auxiliaries

Many authors have treated as 'passive' a number of constructions that are best translated into PDE as passives, most especially indefinite constructions introduced by *man* 'one', cf. (98), (196) and (203), and purposive infinitives such as are illustrated by (97), (190), and:

(80)   ...and hi   hine... of   ðære byrig gelæddon to stænenne
       ...and they him... from that castle led   to stone

(ÆCHom I, 3 46.35)

        ...and they...led him out of the castle to be stoned.

This is because the passive is preferred in PDE if the subject of a clause is indefinite (note that in (80) we do not know whether the same people as led the captive out of the castle were going to stone him; it is quite likely that other unspecified individuals would do that, and indeed that is what the PDE passive implies (contrast *They led him out to stone*). However, this is not the case in OE. Since they are not syntactically passive, such constructions will not concern us here.

The syntactic passive in earlier Indo-European was inflectional. The only survival of the inflection in OE is to be found in the passive form *hatte* 'is/was called' (and the plural *hatton*) of the verb *hatan*.

(81)   on ðæm bocum ðe hatton   Apocalipsin
       in those books PT are-called Apocalypse

(CP 58.445.33)

        in those books which are called the Apocalypse.

Even this verb, however, can occur with a verbal phrase with an auxiliary verb, cf. (15).

The ancestor of the OE syntactic passive with a verbal group consisting of an auxiliary BE-verb and the uninflected past participle is to be found in a construction with a BE-verb and an inflected, originally adjectival, past participle. The inflection is strong; since the strong inflection is zero for masculine and neuter singular, there is always ambiguity between the inflected and noninflected passive where the subject is masculine or neuter singular. Furthermore, the feminine nominative singular was early neutralised with the masculine in many texts.

An example of the inflected passive is:

(82) On þære ilcan tide wurdon twegen æþelingas
      At that same time were   two   athelings
      afliemde (PL) of   Sciþþian
      put-to-flight from Scythia

(Or 1 10 44.24)

At that same time two noblemen were banished from Scythia.

This may be contrasted with the uninflected passive in:

(83) & hu II æþelingas wurdon afliemed   of   Sciþþium
      and how two athelings were   put-to-flight from Scythia

(Or Head 64.10)

and how two noblemen were banished from Scythia.

The inflected as well as the uninflected passive participial may occur with prepositional agentive and instrumental phrases in the prose (the poetry favoured non-prepositional dative and instrumental constructions). The use of agentive and instrumental phrases with both types of passive suggests that the adjectival passive was not entirely stative but rather resultative/stative, since agentives and instrumentals would not be expected with pure statives (e.g. PDE **I was interested by Jim*). As in the case of the development of the phrasal perfect (see §4.3.2.2), the development of the phrasal passive involved the reanalysis of an earlier predicative adjective as part of the verb complex. This means that a construction of the type *he wæs [afliemed]*, where *afliemed* is predicated of *he* as a resultant state, was reanalysed as *he [wæs afliemed]* where the whole verbal complex is the predicate of *hie* (e.g. the difference in PDE between adjectival *It was (quite) closed* and *It was closed by Bill*).

Although no categorial contrast existed between *beon, wesan* and *weorþan* in passive constructions, there appears to have been a tendency to use *weorþan* for activities and changes of state, *beon/wesan* for resultant states. Examples of *weorþan* used for activities include (19), (20) and with *beon/wesan* for resultant states (14) and (29). An example where two momentary changes of state are followed by a more permanent state of affairs resulting from it is:

(84) he gefeaht wiþ   Gotan, & gefliemed   wearð
      he fought against Goths and put-to-flight was
      & bedrifen on anne tun   & þær wearð on anum huse
      and driven   into one fortress and there was   in one   house
      forbærned.   Þær   wæs swiþe ryht dom   geendad
      burned-to-death. There was very   right sentence carried out

(Or 6 34.290.32)

he fought against the Goths and was put to flight and driven into a fortress; and he was burned to death in a house. Very just judgement was carried out there...

This semantic distinction between *weorþan* and *beon/wesan* becomes less and less clear during OE, as is to be expected of a form that was to disappear in ME (*weorþan* was eventually replaced by the *get* passive). Even in OE certain texts contain very few instances of the verb, among them the Bede translation which uses the *beon/wesan* verbs almost exclusively. As has often been noted, Ælfric uses only *beon/wesan* in his discussion of English-Latin equivalents for the passive. However, since he uses *weorþan* extensively in his *Lives of the Saints* and *Homilies*, it is not clear whether he failed to use it in his *Grammar* because he did not regard it as sufficiently 'standard', or because there was no Latin equivalent.

4.3.2.5 Sequencing of auxiliary verbs

In PDE the sequence: Modal – Perfect – Progressive – Passive – V is possible (e.g. *might have been being destroyed*). However, the situation in OE is entirely different. No two auxiliary verbs may occur in sequence except Pre-modal – Passive (e.g. *might be destroyed*), and then only those pre-modals that allow uninflected infinitives are permitted. In other words, there are no equivalents of *may have talked, may be talking, may have been talking, She is being/has been watched*, nor, of course, of *She has been being watched*. However, there are no equivalents of *She is to go* or *She has to go* (the modal meanings of *beon, wesan* and *habban* required inflected infinitives; cf. (71)).

When the pre-modals occur with passives, it is possible to analyse them as main verbs introducing infinitive complements (see §4.5.3.2 on infinitive complements). However, at least in some cases the semantics suggest that the complementiser analysis may not be entirely adequate, since the full main verb meaning is unlikely or even extremely improbable. In (85) it is unlikely that *sceolde* means 'owed' or 'ought'; rather, it seems to have a temporal meaning:

(85) þæt tacnade þæt on his dagum sceolde beon geboren se
      that showed that on his days   should be   born   that
      se   þe us ealle to anum mæggemote   gelaþaþ
      that PT us all   to one   meeting-of-kinsmen bids

                                                  (*Or* 5 14.248.18)

that showed that in his day there would be born he who bids us all to an assembly of kinsmen.

Similarly, as we have seen, it is improbable that the first *wolde* in (75) could have the meaning 'intended, willed'.

4.4 Case assignment and the status of subject and object

As in PDE, predicates in OE may have $\emptyset$, one, two or more 'NP-roles' associated with them, that is, NPs that have such semantic/syntactic relations to the verb or adjective as agent, experiencer/goal, stimulus/source, location, affected being or thing, possessor and identifier. For example, in *John gave a book to Mary*, the verb *give* has associated with it an NP functioning semantically as agent and also as the source or starting-point of the transfer (*John*), an NP functioning as the goal or end-point of the transfer (*Mary*) and an NP functioning as an affected thing (*book*). In *John liked Mary*, the verb *like* has associated with it an experiencer/goal (*John*), and a stimulus/source of the experience (*Mary*).

In PDE, one of the NPs in a finite clause must serve as subject. If there is no NP-role associated with the verb, then a 'dummy subject' must occur, as in *It rained* (*it* in this sentence is not a real subject since it does not replace a noun, cf. **Water rained). Among the few exceptions to the rule that finite clauses must have a subject in PDE are imperatives (e.g. *Leave at once!*) and certain reduced clauses like *John liked Mary but hated Jill*, where the subject of the co-ordinated clause can be said to be deleted. In all the examples beginning with *John*, the NP *John* functions as subject of the sentence, whatever the semantic role assigned to *John*. A 'subject' agrees with the verb in number; furthermore, pronominal subjects are in the 'nominative' or 'non-oblique case', e.g. *he, she, they, I*.

Certain clauses, typically those with verbs known as 'transitive', will also have an 'object'. This is a second NP assigned to the position immediately following the verb, and without a preposition; the pronoun form is 'objective', e.g. *him, her, them, me*. In the examples cited, *Mary* functions as object in *John liked Mary*. However, *Mary* is not the object in *John gave a book to Mary*. In this sentence *a book* is the object and *Mary*, being introduced by the preposition *to*, serves as the 'indirect object'. Sentences like *John gave Mary a book* without a preposition are said to have 'double objects'.

Many predicates in PDE are lexically distinguished according to which semantic role is assigned to the subject function. Thus the same roles are associated with *like* and *please*, but with *like* the experiencer NP is subject, while with *please* the stimulus is the subject, cf. *John liked music*,

Music pleased John. NPs not serving as subject or object usually occur in prepositional phrases, e.g. *The music was pleasing to John.*

OE differs from PDE in three main respects. Subject is not obligatory; few verbs are lexically distinguished according to which role functions as subject; and oblique constructions are marked by genitive, dative and occasionally instrumental case, relatively infrequently by prepositional phrases. This section begins with some generalisations about case assignment, moves on to discussion of 'impersonal' constructions, and then addresses the issue of 'subject' and 'object' in OE, including passives and reflexive constructions.

4.4.1   *Case assignment, prepositional phrases*

The particulars of case morphology have been given in chapter 3. Our concern here is how cases are used, and to what extent case marking correlates with prepositional phrase constructions.

In traditional grammars it is usually pointed out that the grammatical subject in OE is nominative, and the grammatical object accusative, but that in other respects case assignment is largely dependent on individual verbs, adjectives and prepositions, or on adverbial functions. For example, it is noted that some verbs govern more than one case although they mean much the same thing, compare:

(86)   ...onfoh minne gast (ACC)
       ...receive my   soul
                                              (*ÆCHom* I, 29 426.14)

       ...receive my soul.

(87)   Ac ge onfoþ þæm (DAT) mægene Halges Gastes
       But you receive that   power of-Holy Ghost
                                              (*HomS* 46 (*BlHom* 11) 49)

       But you receive the power of the Holy Ghost.

(88)   ... ...   deaðes (GEN) onfoð
       ...he... death   receives
                                              (*ÆCHom* I, 21 308.2)

       ...he...suffers death.

Also, prepositions with essentially the same meaning *vis-à-vis* NP roles may take different cases, cf. *þurh* with the accusative, *fram* with the dative, both introducing oblique agent roles in passive constructions. Or the same preposition may take different cases in different dialects. Furthermore, the case system of later OE was breaking down, allowing for two co-ordinated NPs to be in different cases:

(89) ...ða   ðe þæt tempel (ACC) and þæra
     ...those PT that temple   and those

     goda (GEN) gymdon
     gods   cared-for

(ÆCHom II, 38 281.33)

...those who cared for the temple and the gods.

Taken together, such facts are interpreted as evidence that case assignment in non-nominative NPs was, for the most part, not governed by general syntactic/semantic principles.

Nevertheless, the same grammars also note some general tendencies. For example, it is often noted that the NP expressing the source of an emotion or mental state such as caring, neglecting or enjoying is typically in the genitive; the NP expressing the affected or interested person (the experiencer in the terminology used here) is typically dative with a verb of harming, (dis)pleasing, (dis)believing; and verbs of accusing, asking and depriving typically take the accusative of the person and the genitive of the thing.

It does not seem possible to assign a unique meaning to each case in such a way as to account for every use of case. However, some useful generalisations have recently been proposed for nominative, accusative, dative and genitive as they interact with NP roles, subject and object. These generalisations suggest that case assignment was significantly more subject to regular principles than has been assumed in the past; some will be included in the following outline of case use in OE.

As indicated above, the nominative case is associated with the subject. The semantic significance of this association will be discussed below in §§4.4.2 on 'impersonal verbs' and 4.4.3 on the status of subject. Nominative is also associated with NPs in the identification role, i.e. predicate nominals in constructions of the type NP *is/was* NP, cf. (12). As might be expected from other constructions with verbs translated by PDE *be*, three copula verbs were available for the predicate nominal construction in OE: *beon, wesan* and *weorþan*. It should be noted in passing that in OE the equivalent of the PDE type *It is I/me* was *I am it/I it am*:

(90) Geseoð mine handa &   mine fet, þæt ic sylf   hit eom
      See   my   hands and my   feet, that I (my)self it am

(Lk (WSCp) 24.39)

See from my hands and feet that it is I.

As the translation suggests, the OE construction is closer in meaning to 'I am the one', in other words, identification is paramount. By contrast, in PDE the construction *It is I/me* has come to indicate not so much self-identification as self-presentation.

The accusative case is associated with the grammatical object. However, this does not give us sufficient information to understand the meaning differences between, e.g. (91) and (92) (note the lexical distinctions in the PDE translations, as opposed to the case distinctions in OE):

(91) ond ða   folgode feorhgeniðlan (ACC PL)
      and then followed deadly-foes

(Beo 2928)

and then he pursued his deadly foes

(92) him (DAT) folgiaþ fuglas (NOM)
      him   follow birds

(Phoen 591)

the birds follow him

or between (93) and (94):

(93) ...and þa   unandgytfullan (NOM)... hine (ACC) geefenlacen
      ...and those unintelligent...   him   should-imitate

(BenR 2.24)

...and the unintelligent...may imitate him

(94) Gif he (NOM) geeuenlæcð gode (DAT)
      If he   is-similar-to God

(ÆCHom II, 13 129.71)

If he resembles God.

Such examples have been taken to suggest that accusative signals that the NP is viewed as a participant playing a role antagonistic to or unlike that of other NPs, in this case the subject NP, cf. Plank (1983). In (91) and (93) the accusative NP can also be viewed as highly involved (even if only unconsciously) – the enemy are the focus of the pursuers' attention, as is the individual imitated.

Dative case is typically associated with the experiencer role, with an animate goal (the indirect object), and with other NPs regarded as 'in the scene' but participating in it only minimally. For example, in (20), (92) and (94) the followers, birds and God are not engaged in any strong interaction with the subject. The significance of the semantic difference between accusative and dative will be further clarified in the section on impersonal verbs.

The genitive case is associated with the stimulus/source role, particularly when an experiencer NP is present, cf. (4), (76) and (77) among many others. It is also associated with the possessor role in a possessive phrase. The possessive phrase construction involves a genitive NP, e.g. *mancynnes* in (6), genitive third person pronoun, e.g. *heora* in (11) or the possessive pronoun *sin*. *Sin* occurs almost exclusively in the poetry, which suggests that it is archaic:

(95)   ac   þæt oftor   gecwæð aldor ðeoda   soðum   wordum
         but that more-often said   prince of-people with-true words
         ofer   sin magen
         about his power   (*Dan* 753)

         but the prince of people said that truthfully more often about his power.

Sin is always co-referential with the subject of the same clause and is therefore often used reflexively; unlike other pronouns in the reflexive construction, it cannot be followed by *self*.

An interesting example of a possessive construction is the following (*he* refers to a roof of variable height):

(96)   on sumre stowe he wæs   þæt man mid   his handa nealice
         in one   place   it   was (such) that one   with his hands nearly
         geræcean mihte, in sumre eaþelice mid   heafde
         reach   might, in one   easily   with head
         gehrinan
         strike   (*LS* 25 (MichaelMor) 193

         in one place it was low enough that one could reach it with one's hands, in another low enough that one could strike it with one's head.

This example illustrates the optionality of a demonstrative modifier or a possessive when the possessor of an object is co-referential with the subject. The possessor in both clauses is the indefinite *man* 'one'; *handa* is modified but *heafde* is not, cf. also (8).

When the possessor is human and the possessed thing a body part, the possessor is often expressed not by the genitive but by a dative NP:

(97)   ...he him   het   þæt heafod of aceorfan
         ...he with-regard-to-him commanded that head   off to-cut
                                    (*Or* 5 12.242.16)

         he commanded his head to be cut off.

(98) ... & him self leat forþ þæt him mon aslog þæt heafod of
      ...and himself bent forward that him one struck that head   off

(Or 6 290.10)

...and bent forward so that his head could be struck off.

Alternatively, in constructions of this type, the possessor may also be subject (and therefore nominative) of the verb *habban* 'have':

(99) and Abraham hæfde him on handa fyr and swurd
      and Abraham had   him in hands fire and sword

(ÆCHom II, 4 34.138)

And Abraham had fire and a sword in his hands (= and fire and a sword were in Abraham's hands).

The construction in (99) is very close to the so-called 'dative of interest' construction, where possession is metaphorical rather than actual:

(100) Læcedemonie   hæfdon him   to ladteowe
       Lacaedemonians had   for-them(selves) as leader
       ænne wisne mon
       a   wise   man   (Or 3 1.96.27)

The Lacaedemonians had a wise man as their leader (= the Lacaedemonians' leader was wise).

(101) Se   wæs Karles sunu þe Æþelwulf West Seaxna cyning
       That was Charles' son PT Æthelwulf West Saxons' king
       his dohtor   hæfde him   to cuene
       his daughter had   for-himself as queen   (Chron A (Plummer) 885.18)

He was the son of Charles whose daughter was the queen of Æthelwulf, King of the West Saxons.

So far there has been no discussion of case assignment in adverbial constructions. The details are best checked in the standard handbooks. Very generally: accusative is used in expressions of extent in time (*how long?*) and space (*how far?*), and of motion toward (*where to?*) (for accusative of distance, see (51)). Dative is used in expressions of time in which (*when?*) and place in which (*where?*). In so far as it can be distinguished from the dative (see chapter 3), the instrumental is used in expressions of manner or instrumentality (*how?*), reason (*why?*), accompaniment (*with whom?*) and degree (*how much?*). The genitive is also used in expressions of time, place and degree. The distinction between genitival and accusative/dative/instrumental expressions of time, place and degree is very fine; most often the genitive expressions are not phrasal (e.g. demonstrative or adjective + noun) but rather single word forms that have been frozen into adverbs, cf. *nihtes* 'by night', *geara* 'formerly', *þæs* 'after', *hamweardes* 'homeward', *togeanes* 'back, in return', *ealles* 'completely', *nealles* 'not at all'. Finally, the genitive is used in 'partitive' constructions to mark the whole from which a part has been taken. Signalling measure, quantity and extent, it is used with nouns, adjectives (usually superlatives), pronouns and numerals, cf. *sum dæl þæs felles* 'a part of the rock', *wacost burga* 'weakest of the fortifications', *eower sum* 'one of you', *þara fiftig* 'fifty of them', and see (30) and (62). (Note in (41) *preo wif* without the partitive, but *nigon geara fec* 'nine years' time' with the partitive).

Most adverbial constructions of the type just discussed can also be expressed by a prepositional phrase. Indeed, non-pronominal expressions of place in which, and to which, time, and of accompaniment are typically prepositional, cf. (6), (8), (14), (18), (20), (34), (37), (69), (96) and throughout. Only a few adverbial constructions are not normally expressed by a prepositional phrase, most notably the partitive genitive. Mitchell (1985: §1202) suggests that examples like Matt (Li) 6.29 *an of ðissum* 'one of these' may be Latinisms. It should be noted that *of* in OE meant 'from', cf. (50), (80) and (82), and could not be used to express possession as it is in PDE (cf. *the tail of the cat* beside *the cat's tail*).

Although prepositional phrases are for the most part optional variants of non-prepositional NPs, it appears that agent and instrument NPs in passive sentences were always expressed prepositionally, not by the dative or instrumental alone, except in some of the earlier poetry. For the difference between agent and instrument NPs in passives, consider PDE agentive *by John* in *Mark was killed by John* versus instrumental *by poison* in *Mark was killed by poison*. In the latter case, it is implied that someone killed Mark by using poison, or that poison was in Mark's food and therefore killed him; but poison is not the volitional agent in either interpretation. In OE several prepositions were available for agentive and instrumental NPs in passives. By far the most common personal agentive preposition was *fram*. Derived from the locative *fram* 'from', this preposition highlighted the causal role of the agent in passive constructions, cf. (15) and:

(102) Hu   on Egyptum wurdon on anre niht L   monna
       How in Egypt   were   in one night fifty men
       ofslagen from hiora agnum sunum
       slain   by   their own   sons   (*OrHead* 64.8)

How fifty men were slain by their own sons in one night in Egypt.

The preposition *þurh* could be used for both agent and instrument. An example of the agentive use is:

(103) …and þurh eow (AGENT) me   bið gehalgod manegra
       …and by   you   to-me is   hallowed of-many
       oþre clennysse
       other purity

(*ÆLS* (Julien and Balissa) 16)

…and the purity of many is hallowed for me by you.

The most common instrumental (non-personal agentive) preposition was *mid* 'with', which originated in the comitative 'among, along with', cf. (19) and:

(104) …oð þæt he eall   wæs besæt mid heora scotungum
       …until that he entirely was beset by their missiles

(*ÆLS* (Edmund) 116)

…until he was entirely beset by their missiles.

This preposition was replaced in ME by *with*. In Alfredian prose *þurh* 'through' is especially favoured for the instrumental, although it is used for the agent as well. *Be* 'in proximity', from which *by* is descended, does not apper to have been used in OE in an agentive sense; it is rare even for the instrumental relationship.

4.4.2   'Impersonal verb constructions'

There are a number of constructions in OE that do not require a subject, i.e. they do not require an NP in the nominative case. Furthermore, the verb is always in the third person singular form. Such constructions are usually called 'impersonal', but 'subjectless' might be a more appropriate term.

   Predicates that may have no NPs associated with them are most notably predicates referring to natural phenomena, including weather conditions, e.g. raining, snowing, storming or time changes, e.g. dawning.

(105) Gif on sæternesdæg geðunrað, þæt tacnað   demena and
       If on saturn's-day thunders, that portends judges' and
       gerefena cwealm
       sheriffs' death

(*Prog* 1.2 (Foerst) 7)

If it thunders on a Saturday, that portends the death of judges and sheriffs.

Although constructions of this type do not have a subject in the sense of a lexical NP, they may, and indeed usually do, have an 'empty' third person singular neuter pronoun *hit* in subject-position. This phenomenon will be discussed further in §4.4.3.3.

Verbs with one or more associated NPs are typically verbs of experience, whether sensory or cognitive, e.g. being hungry, liking, etc. Others are metalinguistic verbs of statement, threat, etc. (cf. 'here warns to-us about X' = 'here we are warned about/here there is a warning about').

Verbs of stating and speaking that may be subjectless include *cweðan* 'say', *cyðan* 'make known', *secgan* 'say', *onginnan* 'begin', cf.:

(106)   We leornedon &   on þæm godspelle cwið
         We learned   and in that gospel   says

(HomS 47 (BlHom 12))

We learned, and in the Gospel it says...

(107)   ...swylc her ær   beforan sæde
         ...such-as here earlier before   said

(Or 1 8.40.23)

...such as was said here before.

Verbs of sensory and mental experience that may be subjectless include *behofian* 'need', *eglian* 'ail, be troubled', *hreowan* 'to be sorry', *hyngrian* 'to be hungry', *longian* 'to long', *reccan* 'to care', *sceamian* 'to be ashamed', *swefnian* 'to appear in a dream to someone', *tweogan* 'to doubt', *þyrstan* 'to be thirsty', *þyncan* 'to appear, seem' (cf. archaic PDE *methinks that*...). Semantically they involve an animate experiencer and (often optionally), a stimulus, source or cause expressed by a genitival NP or prepositional phrase: something from which the experience derives, or by which the experience is effected. When there is no subject NP associated with these verbs, the experiencer is generally in the dative or accusative and the stimulus in the genitive:

(108)   and him (DAT) ðæs (GEN) sceamode
         and to-them   of-that   shamed

(ÆCHom I, 1 18.10)

and they were ashamed of that

(109)   þæt hi (ACC PLUR) þæs   metes (GEN) ne recð (SING)
         that to-them   of-that food   not cares

(Met 13.44)

that they take no interest in the food.

When the stimulus is realised by an infinitive or *þæt*-clause, it is often interpreted as a 'subject' (nominative); however, instances such as the following with a demonstrative in the genitive parallel to a *þæt*-clause, suggest that they are, like other stimulus and source roles, in the genitive:

(110) And þæs (GEN) us (ACC) ne scamað na,   ac þæs   us (ACC)
       and of-that   to-us   not shames never, but of-that to-us
       scamað swyþe þæt we bote   aginnan swa... swa bec   tæcan
       shames very   that we atonement begin   as...   as   books teach
                                              (*WHom* 20.3 160)

> and we are not at all ashamed of that, but we are ashamed of this: of beginning atonement in the way that... the books teach.

For further discussion of *þæt*-clauses and infinitive complements of impersonal verbs, see §§4.5.3.

Almost all verbs that occur in impersonal constructions also appear in constructions having either experiencer or stimulus as subject, that is, in non-impersonal constructions. Indeed, for some verbs such as *tweogan* the non-impersonal construction is favoured. This is especially true for *lician* 'please, like', which very rarely occurs in a clearly impersonal construction, but otherwise behaves much like one. Indeed, the only examples which appear to be unambiguously impersonal are those in which the stimulus/cause is a clause, and the experiencer is in the dative, cf. (79). An example of (non-impersonal) *lician* with stimulus as subject is:[3]

(111) ...þæt þu   scealt on æghwylce tid   Godes willan wercan,
       ...that thou shalt at each   time God's will   perform,
       þæt an   þe is selost þæt þu (NOM) Gode (DAT) licie
       that one PT is best   that thou   God   please
                                      (*HomS* 21 (*BlHom* 6) 36)

> ...that you must always carry out God's will and do that one thing that is best, that is, please God.

In such instances the verb has a causal meaning, i.e. 'to please'. Examples of experiencer as subject with *lician* are rare, but do occur in the glosses, perhaps under the influence of Latin:

(112) ðu   arð sunu min leaf, on ðec ic (NOM) wel licade
       thou art son my dear, in thee I   well was-pleased
                                     (*MkGl* (Li) 1.11)

> you are my dear son, in whom I was well pleased.

In cases like this, the verb has a receptive meaning ('like') as opposed to a causal meaning ('please'). Whereas the two meanings are differentiated lexically in Modern English, they are differentiated morphologically and syntactically in OE. (112) and similar examples with *lician* and experiencer as subject all occur in translations of the Bible, and may be influenced by Latin. A similar contrast is provided by *lystan*, which with the dative experiencer means 'cause desire', and with the nominative experiencer means 'feel desire'. This suggests that nominative experiencers with impersonal verbs were not ungrammatical, although unusual, in OE.

A few verbs do not occur with experiencer as subject: these include *gebyrigan* 'be fitting' and *gelimpan* 'befall (someone), happen', for which the receptive-causal distinction is somewhat odd (note these involve neither real sensory nor mental experience). The verb *þyncan*, which is usually glossed as 'appears, seems', rarely occurs with experiencer as subject (this relationship is reserved for *þencan* 'to think'), but it does occur in the passive, thus in a kind of receptive sense. Compare *þyncan* with experiencer as dative:

(113)   him (DAT) selfum ðincð þæt he nænne næbbe
        to-him   self   seems that he none   neg-has

(Bo 29.66.11)

It seems to him that he has nothing.

and the passive:

(114)   se   leoma (NOM)... wæs swiðe lang (NOM) geþuht
        that light...   was very long   thought
        suðeast   scinende
        south-east shining

(Chron E (Plummer) 1097.18)

the light which shone (from it) towards the south east was considered to be very long.

Assignment of dative, genitive, accusative or nominative to a particular NP in the constructions under discussion is therefore not entirely arbitrary, but is correlated at least in part with the perspective taken on the state of affairs described. Although this is not easy to show across the whole class of impersonal verbs, the correlations become clear within subclasses of impersonal verbs (e.g. verbs of rueing, verbs of pleasing, of happening, etc.), and most particularly when comparison is made of contrasting case-assignments with the same verb. The four-way distinction can be shown operating with the one lexical verb root *hreowan*; in OE there are different case possibilities, whereas in PDE there are different lexical forms:

(115) for ði   him (DAT) ofhreow þæs   mannes (GEN)
      for that to-him   pitied   of-that man
      for þan þe he wæs bepæht mid þæs deofles searocræftum
      for that PT he was deceived by that devil's wiles
                                              (*ÆCHom* I, 13 192.16)

he was sorry for the man because he (the man) was deceived by the devil's wiles.

(116) Hreaw hine (ACC) swiðe   þæt...
      Pitied him   very-much that...
                                              (*GenA*, B 1276)

It grieved him very much that...

(117) se   mæssepreost (NOM) þæs   mannes (GEN) ofhreow
      that priest   of-that man   pitied
                                              (*ÆLS* (Oswald) 262)

the priest took pity on the man.

(118) ðurh   his soðan menniscnysse him (DAT)
      through his true   humanity   him
      ofhreow ðæs   folces   meteleast (NOM)
      pitied   of-that people's want-of-food
                                              (*ÆCHom* II, 29 231.32)

because of his true humanity he pitied the people's want of food.

   Some adjectival predicates behave in ways very similar to 'impersonal' verbal predicates. They include adjectives of ease and difficulty, (un)pleasantness, usefulness and necessity, for example:

(119) Swa þonne is me   nu   swiþe earfeðe hiera
      Thus then   is to-me now very   difficult their
      mod to ahwettanne
      spirit to excite
                                              (*Or* 4 13.212.30)

Thus then it is very difficult for me to excite their spirit.

As is true of predicate adjectives like *easy*, *difficult* in PDE, the potential object of the complement clause may be the subject of the sentence. In the following examples, the stimulus (120) and the affected object (121) are subject:

(120) ælc ehtnys   bið earfoðe to þolienne
       each persecution is   difficult to endure

(ÆCHom II, 42 313.110)

every persecution is hard to endure.

(121) & he þonne se   deada   byð uneaþe
       and he then   that dead-man is   difficult
       ælcon   men on neaweste to hæbbenne
       to-each man in nearness to have

(HomS 17 (BlHom 5) 78)

and as for the dead man, it is difficult for everyone to have him in the vicinity.

However, no examples have been noted of adjective of ease or difficulty with the experiencer as subject (cf. PDE *John is easy to please*).

4.4.3   The status of subject

Issues relating to 'subject' in OE have been discussed throughout §4.4. They are summarised here, and then the passive, reflexive and some constructions with 'empty' subject are discussed.

Subject is here defined as a surface grammatical category; it is associated with nominative case, and it agrees with the finite verb (with exceptions mentioned in §4.3.1.1). Most importantly, it was not obligatory in OE (it became so during ME, though a few archaic relics such as *methinks* survived into later periods).

4.4.3.1   Passive constructions

The passive provides supporting evidence for the special syntactic status in OE of nominative and accusative case (as subject and object markers), in contrast to oblique cases (dative and genitive). This is because only NPs that take accusative in active constructions may be passivised, cf. (3), (15), (19), (29), (75), (83) and (102) among others. Verbs with double accusative objects, such as (ge)*læran* 'teach', would appear in principle to permit either object to be subject in a passive sentence. However, Mitchell (1985:§835) says no examples of *gelæran* 'with a retained object of what is taught (MNE *he was taught singing*)' occur in his data.

Verbs with an accusative object and an oblique NP allow only the accusative object to be passivised. An example of *gelæran* with an accusative and a dative object rather than two accusatives is:

(122) ... & fuslice gehyrdon, ða   ðe him gelærde wæron
       ... and readily obeyed,   those PT them taught were

(Bede 4 28,362.23)

... and readily obeyed the (injunctions) they were taught.

Another example of a similar construction is:

(123) Ic secge eow   to soþan þæt sib   is forgifen Godes
       I say to-you in truth that peace is given   to-God's
       gelaðunge (DAT)
       congregation   (ÆLS (Lucy) 127)

I say to you truly that peace is granted to God's congregation.

When a verb is associated with one or more oblique NPs and no nominative or accusative NPs, then the so-called 'impersonal' (or better 'indirect') passive is used; this is a passive construction without a subject, but with a dative or genitive NP, or with a sentential complement.

(124) Ac ðæm (DAT) mæg beon suiðe hraðe   geholpen
       But to-him   may be   very quickly helped
       from his lareowe
       by   his teacher   (CP 33.225.22)

But he may be helped very quickly by his teacher.

(125) Hyt is gecwæden on þære æ   þæt man sceole   lufian
       It is said   in that law that one ought to- love
       hys nehstan   swa swa hyne selfne
       his neighbour so as him self   (Solil 1 19.14)

It is stated in that commandment that one should love one's neighbour as oneself.

In PDE the passive is permitted in constructions with prepositional phrasal verbs such as *laugh at*, *look up* (in the sense of 'visit', or 'check'), cf. *The plan was well thought through*. This construction does not appear to have been possible until early ME. In OE, however, preposition stranding (i.e. separation of the preposition and the NP it governs so that the NP precedes the preposition) was possible in active sentences, for example:

(126) Freond ic gemete   wið
       Friend I may-meet with

(MCharm 11 37)

May I meet with a friend.

and also in relative clauses (see §4.5.2.2). The absence of the passive in constructions of the type illustrated in (126) suggests that in OE the preposition was truly that: an element governing the NP, and therefore construed as introducing an oblique NP (which, like other oblique NPs, could not be passivised). In Middle English many oblique NP constructions were reanalysed so that the preposition became a particle which was part of the verb complex, leaving the NP as an object that could be passivised, as in PDE.

4.4.3.2 Reflexive constructions

Reflexive constructions occur when a non-subject NP refers to the subject NP in the same clause. In OE the reflexive is expressed by the simple personal pronoun. It may be emphasised by the pronoun *self*, used in apposition, cf. (75) and (125), but this is by no means obligatory, cf. (100). Some verbs in OE require a dative NP that is reflexive, but usually not any other kind of NP. These typically do not occur with *self* (as might be expected since no contrast with a non-reflexive NP is possible). They are mainly verbs of rest, bodily movement and emotion, e.g. *faran* 'go, beget oneself', *restan* 'rest', *belgan* 'irritate oneself', *ondrædan* 'fear', cf. (42), (49) and:

(127) Nelle   þu oð ende yrre habban, ne on ecnesse
      Not-may you until end anger have,   nor in eternity
      ðe   awa belgan
      thee ever enrage

(PPs 102.9)

May you not be angry until the end, nor enrage yourself for ever.

Since reflexive requires anaphoric reference to a subject NP in the same clause, the following two sentences must be taken to exemplify emphatic, not reflexive pronoun + *self*.

(128) Hi   þa hrædlice... gewendan eft   ongean þone
      They then quickly... turned   again toward that
      cyning... & hiene selfne gefengon
      king...   and him   himself captured

(Or 1 12.54.4)

Then they quickly... turned again toward the king... and captured even him.

(129) þæt he oðres   mannes ungelimp besargie
      that he another man's misfortune deplore

and ... nanum   gebeodan   þæt him sylfum ne licie
and ... to-no-one to-command that him self   not would-please

(ÆCHom I, 38 584.4)

that he would deplore another man's misfortune and ... not bid
anyone to do what would not please himself to do.

In (128) the object (*hiene selfne*) does not refer to the subject, which is
plural (cf. the plural verb form *gefengon*); as regards (129), if *þæt* is the
subject of *lician*, it is not coreferential with *him*; likewise, if *þæt* is an
accusative NP in an impersonal construction, there is no NP to which
to refer.

4.4.3.3 The development of 'empty' subjects

As has been shown, the surface category subject is clearly not obligatory
in OE. Nevertheless, there is some evidence that already in OE there
was a tendency to fill the subject position and to associate it with
definiteness. This tendency is manifest in two main ways: the occasional
use of *hit* in impersonal constructions (and some others, to be discussed
in §4.5.3), and the use of *þær* in certain copula constructions with an
indefinite subject. Although *hit* and *þær* have different constraints and
are differently motivated, they share the property of not having full
pronominal functions. That is, they do not substitute for a noun phrase,
and therefore have none of the participant semantics associated with
nominative case; furthermore, they are not clearly anaphoric (or
cataphoric). Rather, they appear to have been syntacticised and to
function as 'empty' subjects that simply fill a position.

As we have seen in §4.4.2 there are two major types of impersonal
constructions: those with zero NP-roles, and those with one or more
NPs but no subject. Although the first type can occur without *hit*, e.g.:
(105), *hit* is preferred:

(130) Swa nu   lencten & hærfest: on lencten hit grewð
       Thus now spring and autumn: in spring it grows
       &   on hærfest hit wealwað, & eft   sumer   and winter: on
       and in autumn it   withers, and then summer and winter: in
       sumera hit bið wearm &   on wintra ceald
       summer it is warm and in winter cold

(Bo 21 49.18)

As for spring and autumn: in spring things grow and in autumn they
fade; and then as for summer and winter: in summer it is warm, and
in winter cold.

In impersonal constructions of the second type, *hit* is disfavoured, cf. (113) and (116) among others. However, examples with *hit* can be found, especially in the later period:

(131) ði læs ðe hit ne   genihtsumige us and eow
       lest   it not suffice   us and you
       farað to ðam   syllendum and bicgað eow   ele
       go   to those merchants and buy   yourselves oil

                                              (*ÆCHom* II, 44.327.16)

   lest there is not sufficient for us and you, go to the merchants and buy
   yourselves oil.

Even though *hit* fills the subject slot, the strong preference for it in predicates with zero NP role, compared to its relative scarcity in multi-NP impersonal constructions suggests that occupancy of an NP slot was actually probably more important in OE than occupancy of the subject slot itself: in other words, clauses with zero surface NPs were disfavoured.

Many instances of *hit* in impersonal constructions unambiguously exemplify an empty element without any anaphoric or cataphoric properties. However, when a sentential complement is involved, the syntactic analysis is not always so clear. For example, is *hit* in (132) an empty subject slot filler with no reference to the complement (in which case the complement must be taken to be oblique), or is it a pronoun pointing forward caraphorically to a subject complement which, like all complements, occurs post-verbally?

(132) Lareow, ne ofþingð hit ðe   gif ic þus wer geceos
       Teacher, not displeases it to-you if I thus man choose

                                              (*ApT* 20.6)

   Teacher, it does not displease you if I choose a man thus.

There is no reason based either on semantics or on clause order to require the sentential complement to be subject rather than oblique in this sentence, and indeed most scholars agree that sentential stimulus-cause is usually not subject. So it seems best to analyse (132) as containing an empty *hit* and an oblique complement.

Like *hit*-constructions, *þær*-constructions are optional. Unlike *hit* in impersonals, *þær* occurs with a subject. Its function is not to fill a totally empty subject position, but rather to place a definite element in subject position, where otherwise an indefinite would occur, and thus to correlate subject position with definiteness, at least in copula constructions. In PDE this correlation is obligatory in existential sentences with indefinite subjects, cf. *There's a problem with this analysis* vs. **A problem is with this analysis*. In OE it is optional, compare both the non-use and the use of *þær* in (13).

Þær is derived from the locative adverb meaning 'there', and occasionally the two may be hard to distinguish. The locative is always substitutable by a different adverb of place, but the 'empty' *þær* is not. Of the eight instances of *þær* in the following passage from Wulfstan's description of Estonia in *Orosius*, the first two seem to be clearly locative and substitutable by *on Estlande*, and the last six are at least potentially empty subject-position holders:

(133) Þæt Estland is swyðe mycel, & þær bið swyðe manig
       That Estland is very big,   and there is very   many
       burh,   & on ælcere byrig bið cyningc. &   þær bið
       fortresses, and in each   fortress is king.   And there is
       swyþe mycel hunig... Þær   bið swyðe mycel gewinn betweonan
       very   much honey... There is very   much fighting among
       him.   & ne bið ðær nænig ealo gebrowen mid   Estum, ac
       them. And not is there any   ale brewed   among Ests, but
       þær bið medo genoh. &   þær is mid   Estum ðeaw, þonne
       there is mead enough. And there is among Ests   custom, when
       þær bið man dead, þæt he lið inne   unforbærned mid   his
       there is   man dead, that he lies inside unburned   among his
       magum &   freondum monað... &   ealle þa hwile þe þæt lic
       kin   and friends   month... And all   that time PT that body
       bið inne, þær sceal beon gedrync &   plega
       is inside, there shall be   drink   and play

                                                          (*Or* 1 1.20 14)

The land of the Ests is very large, and there are very many fortresses there, and in each fortress there is a king. And there is very much honey... There is very much conflict between them. And there is no ale brewed among the Ests, but there is enough mead. And there is a custom among the Ests, when there is a man dead, that he lies inside uncremated among his kinsmen and friends for a month... And all the time that the body is inside, there shall be drink and play.

The analysis of the last *þær* as an empty subject-marker rather than a true adverb rests on the assumption that it is unlikely to be anaphoric to *inne* – since drinking and playing were probably not restricted to the very same location in which the body lay at rest.

Although *þær*-constructions are found in *Beowulf*, they are very rare until later OE, especially Ælfric. It is interesting to note that the high preponderance of *þær* in (133) occurs in a section of the text that is usually thought to be a first-hand account (cf. the use of the first person plural pronoun), and may be a feature of speech. This would be consistent with a construction that was to become obligatory later when subject position had to be filled.

4.5 Complex sentences

Complex sentences consist of two or more clauses conjoined. In OE, as in PDE, there are a large number of complex sentence types. Of these only constructions involving the following clause types will be discussed: co-ordinate, relative, sentential complement, purposive, result, causal, conditional, concessive, temporal and comparative. The section will end with some observations about interrogative and negative clauses in both simple and complex sentences. Word order within clauses and clause order will be discussed in §4.6.

The complex clause types of OE are roughly equivalent to PDE co-ordinate and subordinate clauses with similar names. However, in some cases evidence for syntactic as opposed to semantic subordination is not as apparent as in PDE. In PDE there is often a morphological difference between adverbs and conjunctions. It is therefore in most cases possible to tell from form as well as meaning whether a clause is introduced by an adverb or a conjunction, cf. *afterwards* vs. *after*, *therefore* vs. *because*. However, in OE most such pairs are homonymous (with the connective derived from the adverb), cf. *æfter* 'afterwards, after', *for þon* 'therefore, because', *þa*, *þonne* 'then, when', *þær* 'there, where', *swa* 'so, as'. The main exception is the pair *gif...þonne* 'if...then' (as is true in the case of the PDE reflex *if...then*, *þonne* cannot occur alone without *gif* as the marker of a conditional construction). Usually the context invites unambiguous interpretation of a sequence of clauses as a sequence of independent sentences or as connected in a complex sentence. Ambiguities nevertheless do exist, as in:

(134)   Nu   hæbbe we awriten   þære Asian suþdæl,/;
        Now have   we described that Asia's southern-part,/;
        nu   wille we fon to hire norðdæle
        now will   we turn to its   northern-part   (*Or* 1 1.14.5)

Since we have described the southern part of Asia we will turn to the northern part/Up to now we have described the northern part; next we will turn to the southern.

The first *nu* translates Latin *quoniam* 'since' and could be a conjunction (see §4.5.5 on causal uses of *nu*). Alternatively, it could be adverbial ('up to this point...next'). In either case, the second *nu* marks a stage in the development of the argument, as does *now* in PDE. Word order can be a clue to independence or connectedness in the prose, since most adverbs favour Adverb – Verb – Subject...order, while the conjunctions favour Verb-final order. However, there are exceptions (adverbial and connective *nu* 'now, since', *ær* 'beforehand, before', and *siþþan* 'afterwards, after' are both often found with verb-final order). Furthermore, word order is used extensively to express pragmatic factors such as presentation of a new topic, and topicalisation (see §4.6). The most reliable clue is the particle *þe*, which distinctly marks a form as a conjunction.

It should be noted in passing that punctuation cannot be used for establishing independence vs. connectivity. All major OE texts have been edited, and most of the punctuation has been added (see Introduction and Plate).

Once it has been established that a sequence of clauses makes up a complex sentence, the question arises whether the clauses are in a paratactic or hypotactic relation, that is, whether the clauses are linked as equals or asymmetrically, cf. *He went jogging and then left for work* (paratactic) vs. *After he went jogging he went to work* (hypotactic) (here *after he went jogging* is syntactically dependent on *he went to work*). Parataxis is traditionally subdivided into two types. One type, called 'asyndetic', has no overt conjunctions. Typical examples are: *I came, I saw, I conquered*, where no co-ordinating conjunctions are present, and *Do this: take all the forms to room 120*, where a deictic introduces a clause. The second type of parataxis, called 'syndetic', is characterised by overt co-ordinating conjunctions, as in *I came and I conquered*. As these examples illustrate, there is no direct correspondence between parataxis and co-ordination (though co-ordination is subsumed under it). On the other hand, 'hypotaxis' translates fairly readily into 'subordination'.

It is sometimes said that OE syntax, at least in the earlier poetry, was characteristically paratactic (cf. chapter 8). However, the evidence of extant documents, allowing for different style and genre, and different conventions about literacy, suggests that the structure of OE allowed for a great variety of types of hypotaxis. One factor that makes OE seem more paratactic is the greater frequency in formal writing of unco-ordinated and co-ordinated sentences, see (133). Even more significant is the presence of a number of parallel structures that have few analogs in PDE. For example, homonymous adverbs and connectives are often used in correlative constructions. Many, but by no means all, of these are deictic, involving either cataphora, pointing forward to the next proposition, or anaphora, pointing back to the preceding one (cf. *þa...þa* which can be interpreted as 'when...then' or 'then...when', depending on context, and *for þon...for þon* which can be interpreted either as 'for this reason...because' or as 'because...therefore'). Several examples will be given in the sections below.

The problems in understanding complex clause structure in OE are well illustrated by the problem of the status of *þe*. The initial consonant *þ-* suggests that *þe* is ultimately derived from a form of the demonstrative. One possibility is a demonstrative locative adverb **þai*, see Mitchell (1985:§2151), referring to Neckel (1900:60); and also Curme (1911). The particle occurs in a wide number of clause types: relative, complement, causal, temporal, comparative, etc., but not after conditional *gif* or temporal *æfter*. It is sometimes ambiguous:

(135) ...We magon beon getrymeded mid Iohannes cuide
       ...We may   be   strengthened by John's   words
       þæs   godspelleres þe he cuæð...
       of-that evangelist   PT he says

                                                    (CP 14.85.19)

      ...we may be comforted by the words of John the evangelist who [this analysis assumes a resumptive pronoun]/when/because he says...

Recent analyses of *þe* have proposed that its various functions derive from its use as: (i) a relative pronoun referring to an NP in the main clause (see Carkeet 1976); (ii) a relative complementiser signalling a co-reference relation between the main clause NP and either a lower clause NP or the whole lower clause (see Allen 1980); (iii) a complementiser marking the clause as a constituent (see Reddick 1981); or, more loosely, as (iv) a subordinating particle (see Mitchell 1985:§2428). Giving more substance to the analysis of *þe* as a subordinating particle, Wiegand (1987) suggests that *þe* was originally a deictic marking the clause it introduces as a comment on or evaluation of the situation described in the preceding clause; in other words it originally had the discourse function of signalling paratactic connectivity. *Þe* was later reinterpreted as a subordinator in various contexts (relative, complement, causal, etc.). Once this had occurred, it could be used with connectives introducing clauses that precede the main clause. Nevertheless, some more paratactic uses still survived. In the following discussion *þe* is assumed to be a subordinating particle.

4.5.1 Co-ordinate clauses

Co-ordination is signalled by a number of conjunctions including *ond* 'and', *ac* 'but' and *oþþe* 'or', *ne* 'and not' and *naþer* 'neither' (usually with *ne*), and several correlative conjunctions such as *ge...ge* 'both...and', *begen...ge* 'both...and', *ægþer...ge* 'either...or', *ne...ne* 'neither...nor', *nawþer...ne* 'neither...nor'. Such conjunctions may link two or more (a) clauses, cf. (72), (110), (128) and (130); (b) noun phrases: (24) and (130); (c) adjectives: (43); (d) adverbs.

As in PDE, the subject of a co-ordinated clause is normally omitted if it refers to the subject of the first clause, cf. (64), (84) and throughout. The subject may even be omitted when the connective is absent, a construction frequently found in spoken PDE, but not usually permitted in written English:

(136)   Se halga ða het   him   bringan
        That holy-man then commanded to-him to-bring
        sæd; wolde on ðam westene wæstmes tilian
        seed; wanted in that desert   growth   provide

                                        (*ÆCHom* II, 10 86.176)

        The holy man then commanded that seed be brought to him; he wanted to make that desert fertile.

In constructions of this type the second clause is pragmatically subordinated to the first after certain verbs, most especially verbs of saying, requesting and commanding, and *willan* 'intend', *wenan* 'think', *þencan* 'think' in senses involving intention and purpose, see (136). Typically these verbs are used with intentional and causal meanings (cf. 'think = plan, intend') when the co-ordinated subject is absent.

Occasionally, a subject which is anaphoric to a non-subject NP in the preceding clause may also be omitted:

(137)   ...inne on þæm fæstenne   sæton feawa
         ...inside in that stronghold sat   a few
         cirlisce men on, &   wæs sam worht
         country men in, and was half built

                                       (*Chron* A (Plummer) 893.9)

        a few country-men were inside in that stronghold, and it was half built.

For comments on number agreement in the verb when the subject is conjoined, see §4.3.1.1. For comments on conjunction in negative clauses, see §4.5.10.

4.5.2   Relative clauses

There are two main types of relative clauses (also known as 'adjective clauses'). The function of the main one, the so-called 'restrictive' type, is to particularise, or delimit the potential referents of, an antecedent NP (or 'head') in the main clause. The function of the second type, the so-called 'appositive type' is to comment or add parenthetical information, and is marked off in PDE speech by a break in intonation and in writing by commas.[4] The distinction can be seen in the following pair. The restrictive relative restricts the reference of the head to a subset of the possible referents, so *I gave the necklace to my friend who lives in San Francisco* excludes other friends who do not live in San Francisco. By contrast, the appositive only adds descriptive, new information, and so the following implies no contrast with any other friends: *I gave the necklace to my friend, who lives in San Francisco* (indeed, in this sentence 'friend' is interpreted as unique. e.g. 'Jane Smith'). In many varieties of PDE there is a morphological distinction between the two types of relatives. In those varieties where such a distinction occurs, *that* can be used instead of *who* and *which* only in restrictive clauses. No absolute distinction is made in OE, but there is a tendency, to be discussed below, for *þe* to be favoured in certain restrictive relative constructions.

In some languages, there are restrictions on the syntactic function or semantic NP-role of the relativised NP in the surbordinate clause. In PDE, such restrictions are minimal. Relativised NPs can function as the subject or object of the relative clause, or in a variety of other NP roles. Examples are: *The man who has given the book to the woman is here* (the relativised NP is subject of the subordinate clause), *The man whom you wanted to see is here* (the relativised NP is the object), *The man to whom you gave a ride is here* (the relativised NP is the indirect object), *The man by whom you were saved is here* (the relativised NP is instrumental/agent), *The man whose hat you have is here* (the relativised NP is the possessive), etc. The situation is very similar in OE.[5]

Constraints which differ between OE and PDE will be discussed in §4.5.2.2.

4.5.2.1 Types of relativisers

Relative clauses are typically introduced by a grammatical form called a 'relative marker' or 'relativiser'. In OE as in PDE there are two types of relative marker: a pronoun (in PDE *who-whom-whose*), and an invariant form (in PDE *that, which*). Alternatively, there may be no marker at all (as in *That is the woman you met yesterday*).

(a) The pronominal relativiser in OE is the pronoun *se, seo, þæt* 'that'. It is normally inflected for the case of the relativised NP; it may be followed by the invariant particle *þe*. An example of *se* alone is:

(138) Þonne   is an   port on suðeweardum þæm lande (DAT),
      Then   is one port in south-of   that land,
      þone (ACC) man hæt Sciringes heal[6]
      which   one calls Skiringssalr

                                                    (*Or* 1 1.19.10)

Then there is a port in the south of that country which is called Skiringssalr.

(*Hatan* typically has an accusative object.) An example of *se* followed by *þe* and functioning as the subject of the subordinate clause is (85). In (139) *se þe* functions as the object:

(139) ...þæt heo ne woldon heora Gode (DAT) hyran   þone (ACC)
      ...that they not wanted their God   to-obey whom
      þe heo gelyfden
      PT they believed

                                                  (*Bede* 3 15.222.22)

...that they did not want to obey the god in whom they believed.

This type of relativiser occurs in the poetry and prose of all periods. However, *se þe* is rare in the poetry, comprising only some 2.5 per cent of all relatives according to Mitchell (1985: §2173). It appears to be favoured (but by no means obligatory) when the antecedent head has no demonstrative or quantifier. A particularly interesting example from the point of view of PDE is (140), where the antecedent is the plain pronoun *his*. In PDE only the prepositional phrase 'of him', or better 'of the one', could be the antecedent, but in OE such a prepositional phrase was not possible, and the equivalent inflected pronoun could be the antecedent:

(140) ...þæt þu onfo   his (GEN) geleafan & his bebodu
      ...that thou receive his   trust   and his commands

healde, se (NOM) ðe þe   from wilwendlecum earfeðum generede
obey,   that   PT thee from transitory   hardships saved

(Bede 2 9.132.26)

... that you receive the trust of the one who has saved you from earthly
hardships, and obey his commands.

Sometimes the relative pronoun *se* is inflected for the case of the
antecedent (a construction called the 'attracted relative'); it is always
followed by the invariant particle *þe*.[7] Examples are:

(141)   heriað forði   Drihten (ACC), þone (ACC) ðe eardað on Sion
        praise therefore Lord,   whom   PT lives   in Zion

(Ps 9.11)

Praise therefore the Lord, who lives in Zion.

(142)   hi   adulfon gehwylcne dæl þæs   wyrtgeardes (GEN)
        they dug   each   part of-that vegetable-garden
        þæs (GEN) þe þær ær   undolfen was
        of-that   PT there before not-dug was

(GD 202.3)

they dug every part of the vegetable garden that had been left undug
before.

There has been much debate over whether *se* is a demonstrative or a
relativiser in any particular instance under discussion. At issue here is
whether the putative relative clause is actually independent and in
apposition (therefore not relative) or dependent (and relative). As in
other areas of complex sentence structure, neither punctuation nor
word order appears to be much help in making a decision; the only
certain instances of relativisation are those rather rare instances in which
the relative is surrounded by material belonging to the higher clause.
For example, although the following appears to be punctuated as a
demonstrative in the MS, it could equally well be a relative pronoun
without the full stop, especially since there is a tendency in OE to
postpose relatives as part of the process of 'heavy element shifting' (cf.
§4.6):

(143)   Wið   suðan... fylð   swyðe mycel sæ up in on ðæt lond,
        Toward south... penetrates very big   sea up in to that land,
        seo is bradre þonne ænig man ofer   seon mæge
        ?   is broader than any man across see   may

(Or 1 1.19.18)

Toward the south ... a very big body of water penetrates into the land.

> It is broader than anyone can see across / ... a very big mass of water
> penetrates into the land, which is broader than anyone can see across.

Similarly, the first *seo* in (50) may be a demonstrative rather than a
relative. It is precisely the similarity in function between the demonstrative and the relativiser that permits the latter to arise from the
former in many languages of the world. When, as in OE, no
morphological split between the demonstrative and the relative pronoun
occurs, there may be continued association with the demonstrative; it is
presumably such continued association that restricts *se* almost exclusively to third person reference, as opposed to first and second
person reference (Mitchell 1985:§2260).

   (b) The second type of relativiser is an invariant particle, most
typically *þe*, which occurs in prose and poetry from earliest OE on.
Some examples are (60), (68), (101) and:

   (144)   sealde þæm munucum corn genog   þe   wæron æt Hierusalem
           gave those monks   corn enough who were   at Jerusalem

                                                             (*Or* 6 4.260.9)

   Gave enough corn to the monks who were in Jerusalem.

Þe is most frequently used when the relativised NP serves as subject or
object. However, it can also be used when the relativised NP would be
dative, cf. (5), (12) and:

   (145)   ...nyhst þæm tune   ðe se   deada man on lið
           ...next that homestead PT that dead man in lies

                                                             (*Or* 1 1.20.30)

   ...next to the homestead in which the dead man lies.

or even genitive:

   (146)   ...sio hea goodnes þe he full is
           ...that high goodness PT he full is

                                                             (*Bo* 34.84.11)

   ...the great goodness of which he is full.

   There is a tendency for invariant *þe* to be favoured over a pronominal
relativiser if the antecedent is singular and modified by a demonstrative.
This tendency is most noticeable when the antecedent is singular
masculine nominative; thus *se mann þe* 'that man who' is far more likely
to occur than *se mann se*. It is least noticeable when the antecedent is
singular neuter nominative or accusative, in which case a construction
like *þæt iegland þe* 'that island which' is actually less favoured than *þæt*

iegland þæt. Invariant *þe* is also favoured when the antecedent is modified by a quantifier such as *(n)an, manig, eall*. These quantifiers require restrictive relatives in PDE, cf. *No student that/who failed the exam can take it again*, ***No student, who failed the exam, can take it again*. This suggests that invariant *þe* was partially favoured for restrictive relatives. However, this was by no means an absolute constraint.

There are a few instances in OE of *þæt* used invariantly. Invariant *þæt* (as opposed to pronominal *þæt*) can be recognised when the gender, number, or case of neither the antecedent nor the relativised NP is neuter nominative or accusative singular. Like *þe* it requires the preposition to be stranded, which is further proof that it is not a pronoun. An example of *þæt* referring to a feminine antecedent is:

(147) þurh   þa halgo rode (FEM ACC) þet Crist
       through that holy   cross   that Christ
       wæs on þrowod
       was on tortured

                                    (*Chron* E (Plummer) 963.63)

through the holy cross on which Christ suffered.

The presence in OE of invariant *þæt* is of particular interest because *that* totally replaced *þe* in Middle English as the invariant relativiser.

If there is an NP or adverb head with locative adverbial function, an invariant adverbial relative *þær* meaning 'where, in which, to which', occasionally 'from which', may be used:

(148) An   wæs Babylonicum, þær   Ninus ricsade
       One was Babylonia,   where Ninus ruled

                                      (*Or* 2 1.58.28)

One was Babylonia, where Ninus ruled.

(149) þæt sint India gemæro   þær þær Caucasus
       that are India's boundaries there where Caucasus
       se   beorg   is be norþan
       that mountain is in the-north

                                      (*Or* 1 1.10.15)

Those are India's boundaries in the north of which is the mountain Caucasus.

Compare also (252) below. Mitchell (1985: § 2455) notes that in many cases where Ælfric uses *þær þær*, a punctuation mark precedes the first *þær*. This suggests that a double construction is at issue, rather than a construction in which the first *þær* is a constituent of the main clause, and the second is a constituent of the relative clause, i.e. *þæt sint India gemæro* [*þær þær Caucasus*...], rather than *þæt sint India gemæro þær* [*þær Caucasus*...].

(c) Absence of a relative marker results in what are sometimes called 'contact clauses'. Examples in OE are (15) and:

(150) &   on þys ilcan gere forðferde æþered   wæs on
       and in this same year died   Æthered was in
       Defenum ealdorman
       Devon   chief

(Chron A (Plummer) 901.17)

and in this same year Æthered, chief of Devon, died.

Absence of a relativiser is relatively rare in OE, but seems to be a native construction since it is found in the earliest poetry and even in translations of Latin texts where a relativiser is present:

(151) &   sægdon him ða   uundra dyde se   hælend
       and told   them those wonders did   that Saviour

(JnG (Li) 11.46)

and told them the miracles that the Saviour did [Lat. 'et dixerunt eis *quae* fecit iesus'].

It is usually found in relative clauses with predicates such as *hatan* 'to call, name', *wesan* 'to be', *belifan* 'to remain', *nyllan* 'to not want', verbs that either are stative or are used statively in the constructions under discussion, cf. (150) (however, (151) demonstrates that stativity is not required).

4.5.2.2 Constraints on relativisers

There are several analyses of relative clause structures for PDE. The one used here is based on Comrie (1981), since it clarifies some fundamental differences among relative clause patterns in OE. According to this analysis, when the relativiser is a pronoun, it is structurally the relativised NP, and has been moved to clause-initial position. By contrast, when the relativiser is invariant, the clause is marked as a relative, and the position of the relativised NP is not filled, in other words, there is a 'gap'. When the relative marker is absent, the relativised NP is similarly said to be absent, or 'gapped'; the only difference from relative clauses with invariant markers is that the clause is not marked as relative. Thus in PDE *This is the man whom you met* involves a moved pronominal object; by contrast, *This is the man that you met*— and *This is the man you met*— have no pronoun, and the object NP of the relative clause is gapped.

In OE, as in PDE, the pronominal relativiser is case-marked, whereas the invariant relativiser is not. There are additional structural differences between pronominal and invariant relativisers. One has to do with whether or not the 'gap' may be filled by a 'resumptive pronoun'. In PDE this difference is evidenced almost exclusively in spoken English (cf. *He's the kind of fellow that you have trouble liking him*, *He's the man that I know his wife*),[8] but in OE it is evidenced in writing. Pronominal relativisers in OE never permit the relativised NP position to be filled, which is what one would expect if the pronominal relativisers are actually moved relativised NPs (in other words, one would not expect redundancy). However, although the overwhelming majority of OE constructions with invariant relativisers are gapped, they do permit the relativised NP position to be filled by a third person resumptive pronoun. This is what one would expect if there was indeed a 'gap': the pronoun fills the gap and specifies the relativised NPs clause-internal role as subject or object, etc.

Resumptive pronouns are found almost exclusively with the relativiser *þe*, although some instances also occur with *þæt*. In the following example, the relativised NP is an accusative in an impersonal construction:

(152) ... & ic gehwam   wille þærto tæcan þe hiene (ACC)
       and I whomever shall thereto direct PT him
       his lyst   ma to witanne
       of-it would-please more to know

                                                      (Or 3 3.102.22)

   and I shall direct anyone to it who would like to know more about it.

In the following, the relativised NP is a dative:

(153) Swa biõ eac þam   treowum þe him (DAT) gecynde
       So is also to-those trees   PT to-them   natural
       biõ up heah to standanne
       is up high to stand
                                                      (Bo 25.57.20)

   so it is also with trees to which it is natural to stand up straight.

(101) exemplifies relativisation of a genitive NP. In the next example, the relativiser is invariant *þæt* and the relativised NP is nominative; note that the resumptive pronoun is plural but refers to a collective which is grammatically singular:

(154) & þær is mid   Estum an mægð (FEM SG) þæt
       and there is among Ests   a tribe   PT
       hi (NOM PL) magon cyle gewyrcan
       they   can   cold make   (Or 1.21.13)

and there is among the Ests a tribe who are able to freeze (the dead).

In most cases, the resumptive pronoun follows *þe* immediately, whatever its function in the relative clause. However, if the relativised NP is in a non-nominative case and the subject of the relative clause is a pronoun, that subject pronoun may intervene between *þe* and the resumptive pronoun. In the prose, but not the poetry, a noun subject may do so too, cf. (101). In the following example, subject *mon* 'one' intervenes between *þe* and the possessive resumptive pronoun:

(155) Ac gesette þa   men on ænne truman þe mon (SUBJ)
       But put   those men in a   troop   PTone
       hiora (RESUMPT POSS) mægas ær   on ðæm londe slog
       their   kin   before in that land slew
                                                   (Or 2 5.80.19)

But he put those men in a troop whose relatives had earlier been slain in that land.

A second structural difference between pronominal and invariant relativisers has to do with the treatment of prepositions associated with the relativised NP. In PDE if the relativiser is a pronoun which is part of a prepositional phrase, the whole prepositional phrase may be moved to clause initial position, cf. *the house in which Jack lived* and *the girl to whom I told the story*. However, if the relativiser is invariant and the relativised NP is part of a prepositional phrase, the preposition is 'stranded', in other words it must occur in its original position toward the end of the clause, cf. *the house that Jack lived in*, not ***the house in that Jack lived*. In OE the contrast between pronominal and invariant relativisers is stronger. Specifically, pronominal relativisers in OE require the preposition to be moved to clause-initial position with them, see (112). In other words, a construction like **...*dic þæm is iernende stream on* '...ditch wh- a stream is running in' does not appear to be possible in OE. There are some occasional apparent exceptions when the relativiser is *þæt*. For example, in (156) *æfter* follows rather than precedes *þæt*:

(156) gyf ic geseo and habbe þæt ðæt   ic æfter swince
       if I see and have that which I after toil   (Solil 1 26.10)

if I see and have that for which I toil.

This may, however, be an example of a preposition with an invariant
þæt rather than with a relative pronoun of the same form; alternatively,
æfter may be a verbal prefix to *swincan*.

Invariant *þe* requires prepositions to be stranded, as does its successor
in English, *that*, cf. (5), (12) and (145).

In OE the preposition usually precedes the verb. However, in (157)
it follows:

(157) Him is be eastan se   Wendelsæ,   þe man hæt
       Them is to east   that Mediterranean, PT one calls
       Tirrenum, þe Tiber sio ea   ut   scyt on
       Tyrrhenian, PT Tiber that river out pours in

                                      (*Or* 1.1 28.15)

To the east of them is the Mediterranean, which is called the
Tyrrhenian sea, that the River Tiber flows into.

In some languages, including standard PDE, there is a constraint on
relativising out of a subordinate clause. If a language has this constraint,
only NPs in the clause immediately subordinate to the head may be
relativised, but not an NP in another clause which is itself subordinate
to this subordinate clause. Thus the following is not allowed in most
varieties of PDE: **The woman that he knew John thought Bill might want to
meet* (structurally: 'The woman. He knew John thought X: that Bill
might want to meet the woman'). This structure may be more easily
conceptualised in Figure 4.1:[9]

Figure 4.1 Diagrammatic representation of restrictions on extraction called
'island constraints'

Unlike PDE, OE allows an NP to be relativised even if it belongs to a clause which is itself subordinate to the head clause. This is possible with both *se* and *þe* relatives, compare:

(158) Ðis is se rihta geleafa þe æghwylcum men gebyreð
     This is that correct belief PT to-each man behooves
     þæt he wel gehealde & gelæste
     that he well hold and perform

(HomU 20 *(BlHom* 10) 70)

This is the correct belief and it behooves every man to hold and perform it well.

(159) Ic seolfa cuðe sumne broðar ðone ic wolde þæt
     I myself knew a-certain brother whom I wished that
     ic næfre cuðe
     I never knew

(Bede 158 5.15.442.9)

I myself knew a certain brother and I wish that I had never known him.

4.5.2.3 Free relatives

There are a number of examples in OE of constructions which are ambiguous between relatives with a pronominal antecedent and free relatives where one form serves as both antecedent and relativised NP (compare PDE headed 'He who tells lies will be punished' with free 'who(ever) tells lies will be punished'). The ambiguity arises because, as we have seen in §4.5.2.1, it is often difficult to tell whether *se þe* is to be construed as a demonstrative plus invariant relative, or as a relative pronoun plus invariant particle. Note that in these constructions the pronoun is definite in form (*se*), whereas in PDE it is indefinite (*who*). An example of an ambiguous sentence is:

(160) Se þe cinban forslæhð, mid xx scillingum forgelde
     ? ? chin-bone breaks, with 20 shillings pay

(Law Abt 50.1)

He who/Whoever breaks a chin-bone, let him pay for it with twenty shillings.

There are, however, some constructions which are introduced by *se* alone which appear to be unambiguous free relatives, among them (129), which is repeated here for convenience:

(129) þæt he oðres   mannes ungelimp   besargie and ... nanum
      that he another man's misfortune deplore and ... to-no-one
      gebeodan   þæt (ACC NEUT) him sylfum ne   licie
      to-command that him   self   not would-please
                                                    (*ÆCHom* I, 38 584.4)

that he would deplore another man's misfortune and ... not bid
anyone to do what would not please himself to do.

The following may be an instance of an oblique free relative with the
case of the antecedent:

(161) ne   gebelge ic me nawiht wið   þe, ac fagnige
      not anger   I me not   against you, but rejoice
      þæs   þu cwyst
      in-what you say

                                                    (*Solil* 1 36.1)

I am not angry with you but rejoice in what you say.

Ðæs in (161) is a genitive, the case required of NPs expressing the
source argument associated with *fægnian* 'rejoice'; the object of *cwedan*
'say' would be accusative. The only alternative to analysing (129) and
(161) as free relatives (other than emending the text and adding a
relative) is to hypothesise that there is an absent relativiser in these
constructions.

   In addition to free relatives introduced by *se/seo/þæt*, there are also
free relatives introduced by *swa hwa swa*:

(162) Swa hwa swa sylð   ceald wæter drincan anum þurstigum men
      whoever   gives cold water to drink to-a thirsty   man
      þæra   ðe on ure gelyfað: ne bið   his med   forloren
      of-those PT in us believe: not will-be his reward lost
                                                    (*ÆCHom* I, 38 582.23)

Whoever gives cold water to drink to a thirsty man who believes in us
will not lose his reward.

(Note the paratactic construction in the OE here.) The *hwa* in compound
free relatives of this kind can be inflected, and is therefore clearly a
pronoun.

4.5.3   Sentential complements

Sentential complements (also known as 'noun clauses') are clauses that
function as NPs. Like other NPs, they serve NP-roles such as source or

goal, and syntactic functions such as subject or object. They may be either finite (i.e. have a tensed verb) or non-finite. Among non-finite complements are constructions often referred to as 'accusative/dative and infinitive constructions'.

4.5.3.1 Finite complements

Finite complements in OE are introduced by two main types of marker or 'complementiser': *þæt* 'that', and *hwæþer* 'whether'. Occasionally these complementisers may be followed by *þe*. Like PDE *that*, OE *þæt* (*þe*) signals that the complement is definite, and like PDE *whether*, *hwæþer* (*þe*) signals that some element in the clause is open to question. Discussion of *hwæþer* complements occurs in §4.5.9. Here only *þæt*-complements are considered. For discussion of negative syntax in *þæt*-complements, see §4.5.10.

Finite complements are typically associated with nouns, verbs and, occasionally, adjectives that are terms for speech events, e.g. *wedd* 'pledge', *að* 'oath', *andettan* 'think', mental states and activities, desires, obligations, and so forth, e.g. *leaf* 'permission', *hycgan* 'think', *unnan* 'wish, grant', *gedafenian* 'oblige' and *gemyndig* 'mindful'. As in PDE, they may function as complements of NPs or predicates, and as objects, or oblique NPs. However, there is one significant difference from PDE: as will be discussed below, complements that could, on the basis of their equivalents in PDE, be regarded as subjects actually either function as oblique NPs in impersonal constructions, as complements of NPs or predicates, or are undecidable. This is partly because, unlike in PDE, noun clauses cannot occur in sentence-initial position, i.e. there is no equivalent of *That they arrived so late is a problem*.

An example of a finite complement serving as the complement of an NP is:

(163) …þonne beo ic gemyndig mines weddes þæt ic nelle
       …then am I mindful of-my pledge that I not-will
       heonunforð mancyn mid wætere adrencan
       henceforward mankind with water   drown

(ÆChom I, 1 22.11)

and I am mindful of my pledge that henceforward I will not drown mankind with water.

Constructions of this type are much like their equivalents in PDE. The question is whether a construction such as the following, excerpted from (133) (for full example, see above p. 218), involves a complement of an NP, as in (163) or a complement that functions as a subject:

(133a) ... & þær is mid   Estum ðeaw,   þonne þær
       ... and there is among Ests   custom, when there
       bið man dead, þæt he lið inne   unforbærned ... monað
       is man dead, that he lies inside unburned ...   for-month

(Or 1 1.20.14)

and there is among the Estonians a custom that, when a man is dead, he lies inside unburned ... for a month.

In the absence of evidence that the complement in (133a) must be a subject, it is preferable to analyse it as a complement of an NP. Examples of sentential complements serving as objects and oblique NPs are (27), (34), (75), (85) and, with 'impersonal' verbs, (110) and (113). A complex example is to be found in Alfred's famous remarks on the advancement of learning:

(164) Forðy   me ðyncð betre, gif iow swæ ðyncð, ðæt
       Therefore me seems better, if you so seems, that
       we eac sumæ bec,   ða ðe niedbeðearfosta sien   eallum
       we also certain books, which most-necessary may-be to-all
       monnum to wiotonne, ðæt we ða   on ðæt geðiode
       men   to know,   that we those into that language
       wenden   ðe we ealle gecnawan mægen
       should-translate PT we all   know   may

(CPLetWærf 49)

Therefore it seems better to me, provided that it also seems better to you too, that we translate those books which are most necessary for everyone to know into the language that we are all able to understand.

In both (113) and (164) the þæt-clause may be taken to serve the stimulus function without also being subject or object, i.e. it could be an oblique NP. On the other hand, it could be the subject. In most cases with 'impersonal' verbs the analysis is undecidable. This is true also of constructions with a BE-verb and a predicate adjective such as (165) since the clause could be an oblique NP functioning as a stimulus:

(165) dyslic bið þæt hwa   woruldlice speda forhogie for
       foolish is that someone worldly   goods   despise for
       manna herunge
       of-men praise

(ÆCHom I, 4 60.32)

it is foolish to despise worldly goods in order to win the praise of men.

Even the presence of *hit* in an impersonal construction, as for example:

(166) Hit gedafenað þæt alleluia   sy gesungen
       It is-fitting   that Alleluiah be sung

       (ÆCHom II, 9.74.78)

       It is fitting that Alleluiah should be sung,

does not necessarily imply that the complement is functioning as subject, since *hit* can serve as a subject position filler without cataphoric function (cf. the discussion of *hit* as an 'empty subject' marker in §4.4.3.3). On the other hand, the only truly clear cases of complements that are neither subjects nor objects occur when a demonstrative in an oblique case is cataphoric to or parallel with a *þæt*-clause. For an example of the latter, see (110), repeated here:

(110) And þæs (GEN) us (ACC) ne scamað na,   ac þæs
       And of-that   to-us   not shames never, but of-that
       us (ACC) scamað swyþe þæt we bote   aginnan swa...swa
       to-us   shames very that we atonement begin   as...as
       bec   tæcan
       books teach

       (WHom 20.3 160)

       and we are not at all ashamed of that, but we are ashamed of this: of beginning atonement in the way that...the books teach.

In PDE *that* can be omitted after many verbs that govern an object complement, cf. *He decided Bill had left*. In OE *þæt* is usually absent before a complement that represents the exact words of the reported proposition, and when the subjects of the main clause and of the complement are the same. It is only occasionally absent if the complement represents the words indirectly (in the PDE sentence above the representation is indirect, since what was decided was presumably the proposition *Bill has left*) or if the subjects of the main clause and the complement are not the same. An example of omission of *þæt* introducing an indirect report is:

(167) ...and cwæð he wolde   wiðsacan his Criste
       ...and said he intended to-deny his Christ

       (ÆLS (Basil) 371)

       And he said he intended to deny his Christ.

Occasionally, a *þæt*-complement may occur without a full main

clause. Most instances of such constructions are in chapter headings.
Other contexts involve expressions denoting lapse of time:

(168) Þæs   ymb feower niht   þætte Martinus mære   galeorde
       From-that about four   nights that   Martin   borders left

(Men 207)

It was about four nights later that Martin left the country.

Mitchell (1985:§1974) shows that constructions of the type (*Oh*) *that
X might happen* (dependent desires without main clauses), which are
generally thought not to occur in OE, are actually evidenced in at least
a couple of texts, for example:

(169) Þæt sy gehalgod, hygecræftum   fæst, þin nama nu...
       That be blessed,   with-mental-powers firm, thy name now...

(LPr III 3)

Oh may your name be blessed now, you strong in mental power...

which translates the Latin *Sanctificetur nomen tuum* 'Blessed be thy name'.

The exact origin of the complementiser *þæt* is not entirely certain.
However, it seems likely that it originated in a neuter singular
demonstrative pronoun followed by an explanatory clause in apposition,
cf. *That was their custom: they the dead froze, He that said: Abraham was a
holy man.* This assumes that *þæt* as an object preceded the verb; when it
became a complementiser it became associated with the sentential
complement and followed the verb. At the time when the original
demonstrative introduced direct thought or speech, the tense and
person of the quoted sentence were presumably retained (*I/She that said:
I am leaving now*), but when it came to introduce indirect speech, the
tense, person and mood came to be anchored in the reporter's point of
view (with the assumed shift in position of the complementiser, *I/she
said that I/she was leaving then*). Instances of both direct and indirect
speech can be found in OE. However, there are apparently no instances
of free indirect speech in OE, where the person and tense are anchored
in the reporter, but the time and place adverbs are anchored in the
speaker or thinker quoted, and a quotative verb is absent (cf. PDE free
indirect speech *She was leaving now* vs. indirect speech *She said she was
leaving then/at that time*).

Traces of the origin of *þæt* complementisers in a deictic pronoun
referring cataphorically to the following clause are to be found in the use
of 'anticipatory' *þæt*, functioning either as subject or as object. The

pronominal force of an anticipatory object *þæt* is particularly clear when it occurs clause-initially:

(170) þæt gefremede Diulius hiora consul þæt þæt angin
        that arranged   Diulius their consul that that beginning
        wearð tidlice þurhtogen
        was   in-time achieved

                                                    (*Or* 4 6.172.2)

    Their consul Diulius arranged (it) that it was started on time.

(Cf. also the clause-internal object pronoun *þæt* in (227) below.) Traces of other presumably original uses of *þæt*-constructions with less highly integrated syntax than came to be the norm, at least in writing, can also be found in such examples as (90), which is repeated here:

(90) Geseoð mine handa & mine fet, þæt ic sylf   hit eom
      See   my   hands and my   feet, that I (my)self it am
                                    (*Lk* (*WSCp*) 24.39)

    See from my hands and feet that it is I.

As the translation shows, in later English the *that*-clause would not be treated as a double object parallel with 'hands and feet'.

    Whatever its origins, dependence of a *þæt*-clause on a verb governing a non-accusative, e.g. (110), suggests that *þæt* was not a pronoun but a complementiser, at least in some of its uses in OE. Additional evidence that *þæt* was a complementiser in OE is that, if there is a subordinate clause dependent on the *þæt*-clause, this subordinate clause usually precedes it; cf. (164) and:

(171) ...þohte gif he hi   ealle ofsloge, þæt se an ne
      ...thought if he them all   slew,   that that one not
      ætburste   þe he sohte
      would-escape PT he sought
                                  (*ÆCHom* I, 5 82.10)

    he thought that if he slew them all, the one he sought would not escape.

If *þæt* were still an object pronoun, we would expect it either to precede or to follow the verb immediately, and the embedded subordinate clause to follow it.

    Although an embedded subordinate usually precedes the complement clause if it is a conditional or follows the complement clause if it is a relative, it may sometimes be embedded within the complement, cf. (164). Especially if the embedded subordinate clause is lengthy, the complementiser and the subject may then be repeated (the repeated subject is typically in pronominal form):

(172)   Forðæm   hit is awriten ðætte Dauid, ða   he ðone
           Therefore it is written that   David, when he that
           læppan forcorfenne hæfde, ðæt he sloge on his heortan
           lappet cut-off   had,   that he beat on his heart

(CP 28 199.16)

Therefore it is written that, when he had cut off his lappet, David beat his breast.

Tense in *þæt* complements appears to be much as in PDE, in other words, it is dependent on whether the complement is reported or not, and whether it is reported directly or not. Constraints on the meaning of premodals have been discussed in § 4.3.2.3.

Choice of mood (indicative vs. subjunctive) in complements is extremely complex, and is not adequately understood. It depends in part on whether there is a negative or a modal verb in the main clause, in part on whether the report is direct or indirect, and in part on the lexical verb governing the complement. However, there appear to be no or at least few absolute rules. An example of a lexically-based distinction is the fact that *þencan* 'think' favours the subjunctive but *geþencan* the indicative. The distinction may be interpreted as reflecting a difference in meaning between 'I think' and 'I have come to think'. The second meaning is perfective/resultative, which correlates well with the use of the indicative.

The subjunctive is associated with such properties as unreality, potentiality, exhortation, wishes, desires, requests, commands, prohibitions, hypotheses, conjectures and doubts. It follows that the subjunctive is favoured when the main clause contains a negative, or when the governing verb is one of wish or doubt. For examples with mental verbs such as *þencan* and *þyncan*, see (164) and (171); with verbs and adjectives of being appropriate (therefore possible and to be desired) such as *gedafenian* 'be fitting', *gebyrian* 'behoove', *selost beon* 'be best', cf. (111), (158), (165) and (166); with verbs of ordering, and requesting, such as *bebeodan*, *hatan* 'order, bid', see (27). Expressions of desire are especially likely to introduce a subjunctive:

(173)   Forðy   ic wolde ðætte hie ealneg æt ðære stowe wæren (SUBJ)
           Therefore I wanted that   they always at that place were

(CP Let Wærf 73)

Therefore I wanted them always to be there.

The subjunctive is also widely used in reported speech, as is typical in the early Germanic languages. Originally this use may have been of the 'hear-say' type in which the reporter wished to avoid commitment to the truth of what was reported, or wished to cast doubt on it. However, by OE the use of the subjunctive had been conventionalised, cf. (34) and (172) (the latter contains a verb of writing), where there is no evidence that the reporter is casting doubt on the truth of the narrator. The following example is particularly interesting as it starts out with the conventional subjunctive and then switches in the third clause to the indicative:[10]

(174) Wulfstan sæde þæt he gefore (SUBJ) of   Hæðum, þæt
      Wulfstan said that he went   from Hedeby that
      he wære (SUBJ) on Truso on syfan dagum &   nihtum, ðæt þæt
      he was   in Druzno in seven days   and nights, that that
      scip wæs (INDIC) ealne weg yrnende under segle
      ship was   all   way running under sail

                                                        (*Or* 1 1.19.32)

Wulfstan said that he left from Hedeby, that he reached Druzno in seven days and nights, and that the ship was running under full sail all the way.

If there is a real question about the truth of the complement, the modal phrase *scul* + past tense 'was said to' is available, cf. (74) and:

(175) Ic wat   þæt ðu geherdest oft   reccan on ealdum leasum
      I know that you heard   often say   in old   lying
      spellum þætte Iob Saturnes sunu sceolde bion se hehsta god
      stories that Jove Saturn's son should be   the highest god
                                                        (*Bo* 35 98.25)

I know that you often heard tell in ancient false stories that Jove, the son of Saturn, was supposedly the highest god.

The indicative is associated with facts that have occurred, for example in (170). Here the action described in the complement results from action named by the governing verb, *gefremede* 'arranged'. Although, as has been indicated above, desires typically govern the subjunctive, if the desired event actually occurs then it can be expressed in the indicative:

(176) ...bebead   Tituse his suna þæt he towearp (INDIC) þæt
      ...commanded Titus his son that he overthrew   that
      templ
      temple
                                                        (*Or* 67.262.18)

and he commanded Titus his son to overthrow the temple, which he did.[11]

Indicative is also associated with events that are very likely to occur, and with general truths, cf. (133a) (p. 235) and (154). In the context of verbs of saying it is used mainly in direct reports (where the speech is not filtered by the reporter):

(177) Ic ðe   secge, þæt þu eart stænen
       I to-you say   that you are made-of-stone

(ÆCHom I, 26 364.23)

I say to you that you are made of stone.

As might be expected, complements of factive verbs, i.e. verbs and adjectives that govern complements the truth of which is known (e.g. verbs of knowing, remembering, being pleased), are normally indicative. However, they may be subjunctive if the main clause is negative, if the factive verb has a negative meaning such as *sceamian* 'be ashamed of', cf. (110) and (165), or if the reporter wishes to cast some doubt on the truth of the complement:

(178) Þa   geceas he him   ane burg   wiþ   þone sæ
       Then chose he for-them a   fortress facing that sea
       Bizantium wæs hatenu, to ðon þæt him   gelicade þæt hie
       Byzantium was called, to that that to-him pleased that they
       þær mehten (SUBJ) betst frið   binnan habban
       there might   best peace within have

(Or 3 7 116.4)

Then he chose a fortress facing the sea, called Byzantium, because he was pleased with the idea that they might best find peace there.

We may construe (178) as follows: the fact of the possibility pleased them; however, that they were going to have peace was not yet an established fact (and indeed, as Orosius goes on to show, did not come to pass). The function of the subjunctive is to cast doubt on the proposition 'they were going to have peace', and hence to suggest that their pleasure was ill-founded.

4.5.3.2 Non-finite complements
Non-finite complements in OE are infinitive constructions, the precursors of such PDE constructions as *She persuaded John to paint the kitchen, She expected John to paint the kitchen, She wanted to go, She wanted him*

to go, She saw him leave, She may go, etc. They are of two main morphological types:

(a) an infinitive with the suffix *-(i)an*, originally the nominative-accusative case marker for a neuter verbal noun, for example:

(179) He sæde þæt he... wolde fandian   hu longe þæt
       He said that he... wanted to-find-out how long that
       land norþryhte læge
       land northwards lay

                                        (*Or* 1 1.17.7)

(b) an infinitive with prepositional *to*, originally 'toward', and the inflected infinitive suffix *-anne/-enne*, originally the dative case marker for a verbal noun, for example:

(180) ...ne þe nan neod þearf ne lærde to wyrcanne
       ...nor thee no need   not taught to perform
       þæt þæt ðu   worhtest
       that that thou performedst

                                       (*Bo* 33.79.16)

     ...nor did any need teach you to perform what you performed.

Of these, the first (often called the 'bare infinitive') appears in prose and verse from earliest times. The inflected infinitive was of relatively limited occurrence in verse and indeed is quite rare in the earlier OE prose. Nevertheless, a few verbs seem to have required the inflected infinitive from early times, e.g. *agan* 'to possess and have as a duty', *habban* 'to have'. So also did certain constructions such as the infinitive complements of adjectives:

(181) & ða   syndon swyþe fægere... on to seonne
       and those are   very fair...   on to see

                                     (*Or* 1 3.32.12)

     and those are very beautiful... to look at.

Many of the examples in which the inflected infinitive occurs are semantically volitional, even purposive, as in (181), and this may have been the entry-point for the construction. In any event, the development of the inflected infinitive appears to conform to the increasing use of periphrasis found in the OE period, especially with respect to prepositional structures.

Infinitive complements in PDE are considerably constrained with respect to the constituents they may include. In OE, as in PDE, present participles can be constituents of infinitive complements, although this is rare. In OE they are limited to constructions with perception verbs, for example:

(182) Þonne þa   Lapithe gesawon Thesali   þæt folc
       When those Lapiths saw   Thessalians that people
       of   hiora horsum beon feohtende wið   hie...
       from their horses to-be fighting   against them...

(Or 1 9.42.32)

When the Lapiths saw the Thessalians fighting on horse-back against them...

This present participle construction does not occur in the early poetry and is very rare in Early West Saxon. It is, however, relatively frequent by Ælfric's time. It appears that the past participle cannot be a constituent of an active infinitive complement in OE (it can, however, be one in PDE, e.g. *He expected her to have left*).

Unambiguously passive infinitives (i.e. constructions with uninflected participles, see §4.4.3.1) are rare in OE. When they occur, they are always of the bare infinitive type, as in (74) and:

(183) Þa   het   he þysne biscop beon gelæded to þære stowe
       Then commanded he this   bishop to-be led   to that place
(GDPref 3(c) 11.194.17)

Then he commanded this bishop to be led to that place.

In the following example both the main clause and the complement are passive:

(184) ...heo wæron bewered   heora   weorum gemengde beon
       ...they were prevented with-their men   joined   to-be
(Bede 1 16.78.2)

they were prevented from being joined with their husbands.

Passive infinitive complements are generally believed to be calqued from Latin. However, as we have seen in the section on auxiliary verbs, the passive arose in OE out of resultative participial constructions, and often it is difficult to tell whether a construction is passive or resultative. Constructions such as the following with the inflected resultative participial are found relatively frequently:

(185) ðonne magon hie ðeah   weorðan gehælede
       then   may   they nevertheless become healed
(CP 51.399.17)

then may they nevertheless be healed.

This, together with evidence from the growth of auxiliaries and periphrastic constructions in general, suggests that the passive infinitive may have been a native development, though supported by the Latin passive infinitive.

In PDE infinitive complements may serve as subjects or as objects of verbs (cf. *To err is human, to forgive divine, I wanted to leave*). In OE there are a few instances of what might be regarded as subjects in impersonal constructions. But as has been shown in §4.5.3.1, it is usually undecidable whether complements in impersonal constructions are really subjects rather than oblique objects. They are probably oblique:

(186) … þus unc gedafnað ealle rihtwisnesse gefyllan
       … thus us   is-fitting all   righteousness to-fulfil   (*Mt* (*WSCp*) 3.15)

       … thus we ought to do everything that is righteous.

The potential ambiguity of constructions such as (186) may have made the spread and nativisation of subject infinitive complements with copulas possible. Subject infinitives of copula constructions appear originally to have been Latinisms. However, the development in very late OE of constructions with a bare infinitive functioning as the subject of a passive sentence, appears to be native, see (74), which is repeated here:

(74) &   to þam Pentecosten wæs gesewen… blod weallan   of
      and at that Pentecost   was seen…   blood to-well-up from
      eorþan. swa swa mænige sædan þe hit geseon sceoldan
      earth. as as   many   said PT it see   should
                                              (*Chron* E (Plummer) 1100.4)

      and at the Pentecost … blood was seen welling up from the ground, as many said who were supposed to have seen it.

It is likely that such nativisation was not actually wide-spread until after the OE period.

Infinitive complements in OE are for the most part objects of transitive verbs. Most of the work on infinitive complements in OE has focused on the status of the so-called 'accusative and infinitive' and 'dative and infinitive' constructions: those in which there is an accusative or dative NP and an infinitive complement, cf. (182) and (183). The structure can be characterised as NP1 – V – NP2 – INF. The question is what syntactic and semantic relationship holds between NP2 and V on the one hand and between NP2 and INF on the other. In PDE at least three possible relationships can be distinguished:

(a) NP2 functions as both the object of the higher verb and the subject of the lower verb, cf. *She persuaded him to go* = 'She persuaded him that he should go'. Verbs requiring this construction are called 'object control' verbs. Since the subject of the lower clause is required to be referentially the same as the object of the higher clause, the meaning relations between sentences with active and passive complements are not the same. Thus *I persuaded Jim to visit David* is not equivalent in meaning to *I persuaded David to be visited by Jim*. Furthermore, the object of a verb of the object control type must be human or at least animate, compare the oddity of *I persuaded the kitchen to be clean*.

(b) NP2 functions as the subject of the lower clause, and is not a constituent of the higher clause, cf. *She expected Jim to paint the kitchen* = 'She expected that Jim would paint the kitchen'. If the subject of the lower verb is co-referential with the subject of the higher verb, then there is no NP2 (cf. *She expected to paint the kitchen*). This is called 'subject-to-object raising' (the subject of the lower clause appears to be the object of the higher clause). Sentences with active and passive complements mean approximately the same thing, cf. *She expected Jim to paint the kitchen*, *She expected the kitchen to be painted by Jim*. Unlike objects of object-control verbs, objects of subject-to-object raising constructions can be both inanimate and animate, cf. *She expected the kitchen to be clean*. Furthermore, in PDE it is possible for a *there* to occur instead of NP2 if the subject of the lower clause is indefinite, cf. *I expected there to be five cleaners in the building* (but not **I persuaded there to be five cleaners in the building*).

(c) NP2 functions only as the object of the higher verb, and not as a constituent of the lower verb, cf. *She promised Jim to paint the kitchen* = 'She promised Jim that she would paint the kitchen', not **'She promised Jim that he would paint the kitchen'. NP2 cannot be passivised (cf. **Jim was promised to paint the kitchen*). Verbs of this type are called 'subject-control' verbs.

It is difficult to apply all the criteria used for PDE to OE infinitive complements to determine whether the distinction between these three types of construction existed, especially since passive constructions are rare, and without native speakers it is impossible to test whether, for example, a *there* can be inserted into the complement (as in the case of *expect-* but not of *promise-*type verbs). Nevertheless, a number of criteria allow some distinctions to be made, most especially the availability of alternative finite *þæt*-complements, and the negative evidence of the failure of certain constructions to occur. On the basis of such evidence, it is relatively easy to distinguish object-control verb constructions from the other two in OE (see Fischer 1990).

Evidence for the existence of a category of object-control (*persuade*-type) verbs is the availability of alternative finite complement constructions of the type NP1 – V – NP2 – *þæt* complement, and the unavailability of inanimate objects in NP2 position. Thus beside:

(187)   &   ealne þone here   he het   mid þæm scipum
        and all   that   army   he commanded   with those ships
        þonan wendan
        thence to-go   (*Or* 4.10.202.7)

and he commanded the whole army to leave with the ships.

there is:

(188)   ...ða   heht   he his geferan   ðæt hio   sohton sumne
        ...then commanded he his comrades that they sought some
        earmne ðearfan
        poor   needy person   (*Bede* 5 2.388.10)

...then he commanded his comrades to seek out a poor person.

An interesting example of both constructions side by side is:

(189)   ...siþþan gelicade eallum folcum þæt hie   Romanum
        ...after   pleased   all   peoples that they to-Romans
        underþieded wære, &   hiora æ   to behealdanne
        subjected   were, and their law to observe
                                               (*Or* 3 5.106.22)

...afterwards all the peoples were pleased to be subjected to the Romans and to observe their laws.

It should be noted that the verb *hatan* and other verbs of commanding can also occur in constructions of the type:

(190)   Ða   bebead   se   biscop ðeosne   to him lædan
        Then commanded that bishop this-one to him to-lead
                                          (*Bede* 5 2.388.20)

Then the bishop commanded this one to be led to him.

This particular example, like some others, is used to translate a Latin construction with a passive infinitive, in this case:

(190a)   Hunc ergo   adduci   praecipit episcopus
         This   therefore to-be-led ordered   bishop

Therefore the bishop ordered this one to be led (to him).

In (190) no NP referring to the person(s) commanded is present as either the object/oblique NP of the higher clause or as the subject of the lower clause. Therefore what appears as NP2 is actually the object ('this man') of the lower clause: *The bishop commanded someone: someone was to lead this man to him*. Absence of both the object of the higher clause and the object of the lower clause appears to be possible only when they have indefinite reference. Such constructions are therefore often translated as passives; however, they have no passive morphology and should be treated as special cases of NP reduction.

Object control verbs in OE include *hatan* 'command', *biddan* 'command', *forbeodan* 'forbid', *befæstan* 'entrust (to do)', *forgifan* 'give (to do)'. Most are evidenced in constructions with two NP objects (i.e. in 'ditransitive' constructions) as well as with infinitive complements. Thus *bebeodan* can occur with a complement clause as in (190), and also with two objects:

(191) …and him bebead   seofon dagena fæsten
       …and him commanded seven of-days fast

(ÆChom I, 29 434.20)

And commanded him to fast seven days.

(*fæsten* is the accusative object, *him* the oblique object). Most object control verbs take dative (oblique) NP2s, and allow the inflected infinitive. *Hatan* and *biddan*, however, often have accusative objects, and disfavour the inflected infinitive.

In contrast to object control constructions, subject-to-object raising (*expect*-type) constructions in OE have no animacy restrictions on NP2. NP2 is typically accusative, not dative, see (192). Further, in contrast to object-control verbs, many verbs allowing subject-to-object raising may also occur with NP1 – V – *þæt* complement constructions (i.e. the main clause has no object), see (193), or else they have simple transitive instead of ditransitive counterparts, see (194):

(192) þa   hie gesawan þa   deadan men swa þiclice
       when they saw   those dead   men so   thickly
       to eorþan beran
       to earth   to-fall

(Or 3 10.138.23)

when they saw the dead men fall to earth in such thick masses.

(193) …ic geseo þæt þu   will tæcan
       …I see   that thou wilt teach

(ÆGram 150.16)

(194) swa ic nu geseo þa sunnan myd mines lichaman ægan
       so I now see that sun   with my   body's   eyes

(*Solil* 1 31.8)

as I now see the sun with my own eyes.

Fischer (1990) suggests that the verbs in this group include several sets, most especially verbs of physical and mental perception, e.g. *geseon* 'see', *gefrignan* 'learn, find out' and verbs of causation: *lætan* 'allow, cause', *don* 'cause'. There is a constraint on perception verbs that the infinitive can be used only when the time reference of the main clause is the same as that of the complement, a constraint that does not hold with *þæt* complements of the same verb (contrast (192) and (193)). She argues that true mental state verbs like *know*, *believe* did not occur in such constructions until Middle English.

Formal criteria for distinguishing subject-control (*promise*-type) verbs in OE, from object-control verbs and subject-to-object raising verbs are slim. However, some verbs including *behatan* and *gehatan* 'promise' appear to be equivalent to subject-control verbs, primarily on grounds of meaning:

(195)   ...& eallan folce behet   ealle þa   unriht to
        ...and to-all people promised all   those wrongs to
        aleggenne þe on his broðer timan wæran
        reverse   PT in his brother's time were

(*Chron* E (Plummer) 1100.33)

and promised everyone that he would reverse all the wrongs that had occurred in his brother's time.

(196)   ...& griðode   wið þone cyng. & behet   man him þæt
        ...and made-peace with that king. and promised one him that
        he moste worðe beon ælc þæra   þinga þe he ær   ahte
        he could entitled be   to-all of those things PT he before had

(*Chron* E (Plummer) 1046.24)

...and made peace with the king. And he was promised that he would be entitled to all his former possessions.

Other non-finite complement constructions are found in OE, but are considerably less frequent. Only two types will be mentioned here. One is complements of intransitive verbs of motion, most especially *cuman* 'come' and *gewitan* 'go, depart', compare (10) and:

(197) ...þa com þær færlice   yrnan an þearle wod cu
       ...then came there by-chance to-run a very   mad cow

(ÆLS (Martin) 1038)

then by chance there came running a very mad cow.

These occur in the early poetry. By the time of Ælfric, however, the participial construction familiar in PDE was taking over. In continuation of (197) we find:

(198) Heo com þa   yrnende mid egeslicum eagum
       She came then running with terrifying eyes

(ÆLS (Martin) 1043)

She then came running with terrifying eyes.

The second type of construction to be mentioned here is complements of adjectival predicates like *gearu* 'ready' and *geornfull* 'eager', *eaþe* 'easy' and *earfoþe* 'difficult', all of which normally take inflected infinitives, for example:

(199) ...þæt þu   swiðe geornfull wære hit to gehyranne
       ...that thou very eager   wert it to hear

(Bo 22.51.6)

and (119), which is repeated here:

(119) Swa þonne is me   nu   swiþe earfeðe hiera mod to ahwettane
       Thus then   is to-me now very   difficult their spirit to excite

(Or 4 13.212.30)

Thus then it is very difficult for me to excite their spirit.

As the distinction between (199) and (119) reveals, 'eager'- and 'easy'-type verbs are syntactically distinctive in OE. The former have nominative subjects, the latter are impersonal with dative experiencers, and no subject. There is therefore no surface parallelism between the two types such as is found in PDE *John is eager to please*, *John is easy to please*.

One type of non-finite complement construction that occurs in PDE but apparently not in OE is the 'subject-to-subject' raising construction that optionally occurs with verbs like *seem*, and *happen*, e.g. *John seems to like beans* (beside *It seems that John likes beans*), *John happens to be my friend*. In other words, OE *þyncan* 'seem', and *gelimpan* 'happen' appear not to occur in constructions of the type ***Alfred þyncþ min lareow beon* 'Alfred seems to be my teacher'.

4.5.4   Clauses of purpose and result

Clauses of purposes (also called 'final clauses') and of result (also called 'consecutive clauses') share a number of properties. Both can be expressed either by finite clauses or by infinitives.

Finite clauses of purpose and result are for the most part introduced by the same conjunctions, though with some differences in frequency. The commonest conjunction introducing both purpose and result clauses is *þæt*, though there is a slight decline in the frequency of this form in result clauses in the later OE period. Other conjunctions (occurring chiefly in prose) include *swa* (...) *þæt(te)* and prepositional phrases such as *to DEM* (...) *þæt(te)* and *for DEM* (...) *þæt*. An example of a purpose clause with the latter conjunction is:

(200)   Oft   eac becymð se   anwald þisse   worulde to swiðe
        Often also comes that power of-this world   to very
        goodum monnum, forðæm þæt se   anwald þara   yfelena
        good   men,   so-that   that power of-those evil-ones
        weorðe toworpen
        may-be overthrown

                                              (*Bo* 39.133.19)

    Often power over this world is given to very good men, so that the power of evil men may be overthrown.

The only conjunction associated with purpose or result clauses that cannot introduce both is *þy læs* (*þe*) 'lest' which is restricted to negative purpose clauses, cf. (131) and (268) below.

As far as the infinitive forms of purpose and result clauses are concerned, the uninflected form is preferred in poetry, while the inflected form is the norm in prose. An example of the latter is:

(201)   þonon he wæs sended Ongolþeode Godes word to
        thence he was sent   to-English   God's word to
        bodienne & to læranne
        proclaim and to teach

                                        (*Bede* 4 4.272.24)

    he was sent from there to proclaim and teach God's word to the English.

However, the uninflected forms can also occur, especially in formulaic, and therefore probably archaic, phrases, see (33).

In view of the development of the *for to* construction in Middle English, it is interesting to note that Callaway (1913:148) cites one, very late, example of a purposive construction with *for to*, citing it as the only instance in OE:

(202) …oc se   kyng hit dide for to hauene sibbe of   se   eorl
       …but that king it   did   for to have   peace from that earl
       of Angeow. &   for helpe to hauene togænes his neue   Willelm
       of Anjou.   and for help to have   against his nephew William

(*Chron* E (Plummer) 1127.10)

but the king did it to have peace from the Earl of Anjou and to have aid against his nephew William.

As indicated, the evidence for a grammatical distinction between purpose and result clauses is on the whole quite slim. The one area where a partial distinction is made is in mood (provided there is an overt morphological contrast in the verb in question). Subjunctive usually signals a purpose clause, cf. (20), (200) and (203), and indicative a result clause, cf. (204):

(203) Þæt ic wille eac gescadwislecor gesecgean, þæt hit
       That I will also more-wisely say,   that it
       mon geornor   ongietan   mæge (SUBJ)
       one more-exactly understand may   (*Or* 1.60.8)

I will also say it more carefully, so that it may be better understood.

(204) Þa   sume dæge se   niðfulla   deofol… wearp þa
       Then one day that malicious devil… threw then
       ænne stan to ðære bellan, þæt heo eall   tosprang (INDIC)
       one stone at that bell,   that it completely flew-to-pieces

(*ÆCHom* II, 11 93.32)

Then one day the malicious devil…threw a stone at the bell, so that it burst into pieces.

However, the distinction was not rigidly observed. As the last example shows, result is often interpreted as the outcome of purpose, and so the potential mood distinction between purpose and result can be blurred. In OE this pragmatic blurring allowed for purpose clauses to be expressed in the indicative. Conversely, contemplated, hypothetical results could appear in the subjunctive, obscuring any one to one corresponding between result clauses and indicative mood. Example (205) illustrates a subjunctive result clause following a negated antecedent clause:

(205) Nis   þeahhwæðere nan   man to þam dyrstig þæt he on
       Not-is however   not-one man to that rash   that he on

nihtlicere tide binnon þære cyrcan cuman durre (SUBJ)
night   time within that church come   dare

(ÆCHom I, 34 508.30)

However, no one is so rash that he would dare to enter the church at
night.

4.5.5   Causal clauses

Causal clauses in PDE are typically marked by *because/since/as...there-
fore/so...* (or, recently, *the reason...is because...*). Causal clauses are
often distinguished semantically/pragmatically according to a number
of parameters. One possible set of distinctions is according to whether
they are 'external' (based in external reality), 'internal' (based in the
speaker's world of reasoning) or 'rhetorical' (based in the discourse
situation). Examples of the difference are: (a) *He came because he
wanted to see you*, meaning 'His reason for coming was that he wanted
to see you' (external); (b) *He must be here because his bicycle is outside*,
meaning 'The reason I think he is here is that his bicycle is outside'
(internal); and (c) *Since you are so smart, what is 234 times 468*, meaning
'My reason for asking "What is 234 times 468" is that you claim you are
so smart' (rhetorical). Another set of distinctions among causal clauses
is according to whether the information in the causal clause is assumed
to be known ('given') or not. *Since you are so smart, what is 234 times 468?*
is an example of a 'given' causal (it assumes that the addressee has said
something about being smart, or is known to be smart).

In PDE there are morphological and syntactic correlates for these
differences. Most noticeable is the use of *since* and *as* for 'given' causals
(note that neither can be used in answer to a *why* question: *Why are you
late? **Since/As I missed the bus*). Furthermore, the conjunction *for* is
used for those kinds of 'internal' causals that function as explanation
and ground rather than assertion of a true causal relation. *For*-clauses
are restricted to post-main clause position. By contrast, 'rhetorical
causals' of the type exemplified above are restricted to pre-main clause
position. Similar, though not identical, lexical distinctions among causal
connectives have been noted for Latin, cf. *quia* 'because', *quoniam*
'since' and *enim* 'for'.

A striking feature of OE is that such distinctions are difficult to
establish on morphological or even syntactic grounds, except in a few
cases. Instead, the prototypical causal construction in OE consists of a
clause introduced by *for* + DEM + the optional particle *þe*, in either pre-

or post-main clause position. However, it is possible to make explicit such assumptions as givenness; an example is 'because you said that' in (208) below.

It is usually assumed that the 'because'-clause is subordinate in OE, largely because the equivalent clause-type in PDE is subordinate. However, the strongly deictic character of the causal marker, and the optional absence of the particle *þe*, suggest that in OE causal constructions were not as distinctly subordinate as in PDE (see the discussion of the role of *þe* and of hypotaxis vs. parataxis in the introduction to §4.5). Indeed, the original construction in PrOE was probably a paratactic one. *For + DEM* in the 'therefore'-clause was either anaphoric to a preceding sentence, or cataphoric to a following clause, cf. PDE *She left. For that [reason] I was able to finish my work* (referring back), and *The reason I was able to finish my work was that she left* (referring forward). Similarly, the *for + DEM* in the 'because'-clause was either anaphoric (cf. *that* in the last example), or cataphoric (schematically, but not really translatable into PDE, *For that [reason]: she left, for that [reason] I was able to finish my work*). By the earliest OE period, constructions of this type co-existed with others in which the 'because'-clause was clearly subordinate because it was marked with the subordinator *þe*, but we cannot tell whether *for + DEM* in the sense of 'because' had been reanalysed as a subordinator.

The most frequent forms for the 'because'-clause marker are *for þæm / þam / þan / þon (þe)*. A few dozen examples occur of *for þy / þi (þe)*. Both *for þæm* and *for þy* occasionally occur with *þæt* rather than *þe*. Constructions with *þe* seem more likely than those without to express true source or cause rather than explanation. Examples of *forþon þe* in a strictly causal sense, and *forþæm* in an explanatory sense are:

(206) Ða   cwæð ic: Hwy? Ða   cwæð he: Forðon þe we witon
       Then said I: Why? Then said he: For-that PT we know
       swiðe lytel ðæs   þe ær   us wæs buton be gemynde
       very little of-that PT before us was except by reflection

                              (*Bo* 148.7,8)

       Then I said: 'Why?'. Then he said: 'Because we know very little about what preceded us except from thinking about it.'

(207) Sume   men cweþaþ on Englisc þæt hit sie feaxede
       Likewise men say   in English that it is long-haired
       steorra. forþæm þær stent lang leoma of
       star.   because there stands long light from

                       (*Chron* A (Plummer) 892.3)

> Likewise people call it the long-haired star in English because a long ray of light streams from it.

The 'therefore'-clause need not have a causal marker; alternatively, it may be marked by an adverbial *for + DEM*. In the latter case, when there is a conjoined 'because'-clause in the same sentence, the construction is co-relative, and, as in colloquial PDE, the 'therefore'-clause usually precedes the 'because'-clause, cf. (115) and:

(208) Forþam þu   sædest þæt þu   wræccea wære &   bereafod
       For-that thou saidst that thou exile   wert and deprived
       ælces godes forðon þu   nestes   hwæt þu   wære
       of-all wealth for-that thou not-knewest what thou wert

       (Bo 5 13.17)

> The reason you said you were exiled and deprived of all wealth was that you did not know what you were.

Occasionally the co-relative construction is of the form *for + DEM ... þe*, that is, the prepositional connective in the 'because'-clause is absent, and only the subordinating particle *þe* is present. An example with *forðæm ... þe* is:

(209) Ac forðæm hie cueðað ðas   word ðe hie belucað
       But for-that they say   these words PT they close
       hiera modes earan ongean ða   godcundan lare
       their soul's ears   against that divine   teaching

       (CP 45.337.21)

> But the reason they say these words is that they close their soul's ears against the divine teaching.

Among other conjunctions marking cause is *þæs (þe)*, as in:

(210) ...Waa me   þæs   ic swigode
       ...Woe to-me because I was silent

       (CP 49.379.22)

This form may be derived in part from constructions in which the genitive expresses the source (cf. the genitive case associated with the source of pleasure in *brucan* 'enjoy'). Alternatively, it may be derived from temporal *þæs þe* 'after, from the time that', since causal connectives including PDE *since* often derive in the languages of the world from temporals.

The main temporal adverb to be used as a causal connective in OE was *nu* 'now'. Like *since* it indicates a given cause ('now, seeing that ...'); it also indicates that the state of affairs in the causal clause still continues at the time of the main clause. The causal meaning appears originally to have derived from the sense of 'at this starting point in time', but the temporal meaning seems entirely absent in at least a few cases, e.g.

(211) Untwylice   þu lyhst þæt ðu   God
       Without-doubt thou liest that thou God
       sy. nu ðu   nast   manna geþohtas
       art. now thou not-knowest of-men thoughts

(ÆCHom I, 26 378.6)

Certainly you lie saying that you are God, since you do not know men's thoughts.

Other temporals such as *þa* 'than', *þonne* 'then', and *siþþan* 'after' can sometimes be interpreted with causal meanings, but can almost always be construed as temporals as well. For example, it is not possible to tell to what degree *siþþan* must be interpreted as causal rather than temporal in:

(212) Þa,   siþþan   he irre   wæs &   gewundod, he
       Then, after/since he angry was and wounded,   he
       ofslog micel þæs   folces
       slew   much of-that troop

(Or 4 156.11)

(Note that *gewundod* favours a strongly temporal interpretation, but *irre* favours a more causal one.)

'Because'- clauses are typically indicative unless they are negative (i.e. express a denied cause), in which case they are usually subjunctive. A particularly telling example is:

(213) ...ac þæs   wundrodon men, na for ði   þæt hit mare
       ...but of-that wondered   men, not for that that it more
       wundor wære (SUBJ), ac   for ði   þæt hit wæs (INDIC)
       wonder were,   but for that that it was
       ungewunelic
       unaccustomed

(ÆCHom I, 12 184.26)

...but people wondered about that, not because it was a greater mystery, but because it was unaccustomed.

The first 'because'-clause is subjunctive because the proposition is denied, but the second is indicative because it was the real reason for the wonder.

4.5.6   Conditional, concessive conditional and concessive clauses

Conditional (*if…then*), concessive conditional (*even if*) and concessive (*although*) clauses are of great complexity semantically and pragmatically. However, they are relatively straightforward syntactically, and will be dealt with only briefly here.

In conditional clauses, the subordinate 'if'-clause advances a possible or hypothetical state of affairs under which the main 'then'-clause is true. In OE the prototypical conditional sentence is marked by *gif…þonne*, cognate with the PDE prototypical conditional markers. In general, conditionals have indicative in both 'if'- and 'then'-clauses. The following three examples illustrate future, past and present possibilities, respectively.

(214)   …Gif þes bealdwyrda biscop acweald ne bið (INDIC),
        …If this bold   bishop killed   not will-be
(ÆCHom I, 29 420.1)

If this bold bishop is not killed, the fear we bring will not be terrible.

(215)   Þæt is gif   min fot aslad (INDIC), Drihten, ðin
        That is if/whenever my foot slipped,   Lord,   thy
        mildheortnys geheolp (INDIC) me
        mercy   helped   me
(ÆCHom II, 28 227.202)

If my foot slipped, Oh Lord, your mercy aided me.

(216)   And we sceolon (INDIC)… ure mod geclænsian, gif
        And we must…   our spirit cleanse,   if
        we willað (INDIC) Cristes lichaman ðicgan
        we want   Christ's body   to-accept
(ÆCHom II, 15 158.270)

and we must…cleanse our spirit if we want to receive Christ's body.

However, the subjunctive may often be used in the 'if'-clause when the 'then'-clause contains an imperative or an exhortation, especially in the present tense. Mitchell (1985:§§3560–91) shows that the traditional statement that subjunctive is used when there is a volitional in the 'then'-clause is incorrect, since *sculan* and *willan* in the 'if'-clause frequently block use of the subjunctive. For example, (216) has the indicative. Examples (217) and (218) illustrate the subjunctive after an imperative and after a subjunctive of exhortation, respectively:

(217) Fed (IMP) ðonne min sceap, gif ðu   me lufige (SUBJ)
       Feed   then my sheep if thou me love

(CP 43.4)

Then feed my sheep if you love me.

(218) ... Gif hwa   ðenige (SUBJ), ðenige (EXHORT) he suelce
       ... If   someone serve,   serve   he as-if
       he hit of   Godes mægene ðenige
       he it from God's might   serve

(CP 44.323.3)

If someone is to serve, he should serve as if he served through God's
might.

The past subjunctive is also used to express imaginary and unreal
(including counterfactual) conditionality. In this case both clauses are
subjunctive. Since no inflexional distinction is made in OE between
unreality in past, present or future, adverbs may be used to distinguish
specific time-relations, but usually the time-relations are determined
from the context. Example (219) illustrates a counterfactual in the past,
(220) a counterfactual in the present:

(219) ... & ðær frecenlice   gewundod wearð, & eac ofslagen
       ... and there dangerously wounded was,   and even slain
       wære (PAST SUBJ), gif his sunu his ne gehulpe (PAST SUBJ)
       would-have-been,   if his son   him not had-helped

(Or 4 8.186.22)

... and was dangerously wounded there, and would even have been
killed, had his son not helped him.

(220) Hwæt, ge witon þæt ge giet todæge wæron (PAST SUBJ)
       What, you know that you still today were
       Somnitum þeowe, gif ge him ne alugen (PAST SUBJ) iowra
       to-Samnites slaves, if you them not had-belied   your
       wedd
       vows

(Or 3 8.122.11)

Listen, you know that you would still today be the Samnites' slaves,
if you had not betrayed your vows to them.[12]

An alternative for the imaginary or unreal conditional is þær plus the
subjunctive in both clauses:

(221) Ðær we us selfum demden,   ðonne ne demde
       There we our selves had-judged, then not would-have-judged

us no God
us not God

(CP 53 415.7)

If we judged ourselves, then God would not judge us.[13]

Strong evidence that *þær* did indeed have a conditional meaning comes from the fact that *if* and *þær* are sometimes found in parallel conditional constructions. Furthermore, they can be found alternating in different manuscripts of the same work.

As in PDE, a number of non-conditional connectives can be interpreted as conditionals. Among these is the temporal *þonne* in the sense 'whenever'. Also as in PDE, the conditional form can be interpreted in a number of different ways in different contexts. For one, it can be used with the 'factual' meaning of 'if, as you know/say', as in:

(222) Syððan he hæfde hyra fet aþwogene... Gif ic þwoh   eowre
       After he had   their feet washed...   If I washed your
       fet ic eow sealde bysene þæt ge don   swa ic eow   dyde
       feet I you gave   example that you should-do as I to-you did

(Jn (WSCp) 13.12)

After he had washed their feet... If I washed you feet, I gave you an example that you should do to others as I did to you.

It may also occasionally be interpreted as a concessive conditional (*even if*), where the 'then'-clause is asserted to be unexpectedly true despite the fact that the 'if'-clause is true. A possible example of a concessive conditional is:

(223) ...and gif eowere synna wæron wolcnreade ær   ðan, hi
       ...and if your   sins were scarlet   before then, they
       beoð scinende on snawes hwitnysse
       are shining in snow's whiteness

(ÆCHom II, 21 184.139)

...and even if your sins were once scarlet, they are now shining with the whiteness of snow.

In concessive ('even though, although') clauses the main clause is asserted to be true despite the fact that the 'although'-clause is true. The prototypical marker of concession in OE is the conjunction *þeah (þe)*, for example:

(224) & þeah   þæt folc   nolde   ær   Gode   abugan,
       and although that people not-wanted earlier to-God obey,

hy hwæðre þa hyra unðances him gehyrsume
they nevertheless then at-their unwillingness to-him obedient
wæron
were

(Or 1 7.38.17)

and although that people had not wanted to obey God earlier, they
then were nevertheless against their will obedient to him.

Concessives of this type typically take the subjunctive in the 'although'-
clause, even though the factuality of the concessive clause is asserted.

As in many other languages, concession is often not uniquely
marked, but can be interpreted from conditional, causal, comparative
and co-ordinate clause relations. An example of co-ordinate clauses
understood to be in concessive relation is:

(225) Eall þis yfel þu dydest, and ic swugode and þolode
       All this evil thou didst, and I was-silent and endured

(Ps 49.22)

Although you did all this evil, I was silent and endured.

Here the mood of both clauses is indicative. This contrasts with co-
ordinate clauses that can have conditional interpretations. These
typically involve an imperative first clause:

(226) Seceaþ & ge hit findaþ
       Seek   and you it will-find   (Mt (WSCp) 7.7)

Seek and you will find it (If you seek, you will find it).

4.5.7 *Temporal clauses*

The most common temporal conjunctions signifying 'when' in OE are
þa (occasionally þa þa), and, only in the prose, þonne (very rarely þonne
þonne). Þa is almost exclusively associated with past tense and narrative
sequence, i.e. individual events or states of affairs, cf. (1), (75), (172) and:

(227) Ða   on morgenne gehierdun þæt þæs   cyninges þegnas þe
       When in morning heard   that of-the king's thanes PT
       him beæftan wærun þæt se   cyning ofslægen wæs, þa
       him behind were   that that king   slain   was, then
       ridon hie þider
       rode they thither   (Chron A (Plummer) 755.23)

In the morning when the king's thanes who had been left behind
heard that he had been killed, then they rode there.

Þonne has a much wider distribution. It may reference an individual event or state of affairs, cf. (18) and (182), in which case it seems to have the same function as *þa*, which it later replaced, although in some instances it may have a more causal sense than *þa*. However, its main function is to express repeated action, cf. (133a) (see above p. 235) and, from the story of Caedmon:

> (228) ...þonne   he geseah þa hearpan him   nealecan, þonne
> ...whenever he saw   that harp   to-him approach, then
> aras   he forscome from þæm symble... þa   he þæt þa
> arose he for-shame from that feast...   when he þæt on-that
> sumre tide   dyde...
> one   occasion did...
>
> (Bede 4 25.342.20)

> whenever he saw the harp approaching him, he arose for shame from the feast... When he did that on one occasion...

A number of other conjunctions occur with a temporal sense. Among those with the meaning of 'when' is *þær* 'there, when' (in the sense of both 'at that time' and 'whenever'),

> (229) ...ac clummiað mid ceaflum þar   hi   scoldan clipian
> ...but mutter   with jaws   there they should speak-aloud
>
> (WHom 16b 13)

> ...but mutter with their jaws when they should speak aloud.

Others express overlap in time, for example *þenden* 'while' (mainly in poetry), and conjunctions originating as prepositional phrases (used mainly in prose) such as *þa hwile þe* 'while', cf. (21), (133) and *swa lange swa* 'as long as'. The former does not have the concessive meaning 'although' that is found in PDE, but the latter can have a conditional 'if, provided that' interpretation, as in PDE.

The main conjunctions expressing temporal sequence are *siþþan*, and *æfter þæm þe* (used only in prose). *Æfter* alone is not used as a conjunction. *Æfter þæm þe* primarily signals a sequence:

> (230) Þa   on ðam ilcan dæge æfter þæm þe hie   þiss
> Then on that same day   after that PT they this
> gesprecen hæfdon, fuhton Gallie on   þa   burg
> said   had,   fought Gauls against that fortress
>
> (Or 2 8.92.7)

> Then on that same day after they had said this, the Gauls attacked the fortress.

While *siþþan* can also express simple sequencing of events, its main function is to specify the beginning point of an event, and can often be translated as 'from the time that'. Contrast (230) where *æfter* should be translated as 'from the time that' with:

(231) Ac siþþan hie on Sicilium wunnon, hie eac siþþan
       But since they in Sicily   fought,   they also afterwards
       betweonum him selfum winnende wæron, oþ þæt Darius
       among   them selves fighting   were,   until Darius
       Persia   cyning, Læcedemonium on fultume wearþ
       Persians' king, Laecedemonians in help   became

       (*Or* 2 7.90.8)

But from the time that they fought in Sicily, they were also fighting among themselves, until Darius, king of the Persians, came to help the Laecedemonians.

A third conjunction, *þæs þe*, appears to have the function of both *æfter* and *siþþan*. It is relatively rare except in the Chronicle, Orosius and Bede, for example:

(232) & se here   com þa to þeodforda binnon [iii]
       and the enemy-army came then to Thetford within three
       wuca þæs þe hi ær   gehergodon Norðwic
       weeks of-that PT they before ravaged   Norwich

       (*Chron* E 135.11 (1004))

and the enemy army then reached Thetford within three weeks after they had ravaged Norwich.

Immediate sequence is signalled chiefly by *sona* in compound phrases such as *sona swa* 'as soon as' and, in the prose, *sona þa*, *sona mid*, etc.

The conjunctions discussed in the previous paragraph mark the earlier of two or more events as subordinate to the later event. The main conjunctions that mark the later of two events as subordinate to the earlier are *ær* (*þæm* (*þe*)) 'before' and *oþ* (*þæt*) 'until', see (18).

Whereas most subordinate temporal clauses are indicative, except when the main clause is imperative or expresses a wish, subordinate clauses introduced by *ær* are generally subjunctive if the main clause is indicative. It appears that in the older Germanic languages in general, cognates of *ær* introduce subjunctive clauses after a positive main clause, indicative clauses after a negative main clause, but the division is not so clearcut in OE, especially in the prose.[14]

4.5.8   Clauses of comparison

Clauses of comparison can be distinguished according to whether they compare equals (e.g. *John is as tall as Bill* (*is*), *They went the same way we did*), or unequals (e.g. *Mike is taller than Bill* (*is*)). The main conjunctions in OE expressing comparison of equality are *swa* (*swa*) (...*swa*):

> (233)   ne eom ic wyrþe þæt ic swa hangie   swa min drihten
> not am I worthy that I so   should-hang as my lord
> > (*ÆCHom* I, 26, 382.8)
>
> I am not worthy to hang like my Lord.

The main conjunction expressing comparison of inequality is *þonne*:

> (234)   ...ma   manna fægnodon dysiges folces   gedwolan þonne
> ...more men   rejoiced-at foolish people's heresy   than
> hie fægnedon soþra spella
> they rejoiced-at true   words
> > (*BoHead* 30)
>
> ...more people rejoiced at the heresies of foolish people than rejoiced at the truth.

As in PDE clauses of both equal and unequal comparison, if the verb in both clauses refers to a similar event, it may be repeated, as in (234) (note the optionally repeated subject here). Alternatively, it may be substituted by the pro-verb *don* 'to do':

> (235)   ...and hit weox swa swa oðre cild   doð buton   synne anum
> ...and it grew as   other children do without sin   one
> > (*ÆCHom* I, 1 24.33)
>
> and it grew as do other children without any sin.

> (236)   ...for ðan þe he brycð   swiðor on ðone suðdæl
> ...for that PT it breaks-forth more on that south
> þonne he do   on þone norðdæl
> than   it does on that north
> > (*Or* 1 1.24.24)
>
> because it (the Mediterranean) washes more violently on the southern shore than it does on the northern.

Yet again, the verb may be zero as in (233), and:

> (237)   Þone hetolan   deofol he het   middaneardes ealdor,
> That malignant devil   he named middle-earth's prince,
> for ðan þe he hæfð ofer þa   unrihtwisan micelne ealdordom,
> for that PT he has   over those unrighteous great   power,

> þe þisne middaneard   lufiað swiðor þonne þone scyppend þe
> PT this   middle-earth love   more   than   that creator   PT
> gesceop þysne middaneard
> created this   middle-earth
>
> (ÆCHom 7 173)

He named that malignant devil prince of the world, because he has greater power over the unrighteous, who love this world more than the Lord who created this world.

Clauses of comparison of equality (*swa*-clauses) are usually indicative, especially in poetry. However, some examples are found of subjunctive *swa* comparatives subordinated to volitionals, dependent commands and wishes:

> (238)   ...Deme ge nu,   swa swa ge willon (SUBJ) þæt eow   sy
>   ...Judge you now, as   you wish   that to-you be
>   eft   gedemed
>   afterward judged
>
> (HomS 17 (BlHom 5) 130)

Judge now as you wish to be judged later.

Swa and some other conjunctions like *swelc(e)* 'such', occurring either alone or in combination, may be used to express comparatives involving a hypothesis ('as if'), whether merely hypothetical or counterfactual:

> (239)   Hu   Romanum wearð an wundor oþiewed swelce se
>   How to-Romans was   a miracle shown as-if that
>   heofon burne
>   heaven burned
>
> (Head 128.6)

How the Romans were shown a miracle as if heaven burned.

Such comparatives are usually in the subjunctive. Mitchell (1985:§§3378–81) notes that the construction differs from the equivalent in PDE because the present rather than past subjunctive is used with present tense main clauses (i.e. the equivalent of *He runs as if he be tired*, rather than *He runs as if he were tired*):

> (240)   Hu,   ne bið he ðonne swelce he sie (PRES SUBJ) his slaga,
>   What, not is he then as-if he be   his slayer,
>   ðonne he hine mæg gehælan & nyle?
>   when he him may heal   and not-will?
>
> (CP 38.275.9)

What, isn't he as if he were his slayer, if he can heal him and does not wish to?

There is a tendency for the clause of comparison of inequality to be subjunctive if the main clause is positive, and indicative if the main clause is negative. An example of the first case is (236) (*do* is subjunctive). An example of the second case is:

(241) ...ne geortriewe ic na   Gode   þæt he us ne mæge
       ...not distrust   I never to-God that he us not can
       gescildan to beteran tidun þonne we nu   on sint (INDIC)
       shield   for better   times than we now in are

(Or 2 5.86.2)

I do not doubt that God can protect us for better times than we are now in.

There are some examples in OE prose of comparative constructions cognate with PDE *I am the better for it*, *The more the better*. In OE, they are largely constructions with adverbs of comparison, although adjectives occur too. The usual forms are *þon/þy/þe* + comparative + *þe*. In the following examples, *þon/þy/þe* are glossed as COMPAR.

(242)   And sealdon us bysne.   þæt we ne sceolon ...urne geleafan
        And gave   us command. that we not ought   ...our faith
        forlætan, and fram Criste bugan þe   ma   þe hi   dydon
        abandon, and from Christ turn   COMPAR more PT they did

(ÆCHom I, 14.1 212.23)

And commanded us not to abandon our faith and turn from Christ, any more than they did.

Following Small (1930), Mitchell (1985:§3243ff.) argues that the first element (*þon/þy/þe*) derives from an instrumental of comparison meaning 'before that' or 'than before', not an instrumental of cause or measure, as has often been suggested. The reason is that when the standard of comparison is not present, the demonstrative always refers back to something that has been referred to, or can be assumed to be known, rather than to a cause or measure, for example:

(243)   ...Gif hit [blod] swiðe read sie oþþe won þonne bið hit
        ...If it [blood] very red be or   dark then is it
        þy   þe   swiþor to lætanne, gif hit clæne oþþe hluttor
        therefore COMPAR more to let,   if it clean or   clear
        sie læt þy   þe   læsse
        be let therefore COMPAR less

(Lch II(2) 42.1.7)

Here the first COMPAR must mean 'than usual', and the second must mean 'than mentioned above'; neither a causal nor a measure interpretation is semantically plausible. According to Small (1930:384–5), (243) can therefore be translated as: 'If the blood be very red or dark, then it is to be let for that reason more abundantly than usual; if it be clean or clear then because of that, let less than before'.

4.5.9   *Interrogative clauses*

As in PDE, interrogatives clauses can be either main clauses or subordinate clauses. As in PDE they can also be either yes-no interrogatives asking about the truth of the proposition, or content questions asking about the identity of the NP questioned.

In simple clauses, yes-no interrogatives are typically indicative clauses in verb – subject order:

(244)   Hæfst þu   ænigne geferan?
Hast   thou any   companion?

(ÆColl 28)

Do you have any companion?

They may, however, be introduced by the form *hwæþer*, literally 'which of two?'; in this case the order is *hwæþer* – subject – verb. Such constructions are usually in the present subjunctive, though indicative constructions are occasionally found, especially with 'impersonal' verbs. Non-subjunctive *hwæþer* interrogatives may be rhetorical, but they are primarily favoured when the speaker emphasises doubt or incredulity and perhaps even expects the answer 'No', and indeed often translate Latin *num*, which invites a negative answer. Some examples are:

(245)   Hwæðer ge nu   secan gold on treowum?
Whether you now seek gold in trees?

(Bo 32.73.24)

Are you looking for gold in trees?/Surely you aren't looking for gold in trees.

(246)   Hwæþer Romane hit witen nu   ænegum men to secganne,
Whether Romans it know now to-any   men to say,
hwæt   hiera folces... forwurde?
much-many of-their people... perished?

(Or 5 2.220.8)

Do the Romans now know enough to say how many of their people perished?/Surely the Romans know enough...

In complex sentences, *hwæþer* introduces interrogative sentential complements. Like *þæt*-complements, *hwæþer*-complements may be complements of NPs and objects or oblique NPs of verbs and adjectival predicates; there is no unambiguous evidence that they function as subjects, although they may do so in some copula constructions. Also like *þæt*-complements, they clearly have a pronominal origin, thus *hwæþer* is cataphoric to *þe ... þe* 'either ... or' in:

(247) Nat   ic, cwæð Orosius, hwæðer   mare wundor
       Not-know I,   said   Orosius, which-or-two more wonder
       wæs þe þæt he swa mid lytle fultume þone mæstan dæl þisses
       was PT that he so with small help   that greater part of-this
       middangeardes gegan   mehte þe þæt he mid swa lytle werode
       world   conquer might PT that he with so   small troop
       swa micel anginne dorste
       so   large attack   dared

                                                          (*Or* 3 9.124.13)

I do not know, said Orosius, which was the greater marvel, either that he was able to conquer the greater part of this world with such a small troop, or that he dared make such a large attack with such a small troop.

Hwæþer-clauses always follow the main clause. In (248) and (249) the complement serves the source/stimulus function of the impersonal verb *tweonian* 'doubt', and of the adjectival predicate *orwene beon* 'be in despair', respectively:

(248) ...ac us   twynað hwæðer ge magon maran deopnysse
       ...but to-us doubts whether you may   more depth
       þæron þearflice tocnawan
       therein usefully discern

                                                          (*ÆCHom* I, 36 556.13)

...but we doubt whether you may usefully see greater depth in it.

(249) ...for þon þe hie   wæron orwene   hwæðer æfre Romane
       ...because   they were   despairing whether ever Romans
       to heora anwealde becomen
       to their power   would-come

                                                          (*Or* 4 9.192.3)

because they despaired whether the Romans would ever come to succeed over them (Hannibal and his troops).

In the following, the complement is probably the complement of the NP *micel twynung* rather than the subject:

(250) ða wearð micel twynung... hwæðer hi ineodon oððe...
then was great doubt... whether they went-in or...

(ÆCHom I, 34, 506.17)

then there was considerable doubt... whether they should go in or...

Simple content-questions contain one or more interrogative pronouns such as *hwa* 'who', *hwæt* 'what', *hwelc* 'which', *hu* 'how', and *hwær* 'where'. An example is:

(251) Hwæt getacniað ðonne ða twelf oxan buton ða
What signify then those twelve oxen except those
XII apostolas?
XII apostles?

(CP 16.105.5)

What do those twelve oxen signify other than the twelve apostles?

Most content-questions are indicative, but some subjunctive examples are found. These may express surprise or doubt on the part of the speaker, but do not necessarily do so.

Like *hwæþer*-clauses, content questions may be complements of NPs, and objects or oblique NPs of verbs and adjectival predicates of question and doubt. An example with a content question functioning as object is:

(252) ða eode se biscop into þære oþere cyrcan þær se
then went that bishop into that other church where that
martyr inne læig, and befran þone cyrcweard hwær
martyr inside lay, and asked that churchwarden where
þæs halgan wæpnu wæron
of-that holy-man weapons were

(ÆCHom I, 30 452.1)

then the bishop went into the other church in which the martyr lay, and asked the warden where the holy man's weapons were.

4.5.10 *Negative clauses*

Any clause, simple or complex, finite or non-finite, may be negated. Negation in simple clauses ('sentence' negation) in OE is expressed by the preverbal adverb *ne*, which precedes the finite verb (the auxiliary if there is one, otherwise the main verb):

(253) ...ac hie ne dorston þær on cuman
...but they not dared there in come

(Or 1 1.17.27)

...but they did not dare enter there.

Especially in West Saxon, *ne* can be optionally cliticised and attached to a small set of verbs (whether main verbs or auxiliaries) such as *habb-* 'have', *wes-* 'be', *wit-* 'know', *willan* 'want':

(254) He nolde   beon cyning
       He neg-want to-be king

(CP 3.33.19)

He didn't want to be king.

The negated verb is usually in initial position in main clauses, see (247). However, if the subject is a personal pronoun, the latter sometimes precedes (254). Adverbs of place and time, e.g. *þær*, *þa*, exclamations, e.g. *hu* as in (240), and connectives, e.g. *ac* as in (253), and so forth, regularly precede the negative clause. Exceptions are found mainly in poetry.

Negation can also be expressed by use of a negative indefinite pronoun (including adverbial pronoun) or quantifier. It apparently must be so expressed in non-finite clauses. Synchronically, the negative pronouns and quantifiers can be considered to be derived by cliticisation of *ne* to a pronoun. Historically they are derived from earlier *ni*+pronoun or quantifier, cf. neg+*a* 'ever' → *na* 'never, not at all' (often used to introduce contrasting NPs, adjectives, or adverbs, and also non-finite clauses), neg.+*æfre* 'ever' → *næfre* 'never', neg+*a-wiht* 'anything' → *na-wiht/noht* 'nothing' (the earlier form of PDE *not*), neg+*an* 'one' → *nan* 'no'. The constraints on the position of indefinite quantifiers and adverbs dictate the position of these negatives.

Negative concord (also called 'multiple negation') is common, especially in the prose, but not obligatory. Negative adverbs other than *ne* , e.g. *na*, *nalles* (mainly found in poetry), *næfre* may negate finite verbs, with or without *ne*. *Ne* may or may not appear with negative pronouns and quantifiers. Examples with negative concord are:

(255) ...þæt he na   siþþan geboren ne wurde
       ...that he never after   born   not would-be

(Or 6 9.264.13)

that he would not be born afterward.

(256) & ne bið ðær nænig ealo gebrowen mid   Estum
       and not is   there any   ale   brewed   among Ests

(Or 1 1.20.18)

and no ale is brewed among the Ests.

An example of *na* without negative concord is:

(257)   &   cwæð þæt hit na   geweorþan   sceolde þæt...
        and said   that it   never come-to-pass ought that...

(Or 4 6.178.19)

and said that it should never come to pass that...

In PDE a non-negated indefinite quantifier cannot precede the negated verb, cf. ***Anybody didn't come* as opposed to *Nobody came*. But a few examples of an initial non-negative indefinite preceding a negative particle do occur in OE,[15] such as:

(258)   And riht is þæt ænig cristen   man blod   ne   þycge
        And law is that any   Christian man blood not should-drink

(WCan 1.1.2 (Fowler) 53)

And it is a law that no Christian should drink blood.

We turn now to some brief discussion of negation in co-ordination, complementation, and other kinds of complex sentence construction. Negative co-ordination, whether of clauses, NPs, adjectives or adverbs, is typically expressed by *ne* or *naþer* 'neither'. An example of negative adjective co-ordination is:

(259)   ...nu   nit nawþer nyle   beon ne scearp ne heard
        ...now it neither not-will be   not sharp not hard

(Or 4 13.212.29)

now that it [their spirit] wishes to be neither sharp nor hard.

Negative clause co-ordination is illustrated by (72) and:

(260)   Nis   he na gesceapen, ne he nis   na gesceaft
        Not-is he not created,   nor he not-is not creation

(ÆHom 1 169)

He [God] is not created, nor is he a creation.

In contrastive constructions where the first of two elements is negated, the patterns *ne...ac*, *na...ac*, *nalles...ac* 'not...but' are found; of these the first is most frequent in the prose. Negative concord is particularly prevalent in contrastive constructions. The contrastive negative usually immediately precedes the negated element as in:

(261)   ...ac se monandæg nis   na fyrmest daga   on þære
        ...but that Monday   not-is not first   of-days in that
        wucan, ac is se   oþer
        week, but is that second   (*ÆCHom* I, 6 100.23)

        ...but Monday is not the first day of the week, but the second.

However, the negative is sometimes separated from the element it contrasts:

(262)   Ne sind we na Abrahames cynnes flæsclice, ac gastlice
        Not are we not Abraham's of-kin physically, but spiritually
                                                      (*ÆCHom* I, 13 204.21)

        We are of Abraham's kin not in the flesh but in the spirit.

When the second of two alternatives is a constituent of a clause and is negated, it is preceded by (*ond*) *na*, see (263). However, if the alternative is a clause, *ac...ne* is usually found, see (264).

(263)   ...for ðan þe he is god and na gesceaft
        ...because PT he is God and not creature   (*ÆCHom* I, 2 40.12)

        ...because he is God and not created.

(264)   Stanas sind gesceafta,   ac hi   nabbað   nan lif ne
        Stones are created-things, but they not-have no life nor
        hi   naht   ne gefredað
        they nothing not feel   (*ÆCHom* I, 21 302.13)

        Stones are created, but they have no life and do not feel anything.

As far as complementation is concerned, certain verbs which take *þæt*-complements and express negative meanings, such as *forbeodan* 'forbid', *forberan* 'refrain from', *geswican* 'stop', *wiðcweðan* 'deny, refuse', optionally introduce negative forms into complements that are themselves affirmative propositions. An example without a negative marker in the complement is:

(265)   ... & forbead þæt hiene mon god hete
        ...and forbade that him   one God called   (*Or* 6 1.254.6)

        forbade anyone to call him God.

and one with a negative marker is:

(266)   & forbead þæt mon na   ðær eft   ne timbrede
        and forbade that one never there after not built
                                                          (*Or* 6 7.262.21)

        and forbade anyone to build there afterward.

Expressions of doubt like *tweonan* 'doubt', *tweo beon* 'be in doubt', when negated in the main clause, may also introduce negative complements with affirmative meanings, for example:

(267) ...forþon   nis   nan tweo   þæt he forgifnesse syllan
       ...therefore not-is no   doubt that he forgiveness give
       nelle   þam   þe hie geearnian willaþ
       not-will to-them PT it   earn   want   (*HomS* 17 (*BlHom* 5) 178)

> ...therefore there is no doubt that he will give forgiveness to those who want to earn it.

It should be noted that verbs of forbidding, denying, doubting and so forth, have negative properties in PDE, cf. the use of *any* rather than *some* in the complement in *I forbid you to do anything* (not **I forbid you to do something*). Negative concord interacts with these verbs in OE to allow the overt negative in the complement.

There do not appear to be examples of 'negative-raising' as illustrated by PDE *I don't suppose he's coming* which is roughly equivalent to, but pragmatically weaker in meaning than, *I suppose he isn't coming*. However, as will be seen below in connection with (270) and (271), there are some similar-looking constructions in contrastive constructions.

Finite purposive clauses that are negative are either negated like other finite clauses, or are introduced by *þy læs* (*þe*) 'lest, so that... not' (lit. 'by-that less (PT)'), see (131). The particle *þe* is used only in the later period. An example of the construction with *þy læs* alone is:

(268) &   eall his cynn mon ofslog, þy   læs hit monn
       and all his kin one slew,   by-that less it one
       uferan dogore wræcce
       on-later day   avenge   (*Or* 4 5.168.5)

> and all his kindred were slain, lest it might be avenged later.

Negative non-finite purposive clauses of the type *He paid him not to do it* do not appear to occur, but there are instances of contrastive non-finite negative purposives such as:

(269) We sind asende to gecigenne mancynn fram deaðe to life
       We are sent   to call-forth mankind from death to life,
       na to scufenne   fram life to deaðe
       not to deliver-up from life to death   (*ÆCHom* II, 38 283.128)

> We are sent to summon mankind from death to life, not to deliver them up from life to death.

Sometimes a construction may be used with a negative in the main clause as well as in the purposive:

(270)   ac he ne com na to demenne mancynn... ac to gehælenne
         but he not came not to judge   mankind... but to save

                                                                   (*ÆCHom* I, 22 320.5)

        but he came not to judge mankind... but to save them.

This looks rather like the 'raised negative' construction in PDE of the type *He didn't come to bury Caesar but to praise him* (= 'He came not to... but to... '); however, since the purposive is also negative, it may actually be a case of forward-looking concord, as in (262).

    Similar constructions occur in complex sentences involving causals; again, the negative may occur in the main clause, although it logically belongs to the subordinate clause:

(271)   Ne cwæð he ðeah   no ðæt ðæt he cwæð forðæmðe
        Not said he however not that that he said for-that-PT
        he gesinscipe tælde,   ac forðæmðe he wolde ða   sorga
        he marriage censured, but for-that-PT he wanted those sorrows
        awegadrifan ðisse   middangeardes
        away-drive of-this world

                                                     (*CP* 51.401.11)

        he said what he said, however, not because he disapproved of marriage, but because he wanted to drive away the sorrows of this world.

    For negative conditionals, *if... not* can be expressed in OE by *gif... ne*, *nymþe/nemne* 'unless', and *butan* (< preposition 'except' < adverb 'outside'). *Gif... ne* takes the indicative, see (272); however, *nymþe/nemne* usually takes the subjunctive, see (273), and conditional *butan* always does so:

(272)   Gif ðu   þe hraðor ne gewitst (INDIC) fram Iacobe, and buton
        If   thou PT sooner not turnst   from Jacob, and if-not
        ðu   wyrige (SUBJ) Cristes naman, þu   scealt beon beheafdod
        thou curse   Christ's name, thou shalt be   beheaded
        samod   mid him
        together with him

                                              (*ÆCHom* II, 31–32 246.165)

        Unless you turn right away from Jacob, and unless you curse Christ's name, you shall be beheaded together with him.

(273)   ...he bið feorhscyldig,   nimþe se   cyng
        ...he is   liable-for-his-life, if-not that king

alyfan wille (SUBJ) þæt man wergylde alysan mote
allow will,   that one weregild pay   may

(LawGrið 15)

...he is liable for his life, unless the king allows one to pay ransom.

4.6   Word order and the order of clauses

4.6.1   *Word order within the clause*

The types of word order patterns available in the OE period are more
numerous and variable than those of PDE. In the past there has been
little agreement on whether there was a 'basic' word order in OE, or
what the exact word order changes during the OE period were. One
thing that has been fairly well established, however, is that word order
was not free; rather, different word order patterns co-existed, and usage
was consistent within a pattern. One of the main reasons for the lack of
agreement on whether or not there was a basic word order in OE is that
most earlier works on OE word order focused on the order of words in
adjacent phrases rather than in the clause as a whole (see e.g. Bacquet
1962), and therefore missed the extent to which OE word order
conforms to the general typological characteristics of word order
patterns around the world. More recently, it has been shown that the
clause is the proper domain for word order study. Once this approach
is taken, it becomes clear that there was a basic order in OE (see e.g.
Lightfoot (1979), Bean (1983) and Kemenade (1987)).

In this section it is assumed that the observations in Greenberg
(1966), expanded and modified by Hawkins (1983), are essentially
correct, namely that in the languages of the world there are two
fundamentally contrasting word order patterns within the clause: those
that are verb-final, and those that are verb-non-final (proto-typically
verb-initial, but other variants are found, such as verb-second, or verb-
medial). Patterns at the phrase level are strongly correlated with these
two basic types. If a verb-final type changes to a verb-non-final type,
there will naturally be co-existing patterns; there will, however, not be
indeterminate word order. Normally, if change occurs, the pattern of
main clauses changes before that of subordinate clauses.

Verb-final patterns (i.e. of the type *I John saw*) typically involve
[Modifier – Head] order. Among phrases with [Modifier – Head] order,
[Possessor – Head] is a particularly salient construction, e.g. *the cat's
tail*. Languages in which such patterns predominate are usually postpositional (e.g. *herein*) or have case inflections. By contrast, verb-non-

final patterns (i.e. of the type *then saw I him, I saw him*, etc.) typically involve [Head – Modifier] order, including [Head – Possessor], e.g. *the tail of the cat*. Languages in which such patterns predominate are usually prepositional (e.g. *in here*).

A much oversimplified sketch of some major typological contrasts follows. Subject, object, noun, adjective, demonstrative, possessive, preposition and postposition are abbreviated as S, O, N, A, Dem, Poss, Prep and Post respectively, main verb as V and auxiliary verb as Auxil.

	Verb-final			Verb-non-final	
OV	him saw		VO	saw him
V Auxil	gone have		Auxil V	have gone
AN	young thief		NA	thief young
Dem N	that woman		N Dem	woman that
Poss N	bird's feather		N Poss	feather of bird
N + Case	bird's		Prep N	of bird, in London
N Post	London in			

As this sketch suggests, PDE has many verb-non-final characteristics, but by no means all; most notably N A is a very rare order, cf. *the only rivers navigable are…* as opposed to *the only navigable rivers are…* where the first order is used to express a temporal contingency that is expected to change. Furthermore, N Dem does not occur at all in Standard English. PDE also permits the N Poss construction to co-exist and in many cases co-vary with Poss N.

Despite the co-existence of verb-final with verb-non-final characteristics, PDE is basically verb-non-final, or VO in most respects. By contrast, OE is very different. It is basically verb-final, or OV in most respects. The shift from OE word order to modern English word order effectively took place in the Middle English period and will be discussed at length in volume II of this History. The reason why PDE still has some verb-final characteristics is that the change has not gone to completion in all parts of the grammar, but as we will see, basic patterns may be overridden by other phenomena, and so it is far from certain that PDE will ever become rigidly VO. Furthermore, in many respects OE word order patterns are like those in other West Germanic languages such as German and Dutch, and these have not undergone substantial shifts to VO order.

The basic OV word order of OE is most easily observed in

subordinate clauses, cf. the clauses introduced by *nimþe* 'unless' and *þæt* 'that' in (273). In main clauses, it is overridden by two patterns which, although perhaps of independent origin, nevertheless fed each other, and together laid the seeds for the word order change that took place in Middle English.

Most important for OE is what is often called verb-second ('V2') order in most main clauses. By V2 order is meant the placement of finite (i.e. tensed) verbs following an initial constituent, typically an adverb. Pronominal adverbs of locative, temporal or negative origin (e.g. *þær* 'there', *þa* 'then', *na* 'not at all, never', *ne* 'not') in main clauses usually favour the V2, i.e. [Adverb – Finite Verb...] order, cf. (19), (252) and (262). This word order is particularly strongly favoured with *þa* 'then', but less so with other adverbs such as *her* 'here, in this year' (indeed, some adverbs, like *ær* 'before', actually favour [Subject – Verb] order). In *hw-* questions the order is usually [Interrogative – Verb...]. PDE has maintained this order constraint in interrogatives and in some negative constructions, cf. *Why did she leave?, Never had she played so well.*

Although the examples given above involve simple pronominal adverbs, adverbial phrases also often favour V2, as in (14) and (29). The following example emphasises that V2 has nothing to do with the number of words preceding the finite verb, but only with the number of constituents. In this case the initial constituent is an adverbial phrase of time, with its own dependent relative clause:

(274)   On þæs caseres   dagum þe wæs gehaten Licinius wearð
        In that emperor's days   PT was called   Licinius was
        astyred   mycel ehtnys   ofer þa   Cristenan
        stirred-up much persecution over those Christians
(ÆLS (Forty Soldiers))

In the days of the emperor called Licinius there was much persecution of the Christians.

This example also illustrates the point that V2 has nothing to do with subject position. Subject can precede V2 as in numerous examples such as (6) and (12); but it can also follow as in (274) and (277) below.

In transitive main clauses, V2 could lead to the separation of finite auxiliaries from their main verbs, since the finite verb precedes the object which itself precedes the main verb, as would be expected in an OV structure. This is illustrated by (79), which is repeated here:

(79) Hu   wolde þe   nu lician gif…
      How would to-thee now please if…

(Bo 41.142.2)

How would it now please you if…

The second phenomenon that complicates OE word order is the fact that light, i.e. phonologically short, often adverbial or pronominal, forms, were preferred clause-initially, especially in the middle period around 1000, and heavy elements, typically complex phrases or subordinate clauses, were preferred sentence-finally. PDE still favours light elements clause-initially at least in clauses with indefinite subjects (cf. the use of quasi-subject *there*), and there are still remnants of the preference for heavy elements in clause-final position, e.g. *Bill gave Joan a book about the history of pronouns in Germanic* (rather than *Bill gave a book about the history of pronouns in Germanic to Joan*). But in general the light-heavy distibution is no longer a major factor in English word order.

The preference for light elements at the beginning of the clause is presumably an extension of the strong preference in earlier OE for pronominal adverbs like *her* and *þa* to trigger V2. It led, however, to a situation which was not entirely consistent with V2, which is the stacking of pronominal elements at the beginning of the clause. This can be seen in examples like (44), where the order is [Subject – Object – Finite verb]: AECHom I, 1 14.9 *Ic ðe secge* 'I to-you say…'

The preference for heavy elements at the end of the clause likewise led to a situation that was not entirely consistent with OV word order in subordinate clauses. For example, in true verb-final order, the finite verb would be expected to occur at the end after prepositional phrases. However, prepositional phrases often occur clause-finally in subordinate clauses, as in (275) below.

Throughout the OE period, then, we see a gradual shift from greater to lesser use of verb-final patterns. However, object pronouns tend to precede verbs, that is, they occur in [Object – Verb] order, even when most other patterns are verb-non-final. Some researchers argue that the word order change was primarily motivated by the increased role in the middle period of light versus heavy elements (see Strang 1970). Others have suggested that the loss of subject versus object inflection on nouns, but not pronouns, led to potential ambiguity between nominal subjects and objects. This potential ambiguity was avoided by allowing the verb to intervene, so favouring [Verb – Object] order (Bean 1983). Probably both of these factors worked together to contribute to the word order change, but it seems likely that the role of light and heavy elements was the prime factor (Kemenade 1987).

For the classical Alfredian and even Ælfrician periods of OE, we can sum up by generalising and saying that the predominant word order in OE was O V, with V2 in main clauses. The difference between, for example, [þa – Subject ... Verb] and [þa – Verb – Subject ...] can often be used to distinguish a subordinate clause introduced by a conjunction from a main clause introduced by an adverb, as in (1), (75) and:

(275)   Ða   he þiderweard seglode fram Sciringes heale, þa   wæs
           When he thither   sailed from Skiringssalr   then
           him   on þæt bæcbord Denamearc
           to-him on that larboard Denmark   (*Or* 1 1.19.24)

    When he sailed there from Skiringssalr, Denmark was on his larboard side.

However, the distinction was never rigid, and can be regarded only as a tendency. It usually fails to occur in correlative causals, for example, which may have parallel [Subject – Verb] order in both clauses, cf. (208) and (209). It certainly cannot be used as a sure test of main vs. subordinate clause status.

Furthermore, co-ordinate clauses introduced by *and* are V2 if a locative adverbial phrase or an adverb like *ne* or *þær* is present, cf. (13), (74) and (256). Otherwise, they tend to be verb-final, like subordinate clauses, cf. (7) and (56). This characteristic can be attributed to the fact that, from a discourse perspective, co-ordinate clause elaborate on the initial main clause and in this sense modify it, although they are not syntactically subordinate.

In the Chronicle a sequence of events is typically expressed by co-ordinate clauses and no shift of subject. By contrast, events introduced by þa, her, or a similar locative adverb, followed by a verb, signal a new episode in the sequence, typically with a new subject. It has been suggested by Hopper (1986) that differences in word order can therefore be exploited to give pragmatic cues to reference. In PDE we expect nominals to do the work of distinguishing reference, and it has traditionally been thought that OE syntax was somewhat non-literate in so far as referential distinctions are sometimes not made where they would be expected in PDE. However, if word order was used to distinguish reference, then this point of view is incorrect. Hopper suggests that in (276) [þa – Verb ...] signals a change of subject, and so there is no referential ambiguity concerning the *hie* of *budon hie* versus the *hie* of *cwædon hie*. Since [*ond*...Verb] signals continuity of subject reference, there is therefore also no ambiguity about the referent of *hie cwædon*:

(276)   & þa   budon hie hiera   mægum þat hie gesunde
        and then offered they to-their kinsmen that they unharmed
        from eodon; & hie cuædon þat tæt ilce hiera
        away should-go,and they said   that that same to-their
        geferum geboden wære, þe ær   mid þæm cyninge
        comrades offered were, PT earlier with that king
        wærun. Þa   cuædon hie þæt hie hie   þæs   ne
        were. Then said   they that they them-selves of-that not
        ne onmunden...
        not would-regard...

(Chron A (Plummer) 755.21)

And then they (the king's thanes) offered to allow their kinsmen to go away unharmed, and said that the same had been offered to their own comrades who had been with the king earlier (i.e. when he was slain). And then they (the kinsmen) replied that they would not consider it...[16]

If word order had the pragmatic force of indicating topic-shift, as Hopper suggests, this force is most clearly seen in the 755 Chronicle entry, from which (276) is taken. This entry is the story of Cynewulf and Cyneheard, and is usually thought to be somewhat archaic. During the Old English period, the putative pragmatic force of [þa – Verb...] versus [*ond*...Verb] order diminished, most especially in non-narrative contexts, primarily because verb-final order was in recession. However, in narrative contexts there continue to be some striking examples of the use of verb-initial word order to convey pragmatic information similar to that discussed above. In Bede's story of Cædmon, the hero is introduced as follows:

(277)   In ðeosse abbudissan mynstre wæs sum broðor syndriglice
        In this   abbess'   minster was a   brother specially
        mid godcundre gife gemæred &   geweorðad
        with divine   gift celebrated and honoured

(Bede 4 25.342.3)

In this abbess' minster one brother was especially proclaimed and honoured for having a divine gift.

Here the adverbial phrase of location ('in this abbess' minster'), although not pronominal, refers back to a given topic (the abbess); the verb follows the adverbial phrase, as is typical after locative adverbs; and then a new character (the brother) is introduced. Here we see the continued function of the [Adverb – Verb...] construction illustrated in (276): to introduce a new subject. Several co-ordinate clauses follow (277) describing the nature of the divine gift: to compose songs of praise to the Lord without any prior education. These are verb-final and descriptive, but do not convey the same pragmatic function of topic-continuity as in the 755 Chronicle, since the subjects change. When the description is complete, Bede starts to tell the story of how this gift came to Cædmon. This new section begins:

(278) Wæs he se   mon in weoruldhade geseted
       Was he that man in secular life   placed

(Bede 4 25.342.19)

This man was of the secular order.

Here we have a verb-initial clause followed by a pronoun referring forward to a full NP. The word order signals that a new segment of information is beginning, and is a device for reintroducing for renewed attention a topic that has already been mentioned.

The pragmatic use of word order is particularly clearly seen in topicalised NP constructions. In PDE a topicalised NP is a clause-initial NP that refers to material that is already evoked in the discourse or that belongs semantically to a set that has been evoked. The pragmatic effect of topicalisation is to draw particular attention to the NP, often as a contrastive instance of a given category. In *Beans I like*, *beans* is the topicalised NP.[17] The sentence is appropriate either if a number of vegetables have already been mentioned, or if the set of vegetables has been mentioned; for example, it could be used as an answer to *Do you like beans, peas and avocados?* or to *Do you like vegetables?* The identifying and highlighting function of topicalisation is often made overt by the presence of a relative clause (cf. *It is that same city which was ruthlessly destroyed later that year*). In OE as in PDE the topicalised NP is fronted to the beginning of the clause (it can, however, be preceded by a conjunction or an adverb). Examples of topicalised subject are (24) and:

(279) Seo ilce burg Babylonia, seo ðe mæst   wæs & ærest
       That same city Babylon,   REL PT greatest was and first
       ealra burga, seo is nu   læst &   westast
       of-all cities, it is now least and most-deserted

(Or 2 4.74.22)

> As for that same city of Babylon, which was the greatest and first among all cities, it is now the least and the most deserted.

In these examples, the topicalised NP does not leave a gap but rather, the clausal position is filled with a 'resumptive' demonstrative pronoun (see also (281) below). Indeed, topicalised NPs typically do not leave a gap in OE, although they may do so.

Usually the topicalised NP carries the case required by its grammatical function in the clause. Examples of a topicalised genitive NP are (110) and:

(280) Ðara   iglanda (GEN) þe man hæt Ciclades
      Of-those islands   PT one calls Cyclades
      þara (GEN) sindon þreo &   fiftig
      of-them   are   three and fifty
                                                        (*Or* 1 1.26.35)

Of the islands that one calls the Cyclades, there are fifty-three.

There are, however, instances of topicalised NPs that do not carry the expected oblique case, but are in the nominative:

(281) Þa   land (NOM) þe man hæt Gallia Bellica, be eastan
      Those lands   PT one calls Gaul Belgic, at east
      þæm (DAT) is sio ea   þe man hæt Rin
      to-them   is that river PT one calls Rhine
                                                        (*Or* 1 1.22.22)

Those lands which are called Belgic Gaul, east of them is the river called Rhine.

(282) ...þas   Godes þegnas (NOM)... hwyder gescyt þonne
      ...those God's thanes...   whither falls   then
      heora (POSS) endebyrdnys?
      their   order?
                                                        (*ÆCHom* I, 24 346.1)

...as regards those thanes of God...where is their order allotted to be?

Mitchell remarks (1985:§1486) that there are no instances in OE of constructions with anticipatory *it* as in PDE *It's food that I want* because the same emphasis is achieved in OE by fronting the NP alone. However, Visser I.63 cites a few examples with *þæt*:

(283) Þæt is laðlic   lif þæt hi   swa maciað
      That is loathsome life that they thus make   (*WPol* 2.1.1 (Jost) 183)

It is a loathsome life that they thus create.

It should be noted that topicalised NPs (rather than pronouns) bring heavy material to the beginning of the clause. The contrastive effect of topicalised NPs must therefore have been even stronger than in PDE, because of the tendency for light (therefore usually pronominal, and usually 'given') material to occur clause initially in OE.

Several other notable properties of word order have been mentioned in the course of earlier sections, and will not be elaborated on here. Most important among these is preposition stranding, whereby prepositions are detached from their NPs (including pronouns), exemplified in example (157), which is repeated here:

(157) Him is be eastan se Wendelsæ,   þe mon het
       Them is to east   that Mediterranean, PT man calls
       Tirrenum, þe Tiber sio ea   ut scyt on
       Tyrrhenian, PT Tiber that river out pours in

                                                (*Or* 1.1 28.15)

east of them is the Mediterranean, which is called the Tyrrhenian Sea, into which the river Tiber flows.

Preposition stranding is not limited to relative clauses but may also occur in main clauses, probably triggered by the preference for light (especially pronominal) material in clause-initial position, as in:

(284) and him com þæt leoht to þurh   Paules lare   siðan
       and him came that light to through Paul's teaching afterwards
                                                (*ÆLS* (Denis) 17

and afterwards he was enlighted through Paul's teachings.

Another notable property of word order is splitting of the co-ordinated constituents such as is illustrated by (27), repeated here:

(27) God bebead   Abrahame   þæt he sceolde and
      God commanded to-Abraham that he ought and
      his ofspring his wed   healdan
      his offspring his covenant keep

                                                (*ÆCHom* I, 92.30)

God commanded Abraham, that he and his sons should keep his convenant.

4.6.2   Word order within the NP

We turn now to word-order within the NP. Carlton (1970:780) shows that NP-internal word-order is as follows in original charters from 805 to 1066:[18]

6th position (*eall, sum, manig*)	5th position (pron.)	4th position (numeral)	3rd position (*oþer*)	2nd position (adj. and part.)	1st position (noun in gen. case)	Head word (noun)
	þære			geættredan	deofles	lare
		an	oþer	healf		gear
		ænne		blacne		stedan
	þæm	þriim				dælum
	min	twa				wergeld
	þa		oþoro			lond
mænig			oþer	god		man
allum	þæm					halgum
ealle	his			leofan		halgan
sum	þæt					lond
ealle	mine					freondum
			oþrum	sue miclum		lande

It should be noted that the full array of positions is not filled in actual use in any given NP, and therefore the tables represent extrapolations of possible orders rather than attested sequences.

Some orders not specified in Carlton's table include the expansion of the fifth position into possessive + demonstrative. As was mentioned in §4.2.1, this is particularly common when an adjective is also present, cf. (9) and *ÆCHom* I, 11 168.1 *urne þone ecan deað* 'our that eternal death'/'our eternal death'. Another order not specified in the chart pertains to proper name augments: expansions by NPs designating natural category, rank, title, occupation, sex or relationship, such as *Tiber ea*, *Ælfred cyning*, *Gregorius se halga biscop* and, in the following example:

(285)   Ælfred kyning hateð gretan Wærferð biscep his
        Alfred king   bids greet Werferth bishop with-his
        wordum luflice
        words   lovingly

(CPLetWærf 1)

King Alfred bids Bishop Werferth be greeted with words full of good will.

The normal order appears to be proper name + rank, as in (285). Examples like *se cyning Ælfred* (with demonstrative) occur, but not of *cyning Ælfred* without the demonstrative. The demonstrative + rank + name order is favoured in writings strongly influenced by Latin.

As (285) and *Ælfred se cyning* show, it is possible for NP modifiers to follow the noun in OE, and when they do so, the word order is the same as in the table, cf. *HomS* 17 (*BlHom* 5) 136 *cyle þone grimmestan* 'cold that grimmest'. Furthermore, although when two adjectives occur, both may precede the N or both may follow, it is also possible for one to precede and one to follow, with or without a conjunction, compare:

(286)   &   berenne kyrtel oððe yterenne
        and bear   tunic or   of-otter-skin

(Or 1 1.18.19)

and a bear- or otter-skin tunic.

(287)   tamra   deora   unbebohtra syx hund
        of-tame animals unsold   six hundred

six hundred unsold tame animals.   (Or 1 1.18.9)

This is in keeping with the splitting of co-ordinate constructions mentioned at the end of §4.6.1.

The word order patterns outlined in the table are essentially characteristic of verb-final languages. The most salient evidence is the [Possessive – Head] order (although listed in the table, such constructions as *sunu min* 'son mine' are rare in prose, especially in the vocative). The word order patterns within NPs have remained relatively constant in the history of English. It is only in the domain of the [Possessive – Head] construction that there have been major changes in word order. In this one instance (and then primarily only in constructions with inaminate heads), [Head – Possessive], which is correlated with verb-internal order, has become predominant. Thus in PDE the older order [Possessive – Head] as in *the cat's tail* co-exists with, and may be preferred to, the newer order [Head – Possessive] as in *the tail of the cat*; however, *the leg of the table* is preferred to *the table's leg*.

4.6.3   Clause order

Clause order is rather different from that in PDE. The difference is primarily related to the principle that heavy elements are favoured in clause-final position. In this case the heavy element is the clause, and it tends to be sentence-final.

Relative clauses may follow their heads immediately, as in the case of (153) and (154). Alternatively, they may be shifted to the right of the NP head if they modify a dependent phrase, as in the case of (274), or to the right of the main clause, as in the case of (140), (143), (144) and (155). (144) is repeated here:

(144)   sealde þæm munucum corn genog   þe wæron æt Hierusalem
        gave   those monks   corn enough PT were   at Jerusalem

(Or 6 4.260.9)

gave enough corn to those monks who were in Jerusalem.

The splitting of the modifying relative from its head seems to be motivated by the heavy element shift.

In PDE a sentential complement serving as subject may occur either in subject position or it may be 'extraposed' (with *it* in subject position), as in the variants *That she had lied was obvious, It was obvious that she had lied*. However, in OE subject sentential clauses can only occur after the main clause (and a pronoun is not necessary in subject position). As discussed at some length in §§ 4.4.3.3 and 4.5.3.1, this constraint on subject clause order often makes it impossible to tell whether a clause in a predicate copula or a potential impersonal construction is a subject, rather than an object, or oblique NP. Another notable feature of sentential complements is that if a conditional or temporal clause is subordinate to a *þæt*-complement, the conditional usually precedes the *þæt*-complement, see (171). However, a subordinate relative clause usually follows the complement.

As in PDE certain elements can be moved out of the lower clause into the higher. Some examples of negatives that logically belong in the lower clause occurring in the higher clause have been cited in §4.5.10, see especially (270) and (271). Occasionally other adverbs or adverbial phrases may also be moved out of a lower clause, as in (288) where the directional adverb appears to have been moved out of the lower clause into sentence-initial position:

(288) Þyder   he cwæð þæt man mihte geseglian on anum monðe
       Thither he said   that one might sail   in one   month

(Or 1 1.19.12)

He said that one might sail thither in one month.

4.7   Summary of changes

As indicated in §4.1, this study has been primarily synchronic because
the main prose texts in OE were written within a rather limited period
of time between the end of the ninth century and the beginning of the
eleventh. Such changes as were evidenced during the historical period
of OE are tendencies rather than radical changes. The main changes that
have been discussed are summarised here in the order of presentation in
this chapter:

(a)   The demonstrative *se, seo, þæt* and the numeral *an* developed
       semantic characteristics of articles in certain contexts (§4.2.1).

(b)   Distinctions between indicative and subjunctive mood became
       blurred (§4.3.1.3).

(c)   Periphrastic (i.e. phrasal) verbal constructions, specifically, the
       origins of auxiliary progressive, perfect and pluperfect tense
       and aspect came to be more widely used (§§4.3.2.1 and 4.3.2.2).

(d)   There is some evidence in the later period of incipient auxiliary
       verb uses of the pre-modals (§4.3.2.3).

(e)   Distinctions between the three BE-verbs, *beon, wesan* and *weorþan*
       became weaker, most especially in passive constructions
       (§4.3.2.4).

(f)   As morphological distinctions between case markers became
       less distinct, some of the earlier semantic distinctions among
       cases became eroded. At the same time, the use of prepositions
       to express certain case relations was increasing (§4.4.1).

(g)   A tendency to fill the subject position with a quasi-definite (*hit,
       þæt, þær*) became more marked (§4.4.3.3).

(h)   Nativisation may have begun at the very end of the OE period
       of subject infinitive complements (§4.5.3.2).

(i)   The construction *He came running*, as opposed to *He came to-run*,
       became common by Alfred's time (§4.5.3.2).

(j)   The frequency of verb-non-final word order increased, partly
       because of the effects of V2 and of heavy NP shift (§4.6).

It is important for the history of English to note that many of the characteristics usually associated with Middle English syntax were incipiently present in OE, for example the use of prepositions, auxiliary verbs, verb-non-final word order and of a subject-position filler. However, they were for the most part not predominant, and all were in variation with other structures (specifically, case inflections, tense and mood inflections, verb-final order and 'impersonal' constructions without subject-slot filler). The changes that led to the predominance in Middle English of the structures that were largely incipient in OE will be discussed in volume II of this History.

FURTHER READING

Extensive bibliographical references are provided in Mitchell (1985). The references below are intended to identify major works already cited in Mitchell as well as some more recent works.

4.1 Old English syntax has been covered in very great detail in Mitchell (1985) and, more discursively, in Visser (1963–73). The present chapter is substantially based on Mitchell; however, the interpretations of the data are sometimes different from Mitchell's.

Other general sources of information on OE syntax include Brunner, vol. II (1962), McLaughlin (1963), Mitchell & Robinson (1986), Mosse, vol. I (1950), Quirk & Wrenn (1957), Traugott (1972) and Kemenade (1987).

The syntactic approach is relatively informal; my aim has been to answer questions about OE syntax that might be raised in syntactic traditions such as are developed in Quirk *et al.* (1972) and in Radford (1981), Newmeyer (1986) and Sells (1986).

4.2 Major studies of definite and indefinite constructions are Christopherson (1939) and Rissanen (1967). A recent analysis, with focus on pragmatic factors, is Hopper (1986). For issues in gender agreement see Jones (1967) and Wyss (1983).

4.3 For further discussion of the imperative, see Millward (1971); for the progressive, Nickel (1966) and Dal (1952).

The pre-modals are discussed in Standop (1957), Lightfoot (1979) and Plank (1984). A so far unresolved question is the extent to which epistemic meanings of the pre-modals can be identified in OE; Goossens (1982) and Plank (1984) discuss the relative lack of epistemics; Denison (1990b) shows that the epistemic colouring is most prevalent in impersonal constructions; Warner (1987), shows that epistemic colouring was relatively more advanced in OE than has been thought.

For more on the passive, see Frary (1929) and Klingebiel (1937).

A major theoretical issue that has been discussed recently is whether there is any evidence that, even if there were auxiliary verbs in Old English, they had such unique syntactic properties that they can be considered to be members of the category AUX. In PDE, this category is postulated on largely distributional grounds, including the fact that the modals (*will, would, must*, etc.), the perfect (*have-en*), the progressive (*be-ing*), and the passive (*be-en*), do not co-occur with *do* (cf. *I might not go, *I might do/did not go* vs. *I didn't go*), and furthermore, may occur in tag-questions (cf. *She could leave, couldn't she?*; **She left, leftn't she?*; *She left, didn't she?*). Lightfoot argues that there was no category AUX until the sixteenth century when the pre-modals ceased (at least in Standard English) to appear in certain constructions, such as infinitival *to* constructions (e.g. *appeared to mow* [+ '*may*'] *stande the realm in great stede*); and when *do* became firmly established (Lightfoot (1979:110). The status of AUX in the history of English depends heavily on the theoretical model adopted. For example, Akmajian, Steele & Wasow (1979) argue that AUX is a universal of grammar, and is realised in all languages as at least Tense or Modal; if so, OE must have had at least one of these. On the other hand, Gazdar, Pullum & Sag (1982) argue that AUX is not a category; instead, they account for the distributional properties of PDE auxiliary verbs in terms of features on verbs; these trigger certain morphosyntactic phenomena such as past participle (on perfect and passive), and block certain syntactic structures (e.g. modals and other auxiliaries cannot be passivised). Such an analysis is more coherent with the historical facts than an analysis that postulates a separate category AUX, since it does not make such a radical distinction between main and auxiliary; it therefore potentially allows for an account of step by step change during the history of English, and does not require a 'catastrophic' change from non-AUX to AUX such as Lightfoot postulates.

4.4 The analysis presented here of NP-roles depends largely on Jackendoff (1983, 1987).

Kemenade (1987) is an important study of syntactic and morphological case in OE. Generalisations about the semantics of case assignment in OE are proposed in Plank (1983), Anderson (1986) and Fischer & van der Leek (1983, 1987).

For detailed studies of impersonal constructions, see Mitchell (1985:§§1025–51); also van der Gaaf (1904), Wahlen (1925), Elmer (1981), Fischer & van der Leek (1983, 1987), Anderson (1986), Ogura (1986), Denison (1987) and forthcoming); and further Lightfoot (1979) and Allen (1986a). Allen (1986b) discusses the status of dummy subject *hit*.

The non-existence of verb-particle passives in OE is discussed in Denison (1985).

4.5 OE Relative clause structures are discussed in Andrew (1940), Allen (1980), Simons (1987) and Dekeyser (1987).

For non-finite complements in general, see Callaway (1913) and Fischer (1990).

For causal clauses see Van Dam (1957), Liggins (1955) and Wiegand (1987). The pragmatics of PDE causals are discussed in Sweetser (1984).

The distinction between conditionals, concessive conditionals and concessives is made by König (1986).

For clauses of comparison, see Small (1924) and Allen (1980).

Negative constructions, especially of the contrastive type, are discussed in LaBrum (1982).

4.6 Among major traditional studies of word order are Andrew (1934), Fries (1940), Bacquet (1962), Shannon (1964), Reszkiewicz (1966), Pillsbury (1967), Brown (1970), Carlton (1970) and Gardner (1971). More recent studies which focus on word order within the clause, and on typology and/or issues of base structure include Haiman (1974), Stockwell (1977), Canale (1978), Kohonen (1978), Butler (1980), Bean (1983; criticized in Denison (1986), Kemenade (1987) and Pintsuk & Kroch (1989). For the pragmatics of word order in OE, see Hopper (1979, 1986) and (Butler (1980).

ENDNOTES

1 Translations of personal and place names in *Orosius* are taken from Bately (1980).

2 The OE development of periphrastic *have* followed a different path from that of the rather similar *habere* construction in Late Latin. In Latin the resultant states were mental states, not actions, see Benveniste (1968).

3 Another possible example is (129) below. However, *þæt* may be playing a double role here as both object of *geboden* and either nominative subject of *lician* or accusative oblique NP.

4 Occasionally, in OE as well as PDE the relative clause modifies a whole antecedent clause, as in *She threatened to leave, which would be a disaster*. This kind of relative will not be discussed here.

5 Comrie (1981). The only relative head role not permitted in OE and PDE is the object of comparison: **The man who John is taller than*.

6 MS *þonne* is presumably a scribal error for *þone*.

7 Mitchell writes the 'attracted' relativiser as *se'þe*, to differentiate it from the non-attracted type, which he writes as *'seþe*. A third orthographic form *seþe* is used for instances where the case of the antecedent and of the relative head are the same, and it is therefore not possible to tell which type is involved.

8 Although it has been claimed that such constructions are impossible in PDE (see Kroch 1981), they are sporadically mentioned in the literature and are relatively widely attested. Dwight Bolinger and Dovie Wylie (both personal communications) report hearing the following: *He's a man that I know his wife*, and (with reference to a television show) *There's one trashy female that I just love her*; see also Menner (1930–1).

9 Such restrictions on extraction are called 'island constraints'. For discussion of examples in spoken PDE of violation of these island constraints as in *There's one guy that I didn't think he would come*, see Kroch (1981).

10 There is a certain similarity here to the switches in gender-agreement: greater distance from the head permits freer use of the 'unmarked' or less specialised form.

11 The Venezky & Healey (1980) concordance has *þæt to towearp*. This seems to be a mistake.

12 In Orosius, *wæron* can be used for both indicative and subjunctive, see chapter 3.

13 In his translation of the *Cura pastoralis*, Sweet renders this as 'When we judged ourselves, God judged us not' (Sweet 1871:414), but the conditional reading seems preferable since the context is an explanation in indirect quotation form of Christ's proclamations about how he would treat those who repented and confessed in life.

14 Muxin (1958: a Russian work cited in Mitchell 1985:§2739) has suggested that the indicative signals that two events are in immediate (chained) sequence in a narrative, while the subjunctive is used when there is no immediate link between the events.

15 There appear to be no examples of negative definite constructions of the type *Not came someone* 'Someone didn't come'.

16 This interpretation diverges from Earle and Plummer's (1899, vol. II, p. 46), which reads as follows (K = king's thanes, E = the kinsmen): 'And then they (K) offered their kinsmen that they might depart unscathed. And they (E) said that the same offer had been made to their (K) comrades, who had been with the king before. Then said they (E) that they (E) regarded it [the offer] not a whit more than...' This translation is preceded by the comment: 'The poverty of the English language in demonstrative pronouns as compared with the Latin *hic, ille, is, iste, ipse* appears very strongly in this passage and makes it difficult to follow.' Plummer's translation is consistent with the view that the Thanes had just arrived and might not have known about prior negotiations. Hopper's is consistent with the view that one and the same group of individuals would extend the same terms.

17 The exact distinctions between 'topicalised', 'focused' and other kinds of pragmatically highlighted NPs are still a matter of some debate and terminological inexactitude. For an attempt to sort out the distinctions, see Prince (1981). The term 'topicalised' is used here in a broad sense to cover a number of highlighting phenomena brought about by 'fronting' of an NP or of the verb.

18 Reprinted with permission. See Mitchell (1985:§149) for a similar chart for the poetry.

5 SEMANTICS AND VOCABULARY

Dieter Kastovsky

5.1 Introduction

5.1.1 One linguistic concept, although fundamental and constantly referred to, is often taken for granted: the concept of 'word'. The word is the domain of many phonological statements; it is the implicit ordering principle in morphology; and the word is a central, though again implicit concept of syntax in so far as the latter describes the patterns or rules according to which words are combined into larger linguistic structures. It is therefore necessary to be somewhat more explicit about this linguistic category, not only because words – more precisely, the aggregate of words making up the vocabulary (= dictionary = lexicon) of a language – are the topic of this chapter, but also because the term is familiar from non-technical, everyday language, where it is often employed in a variety of senses, while as a technical term it ought to be unambiguous. Thus, when talking about inflectional paradigms, the term 'word' might be used to refer both to each individual member of the paradigm, and to the global entity each member of the paradigm is a form of, as well as to the entity that is bounded by spaces to its left and right in a text. This, then, might lead to a seemingly contradictory statement such as

(1) The word *heah steap* is written as two words.

In actual fact, there is a sequence *heah steap reced* 'very high house' (lit. 'high lofty house') in *Gen.* 2840 (Sauer 1985:270), where *heah steap* is normally interpreted as an adjectival compound, which, however, is written in the manuscript as two separate words. It is therefore not just terminological hypertrophy that in modern linguistics these three meanings of 'word' are systematically kept apart along the following lines (cf. Matthews 1974:20ff., Lyons 1977:18ff., Kastovsky 1982:70ff.).

The terms 'lexeme' or 'lexical item' are used to refer to words in the sense of 'dictionary entry' or 'lemma', which at the same time implies reference to the inflectional paradigm as a whole. An individual inflected form of such a lexical item is then called a 'word-form', while the term 'word' is reserved for any actual sequence of letters bounded by a space to its right and left in a text, i.e.

2(a)   stan 'stone': lexeme/lexical item
stan, stanes, stane, stanas, stana, stanum: word-forms/words in texts

(b)   dem(-an) 'to judge': lexeme/lexical item
deman, deme, demst, demde, gedemed, etc.: word-forms/words in texts

The form used to refer to the lexical item as such, its 'citation form', is by convention the nominative singular with nouns and adjectives, and the infinitive with verbs. Thus, it may be a form with or without an inflectional ending, cf. *dem-an* vs. *stan*. As we shall see in the section on word-formation below (§5.4.7), this duality, absent in present-day English, where all quotation forms are at the same time uninflected base forms, is the cause of the typologically mixed status of Old English inflexion and word-formation.

5.1.2   It is the basic function of lexemes to serve as labels for segments of extralinguistic reality that for some reason or another a speech community finds nameworthy. Therefore it is no surprise that even closely related languages will differ considerably as to the overall structure of their vocabulary, and the same holds for different historical stages of one and the same language. Looked at from this point of view, the vocabulary of a language is as much a reflection of deep-seated cultural, intellectual and emotional interests, perhaps even of the whole *Weltbild* of a speech community as the texts that have been produced by its members. The systematic study of the overall vocabulary of a language is thus an important contribution to the understanding of the culture and civilization of a speech community over and above the analysis of the texts in which this vocabulary is put to communicative use. This aspect is to a certain extent even more important in the case of dead languages such as Latin or the historical stages of a living language, where the textual basis is more or less limited. But a word of caution might not be inappropriate at this point. We must not forget that the vocabulary of a living language, accessible to direct observation, exhibits a complex, multidimensional stratification, whereas the textual material available from earlier periods is usually extremely restricted as to the varieties making up what Coseriu (1966) has called the 'architecture' of a language.

The following dimensions of linguistic variation have become established as major factors leading to differences at the phonological, morphological, syntactic and/or lexical level within a speech community:

(a)   region, (b) social group, (c) field of discourse, (d) medium,
(e)   attitude (Quirk *et al.* 1985:16ff.)

Regional differences are usually equated with the notion of (regional) dialect, e.g. Scots, Midland or Cockney, which is normally contrasted with a supraregional standard. But in present-day English, we might also want to recognise regionally definable standards, e.g. British English (e.g. *lorry, bumper, bonnet, railway, luggage*) vs. General American (*truck, fender, hood, railroad, baggage*), which do not really conform to the traditional notion of dialect. Social differences basically result from the affiliation to specific socio-economic groups, the kind of education one has received, one's age and sex, and they frequently interact with regional variation: certain socio-economically definable groups are more prone to use regionally restricted varieties (dialects) than others. Varieties according to the field of discourse reflect 'the type of activity engaged in through language' (Quirk *et al.* 1985:23) and manifest themselves in labels such as 'technical', 'legal', 'religious', 'literary', 'bureaucratic', etc., i.e. they are intimately connected with the subject matter of the discourse. Varieties according to medium are mainly related to the difference between spoken and written language, while varieties according to attitude refer to the degree of formality reflected by the utterance in question.

Obviously, these five dimensions are to a certain extent interdependent, i.e. informal language use is more often than not tied to the oral medium and to a certain field of discourse. Furthermore, every fluent native speaker will both actively and passively know more than one variety within each dimension.

There is no reason to assume that the situation was radically different in Old English. We know that there were dialectal differences, not only in phonology and morphology, but also in the lexicon (cf. §5.3, below, and ch. 6). There certainly were differences according to the field of discourse, in so far as poetic diction differs considerably from prose diction, both on the levels of syntax and the lexicon, and possibly even at the levels of orthography and phonology, see chapter 8.

Within prose diction we of course find further differences according to the subject matter of the text, e.g. between legal documents, laws, religious-didactic prose, botanical or medical treatises and even according to text-type, i.e. whether the text is an original piece of OE prose, a translation of a Latin original in the form of an independent text, as with Orosius, Bede, Boethius, or an interlinear gloss of a Latin text. But variation along the other dimensions, although it unquestionably existed, is much more difficult to discover, if it is ascertainable at all in view of the type of texts that have come down to us. Practically all are of a literary, religious-didactic or technical character or are poetic records. We cannot expect that they reflect linguistic differences based on affiliation to different social groups. Authors and scribes on the whole belonged to a fairly homogeneous set, the highly educated elite of the country. And poetic texts, whose authors are only partly known, follow a stylised diction that may throw some light on the social situation of the period in which this art form came into being, but do not tell us too much about the later OE period. Moreover, they again only reflect the usage of the social elite. Nor would we expect much variation as to medium, because practically all texts reflect the written usage of the period. Some authors have tried to establish Old English colloquialisms (Magoun 1937; von Lindheim 1951), but the results are rather meagre and problematic (see §5.3.3 below). The same holds for the dimension of attitude; all texts, with the exception of Ælfric's *Colloquy*, are formal, and even in the latter, the language is stylised rather than genuinely informal.

Thus, what we have in the way of OE vocabulary – according to some rough counts between 23,000 and 24,000 lexical items (Scheler 1977:14, 74n.45) – represents a fairly restricted spectrum of the overall vocabulary, and any general conclusions as to its overall structure and organisation will have to be drawn with due care. On the other hand, this sample will still contain a substantial number of items that belong to what Quirk *et al.* (1985:161) have called the 'common core of the language', so that general conclusions as to certain structural properties of the vocabulary, e.g. within the domain of word-formation, the structure of semantic fields, the attitude towards borrowing, etc., are not without a sufficiently large empirical basis.

5.1.3.1   When we take a bird's eye view of the OE vocabulary as listed in the existing major dictionaries (e.g. Bosworth & Toller 1898; 1921; 1972; Clark Hall & Merritt 1969) – the forthcoming *Dictionary of Old English* prepared in Toronto will probably add details but not change the general impression – we are immediately struck by a number of features that put it into sharp contrast with present-day English.

First of all, there is an extremely low percentage of loan words: roughly 3 per cent as against estimated 70 per cent or even more for present-day English (Scheler 1977:74). Thus OE is, from the point of view of its vocabulary, a thoroughly Germanic language. This immediately leads to a second, closely related observation: the vocabulary is characterised by large morphologically related word-families, where the relationship is transparent not only formally but most often also semantically. Put differently, much of the OE vocabulary is derivationally related by productive word-formation patterns, and, as we shall see below, instead of borrowing a foreign, usually Latin word, the corresponding notion is often expressed by activating one of the indigenous word-formation rules, producing a so-called loan trans-lation, cf. as a typical example Ælfric's translations of Latin technical terms in his grammar, e.g. *praepositio = foresetnys* 'preposition', *interiectio = betwuxalegednys* 'interjection', *significatio = getacnung* 'signification'; all are derivatives from corresponding OE verbs (*forsettan* 'put before', *alecgan* 'put down' + *betwux* 'between', *tacnian* 'mark, indicate, signify' < *tacen* 'sign').

The OE vocabulary thus is 'associative', the present-day English vocabulary is 'dissociated', because very often besides a Germanic lexical item there are semantically related non-Germanic derivatives, as in *mouth*:*oral*, *father*:*paternal*, *sun*:*solar*.

The following example, a selected list of compounds and derivatives related to the verbs *gan*/*gangan* 'go' is typical for the overall situation:

(1)   *gan*/*gangan* 'go, come, move, proceed, depart; happen'
(2)   derivatives:
   (a)   *gang* 'going, journey; track, footprint; passage, way; privy; steps, platform'; compounds: *ciricgang* 'churchgoing', *earsgang* 'excrement', *faldgang* 'going into the sheep-fold', *feþegang* 'foot journey', *forlig-gang* 'adultery', *hingang* 'a going hence, death', *hlafgang* 'a going to eat bread', *huselgang* 'partaking in the sacrament', *mynstergang* 'the entering on a monastic life', *oxangang* 'hide, eighth of a plough-land', *sulhgang* 'plough-gang

= as much land as can properly be tilled by one plough in one day'; *gangern*, *gangþytt*, *gangsetl*, *gangstol*, *gangtun*, all 'privy'

(b) *genge* n., sb. 'troops, company'

(c) *-genge* f., sb. in *nightgenge* 'hyena, i.e. an animal that prowls at night'

(d) *-genga* m., sb. in *angenga* 'a solitary, lone goer', *æftergenga* 'one who follows', *hindergenga* 'one that goes backwards, a crab', *huselgenga* 'one who goes to the Lord's supper', *mangenga* 'one practising evil', *nihtgenga* 'one who goes by night, goblin', *rapgenga* 'rope-dancer', *sægenga* 'sea-goer, mariner; ship'

(e) *genge* adj. 'prevailing, going, effectual, agreeable'

(f) *-gengel* sb. in *æftergengel* 'successor' (perhaps from *æftergengan*, wk. vb. 'to go')

(3) compounds with verbal first constituent, i.e. V + N (some of them might, however, also be treated as N + N, i.e. with *gang* as in (2a): *gangdæg* 'Rogation day, one of the three processional days before Ascension day', *gangewifre* 'spider, i.e. a weaver that goes', *ganggeteld* 'portable tent', *ganghere* 'army of foot-soldiers', *gangwucu* 'the week of Holy Thursday, Rogation week'

(4) *gengan* wk. vb. 'to go' < *gang-j-an*: *æftergengness* 'succession, posterity'

(5) prefixations of *gan/gangan*:

(a) *agan* 'go, go by, pass, pass into possession, occur, befall, come forth'

(b) *began/begangan* 'go over, go to, visit; cultivate; surround; honour, worship' with derivatives *begáng/bígang* 'practice, exercise, worship, cultivation'; *begánga/bígenga* 'inhabitant, cultivator' and numerous compounds of both; *begenge* n. 'practice, worship', *bigengere* 'worker, worshipper'; *bigengestre* 'hand maiden, attendant, worshipper'; *begangness* 'calendae, celebration'

(c) *foregan* 'go before, precede' with derivatives *foregenga* 'fore-runner, predecessor', *foregengel* 'predecessor'

(d) *forgan* 'pass over, abstain from'

(e) *forþgan* 'to go forth' with *forþgang* 'progress, purging, privy'

(f) *ingan* 'go in' with *ingang* 'entrance(-fee), ingression', *ingenga* 'visitor, intruder'

(g) *niþergan* 'to descend' with *niþergang* 'descent'

(h) *ofgan* 'to demand, extort; obtain; begin, start' with *ofgangende* 'derivative'

(i) *ofergan* 'pass over, go across, overcome, overreach' with *ofergenga* 'traveller'

(j) *ongan* 'to approach, enter into' with *ongang* 'entrance, assault'

(k) *ofgan* 'go away, escape'

(l) *togan* 'go to, go into; happen; separate, depart' with *togang* 'approach, attack'

(m) *þurhgan* 'go through'

(n) *undergan* 'undermine, undergo'

(o) *upgan* 'go up; raise' with *upgang* 'rising, sunrise, ascent', *upgange* 'landing'

(p) *utgan* 'go out' with *utgang* 'exit, departure; privy; excrement; anus'; *?utgenge* 'exit'

(q) *wiþgan* 'go against, oppose; pass away, disappear'

(r) *ymbgan* 'go round, surround' with *ymbgang* 'circumference, circuit, going about'.

5.1.3.2   Another consequence of the thoroughly Germanic character of the vocabulary is the preservation of ablaut not only as a feature characterising verbal inflexion with strong verbs, but also within the derivational system. It was probably no longer really productive in the OE period, but it permeates the vocabulary in so far as deverbal nouns, adjectives and verbs very often exhibit the same ablaut alternations as found in their verbal bases (for the Indo-European and Germanic ablaut patterns see chapter 2). The situation is similar to that in Modern High German but was given up completely in the course of the ME period, cases such as *song* being rare exceptions. A more detailed description and evaluation of this phenomenon will be given in § 5.4 on word-formation, but a few examples are perhaps not inappropriate at this stage.

Thus, from the verb *brecan* 'break, shatter, violate; roar', a strong verb of class IV with the forms *bræc*, *bræcon*, *gebrocen*, we get the following derivatives:

(a)   normal grade: *æbrecþ* f. 'sacrilege', *æwbreca* 'adulterer', *brecness* f. 'breach', *brecþa* m. 'broken condition'

(b)   IE *o*-grade (Gmc *a*-grade): *(ge-)bræc* n. 'noise, sound'

(c)   lengthened grade: *bræc* f. 'breaking, destruction', *æwbræce* adj. 'adulterous, despising the law'

(d) $\begin{bmatrix} \text{zero grade} \\ \pm \text{ umlaut} \end{bmatrix}$: *æbrucol* 'sacrilegious', *broc* m. 'breach, fragment', *bryce* m. 'break, fragment', *husbryce* 'burglary', *husbrycel* adj. 'burglarious', *bryce* adj. 'fragile, brittle'.

The strong class II verb *ceosan* 'choose, approve' with the forms *ceas*, *curon*, *gecoren* yields the derivatives:

(a) $\begin{bmatrix} \text{zero grade} \\ +\text{Verner's Law} \\ -\text{Umlaut} \end{bmatrix}$: *gecor* n. 'decision', *gecorenness* 'choice, election, goodness', *gecorenscipe* 'election, excellence', *gecorenlic* 'elegant'

(b) $\begin{bmatrix} \text{zero grade} \\ +\text{Verner's Law} \\ +\text{Umlaut} \end{bmatrix}$: *cyre* m. 'choice, free will'

(c) $\begin{bmatrix} \text{zero grade} \\ -\text{Verner's Law} \\ +\text{Umlaut} \end{bmatrix}$: *cyst* f., m. (< **kus+ti-*) 'free will, choice, election; the choicest'

(d) $\begin{bmatrix} \text{zero grade} \\ -\text{Verner's Law} \\ -\text{Umlaut} \end{bmatrix}$: *cost* m. 'option, choice'; *cost* adj. 'tried, chosen; excellent'.

The strong class III *drincan* 'drink' with the forms *dranc*, *druncon*, *gedruncen* is associated with the following derivatives:

(a) normal grade: *drinc* m. 'drink, drinking', *gedrinca* m. 'one who drinks with another; cupbearer', *drincere* m. 'drinker, drunkard'

(b) [*o*-grade, +umlaut]: *drenc* m. (< **drank+iz*) 'drink, drinking'; *drencan* wk.vb. 1 (< **drank+j+an-*) 'give to drink, soak', *drenchus* 'drinking-house'

(c) [zero grade, ±umlaut]: *druncen* n. 'drunkenness', *druncennis* f. 'drunkenness', *druncnian* wk.vb. cl.2 'be, get drunk', *druncning* 'drinking', *drync* m. 'drink, potion, drinking'.

As these examples show, strong verbs, or, rather, the various stem allomorphs of strong verbs with their different ablaut grades form the basis for both suffixal and suffixless derivatives, which in turn may act as the starting-point for further derivational series, as in *drincan drunc(en)* → *drunc+n+ian* → *drunc+n+ing*, or *faran* 'travel' → *for* f. 'journey' ⇒ *fer+an* (< **for+j+an-*) 'go on a journey, travel, set out' → *fer+end* m. 'sailor', *fer+ness* f. 'passage, transition, passing away'. Hinderling's (1967:2) claim that a description of word-formation in the Germanic languages has to take the strong verbs as its starting-point is thus fully justified.

5.1.3.3 But these examples have also demonstrated a further striking property of the OE word-formation system, and consequently of the overall OE vocabulary as far as it is inter-related by word-formation patterns: the pervasiveness of morphophonemic alternations, which is also characteristic of the inflectional system, and which is a synchronic reflex of the various sound changes that have taken place in the Germanic and early OE period, such as Verner's Law (cf. *ceosan* ~ *cyre*), West-Germanic Consonant Lengthening (*gram* 'angry' ~ *gremman* (< *gram + j + an-*) 'make angry' besides *gremian* from *grem + e + de*), *i*-umlaut (*cyre* < *kur + iz*, *gremman*) or palatalisation/assibilation (*ceosan* ~ *cyre*, *sprecan* ~ *spræc* 'speech').

One striking property of the OE vocabulary is thus the widespread stem-variability present both in inflexion and word-formation, a variability which obviously originated in the combination of inherited ablaut alternations and morphophonemic alternations newly emerging as relics of certain sound-changes in the Germanic and early OE period. One of the most noteworthy changes at the end of the OE period and throughout ME, therefore, was the almost total loss of this stem-variability, or at least its loss as a system-defining property, and its replacement by stem-invariancy as a new morphological principle. This change was brought about by the complete collapse of the OE morphophonemic system because of its rapidly growing opacity (Kastovsky 1988a,b, 1990a), and the ensuing phonological, morphophonemic and morphological restructuring at the end of the OE and the beginning of the ME period, whose details still await a systematic investigation. It is perhaps not unimportant to add that the present-day English alternations of the type *sincere* ~ *sincerity*, *divine* ~ *divinity*, *electric* ~ *electricity*, *produce* ~ *production*, etc., which are predominantly characteristic of the Latino-Romance part of the vocabulary, came about much later and are mainly due to the Great Vowel Shift in conjunction with stress alternations. They thus are in no way a continuation of the OE type of stem-variability.

5.1.3.4   There is one further conspicuous feature of the OE vocabulary, however, which seems to be primarily due to the type of texts that have been preserved, and in particular to the high proportion of poetic records among them, because there the phenomenon in question is one of the main artistic devices: lexical variation. As a consequence, there are certain areas in the vocabulary that abound in near-synonyms or even complete synonyms, at least from our rather distant point of view, which does not always enable us to establish minimal meaning differences between such items. Typical examples of such densely populated lexical fields are expressions for 'man' and 'warrior' (*beorn, guma, hæleþ, rinc, secg; man, wiga*), 'battle' (*guþ, hild, beadu; wig*), or 'heart, mind' (*sefa, ferhþ, hyg; mod*), where the lexical items before the semicolon are predominantly or exclusively used in poetry, while those after the semicolon are of general currency (cf. also ch. 8 below). This kind of synonymy, based on the inherent denotative meaning of the lexical items involved, should be kept apart from another, equally striking phenomenon, the widespread metaphorical use of simple or complex lexical items with different meanings as coreferential designations, i.e. the so-called *kenningar*. Thus, a lord or king will not only be referred to by *frea* 'ruler, lord' or *cyning* 'king', but also by epithets such as *burh-agend* 'city-owner', *beag-gifa* 'ring-giver', *eþel-weard* 'lord of the realm', etc. And the sea is not just called *sæ, geofon, heafu, mere, lagu* or just *wæter*, but also *fam* 'foam', *wæg* 'wave' or *hrycg* 'back, ridge', as well as *ar-gebland* 'waveblend, surge', *stream-gewinn* 'strife of waters', *hwæl-weg* 'whale-way', *seolh-bæþ* 'seal-bath', etc. I will return to these phenomena in §§ 5.3 and 5.5 below.

These examples have again demonstrated the importance of word-formation patterns for the structure of the OE vocabulary. For this reason, the greater part of this chapter will be devoted to an outline of the major OE word-formation patterns, especially since there still does not exist a comprehensive treatment of OE word-formation, comparable to Marchand's (1969) treatment of the subject for present-day English. But before I turn to these morphological aspects of the OE vocabulary, a few more detailed remarks should be made about the etymological sources of the OE vocabulary, notably the loan-words forming part of it, and its diatopic and diaphasic stratification.

5.2   Foreign influence

5.2.0.1   As has already been mentioned, the OE vocabulary is, etymologically speaking, extremely homogeneous, especially if compared with present-day English. Nevertheless, contacts with other languages in the PrOE and OE periods have left some traces, which provide interesting insights into the external history of the language, in so far as they reflect cultural, religious and/or political changes. Such traces are basically of two types:

(1) A lexical item is borrowed as such from the donor language, usually together with the concept or object it refers to, and is integrated into the receptor language; the degree of integration may vary considerably,

however, cf., for example, the non-integrated OE loans *circul zodiacus*, *bissextus*, *firmamentum*, *terminus* from Ælfric's version of Bede's *De temporibus* quoted in Funke (1914:171), or the terms for liturgical books *sacramentor(i)um*, *antiphonaria*, *pistelari*, *collectaneum*, *capitularia*, *martirlogium* (Gneuss 1985:121ff.), as against integrated *antefnere* 'gradual', *tropere* 'troper', *(p)salter(e)* 'psalter', or *cyse* 'cheese' < L *caseus*, *pytt* 'hole, well' < Lat. *puteus*, *turnian* 'turn' < Lat. *turnare*, *fersian* 'versify' < L *versus* etc.

(2) Only the meaning of a lexical item of the donor language is transferred to the receptor language, when either: (a) the meaning of some lexical item of the donor language influences the meaning of an already existing native word by being added to it (semantic loan); thus OE *synn* 'injury, enmity, feud' adopted the additional meaning 'sin, crime' of Lat. *peccatum* or *cniht* 'boy, servant' took over the additional meaning 'disciple' of Lat. *discipulus (Christi)* (Gneuss 1955:20–1); or (b) the meaning of some lexical item of the donor language is translated into a complex expression consisting of linguistic material of the receptor language. If the translation directly imitates the original, we speak of a loan translation, as with Ælfric's grammatical terminology, e.g. *participium = dæl-nimend* 'something taking part' *praepositio = forsetnys* 'that which is put before', *interiectio = betwuxaworpennys/betwuxalegednys* 'that which is thrown/placed between'. If the translation is relatively free and does not structurally–morphologically follow the original, one usually speaks of a loan-creation, cf. Ælfric's *pronomen = þæs naman spelȝend* 'substitute for the name', or *fahwyrm* 'variegated reptile' rendering Lat. *basiliscus*.

Loan words are of course much easier to establish than semantic loans, loan translations or loan creations, but these latter are perhaps even more important for OE, where native means for extending the vocabulary were clearly preferred to borrowing. Unfortunately, with the exception of Gneuss (1955) there is no comprehensive study for the whole of the OE period.

5.2.0.2 The largest number of loans, whether direct or indirect (semantic loans, loan translations), in OE is due to the influence of Latin, which had already started at the time when the ancestors of the Anglo-Saxons were still on the Continent. At this stage Latin may also have acted as an intermediary for the adoption of some loans from Greek, although direct borrowing, perhaps via Gothic, is perhaps phonologically more likely in the following cases: OE *deofol* 'devil', Gk διάβολος, Lat. *diabolus* with [v] rendering the Greek bilabial fricative, whereas Latin has [b]; OE *Crecas* 'Greeks' cf. Goth. *Krekos* for Gk Γραικοί with substitution of Gmc [k] for [g], because at this stage [g] in the Germanic dialects only occurred as a geminate or as [g]; OE *engel* 'angel' (as against the later loan *angel* in the Lindisfarne gospels, e.g. Luke I, 26; I, 35; cf. Funke 1914:137) from Gk ἄγγελος > Gmc *angil-, and OE *cirice* 'church', Gr. κυριακόν.

The second largest group of loans comes from Scandinavian (Danish and Norwegian) after the settlement of the Vikings in England, although the bulk of the Scandinavian loans was adopted only in the early ME period. Apart from these two languages, there are some Celtic and perhaps a few French loans alongside a handful from the continental Germanic languages.

5.2.1   Latin influence

5.2.1.1   Following Serjeantson (1935:1ff.), the classical handbooks usually speak of 'three distinct occasions on which borrowing from Latin occurred before the end of the Old English period' (Baugh & Cable 1978:75): (1) continental borrowing before the migration of the Anglo-Saxons to England; (2) early Latin borrowings during the settlement period ('Latin through Celtic transmission', Baugh & Cable 1978:79); (3) borrowings in connection with the Christianisation of the Anglo-Saxons after ca 600/650. This last period in turn might be subdivided into the time before and after the Benedictine Reform, led by Dunstan, Æthelwold and Oswald, see chapter 1. The demarcation line between these periods is of course not sharp, and there are quite a number of loans for which it is somewhat difficult to decide to which period they belong. Nevertheless, each period is distinctly marked off by the specific character of the loan words adopted, apart from other criteria, e.g. sound changes, so that such a division seems justified.

5.2.1.2   Contacts between the Germanic and the Latin peoples existed from the days of Julius Caesar, and although these contacts were not always peaceful in the beginning, they gradually developed into peaceful co-existence, and more and more members of Germanic tribes joined the Roman army, even forming cohorts of their own. These soldiers and their families thus became familiar with Latin military terminology, with the names of everyday objects in use in camp and town, and of plants and animals they had not seen before or had no name for, and thus gradually several hundred Latin words penetrated into the various Germanic dialects. Some were adopted in only one dialect, others in several or even all. The army was followed by the Roman merchant, who came into the pacified regions and sold his superior goods, e.g. household vessels, plant products, dresses, ornaments and jewels from the south, and gradually also settlers stayed, introducing building terms. Borrowing was of course heavier in the southern provinces, but in principle the northern Germanic tribes that were eventually to migrate to England were affected in the same way. It is estimated that about 170 lexical items were borrowed during this continental period (Williams 1975:57; Serjeantson 1935:271–7), of which roughly 30 per cent denote plants and animals, 20 per cent food, vessels, household items, 12 per cent buildings, building material, settlements, 12 per cent dress, 9 per cent military and legal institutions, 9 per cent commercial activities, 3 per cent miscellaneous other phenomena (Williams 1975:57).

Examples for these various groups are: *box* 'box-tree' < *buxum, -s, cipe* 'onion' < *cepe, cesten-beam,* 'chestnut tree' < *castanea, ciris* 'cherry' < VLat. *ceresia, cyrfet* 'gourd' < *cucurbita, cymen* 'cumin' < *cuminum, minte* 'mint' < *menta, pise* 'pea' < *pisum, piper* 'pepper' < *piper, rædic* 'radish' < *radic-em, plante* 'plant' < *planta, caw(e)l* 'cabbage' < *caulis, win* 'wine' < *vinum*; *catt(e)* 'cat' < Late Lat. *cattus, draca* 'dragon' < *draco, elpend/ylpend* 'elephant' < *elephant-, pea/pawa* 'peacock' < *pavo, struta/stryte* 'ostrich' < *struthio; turtle/turtla* 'turtle-dove' < *turtur; butere* 'butter' < *butyrum, cyse* 'cheese' < *caseus, must* 'must, new wine' < *mustum; bytt* 'bottle' < VLat. *bottis, celc* 'cup' < *calic-em; cetel* 'kettle' < *catillus; cupp(e)* 'cup' < *cuppa, disc* 'plate, dish' < *discus, lebil/læfel* 'cup, bowl' < *labellum, panne* 'pan' < VLat. *panna* < Lat. *patina, scrin* 'chest' < *scrinium; candel* 'candle' < *candela, fifele* 'buckle' < *fibula, fæcele* 'torch' < *facula, mise* 'table' < VLat. *mesa* < L *mensa; pipe* 'pipe' < VLat. *pipa, scamol* 'bench, stool' < *scamellum, mylen* 'mill' < *molinus, -a.; belt* 'belt' < *balteus, cemes* 'shirt' < *camisia, fullere* 'fuller of cloth' < *fullo* (with adaptation of the suffix), *pæll* 'rich robe, purple robe' < *pallium, pihten* 'reed' < *pecten* 'comb', *pilece* 'robe of skin' < VLat. *pellicea, purpur* 'purple garment' < *purpura; pyl(w)e* 'pillow' < *pulvinus, sacc* 'sack, bag' < *saccus, sæcc* 'sack, bag' < VLat. **saccium, side* 'silk' < VLat. *seda* < Lat. *seta, sutere* 'shoemaker' < *sutor; cruft(e)* 'vault, crypt' < *crupta/crypta, cylen* 'kiln' < *culina, pile* 'mortar' < *pila, pinn* 'pin, peg', *port* 'gate, door' < *porta, regol* 'wooden ruler' < *regula, scindel* 'roof-shingle' < *scindula, tigle* 'tile, brick' < *tegula, weall* 'wall' < *vallum, ynce* 'inch' < *uncia; ceaster* 'city' < *castra, ceosol* 'hut' < *casula,* *cluse* 'enclosure' < VLat. *clusa*, *cycene* 'kitchen' < *coquina*, *port* 'harbour, port' < *portus*, *wic* 'dwelling, village, camp' < *vicus*; *camp* 'field, battle' (and *campian* 'to fight', *cempa* 'warrior') < *campus*, *diht* 'saying, direction' < *dictum*; *dihtan* 'set in order' < *dictare*; *scrifan* 'allot, decree' < *scribere* (one of the few verbal loans that entered into the category of strong verbs, cf. PDE *shrive* – *shrove* – *shriven*), *sinoð* 'council, synod' < *synodus*, *stræt* 'road' < (*via*) *strata*; *ceap* 'goods, price, market', *ceapian*/*ciepan* 'buy' < *caupo* 'innkeeper, wine-seller', *mangere* 'merchant, trader', *mangian* 'to trade' < *mango* 'dealer in slaves and other goods'; *mil* 'mile' < *mille* (*passuum*), *mydd* 'bushel' < *modius*, *pund* 'pound' < *pondo*, *toll* 'toll' < *teloneum*; *predician* 'preach' < *praedicare*, *mynster* 'minster' < *monasterium*; *mæsse* 'mass' < *missa*, *abbud* 'abbot' < *abbat-em*; *munuc* 'monk' < *monachus*; *scol* 'school' < *scola* (thus Berndt 1982:52; Serjeantson 1935:281, 286 and Strang 1970:367 place these in the 2nd and partly even in the 3rd period).

Loans of this and the next period were mainly introduced via the spoken language, i.e. their source was not the classical, written Latin used for scholarly and religious purposes, but the popular form, called Vulgar Latin. This began gradually to undergo sound changes (e.g. *i* > *é*, *ú* > *ó*) by which it came to differ from Classical Latin. Whether a loan exhibits such changes or not is thus one criterion to determine its age. Thus, the loans *disc* 'dish' < *discus*, *pic* 'pitch' < *picem*, *trifetum* d.pl. 'tributes' < *tributum*, *cugele* 'cowl' < *cuculla* (with VLat [k] > [g]), *culter* 'knife' < *culter*, *must* 'must' < *mustum* are early loans, while *cest*, WS *cyst* 'box' < *cista*, *peru* 'pear' < *pirum*, *segn* 'banner' < *signum*, *insegel* 'seal' < **insigillum*, *copor* 'copper' < *cuprum*, *torr* 'tower' < *turris* are later and show the VLat. development of [i] > [e], [u] > [o] dating back to the third century.

Another criterion for the establishment of the age of a loan is whether it has undergone sound changes that are relevant also for the history of native words. Thus, *i*-umlaut and/or palatalisation/assibilation are fairly safe criteria according to which *tyrnan* 'turn, revolve' < *tornare*/*turnare*, *ciepan* 'buy' < *caupo* 'innkeeper, wine-seller', *mydd* 'bushel' < *modius*, *mynet* 'coin, money' < *moneta*, *cemes* 'shirt' < *camisia*, *celc* 'cup' < *calicem*, *cyse* 'cheese' < *caseus* are old loans, while *calic* 'cup' < *calicem*, *tunece* 'tunic' < *tunica*, *pic* 'pike' < *picus*, *castel* 'village, small town' are much later. Of particular interest are doublets such as *celc*/*calic* 'cup' < *calicem*, *cliroc*/*cleric* 'clerk, clergyman' < *clericus*, *cellendre*/*coryandre* 'coriander' < *coriandrum*, *leahtric*/*lactuca* 'lettuce' < *lactuca*, *spynge*/*sponge* 'sponge' < *spongea*, *læden*/*latin* 'Latin' < *latinus*, *lempedu/lamprede* 'lamprey' < *lampreta*, *minte/menta* 'mint' < *menta*, etc., where the second form was reborrowed in the 3rd period.

5.2.1.3   The second period of Latin influence on the OE vocabulary is usually identified with the settlement period after ca 450 until the Christianisation of the Anglo-Saxons, which began at the end of the sixth century. How many Latin loans were incorporated by the Germanic settlers in this period is a matter of dispute and much depends on the assessment of the linguistic situation that prevailed in Britain when the Anglo-Saxons arrived. Baugh & Cable (1978:45–6, 79–80) assume that after about 410, with the official withdrawal of the last of the Roman troops from Britain, the use of Latin began to decline, since it had at best been used by Britons belonging to the upper classes and inhabitants of the cities and towns. They therefore conclude that there was 'no opportunity for direct contact between Latin and Old English in England, and such Latin words as could have found their way into English would have had to come in through Celtic transmission' (Baugh & Cable 1978:80). But since the Celtic influence on the OE vocabulary has been very slight, (see below §5.2.2), Baugh & Cable conclude that the number of Latin loans transmitted by the Britons also was very small. As relatively certain candidates they only mention *ceaster* < *castra* as a frequent place-name element, cf. *Chester*, *Colchester*, *Manchester*, *Winchester*, etc., *port* 'harbour, town' and 'gate' < *portus/porta*, *wic* 'village' < *vicus* (all three are classified as continental borrowings by Serjeantson 1935:271ff.), *munt* 'mountain' < *mont-em* and *torr* 'tower, rock' < *turris*. Strang (1970:390), on the other hand, following Jackson (1953:ch. 3), assumes that Latin was still the official language of Britain in the first half of the fifth century, although for everyday purposes British was used, and that it even survived among the upper classes and rulers of the Highland zone during the sixth century, i.e. during the settlement period. She then claims that 'very many Latin words passed into OE at this stage', but admits that it is in many cases difficult to decide 'how far the early English loans from Latin represent direct borrowings from Latin-speaking Britons who remained among them, how far they are words which have passed through British to enter OE, or even how far they are really continental loans resulting from the close contacts the English still maintained with Europe' (Strang 1970:390). As examples she quotes *cyrtel* 'garment, kirtle' < *cyrtan* 'to shorten' < *curt-us* 'short', *stropp* 'strap' < *stroppus*, *ancor* 'anchor' < *anchora*, *punt* 'punt' < *ponto*, *oele* 'oil' < *oleum*, *cest* 'box' < VLat. *cesta* < *cista*, *mortere* 'mortar' < *mortarium*, *pægel* 'pail' < VLat. *pagella*, *pott* 'pot' < VLat. ?*pottus*, *tunne* 'cask' < VLat. *tunne*, *cæster* (earlier *ceaster*) < *castra*, *cerfelle* 'chervil' < *cerefolium*, *coccel* 'corn-cockle' < VLat. *cocculus*, *petersilie* 'parsley' (the modern form is from F *persil*) < *petroselinium*, *fann* 'winnowing fan' < *vannum*, *forca* 'fork' < *furca*, *catt(e)* 'cat' < VLat. *cattus, -a, cocc* 'cock' < *coccus, truht* 'trout' < *tructa, muscelle* 'mussel' < *musculus, læden* 'Latin; a language' < VLat. *Ladinus* < *Latinus, munuc* 'monk' < *monachus, mynster* 'monastery, minster' < *monasterium, nunne* 'nun' < Late Lat. *nonna, sætern-* 'Saturn' in *sæterndæg* 'Saturday' < *Saturni dies*.

Most of these are also contained in Serjeantson's list B 'Words probably borrowed in Britain, 450–650' (Serjeantson 1935:277–81), which includes 112 lexical items. *Catte, munuc, mynster* are continental loans according to Serjeantson. The largest group are again plant names and words for vessels and agriculture; but as in the preceding period we find words for dresses and textiles, food and cooking expressions, animals, and a larger number of words having to do with religion and learning. Thus we might add the following from Serjeantson's list: *mægester* 'master' < *magister, prafost/profost* 'officer, steward' < *prae-positus, segn* 'mark, sign' < *signum, cugle* 'cowl' < VLat. *cuculla, mentel* 'cloak' < *mantellum, cæfestre* 'halter' < *capistrum, teosol* 'die' < *tessella, tasol* 'mosaic stone' < **tassellus, -a, -um* (cf. Dietz 1985, according to whom *teosol* and *tasol*, usually listed as variants, should be treated as different lexical items with different etyma), *trefet* 'tripod' < *tripod-em, cocer* 'quiver' < VLat. *cucurum, eced* 'vinegar' < *acetum, mur* 'wall' < *murus, æbs* 'fir-tree' < *abies, humele,* 'hop-plant' < VLat. *humulus, leahtric* 'lettuce' < *lactuca, lent* 'lentil' < *lent-em, lufestic* 'lovage' < VLat. *luvestica* < *ligusticum, sæppe* 'spruce fir' < *sappinus, senap* 'mustard' < *sinapis* (cf. earlier *sinop*), *solsece* 'heliotrope' < *solsequia, renge* 'spider' < *aranea, lafian* 'to bathe, wash' < *lavare, trifulian* 'to grind to powder' < *tribulare, dilegian* 'to cancel, blot out, destroy' < *delere, græf* 'stylus' < *graphium, mynecen* 'nun' < VLat. *monic-* < *monachus* + Gmc feminine suffix *-en, pinsian* 'reflect, consider' < *pensare*.

5.2.1.4.1 In the third period, the type of loans as well as the way in which they were adopted differed rather markedly from that of the previous two. The church became the dominant vehicle for the introduction of loans, and so we notice a considerable increase of loans having to do with religion and learning, although borrowing in the domain of material culture, which had dominated earlier on, did continue. The introduction of the Benedictine Reform at the end of the tenth century is an important dividing line within this period, not only because after its implementation the majority of loans take on a distinctly learned character and are therefore less integrated into the vocabulary, but also because the spiritual renaissance sparked off by it was one of the causes for the establishment of a supraregional written standard in Wessex.

The loans of the first two periods had come into English mainly through the oral medium. Now they were more and more introduced into the written language, before they entered the spoken register, if they in fact ever did, since many of them, especially towards the end of this period, remained confined to written language. This change is not really surprising in view of the cultural and social situation in which the Anglo-Saxons found themselves, for which see the remarks in chapter 1. Latin played a central role in these developments, because it was the language of the church and of learning and scholarship. On the other hand, the new faith had to be propagated in the vernacular, which thus had to be adapted to the task of expressing many new concepts. Had English then behaved with regard to borrowing in the same way as it did under similar circumstances in later centuries, the number of loans would have been tremendous. But, although it is higher than in the previous periods, it is much lower than one would expect, because other means of extending the vocabulary – semantic loans, loan translation and loan creations – were preferred (cf. 5.2.1.5 below).

Loans in the religious sphere predominantly refer to church organization, ranks and functions, less to the central notions of the faith, e.g. *abbod* 'abbot' < VLat. *abbad-em* < *abbat-em*, *abudesse* 'abbess' < VLat. *abbadissa*, *alter* 'altar' < *altar*, *(a)postol* 'apostle' < *apostolus*, *ælmæsse* 'alms' < VLat. *almosina*, *bæȝere/bæðȝere* 'baptist' < *baptista* (a case of folk etymology, the first part being mistakenly associated with *bæþ* 'bath'), *culpe* 'guilt, fault' < *culpa*, *cumædre/cumpæder* 'god-mother/godfather' < Late Lat. *commater/compater* (with partial anglicisation of the second part), *mæslere* 'sacristan' < VLat. *mansion-arius*, *messe/mæsse* 'mass' < VLat. *messa* < *missa*, *nonn(e)* 'monk' < *nonnus*, *offrian* 'sacrifice, offer' < *offerre*, *oflæte* 'oblation' < *oblata*, *papa* 'pope' < *papa*, *predician* 'preach' < *praedicare*, *sacerd* 'priest' < *sacerdos*, *regol* 'rule of religious life' < *regula*. There are also several loans referring to books and learning, e.g. *canon* 'canon of scripture' < *canon*, *calend* 'month' < *calendae*, *fers* 'verse' < *versus*, *cranic* 'chronicle' < *chronica*, *(e)pistol* 'letter' < *epistula*, *graðul* 'gradual, mass-book' <

graduale, *scol* 'school' < *scola*, *studdian* 'to see, take care of' < *studere*.

Other areas are plants, e.g. *balsam* 'balsam, balm' < *balsamum*, *bete* 'beetroot' < *beta*, *caul/cawel* 'cole, cabbage' < *caulis*, *lilie* 'lily' < *lilium*, *laur* 'laurel' < *laurus*, *menta* 'mint' < *minta* (for earlier *mint*), *rose* 'rose' < *rosa*, *sigle* 'rye' < *secale*, and *plant* 'plant' < *planta* itself; household items, vessels, etc., some examples being *ferele* 'rod' < *ferula*, *pic* 'pike' < *picus*, *caul* 'basket' < *cavellum*; music, hence *citere* 'cither' < *cithara*, *fipele* 'fiddle' < VLat. *vitula*, *orgel* 'organ' < *organum*; and buildings, thus *fenester* 'window' < *fenestra*, *palentse* 'palace' < VLat. *palantium*, *plætse* 'open place in a town, street' < *platea*.

5.2.1.4.2 The loans adopted during these first two centuries of Christian and ecclesiastical influence still came in, at least partly, via the spoken language. This is confirmed by the fact that quite a few show the phonological changes characteristic of Vulgar Latin or had not been part of the Classical Latin vocabulary. Thus they reflect, to a certain extent, the kind of Latin apparently spoken at the monasteries, which obviously was not the pure Classical variety. Things became radically different in the subsequent centuries, when Classical Latin was more or less the exclusive source of the loans and the borrowing process primarily involved the written language. The reasons for this are again closely related to the external history of the country between 800 and 1050, notably the invasions and settlements of the Vikings, Alfred's educational reforms and, above all, the Benedictine monastic revival, see chapter 1 for further details. It is in the period of the Benedictine reforms, when learning and scholarship were re-established, that once more a considerable number of loans were introduced into English, according to Strang (1970:314) roughly 150. But their character was different now. They were all drawn from Classical Latin, reflect the scholarly interests of the writers, and were not really integrated into the native linguistic system. Very often, they are technical terms, and more often than not they would even keep their Latin ending rather than adopt the appropriate West Saxon one, as had been the case earlier. This is the period where often an older, integrated loan was duplicated by a new, learned loan, cf. the examples at the end of §5.2.1.2, or *corona* besides earlier *coren* 'crown', *tabele/tablu* 'table, tablet' besides earlier *tæfl*, *clauster* 'cloister' besides earlier *clustor* < *claustrum*, *cucurbite* instead of earlier *cyrfet* < *cucurbita*, *turtur* instead of *turtle* 'turtle-dove' < *turtur*, *magister* instead of *mægester* < *magister* or Ælfric's *cuppe* 'cup' < *cuppa* instead of the integrated *copp*. A fairly comprehensive survey of these loans was made by Funke (1914). As Strang (1970:314) aptly puts it, the loans of this period fill gaps 'mainly relevant to the concerns of the educated professed man of religion, for whom linguistic concessions do not need to be made'; moreover, 'many reflect growing curiosity about branches of learning and about distant places and their products'.

Typical examples of religious loans from this period include: *acolitus* 'acolyte' < *acoluthus*, *apostata* 'apostate', *cleric* 'clerk, clergyman' < *clericus*, *creda* 'creed, belief' < *credo*, *crisma* 'chrism' < *chrisma*, *cruc* 'cross' < *cruc-em*, *demon* 'demon' < *daemon*, *discipul* 'disciple' < *discipulus*, *paradis* 'paradise' < *paradisus*, *prior* 'prior' < *prior*, *sabbat* 'sabbath' < *sabbatum*, and certain terms for liturgical books, see Gneuss (1985), e.g. *sacramentor(i)um*, *antiphonaria*, *collectaneum*, *passionale*, *martyrlina*.

Loans of this period are also found pertaining to scholarship, learning, culture and recreation, and science. Amongst some of the more interesting examples are: *bibliopece* 'library' < *bibliotheca*, *capitol(a)* 'chapter' < *capitolum*, *declinian* 'decline' < *declinare*, *grammatic(-cræft)* 'grammar' < *(ars) grammatica*, *mechanisc* 'mechanical' < *mechanicus* (with suffix adaptation), *philosoph* 'philosopher' < *philosophus*, *paper* 'paper' < *papyrus*, *bises* 'leap-year' < *bissextus*, *cometa* 'comet' < *cometa* (but also glossed as *feaxede steorra* 'haired star'), *cantere* 'singer' < *cantor* (with suffix adaptation), *chor* 'dance, choir, chorus' < *chorus*, *cimbal(a)* 'cymbal' < *cymbalum*, *ymen* 'hymn' < *hymnus*, *coc/cocere* 'cook' < VLat. *cocus* < *coquus*, *press* 'wine-press' < *pressa*, *scutel* 'dish, scuttle' < *scutula*, *cucumer* 'cucumber' < *cucumer*, *organe* 'marjoram' < *origanum*, *persic* 'peach' < *persicum*, *rosmarin* 'rosemary' < *rosmarinus*, *salfie* 'sage' < *salvia*, *ysope* 'hyssop' < *hyssopum*, *aspide* 'asp, viper' < *aspid-*, *basilisca* 'basilisk' < *basiliscus* (also glossed as *fahwyrm*), *cancer* 'crab' < *cancer*, *delfin* 'dolphin' < *delphinus*, *leo* 'lion' < *leo*, *lopust* 'locust' < *locusta* (influenced by OE *loppestre* 'lobster'), *pard* 'leopard' < *pardus*, *mamma* 'breast' < *mamma*, *plaster*, 'plaster' < *emplastrum*, *rabbian* 'be mad, rage' < *rabiare*, *scrofel* 'scrofula' < *scrofula*.

As in the previous periods, the overwhelming majority of these loans are nouns. Borrowed adjectives and verbs are rare, but very often we find that denominal adjectives and verbs are coined according to the OE word-formation patterns. Many of the loans had thus been integrated fairly well into the OE linguistic system. At the same time, this tendency once again illustrates the resourcefulness of indigenous means for extending the vocabulary.

5.2.1.5.1 Given the impact Roman culture and Christianisation had on the Anglo-Saxons, on their way of thinking and their material culture, the number of Latin loans borrowed in the OE period is relatively small, in particular when compared to the number of Latin loans that came in during Middle and Early Modern English. The main reason for this is the astonishing versatility with which the native vocabulary could be used in order to render a foreign concept. We still lack a full-scale investigation of semantic loans, loan translation and loan-creation for the OE period, but the observations in Kroesch (1929), and Gneuss (1955, 1982, 1985) indicate that these processes were all-pervasive in the OE lexicon and by far outweigh the loans described in the previous sections. On the other hand, it cannot be denied that loans are much easier to recognise, and that it is not always easy to prove whether a given lexical item has been modelled after a foreign original. But, as Gneuss has shown, it can be done.

Semantic loans, where existing native lexemes adopt the meaning or part of the meaning of a foreign model, are probably the most frequent instances of borrowing, but also the most difficult to prove. It is tempting for the translator to have recourse to this solution rather than to either direct borrowing or a loan translation, because the former usually requires an additional explanation, while the latter may violate restrictions on the productivity of a word-formation pattern and may therefore not be fully acceptable. There is, of course, always the danger of misunderstanding: the translator may have intended the word to be understood in a non-usual sense, taken over from the Latin model, but the reader, not knowing this, might still interpret the word in its original, native sense. Thus, as Gneuss (1955:21) has pointed out, it is difficult to know whether *synn* as a semantic loan for *peccatum* really had adopted all its semantic features for all members of the speech community in view of its use in Beowulf (*Beo* 2472) *þa wæs synn ond sacu Sweona ond Geota* 'there was feud and strife between Swedes and Geats', where *synn* can hardly be interpreted in the Christian sense as 'violation of God's law'. Bosworth & Toller's translation (s.v. *synn* I. 'with reference to human law or obligation: *misdeed, fault, crime, wrong*') as 'then there was wrongdoing and strife between Swedes and Geats' seems to have been influenced by such a misunderstanding.

Semantic borrowing is an instance of semantic change, since no matter whether the old meaning is preserved or not, there is a change of meaning involved. Two subtypes may be distinguished.

(1) The original and the native lexical item share one reading, and an

additional reading is taken over from the original. This might be termed 'analogical semantic borrowing' and can be illustrated by *passio* 'suffering, Christ's Passion' ∼ *þrowung* 'suffering' (< *þrowian*) → 'Christ's Passion'; *lingua* 'tongue, language' ∼ *tunge* 'tongue' → 'language'; *pastor* 'shepherd, guardian of the soul' ∼ *hierde* 'shepherd' (< *heord* 'flock') → 'pastor'; *getimbran* 'build, construct, erect' (< *timber* 'building material, structure, building') → 'edify (spiritually)' from *aedificare* and 'instruct' from *instruere*; *mægen* 'bodily strength, might, valour, power; troops, army' → 'miracle, good deed' and 'heavenly host' from *virtus/virtutes* with these additional meanings.

(2) The foreign meaning is transferred without a shared reading; this might be called 'substitutive semantic borrowing' (Gneuss 1955:21ff.). An example already mentioned is the addition of the reading 'disciple, follower of Christ' of *discipulus* to the original meaning of *cniht* 'child, servant, retainer'. Here the imagination and creativity of the translator play a decisive role. Substitutive semantic borrowing is particularly frequent in the religious vocabulary, since in using a native ('heathen') word for a Christian concept, the pagan interpretation had to be replaced by the Christian concept and all its theological associations. A good example is the word *God* as used for *Deus* (cf. Strang 1970:368). Originally it seemed to have meant 'that which is invoked', 'that to which libation is poured', was a neuter noun and could form a plural, since the Germanic peoples had a polytheistic religion. The missionaries, however, had to convey the notion of a single Deity, a Person or One of the Persons of the Trinity. Instead of adopting the lexical item *Deus*, its meaning was substituted for the old meaning of *god*, which, in this case, even produced a grammatical change: *God* as a singular noun became masculine; if it occurred in the plural, it only referred to pagan gods and remained neuter.

But such substitutions were not restricted to religion; whenever Germanic words were used to render institutions of a different society, similar substitutions took place. Compare, for example, the equivalents of Roman institutions or positions such as *censor* ∼ *geroefa* 'sheriff, steward', *gladiator* ∼ *cempa* 'fighter', *dictator* ∼ *aldur* 'chief, leader', *res publica* ∼ *cynedom* in glosses, or *consul* ∼ *heretoga* 'commander, chieftain' ∼ *ladteowa* 'leader, general' ∼ *cyning* 'king' in Boethius, *præfectus* ∼ *cyning*, *ealdorman* 'ruler, prince, chief', *praetor* ∼ *ealdorman* in Orosius, where the OE lexical items also denote functions in the Anglo-Saxon political system.

There is no clear-cut boundary between these two groups, since the latter still presupposes a certain similarity between the meanings of the model and that of the native word; after all, such substitutions are not completely arbitrary. But the similarity, the semantic fit, is less obvious than in the first group. A reanalysis of these phenomena in the light of more recent semantic theories might provide better criteria for a delimitation, but has not yet been undertaken. In view of this, the following additional examples taken from Gneuss' (1955:49ff.) material culled from the Vespasian Psalter are not sub-classified into analogical and substitutive semantic loans: *dryhten* 'ruler, king' → 'Lord God' < *Dominus*; *gast* orig. 'demon, evil spirit' → 'soul; Holy Ghost; breath; wind, storm' < *spiritus*, *eadig* 'rich, wealthy, fortunate' → 'happy, blessed' < *beatus*, *alesan* 'to loosen, free, release', 'redeem, absolve' < *redimere* (but *alesnis* ∼ *redemptio* is probably a loan translation), *arisan* 'rise, get up' → 'rise from the dead' < *resurgere*, *rod* orig. 'rod, pole, measure of land' → 'cross, rood' < *crux*, *forgiefan* 'give, grant, allow', *forlætan* 'let go, relinguish, release' → 'forgive, pardon (sins)' < *dimittere*, *remittere*, *ignoscere* (similarly the nouns *forgefennis*, *forletnis* < *remissio*, *indulgentia*), *becn* 'beacon, sign,' → 'portent' < *prodigium*, *forþrested* 'crushed, oppressed, destroyed' → 'contrite' < *contritus*, *wit(e)ga* 'wise man, soothsayer' → 'prophet' < *propheta*.

Some further examples from Kroesch (1929) illustrate other, non-religious domains: *bite* 'bite' → 'pain of wound' < *morsus*, *clæne* 'pure, clean' → 'chaste, innocent' < *purus* (although in both instances independent metaphorical extension cannot be ruled out), *cræft* 'strength, art, skill' → 'trick, deceit' < *artificium*, *dæl* 'part, portion, share' → 'part of speech' < *pars orationis*, *gebygan* 'bow, bend' → 'inflect, decline a part of speech' < *inflectere*, *declinare*, *mod* 'heart, mind, spirit' → 'courage, arrogance, pride' < *animus*, *ramm* 'ram' → 'instrument for pounding or battering' < *aries*, *sellend* 'giver' → 'betrayer' < *traditor*.

5.2.1.5.2 Semantic borrowing always involves a pre-existing native lexical recipient to which the borrowed meaning is attached; this recipient may be either simple, as with *cniht*, or complex, i.e. a compound or derivative, as in *eadig*, *alesan*, *bite*. Loan-formations, on the other hand, are in principle new formations and therefore necessarily complex, i.e. compounds or derivatives. They involve the activation of some productive word-formation pattern in the recipient language, and they allow the hearer/reader to reconstruct the meaning of the lexical item from its external form (see below §5.4.1). This principle of compositionality or motivation is the basic *raison d'être* of word-formation, because it reduces the memory load by providing for transparent, i.e. analysable, lexical items, whose meanings do not have to be remembered but can be deduced even when one encounters them for the first time. Thus *regnlic* 'rainy' as a translation of *pluvialis* (*ÆGram* 54.8), or in *þa regenlican weter* 'the rainy waters' for *pluviales aquas* in *Ps* (A) 77.44 is wholly transparent to anyone who comes across it for the first time; in Marchand's (1969:228ff.) terminology it is a 'transpositional adjective', which simply transposes a noun (e.g. *regn*) into the category of adjective, without adding anything else to it. Similarly transparent are *eft-cerran* (from *eft-* 'again' and *cerran* 'turn, go') 'turn back, return' as a translation of *redire, reverti*, parallel to *eftcuman* 'come again', *efthweorfan* 'return, recur', *eftsceogian* 'put one's shoe on again'; or *gescild-end* 'defender, protector' for *defensor, protector* parallel to the many agent nouns in *-end* (e.g. *hienend* 'accuser', *hierwend* 'blasphemer', *hliniend* 'one who reclines'). Unfortunately, however, not all wordformations are as straightforward as these because of the phenomenon of 'lexicalisation' or 'idiomatisation', which refers to the fact that word-formations may adopt meanings, meaning elements or referential specifications that can no longer be reconstructed from the constituents. Thus, *dælnimend* literally means 'someone or something taking part in', but from this it cannot be deduced that it glosses *participium*, except when Ælfric's explanation is added:

> he nymð anne dæl of naman and oðerne of worde, of naman he nymð CASUS, þæt is, declinunge, and of worde he nymð tide and getacnunge. of him bam he nymð getel and hiw.

> It takes one part from the noun (= 'name') and the other from the verb ('word') [both are examples of semantic loans]; from the noun it takes case, i.e. declination, and from the verb it takes tense (= 'time') and meaning/signification; from both it takes number and form.

Here the Latin form has been translated bit by bit, and the special meaning inherent in *participium*, but not part of the basic, literal meaning of *dælnimend*, has also been adopted. The result is a lexicalised or idiomatised loan translation, Betz's (1949:27) 'bereichernde Lehnübersetzung', where loan-formation is accompanied by semantic borrowing. The major difference between loan-formation and semantic loans is thus the creation of a morphological neologism by the former, but not by the latter; this creation, however, may in turn be accompanied by semantic borrowing, in which case the neologism adopts a special reading from the original which is not predictable, i.e. it is immediately lexicalised/idiomatised.

Loan-formations are sometimes subdivided into loan-translations or 'calques' (*Lehnübersetzungen*), loan-renditions (*Lehnübertragungen*) and loan-creations (*Lehnschöpfungen*) (cf. Gneuss 1955:31ff., 1985:119), although these divisions are not completely unproblematic.

5.2.1.5.3   In a loan-translation each element of the model is reproduced by a semantically corresponding element of the borrowing language. The model is thus itself complex, i.e. a compound or derivative or a syntactic group. Thus, *liber evangelii* and *liber benedictionum* are rendered by the compounds *godspellboc* 'gospel book' and *bletsungboc* 'book of blessings'; *liber missalis* and *liber epistolaris* have as equivalents *mæsseboc* 'mass-book' and *pistolboc* 'epistle-book'. Similarly, *ascensor* is translated as *upstigend*, *onstigend* 'one who mounts up, rider', *dominatio* as *waldnis* 'rule', *monarchia* as *anweald* 'single power'. Somewhat problematic in this respect are the numerous Latin verbs of the type *instruere*, *decipere*, *continere*, etc., where 'prefix' and 'base' have lost their original meaning, so that it is questionable in how far such lexical items should still be regarded as complex. The problem is exactly parallel to the handling of PDE verbs such as *receive*, *deceive*, *conceive*; *commit*, *submit*, *transmit*, etc., where some linguists would argue that they are bimorphemic, whereas others would reject such an analysis (cf. Marchand 1969:5–6). Often, such 'prefixal' verbs are translated by OE verbs that are also characterised by a prefix, the prefix being redundant, or at least without any specific meaning: cf., e.g. *instruere* ∼ *ontimbran* 'instruct' (*timbran* = 'build, construct, erect, instruct', i.e. *timbran* = *ontimbran* in this sense), *praeferre* 'prefer' ∼ *foreberan* lit. 'carry before', probably also *accendere*, *incendere* 'set fire to, burn' and *incensio* 'burning, kindling', which are rendered by *onælan* and *onal* (but *ælan*, *al* seem to have the same meaning as the prefixations), and cf. also *incensio* 'incense' ∼ *onbærning*, *onbærnness*. In such cases, the loan-translation process seems to have operated purely mechanically, only taking account of the formal make-up of the model, which the translator tried to replicate in the receptor language, but disregarding its lack of semantic compositionality. Since such instances seem to be rather frequent, it would be interesting to find out whether or not such purely formal correspondences were only possible because many OE prefixes had already lost their meaning to a considerable extent at the time when these formations were coined. In that case the status of numerous native prefix formations would have already been more or less the same as that of the semantically opaque Latin models, and the translator simply tried to mechanically find a morphological one-to-one correspondence. Alternatively, it is of course possible that this mechanical procedure created havoc among prefixations and accelerated their decline by adding more and more instances of morphosemantically opaque formations to the numerous already existing ones, since many OE prefix formations of old standing were certainly no longer analysable in OE, e.g. *onginnan* 'begin', *forgietan* 'forget', etc. Probably these are not really alternatives but concurrent factors that supported each other. The question has, to my knowledge, not yet been looked at from this point of view, but considering the radical loss of OE verbal prefixes in the subsequent period, which has so far been explained only partly, this aspect might be worth considering.

Loan translations abound in OE, as the following highly selective examples from *Ps(A)* in Gneuss (1955:51ff.) show. Many more can be found in practically every OE translation; a particularly rich source is Ælfric's *Grammar*.

Compounds: *bene-placitum* ~ *wel-gelicod* 'God's pleasure', *misericors* ~ *mildheort* adj. 'merciful = mildhearted' (with derivative *mildheortness misericordia*), although Gneuss (1982:155), in view of the series *bliþheort* 'happy, joyful', *cealdheort* 'cruel', *gramheort* 'hostile-minded', *hatheort* 'wrathful, furious', etc., doubts whether this is really a loan-translation; a further argument adduced by him is the non-correspondence of *miser* 'poor' and *mild*; *pusillanimus* ~ *lytelmod* 'having little courage, pusillanimous', besides *wacmod* in the same meaning, *maledicere* ~ *wergcweoðan* 'speak badly, maledict, curse', *unicornis/unicornuus* ~ *anhorn/anhyrne* 'unicorn'/'having one horn', *nocticorax* ~ *næhthrefn* 'nightraven', *particeps* ~ *dælnimend* 'one who takes part'.

Prefixations: *col-laudare* ~ *efen-herian* 'praise together', *aspergere* ~ *on-stregdan* 'sprinkle' (*stregdan* 'strew, sprinkle'), *enuntiare* ~ *forþcyðan* 'announce, declare', *advocare* ~ *togecegan* 'to call together', *providere/praevidere* ~ *foreseon* 'foresee', *in-noc-en-s* ~ *un-sceðð-end-e* 'innocent, harmless', *inebriare* ~ *indrencan* 'make drunk', *inhabitare* ~ *ineardian* (= *eardian*) 'inhabit', *circumhabitare* ~ *ymbeardian* 'dwell around', *regredi* ~ *eftgan* 'go back', *provehere* ~ *forþwegan* 'go forth, progress'.

Suffixations: *trinitas* ~ *þriness* 'trinity', *libera-tor* ~ *gefrig-end* 'liberator', *salvator* ~ *hælend* 'saviour', *miserator* ~ *mildsiend* 'pitier', *il-lumina-tio* ~ *in-liht-nis* 'illumination', *episcopatus* ~ *biscophad* 'office of bishop, episcopate', *sanctitas, sanctimonium* ~ *halignis* 'sanctity', *sanctificatio* ~ *hal-*

igung 'consecration', *contra-dic-tio* ~ *wið-cweden-nis* 'contradiction', etc. Compare also the following examples from *ÆGram*: *coniunctio* ~ *geðeodnys* 'joining' < *(ge)ðeodan* 'join', *praepositio* ~ *foresetnys* 'that which is put before', *in-corpor-al-ia* ~ *un-licham-lic-u* 'incorporeal', *possessivum* ~ *geagniendlic* 'possessive', *comparativus* ~ *wiðmetendlic* 'comparative', *comparatio* ~ *wiðmetenness* 'comparison' < *wiðmetan* ~ *comparare*, *diminutivum* ~ *wanjendlic* 'diminutive' < *wanian* 'diminish' and many more.

5.2.1.5.4 Unlike loan-translations, loan-renditions do not correspond in all their elements to the foreign model, but at least one morphological constituent must be semantically equivalent to some part of the model (Gneuss 1985:119). Thus, a derivative may be rendered by a compound, as, e.g. *discipulus* ~ *leorningcniht* 'disciple' (besides the loan-translation *leornere*), or *nocturnale* ~ *nihtsang* 'nocturn = night song', *liber manualis* ~ *handboc*, etc., or a simple lexical item by a complex one, e.g. *domus* in the sense of 'family, race' by *gehusscipe* lit. 'houseship'. Loan-renditions are rarer than loan-translations and more difficult to spot. Moreover, they are not always easy to distinguish from the latter, and in individual cases it may be difficult to decide which category a given formation belongs to. Thus, the compounds *bletsungboc* and *mæsseboc* were treated as loan-translations above on the assumption that they rendered the Latin syntactic groups *liber benedictionum* and *liber missale*. But Latin has also the terms *benedictionale* and *missale*, which, morphologically speaking, are derivatives, and could also have acted as models. In this case, *bletsungboc* and *mæsseboc* would count as loan-renditions. Without knowing which model actually prompted the OE formation any decision seems to be arbitrary. Similarly, *calumni-are* and *calumnia-tor* are matched by the loan-formations *hearm-cwepan* 'calumniate' and *hearm-cwep-end* 'calumniator'. The verb clearly is a case of loan-rendition, since the Latin form is a derivative, while the OE form is a compound, at least superficially, but see §5.4.3. Derivationally speaking, the noun *hearm-cwep-end* is a loan-translation, because it matches *calumnia-tor* in this respect: both are deverbal derivatives. But structurally speaking, it has to be treated as a loan-rendition because of the divergent morphological make-up. Thus, for some of the following examples, again taken from Gneuss's material, the classification may be disputable.

Investiga-tor ~ *aspyrg-end* 'investigator' (*aspyrian* = *spyrian* 'investigate', probably another case where an apparent Latin prefix was 'translated'), *prosperari* ~ *gesundfullian* 'prosper' (*prosperus* ~ *gesund*), *iustificatio* ~ *gerehtwisung* 'justification', *sabbatum* ~ *restedæg* 'day of rest'

(< Heb. *schabbath* 'to rest'), *praevaricatio* ~ *oferleornis* 'transgression'
(< *oferleoran* 'transgress', in this sense a semantic loan, the normal
meaning is 'pass over, by'; the noun could therefore also be interpreted
as a loan-translation), *index* ~ *gebecnend* 'indicator' (< *gebecnan* 'indicate'), *parabola* ~ *bispell* 'proverb' (the meaning 'parable' is probably
a secondary semantic loan, cf. Gneuss (1955:96)), *ignorantia* ~ *unond-
cyðignes* 'ignorance, lit. state of not knowing' (< *oncyðig* 'conscious,
understanding'), *superbire* ~ *oferhygdian* 'be proud' (< *oferhygd*
'proud'), *alienatio* ~ *afremðung*, *ælfremedung* 'alienation' (*ā* + *fremde* 'foreign' > *afremdian* 'to estrange', *ælfremed* 'strange'), *locquacitas* ~ *fela-
sprec-ol-ness* 'loquacity, much-speakingness' (*LibSc* 79,9; 170, 18), *captio*
~ *geheftedness* 'trap' (in *Ps(DEGH) gegripennis*), *irreprehensibilis* ~ *un-
telwyrde* 'lit. unblameworthy' (< *tæl* 'blame'), *innocens* ~ *unsceðful*
'innocent' (≠ 'not harmful', which would be the literal meaning),
retribuere ~ *geedleanian* 'reward' (< *edlean* 'reward'), *legislator* ~ *ælad-
teow* 'legislator' (< *æ* 'law' + *ladteow* 'prince, leader'), *domus* in the
sense 'family, race' ~ *gehusscipe* lit. 'houseship', *lactans* ~ *milcdeond*
'suckling, i.e. someone who sucks milk', also *milsucend*, and many more.

Occasionally, the literalmindedness of glossators and translators leads
to errors that illustrate the creativity of this process – and with it that of
OE word-formation – even more drastically than the appropriate
translations quoted so far. In Canticum 4, 10 of *Ps(A)* we find the phrase
et familici saturati sunt. Comparison with other versions shows that
familici is a scribal error for *famelici* 'the hungry ones', and accordingly
in other manuscripts we get glosses such as *þa hungrigan, þa hungriendan*,
i.e. the passage means 'the hungry shall be fed'. The glossator of *Ps(A)*,
however, did not notice the error, interpreted *familici* as a diminutive of
famulus 'servant' and translated it as *ðiowincel* 'little servant', thus
demonstrating the productivity of the diminutive suffix + *incel*.

5.2.1.5.5 The last category, also the rarest and most difficult to
establish, comprises loan-creations, where no element of the newly
formed lexical item corresponds directly to those of the word it
translates. The following examples may suffice to illustrate the process:
basiliscus ~ *fahwyrm* 'basilisk, lit. variegated snake or reptile', *diluvium*
~ *cwildeflod* 'deluge, lit. flood that brings death', *baptismum* ~ *ful-
wiht/baptizare* ~ *fulwian* 'baptise, lit. consecrate fully', *cives* ~
ceasterwaran 'citizens, lit. inhabitants of the city', *inferi* ~ *helwearan*
'inhabitants of hell', *rectus corde* ~ *rehtheort* 'someone who is righteous',
usura ~ *westmsceat* 'usury, interest, lit. benefit-wealth' (*wæstm* 'benefit,

product, interest', *sceat* 'wealth, property'), *solium* ~ *sundurseld* 'throne = special seat', *incolatus* ~ *londbigang* 'pilgrimage, stay in a (foreign) country'.

5.2.1.5.6 The examples used to illustrate these three categories of loan-formations together with those documenting semantic loans are only a very small selection of the material, but they document how deeply the Anglo-Saxon way of thinking had been influenced not only by the impact of Christianity, but also by the language through which it had been brought to them, Latin. On the other hand, they also testify to the resourcefulness of the native language, whose word-formational flexibility by far surpasses that of present-day English. It is all the more regrettable that so far we have no comprehensive study of Old English word-formation, and in particular no systematic study of Old English word-formations and their relationship to Latin models in translations, since this could also tell us something about the relative productivity of the various Old English patterns. It is to be hoped, however, that this gap will be closed in the near future.

5.2.2 *Celtic influence*

When one people conquers another and subsequently the two peoples mix by intermarriage, the resulting contact situation normally has important linguistic consequences. Usually, one of the two languages, either that of the conquerors, but sometimes that of the conquered people, will eventually prevail, but it will always exhibit deep influences of the other language. Thus in France, Latin was greatly modified by the Celtic substratum, and in England the languages of the two conquerors, the Scandinavians and the Normans, have also left indelible traces, so much so that some linguists even assume a stage of creolisation in ME, for English–Scandinavian recently, e.g. Poussa (1982), and for English–French e.g. Bailey & Maroldt (1977), hypotheses that are rejected by many because of the rather wide notion of 'creole' assumed in both cases (e.g. Görlach 1986).

One would expect that the same kind of development took place when the Angles, Saxons, Jutes and other Germanic tribes gradually took over Britain in the fifth and sixth centuries. As far as we can tell, the Celts were by no means generally exterminated by the invaders, as the place-name evidence shows. Many fled to the west and the north, where a considerable Celtic-speaking population survived until fairly late times; thus there is a whole cluster of Celtic place-names in the northeastern part of Dorset (Zachrisson 1927:55), and there is also evidence that Celtic must have lingered on in Northumbria because of certain loans found only in Northumbrian texts (*bratt* 'cloak', *carr* 'rock', *luh* 'lake'). Moreover, it is not unlikely that Celts were held as slaves by the conquerors, cf. the semantic development of the form *wealh*, which came to mean 'slave', and certainly many of the Anglo-Saxons married Celtic women. Thus, at least in parts of England, contact between the two peoples must have been fairly intimate and must have persisted over several generations. Nevertheless, the traces Celtic has left on the emerging Anglo-Saxon dialects are minimal – not even a definable phonological substratum has been established. And as to loans, the number of those that have been identified with certainty is so low that we can afford to give a complete list. It is only in the domain of place-names that the influence is substantial, see chapter 8, and, moreover, there are regional differences; thus the West-Midland areas show a higher proportion of Welsh loans, which is particularly noticeable in the field-naming of the Welsh marches (see Dodgson 1985b).

The Celtic loans found in OE can be attributed to three different strata: continental loans, loans taken over after the settlement and loans adopted in the course of Christianisation, probably from Irish missionaries, which is why these are mainly ecclesiastic and religious terms. Almost all Celtic loan words became established as popular words, and all, with the exception of those from the last stratum, were taken over via the spoken language. Only the religious terms probably came in through writing.

Words usually regarded as continental loans, which also occur in other Gmc languages, are *rice* 'rule, reign, empire' (but cf. Kluge 1967: s.v. *Reich*, who opts for a native origin) and *ambeht* 'servant, service, office' (possibly via Latin *ambactus*).

The following loans are due to the period after the settlement: *binn* 'bin' < OBrit. *benna (although this might have been borrowed from Gallo-Roman on the continent); *bannoc* 'a bit, piece (of a cake or a loaf)' < OBrit. *bannoc 'a bit, drop', occurring only in a gloss to one of Aldhelm's works; *gafeluc* 'a small spear' in Ælfric's *Vocabulary* 143 is questionable; *dunn* 'dark-coloured, grey, dunn', qualifying *tunecan* 'tunic' and *stan* in some charters; *broc* 'badger' in Ælfric's *Vocabulary* 119; *assen* 'ass', originally from Latin *asinus*, may have come in through Old Welsh *assen. Three more items occur in the Lindisfarne Gospels:

bratt 'cloak', together with *hrægl* and *hæcla* glossing *pallium*; *carr* 'rock'; and *luh* < OWelsh **luch* (cf. *loch*) 'lake, inland sea, strait'. Finally, there are some cases which are frequent as place-name elements, but also occur as independent lexical items: *torr* 'rock, rocky peak, hill' < OBrit. *torr* in Ælfric's *Vocabulary* 147 glossing *scopulum*; it occurs also in other glosses, and is frequent in charters; *cumb* 'deep valley' < OBrit. **kumba* (cf. place-names like *Ilfracombe*, etc.); and finally *funta*, which is originally Latin but may have come into English via Celtic, cf. place-names such as *Chalfont*.

Loans probably borrowed from the Irish missionaries that brought Christianity from the North are: *dry* 'magician, sorcerer' < OIr. *drui* (pl. *druid*), from which a feminine was derived by means of the native suffix *-icge*: *dryegge* in *þæt heo wære dryegge ond scinlæce* 'that she was a sorceress and a witch' (*Mart* 28); *clucge* 'bell' is recorded only once in the translation of Bede, and is replaced in other manuscripts by the native *bell*; *ancor* 'hermit, anchorite' < OIr. *anchara*, is originally from Latin. Also ultimately Latin are frequent *stær* 'history' (Irish *stoir* < VLat. *storia* < *historia*), where, however, the phonological development *o* > *æ* is unclear; the *hapax legomenon æstel* 'bookmark' in Alfred's Preface to his *Cura pastoralis* translation < Lat. *hastela* 'slip of wood' and *cine* 'gathering of parchment leaves' < OIr. *cin* < Lat. *quina* 'five each'. The last word of this set is *cross*, which is extremely rare in OE, the native word being *rod*. It is found in the name *Normannes cros* (a hundred name near Peterborough, today *Norman Cross*), which may, however, be a post-Viking coinage because of the naming pattern involved, and occurs three times in the tenth century; other Cross names are from the eleventh century. In view of its late appearance it has been argued that this word was borrowed from the Scandinavians; on the other hand, there is the well-known popularity of the stone-cross in Ireland, and the influence of Celtic art on the stone crosses of England. Moreover, there are hardly any religious terms borrowed from the Scandinavians, so Celtic origin is after all not completely unlikely. But the matter is not yet definitely settled one way or the other.

With the exception of the numerous place-names, the Celts have left remarkably little behind in English, a phenomenon that so far has not really been explained satisfactorily. True, the surviving Celts were a conquered race, but their culture must have been more developed than that of the German invaders due to the 400 years of Romanisation, and from that point of view more loans would not have been completely unlikely. Perhaps one reason may be that the Germanic tribes coming into England had already been familiar with Latin and preferred to borrow a Latin term if necessary, because they had come across it on the Continent, rather than borrow it from the Celts in a different guise. But this is mere speculation, and hardly possible to prove. So we can only state that Celtic, contrary to all expectations, has not really left its mark on the English language.

5.2.3   Scandinavian influence

5.2.3.1.1   When we now turn to the influence of the Scandinavian languages Danish and Norwegian (as to the relevance of this distinction cf. §5.2.3.2) on English subsequent to the Viking invasions, we are confronted with another problem that still awaits a definite solution. In connection with the Celts, it was their relative lack of influence that required explanation, it is now the intensity of the influence – but also its temporal deployment – that has to be explained. Thus, in OE we come across ca 150 loans, but in ME 'several thousands' (Hansen 1984:63) crop up in various manuscripts, especially of northern and western provenance, of which between 400 and 900 (Hansen 1984:60; Geipel 1971:70: 'some 400 items') have survived in Standard English and a further 600 or more in the dialects. Moreover, among these loans we find not only the expected share of technical vocabulary such as words for ships, money, legal institutions, warfare, etc. (cf. §5.2.3.4), we also meet with numerous everyday nouns such as PDE *band, bank, birth, crook, dirt, dregs, egg, fellow*, or adjectives such as *odd, rotten, rugged, scant, seemly, sly, tattered, tight, weak*, and even numerous verbs, e.g. *call, cast, clip, crave, crawl, die, droop, gape, gasp, get, give, glitter, raise, rake, rid, scare, scowl*. Furthermore, the phrasal verb type *come on, make up* – including *muck up, muck about*, where the verbs themselves are of Scandinavian origin (Poussa 1982:73) – seems to be due to Scandinavian influence (Logeman 1906), or was at least strengthened by a parallel Scandinavian pattern (Hiltunen 1983:42–4), while its ultimate origin has been attributed to a Celtic substratum (de la Cruz 1972:171ff.). And, even more important, not only lexical items were borrowed, but also grammatical items (form words) such as the pronouns *they, them, their, both, same*, or the prepositions *till* (in the sense of *to*), *fro* (cf. *to and fro*), *though* (the phonological form, replacing OE *þeah*); and, possibly, the spread of Northern *are* (vs. Southern *sindon*, pl. of *to be*, OE *beon*), as well as the *s*-suffix of the 3rd pers. sg. instead of original *-ð* (i.e. *he drifð > he drifes*) are also due to Scandinavian influence.

5.2.3.1.2   The Scandinavian influence on English has thus been very far-reaching indeed, and requires an explanation in terms of the type of language contact most likely to bring it about. But this involves an additional difficulty, one that also affects the presentation of the material in this volume: the temporal dimension of the borrowing process. According to the official historical sources – the Anglo-Saxon Chronicle – the Viking raids began in 787, when three shiploads of 'Danes' (according to Geipel 1971:32 more likely Norwegians), probably coming from France, descended upon Portland in Dorset (belonging to Wessex) and killed Beaduheard, the king's reeve, who had come to ask who they were. Regular settlement, one pre-requisite for large-scale borrowing, seems to have begun in the East and North in the second half of the ninth century, especially after the establishment of the Danelaw in 886 by the Treaty of Wedmore. By chance, the treaty between Alfred the Great and Guthrum also contains the first Scandinavian loans found in an Anglo-Saxon text: the items *healfmearc* 'half a mark' (adopting the Scandinavian monetary unit *mǫrk*) and *liesing* (in *heora liesengum* 'their freedmen') from ON *leysingiar* 'freedman'. What now causes the problem is the fact that in the OE texts up to ca 1100 only some 150 Scandinavian loans have been identified, many of them technical terms, while the overwhelming majority of the Scandinavian loans are found for the first time in early ME northern and eastern manuscripts such as *Orrmulum* (ca 1200) or *Havelock the Dane* (thirteenth century), i.e. about 300 years after the first *landnam*. We thus have to explain the time lag between the major settlement period, which was undoubtedly the tenth century, and the first appearance in manuscripts of the majority of the loans in ME, a phenomenon, incidentally, that will recur with the Norman French loans after the Conquest. This involves a decision as to where the Scandinavian influence should mainly be dealt with, in this or the next volume. The OE period is responsible for the extralinguistic situation that made borrowing on such a large scale possible, but the results of the process only become visible in ME. Any decision as to splitting up this process will be to some extent arbitrary, and must be a compromise. The following solution has been adopted. As to the loan words themselves, only those found in OE texts up to ca 1100 will be dealt with in this volume in greater detail. The general contact situation responsible for the borrowing process and the events leading up to it will be discussed briefly here, because this was established during the Danelaw period, and later during the period of Danish rule between 1016 and 1035, and consequently falls within the OE period. But we will also take at least a brief look at the contact situation after 1100 in order to shed some light on the later borrowings, since, as will be shown below, the subsequent developments are an immediate consequence of the state of affairs in the eleventh century.

5.2.3.2   For a brief summary of the historical events leading up to the Scandinavian settlement see chapter 1. According to Geipel (1971:34) the participants in the earliest raids were mainly Norwegians, who not only had been peacefully settling in substantial numbers on the Shetlands and Orkneys earlier on, but who now also appeared further south, driven by 'the same westward movement from Norway as that which led to the Scandinavian settlement of the Scottish Isles and Ireland, and eventually to the colonisation of Iceland and Greenland and the discovery of North America' (Geipel 1971:34). In these early reports, usually no distinction is made between Norwegians and Danes, both being lumped together under the cover-term 'Danes'. It is indeed questionable whether the distinction is of linguistic relevance for this period. Geipel (1971:27) assumes that 'the bulk of the Norse expressions in our language entered it at a time when regional discrepancies within the Scandinavian speech community must have been scarcely perceptible'. Be that as it may, demonstrably Danish rather than Norwegian activities at the British coast began around 835, marking the beginning of a series of raids which went on year after year for the next thirty years. These attacks seem to have been launched mainly from the Continent. At the same time, the Norwegians had continued their attacks on Ireland and finally, in 836, had captured Dublin, where they established a fortified base. From there, raids were undertaken into Ireland itself, but also to the Scottish Isles and Scotland, Northern and Western England and Wales.

In England, the yearly raids continued until 850. But in this year for the first time a Danish force overwintered on Thanet, an island in the Thames estuary, and captured London and Canterbury in the following spring. Winter camps on Thanet and Sheppey from now on became customary, but the Danish activities were still basically restricted to individual raids, which did not escalate into a real campaign. This changed in 860 (Geipel 1971:40; Strang 1970:318 and Baugh & Cable 1978:92 give 865/866 as crucial dates), when a Danish army – called *se mycel hæþen here* ('the great heathen army') in the Chronicle – appeared in East Anglia. This force proved to be singularly aggressive and well-disciplined, and remained active for about 15 years, crossing and recrossing England from East to West and North to South, plundering and ravaging wherever they went, until, finally, part of it settled in what was to become the Danelaw after 886. In 886, Alfred recaptured London, and in the same year he concluded the Treaty of Wedmore with Guthrum, in which the Danish leader swore to confine the activities of his followers to the parts of England lying east of Watling Street and north of the Thames, i.e. roughly east of a line stretching from London to Chester: the Danelaw. The treaty explicitly stated that no slave or freeman was to cross the border without permission, and *The Parker Chronicle* annal for the year 894 shows us that the East Anglian border was closed to Alfred's army then (Bately 1986:58; Poussa 1982:73). Traditionally, it is assumed that the agreement between Alfred and Guthrum and the establishment of the Danelaw was followed by a wave of immigrants from Denmark, who were pressing inland from the Lincolnshire coast and the Humber estuary. These colonists apparently were not necessarily displacing the established Anglian population, but were founding new settlements in less favourable, more sparsely populated areas, such as the flanks of the Lincolnshire Wolds, the low bottomlands of Kesteven, or the Wreak Valley in Leicestershire. This assumption was based mainly on place-name evidence (thus, parish-names of Scandinavian origin are virtually confined to the Danelaw), the personal names in the *Domesday Book* of 1086, and the corresponding statements in the Anglo-Saxon Chronicle (see e.g., Stenton 1947:241, 495–518; Ekwall 1930, 1936a, 1937). And it is indeed rather unlikely that only the remnants of the *mycel here*, which originally did not count more than about 1,000 men, should be held responsible not only for some 2,000 Scandinavian place-names so far identified in England, but also for the number and type of loans that have been taken over in the English language. Nevertheless, Davis (1955) and Sawyer (1958) question the validity of this evidence: the Anglo-Saxon Chronicle is said to be heavily biased in favour of Wessex and does not really provide any reliable information about the scale and nature of the Danish settlement in the Danelaw, which is undoubtedly true. The evidence of the *Domesday Book* is allegedly not unambiguous: the distribution of so-called *sochemanni* and *liberi homines* originally seemed to correspond with the Danelaw extension of 875, but on closer inspection is not confirmed by the place-name evidence. Thus, a direct connection between the original settlement and the place-names first attested 150 or 200 years later is rejected. The place names are potentially attributable also to internal colonisation and linguistic influence on the native English population. The Scandinavian names might be due to a change in the fashion of name-giving. All that in fact is required to account for the linguistic influence would be the existence of a small but prestigious Danish aristocracy, as in the case of the Norman-French loans after the Conquest. But Cameron (1965, 1970, 1971) and Fellows Jensen (1972, 1978a,c), having investigated the patterns of distribution of a large number of place-names including the geographical as well as the geological and topographical characteristics of the sites, come to the conclusion that the original settlement hypothesis is correct: numerous settlers had come as colonists and had settled on whatever land had been left vacant by the English (but see now Fellows Jensen 1982, who suggests that place-names in *-by*, *-thorpe(e)* and the *Grimston*-hybrids may have been given to already existing English villages, which originally had a different name, and were rechristened when small parcels of land passed into private ownership in the tenth century; they may thus have nothing to do with the Danish colonisation as such, although they of course reflect Scandinavian influence). This conclusion is corroborated by Hansen (1984) on the basis of an evaluation of the Scandinavian loans: although the OE loans are compatible with a socially superior, more prestigious status of Scandinavian in the Danelaw – cf. their mainly technical character that marks them as 'cultural loans' (Bloomfield 1935:461) – the character and number of the ME loans can only be accounted for by assuming the existence of a mixed speech community operating on the basis of social and cultural equality, i.e. in addition to a small aristocracy we shall have to allow for a large number of possibly secondary Danish immigrants living side by side with the native population (Hansen 1984:79). This does not mean that Stenton's figure of 40–50,000 settlers is likely – in fact it is not, but Sawyer's 400 aristocrats are certainly far too few to account for the type of loans we find in ME.

As the name already indicates, the Danelaw was to be governed by Danish law, and consequently a Danish legal system and other distinctively Scandinavian institutions were soon established in the north and east Midlands. The monetary units were now *øre* and *mark* instead of *shillings* and *pounds*, and Danish measures such as *oxgangs* and *ploughlands* were applied to measure out land. Administrative districts were now the *wapentake*, OE *wæpen-tæc* (instead of the 'hundred') or the *þriding* (cf. the Ridings in Yorkshire), which were governed by jarls and their twelve lawmen (ON *logmenn*).

In the meantime, Norwegians coming from the Orkneys had settled in the north of Scotland; these settlements were to survive well into the seventeenth century. Another wave of Norwegians early in the tenth century came from Ireland and settled in western Scotland (cf. *Galloway*, from *Gall-Gæl*, the name of the Irish-Norwegian halfbreeds), in north-west England (especially in Lancashire, Westmoreland and Cumberland), and near Chester.

The Danelaw was gradually reconquered by the West Saxons, but Viking fleets began to reappear towards the end of the tenth century, and in 991 Olaf Tryggvasson arrived with a fleet of 93 ships in Essex. Æthelred's troops, led by Byrhtnoth, Earl of the East Saxons, were defeated in a battle celebrated in the poem *The Battle of Maldon*. The Danish army, strengthened by second- and third-generation Danes from the Danelaw – the Danish ties in this area thus must still have been rather strong – marched north towards York, collecting large sums to refrain from plunder. In retaliation Æthelred ordered the massacre of all foreigners outside the Danelaw. One of the victims was Gunnhildr, sister of the Danish king Sveinn Forkbeard. Sveinn, after hearing of this atrocity, landed in East Anglia in 1008 with a great fleet, and the Danes once again ransacked the eastern and northern parts of the country, except when they were bought off by larger and larger sums (in 1012 the amount necessary was £48,000). In 1009 reinforcements from Denmark went up the Thames and plundered Oxford, while Sveinn took Winchester. Both armies now continued to harass the country until Sveinn's death in 1014. Æthelred, who had fled to France, returned and started to brutally eliminate the pro-Danish element in the north and east. As a reaction, Sveinn's son Canute, only recently driven from England on account of his atrocities, was called back by the Danes. He arrived in 1015 with a large fleet and within months the whole country, save for London, was in Danish hands. When Æthelred died in 1016, Canute was proclaimed king of all England. England, Denmark and Norway were thus united in one single but short-lived kingdom.

After Canute's victory, many of his men returned to Scandinavia, but others stayed in England, again adding to the number of Scandinavian settlers, this time not only in the Danelaw, but also in other parts of the country. Under Canute's rule, many Danes held high positions at court, which must have had consequences also for the linguistic situation in the country, and especially in the Danelaw, cf. §5.2.3.3. Canute died in 1035, and after the death of his son Hardecanute in 1042, the half-English, half-Norman son of Æthelred, Edward the Confessor, was elected king. Edward brought with him a number of Norman friends and attempted to install them in key posts in church and state. On the other hand, his principal adviser was Godwine, the earl of the West-Saxons, probably of English descent but decidedly pro-Danish, who saw to it that the Norman influence was kept within limits. Interestingly, the assessment of the situation at the court varies considerably. Baugh & Cable (1978:108) claim that a 'strong French atmosphere pervaded the English court during the twenty-four years of his reign', while Poussa (1982:76), following Stenton (1947:419) remarks that 'Edward the Confessor's court was very Scandinavian in character'. Probably both assumptions are correct in view of the fact that two factions at the court were striving for the supremacy.

In 1066, Edward died childless, and Harold, the son and successor of Godwine, was elected king. He had just been fighting at the Battle of Stamford Bridge, when the news reached him that William of Normandy had landed in Kent in order to claim what Edward the Confessor apparently had promised him and what Harold once seemed to have confirmed by a forced oath: that William would succeed to the throne of England. The outcome of the subsequent events is well-known: William Duke of Normandy became William the Conqueror, and from now on (Norman) French was to be the dominant linguistic factor in the further development of the English language. There were some abortive Danish attempts to reclaim the English throne both from outside and inside, and the continued resistance of the Northumbrian earls Edwin and Morcar, the latter of Scandinavian descent, brought about William's retaliation known as the 'Harrying of the North', during which large areas in Northumbria were depopulated and devastated. The area was later repopulated by settlers of mixed Scandinavian/Irish parentage from the Norwegian colonies west of the Pennines, as can be inferred from the place-name evidence.

But this defeat was by no means the end of Scandinavian influence on the English language. On the contrary, some 150 to 200 years after these events we witness the surfacing of numerous everyday Scandinavian loan-words in written documents, and in many cases 'a good Old English word was lost, since it expressed the same idea as the foreign word. Thus the verb *take* replaced the OE *niman*' (Baugh & Cable 1978:100). Whether these words had been part of the spoken language earlier on we do not know, but general experience would suggest that they had. One reason for the delay is certainly the lack of documents from the Danelaw before 1200–50, coupled with the dominance of the south-western written standard, which continued to hold its position until the beginning of the twelfth century. But there obviously were other reasons as well, reasons which had to do with the overall linguistic situation in the Danelaw, to which we will now turn.

5.2.3.3.1   When we talk about the Danelaw and its impact on the history of English, we are necessarily talking about a 'languages-in-contact' situation. This has always been recognised, since terms such as 'amalgamation of Scandinavian and English dialects' (Björkman 1900–2:5), 'Sprachmischung' (Hofmann 1955:175, although with a *caveat*), 'fusion' (Geipel 1971:14) or 'intimate mingling' (Baugh & Cable 1978:101) are usually employed to describe the relationship of OE and Scandinavian. The problem, however, is that these terms are used rather loosely and are usually never really defined, nor are their theoretical implications made clear (Hansen 1984:69ff.). On the other hand, it is precisely this linguistic situation – however it may be described and whatever it may be called – that is held responsible for accelerating or even initiating, certain major restructurings of the English language at the end of the OE and the beginning of the ME period. There is no doubt that the Danelaw area, and notably Northumbria, see the glosses of the Lindisfarne Gospels, was much more progressive linguistically than the rest of the country, and that the changes that had started there were gradually radiating into the rest of the country. These changes are mainly of a morphological kind and basically result in a simplification of the morphological system: for example, loss of grammatical gender, reduction of inflectional endings, see chapter 4. This has even been taken as an indication of creolisation (Poussa 1982), but since the term 'creole' begs as many questions as terms such as 'amalgamation', 'Sprachmischung' or 'fusion', such an interpretation has been met with considerable scepticism (cf. Hansen 1984, Görlach 1986).

We thus have to ask: what was it that made this type of intimate influence possible? The answer – or answers – will necessarily have to be tentative, because we lack reliable direct evidence as to the linguistic situation obtaining in the Danelaw between, say, 900 and 1200. We can only make inferences on the basis of linguistic and extralinguistic data, which, of course, are open to interpretation, and on the basis of what we generally know about contact-situations.

5.2.3.3.2   Let me begin with the last aspect. Borrowings of the type encountered here normally presuppose either a fair amount of mutual intelligibility or relatively widespread biligualism, and a considerable period of coexistence of the two languages involved. Unfortunately, none of these can be established with certainty.

A certain amount of mutual intelligibility probably existed, given that the Scandinavian and the OE dialects are part of the Germanic language family and that 'at the time of the early Scandinavian settlements in England the period of separation had only been slightly longer than between British and American English today, and the communities had been in touch with one another for much of the time' (Strang 1970:282). But the degree of mutual intelligibility is a matter of dispute – and will have to remain so for lack of conclusive evidence. Strang obviously believes in a fairly high degree, although perhaps not as high as is implied in the Saga of Gunnlaugr Serpent's Tongue, where we read: 'The language in Norway and England was one and the same when William the Bastard won England' (Geipel 1971:57; for a different interpretation cf. Poussa 1982:77). Geipel is somewhat more reserved, when he states that

> ...the Danes would sooner or later have found it expedient to acquire at least a smattering of English for everyday purposes. The learning process need not have involved undue effort, and in the Anglian north and east, where the language was somewhat closer to Norse than was West Saxon, communication between settlers and natives must have been particularly simple.
>
> (Geipel 1971:57)

Baugh & Cable (1978:95) are even more careful: 'The two [i.e. Anglian and Scandinavian] may even have been mutually intelligible to a limited extent'. Poussa, on the other hand, is more optimistic – not surprisingly in view of her creolisation hypothesis – when she comments on Strang's evaluation quoted above:

> I think myself that a closer analogy would be the divergence of the spoken forms of the modern Standard Scandinavian languages. In this case, as we see in pan-Scandinavian conferences, communication between speakers of the different languages is possible, but not easy.
>
> (Poussa 1982:72)

Hansen (1984:88), finally, is extremely sceptical and excludes immediate mutual intelligibility as a cause for the many borrowings of everyday words, settling rather for bilingualism 'combined with the affinity between the two languages'. Given that at ca 900 at least 400 to 500 years had passed since the two languages had been direct neighbours and probably mutually intelligible in the same way as two not too distant dialects of the same language, it is indeed likely that the degree of mutual intelligibility now had become rather limited, though certainly not zero. Thus a native speaker of Standard High German, e.g. the author of this chapter, will usually manage to understand about 40 per cent to 60 per cent of a Dutch conversation, provided he knows what it is all about, but probably no more. Presumably, the mutual intelligibility of Anglian and Scandinavian was even lower, given the syntactic and morphological differences (e.g. word order, position of the article, etc.) between the latter; people could make themselves understood to a certain extent in everyday standard situations, but would probably have found it rather tiresome to carry on a reasonably fluent conversation.

Thus the main vehicle for linguistic influence of the kind at issue here must have been bilingualism, which has been postulated more or less by all authors dealing with this period. Where there is some disagreement, however, is the question as to who was or became bilingual, the English, the Danes, or both. What causes bilingualism? Usually the necessity to communicate effectively with members of two different, partly monolingual speech communities. One frequent, although not indispensible direct cause is, of course, intermarriage. Now at the beginning the Danes came as invaders, as conquerors, and certainly were regarded as such by the English in the Danelaw. Consequently, the pressure to learn Scandinavian was greater for the English, than for the Scandinavians to learn English, although some Danes probably also tried to pick up some English, especially when they did not settle within larger Danish-speaking communities, cf. the side-by-side appearance of Scandinavian and English personal names within families of minor land-holding status in the mid-tenth century. Intermarriage, which certainly was common enough, probably produced a lot of bilingualism in the second and any following generation. But it must not be forgotten that, if the hypothesis of peaceful Scandinavian immigration is correct, there was a constant flow of monolingual Scandinavian speakers until the middle of the eleventh century coming to England. The type of loans found in the OE period (cf. §5.2.3.4) corroborates this assumption: they are mainly technical terms that would be adopted from a speech community that is socially more prestigious. This situation was of course consolidated when Canute became king of England. Poussa (1982:74ff.) assumes that the creole that according to her had developed in the Midlands out of the contact situation between English and Danish was stabilised by this political event and was even raised to a supraregional spoken koiné, among other things because it was equally understandable in the North and the South, although southerners might have had certain lexical problems beyond the usual dialect variation. There would thus have existed a *diglossia* situation: Late West Saxon was continued as the written standard, while the Midland creole koiné was used for everyday spoken communication at court and between people of different regional dialects (Poussa 1982:76). Being a spoken variety, there is of course no real evidence for the existence of such a creole koiné, but it must be admitted that in order to govern England in those days a kind of *lingua franca* would indeed have been useful. And this Midland dialect, whether it was just a somewhat modified Anglian or whether it really was a Danish–English interlanguage as Poussa claims, would have been a good candidate because of its geographically intermediate position. After all, it later on became the basis of the emerging standard in London.

Since we lack direct evidence, however, all this must remain speculative, and we will have to content ourselves with some rather minimal assumptions. Thus it seems reasonable to conclude that there was a certain amount of bilingualism, notably with offspring of mixed marriages or second- and third-generation settlers; that the tendency towards bilingualism, or at least towards the acquisition of a working knowledge of the other language was probably somewhat stronger among the Anglo-Saxons than among the Danes, although Hofmann (1955:21–148, 261–7) has shown that Icelandic scaldic poetry contains Anglo-Saxon loans, which might be interpreted as reflecting some bilingualism among the Danes in the Danelaw in the tenth century too (one decisive factor probably was the relative number of speakers of each language within a community, which varied from district to district); and that the position of Danish was strengthened by continuous immigration and the role it played at the court between 1016 and 1066, although from 1035 on in a somewhat reduced form. This scenario is probably sufficient to account for the loans that came into the language during the OE period, because they conform to what one would expect from such a situation. For the ME loans, however, we require a different scenario, and it seems that the one discussed in Hansen (1984:83ff.) involving language death and language shift as major factors (cf. also already Björkman 1900–2:21–2) is a fairly plausible explanation of the linguistic facts.

After 1066, the situation of Scandinavian must have changed radically. Already, in 1042, with the accession of Edward the Confessor to the throne, it must have lost considerable ground at court; but after 1066 Norman French became the general court language, and with the elimination of the native (including Scandinavian) higher nobility and clergy it lost its prestigious status, becoming as much the language of a conquered people as the native OE dialects. It also lost its other supportive factor: immigration from Scandinavia stopped, and the ties between England and Scandinavia were disrupted. Scandinavian thus had become a normal minority language and was more and more threatened by English, simply because of the numerical superiority of the speakers of OE dialects. To this has to be added the fact that both speech communities now had to cope with a third language, French. Now we are probably justified in assuming that Scandinavian for a certain period of time was a spoken language in England, although we do not know quite for how long, because the only direct evidence, runic inscriptions and other epigraphical material, is too fragmentary and ambiguous to allow any definite conclusions (cf. Page 1971). But we do know that at some point before 1200–1300 Scandinavian must have been replaced by English, since there are no Scandinavian manuscripts in the Danelaw. We are thus faced with a typical case of language death with concurrent language shift. And in this case it may be assumed that the speakers of the dying language were primarily responsible for the ME borrowings, since they probably first became bilingual, then restricted Scandinavian more and more to certain (intimate) situations, i.e. Scandinavian became monostylistic, until they finally stopped speaking it altogether, switching to English for all situations. In view of the fact that practically no Scandinavian manuscripts exist, we must assume that Danish was more or less exclusively a spoken language, so that this shift was not in any way hampered or delayed by the existence of a written language. This scenario, I think, not only explains the number of loans, but also their everyday character.

If these considerations are correct, then we have two completely different contact situations, with, quite obviously, completely different effects. The early OE loans were basically adopted by bilingual (and possibly monolingual) speakers for whom English was the basic language; Scandinavian at that stage had a somewhat more prestigious status than English, at least temporarily. The ME loans are primarily, although certainly not exclusively, due to speakers of Scandinavian descent and their switch from Danish to English in connection with the death of Scandinavian in the Danelaw.

5.2.3.4 When we now turn to the Scandinavian loans in Old English, it is perhaps useful to first discuss some criteria by which these can be recognised. Thus, on account of the genetic relationship between Scandinavian and OE there is a considerable overlap of the core vocabulary of these two languages, and it is therefore necessary to have some criteria that allow us to distinguish loans from native OE lexical items. Fairly safe criteria are phonological differences resulting from different phonological developments in the two languages (see further chapter 3). The most noticeable feature in this respect is the lack of palatalisation/assibilation of velar stops in front of original palatal vowels and initial /sk/, i.e. the pre-OE/OE changes /g/ > /j/, /k/ > /tʃ/, /gg/ > /ddʒ/, /kk/ > /ttʃ/, /sk/ > /ʃ/. Unfortunately, however, OE spelling did not consistently distinguish all these sounds, so that an OE manuscript spelling, taken at face value, is not an absolute criterion. This is true especially in those cases in which the OE form has been replaced by the cognate Scandinavian one (cf. *give* vs. OE *giefan*, *get* vs. OE *gietan*, *begin* vs. OE *onginnan*, *kettle* vs. OE *cetel*, etc.), or when both forms have come down to us, as with *shirt* (OE *scyrte*) and *skirt* (ON *skyrta*), or *ditch* (OE *dic*) and *dike* (ON *dík*). But on account of the PDE pronunciation, *scab*, *scant*, *scare*, *score*, *scrub*, *skill*, *skin*, *sky*, *gate*, *gape*, *again*, *anger*, *guest*, *gear*, *gift* can unambiguously be identified as Scandinavian loans. Another safe criterion is the development of Germanic /ai/, which in OE became /ɑː/, PDE/əʊ/, while in Scandinavian it became /ei/, /eː/, PDE /eɪ/, cf. the pairs *no/nay*, *whole/hale*. In cases where phonological criteria are not applicable, because the two languages had the same phonological development, criteria such as manuscript location, semantic field affiliation, date of first appearance, or meaning have to be resorted to. Thus, PDE *bloom* goes back to Scandinavian *blóm* 'flower, bloom', since OE *bloma* meant 'ingot of iron'; similarly, PDE *plough* represents ON *plógr* 'plough', not OE *plow* 'measure of land'; the OE word for 'plough' was *sulh*.

The earliest Scandinavian loans occur in the treaty between Alfred and Guthrum, then in the Anglo-Saxon Chronicle, especially in the D and E manuscripts, which come from York and Peterborough respectively, in some of Æthelred's laws, in vocabularies, in the Lindisfarne and Rushworth Gospels, and in the Durham Ritual. The following selection is based on the material in Peters (1981a,b), who not only lists direct loans, but also semantic loans and loan-translations. For convenience's sake the usual Old Norse/Old Icelandic equivalents will be used below, even if they could not have been the direct input to Old English, but were the result of Scandinavian sound changes.

(1) Seafaring terms: *barð* 'barque' < ON *barð* 'armed prow, stem', *barða, barda* 'beaked ship' < ON *barði* 'kind of ship, ram', *cnearr* 'small ship' < ON *knǫrr* 'ship, merchant ship', *flege, flæge* 'little ship' < ON *fløy* 'little ship', *scegð, scæd* 'light ship, vessel' < ON *skeið* 'kind of swift-sailing ship of war of the class *langskip*', *snacc* 'small vessel, warship' < ON *snekkja* 'swift-sailing ship'. To these should be added the semantic loan *æsc* 'ash > warship' < ON *askr* 'ash; small ship, barque' as the usual term for the Scandinavian boats; *ha* 'oar-thole' < ON *hár* 'thole', *hamele* 'rowlock' < ON *hamla* 'oarloop', *wrang(a)* 'hold of a ship < ON *vrǫng* 'rib in a ship'; *hæfene* 'haven, port' < ON *hǫn* 'port', *lænding* 'landing-site < ON *lending*, the semantic loan *healdan* in the sense 'proceed, steer' < *halda (skipi)* 'to hold in a certain direction', and the loan-translation *wederfæst* 'weatherbound < ON *veðrfastr* 'weatherbound'; *butsecarl* 'sailor, boatsman' < ON *búza* 'boat' + *carl* 'man', the loan-translations *steor(es)mann* 'pilot' < ON *stýrismaðr* 'steersman, skipper', *hasæta* 'oarsman, rower' < ON *háseti* 'oarsman', and the compounds *æschere* 'Viking army', *æscman* 'Viking, pirate', *scegðmann* 'Viking', which were probably prompted by foreign models.

(2) Legal terms: not surprisingly, this set contains the largest number of items, since, after all, one of the crucial features of the Danelaw was its Danish legislation. Direct loans: *feolaga* 'fellow, partner' < ON *félagi* 'fellow, comrade', *formæl/formal* 'negotiation, treaty' ON *formáli* 'preamble' (*mæl* instead of *mal* indicates partial loan-translation), *friðmal* 'article of peace' < ON *friðmál* 'words of peace', *grið* 'truce, sanctuary, temporary peace' < ON *grið* 'truce' (cf. also Weimann 1966), *husting* 'tribunal, court' < ON *húsþing* 'council, meeting called by the king or earl', *lagu* 'law' < ON *lǫg* 'law' (first restricting native *æ* to 'spiritual law', and finally replacing it altogether), together with several compounds (partly native, partly loan-translations), e.g. *lahbreca* 'law-breaker', *lahbryce* 'breach of the law' < ON *logbrót* 'breach of the law', *lahmenn* 'law-men' < ON *lǫgmenn* 'men who have knowledge of law', *lahriht* 'legal right' < ON *logréttr* 'legal personal right', *lahwita* 'lawyer', *mal* 'law-suit' < ON *mál*, *niþing* 'villain, outlaw' < ON *niðingr* 'villain', *sac* 'guilty' < ON *sekr* 'guilty', with the loan-translations *sacleas* 'innocent' < ON *saklauss* 'innocent', *unsac*

'innocent' < ON *ósekr* 'innocent', *sehtan, sehtian* 'to conciliate, settle', *seht* 'settlement', adj. 'reconciled' < ON *sætt* < **sahti, utlah* 'outlawed', *utlaga* 'outlaw', *utlagian* 'to banish' < ON *útlagr* 'outlawed', *unlagu* 'abuse of law' < ON *ólǫg* 'violation of law', *wrang* 'wrong' < ON *vrangr* 'wrong, unjust'. Semantic loans: *mund* 'money paid by bride-groom to bride's father' (OE *mund* 'hand, palm, trust, security'), *cwiddian* 'to make a claim against' (OE 'to talk, say, discuss') < ON *kveðia* 'to summon', *stefn* 'summons', *stefnian* 'to summon' (OE 'voice, sound; call on a person to act'). Loan-translations: *drincelean* 'enter-tainment given by the lord to his tenants' < ON *drekkulaun* 'gratifi-cation (by the king)', *landceap/landcop* 'fine paid to the lord on the alienation of land' < ON *landkaup, festermenn* 'bondsmen', as well as the ones mentioned above, i.e. *lahbryce, lahriht*, etc.

(3) Ranks: *bond, bunda, husbonda* 'householder, husbandman, < ON *bóndi, búandi* 'husbandman' (cf. Schabram 1975), *huscarl* 'member of the king's bodyguard' < ON *húscarl, hold* 'vassal, holder of allodial land, ranking below a jarl' < ON *holdr* 'owner of allodial land', *liesing* 'freedman' < ON *leysingr, þræll* 'slave'; very important is the semantic loan *eorl* 'nobleman, chief' replacing *ealdorman* < ON *jarl* 'nobleman' (OE *eorl* 'warrior, free man').

(4) War terms: *brynige* 'mail-shirt' < ON *brynja, cnif* 'knife' < ON *knífr, fesian, fysian* 'put to flight, banish' < ON **feysa, genge* 'troop' < ON *gengi* 'help, support, troops', *lið* 'fleet' < ON *lið* 'host, fleet' (with the loan-translation *liðsmann* 'follower, sailor' < ON *liðsmaðr* 'follower, warrior'), *mal* 'soldier's pay' < ON *máli* 'soldier's pay', *rædan on* 'attack' < ON *rápa* 'attack', *targe* 'small shield' < ON *targa* 'small round shield'; to these is to be added the loan-translation *heafodmann, heafdesmann* 'captain' < ON *hofudsmaðr* 'captain, leader'.

(5) Measures and coins: *marc* 'marc, half a pound' < ON *mork* 'mark', *ora* 'Danish coin' < ON *aurar/eyrir, oxangang, oxnagang* 'eighth of a plough-land, hide' < ON *oxnagang, ploh, plogesland* 'plough-land, land-measure = what a yoke of oxen can plough in a day', *sceppe* 'measure of wheat or malt' < ON *skep* 'bushel', *scoru* 'score' < ON *skor* 'score', *ðrefe* 'measure of corn or fodder' < ON *þrefi* 'measure'.

(6) Other semantic areas:

  (a) Nouns: *becc* 'brook, beck' < ON *bekkr* 'brook', *carl* 'man' < ON *carl* 'man', *gærsum* 'treasure' < ON *gersemi, gørsum* 'costly thing, jewel' *hofding* 'chief, ringleader, leader' < ON *hofþingi* 'ringleader, commander', *læst* 'fault, sin' < ON *lostr* 'fault, misbehaviour, vice', *loft* 'air' < ON *loft, lopt* 'air', *mæl,* 'speech' < ON *mál* 'faculty of speech, language, tale', *rot* 'root' < ON *rót*, *sala* 'sale' < ON *sala* 'sale', *scinn* 'skin, fur' < ON *skinn*, *þriðing* 'third part of a county' < ON *þriðjungr* 'third part', *þweng* 'thong' < *þwengr* 'thong, latchet', *wæpengetæc* 'district' < ON *vápnatak*, *wæð* 'ford' < ON *vað*. To these can be added the (partial) loan-translations *brydhlop*, *brydlop* 'ceremony of conducting a bride to her new home, wedding' < ON *bruðhlaup*, *rædesmann* 'counsellor; steward' < ON *rædismaðr* 'manager, steward', *taperæx*, *taperæx* 'small ax' < ON *taparøx* 'small tapering axe' < Slav. (cf. OCS *toporu*, probably the first Slavonic loan in English, transmitted through the Vikings).

(b) Adjectives: *dearf* 'bold' (with the derivatives *dearflic* 'bold, presumptuous', *dearfscipe* 'boldness, presumption') < ON *diarfr*, *fere* 'fit for military service', *unfere* 'unfit, disabled' < ON *færr* 'able, capable, fit', *ræggig* 'rough, shaggy' < ON *raggigr*, *stor* 'strong, great' < ON *storr* 'big, great, important' and the loan-translation *goldwrecen* 'covered with gold' < ON *gullrekinn* 'gilded or inlaid with gold'.

(c) Verbs: *farnian* 'prosper' < ON *farnask* 'speed well', *geeggian* 'egg on, incite' < ON *eggia* 'egg on', *hittan* 'hit' < ON *hit*, *serðan* 'rape, lie with' < ON *serða* 'violate', *tacan* 'take' < ON *taka*.

While these and other instances, according to Peters (1981a,b) can be regarded as certain, the following are somewhat questionable and might also be taken as originally native: (1) *bȳ* 'dwelling' (cf. Hofmann 1955:175, who opts for a native origin because of the meaning difference (OE *by* 'dwelling' vs. ON *byr* 'farm, landed estate') and draws attention to the northern verb *bya* 'dwell' instead of southern *buan* and ON *búa*; Peters (1981a:104), on the other hand, on account of the parallelism of *by* (Mk(Li) V.3) ~ *bying* (Mk(Ru) V.3) thinks Scandinavian origin still likely; moreover, as a place-name element *-by* is virtually confined to the Danelaw, which makes Scandinavian origin even more likely); (2) *ceallian* 'call', *calla* in *hildecalla* 'war-herald' < ON *kalla* as replacement of synonymous OE *clypian* and *cegan*, *cigan* (cf. Stanley 1969b, who suggests that *hildecalla* is an Anglian form preserved in poetic diction comparable to *cald*; Björkman (1902:214) separates *hildecalla* from *ceallian* and treats only the latter as loan; Peters (1981a:106) follows Stanley, pointing out that the phrase *onginnan ceallian*, occurring in *Mald* 91, is also found in ME texts localised in London, i.e. the King Alisaunder Group (MS Auchinleck), which would make Scandinavian origin rather implausible); (3) *diegan*, *degan* 'die' < ON *deyja* (but cf. Luick 1914–40:§384, n.5, who points out that *e* of *degan* is not a possible rendering of ON *ey*; therefore, an unrecorded

OE verb *degan < West Gmc *dauwjan is more likely as source); (4) scipere 'sailor', scipian 'man a ship', occurring in the Anglo Saxon Chronicle (1052C, 1075D) (according to Hofmann (1955:222–3, 233) from ON skipari, skipa, but according to de Vries (1962:493) a native OE formation, which is also accepted by Peters (1981a:115)); (5) sumorlida 'summer-army, summer-fleet' (in Björkman (1900–2) and Kluge (1891) classified as a loan, questioned by Hofmann (1955:161–2) in view of yðlida 'ship', sælida 'seafarer', which are definitely OE, cf. OE liðan 'travel by sea'; Peters (1981a:118) suggests an incorrect loan-translation of ON sumerliði, where the second element was identified with OE lida).

Thus, on the one hand, the number of early Scandinavian loans is fairly high, but on the other, as Peters (1981b) has shown, most of them did not really get established in the OE onomasiological system (major exceptions are lagu and tacan) and therefore are no longer found in ME or PDE. This is to be expected, since most of the loans discussed here are technical terms that have to do with Scandinavian culture. Once the denotata lose their relevance – and many do after the Conquest – their names will also gradually be forgotten.

5.2.4 Other influences

Latin, Scandinavian and to a certain extent Celtic, are the languages that unquestionably exerted the greatest influence on the OE vocabulary. But two other languages, Old Saxon and Old French, should be mentioned briefly, because they, too, contributed to the OE vocabulary, although on a much more limited scale.

The Anglo-Saxons always kept in touch with their continental cousins, especially the Frisians, and it seems that at least the compound iegland 'island' is of Frisian origin. But more important is the fact that King Alfred in his educational revival not only fell back on native Mercian help, but also engaged people from the continent, e.g. Saxons. Thus, one of his mass-priests, John the Old Saxon, came, as the name suggests, from Saxony, and Kuhn (1986:49ff.) speculates that he may have been the source of the verbs macian/gemacian occurring five times in Cura pastoralis and Boethius' Consolatio. The only other contemporary occurrence is in Genesis B, which is a translation from Old Saxon. Macian/gemacian occur for the first time in Alfred's prose, and subsequently remain more or less restricted to the West Saxon dialect. Kuhn provides conclusive evidence that these words were borrowed into West Saxon from Old Saxon, which in turn had adopted them from Old High German.

Further Old Saxon loans are found especially in *Genesis B*, a translation from an Old Saxon original in the second half of the ninth century. The following list has been established by Klaeber (1931:49) with the help of Siever's Heliand edition: *wær* 'true, correct' (for *soþ*), *suht* 'illness', *strið* 'struggle', *hearra* 'lord, master', *sima* 'band, chain', *sæl(i)ð* 'dwelling, house', *romi(g)an* 'possess?', *hearmscearu* 'affliction, punishment', *hygesceaft* 'mind, heart', *landscipe* 'region', *heodæg* 'today', to which the following semantic loans should be added: *þegnscipe* 'allegiance' (otherwise 'service, duty, manliness, valour'), *sceaða* 'injury' (otherwise 'injurious person, criminal'), *onwendan* 'take away from' (otherwise 'change, exchange, amend'), *freo* 'woman' (otherwise 'free, glad, joyful').

Furthermore, Schabram (1960) has identified *gal*, *galscipe* (*GenB* 327, 341) as semantic loans from Old Saxon, since in these passages the only appropriate meaning is *superbia* 'pride', i.e. the one associated with Old Saxon *gêl* and its compounds, and not the one usually attributed to OE *gal*, 'lust'. Influences of this kind are not surprising, however, if one realises that a copy of the Old Saxon *Heliand* (London, British Library, Cotton Caligula A. vii), was probably produced in southern England in the late tenth century (Gneuss 1982:165n.11). Thus Old Saxon texts were by no means unknown in the later Anglo-Saxon period. In view of the close genetic relationship, many more possible loans may as yet be unidentified.

The other minor source of loans in the later OE period was Old French. It will be remembered that the religious revival in the late tenth and the eleventh centuries had its starting point in France, and that many of those responsible for its implementation in England had spent some time in French monasteries. Moreover, Edward the Confessor, son of Æthelred the Unready and the daughter of a Norman duke, was brought up in Normandy during the exile of his father and while the Scandinavians ruled England. When he came to the throne in 1042, he brought his French friends to England and tried to provide them with appropriate positions.

Consequently a handful of French loans are already found in pre-Conquest OE texts. The most noticeable is *prud*, *prut* 'proud' with the derivatives *prutlic*, *prutlice*, *pryto*/*pryte*, *prytscipe*, and *prutness* 'pride', and the compounds *oferprut* 'haughty' *prutswongor* 'overburdened with pride', *woruldpryde* 'worldly pride' and *oferprydo* 'excessive pride'

(Schabram 1965:14–16), which encroach on the territory of West Saxon *ofermod* and *modig*. Probably taken over in connection with the Benedictine reform, it is also remarkable for the analogical *i*-umlaut in the deadjectival noun *pryto*, matching the pattern *full* ~ *fyllu*, *hal* ~ *hælu*, which seems to indicate that at least at the time of the borrowing, i.e. late tenth, early eleventh century, *i*-mutation was still a living morpho-phonemic factor (see §5.4). Other early French loans are *sot* 'foolish' (although this might also be directly from VLat.), *tur* 'tower' (Funke 1914:167, however, rejects French as a possible source and suggests direct borrowing from Latin), *capun* 'capon', *tumbere* 'dancer' < OF *tomber* 'fall', possibly *fræpgian* < OF *frapper* translating *accusare* (*Mt(Li)* XII.10) and *reverebuntur* (perhaps a confusion with *reverberare* 'hit'), *servian* 'serve', *gingifer* 'ginger', *bacun* 'bacon', *arblast* 'weapon', *serfise* 'service', *prisun* 'prison', *castel* 'castle', *market*, *cancelere* 'chancellor', these latter in the Chronicle between 1048 and 1100. The real influx of French loans, however, begins in the second half of the twelfth century.

Compared to the present-day English situation, the number of loans in OE is small, and the majority do not really form part of the everyday vocabulary – with the exception perhaps of some of the earlier Latin borrowings. Nevertheless, it was a beginning, on which later periods could build when the trickle characterising OE gradually turned into a flood in ME.

5.3 The stratification of the Old English vocabulary

5.3.1 *Diatopic variation*

5.3.1.1 Dialects are usually established on the basis of phonological, and to a certain extent inflectional criteria, while lexical differences only play a supplementary role, or, not infrequently, are disregarded altogether. Thus, not untypically, the chapter on OE dialects in this volume basically concentrates on phonological data and their interpretation. Crowley (1986) in his survey lists seven major OE dialect criteria, of which six are phonological; the seventh, 'dialectal vocabulary', is discussed in merely ten lines (Crowley 1986:110); it is given a more extensive treatment, however, in his dissertation (Crowley 1980:275–88). And Hogg (1988) also bases his rather critical assessment of our present 'too inflexible' (1988:198) concepts of Old English dialects exclusively on phonological studies.

But alongside this phonologically dominated OE dialectology, an OE word-geography has gradually evolved which investigates the dialectal (and chronological) distribution of the OE vocabulary, and whose recent results have provided a number of extremely useful additional criteria for localising manuscripts (cf., for example, Schabram 1965; Wenisch 1979 and Hofstetter 1987) or determining the authorship of certain works (Gneuss 1972, 1982; Hofstetter 1987). One of the first to point to lexical peculiarities in the diction of Ælfric was Dietrich (1855:544–5, no.140), who noted that he seemed consciously to avoid the commonly used words *fremde* 'strange, foreign', *(ge)gearwian* 'prepare, procure, supply' or *(ge) felan*, 'feel, perceive', replacing them by *ælfremed*, *(ge)gearcnian*, *(ge) fredan* (*fremde* occurs once in *ÆCHom* II 142.26 and according to Hofstetter (1987:39–41) is probably due to syntactic and metrical considerations). These items belong to the set called 'Winchester words' by Gneuss (1972), which are characteristic of the Late West Saxon standard that evolved in the Winchester school under Æthelwold and Ælfric in the late tenth and early eleventh century.

Observations such as these remained isolated for some time, but their number increased at the end of the nineteenth century, compare the dialect labels in Sweet (1889), and the contributions by Deutschbein (1901), Klaeber (1902/1904), or Wildhagen (1905). The first, methodologically still valid, really systematic investigation was Jordan's (1906) *Eigentümlichkeiten des anglischen Wortschatzes*, which remained the only fairly reliable work in this field for a long time, since the theses by Scherer (1928) and Rauh (1936) are only of rather limited reliability, while Meißner (1934/5) is completely useless (cf. the summaries in Funke (1958), Schabram's (1965:17) statement that these publications have discredited OE word-geography rather than advanced it, as well as Schabram's (1969) devastating review of Meißner and Wenisch's (1978) evaluation of Rauh). The major flaw of these publications was their exclusive reliance on dictionaries and glossaries, because these do not contain all occurrences of the items in question. But only a complete coverage of the material available can provide a sound basis for reliable conclusions as to the dialectal and diachronic distribution of the OE vocabulary, something which had already been postulated by Jordan (1906:4; cf. also Schabram 1965:16ff., 1969:101ff.). The more recent publications by Menner (1947, 1948, 1949, 1951/52), J. J. Campbell (1951, 1952) or Clark (1952/3), although on the whole more reliable, still suffer from basically the same shortcomings. Thus, Campbell restrict his investigations to the various revisions of the Bede translation (already mentioned in Jordan (1906:6) as a useful source), and Clark relies on ME rather than on further contemporary OE evidence, which is not unproblematic. Schabram (1965:17) therefore estimated that at the time when he wrote his monograph about two thirds of the statements about the dialectal and chronological distribution of the OE vocabulary were incorrect.

It was Schabram's (1965) study of the dialectal and chronological distribution of the words covering the semantic field *superbia* 'pride' and Gneuss' work on the Winchester School (Gneuss 1972) that provided new impulses for OE word-geography by finally complying with the requirement of covering the whole OE material before drawing conclusions about the distribution of lexical items (a condition more easily met now with the availability of the Toronto microfiche concordance). These were followed among others by Wenisch's (1979) investigation of the Anglian vocabulary in the glosses of the Gospel of St Luke in the Northumbrian Lindisfarne Gospels, and Hofstetter's (1987) meticulous analysis of part of the vocabulary of the texts originating in the Winchester school and its comparison with the equivalent lexical items used elsewhere. The results of these investigations not only established for the first time conclusive evidence for the Anglian or Late West Saxon status of a large number of lexical items; but at the same time provided additional, and perhaps even more reliable, criteria than phonology for the dialectal classification of manuscripts whose dialectal provenance so far was unknown or doubtful. But before these results are discussed in greater detail, something should be said about the basic assumptions and the methodology applied in these studies, and also about the material they deal with.

5.3.1.2 Four major dialects are usually recognised for OE, Northumbrian, Mercian (both subsumed under the cover term Anglian), West Saxon and Kentish, although there may have been more (see chapter 6 and also Hogg (1988:186)). Of these, Kentish is too poorly documented to play a major role in OE word geography; moreover, the manuscripts identified as Kentish are all of mixed dialectal character, making it extremely difficult to isolate genuinely Kentish vocabulary features. Consequently, the central issue of OE word geography has always been the contrast between Anglian and West Saxon, and more precisely the identification of specifically Anglian (Mercian, Northumbrian) lexical items. Only recently, following Gneuss (1972), have attempts been made to isolate systematically the specific Late West

Saxon (Winchester) vocabulary, see Hofstetter (1987). The dominance of Anglian is probably due to the textual situation. We have many more West Saxon and dialectally mixed manuscripts than pure Anglian ones, because of the political supremacy of Wessex from the end of the ninth century onwards; moreover, many originally Anglian texts only exist in West Saxon copies, e.g. the early poetic records, and in the copying process have undergone various degrees of Saxonisation. It would therefore seem to be a useful first step to identify those words that are found only in Anglian texts, since in West Saxon texts the non-occurrence of a lexeme found elsewhere is less likely to be fortuitious because of the bulk of the material. But, as Jordan (1906:4) points out, this can only be a first hint at dialectal status. Nor does the sporadic occurrence of a lexical item in West Saxon automatically qualify it as West Saxon or general OE, since we must assume that the West Saxons were to some extent familiar with Anglian vocabulary, cf. the use of Anglianisms by Alfred, e.g. *oferhygfd* (*CP* 111.22, etc.), *oferhygdig* (*CP* 301.8), which Schabram sees as unquestionably Anglian.

The dialectal status of a lexeme can only be established with reasonable certainty if the empirical basis is sufficiently large, preferably comprising the whole available OE text corpus, as postulated by Schabram (1965:17), Wenisch (1976:16) and Hofstetter (1987:4). The further criteria and the basic methodology were already sketched by Jordan (1906:4ff.) and have been adopted with suitable modifications in the studies just mentioned. The best test is the existence of synonyms with different dialectal distributions. This distribution may either be complementary, as in the case of Angl. *fæs*, WS *fnæd* 'fringe, border', or Angl. *bebycgan*, WS *sellan* 'sell', where one item occurs only in Anglian, the other only in West Saxon manuscripts (dialectally mixed manuscripts are of course to be disregarded for this purpose). Or the distribution may be overlapping, in which case one of two (or more) Anglian synonyms also occurs outside Anglian texts, where it is used exclusively, however; this lexeme can then be regarded as common OE, e.g. Angl. *nymþe*, *nemne*, common OE *buton* 'unless, except', or Angl. *gen*, common OE *giet* 'yet'. As a safeguard Jordan requires that a lexeme should be found in at least two independent Anglian sources, before one regards it as Anglian (see also §5.3.3.3). An important source of information are West Saxon copies of known Anglian originals, especially the vocabulary substitutions in the Saxonised manuscripts, e.g. Bede, Gregory's *Dialogues* (see the long list in Hecht (1907:134–70)), the *Martyrologium* or the Northumbrian interlinear versions and West

Saxon translations of the gospels (see Wenisch). But great care has to be taken for two reasons. First, there is always a time lag between the original and the copy, so that the lexical substitution may be due to the obsolescence of the original and not to its dialectal status. Second, the revisers were hardly ever consistent. Thus, such revisions on their own are insufficient as a criterion. Finally, Jordan mentions as supplementary criteria the evidence of Middle and present-day English dialects. But in view of the possibility of dialect mixture and interdialectal borrowing, this criterion is treated with considerable reservation in more recent studies (see Wenisch 1979:13n18).

There is one fundamental precondition that has been taken for granted so far, but should be mentioned, even if it is self-evident. All these investigations start from the assumption that there are at least some manuscripts that can be localised unambiguously and that represent the dialect in question in relatively pure form. This is true of several manuscripts, e.g. the Lindisfarne Gospels, the Durham Ritual, etc., as well as a considerable number of West Saxon manuscripts. Once a certain number of lexemes have been identified as dialect-specific on that basis, one can proceed by manner of triangulation, using these items as indicators. And the more lexemes are identified as dialect-specific, the more texts will eventually be localised, and the more reliable this localization will be.

5.3.1.3 On the basis of the above criteria, Jordan establishes three groups: (1) lexemes identified as Anglian on the basis of internal OE evidence (criterion: at least two independent prose instances); (2) lexemes identified on the basis of ME and PDE dialect evidence, where the above criterion is not satisfied; (3) uncertain cases, e.g. *hapax legomena*, without ME/PDE corroboration. He also separates prose vocabulary from lexemes occurring also in poetry. These distinctions will be disregarded in the following selective list, which will only quote examples from the first group; WS or common OE equivalents are given in parentheses.

(a) Common Anglian: *in* (*on*) 'in', *nemne, nymþe* (*buton*) 'unless, except', *gen, ge(o)na* (*giet*) 'yet'; *acwinan* (*acwincan*) 'disappear, dwindle', *alan* (*fedan*) 'feed', *bebycgan* (*sellan*) 'sell', *bisene* (*blind*) 'blind', *cælc* (*calic*) 'chalice', *clucge* (*bell*) 'bell', *dian, deon* (*sucan*) 'suck', *efolsian* (*bysmerian, dysegian*) 'blaspheme', *eþian* (*orþian*) 'breathe', *fæs* (*fnæd*) 'fringe, border', *grornian* (*gnornian*) 'be sad, complain, murmur', *leoran* (*forþgewitan, forþfaran, feran*) 'depart, die', *los* (*lor*) 'loss, destruction', *lygge* (*leas*) 'false', *spittan* (*spætan, spiwan*) 'spit', *stylan, styllan* (*wundrian, forhtian*) 'be amazed, hesitate', *sunor* (*swina heord*) 'herd of swine', *þorf(f)æst* (*nytt, behefe*) 'useful', *wælan* (*gedreccan, geþreagan*) 'vex, torment', *wiþerbreca* (*wiþerwinna, wiþersaca*) 'adversary'.

(b) Specifically Northumbrian: *deþa* (*diedan*) 'kill', *drysnia* (*acwencan, adwæscan*) 'extinguish', *ear-lipric(a)* (*ear-læppa*) 'flap of the ear', *giwiga* (*biddan*) 'ask', *hoga* (*snottor*, WS *gleaw*) 'careful, prudent'.

(c) Specifically Mercian: *sehðe, sihðe* (*efne*) '*ecce!* look', *semninga* 'at once, suddenly'.

Jordan's findings were largely substantiated by subsequent investigations based on more extensive material, e.g. Schabram (1965) and Wenisch (1979), which added a substantial number of indubitably Anglian lexemes to Jordan's list. Schabram (1965) contains a meticulous analysis of all the occurrences of the lexemes related to the semantic field *superbia* 'pride, haughtiness' in all pre-1100 texts available in edited or facsimile form. The forty-one lexemes investigated make up four different lexical families:

(1)   *oferhygd-*: *oferhygd(u), oferhyg(e)dness* (sb.), *oferhygdig, oferhygd, oferhygdlic* (adj.); *oferhygdlice* (adv.)

(2)   *ofermod-*: *ofermod, ofermodness, ofermodigness, ofermodgung, ofermettu, ofermedu, ofermedla* (sb.); *ofermod, ofermodlic, ofermodig, ofermede* (adj.); *ofermodlice, ofermodiglice* (adv.); *ofermod(i)gian* (vb.)

(3)   *modig-*: *modigness* (sb.); *modig, modiglic* (adj.), *modiglice* (adv.); *mod(i)gian* (vb.)

(4)   *prut-/prud-*: *pryto/pryte, prutscipe, prutness, prutung* (sb.); *prut/prutlic* (adj.); *prutlice* (adv.); *prutian* (vb.).

There is a remarkable dialectal split between these families: *oferhygd-* is exclusively Anglian, while the other three are only found in West Saxon and Kentish, except for *modig-*, which frequently occurs in Anglian-based poetry, but only in the completely different, positively evaluative sense 'spirited, brave, high-souled, magnanimous', and never in the negatively evaluative religious sense referring to the mortal sin of *superbia*. Thus *modig-* is non-Anglian only in religious usage. Furthermore, there is a diachronic difference in the distribution of the three southern families: *ofermod-* dominates in Early West Saxon; *modig-* comes in in connection with the translation of the Benedictine Rule, and begins to dominate from ca 1000 onwards without, however, completely replacing *ofermod-*, and from ca 950 on we also find *prut-*, which in PDE is the only survivor in this field. Not surprisingly, there is also a stylistic difference: *oferhygd-* and *ofermod-* play a role in poetry, as well as *modig-* in the sense of 'brave', while *prut* and *modig-* in the sense of 'proud' are only found in prose.

This precise dialectal and diachronic classification by Schabram (1965:130ff.) of the *superbia*-vocabulary provides a valuable criterion for the dialectal and chronological localisation of doubtful manuscripts. Thus, Alcuin's translation *De virtutibus et vitiis* is clearly of Anglian origin, as shown by the *superbia*-vocabulary, similarly several homilies, which only exist in Late West Saxon copies. Also, the *superbia*-vocabulary found in the translation of Bede's *Historia ecclesiastica* provides a further argument against the hypothesis that it had been translated by King Alfred, and the same argument applies to Orosius, where Alfred's authorship had already been questioned for some time (Schabram 1973:279).

Even more material is provided by Wenisch (1979), who has investigated the interlinear gloss to St Luke in the Lindisfarne Gospels as to its dialect vocabulary. The investigation, which follows the principles established by Jordan and further refined by Schabram, was particularly fruitful, because the Northumbrian, Lindisfarne and Rushworth[2] glosses are matched by an almost contemporaneous West Saxon version of the gospels. Wenisch first compared the Northumbrian translations of every Latin word with the WS correspondences; this provided 14,000 lexical variants in 7,000 places consisting of altogether 3,000 OE lexemes. On the basis of glossaries and dictionaries, ca 2,000 lexemes turned out to be common OE. The remaining 1,000 were checked in the whole OE corpus; as a result, 350 lexemes were identified as genuinely Anglian. Thus, the following lexemes, which had sometimes been regarded as specifically Anglian, are common OE: *denu* 'valley, dale', *diegol* 'secret, hidden', *gieman* 'care for, regard, control', *hienan* 'fall, prostrate, abase, accuse', *hiwan* 'members of a family', *iecan* 'increase', *reordian* 'feed, refresh', *risan* 'be fit, proper', *seað* 'hole, pit, well, cistern' (against Jordan 1906:97), *smeagan* 'think, deliberate', *gestreon* 'treasure', *tælan* 'blame', *weorcmann* 'workman'. One hundred and forty-one lexemes, which had already been identified as Anglian, were confirmed and their distribution made more precise. Seventy-four of them turned out to be common Anglian, e.g. *acweþan* 'say, speak', *bewerian* 'prohibit', *cofa* 'closet, cave', *edwitan* 'reproach', *forhwon* 'wherefore', *geornness* 'desire, zeal', *hrerness* 'disturbance', *lixan* 'shine', *morþor* 'murder, mortal sin', *nænig* 'no one, none', *symbel* 'feast-day', *þeostrig* 'dark, obscure', *wæccan* 'watch'. Ten lexemes were common Anglian from the tenth century onwards, but common OE earlier: *blinnan* 'cease', *carcern* 'prison', *feogan* 'hate', *feon* 'rejoice', *feoung* 'hatred', *frignan* 'ask, inquire', *hwilchwugu* 'any, some, anything', *snytru* 'wisdom, prudence', *to hwon* 'wherefore, why', *tynan* 'enclose, shut'. And 57 of the 141 were restricted to Northumbrian, e.g. *astyltan* 'be astonished', *brydhlop* 'wedding', *carr* 'stone, rock' (Celtic), *deadian* 'die', *eftersona* 'afterwards, soon', *fellread* 'purple', *hoga* 'prudent', *inlihtan* 'enlighten', *leohtisern* 'candlestick', *luh* 'pond, loch' (Celtic), *morsceaþa* 'robber', *nestan* 'spin', *oferufa* 'upon, on', *portcwen* 'prostitute', *rendan* 'rend, tear', *screadung* 'fragment', *tocymende* 'coming', *utacund* 'foreign'.

Finally, Wenisch (1979:326) added 216 new Anglianisms to the known ones. Of these, 139 occur only in *Mk(Li)* and/or *Mk(Ru2)*, *Mk(Ru1)* I.1–2, 15, examples being: *awisnian* 'wither', *bebregdan* 'pretend', *cwicfyr* 'sulphur', *deofolgitsung* 'unrighteous mammon', many *efen*-combinations, e.g. *efneawendan* 'convert', *efnegebiegan* 'conclude', *efne(ge)brengan* 'confer', (obviously in many instances literal translations of Lat. *con*-, see p. 313 above), similarly *eftlifgan* 'revive', *efttoseleness* 'retribution', *eftwunian* 'remain' (with *eft*-rendering Lat. *re*-), *inawritan* 'inscribe', *inbewindan* 'involve', *infrignan* 'interrogate' (*in-* = Lat. *in*-); *ofasettan* 'deposit', *ofgemearcian* 'designate' (*of*- translating Lat. *de*-), *underbrædan* 'spread under', *undercierran* 'subvert' (*under*- = Lat. *sub*-), *wætness* 'moisture'. Twenty-three lexemes are Northumbrian, i.e. occur outside *Li/Ru*, e.g. *afreon* 'free', *begangol* 'cultivator', *bodere* 'teacher', *efnegemynd* 'commemoration', *hæsere* 'lord, master', *liesing* 'redemption'. Fifty-two of these 216 lexemes are common Anglian, e.g. *awundrian* 'wonder (at)', *bereflor* 'barnfloor', *bid* 'hesitation, delay', *clynnan* 'sound, resound', *dyrnlicgan* 'fornicate'. Two lexemes, *dieglan* 'hide' and *gierwan* 'clothe, adorn' are Anglian from the tenth century onwards.

Wenisch (1979:327) demonstrates that several southern texts exhibit Anglian influence which so far had not been noted, among others *AldV* 1, *Chron C* (early parts), *Mem*, *Ben R*, *Chrod R*, several charters, *Ant Gl*, *Med* 1.1. (*HerbA*), *ThCap* 1, *Th Cap* 2, *Kentish glosses*, *Or*, *Ps(P)*, *RegCGl*, *LibSc*, *WS*. Further, he identifies a number of so far unlocalised texts as probably of Anglian origin, thus several charters (Harmer 13, Robertson 64, 104), various homilies (*HomS* 31, *Assmann* XIV, *Napier* XLIII, XLIV, XLV, *Tristram* I, II, IV, *Skeat* 23 B, *Macarius Homily*), *Med* 1.1, *Old English Glosses* (ed. H. D. Meritt) C 4,8,70, *HomM*8 (*SlBPr* I), *VercHom* 1,7,8,9,11,12,17,19,22; *VL* (*Vision of Leofric*).

Using the same type of methodology, Wenisch (1978) showed that the lexemes *astreccan* 'stretch out', *beren* (= *berer*), **bereærn* 'barn', *candelstæf* 'candlestick', *cnucian* 'knock', *cruma* 'crumb', *dædbot* 'amends', *deofolseocness* 'demoniacal possession', *geferræden* 'companionship', *fordeman* 'condemn', classified as 'West Saxon' or 'possibly West

Saxon' by Rauh (1936) are in fact common Old English. In another study (Wenisch 1985), he confirmed that (*ge*)*fægnian* 'rejoice, be glad', was restricted to West Saxon, while its synonyms *gefeon* and *blissian*/*blīþsian* were Anglian (Wenisch 1979:137ff.) and common OE (Hallander 1966:289–91), respectively.

5.3.1.4 An investigation of the West Saxon vocabulary inevitably has also to deal with the literary standard originating in Æthelwold's school at Winchester and characterised inter alia by its 'regulated' vocabulary in several semantic domains, which was employed with remarkable consistency (Gneuss 1972:80). This also raises the problem of distinguishing between diachronic and diatopic differences and the question of the homogeneity of OE dialects discussed in chapter 6 and in Hogg (1988:185ff.). The terms 'Early West Saxon' (= Alfredian West Saxon) and 'Late West Saxon' (= Æthelwoldian/Ælfrician West Saxon) commonly used in the handbooks to refer to the ninth-century and tenth/eleventh-century varieties of WS suggest a purely chronological difference. On the other hand, when discussing the development of EWS *ie* in LWS, Campbell (1959:128) observes that 'the type of language found in the manuscripts accepted as eW-S differed considerably from that which contributed most to the formation of lW-S'. This would seem to imply that diatopic variation is involved as well as diachronic variation. Recent vocabulary studies corroborate this. Thus, Alfred's and Ælfric's usage in the semantic domains investigated by Hofstetter (1987) are radically different: Alfred uses practically no 'Winchester words', which on the other hand dominate in Ælfric's texts, cf. Table 5.1 based on Hofstetter (1987:38–66; 305–11). The differences are so remarkable that more than diachronic variation must be involved. This was already suggested by Seebold (1974:323–33) on the basis of an investigation of the semantic fields of *sapiens* 'wise' and *prudens* 'prudent' and their comparison with Schabram's findings, which patterned in a similar manner. The distributional facts led Seebold to postulate four text-groups: the Benedictine group (basically equivalent with Gneuss' Winchester texts), Alfred and Wulfstan, the Bible translation, and *Orosius*:

(a) *sapiens*:   Anglian *snottur* (occ. *wis* as a loan), WS *wis*, *wita* (sb.)
                  (occ. *snotor* as a loan)

   insipiens: Anglian *unwis*, *unsnottur*, WS *unwis* (occ. *unsnotor*)

(b) *prudens*:   Anglian (Ru[1], EP) *snottur*, elsewhere also *hoga*, *gleaw*, *wis*

Table 5.1

A typical Winchester words

B unspecific words which occur in Winchester texts as synonyms of A and also elsewhere

C typically non-Winchester words, i.e. common OE (e.g. *fremde*), Anglian (e.g. |oferhygd|) or specifically WS (e.g. *ofermod*), where they are the equivalent of Winchester words. | | denotes a whole word-family; the figures refer to the number of instances.

Alfred's vocabulary	(*CP, Bo, Sol*)		
	A	B	C
foreign, strange	—	—	fremde 17
martyr	—	martir 1	—
		martirdom	
dare	—	—	þristlæcan 1
prepare, supply	—	—	(ge)gearwian 7
			fullgearwian 2
			(ge)gierwan 4
			ongierwan 3
			ungierwan 1
church in the sense of community of people	—	—	cirice 8
			gesamung 9
Lat. virtus = virtue	—	mægen[a] 23	cræft[a] 77
			strengu[a] 1
Lat. virtus = power, might, heavenly powers	—	—	cræft[b] 8
			mægen[b] 9
terror, fright	—	broga 4	—
		ege 72	
correct, mend one's way	rihtlæcing 1	(ge)rihtan 4	—
		rihting 1	
regret, repent	—	—	hreow 2
			hreowsian 40
			hreowsung 43
proud	modig 4	—	|oferhygd|4
			|ofermod|84
crown	—	—	beag 3
			heafodbeag 2

Ælfric's vocabulary

	A	B	C
foreign, strange	ælfremed 21 geælfremod 2	—	fremde 1
martyr	cyþere 4	martir 113 martirdom 53	—
dare	gedyrstlæcan 17	dyrstigness 30	—
prepare, supply	(ge)gearcian 121 gearcung 4	—	—
church in the sense of community of people	gelaþung 223	—	cirice 3
Lat. virtus = virtue	miht^a 38	mægen^a 40 heafodmægen 1 heahmægen 1	—
Lat. virtus = power, might, heavenly powers	miht^b 94	—	mægen^b 2
terror, fright	oga 37	broga 2 ege 71 fyrhto 25	egesa 2 gryre 1
correct, mend one's way	(ge)rihtlæcan 57 rihtlæcung 1	gerihtan 18 rihting 12	—
regret, repent	|behreowsian|103	—	—
proud	|modig| 133	pryte 1	oferhygdig 1 ofermod 3
crown	|wuldorbeag|15	cynehelm^a 25 helm 5	cynehelm^b 3

WS	*prudens*	*superbus*
Alfred	*wær(scipe)*	*ofermod/-mettu*
Wulfstan	*wær(scipe)*	*ofermod/-mettu* *ofermodigness*
Bible-translations		
early	*gleaw(ness)*	*ofermod(ness)*
late	*gleaw(ness)*	*ofermod(ness)*
	gleaw(scipe) *snoter(ness)*	*ofermodig(ness)*
Orosius	*(snyttru)*	*ofermodig/-mettu*
Benedictine group	*snotor(ness)*	*modig(ness)*

Seebold (1974:320) suggests that the difference between the Benedictine group and the other three groups is almost certainly due to dialectal variation, and not just a matter of diachrony within a single dialect. Thus the Benedictine group must have relied rather heavily on a local southern dialect when establishing their written norm, which also spread to the area of the Bible translations (possibly Canterbury). This conclusion basically agrees with the findings of Gneuss (1972), except that the latter regards the 'Winchester standard' not as a dialectal phenomenon but as an instance of language planning, involving 'a specific and planned vocabulary, prevalent in one school and restricted to a certain area, and not just a modern trend in general usage' (Gneuss 1972:78). Hofstetter (1987:545), on the other hand, following Seebold, also thinks that the local dialect of Winchester and/or its surroundings had some decisive influence. In any case, it is obvious that West Saxon was no homogeneous dialect but must be seen as a set of (more or less overlapping) subdialects sharing common features that distinguished them from the various Anglian sub-dialects.

To the examples of 'Winchester words' listed as part of Ælfric's vocabulary can be added: *undergytan* 'understand' instead of *ongietan* (Alfred, and Anglian), *understandan* (Wulfstan) (Ono 1986), *leorningcniht* 'disciple', *weofod* 'altar' (vs. *alter*, *altare*), *sunu* 'son' (vs. *bearn*), *cnapa* 'boy' (vs. *cniht*), *gylt* 'guilt' (vs. *scyld*), *(ge)blissian* 'rejoice' (vs. *gefægnian*), and others, see Hofstetter (1987:16), Gneuss (1972:76–7).

Other, general Late West Saxon words that are not restricted to the 'Winchester school' include *angsum* 'narrow, anxious', *besargian* 'lament', *eornostlice* 'therefore, indeed', *gedeorf* 'labour', *mærsian* 'praise', *scrudnian* 'examine, consider', *þæslic* 'suitable', *wæfels* 'dress, cloak' (Gneuss 1972:80), *behatan* 'promise', *hundfeald* 'hundredfold', *wiþæftan* 'from behind', *tima* 'time', *wiþerwinna* 'opponent' (Wenisch 1978:21).

5.3.1.5 Dialects tend to differ not only at the level of the individual lexeme, but also at the more general level of word-formation, in that they select or at least favour certain patterns over other functionally equivalent ones. This is corroborated by a number of observations, although a systematic investigation of this aspect of OE word-formation does not yet exist.

One clear-cut difference between Anglian and non-Anglian dialects is the employment of *-icge* vs. *-estre* for the formation of female agent nouns (von Lindheim 1958, 1969; Schabram 1970). For example, *byrdicge* 'embroideress', *dryicge* 'sorceress', *hunticge* 'huntress', *scernicge* 'actress', *synnicge* 'sinner', *a-, ge-, sunu-cennicge* 'mother' occur only in texts whose Anglian origin is certain or at least highly likely (Schabram 1970:97), and not in WS texts. On the other hand, *bepæcestre* 'whore', *berþestre* 'female carrier', *cempestre* 'female warrior', *forgifestre* 'female giver', *hearpestre* 'female harper', *huntigestre* 'huntress', *lufestre* 'female lover', etc., occur only in WS texts.

Similarly, the suffixoids (Sauer 1985:283) *-berende* and *-bære* acting as equivalents of Lat. *-fer/-ger* (cf. Lat. *lucifer, floriger*) seem to occur in complementary dialectal distribution (von Lindheim 1972). Thus *-berende* (in *adlberende* 'carrying illness', *æppelberende* 'apple-bearing', *atorberende* 'poisonous', *blostmberende* 'flower-bearing', etc.) is practically exclusively Anglian; only *deaþberende* 'death-bearing' *CP* 280.7, *leohtberende* 'light-carrying' *Hept Gen* XV.17, *wæstmberende* 'fertile' are attested in WS texts. On the other hand, *-bære* (in *atorbære, blostmbære, cornbære*, etc.) seems to be WS; it was particularly productive in LWS and was a favourite with Ælfric.

While these cases of dialectal word-formation patterns can be taken as definitely established because of the scope of the material covered, other instances need reinvestigation. Jordan (1906:103) mentions the Anglian, especially Northumbrian employment of the adjectival suffix *-ig* also for deriving deadjectival adjectives, e.g. *druncenig* 'drunk' < *druncen* 'drunk', *untrymig* 'infirm' < *untrum, þiostrig/þystrig* 'obscure, dark' < *þeostor* 'dark', *gesyndig* 'sound' < *gesund, cyþig* 'known' < *cuþ*. He also points to the Northumbrian compounds in *-welle*, e.g. *lifwelle* 'living', *harwelle* 'hoary', *hundwelle* 'a hundredfold', *rumwelle* 'spacious', *deadwelle* 'barren' (Jordan 1906:109), which are not found in the south.

Another example is *-nis/-nes*, forming abstract nouns, which according to Jordan (1906:101) 'in WS in general is only denominal, i.e. is added to the participle (mainly pret. part.), while in Anglian it is added to the verbal stem. EWS has more formations derived from the verbal stem than LWS' [my translation]. There are indeed many doublets (Jordan lists *acennis/acennedness* 'birth', *gecignes, cignes/gecyg(e)dness* 'calling', *gedrefnis/gedrefednis* 'tempest', *gemengnis/gemengednys* 'mingling', *tostencnis/tostencednis* 'dispersion, destruction', *geswencnes/geswencednes* 'affliction', *æteawnis/ætywednis* 'appearance', *flownis/flowendnys/flowednys*), and J. J. Campbell (1951:367), who adopts Jordan's analysis, points out that in the later Bede-version in many instances the original *-nis*-formations derived from the verb stem are replaced by participial derivatives or other formations. Weyhe (1911:9ff.) corroborates the increase of participial derivatives in LWS, but since in EWS we find both derivatives from verb stems and from participles, it is not improbable that the distribution reflects a diachronic change rather than a dialectal split. Another area where dialectal and/or chronological factors may be at work is the distribution of *-ing*/*-ung*-formations (cf. Weyhe 1911:28): in LWS *-ing*-derivatives from short-stemmed class 1 weak verbs and from those ending in a stop + liquid or nasal are replaced by the corresponding *-ung*-formations, e.g. *hering* > *herung* 'praise', *styring* > *styrung* 'motion', *bytling* > *bytlung* 'building', *gebicning* > *gebicnung* 'beckoning', etc. But as in the previous case, only an analysis of the whole OE corpus can show whether this is a diachronic or a diatopic phenomenon.

5.3.2 Diaphasic variation

5.3.2.1   As pointed out in §5.1.2, there are various dimensions of variation besides 'region' that affect the structure of the OE vocabulary. Of these, 'social group' (or 'diastratic variation') and 'medium' are necessarily monostratal because of the nature of the OE texts, which all come from the same type of social group and represent only the written language. At the same time this limits the dimension of 'attitude' to the formal level. There have been some attempts to discover OE colloquialisms in vocabulary and meaning on the basis of the OE Riddles and of native words that appear for the first time in early ME. Thus, von Lindheim (1951/2) suggests that *wamb* 'womb', *neb* 'nose', *þyrel* 'hole', *steort* 'tail', all typical riddle-words with possibly obscene connotations and not occurring in other types of poetry, as well as the meaning 'lust' of *wlonc* and *gal* might have been colloquial in OE. But both the method and the available material have strong limitations, and the conclusion must necessarily remain rather tentative. Within the formal level, however, there are remarkable differences between poetry and prose, and even within these categories, e.g. between heroic and Christian poetry, or between didactic, legal or scientific prose, see also chapter 8 below.

5.3.2.2   There are basically three categories of lexemes in OE: (1) those that are common OE and occur both in prose and poetry, e.g. *man* 'man', *hus* 'house', *blod* 'blood', *heofon* 'heaven'; (2) those that only or predominantly occur in poetry, e.g. *hæleþ*, *beorn*, *freca*, *rinc*, *secg*, 'hero, warrior, man', *þengel*, *fengel*, *brego*, *eodor*, *ræswa* 'prince, king', *ides* 'woman, queen'; (3) those that only or predominantly occur in prose, e.g. *abbod* 'abbot', *borg* 'surety', *ege* 'fright', *hopa* 'hope', nouns in *-ere*, verbs in *-læcan*, loan-translations, later loans from Latin, etc. (cf. Stanley 1971). Purely poetic words have always received special attention and are usually also given specific labels in dictionaries (cf. Clark Hall 1960) or editions (cf. Klaeber 1950: lxiii, 293ff.). But, as Schabram (1966: 85, 1969: 101) has pointed out, such indications are far from reliable, because they are usually not based on a complete survey of the prose texts. The existence of specifically prosaic words has also been known for quite a long time, but the first systematic study was Stanley (1971), who investigated those specifically prosaic words that occasionally also occur in strict verse (cf. also Gneuss 1982: 158).

5.3.2.3 The existence of specifically poetic words as such is not too surprising, because poetry not infrequently tries to use a diction that differs from everyday language, for example, by employing rare, frequently archaic words. The same is of course true of OE, and many poetic words seem to be archaisms, e.g. *heoru*, *mece* 'sword', *guþ*, *hild* 'battle' (possibly originally Valkyrie-names, cf. Marquardt 1938: 119), or *gamol* 'old', *firas* 'men' (Schücking 1915: 6). Others are, or originated as, metonymic or metaphorical expressions, e.g. *ceol* 'keel', *flota* 'floater' for 'ship' (instead of *scip*, *bat*) or *lind* 'shield', *æsc* 'spear' (referring to the material they consist of), or *freca* 'warrior' (*frec* adj. 'eager, bold, daring'). This may have the effect that the meanings of such poetic words are not always completely clear, which is why Schücking (1915: 6) speaks of 'thick veils' obscuring what is described in these poems.

Another source of the semantic problem of meaning-specification is intimately related to 'the most important rhetorical figure, in fact the very soul of the Old English poetical style' (Klaeber 1950: lxv), variation. Variation can be defined as 'a double or multiple statement of the same concept or idea in different words, with a more or less perceptible shift in stress' (Brodeur 1959: 40). For example, in *Beowulf* we find the lines

> Ic þæs wine Deniga,
> frean Scyldinga   frinan wille,
> beaga bryttan   swa þu bena eart
> þeoden mærne   ymb þinne sið...

'I shall ask the lord of Danes, the ruler of the Scyldings, giver of rings, as you make petition, ask the famous prince concerning your visit...'

Here, *wine Deniga* 'lord of the Danes', *frean Scyldinga* 'ruler of the Scyldings', *beaga bryttan* 'giver of rings', *þeoden mærne* 'famous prince' all refer to King Hrothgar, but describe him from different points of view, attributing different properties to him. This rhetorical figure obviously requires a large number of synonyms, either simple or complex, especially in those areas that form the central topics of the OE poetic literature. It is not surprising, therefore, that there are so many (partial) synonyms for notions such as 'sea' (see Buckhurst 1929) (e.g. *sæ, geofon, heafu, mere, lagu, wæter, flod, holm, sund, brim, fam, sæstream, sæwæg, sæholm, lagustreamas, brimstreamas, lagoflodas, drencflod, wægþreat, yþa wylm*), 'ship' (*scip, ceol, wægflota, hringed-stefna, sægenga, brimwudu, merehus, sæhengest, yþmearh, sundhengest*), 'hall, house' (*hus, earn, reced, flet, heall, sæl, sele, bold, burh, geard, hof, wic*), 'man, warrior' (*monn, eorl, ceorl, wer, guma, rinc, beorn, secg, hæleþ, firas, niþþas, ylde, landbuend, grundbuend, foldbuend, sawlberend*) and many others. And this is also the reason why the determination of the precise shade of meaning of those synonyms is so difficult, at least as far as simple lexical items are concerned. Items such as *brimwudu, sæhengest* at the same time represent another phenomenon characteristic of Germanic poetry in general and also directly related to the principle of variation: the systematic use of simple and complex metaphorical expressions called *heiti* and *kenningar* (cf. Marquardt 1938; Brodeur 1959:247–59). Following Snorri Sturluson's categorisation in *Skáldskaparmál* (see Brodeur 1952; 1959:247ff.), three categories may be distinguished.

The *ókend heiti* ('uncharacterised terms') are simple, unqualified nouns with a literal (e.g. *scip, bat*) or a metaphorical/figurative (e.g. *flota* 'that which floats = ship', *ceol* 'keel = ship') interpretation; the *kend heiti* and the *kenningar* are complex expressions serving as metaphorical periphrases of the referent in question, replacing the lexical item that would normally be used. They are nominal in structure, i.e. nominal compounds or groups, for example, a noun modified by a genitive, which is functionally equivalent to a compound (e.g. *yðgewinn = yða gewinn* 'wave strife = strife of the waves = sea'). They differ in that the *kend heiti* ('characterised terms') identify the referent as something which it is by emphasising a certain quality, aspect or function of it, while in the *kenningar* 'the base word identifies the referent with something it is not, except in relation to the concept expressed in the limiting word' (Brodeur 1959:250). Thus, a ship really is a *sægenga* 'sea-goer', or *wægflota* 'wave-floater', but it is not a *wæghengest* 'sea-steed' or *brimwudu* 'sea-wood'; the sun really is a *heofonleoma* or *swegles leoht* 'light of heaven', but it is not a *rodores candel* 'heaven-candle' or *heofnes gim* 'heavenly gem', except in a metaphorical sense (but cf. Marquardt 1938:116ff., who rejects this distinction and treats both types as *kenningar*). In the kennings, there is thus 'a tension between the concept and the base-word; the limiting word partially resolves the unreality of that relation...it depends on the hearer's ability and willingness to see likeness within unlikeness' (Brodeur 1959:150–1).

Both types of periphrasis, typically associated with variation structures, are extremely frequent in OE poetry. Further examples of *kend heiti* are expressions for earth (*hæleþa eþel* 'home of men', *fæder ealdgeweorc* 'ancient work of the Father'), the sea (*fisces eþel* 'home of the fish', *seolhbæþ* 'seal-bath', *yþa geswing* 'surge of the waves'), thunder (*wolcna sweg* 'sound of the clouds'), dragon (*lyftfloga* 'flier in the air', *goldweard, hordes hyrde* 'keeper of gold, treasure'), or the many expressions for lord, prince, king (*ealdor þegna* 'lord of the warriors', *hæleþa brego* 'ruler of men', *folces weard* 'protector of the people', *beaggifa* 'ring-giver', etc.). The following are genuine kennings: *beadoleoma, hildeleoma* 'battle-light = sword', *mere-hrægl* 'sea-dress = sail', *guþwine* 'battle-friend = sword', *banhus, bancofa* 'bone-coffer, bone-chamber = body' (all in *Beowulf*), or *hildenædre* 'battle-adder = javelin, arrow', *garbeam* 'spear-tree = warrior', *heafodgim* 'head-gem = eye'. These latter come from religious poems such as *Genesis, Exodus, Elene* or *Andreas*, and are regarded as 'riddle-like and far-fetched' by Brodeur (1959:35), who sees in these more extravagant formations a typical feature of the later religious poems, i.e. there seems to be a difference in this respect between the traditional heroic and the later religious poems which have adopted but also modified the format of heroic poetry.

The phenomenon in question highlights a property of OE repeatedly mentioned already, the prolificness of its word-formation patterns, because many, although by no means all of the *kend heiti* and *kenningar* are compounds. It is certainly no accident that, for example, in *Beowulf* about one third of the entire vocabulary consists of compounds. In the 3,182 lines of the poem, Brodeur (1959:7) has counted 903 distinct substantive compounds, 518 of which occur only in *Beowulf*, and 578 are found only once in the poem; there are 86 Adj + Adj or Advb + Adj compounds (e.g. *brunfag* 'brown-hued', *gramhydig* 'hostile-thinking'; *feorrancund* 'come from afar'), of which 36 occur only here; 164 items are N + Adj compounds (e.g. *lagu-cræftig* 'skilled in seafaring', *morgenceald* 'morning-cold'), of which 86 are unique; and 36 are bahuvrihi-compounds of the structure Adj + N (e.g. *blodigtoð* 'bloody-toothed', *blondenfeax* 'grizzly-haired', *famigheals* 'foamy-necked'), of which 15 are pecular to *Beowulf*. *Beowulf* certainly is an extreme, but it is nevertheless representative of the OE poetic diction and its vocabulary and thus demonstrates, perhaps most clearly, how strongly poetic diction is based on a specific type of vocabulary.

5.3.2.4 Compared to poetic diction, the prose vocabulary is less striking. According to the subject matter dealt with in the existing texts, we will of course come across differences, e.g. between legal terminology in the Anglo-Saxon laws (cf. Liebermann 1903–16), medical and biological terminology in the *Leechbook* (cf. Bierbaumer 1975/6) or grammatical terminology in Ælfric's *Grammar*. One feature which must have had a considerable influence on the formation of the OE vocabulary should be mentioned again in this connection, namely the dependence of many OE texts on a Latin original. In §5.2.1.5 the phenomena of semantic loans, loan-translations and loan-creations have already been discussed extensively, and it is quite obvious that they play a much greater role in the prose vocabulary (and even more so in the glosses) than in poetry. Unfortunately, besides Gneuss' (1955) investigation of the Vespasian Psalter there has been no further large-scale attempt at describing this area. One domain that would profit greatly from further studies of loan-translations is OE word-formation, because it is quite clear that many OE formations were prompted by Latin originals. And even if many OE translations may have had a rather esoteric status – cf. e.g. the grammatical terminology in Ælfric's *Grammar* – they still provide clues as to the productivity of OE word-formation patterns. But there again, a comprehensive description has still to be written.

5.4 Word-formation

5.4.1 General aspects

5.4.1.1 Every language requires patterns according to which new lexemes can be formed on the basis of already existing lexical material. The most basic property of such new formations is their transparent, motivated status: on the basis of their structure and the meaning of the constituents their meaning can be computed. Thus, *wæter-berere* 'water-bearer', *pening-mangere* 'money-dealer', *lagu-swimmend* 'sea-swimmer = fish', *aþ-swerung* 'oath-swearing' are easily interpreted on this basis even when coming across them for the first time. This, certainly, was one reason why loan-translations were preferred to loans in the earlier OE period.

Word-formations are lexical syntagmas based on a determinant (modifier)/determinatum (head) relation (Marchand 1969:3); in the Germanic languages, the determinant always precedes the determinatum. This holds for compounds as well as for prefixations and suffixations, cf.

dt	/	dm	
wæter	/	berere	'bearer of water'
winter	/	setl	'winter-quarters'
forþ	/	faran	'go forth, depart'
sin	/	cald	'perpetually (*sin-*) cold'
feond	/	scipe	'hostility = state (*-scipe*) of being an enemy (*feond-*)'
lær	/	end	'teacher = someone (*-end*) who teaches (*lær-*)'

The principle of transparency/motivation can be impaired by the process of lexicalisation: once formed, a lexeme may adopt additional semantic properties that are not predictable from the meanings of the constituents and the pattern underlying the combination. Thus *morgengifu* is not simply a gift given at some morning, but a gift given to the bride by her husband after the wedding-night; *cyningeswyrt* is not simply a herb that has something to do with a/the king, but refers to marjoram; and *forþfaran* does not only mean 'go away' in the literal, but also the figurative sense, 'die'. Lexicalisation is not an all-or-nothing phenomenon, but a scale, and lexemes may move along this scale in the course of time. When dealing with an historical period, therefore, it is not always easy to determine whether a given formation is lexicalised or not.

Sometimes lexicalisation itself may be pattern-forming, when some element of a series of formations loses its original meaning (usually by a process of meaning generalisation) and is only employed with this new meaning in new formations. This may in time lead to the status of an affix, e.g. with *-scipe* 'state, status', *-bære* 'carrying', *-wende* 'conducing', or at least an affixoid, as with *-dom, -lac, -ræden* 'state, status' (Sauer 1985:283). A slightly different development took place with *leod, þeod* 'people', which in *leodcyning, þeodcyning* 'king of the people = mighty king' have still preserved their original meaning, although with an additional intensifying function, whilst in *þeodloga* 'arch-lier', *þeodwiga* 'great warrior', *leodbealu* 'terrible calamity', *leodgryre* 'general terror', the determinant has merely intensifying function. But in view of the existence of combinations with a literal meaning, we should not treat *leod*, *þeod* as prefixoids (with respect to Sauer 1985:284). The morpheme *cyne-*, alternant of *cyning* 'king', on the other hand, has probably progressed further in this direction, cf. *cynebænd* 'diadem', *cynebot* 'king's compensation', *cynegierela* 'royal robe', although a formation like *cynescipe* 'royalty, majesty' confirms that *cyne-* must still have had word-status, because *-scipe* in OE was definitely a suffix, and combinations of the type **prefix + suffix have never existed in English.

5.4.1.2   Marchand (1969:2) defines word-formation as 'that branch of the science of language which studies the patterns on which a language forms new lexical units'. Applying this definition to a language no longer spoken raises a number of serious problems.

Firstly, there is no way of testing productivity directly; all we have is circumstantial evidence such as the number of new formations occurring in texts of a given period, their semantic quality (i.e. their semantic regularity, homogeneity, degree of lexicalisation), the correlation of morphophonemic alternations with the overall morphophonemic system operating also in inflexion (i.e. the degree of morphological transparency, the type of conditioning, etc.) or continued productivity in subsequent periods. Taken together, these factors will give us a reasonably good indication as to whether a pattern was productive or not, but no more than that. Moreover, productivity is a cline, and we have to determine a cut-off point after which we should no longer include the respective formations.

Secondly, neither productivity nor transparency are static phenomena; they can vary diachronically, cf. *-nis*, which apparently lost the ability to combine with verb-stems and came to be restricted to participles and adjectives in LWS (see §5.3.1.5). When one has to deal with a linguistic period such as OE, stretching over some 600 years, there are bound to have been many such changes, not all of which can be reconstructed because of our limited evidence, which covers only the last 200 to 250 years and is rather fragmentary at that. Much of what would actually constitute various historical layers within a given pattern will therefore inevitably appear projected onto a two-dimensional plane, since only the output of the patterns as recorded in the later documents is available for study.

Thirdly, and perhaps more importantly, even when a given pattern loses its productivity, it leaves behind at least some of its output as an integral part of the vocabulary. It is true that loss of productivity usually increases the tendency towards lexicalisation, with subsequent reduction and perhaps even obliteration of semantic and morphological transparency. Still, very often many formations remain fully transparent and by virtue of this property constitute an important factor in the overall structure of the vocabulary which should not be disregarded. For a diachronic study, therefore, transparency/analysability will have to be regarded as more important than productivity, although the latter cannot of course be completely disregarded.

Unfortunately, this does not solve the demarcation problem, because we do not want to include all residues of unproductive patterns indiscriminately. Thus the ablaut formations mentioned in § 5.1.3.2 will have to be treated, because their number makes them a significant, even typologically relevant, feature of the OE vocabulary despite their basic lack of productivity. The derivatives

(1) *æs* n. 'food, meat, carrion' < *et-(an)* ~ *æt-(on)* 'eat'
blæs m. 'blowing, blast' < *blaw-(an)* 'blow'
hæs f. 'command, bidding' < *hat-(an)* 'command'
læs f. 'letting of blodd' < *læt-(an)* 'let'
ræs f. 'counsel, deliberation' < *ræd-(an)* 'advise'

on the other hand, constitute the limiting case and should probably be disregarded because of semantic and morphological irregularities.

But there are more complicated situations such as the following four groups of deverbal nouns (see also Kastovsky 1985:231ff.):

(2)(a) m.   *han-cred* 'cock-crow' < *craw-(an)*, *geblæd* 'blister < *blaw-(an)*

n.   *aþ-swyrd* 'oath' < *swer-(ian)* 'swear', *sæd* 'seed' < *saw-(an)* 'sow'

f.   *fierd* 'national levy or army' < *far-(an)* 'travel, go'; *byrd* 'birth, burden' < *ber-(an)* ~ *bor(en)* 'carry', *bled* 'flower, blossom' < *blow-(an)* 'blossom', *flode* 'channel, a place where anything flows' < *flow-(an)* 'flow'

m/n *flod* 'flood' < *flow-(an)*

m/f *cwild* 'death, destruction' < *cwel-(an)* 'die'

(b) m.   *ymbhwyrft* 'circuit, bend, turn' < *ymbhweorf-(an)* ~ *-hwurf-(on)* 'revolve', *slieht* 'striking, animals for slaughter' < *sle-(an)* ~ *slæg-(en)* 'slay', *scrift* 'one who shrives, confessor; penalty' < *scrif-(an)* ~ *scrif-(en)* 'shrive', *wælslihta* 'murderer' < *sle-(an)* ~ *slæg-(en)* 'slay', *wyrhta* 'workman' < *wyrc-(an)* 'work'

f. *æht* 'possessions, serf' < *ag-(an)* 'own', *iht* 'increase' < *eac-(an)/ic-(an)* 'increase', *næft* 'need, want' < *nabb-(an)* 'have not, want', *gesiht/gesihþ* 'slight' < *seon* ~ *seg-(en)* 'see', *þeoft/þiefþ/þeofþ* 'stolen goods' < *þeof-(ian)* 'steal', *wist* 'food, sustenance' < *wes-(an)* 'be, exist'

m/f/n *cyst* 'what is chosen' < *ceos-(an)* ~ *cur-(on)* 'choose', *gift* 'giving, gift' < *gief-(an)* 'give', *gesceaft* 'what is created' < *sciepp-(an)* ~ *sceap-(en)* 'create', *weft(a)* 'weft' < *wef-(an)* 'weave'

(c) f. *æbrecþ* 'sacrilege' < *brec-(an)* 'break', *fyrmþ* 'washing'; pl. 'sweepings, rubbish' < *feorm-(ian)* 'scour, clean', *geþingþ* 'intercession; court' < *þing-(ian)* 'determine, intercede', *ripþ* 'harvest' < *rip-(an)* 'reap'

n *gewilcþ* 'rolling' < *(ge)wealc-(an)* 'roll'

(d) m. *fiscoþ* 'fishing; place for fishing' < *fisc-(ian)* 'fish', *hergaþ* 'harrying' < *herg-(ian)* 'harry', *hæletoþ* 'greeting' < *hælett-(an)* 'greet', *huntoþ* 'what is hunted' < *hunt-(ian)* 'hunt', *folgaþ* 'train, retinue' < *folg-(ian)* 'follow', *migoþa* 'urine' < *mig-(an)* 'make water', *spiweþa* 'what is vomited, vomit' < *spiw-(an)* 'vomit', *sweoloþ(a)* 'heat, burning' < *swel-(an)* 'burn', *sceafoþa* 'chip' < *sceaf-(an)* 'shave'

n. *gifeþe* 'what is granted by fate' < *gief-(an)* 'give'.

It would seem that *-d* in (2a) was no longer productive in OE, because there are no derivatives from weak verbs in contradistinction to the other three groups; but the derivatives are fairly transparent and semantically regular. Present-day English derivatives like *spilth*, *growth* suggest that *-þ* was productive in OE; the same is probably true of *-oþa*, because it combines with weak class 2 verbs, a category of more recent origin than the strong verbs; the status of *-t* is not quite clear, but the existence of derivatives from weak verbs also suggests that it may still have been productive.

The main question to be asked in this case, however, is whether these four groups should be treated as independent derivational patterns, in turn consisting of gender-specific sub-patterns, because only (2d) is homogeneous as to gender-affiliation. It would seem that each gender, and also each inflexional class should constitute a separate pattern (see Pilch 1985:423), although this causes problems with those instances having multiple gender-affiliation without any meaning-difference (e.g. *gift*, *cyst*).

As to the treatment of *-d*, *-t(a,e)*, *-þ* and *-oþa* as independent suffixes, it should be noted that a fairly systematic complementary distribution seems to obtain, -*d* occurring after roots ending in a glide, liquid or nasal, -*t* after roots ending in a fricative, -*þ* after roots ending in a stop, -*oþ* with weak class 2 verbs, -*oþa* with strong verbs. There are a few exceptions, e.g. the doublets *gesiht/gesihþ*, *þeoft/þeofþ*, *þiefþ* or *hæletoþ* (with a class 1 base), but these might be explained as analogical reformations indicating that the complementary distribution was no longer fully effective. Since none of these suffixes is tied to a specific meaning but all have roughly the same semantic range, we can probably treat them as partly morphologically, partly phonologically conditioned alternants. This in fact corresponds to their historical origin, a ProtoIE suffix family clustering around the formative -*t*- (Krahe and Meid 1967:19ff.), to which various vocalic extensions functioning as stem-formatives were added (-*to*-, -*ta*-, -*tio*-, -*tia*-, -*ti*-, -*tu*-, etc.). These stem formatives originally determined gender and class affiliation, but were lost in PrOE; they were responsible for the gender differences in (2a–c). The consonantal alternation reflects Pre-Germanic stress differences (root vs. suffixal stress) and the effects of Grimm's and Verner's Laws. It is thus quite obvious that we have to do with various derivational layers, of which only -*þ*/-*oþ*, and perhaps -*t* (without *i*-mutation, cf. *þeoft*) were still productive. In the existing literature, such derivational layers are discussed only exceptionally, e.g. in von Lindheim (1958), Kärre's (1915) study on agent-nouns in -*el*/-*ol* and -*end*, Weyhe's (1911) treatment of -*ness* and -*ing*/*ung*, or Hinderling's (1967) study of the Germanic strong abstract nouns. Here, much work still remains to be done. The example has demonstrated, however, that a full-scale description of OE word-formation will have to strike a balance between a purely synchronic and a purely historical-etymological approach by also including unproductive patterns, as long as their output is still transparent.

5.4.1.3 OE word-formation is characterised by widespread stem-allomorphy, i.e. we find the same kind of morphophonemic alternations as in inflexion. Besides ablaut (cf. §5.1.3.2), the following alternations occur:

1   *i*-mutation: *full* ~ *fyllan* < */full-j-an/ 'fill', *curon* (~ *ceosan*) ~ *cyre* 'choice', *gram* ~ *gremman* 'enrage', *sæt* (~ *sittan*) ~ *settan* < */sat-j-an/ 'set', *trum* ~ *trymþ* 'trimness'

2   consonant gemination (accompanied by *i*-mutation): *gram* ~

gremman, wefan ~ webba, secgan ~ sagu 'saying' (reverse alternation)

3   palatalisation/assibilation: *ċeosan/curon ~ cyre, lugon ~ lyġen, bre-
can/brucon ~ bryċe* 'breach', *gangan ~ genġa* 'goer', *fon/fangen ~
fenġ* 'grasp'

4   /æ/ ~ /ɑ/: *faran ~ fær* 'journey', *grafan ~ græf* 'style for
writing', *græft* 'carved object', *bacan ~ gebæc* 'baking' (with
internal paradigmatic alternation as well, cf. *fær ~ farum*)

5   Verner's Law: *ceosan ~ cyre* < */kur-i/, *risan/ras ~ ræran* <
/rɑːz-j-an/ 'raise'.

How these alternations are handled depends on one's phonological
analysis, i.e. whether one allows abstract underlying representations or
not, see chapter 3. If one does (cf. Lass & Anderson 1975), *i*-mutation,
consonant gemination and palatalisation/assibilation can be analysed as
phonologically conditioned, as long as the element (-*i*-, -*j*-) triggering
these processes is part of the underlying representation (see also
§5.4.4.1). It would seem, however, that in classical OE at the latest,
these three alternations were also morphologically conditioned, cf.
analogical formations without *i*-mutation such as *stanig* 'stony' besides
stænig, þorniht/þyrniht 'thorny', *eorlisc* 'noble' besides *mennisc* (< *man*)
'human', etc. The status of /æ/ ~ ɑ/ is questionable but was probably
still phonologically conditioned.

Certain prefixes exhibit stress-conditioned alternations; in verbs they
are unstressed or have secondary stress, in nouns they have full stress.
This is also accompanied by allomorphy, cf. *àwéorpan* 'throw away' ~
ǽwỳrp 'what is cast away', *ònsácan* 'contest' ~ *ándsæc* 'denial', *ándsàca*
'adversary', *begán* 'go over, worship' ~ *bíġèng* 'worship', *bíġènga*
'worshipper', besides homological *ónsæc, begáng, begánga*. This is the
source of Modern English *recórd* vb. ~ *récord* n. and goes back to the
proto-Germanic period, when word-stress came to be fixed on the first
syllable. At this stage, prefixed nouns already existed, whereas
inseparable prefixed verbs apparently are a later development, and
therefore kept the stress on the root, cf. the chapters on phonology in
volumes I and II.

5.4.2   Compounding

5.4.2.1   Introduction

As we have seen in §5.3, compounds were one of the most important stylistic devices of poetry, but were of course not restricted to poetic language. Accordingly, their number is substantial and the following can only provide a brief outline of the major features.

Compounds are complex lexical items consisting of two or more lexemes, e.g. *deofol-gyld-hus* 'heathen temple', *god-spell-bodung* 'gospel preaching'. There are substantival, adjectival and verbal compounds; the latter, however, are restricted to adverbs and prepositions as first members, e.g. *forþ-feran* 'depart', *ofer-lecgan* 'place over', *under-lecgan* 'underlay'; verbs such as *cyne-helm-ian* 'crown', *grist-bit(i)an* 'gnash the teeth', etc. are derivatives from nominal compounds (*cyne-helm* 'crown') or back derivations from deverbal compounds (*grist-bite* 'gnashing').

One major problem is the delimitation of compounds from corresponding syntactic groups. Spelling or semantic isolation (lexicalisation), sometimes suggested as appropriate criteria, do not work. Spelling in OE was as erratic in this respect as it is in present-day English, and according to the other criterion, *morgengifu* as well as *halig gast* 'Holy Ghost', *se hwita sunnandæg* 'Whit Sunday' would count as compounds, while *morgenleoht* 'morning-light', *morgensweg* 'morning-cry' would not, which is certainly counter-intuitive. According to Marchand (1969:21), the only decisive criterion is the morphological isolation of the compound from the corresponding syntactic group; this isolation can take various forms. Stress is one possibility, cf. the compound type *snówbàll* vs. the group type *stòne wáll*. But for OE, this criterion is not very helpful, because in prose texts stress cannot be established, and in poetry both elements of a compound may receive a main stress for metrical reasons, cf. *wúndenstéfna* 'ship with curved prow' *Beo* 220, *héorðgenéatas* 'retainers' *Beo* 261 (cf. Sauer 1985:271). Another criterion is the lack of a parallel syntactic group or its different formal make-up, as in the case of copulative compounds like *aþumswerian* 'son-in-law and father-in-law', *cnihtcild* 'boy, lit. boy-child', V + N compounds like *hereword* 'word of praise', *rædeboc* 'reading-book', and exocentric compounds like *bærfot* 'barefoot', *heardheort* 'hard-hearted'. Adj-N compounds are easily recognisable in their inflected forms, because the adjective is not inflected, cf. *heahenglas* 'archangels', *wilddeora* 'wild beasts', *heahcyninges* (gen.) 'high-king'; but occasionally there are syntactic group doublets with an inflected adjective, e.g. *wilde deor, þone hean cyninge*, and in the nominative singular, where the adjective may be uninflected – cf. *heah engel*, *heah cyning* – the criterion is neutralised. Thus, since *idel gylþ*, *idel wuldor* 'vainglory' in their inflected forms occur only with an inflected adjective (*for*, *mid idelum gylpe/wuldre*, etc.), these items are syntactic groups and not compounds as assumed in Clark Hall and Bosworth/Toller (Sauer 1985:275). Inflexion of the determinant is no criterion with genitive compounds, however, as in *Sunnandæg* 'Sunday', *cyningeswyrt* 'marjoram', *dægeseage* 'daisy'. Here the whole NP has to be checked; if the article refers to the determinatum (head), we have a compound, as in *se egesfullica domesdæge* 'the terrible doomsday'; if it refers to the determinant (modifier), we have a syntactic group, as in *þære sweartan helle grundes* 'bottom of the black hell', whereas *hatne helle-grund* 'hot hell-bottom' probably has to be regarded as a compound.

In a number of cases, e.g. *hildecalla* 'war-herald', *hildegeatwe* 'war-harness', *stanegella* (besides *stangella*) 'pelican', *goldefrætwe* 'gold ornaments', *drencefæt* 'drinking-vessel', *yrfeweard* 'heir', the internal vowel should not be regarded as a genitive ending, but as a linking element like the German *Fugen-s* in *Liebesbrief* 'love-letter'. For a detailed treatment of these linking elements or 'bridge-vowels' see Carr (1939:281–98).

Compounds must also be kept apart from prefixations and suffixations, but the delimitation is not absolute, there being a number of borderline cases. Thus, *cyne-* 'royal' in *cynegild* 'king's compensation', *cynestol* 'throne', *cynecynn* 'royal race' only occurs as a determinant in compounds and might therefore be interpreted as a prefix. But since it is in complementary distribution with *cyning*, *cyning* being extremely rare as a determinant in compounds (save for *cyninggereordu* 'royal meal', *cyn(in)gestun* 'royal town'), and since there are formations like *cynelic* 'royal', *cynescipe* 'kingship', where *-lic* and *scipe* have to be regarded as suffixes, *cyne-* should be analysed as an allomorph of *cyning*. Its occurrence as a prototheme in personal names also argues against an interpretation as prefix. *Twi-* is subject to the same restriction, cf. *twidæl* 'two thirds', *twifeald* 'twofold', *twiræde* 'uncertain', *twiecge* 'two-edged', *twideagod* 'twice-dyed', and might be regarded as an allomorph of *twa* 'two'. More difficult is the classification of *-dom*, *-had*, *-lac*, *-ræden* (nominal), and *-fæst*, *-ful(l)*, *-leas* (adjectival), which also occur as words, and of *-bære*, *-feald*, *-wende*, which only occur as determinata. Sauer (1985:282ff.) classifies *had*-combinations as compounds, because *-had* in *bisceophad*, *martyrhad* 'state, rank of a bishop, martyr' still has basically the same meaning as the lexeme *had*, whereas the other morphemes are regarded as suffixoids with more or less pronounced suffixal character. I shall follow Sauer and treat these elements in the section on suffixation.

There are two basic types of word-formation patterns, expansions and derivations. Expansions satisfy the condition AB = B, i.e. the determinatum (head) is a lexeme, and the combination as a whole belongs to the same word-class and lexical class as the determinatum (Marchand 1969:11); derivations do not satisfy this criterion. On the basis of this criterion, both compounds and prefixations qualify as expansions. Thus, *bedstreaw* 'straw for bedding' is a subcategory of *streaw*, *swefen-reccere* 'interpreter of dreams' is a kind of *reccere* 'interpreter', *edlean* 'reward' is a kind of *lean* 'gift, loan', etc.

On the basis of this criterion certain combinations that look like compounds in that they consist of two lexemes do not qualify as expansions: an *anhorn* 'unicorn' is not a horn, but an animal with one horn, a *hundestunge* 'hound's tongue' is not a *tunge* but a plant with leaves like a dog's tongue; and *bærfot* 'barefoot', *rihtheort* 'righteous', *yfelwille* 'malevolent' should be nouns, but are actually adjectives. Traditionally, these are called *bahuvrihi* or exocentric compounds, because the determinatum lies outside the formation. Marchand uses the term pseudo-compound (1969:13ff., 386–9) and treats them as zero-derivatives with the structure $anhorn_N/\emptyset_N$ 'something ($= \emptyset_N$) which has one (*an*) horn (*horn*)', $bærfot_N/\emptyset_{Adj}$ 'having ($= \emptyset_{Adj}$) a bare foot (*bærfot*)', cf. *anhyrned* = 'having ($= ed_{Adj}$) one horn'. I shall follow this practice and discuss such formations in §5.4.5 together with other types of zero-derivation.

Since the explicit morphological structure of such formations did not agree with their function, they were often reformed by either changing the inflexional class (usually to the weak declension), cf. *anhorna*, *bundenstefna* m. 'ship with an ornamented prow' (*stefn* was probably originally an *i*-stem, cf. Campbell 1959:74n.4), or by adding a derivational suffix, cf. *cliferfete* 'cloven-footed' (*-ja*-suffix), *eaþmodig*, *eaþmodlic* 'humble' (besides *eaþmod*), etc. These are usually called 'extended *bahuvrihi* compounds' (Carr 1939:252ff.), but in actual fact are clearly derivatives and not compounds. They will therefore be treated under the corresponding suffixes.

One further type of compound deserves special consideration, formations such as *wæter-berere* 'water-carrier', *aþ-swerung* 'oath-swearing', *feþer-berend* 'feather-bearing creature', *ælmesgifa* 'almsgiver'. These are characterised by the fact that the determinatum itself is a derived, usually deverbal noun, and that the determinant can be regarded as one of the arguments of the underlying predicate, i.e. *wæter-berere* 'someone (*-ere* = Subj.) carrying (*ber-*v) water (*wæter* = Obj.)'. Such combinations are fairly frequent. They belong to Marchand's (1969:31ff.) category of 'verbal-nexus-combinations' and are among other things characterised by the fact that the determinatum need not necessarily occur as an independent lexeme, as long as it represents a possible deverbal derivative, cf. instances such as *nihtegale* 'night-singer = nightingale', *yrfenuma* 'heir-taker = heir'. This property has given them the name 'synthetic compound'. Consequently there is no need to regard *-bora* 'carrier' in *candelbora* 'candlebearer', *mundbora* 'guardian', lit. 'protection-bearer', *tacnbora* 'standard-bearer' as a suffix, because it does not occur outside such compounds (cf. Sprockel 1973:II, 41ff., Quirk & Wrenn 1957:115). Such formations should also be treated as synthetic compounds, cf. PDE formations such as *nutcracker, chimney sweep*.

A further subclassification and description of compounds is best based on the word-class affiliation of the determinatum (noun, adjective including participles, verb; other categories are marginal), and of the determinant (noun, adjective including participles, verb, particle), on the distinction between simple and derived determinata, on further morphological distinctions, e.g. between stem vs. genitive compounds, and on semantic-syntactic criteria, see, for example, the classification in Marchand (1969:ch. 2), or Kastovsky (1985) for deverbal nouns. The semantic description of word-formation syntagmas, especially compounds, has been a much-discussed topic, which cannot be taken up here. The labels used in the following are not intended to represent a particular theoretical framework, but are used in their traditional signification to provide a frame of reference for something that in view of space limitations can only exemplify the possibilities but cannot be an exhaustive description.

5.4.2.2 Compound nouns

5.4.2.2.1 **Noun + Noun** compounds represent the most frequent pattern. The relationship between the two immediate constituents – determinant and determinatum – can be reduced to three basic types: additive, copulative, rectional (Marchand 1969:40), although the additive type is only represented by two examples from poetry – *aþumswerian* 'son-in-law and father-in-law' and *suhtorgefædran* 'nephew and uncle' – and was obviously unproductive in Old English. These should actually be treated as exocentric compounds with the semantic-morphological structure 'something (= -∅) consisting of *son-in-law* and *father-in-law*', etc. Numerals from 13 onwards (*þreotine*) follow the same pattern.

The copulative compounds can be paraphrased by a construction containing the copula *be*, e.g. *eoforswin* 'pig (*swin*) which is a boar (*eofor*)', *freawine* 'friend (*wine*) who is also a lord (*frea*)'. There are two subgroups, attributive and subsumptive compounds (Marchand 1969:40ff.).

In attributive compounds, the determinant attributes a specific property to the determinatum, while with subsumptive compounds, the determinant denotes a subclass of the determinatum. Typical examples of attributive compounds are sex-denoting nouns, e.g. *cilforlamb* 'ewe-lamb', *cnihtcild* 'boy', *cucealf* 'heifer-calf', *fearhryþer* 'bull', *mægþmann* 'maiden', *gummann* 'man', *wifmann* 'woman'. The reverse order occurs in *assmyre* 'she-ass', *gatbucca* 'billy-goat', *olfendmyre* 'camel', *rahdeor* 'roe-buck', i.e. these have the same structure as derivatives with a sex-denoting suffix, e.g. *gyden* 'goddess', *dryicge* 'sorceress', *lufestre* 'female lover'. The same possibilities exist for nouns denoting the young of an animal or person, e.g. *steoroxa* 'young ox' vs. *hindcealf* 'fawn', *leonhwelp* 'lion's cub'. Profession is another concept belonging here, e.g. *weardmann* 'guard', *ambehtmann* 'servant'.

Among the subsumptive compounds, the following subgroups can be distinguished (cf. Carr 1939:324ff., whose subclassification differs somewhat from the one adopted here, because he includes sex-denoting compounds among the subsumptive type).

(a) The determinant denotes a concept with which the determinatum is compared: *colmase* 'coal-tit', *goldfinc* 'goldfinch', *ælepute* 'eel-pout', *sperewyrt* 'spearwort'.

(b) The determinant denotes the species, the determinatum the *genus proximum*: *cederbeam* 'cedar', *cirisbeam* 'cherry-tree', *marmanstan* 'marble', *hwætecorn* 'grain of wheat', *piporcorn* 'peppercorn', *regenscur* 'rain-shower', *eagæpple* 'eyeball', *fugolcynn* 'birds', *æfentid* 'evening'.

(c) Both constituents denote different aspects of the same thing, e.g. *werewulf* 'a being which is both a wolf and a man'; there is a close relationship to the preceding group: *agendfrea* 'lord and owner', *ealdorbisceop*, *bisceopealdor* 'chief bishop', *dryhtenweard* 'lord and guardian', *mægwine*, *winemæg* 'relative and friend', *hleodryhten* 'lord and protector'.

(d) The meaning of the determinant is already contained more or less in the determinatum (pleonastic compounds), e.g. *eorþstede*, *eorþweg* 'earth', *lagustream*, *merestream*, *sæstream* 'sea'.

In many instances, the two constituents are practically synonymous, although one should probably not regard such compounds, which mainly, although not exclusively, occur in poetry, as mere tautologies (Marchand 1969:62): *æledfyr* 'fire', *deaþcwealm* 'death', *dolgbenn* 'wound', *feondsceaþa* 'enemy, robber', *feorhlif* 'life', *holtwudu* 'wood', *wuduholt* 'wood', *mægencræft* 'strength', *willspring* 'spring'. Many of these compounds also occur in reversed order without any apparent change of meaning, cf. *bealucwealm/cwealmbealu* 'violent death', *beotword/wordbeot* 'boast, threat', *cearsorg/sorgcearu* 'anxiety', *rimgetæl/getælrim* 'number'.

Rectional compounds are best defined negatively as those that do not allow a copulative paraphrase. Morphologically, we can distinguish two subcategories, pure nominal compounds and synthetic compounds, i.e. those having a deverbal noun as the determinatum. Semantically speaking, both groups can express the same kinds of relationship (cf. Marchand 1969:31ff.). The following examples are extremely selective; a comprehensive description is not possible in this connection.

1 Synthetic compounds

(a) The determinatum is an agent noun, the determinant denotes the goal (object), place, instrument or time of the action, e.g. *man-swara* 'perjurer', *freols-gifa* 'giver of freedom', *wudu-heawere* 'wood-cutter', *blod-lætere* 'blood-letter', *sweord-bora* 'sword-bearer', *reord-berend* 'speech-bearer = human being', *eorþ-buend* 'earth-dweller', *land-buend* 'land-dweller', *sæ-liþend* 'sailor', *sæ-genga* 'sailor', *sæ-lida* 'sailor, pirate', *garwigend* 'spear-fighter', *nid-nima* 'one who takes by force', *æsc-wiga* 'spear-fighter', *mete-rædere* 'monk reading at meals', *nihte-gale* 'nightingale', *niht-genga* 'a creature that goes by night, goblin', etc.

(b) The determinatum is an action noun, the determinant denotes the agent, goal, place, instrument or time of the action: *hancred* 'cockcrow', *sæ-ebbing* 'ebbing of the sea', *eorþbeofung* 'earthquake', *feaxfalling* 'shedding of hair', *bec-ræding/boc-ræding* 'reading of books', *hlaford-swicung* 'treachery to a lord', *wæterfyrhtness* 'fear of water, hydrophobia', *ciricgang* 'church-going', *wægfaru* 'passage through the sea', *wordbeotung* 'promise', *handgripe* 'hand-grasp', *nidnæm* 'forcible seizure', *æfenræding* 'evening reading', *nihtfeormung* 'hospitality for the night', *morgensweg* 'cry at morn'.

The demarcation between synthetic and regular nominal compounds is not without problems (cf. Kastovsky 1968:8ff., 96; Marchand 1969:15ff.). The basic criterion used here is the derived status of the determinatum and the function of the determinant as one of the arguments of the underlying predicate.

2 Regular compounds

(a) The determinatum represents an agent, the determinant a goal (object), place, instrument or time connected with some implied activity, or this activity itself: *broþorbana* 'fratricide', *dureweard* 'janitor', *æcermann* 'ploughman', *gathyrde* 'goatherd', *sæfisc* 'seafish', *sæmann* 'seaman', *hereflyma* 'deserter', *sweordfreca* 'a warrior who uses his sword', *nihthræfn* 'night raven', *ceapmann* 'merchant', *fæstingmann* 'retainer'.

(b) The determinatum represents some object or phenomenon that could be regarded as in some sense affected or effected by an implied action or being in some state or position; the determinant specifies an agent, source, material, place, time, instrument or the action itself: *beobræd* 'honey', *smiþbelg* 'bellows', *sweostorsunu* 'sister's son', *fotspor* 'footprints', *hwætemelo* 'wheatflour', *arfæt* 'bronze vessel', *sigelean* 'reward for victory', *heafodwærc* 'headache', *æfensteorra* 'evening star', *sumorhæte* 'summer heat', *rædhors* 'riding-horse', *bletsingboc* 'benedictional', *eringland* 'arable land'.

(c) The determinatum is part of the determinant: *bordrima* 'edge of a plank', *cawelstela* 'cabbage-stem', *earlæppa* 'earlobe', *earmsceanca* 'armbone', *hearpestreng* 'harpstring'.

(d) The determinatum represents a place to which the determinant is related as object or action: *sealtfæt* 'salt-cellar', *beorsele* 'beer-hall', *ealuhus* 'alehouse', *melcingfæt* 'milkpail', *witungstow* 'place of punishment', *rædinsceamol* 'lectern', *eardungstow* 'dwelling-place, tabernacle'.

(e) The determinatum represents an instrument, the determinant an object or action related to it: *blæstbelg* 'bellows', *breostbeorg* 'breastplate', *fiscnett* 'fishing-net', *fugellim* 'birdlime', *snidisen* 'lancet', *blæshorn* 'trumpet', *þrawing-spinel* 'curling-iron', *writing-feþer* 'quill', *brædingpanne* 'frying-pan'.

(f) The determinatum represents a time, the determinant an action related to it: *hærfestmonaþ* 'harvest-month', *sædtima* 'sowing-time', *clænsungdæg* 'day for purging'.

(g) The determinant functions as intensifier and has partially or totally lost its literal meaning: *firenþearf* 'dire distress', *firensynn* 'great sin' (*firen* 'sin, crime'), *mægenbyrþen* 'huge burden', *mægenfultum* 'great help', (*mægen* 'strength, power'), *þeodbealu* 'great calamity', *þeodwiga* 'great warrior (= panther)' (*þeod* 'people, nation'). Carr (1939:351) also lists *heoru* 'sword' as an intensifying element of alliterative poetry, but his gloss 'fearsome, dangerous, cruel' (cf. *heoruwearg* 'bloodthirsty wolf', etc.) indicates that although *heoru* may have been subject to some meaning generalisation (e.g. towards 'battle, fight, war'), it has not been sufficiently bleached to be regarded as a mere intensifier.

While *firen*, *mægen* and *þeod* may be regarded as pattern-forming in their intensifying function, the other examples listed in Carr (1939:351ff.), e.g. *beaducwealm* 'violent death' (*beadu* 'battle'), *færcyle* 'intense cold' (*fær* 'sudden danger'), *folcegsa* 'great terror', *leodbealu* 'great calamity' (*folc*, *leod* 'people', cf. *þeod* above), *heaþufyr* 'cruel fire' (*heaþu* 'battle'), *hildeswat* 'destructive vapour' (*hilde* 'battle'), should best be treated as individual lexicalisations, in so far as the determinants have also partly, but not completely, lost their original meanings. Most of them were probably coined in analogy to the more frequent intensifying patterns with *firen*, *mægen*, *þeod* as attempts at variation and perhaps also under the pressure of metre and alliteration.

There are also compounds consisting of three lexemes, i.e. having either a compound determinant (e.g. *eaforheafod-segn* 'boarhead banner', *deofolgyld-hus* 'heathen temple', *godspell-bodung* 'gospel preaching', *godweb-wyrhta* 'weaver of purple' or a compound determinatum (e.g. *bisceop-heafodlin* 'bishop's head ornament', *niht-butorfleoge* 'moth'). Compounds with more than three members do not seem to exist.

The above description is by no means exhaustive and covers only some of the more frequent patterns; for more detailed surveys cf. Carr (1939), Rubke (1953), Reibel (1963), Gardner (1968), Talentino (1970) or Sauer (1985).

5.4.2.2.2   For **Noun (genitive)** + **Noun** combinations it cannot always be decided with absolute certainty whether a given combination should be treated as a syntactic group or a genitive compound ('secondary compound' in Carr 1939:309ff.) but it would seem unjustified to deny the existence of genitive compounds (see Nickel *et al.*, 1976:II, 20) in view of the behaviour of words such as *domesdæg*, *cristesboc*. These never appear with a modified determinant, i.e. we only find *se egesfullica domesdæg*, 'the terrible judgment day', but never *se/þæs egesfullican domesdæg* (Sauer 1985:275).

Another problem is the treatment of cases such as *restedæg* 'rest day', *æhtemann* 'farmer', *hyldemæg* 'near kinsman', *hellefyr* 'hell-fire' (vs. *hellcwalu* 'pains of hell'), where the intermediate vowel could be interpreted either as a genitive marker, a 'linking vowel' or *Fugenelement* (empty morph), or as the stem formative of the determinant (see Bammesberger 1980 with regard to *hild/hilde*, the latter being the expected compound form according to the Germanic stem-formation rules). Since we cannot apply operational tests as in Modern English, the demarcation of genitive compounds will have to remain fuzzy, but at least some semantic patterns seem to unambiguously belong here. These are: (a) the (lexicalised) days of the week (*Sunnandæg, Monandæg, Tiwesdæg, Sæter(n)(es)dæg*, etc.), and some analogical formations either also involving a temporal relationship, e.g. *gebyrdetid* 'time of birth', *restedæg* 'rest day', *uht(an)tid* 'time of dawn, twilight', or just formal parallelism, e.g. *sunnanleoma* 'sunray', *sunnanscima* 'sunshine', *sunnansetlgong* 'sunset'; (b) a set of person-denoting nouns, e.g. *cynnesmann* 'kinsman' (alongside the group *heora agenes cynnes mannum* Chron C and D 1052), *landesmann* 'native', *rædesmann* 'counsellor', *æhtemann* 'farmer', *gatahierde* 'goatherd', *oxanhyrde* 'herdsman', etc.; (c) place-names, e.g. *cyn(in)gestun > Kingston*, etc.; (d) plant-names, e.g. *dægeseage* 'daisy', *oxan-slyppe* 'oxlip', etc.; some of the latter could also be interpreted as *bahuvrihi* compounds. Other instances are less easily associated with specific semantic areas, e.g. *bogenstreng* 'bow-string', *byttehlid* 'butt-lid', *tunnebotm* 'bottom of a cask', *æhteland* 'territory', *feormeham* 'farm', *nunn(an)mynster* 'convent', *hellehus* 'hell-house', *æweweard* 'priest', *mihtesete* 'seat of power', etc., many of which are only found in late texts; in these, the vowel is probably a 'bridge-vowel' (*Fugenelement*) rather than a genitive marker. Clearly, as in Modern English the semantic range of genitive compounds is much more restricted than that of the stem compounds.

5.4.2.2.3   With **Adjective + Noun** compounds, the relationship between the determinatum and the determinant is that of attribution (the type *madhouse* 'house for mad (people)' does not seem to exist in OE). Examples of this fairly productive pattern are *cwic-seolfor* 'mercury', *efenniht* 'equinox', *ealdfæder* 'ancestor', *gyldenbeag* 'golden crown', *heahbeorg* 'high mountain', *haligdæg* 'holy day', *surmeolc* 'sour milk', *wildgos* 'wild goose', etc. The pattern was also very productive with *bahuvrihi* compounds of the type *heardheort* 'hard-hearted', see §5.4.5.

5.4.2.2.4   The pattern **V (verbal stem) + N** was a recent development in the Germanic languages (Carr 1939:162) and resulted from instances where the determinant was a deverbal noun which was formally identical with the verb stem, as in *delf-isen* 'spade' (*delf* 'digging' and stem of *delfan* 'dig'). Consequently, many OE formations are ambiguous between an N + N and a V + N interpretation, although it would seem that the latter is preferable in all those instances where the determinatum can unambiguously be analysed as a potential argument of the verbal determinant. Thus *isen* in *delfisen* is interpretable as an Instrumental with regard to *delfan*, and the compound therefore qualifies as V + N. After the merger of the verbal nouns (*-ing/-ung*) and the present participle (*-ende*) in ME, the V + N pattern is rivalled by the semantically equivalent pattern *writing-table*, where *writing* can be analysed either as a present participle or a verbal noun. In OE, *-end*-formations in the determinant, e.g. in *sceawendspræc* 'buffoonery', *sceawendwise* 'buffoon's song', *agendfrea* 'lord and owner', *Wealdendgod* 'Lord God', have to be regarded as agent nouns, not as participles; the combinations thus belong to the N + N pattern.

Both strong and weak verbs occur as determinants. The strong verbs usually appear as pure stems, but sometimes a non-etymological linking vowel may be found (e.g. *bæcering* 'gridiron', vs. *bæchus* 'bakery', *eteland* 'pasture'); for these cases, alternative interpretations (verb, *bæcan*, noun *ete*) have been suggested (Holthausen 1963: s.v. *bæcering, eteland*). But since the weak verbs, as well as the strong verbs having a *-j*-present, preserve their stem-formative *-j-* as *-e-*, although not completely systematically (cf. *hwetestan* 'whetstone', *wecedrenc* 'emetic', *steppescoh* 'slipper' vs. *tyrngeat* 'turnstile'), analogical extension of *-e-* as a linking vowel is also a plausible explanation. The major semantic types are: V + Agent/Subject: *wigmann* 'warrior', *ridwiga* 'mounted soldier', *spyremann* 'tracker'; V + Object: *fealdestol* 'folding-stool', *bærnelac* 'burnt offering', *tyrngeat* 'turnstile'; V + Locative: *bæchus* 'bakery', *ærneweg* 'racecourse', *writbred* 'writing-tablet'; V + Instrumental: *bærnisen* 'branding iron', *scearseax* 'razor', *hwetestan* 'whetstone'; V + Temporal: *restedæg* 'rest day'; V + Cause, i.e. the noun causes the action denoted by the verb: *spiwdrenc, wecedrenc* 'emetic', *fielleseocness, fiellewærc* 'epilepsy, falling sickness'.

5.4.2.2.5 The pattern of **Past participle + Noun** is relatively weak and is mainly represented by *bahuvrihis* of the type *wundenfeax* 'with plaited mane'. Regular compounds are *broden-, sceaden-, wundenmæl* 'damascened sword', *nægledcnearr* 'nail-fastened vessel', *etenlæs* 'pasture'.

5.4.2.2.6   For **Adverb + N compounds** in principle two different cases have to be distinguished: (a) the adverb is combined with an independent primary or derived noun, e.g. *oferealdorman* 'chief officer', *oferbiterness* 'excessive bitterness'; (b) the combination is a derivative from a verbal compound, e.g. *oferleornes* 'transgression' < *oferleoran* 'transgress', *ofersceawigend* 'overseer, bishop' < *ofersceawian* 'superintend'. But in practice this distinction cannot always be upheld, for sometimes both analyses seem possible, e.g. *oferfæreld* 'passage over' could be either *ofer + færeld* 'travel' or a derivative of *oferfaran* 'cross, go over'. Moreover, the absence of a verb corresponding to instances such as *oferæt*, 'gluttony', *ofercyme* 'arrival', *ofermearcung* 'superscription' might only constitute an accidental gap in the data. Formations containing a deverbal determinatum thus must always be regarded as potentially ambiguous between these two interpretations.

Adverbs which appear as the first element of such compounds are: *æt* 'at, to, near', *an* 'single, alone, only; numeral one', *eft* 'again, anew', *fore* 'front; beforehand (local and temporal)', *forþ* 'forth, forward, away, front', *in* 'within, inside', *innan* 'inside', *mid* 'together', *ofer* 'over, above (local); very much, in excess', *on* 'forward, onward', *ongean* 'again, against', *samod* 'simultaneous, together', *under* 'under (local); inferior, secondary', *wiþer* 'against', *ymb* 'about, around'. Typical examples of compounds with these elements are: *æteaca* 'addition', *anbuend* 'hermit', *eftlean* 'recompense', *forebreost* 'chest', *forebysen* 'example', *forþweg* 'departure', *forþfæder* 'forefather', *inadl* 'internal disease', *inflæscness* 'incarnation', *innanearm* 'inner side of arm', *midgesiþ* 'companion', *oferbraw* 'eye-brow', *oferlufu* 'too great love', *onbring* 'instigation', *ongeancyme* 'return', *ongeansprecend* 'one who reproaches', *samodeard* 'common home', *underhwitel* 'undergarment', *undercyning* 'underking', *wiþersteall* 'resistance', *ymbhoga* 'care, anxiety'.

5.4.2.3   Compound adjectives

5.4.2.3.1   In **Noun + Adjective compounds** the following semantic types dominate: firstly, the determinant can be regarded as a complement of the adjective: *eagsyne* 'visible to the eye', *ellenrof* 'famed for strength', *æcræftig* 'learned in the law'; secondly, the determinatum is compared to an implicit property of the determinant, where the comparison can be bleached to mere intensification: *blodread* 'blood-red', *dæglang* 'all day long', *hunigswete* 'sweet as honey', *hetegrim* 'fierce'; thirdly, the formal determinatum is an attribute of the determinant. This type probably arose as a reversed *bahuvrihi* compound (Carr 1939:260,

341), i.e. *seocmod* 'having a sick heart' > *modseoc* 'sick with regard to the heart, sick at heart' > 'heartsick', and this leads to their analysis as pseudo-compounds (Marchand 1969:85ff.): *ferþgleaw* 'prudent' (cf. *gleaw-ferþ*), *ferþwerig* 'soul-weary' (cf. *werigferþ*), *modglæd* 'joyful' (cf. *glædmod*), *leoþuwac* 'flexible', *earmstrang* 'strong of arm'.

5.4.2.3.2   In **Adjective + Adjective** combinations the following semantic relations occur:

(a) Additive: *nearofah* 'difficult and hostile', *earmcearig* 'poor and sorrowful'

(b) Subordinative (mainly colour-terms): *brunwann* 'dusky', *deorcegræg* 'dark grey', *blæhæwen* 'light blue', *heardsælig* 'unhappy'

(c) Intensifying/downtoning: *ealmihtig* 'almighty', *felafæcne* 'very treacherous', *efeneald* 'of equal age', *healfdead* 'half-dead', *widmære* 'far-famed', *gearosnotor* 'very skilful'

(d) The determinant functions as the goal of the determinatum: *clængeorne* 'yearning after purity', *ellorfus* 'ready to depart', *druncengeorn* 'drunken'

(e) The determinant is equivalent to a manner adverb modifying the verb contained in the determinatum, which is a deverbal adjective. These formations are synthetic compounds: *deoþþancol* 'contemplative', *fæstgangol* 'steady, faithful', *hearmcwidol* 'evil-speaking', *earfoþrime* 'hard to enumerate', *eaþbede* 'easy to be entreated', *eaþhylige* 'easily irritated', *eaþcnæwe* 'easy to recognise', *eaþgesyne* 'easily seen', *felaspræce* 'talkative'. This type does not seem to have any counterpart in Modern English, where manner adverbs do not occur as determinants in adjectival or nominal compounds. In principle, the participial formations could also be treated here, but in view of the wider range of the functions of their determinants they have been treated separately.

5.4.2.3.3   **Noun/Adjective + present participle** formations, many of which are typical kennings, are not always easy to distinguish from synthetic agent nouns of the type *landbuend* (cf. §5.4.2.2.1), and often we find nominal and adjectival doublets (cf. Kärre 1915:77ff., Carr 1939:211ff.). The determinant functions as an argument of the verb; if it is an adjective, it has adverbial function. Types of argument include:
Subject: *hunigflowende* 'flowing with honey', *blodiernende* 'having an issue of blood' (parallel to the reversed *bahuvrihis* in §5.4.2.3.1 above)
Object: *ealodrincende* 'beer-drinking', *bord-*, *lind-hæbbende* 'shield-bearing', *rihtfremmende* 'acting rightly'

Locative: *bencsittende* 'sitting on a bench', *brim-*, *mere-*, *sæliþende* 'seafaring', *foldbuende* 'earth-inhabiting'
Instrumental: *rond-*, *lindwigende* 'fighting with a shield'
Adjective: *anbuende* 'dwelling alone', *feorbuende* 'dwelling far off', *gramhycgende* 'hostile', *fulstincende* 'foul-smelling', *welwyrcende* 'doing good', *widferende* 'travelling far'.

5.4.2.3.4 In **Noun/Adjective + past participle** combinations the determinant functions as argument of the verb and can represent:
Subject: *bearneacnod* 'pregnant', *ceorlboren* 'low-born', *cifesboren* 'bastard' (*cifes* 'harlot, concubine'), *windfylled* 'blown down by the wind'
Instrumental: *beaghroden* 'adorned with rings', *goldhlæden* 'adorned with gold', *handgewriþen* 'hand-woven'
Locative: *æhtboren* 'born in bondage', *heofoncenned* 'heaven-born'
Manner: *æwumboren* 'legally born', *wundor-agræfen* 'wondrously engraved'
Adjective (in complement or adverbial function): *æþelboren* 'of noble birth', *dierneforlegen* 'adulterous', *ealdbacen* 'stale', *heahgetimbrad* 'high-built', *healfbrocen* 'half-broken', *fullmannod* 'fully peopled'. Notice the difference between the latter and formations such as *feowerhweolod* 'four-wheeled', which are extended *bahuvrihi* compounds and have to be analysed into the constituents [[feower-hweol]$_{dt}$/od$_{dm}$], as against [[full$_{dt}$]/[mann-od]$_{dm}$], where *mannod* is the participle of *mannian* 'to man'.

5.4.2.3.5 In **Adverb + Adjective** combinations the following adverbs occur as first elements: *æfter* 'later, afterwards', *ær* 'earlier, before', *eft* 'again', *fore* 'before, very', *forþ* 'very', *in* 'very', *ofer* 'over, above (local); too, very much', *samod* 'together', *þurh* 'through, very', *up* 'up', *wiþer* 'against, opposing'. Typical examples of such compounds are: *ærboren* 'earlier born', *eftboren* 'born again', *forecweden* 'aforesaid', *foremanig* 'very many', *forþsnotor* 'very wise', *ingemynde* 'well-remembered', *oferhangen* 'covered', *ofereald* 'very old', *samodfæst* 'joined together', *þurhsyne* 'transparent', *þurhlæred* 'thoroughly learned', *upheah* 'uplifted', *wiþermede* 'antagonistic'.

5.4.2.4 Compound verbs
5.4.2.4.1 In the Germanic languages verbal composition is basically restricted to combinations with adverbs or prepositions as determinants (Marchand 1969:100). There are a number of combinations, however,

e.g. *nidniman* 'take by force', *gecynehelmian* 'crown', *rihtwisian* 'justify', that seem to contradict this assumption. These can be subdivided into two groups. The first, illustrated by the examples above, consists of derivatives from nominal compounds (*cynehelm* 'crown', *rihtwis* 'justifiable, just') or back-derivations from synthetic compounds (*nidnimung* 'taking by force' > *nidniman* 'commit *nidnimung*'). These should be treated as genuine derivatives, not as compounds. The status of the other group is less clear, since there does not seem to exist a corresponding nominal basis. This may of course be due to the fragmentary nature of the evidence, but it is also possible that at least some of these instances represent sporadic attempts at verbal composition. Examples are *ellencampian* 'campaign vigorously', *gecwealmbæran* 'torture to death', *geþancmetian* 'deliberate', *morgenwacian* 'rise early', *wea-cwanian* 'lament'.

Combinations with adverbs/prepositions also represent two patterns, so-called 'inseparable' and 'separable' compounds, compare inseparable *to oferfeohtanne* 'conquer', *þu ne oferbrec* 'you don't violate' vs. separable *forþ to brenganne* 'bring forth', *hie ut ne sprecaþ* 'they do not speak out'. With the separable compounds, the particle may be separated from the verb by the negative particle or other elements, and it may also occur positioned after the verb. Traditionally it is assumed that the particles in the inseparable compounds are unstressed (*understándan* 'understand') and tend towards a less literal interpretation, while they receive the main stress and more often than not preserve their original locative meaning in separable compounds (*únderstàndan* 'stand under'). Unfortunately, however, in the individual textual examples it is not always easy to determine which of the two possibilities obtains, and Hiltunen (1983:25ff.) therefore regards the distinction as a cline rather than a neat dichotomy. This is probably justified, because the inseparable pattern was more and more replaced by the postpositional phrasal verb pattern *fly over*, *walk under*, etc. In the following, therefore, no attempt will be made to keep separable and inseparable combinations apart, nor will we make a distinction between phrasal adverbs, prepositional adverbs and prepositions, which also seem to constitute a cline (cf. Hiltunen 1983:20ff.). On the other hand, genuine prefixes, i.e. those elements that do not occur independently, such as *a-*, *ge-*, etc., will be treated in the section on prefixes. Incidentally, this distinction is not made by Pilch (1970:126ff.), who regards *be*, *æt*, *ofer*, *wiþ* as prefixes on a par with *a-*, *ge-*.

5.4.2.4.2   The principal particles, together with an example of each in their most important meanings, are: *adun(e)* (separable): *adunfeallan* 'fall down'; *æfter* 'after (local/temporal)' (separable): *æfterfolgian* 'succeed, pursue'; *æt* 'at, near, on (locative/temporal)' (separable/inseparable): *ætbeon* 'be present'; *aweg* 'away' (separable): *aweggan* 'go away'; *be* 'around, to, together' (inseparable): *bebugan* 'flow around'; often, however, without a clear meaning, and not easily distinguishable from the prefix *be-*, cf. *bebeodan* 'offer, announce'; *efen* 'together, equally' (inseparable): *efencuman* 'come together, agree'; *eft* 'again, back' (inseparable): *eftcuman* 'come back'; *for* 'before' (inseparable, not to be confused with the prefix *for-* of *forbærnan*, etc.): *forcuman* 'come before'; *fore* 'before' (separable): *foresittan* 'preside'; *forþ* 'forth, forwards' (separable): *forþberan* 'bring forth'; *fram* 'from, away' (separable): *framswengan* 'swing away'; *full* 'completely' (inseparable): *fullfremman* 'fulfil, perfect', *fullgrowan* 'grow to perfection'; *geond* 'completely, entirely' (usually inseparable): *geonddrencan* 'drink excessively'; 'through, over, beyond': *geondfaran* 'traverse'; *in(n)* 'in, into' (separable): *infaran* 'enter'; *niþer* 'down' (separable/inseparable): *niþerascufan* 'push down'; *of* 'off, from' (inseparable/separable): *ofgiefan* 'give up'; 'result': *ofacsian* 'find out by asking'; 'intensifying': *ofdrædan* 'fear'; *ofer* 'over' (inseparable/separable): *oferfaran* 'go over'; 'too much': *oferdon* 'overdo'; *on* 'on, in' (inseparable/separable): *onlihtan* 'illuminate'; 'off, away': *onsceacan* 'shake off'; *onweg* 'away' (separable): *onwegadrifan* 'drive away'; *to* 'to' (separable, stressed): *toclifian* 'cleave to'; 'apart, away' (inseparable, unstressed): *toberan* 'carry off'; *þurh* 'through' (separable/inseparable): *þurhseon* 'see through'; 'intensively': *þurhleornian* 'learn thoroughly'; *under* 'under' (separable/inseparable): *underdelfan* 'dig under'; metaphorical: *undergietan* 'understand'; *up* 'up' (separable/inseparable): *upgan* 'go up'; *ut* 'out' (separable/inseparable): *utgan* 'go out'; *wiþ* 'against' (separable/inseparable): *wiþcweþan* 'speak against'; *wiþer* 'against' (separable/inseparable): *wiþerstandan* 'withstand'; *ymbe* 'about, round' *ymbfaran* 'surround'.

As with the verbal prefixes (see below), the system is far from optimal, since in a number of cases the particle may express opposite meanings, cf. *æt* 'at, near' vs. 'from, away', *on* 'on, in' vs. 'off, away', or *to* 'to' vs. 'off'. Moreover, there are many formations, which have not been listed above, where the particle no longer seems to have any identifiable meaning. It is therefore not surprising that many of these particles lost their productivity, so that only *out-*, *over-* and *under-* have remained productive in Modern English.

5.4.3   Prefixation

5.4.3.1 Prefixes are bound morphemes occurring in initial position in word-formations. Functionally speaking they are equivalent to an adjective when they modify a noun (e.g. *sin-* in *sindream* 'everlasting joy'), or to an adverb when they modify an adjective (*sin-* in *sinceald* 'perpetually cold') or a verb (*mis-* in *miscweþan* 'speak ill'). In both functions they act as determinants, and the combinations are expansions. A third function is that of preposition, e.g. *æ-* 'without' in *æfelle* 'without skin', *ænote* 'useless'; in this case, we have to do with derivations (here without an explicit suffix), since the prefix as such does not change the word-class. The pattern is probably best regarded as the negative counterpart of *bahuvrihis* such as *flohtenfote* 'webfooted', *anhyrne* 'having one horn', and formations such as *gebirde* 'bearded', *gecladed* 'clothed'.

As mentioned in §5.4.1.3, certain prefixes exhibit allomorphic variation in connexion with stress alternation: with verbs the prefix has reduced stress, with nouns it is stressed, cf. *àspríngan* 'spring forth': *ǽsprìng* 'spring', *begán* 'worship': *bígèncga* 'worshipper', *ònfón* 'take, receive': *ándfèncga* 'receiver'. In other instances, the stress alternation is not accompanied by allomorphic variation, cf. *míslìmpan* 'turn out badly': *míslìmp* 'misfortune'. The prefixes *for-* and *ge-*, however, do not seem to be subject to stress alternation and are always unstressed.

As Horgan (1980) and Hiltunen (1983) have shown, the system of OE prefixes, in particular those occurring with verbs, was already at the end of the tenth century in a state of advanced decay, because many prefix-verb combinations were no longer transparent. With many verbal prefixes, e.g. *a-*, *ge-*, *oþ-*, it is impossible to establish consistent meanings, and frequently there does not seem to be any meaning difference at all between the simplex and the prefixed form. This is confirmed by the observation that in subsequent copies of one and the same text prefixes are often omitted, added or exchanged for other prefixes without any apparent semantic effect (see Horgan 1980; Hiltunen 1983:54ff.). This points to a considerable weakening of the meaning of these prefixes, especially of *a-*, *be-*, *ge-*, and the prepositions/adverbs *for* and *of*. It is not surprising, therefore, that the OE prefix and preparticle system was an easy victim both for the Romance invasion of the lexicon and the rise of postparticle (phrasal) verbs in ME.

5.4.3.2   There was widespread use of prefixation in Old English, and the following discussion and exemplification of individual prefixes aims to do no more than provide a first indication of the type, range and frequency of the processes. Amongst the prefixes which are most regularly attested in the texts of the period are the following: *a-*, *æ-*, *æf-*, *and-*, *be-*, *bi-*, *ed-*, *fær-*, *for-*, *ge-*, *mis-*, *or-*, *sam-*, *sin-*, *un-*, *wan-*.

It is questionable whether *a-* was still productive in OE in view of its many shades of meaning reflecting its different origins, namely as a reduced form of *of-*, *on-*, *un-*. It is also uncertain whether the prefix had a long or short vowel. Bosworth (1898:s.v. *a-*) opts for the short alternative, the supplement (1927) and Clark Hall (1969) treat the prefix as long; Hiltunen (1983:48) assumes both an accented (long) and an unaccented (short) prefix, but admits 'that it is not easy to draw the line between the accented and unaccented variant in practice' and therefore decides to ignore the distinction. In any case, even if it was stressed, it would only have had secondary stress, the stem carrying the main stress as with all verbal prefix-formations.

In view of the vagueness of the meaning of this prefix, which only occurs with verbs or deverbal derivatives, it is difficult to give precise semantic patterns, and in many instances it does not seem to have added anything to the meaning of the stem, cf. *abacan/bacan* 'bake', *abarian/barian* 'lay bare', *aberan/beran* 'bear'. In some instances it seems to denote 'out', e.g. *aberstan* 'burst out', *abrædan* 'spread out', *acleopian* 'call out'; in others, it seems to add an intensifying or completive element, e.g. *abeatan* 'beat to pieces', *acalan* 'become frost-bitten', *adrygan* 'dry up'. But in the overwhelming majority of instances, its meaning is no longer transparent.

Æ- was, firstly, the stressed alternant of *a-* in deverbal derivatives with the same range of meanings as *a-*: *æbylga* 'anger, offence', *æcyrf* 'wood-choppings', *ærist* 'rising, resurrection'. Secondly, *æ-* was used in suffixless (zero-derived) adjectives with *bahuvrihi*-character, where it has the meaning 'without', e.g. *æblæce* 'lustreless, pale', *æfelle* 'without skin, peeled', *æwæde* 'without clothes'.

The prefix *æf-* was a variant of *of-* denoting negativity, as in *æfgrynde* 'abyss', *æfþanc(a)* 'insult'; *æfweard* 'absent'.

And- was the stressed variant of the verbal prefix *on-*, which, however, in many instances had lost its semantic transparency. There are many examples of deverbal nouns of the type *andcwiss* 'answer', *andgiet* 'understanding', *andsaca* 'adversary', together with the primary *andlean* 'retribution'. It is also found as a verbal prefix with the meaning 'against, to' in forms such as: *andcweþan* 'contradict', *andhweorfan* 'move against', *andspurnan* 'stumble against'.

As already mentioned, the status of *be-* as preposition or prefix is not quite clear; it seems, however, that the following examples are best treated as prefixal: (a) transitivisation: *befeohtan* 'take by fighting', *befleogan* 'fly upon', *besprengan* 'besprinkle'; (b) intensification: *bebrecan* 'break to pieces', *begnidan* 'rub thoroughly'; (c) often without specific meaning: *bebeodan* 'offer, announce', *beceapian* 'sell'. The instances in which *be-* occurs in nouns are all deverbal derivatives, e.g. *beclypping* 'embrace' < *beclyppan*, *befrinung* 'inquiry' < *befrinan*, *begimen* 'attention' < *begiman*.

The stressed form of *be-* both in its prepositional and prefixal functions is *bi-*. It is found firstly in the meaning 'about, around', as in: *bifylce* 'neighbouring people', *bigyrdel* 'girdle, belt', *binama* 'pronoun'. Secondly, it is found in deverbal nouns derived from *be-* verbs, e.g. *bigeng*, *bigenge* 'practice, worship', *bigenga* 'inhabitant, cultivator', *bisæc* 'visit'.

The prefix *ed-* 'back, again' occurs with primary and derived nouns, adjectives and verbs, in the latter case frequently in conjunction with the prefix *ge-*. Typical examples are: (a) nouns: *geedcucoda* 'man restored to life', *edgift* 'restitution', *edlean* 'reward'; (b) adjectives: *edcwic* 'regenerated, restored to life', *edgeong* 'becoming, being young again', *edniwe* 'renewed'; (c) verbs: *geedciegan* 'recall', *edgyldan* 'remunerate', *edhwierfan* 'return'.

The element *fær-* is a typical borderline case between compounding and prefixation. *Fær* as an independent noun is listed with the meanings 'calamity, sudden danger, peril, sudden attack, terrible sight' in Clark Hall, and above (§5.4.2.2.1) instances such as *færbyrne*, where it has merely intensifying function, were treated as lexicalised compounds. But in the following type of examples with the meaning 'sudden', *fær-* seems to already have reached the status of a prefixoid: *færblæd* 'sudden blast', *færcwealm* 'sudden pestilence', *færgripe* 'sudden grip', *færræs* 'sudden rush'.

The prefix *for-* occurs with verbs and deverbal derivatives, as well as with adjectives. It may have the meaning 'loss, destruction', as in *forberstan* 'burst asunder', *fordon* 'destroy', *forweorþan* 'perish' (cf. also German *ver-* in *verspielen*, *vertrinken* 'lose by gambling, drinking, etc.), or it may signify intensification or perfectivity, as in *forbærnan* 'burn up', *forbitan* 'bite through', *forceorfan* 'cut out, down', and, in adjectives, *forgeare* 'very certainly', *forheard* 'very hard', *formanig* 'very many', *foroft* 'very often'. Often, however, it has already lost its basic meaning, e.g. *forbeodan* 'forbid, refuse, annul', *forgiefan* 'give up, forgive', *forgietan* 'forget'.

One of the most frequent prefixes in Old English was *ge-*, where two basic functions have to be distinguished, a verbal and a nominal one, which differ semantically.

In the case of verbal *ge-* in those instances where *ge-* can still be attributed a specific meaning, it denotes 'perfectivity', 'result', often in connection with transitivisation, e.g. *geærnan* 'gain by running', *geascian* 'learn by asking', *gesittan* 'inhabit'. But in many instances, the meaning of *ge*-verbs is idiosyncratic, e.g. *gestandan* 'endure, last', *gebæran* 'behave' (no simplex), *geweorþan* 'agree', or there does not seem to be any meaning difference between a simplex and a *ge*-prefixation, cf. *(ge)adlian* 'be, become ill', *(ge)æmtian* 'to empty', *(ge)campian* 'strive, fight', etc. Incidentally, this carries over to corresponding deverbal derivatives, e.g. *gecid* 'strife, altercation'.

With nouns other than derivatives from *ge*-verbs, two related meanings are rather frequent: 'collectivity' and 'associativity' (Kastovsky 1968:488). The first implies a collectivity of persons or objects, e.g. *gegeng* 'body of fellow-travellers', or a repetitive action, e.g. *gebeorc* 'barking' (cf. G *Gebell, Geschrei*). Further typical examples are: *gebroþor* 'brethren', *gefylce* 'collection of people, army', *gesceaft* 'creation', *gescy* 'pair of shoes'. The second, associativity, indicates that the subject performs an overt or implied action in conjunction with somebody else; *ge-* here corresponds to Lat. *con-*, e.g. *gefara, gegenga* 'one who travels with another', *gebedda* 'one who lies in bed with another', *gehada* 'brother-monk', *gehlytta* 'partner', *gefera* 'companion', *gesiþ* 'fellowship'.

With adjectives, *ge-* mainly indicates 'having, provided with', which may be compared with the basic verbal function. It occurs partly without additional explicit derivative suffix, e.g. *gebird(e)* 'bearded', *gecelfe* 'great with calf', *gecnæwe* 'knowing, aware', *gefræge* 'known', partly with an additional suffix, usually *-ed/-od*, e.g. *gecladed* 'clothed', *geglofed* 'gloved', *geheafod* 'having a head'. Occasionally in these cases, *ge-* also denotes 'associativity', e.g. *gefederen* 'having the same father', *gemod* 'of one mind, agreed' (as against *gemodod* 'minded, disposed').

Mis- 'bad, badly' occurs frequently with verbs, nouns and participial adjectives, e.g. *miscweþan* 'speak ill', *misdon* 'do evil', *misfaran* 'go wrong'; *misdæd* 'misdeed', *misgehygd* 'evil thought', *mis(ge)widere* 'bad weather'; *misboren* 'abortive', *mishæbbende* 'being ill'; *misscrence* 'distorted, shrivelled'.

The prefix *or-* has both the meaning 'without, lack of', as in *orblede* 'without blood', *orsawle* 'lifeless', *orwurþ* 'ignominy', and an intensifying sense, as in *orcnæwe* 'evident, well-known', *oreald* 'very old', *orgyte* 'well-known'.

Sam- 'together' occurs with adjectives, e.g. *samheort* 'unanimous', *sammæle* 'agreed', *samrad* 'harmonious' (partly *bahuvrihi*-type formations, i.e. basically zero-derivatives), and nouns, e.g. *samræden* 'married state', *samwist* 'living together', *samwrædness* 'union'.

The next prefix, *sam-* 'half', is distinguished from the immediately preceding by having a long vowel, i.e. *sām-*. It occurs most often with adjectives, e.g. *samcwic* 'half-dead', *samgrene* 'half-green', *samlæred* 'half-taught', but also with nouns, e.g. *sambryce* 'partial breach' and verbs, e.g. *samwyrcan* 'to half do a thing'.

Sin- 'perpetual, lasting, excessive' modifies adjectives, e.g. *sinbyrnende* 'ever burning', *sincald* 'perpetually cold', *singrim* 'exceedingly fierce', and nouns, e.g. *sinfrea* 'overlord, husband', *sinhiwan* 'wedded couple', *sinniþ* 'perpetual misery'.

Another extremely frequent prefix is *un-*, whose basic meaning comprises negativity ('not, opposite'), i.e. the formation of complementaries and antonyms with adjectives and corresponding deadjectival nouns, e.g. *unæþele* 'of low birth', *unawemmed* 'unstained', *unberende* 'unbearable, unfruitful', *unbrad* 'narrow'. It also has the same meaning with nouns not derived from adjectives, e.g. *unar* 'dishonour', *unbealu* 'innocence', *unfriþ* 'enmity', *unlif* 'death'. From this basic meaning there stems a development to a pejorative meaning, i.e. 'bad(ly), excessive(ly)'. This is found both with adjectives, e.g. *unforht* 'afraid', *unhar* 'very grey', and nouns, e.g. *unæt* 'gluttony', *undæd* 'wicked deed', *unlæce* 'bad physician', *unlagu* 'bad law, injustice'. Finally, in the case of verbs only, there is a third, reversative, meaning, denoting the undoing of the result of a pre-action, e.g. *unbindan* 'unbind, loosen', *undon* 'undo', *unlucan* 'unlock', *unwreon* 'uncover'.

The last prefix I shall mention is *wan-* 'lacking, not', which modifies nouns, e.g. *wanhælþ* 'weakness, sickness', *wanhafa* 'poor man', *wanhoga* 'thoughtless one', *wansped* 'poverty', and adjectives, e.g. *wanhafol* 'needy', *wanhal* 'unsound', *wanscryd* 'poorly clad'.

5.4.4 Suffixation

5.4.4.1 Introduction

While prefixes do not cause morphophonemic alternations in the lexemes to which they are added, suffixes may do so, the most notable alternation being *i*-mutation, cf. *stan*:*stænig*, *wealcan*:*gewilcþ* 'rolling', *feallan*:*fillen* 'falling'. But from the point of view of late Old English none of these suffixes produces *i*-mutation completely consistently in all possible instances; there are always at least some (analogical re-) formations without umlaut. Given that the occurrence of umlaut in derivational patterns is no longer really predictable, we have to assume a shift from phonological to morphological conditioning with a concomitant restructuring of the morphophonemic system during the Old English period. Exactly when this restructuring took place is difficult to determine and will, at least to a certain extent, also depend on the degree of abstractness that one allows in one's description, i.e. whether one accepts underlying segments that never surface in their underlying form or are deleted in the majority of cases. The early generative phonologists assumed a rather late date, while Hogg in chapter 3 (see §3.4.2.3) opts for a rather early date before the emergence of Early West Saxon. This restructuring does not mean, however, that the alternation was no longer productive, at least as an analogical, though not exceptionless process, cf. the LWS deadjectival noun *pryto/pryte* 'pride', derived from the French loan *prut* 'proud', in analogy to *hat* 'hot':*hætu* 'heat', *eald* 'old':*yldo* 'old age', *strang* 'strong':*strengu* 'strength', etc. On the other hand, there seems to have been a growing preference for non-alternating derivation, probably because of the progressively increasing opacity and eventual breakdown of the Old English morphophonemic system, and this homological principle eventually prevails (see Kastovsky 1988a,b).

The reduction of final unstressed syllables, which in the last resort was responsible for the morphologisation of *i*-umlaut, also results in a change of the morphological status of a number of word-formation patterns from suffixation to zero-derivation (conversion, affixless derivation, see §5.4.5). A typical example is the analysis of deadjectival and denominal weak verbs of the type *trum* 'strong':*trymman* 'strengthen', *lufu* 'love' sb.:*lufian* 'love' vb., *prut*:*prutian* 'be proud' in Germanic, Early and Late OE (see Hogg §3.4.2.3). The original structure of these verbs is:

	stem (base)	+	derivational affix	+	inflexion
class 1	*trum	+	j	+	an Inf.
	*trum	+	i	+	d + a Pret.
class 2	*luf	+	o:j	+	an Inf.
	*luf	+	o:	+	d + a Pret.

The elements */j ~ i/, */o:j ~ o:/ are usually referred to as stem-formatives or stem-extensions, which have the function of indicating inflexional class, but on top of that they also have to be regarded as derivational suffixes, as Hogg quite rightly points out. As his paradigms indicate, this morphological structure is still fully transparent in the fifth century (see Hogg pp. 157–8, 160), but it gradually loses this transparency with the loss of */i, j/ or their reduction to /e/ (cf. *trymman, trymede*), and the reduction of */o:j ~ o:/ to /i/, /a/, /o/ (cf. *lufian, lufast, lufode*). At the beginning we might still postulate an underlying /j/ with subsequent deletion, at least as long as mutated vowels unambiguously correlate with unmutated ones. But with the un-rounding of /ø:, ø/ to /e:, e/, this systematic correlation was lost, and *i*-umlaut became morphologised, a process which according to Hogg must have taken place before the emergence of Early West Saxon. This restructuring, however, does not only affect the phonological level, it has morphological consequences: the derivational suffix is eliminated, and derivation shifts from suffixal to affixless derivation (or zero-derivation), because the remaining inflexional endings do not have derivational function. A similar reanalysis probably also took place for class 2 verbs, where the /i ~ a ~ o/ alternation could no longer be identified with a derivational element, and the vowels became part of the inflexional endings in the same way as /e/ in *trym+ed+e*, i.e. *luf+o+d+e > luf+od+e*.

Similar developments have to be postulated, for example, for deverbal nouns of the type *lyge < lug+i+∅* (: *leogan*) or deadjectival nouns like *hæte < hat+i+∅*, etc., where -*i*- was originally a derivational suffix, which subsequently was reinterpreted as part of the stem. For all these derivational patterns we have to assume a shift from suffixal to affixless (= zero) derivation in the PROE or earliest OE period, which is why these patterns are not treated here, but in §4.5 together with *bahuvrihi* adjectives of the type *bærfot* 'barefoot', *anbieme* 'made of one trunk'.

5.4.4.2 Nominal suffixes

The principal nominal suffixes are: *-d/-t/-(o)þ*, *-dom*, *-el(e)/-l(a)/-ol*, *-els*, *-en*, *-end*, *-ere*, *-estre*, *-et(t)*, *-had*, *-incel*, *-ing*, *-lac*, *-ling*, *-ness*, *-ræden*, *-scipe*, *-þ(o)/-t*, *-ung/-ing*, and *-wist*.

As pointed out in §5.4.1.2, the affixes *-d/-t/-þ* constitute a suffix family, historically based on *-t-*, which derives various types of deverbal nouns, cf. the examples given in (4). The suffix *-oþ* as in *fiscoþ* 'fishing', *huntoþ* 'hunting', also listed in (4), might either be included here, or it could be treated as an independent suffix.

The source of *-dom* is the lexeme *dom* 'judgement', but the semantic development has progressed so far that it has to be regarded at least as a suffixoid if not a genuine suffix. It derives denominal and deadjectival abstract nouns with the meanings 'state, condition, fact of being, action of'. Denominal examples include *caserdom* 'empire', *martyrdom* 'martyrdom', *campdom* 'contest', *læcedom* 'medicine'; deadjectival examples are *freodom* 'freedom', *haligdom* 'holiness, sanctuary', *wisdom* 'wisdom'.

As in the case of *-d/-t/-(o)þ*, the group *-ele(e)/-l(a)/-ol* form a suffix family that includes several subgroups distinguished as to gender and/or inflexional class; these should probably also be regarded as independent derivational patterns, but have been grouped together in the following for convenience's sake. All of them form nouns from verbs with the typical semantic characteristics of this category (i.e. denoting action, agent, object, result, instrument, etc.). Thus we find Action nouns such as *scendle* f. 'reproach', *þreal* f. 'reproof'; *hwyrfel* m. 'circuit, whirlpool', *þweal* n. 'washing'; Agent nouns such as *æftergengel* m. 'successor', *bydel* m. 'herald', *bæcslitol* m. 'backbiter'; Object/Result nouns such as *scytel* m. 'dart, missile', *fyndel* m. 'invention', *hangelle* f. 'implement that hangs', *bitol* n. 'bridle'; Instrumental nouns such as *sceacel* m. 'shackle', *tredel* m. 'sole of the foot', *spinel* f. 'spindle', *swingel(e)* f. 'scourge', *þweal* n. 'ointment'; and Locative nouns such as *smygel* m. 'burrow, retreat', *stigel* m. 'stile', *setl* n. 'seat'.

All genders are represented, but there is a definite preponderance of the feminines among the Action nouns, and of the masculines among the Agent and Instrumental nouns; neuter nouns are rare. Masculines and neuters mainly belong to the strong declension, feminines mainly follow the weak declension.

Many derivatives exhibit *i*-umlaut, cf. *hwyrfel*, *bydel*, but others do not, cf. *þweal*, *scendle*. The overwhelming majority of the derivatives are based on strong verbs, partly on the full grade of the present (*swingel(e)*-type), partly on the reduced grade (*bydel*-type), but there are also some derivatives from weak verbs (*þreal*-type). The preponderance of strong verbs as bases suggests that many formations are probably already quite old. On the other hand, there are also some formations based on weak verbs. Since these latter tend to be younger than the strong verbs, it is quite likely that the pattern was still productive in OE. This is confirmed by the fact that at least a few derivatives were formed in the later stages of the language, e.g. *spittle*, *swivel*, etc.

The suffix *-els* forms masculine deverbal nouns of the same semantic types as the preceding suffix group from strong and weak verbs, e.g. *rædels* 'counsel', *brædels* 'carpet', *gyrdels* 'girdle', *hydels* 'hiding-place'. Wherever possible, derivatives from strong verbs have *i*-umlaut.

In the case of *-en* there are two basic patterns, both deriving feminine nouns. The first produce feminines from nouns denoting male beings, e.g. *fyxen* 'vixen', *gyden* 'goddess', *mynecen* f. 'nun'. The second pattern produces abstract and concrete deverbal and denominal derivatives. Deverbal nouns may be Action nouns, e.g. *sien* f. 'sight', *fillen* f. 'falling', *swefen* n. 'sleep, dream'; Object/Result nouns, e.g. *rædenn* f. 'reckoning, estimation', *sel(l)en* f. 'gift', *fæsten* f. 'fortress'; or Instrumental nouns, e.g. *hlæden* m. 'bucket', *lifen* f. 'sustenance', *fæsten* n. 'fastener'; or Locative nouns, e.g. *hengen* f. 'rack, cross', *byrgen* f., n. 'grave'. The strongest group by far is that of feminine Action nouns. Umlaut occurs sporadically; derivation is made both from strong (classes I–III: reduced grade, classes V–VII: full grade) and weak verbs, and the pattern was probably still productive in Old English. Denominal nouns with *-en* probably constituted a residual pattern in view of the semantic irregularities, cf. *þeoden* m. 'prince', *dryhten* m. 'lord', *nyten* 'animal'.

One of the most productive OE suffixes is *-end*, which primarily forms deverbal Agent nouns from both weak and strong verbs. Other semantic types are rare. The Agent nouns are strong masculines, the Action nouns are feminines. The suffix does not cause *i*-umlaut and is always added to the infinitive stem. Examples of Agent nouns are: *biddend* 'petitioner', *lærend* 'teacher', *dælnimend* 'participle'. Examples of Object nouns (all masculine) are: *belifend* 'survivor', *gehæftend* 'prisoner'; Instrumental nouns: *(ge)bicnined* 'forefinger'. Examples of Action nouns are: *nidnimend* 'rapine', *blinnende* 'rest, ceasing', *þeofend* 'theft'.

Another extremely productive Agent-noun-forming suffix is *-ere*, which originally was added to nouns, but was subsequently extended also to deverbal derivatives (cf. Kastovsky 1971). It does not cause *i*-

umlaut and is added to the infinitive stem of both strong and weak verbs. Most derivatives are masculine, but a few are neuter. With deverbal nouns it is found in all the usual semantic categories, i.e. Agent, Object/Result, Instrumental, Locative and Action. Examples of each are: *leornere* 'disciple', *sceawere* 'mirror', *punere* 'pestle', *word-samnere* 'catalogue', (*dirne*)-*geligere* n. 'adultery'. Denominal nouns so formed are Agent nouns, e.g. *scipere* 'sailor', *sco(h)ere* 'shoemaker', *sædere* 'sower'.

The suffix *-estre* derives deverbal and denominal feminine agent nouns denoting females. It is West Saxon as against Anglian *-icge* (see §5.3.1.5). Deverbal examples are: *hleapestre* 'female dancer', *wæscestre* 'washer', *tæppestre* 'female tavern-keeper', and denominal examples are: *byrþestre* 'female carrier', *fiþelestre* 'female fiddler', *lybbestre* 'sorceress'.

The suffix *-et(t)* forms abstract and concrete deverbal and denominal nouns and usually causes *i*-umlaut. The derivatives are all strong neuters and examples include *rewett* 'rowing', *hiwett* 'hewing', *bærnett* 'burning' from verbs, and *nierwett* 'narrowness', *þiccett* 'thicket', *rymet* 'space, extent' from nouns.

The status of *-had* is not quite clear. Marchand (1969:293) and Sauer (1985:282ff.) regard it as the second element of compounds, while Quirk and Wrenn (1957:116) and Wright and Wright (1925:316) treat it as a suffix. As an independent word, *had* had the meaning 'state, rank, order, condition, character' and this is more or less also the meaning it would have as a 'suffix', e.g. *abbudhad* 'rank of an abbot', *camphad* 'warfare', *cildhad* 'childhood', *geoguþhad* 'youth', etc. It is probably justified, therefore, to follow Marchand and Sauer and assume that the development towards a suffix took place in the post-OE period.

The suffix *-incel* derives neuter denominal diminutives, e.g. *bogincel* 'small bough', *husincel* 'little house' (incorrect translation of Lat. *domicilium*, *tabernaculum*), *scipincel* 'little ship'.

The suffix *-ing* forms masculine nouns denoting 'proceeding or derived from (the stem', 'associated with (the stem))', often with patronymic function. Such nouns are derived either from adjectives, e.g. *æþeling* 'son of a noble, prince', *ierming* 'poor wretch', *lytling* 'child', or nouns, e.g. *wicing* 'pirate', *Scylding* 'descendant of the Scylds', or verbs, e.g. *fostring* 'fosterchild', *lising* 'free man', *wædling* 'needy person'.

Originally an independent lexeme, *-lac* was already in OE functioning as a suffixoid, forming masculine abstract nouns with the meaning 'state, act, quality, nature of' from nouns and verbs. Examples of derivatives from nouns are: *bodlac* 'decree', *brydlac* 'marriage, marriage gift', *lyblac* 'witchcraft'. Rather less frequent are examples from verbs of the type *breowlac* 'brewing'.

The suffix -*ling* originated from derivatives like *æþeling*, *lytling* (see above) by misanalysis and it too derives mainly personal nouns, originally from adjectives and nouns, and, via denominal verbs, subsequently also from verbs. Examples of each are: *deorling* 'favourite', *geongling* 'youth'; *cnæpling* 'youth', *fostorling* 'fosterchild', *þeowling* 'slave'; *hyrling* 'hireling', *ræpling* 'prisoner', *hwirfling* 'that which turns'.

The suffix -*ness* is used very frequently to derive feminine, mainly abstract, nouns from adjectives and verbs. The handbooks usually only list the deadjectival function, incorrectly, because there are numerous derivatives from verbal stems, particularly in Anglian. On the other hand, it is correct that in Late West Saxon derivation from participial bases supersedes derivation from the infinitive stem (see §5.3.1.5). Typical examples of the many deadjectival nouns are: *æþelness* 'nobility', *beorhtness* 'brightness', *biterness* 'bitterness', *clænness* 'purity'. In the case of deverbal nouns there are derivatives from infinitives, and present and past participles, see the remarks above. Thus we find Action nouns such as *blinness* 'cessation', *brecness* 'breach', *costness* 'temptation', all from infinitives, alongside *ablinnendness* 'cessation', *astandendness* 'continuance', *gebetendness* 'emendation, correction', from present participles, and *agotenness* 'effusion', *uparisenness* 'resurrection', *cirredness* 'turning', from past participles. Similar patterns occur with Object/Result nouns, e.g. *onbærnness* 'incense', (*a-/in-*)*setness* 'ordinance, regulation', *streowness* 'bed, mattress'; *agendness* 'property'; *alegedness* 'interjection', *forset(ed)ness* 'preposition', *afundenness* 'device, invention', *gegaderedness* 'gathering of diseased matter, abscess'. The same applies to Instrumental and Locative nouns, although the numbers are fewer. So we find *fedness* 'nourishment', *gereordness* 'food', *smireness* 'ointment', *gefegedness* 'conjunction', and *wuneness* 'dwelling', besides *behydedness* 'secret place'.

As these examples show, there is no functional difference between derivatives from the infinitive stem and from participles. Consequently, we find quite a few doublets or even triplets, e.g. *tocnawness/tocnawenness* 'knowledge, understanding', *forgifness/forgifenness* 'forgiveness', *onginness/ongunnenness* 'undertaking', *ongitness/ongitenness* 'understanding', *leorness/leorendness/leoredness* 'departure, passing away', *alisness/alisendness/alisedness* 'redemption', and others. Clearly, all of these exhibit typical Action noun meanings, and not the meanings of 'passive state' which one would associate with a past participle, if this was the deriving base from a semantic point of view (cf. Modern English *-ness*). Obviously, semantically speaking, the verbal stem as such acts as basis, regardless of whether this is represented morphologically by the infinitive stem or one of the participles. As has been pointed out in § 5.3.1.5, Jordan (1906) and Weyhe (1911) assumed a dialectal split with regard to the derivational basis, Anglian selecting the infinitive, and West Saxon, in particular Late West Saxon, opting for the participle. This may, however, also reflect a diachronic change, especially since in EWS we find both types side by side. Here, a more detailed reinvestigation on the basis of Venezky & Healey (1980) seems to be called for.

The suffix *-ræden* derives feminine denominal nouns with the meaning 'state, act, condition of', e.g. *bebodræden* 'command, authority', *broþorræden* 'fellowship, brotherhood', *campræden* 'war, warfare'.

The suffix *-scipe* forms masculine abstract nouns from adjectives and nouns with the meaning 'state, act, fact, condition'. Denominal examples are of the type *bodscipe* 'message', *freondscipe* 'friendship', *leodscipe* 'nation, people', while deadjectival examples include *gecorenscipe* 'election, excellence', *unwærscipe* 'carelessness', *hwætscipe* 'activity, vigour'.

The suffix *-þ(o)/-t* is obviously related to the group *-d/-t/-(o)þ* discussed earlier and derives feminine deadjectival abstract nouns (with and without *i*-umlaut), e.g. *fylþ* 'filth', *hiehþ(o)* 'height', *iermþ(o)* 'poverty', *læþþo* 'hatred', and the many derivatives from *-leas*-adjectives, e.g. *larleast/larliest* 'ignorance', *lifleast* 'death', *slæpleast* 'sleeplessness'.

What may be regarded as the single suffix *-ung/-ing* forms deverbal nouns from both strong and weak verbs, *-ung* primarily occurring with weak class 2 verbs, and *-ing* elsewhere, although this originally complementary distribution is no longer fully observed in late OE (see Weyhe 1911 for details). As with many of the other deverbal suffixes, the derived nouns may be classified into the categories of Action, Agent (collectives), Object/Result, Instrumental and Locative. Two examples of each category follow: *binding* 'binding', *huntung* 'hunting'; *gaderung* 'gathering, assembly', *(ge)meting* 'meeting, assembly'; *beorning* 'incense', *agnung* 'possessions'; *lacnung* 'medicine', *wering* 'dam'; *cyping* 'market', *wunung* 'dwelling'.

Finally, *-wist* as an independent lexeme meaning 'being, existence' also developed into a suffixoid deriving denominal, deadjectival and deadverbial feminine abstract nouns, e.g. *huswist* 'household', *loswist* 'loss', *stedewist* 'constancy', *midwist* 'presence'.

5.4.4.3 Adjectival suffixes

In this section the following adjectival suffixes are discussed and exemplified; *-bære*, *-cund*, *-ed(e)/-od(e)*, *-en*, *-fæst*, *-feald*, *-full*, *-ig*, *-iht*, *-isc*, *-leas*, *-lic*, *-ol*, *-sum*, *-weard*, *-wende*.

Sauer (1985:283) regards both *-bære*, which is mainly West Saxon, and its Anglian counterpart *-berende* (see § 5.3.1.5), as suffixoids. It seems, however, that the *-berende*-formations have preserved their original compound status to a much greater extent than the *-bære*-adjectives, given the productivity of the pattern N + present participle (see § 5.4.2.3), so that *-berende* formations should be regarded as compounds rather than as derivatives, while *-bære* indeed qualifies as a suffixoid with the meaning 'productive of, having, carrying', e.g. *æppelbære* 'apple-bearing', *atorbære* 'poisonous', *cornbære* 'corn-bearing' and many others.

The suffix *-cund* derives denominal and deadjectival adjectives with the meaning 'of the nature of, originating from'. Thus we find from nouns examples such as: *engelcund* 'angelic', *gastcund* 'spiritual', *godcund* 'divine'; and from adjectives we find *æþelcund* 'of noble birth', *innancund* 'internal', *yfelcund* 'evil'.

Clearly related to the weak past participle is the suffix *-ed(e)/-od(e)*, which derives possessive adjectives with the meaning 'provided with' from simple and compound nouns; in the latter case, the formations have to be regarded as extended *bahuvrihi*-compounds, i.e. to the *bahuvrihi*-compound an adjectival suffix has been added, cf. *feowerfote, feowerfete* vs. *feowerfotede* 'four-footed'. Therefore, we find many *bahuvrihi* and extended *bahuvrihi* doublets, as, for example, with the suffix *-ig*. Other meanings are 'resembling, having the character of'. The distribution of *-ede(e)/-od(e)* has not yet been investigated in detail. Examples of this common suffixation are: *agimmed* 'set with precious stones', *gebleod* 'beautiful, variegated', *anhyrned* 'having one horn'; *acæglod* 'studded with pegs', *gebyrnod* 'corseleted', *feowerhweolod* 'four-wheeled'.

The adjectival suffix *-en* derives denominal adjectives with the meanings 'made of, consisting of, characterised by, manifesting'. Older formations have umlaut, more recent ones lack this alternation. Typical examples are: *æscen* 'made of ash-wood', *ceoslen* 'gravelly', *hyrnen* 'made of horn'.

The suffix *-fæst* derives adjectives from nouns and adjectives with the meaning 'having, characterised by, being', e.g. *arfæst* 'virtuous', *blædfæst* 'glorious, prosperous', *domfæst* 'just, renowned', all from nouns, and *hogfæst* 'prudent', *soþfæst* 'truthful', *wisfæst* 'wise', from adjectives.

The suffix *-feald* is used to form adjectives with the meaning '-fold' from numerals and quantifiers, e.g. *anfeald* 'single', *þrifeald* 'threefold', *manigfeald* 'manifold', *hundfeald* 'hundredfold'.

The suffix *-full* derives adjectives from nouns, adjectives and occasionally, verbs with the meaning 'having'. Derivatives from nouns include *andgietfull* 'intelligent', *bealoful* 'wicked', *bismerful* 'shameful'; from adjectives *earmful* 'wretched, miserable', *geornful* 'eager', *gesundful* 'unimpaired'; whilst from verbs there is *hyspful* 'contumelious, ridiculous'.

The frequently used suffix *-ig* derives denominal, deadjectival and deverbal adjectives with the meaning 'characterized by, having'. As with *-ede/-ode*, many of these are extended *bahuvrihis*. In many instances, there is a doublet in *-lic*. Since OE *-ig* is the continuation of both Gmc *$*$-ig* and *$*$-ag*, we find forms both with and without *i*-umlaut. Typical examples from nouns, adjectives and verbs respectively are: *adlig* 'sick', *blissig* 'joyful', *blodig* 'bloody'; *untrymig* 'infirm', *þystrig* 'obscure, dark', *gesyndig* 'sound' (see §5.3.1.5); *ceorig* 'querulous', *cwamig* 'sad, sorrowful', *gefyndig* 'capable'.

The suffix *-iht* has the same meaning as *-ig* – 'having, characterised by' – and derives denominal adjectives with and without *i*-umlaut, e.g. *adeliht* 'filthy', *flaniht* 'related to darts', *hæriht* 'hairy', *stæniht/staniht* 'stony', *þorniht/þyrniht* 'thorny'.

The suffix *-isc* forms denominal adjectives with and without *i*-umlaut with the meaning 'being like, having the character of', e.g. *ceorlisc* 'of a churl, common', *cildisc* 'childish', *mennisc* 'human'. The suffix is also frequently used for the derivation of ethnic adjectives, e.g. *denisc* 'Danish', *englisc* 'English', *scyttisc* 'Scottish', *wielisc* 'Welsh, foreign'.

The counterpart of *-ful* is *-leas*, denoting 'lack of'. It derives denominal adjectives such as *bismerleas* 'blameless', *blodleas* 'bloodless', *broþorleas* 'brotherless' and many more.

The suffix *-lic* derives denominal, deadjectival and deverbal adjectives with the meanings 'being, characterised by, having', in the latter function also forming extended *bahuvrihi*-adjectives. It is a rival of *-ig*, which is why we find many *-ig/-lic* doublets. There are many examples of denominal and deadjectival derivations, but fewer deverbal ones. Typical denominal forms are: *ælmeslic* 'charitable, depending on alms', *andgietlic* 'intelligible', *cildlic* 'childish'; typical deadjectival forms are: *æþellic* 'noble', *deoplic* 'deep', *bewependlic* 'lamentable'; for deverbal forms we may cite: *cieplic* 'for sale', *(ge)cwemlic* 'pleasing, satisfying'.

The suffix *-ol* derives adjectives with the meaning 'being, prone to' from deverbal nouns and directly from verbs; derivatives from strong verbs often have the reduced grade, and sometimes *i*-umlaut. Denominal examples are: *deopþancol* 'contemplative', *gearoþancol* 'ready-witted', *heteþancol* 'hostile'; and deverbal examples include: *beswicol* 'deceitful', *cwedol* 'talkative, eloquent', *forgitol* 'forgetful'.

The suffix *-sum* derives adjectives with the meaning 'being (characterised by)'. These may be from nouns, e.g. *friþsum* 'peaceful', *geleafsum* 'believing', *gedeorfsum* 'troublesome'; adjectives, e.g. *ansum* 'whole', *fremsum* 'beneficial', *genyhtsum* 'abundant'; or verbs, e.g. *(g)hiersum* 'obedient', *gecwemsum* 'pleasing', *healdsum* 'careful'.

The suffix *-weard* '-wards' is found in *æfterweard* 'following', *heononweard* 'transitory, going hence', *norþe(e)weard* 'northward', and similar forms.

Finally, *-wende* derives deadjectival and denominal adjectives with the meaning 'conducive to, consisting of'. Examples of the two types are: *halwende* 'healthful', *hatwende* 'hot'; and *lufwende* 'amiable', *hwilwende* 'temporary'.

5.4.4.4   Verbal suffixes

Verbal derivation in OE is primarily affixless: the few overt derivational suffixes, therefore, do not exhibit large-scale productivity. The suffixes which are regularly attested are: *-ett(an)*, *-læc(an)*, *-n(ian)* and *-s(ian)*.

Of these *-ett(an)* seems to have frequentative or intensifying meaning, and is added to nominal and adjectival, but primarily to verbal bases. From nouns we have *sarettan* 'lament', *botettan* 'repair'; deadjectival examples are: *agnettan* 'appropriate, usurp', *halettan* 'greet, hail'; examples of the more frequent derivatives from verbs are: *blicettan* 'glitter, quiver', *dropettan* 'drop, drip', *hleapettan* 'leap up'.

-Læc(an) forms deadjectival verbs with the meaning 'be, become, make' and denominal verbs with the meaning 'produce, grow, become'. Examples of the former are: *dyrstlæcan* 'dare', *geanlæcan* 'make one, join', *rihtlæcan* 'put right'; examples of the latter are:

æfenlæcan 'become evening', *loflæcan* 'promise', *sumorlæcan* 'become summer'.

The suffix *-n(ian)* results from misanalysis of zero-derived verbs such as *fægenian* 'rejoice' < *fægen*, *openian* 'open' < *open*, *tacenian* 'make a sign' < *tacen*, and leads to a few analogical formations such as *berhtnian* 'glorify', *lacnian* 'heal', *þreatnian* 'threaten' (see Marchand 1969:271, Raith 1931).

The quite frequent suffix *-s(ian)* derives deadjectival and denominal verbs (see Hallander 1966). Denominal examples are: *cildsian* 'be childish', *(g)eg(e)sian* 'terrify, inspire with fear, awe', *metsian* 'feed, furnish with provisions'; deadjectival examples are: *blipsian* 'make glad', *brycsian* 'be, become useful', *clænsian* 'make clean' and many others.

5.4.5 *Zero derivation (affixless derivation)*

5.4.5.1 The bases for the postulation of a separate category of zero or affixless derivation – the choice between these two is theory-dependent – are the distinction between inflexional and derivational morphology on the one hand and between expansions and derivations on the other. Inflexional morphemes mark grammatical functions and derive word-forms (see §5.1.1), but do not create new lexemes; this is the function of derivational morphemes. Thus, in a paradigm like *gum-a, gum-an, gum-ena, gum-um*, the morphemes *-a, -an, -ena, -um* have purely inflexional function; and they have exactly the same function in *cum + a* 'guest' < $cum(+an_{inf})$ 'come' (and *cum-an, cum + ena, cum + um*), i.e. they cannot be regarded as derivational affixes. Since *cum(+an)* is basically a verb, *cum(+a)* a noun and *-a, -an, -ena, -um* inflexional morphemes, there is no overt derivational (nominalising) morpheme, i.e. we have to assume affixless derivation. In a word-formation theory which is based on the syntagma principle, i.e. where word-formations in principle are binary and consist of a determinant and a determinatum (see §5.4.1.1), however, one would not speak of affixless derivation but rather of zero-derivation, that is, one would still assume a binary morphological structure, with the suffix assuming the form of a zero-morpheme. This move makes it possible to capture the semantic parallelism with explicit derivation, e.g. *gief(+an)*:*gief+end* 'someone (-*end*) who gives' = *gief(+an)*:*gief+$\emptyset$(+a)* 'someone (-$\emptyset$-) who gives'; *brec(+an)*:*brec+ung* 'act (-*ung*) of breaking' = *brec(+an)*:*bryc+$\emptyset$(+e)* 'act (-$\emptyset$-) of breaking'. This parallelism is essential, and it is therefore misleading to characterise this type of derivational process merely as functional shift, as is sometimes done (cf. Lee 1948, Quirk & Wrenn 1957:105ff. as against Biese 1941, Kastovsky 1968). Moreover, this analysis also captures the diachronic loss of a derivational affix (see §5.4.4.1), e.g. the loss of the stem formatives of nouns and verbs, which coalesced with the inflexional endings denoting case/number, or person/number/ tense. It should be added here that the ablaut alternations found in derivatives such as *gripe* 'grip' (< *gripan*), *cyre* 'choice' (< *ceosan*), do not have any derivational force, just as they do not have any derivational force in suffixal derivatives. Moreover, it would seem that derivation other than from the infinitive was no longer productive, at least in the later OE period. The general implications of the ablaut alternations will be discussed in §5.4.7.

Finally, the distinction between expansions and derivations (see §5.4.2.1) is responsible for treating the so-called *bahuvrihi*-compounds like *bærfot, anhorn* here rather than in the section on compounding; they do not conform to the structure AB = B, which is why in many cases the adjectival *bahuvrihi*-compounds have been converted into suffixal derivatives proper by adding one of the adjectival suffixes -*ed(e)*, -*ig*, -*lic*, -*ol*.

5.4.5.2 Nominal derivatives

For deverbal nouns on the whole, all the typical deverbal semantic types (Agent, Action, Object/Result, etc.) are represented, although Action and Agent nouns dominate. All genders occur, and most inflexional classes within them, which means that a considerable number of derivatives are also affected by alternations such as *i*-umlaut. But there is no absolute correlation between semantic type, gender, inflexional class and ablaut grade, although some preferences reflecting earlier regularities are discernible; thus agent nouns tend to be masculine and to have reduced grade; masculine action nouns frequently have a full-grade base, while neuter ones often go with reduced bases. It should also be mentioned that derivation is made from both strong and weak verbs. The latter point requires some explanation. Historically speaking, weak verbs were denominal, deadjectival and deverbal derivatives, but in quite a few cases the direction of derivation came to be reversed in the course of time in analogy with other patterns. Thus, semantically speaking, it is more natural for an action noun to be interpeted as being derived from a verb (e.g. *gnorn* 'affliction, sorrow' < *gnornian* 'grieve, mourn, be sad') than for a verb to be derived from a primary action noun (*gnorn* > *gnornian*). Consequently, the 'unnatural' direction of derivation was replaced by the more natural one. This kind of reinterpretation is the same as that observed with back-derivations of the type *pedlar* > *peddle* 'act as a peddlar' → *to peddle* > *peddler* 'someone who peddles' (see Marchand 1969:391ff., Kastovsky 1968:93ff.).

In the space available it is impossible to give a full summary of the range of deverbal derivatives, for which see Kastovsky (1968). Instead the process is exemplified below by examples of derived Action nouns only. Here we find strong masculines from strong verbs, e.g. *drepe* 'slaying', *drinc* 'drink', *cyme* 'coming'; and from weak verbs, e.g. *bælc* 'belch', *drenc* 'drowning'; weak masculines from strong and weak verbs, e.g. *steorfa* 'mortality', *sceaþa* 'harm'; *hopa* 'hope, expectation', *plega* 'play, fight'; strong feminines from strong and weak verbs, e.g. *hreow* 'sorrow', *faru* 'journey, going', *giefu/giefe* 'gift, favour'; *hunt* 'hunt', *lufu* 'love'; weak feminines from strong and weak verbs, e.g. *birce* 'barking', *feohte* 'fight'; *æsce* 'search, inquisition', *gicce* 'itch'; and strong neuters from strong and weak verbs, e.g. *beorc* 'bark(ing)', *geberst* 'eruption', *delf* 'digging'; *gebirg* 'tasting', *gecid* 'strife'.

Deadjectival nouns of this type are strong feminines; their meaning is usually 'quality, fact, state of being'; if possible, they have *i*-umlaut. The process must have been productive even in late OE, cf. *pryto* 'pride', derived from the French loan *prut*. Typical examples are: *bieldu* 'boldness', *birhtu* 'brightness', *cieldu* 'cold', and a number of others.

Denominal nouns are nominal *bahuvrihi*-compounds with the meaning 'someone, something having', i.e. *anhorn/ø* 'animal having one horn'; for the history of this type see Carr (1939:164ff.), for its analysis Marchand (1969:386ff.). This type is much weaker than the adjectival *bahuvrihis* in §5.4.5.3. below. Many OE formations are loan-translations from Latin; the most frequent patterns are Adj + N, Num + N; some instances of N(Gen) + N also occur. Not infrequently the morphological (overt) head belongs to a different gender and inflexional class than the independent lexeme, and sometimes the derivation involves *i*-umlaut, cf. *leaf* (strong neuter), but *fifleafe* 'quinquefolium' (weak feminine) beside *fifleaf*; *horn* (strong neuter), but *anhorna* 'unicorn' (weak masculine), *anhyrne* (strong masculine with umlaut) besides *anhorn* (strong neuter). Further examples include *belcedsweora* 'one having a swollen neck', *bundenstefna* 'ship with an ornamented prow', *hyrnednebba* 'horny-beaked bird, eagle'.

5.4.5.3 Adjectival derivatives

Affixless deverbal adjectives are primarily, although not exclusively, derived from strong verbs, mainly from the reduced, sometimes also the lengthened, and with class VII from the basic grade, with and without *i*-umlaut. The derivatives frequently occur as second members of compounds, see §5.4.2.3. Their meaning is typically 'prone to do, doing, being...(ed)', as in *swice* 'deceitful', *eaþfynde* 'easy to find', *æþryt* 'troublesome', *cweme* 'pleasant, agreeable'.

The numerous simple and complex zero-derived denominal adjectives can be divided into two basic categories: those having the masc. nom. sg. in *-e*, and those without an ending. The former category is derived from a simple or a compound noun, with or without *i*-umlaut, e.g. *fielde* 'field-like', *anbieme* 'made of one trunk', *aneage* 'one-eyed', and is characterised by typically adjectival meanings such as 'having, being like, being characterised by, being made of'. The second category is endingless and consists of *bahuvrihi*-compounds proper, e.g. *bærfot* 'barefoot', *langmod* 'patient', *blandenfeax* 'grey-haired'.

5.4.5.4 Verbal derivatives

As has been mentioned, affixless derivation is the major source of new verbs in Old English, because all verbal suffixes are fairly unproductive. The only really productive patterns in Old English are denominal deadjectival and deadverbial derivations; deverbal derivation (resulting in causatives) is no longer productive, although its results are still transparent. The results are weak verbs. Pilch (1970:132) lists the following strong class VII verbs as denominal: *rædan* 'advise' < *ræd* 'advice', *slæpan* 'sleep' < *slæp* 'sleep', *bland* 'mix' < *gebland* 'mixture', *hropan* 'shout' < *hrop* 'clamour'. It would seem, however, that even if this assumption really represents the historical development, in Old English the verbs have to be regarded as basic and the nouns as derived, so from the OE point of view there are no derived strong verbs. As to weak verbs, only class 2 (type *beorht*:*beorhtian* 'be, make bright', *wuldor*:*wuldrian* 'glorify) was fully productive throughout the OE period. Derivation of class 1 weak verbs (type *full*:*fyllan* 'fill', *scrud*:*scrydan* 'clothe') was certainly productive as long as *i*-umlaut was fully transparent, but it apparently lost its productivity early in the OE period, and gradually also lost its transparency; as a consequence many of the class 1 verbs joined class 2, so there are numerous doublets.

For denominal verbs the following semantic groups dominate. The sense 'be, act like, become' is found in verbs such as *ambehtan* 'minister, serve', *bisceopian* 'confirm', *dagian* 'dawn'. A rather larger number of verbs share the sense 'provide with, add, treat with': *frefran* 'comfort', *scrydan* 'clothe', *arian* 'give honour to'. *Heafdian* 'behead' has the sense 'remove', whilst the sense 'produce' is found in, for example, *bledan* 'emit blood', *betan* 'make good, repair', *blostmian* 'blossom'. *Heapian* 'heap up', *clynian* 'make into a ball', *munucian* 'make a person into a monk' bear the sense 'make into', whilst the sense 'perform' is found in, e.g. *cræftan* 'perform a craft', *deman* 'judge', *cossian* 'kiss'. Finally, *gryndan* 'come to the ground, set', *hæftan* 'bind, arrest, imprison', *husian* 'house' and others share the sense 'put (in)to, go to'.

The possible meanings of deadjectival verbs are 'be, become, make into + adjective'; many derivatives have more than one of these meanings. Typical examples from this fairly common group are *byldan* 'make bold', *blæcan* 'bleach', *brædan* 'broaden', *cypan* 'make known', *blodigian* 'make bloody', *deopian* 'become deep'.

The cateogory of deverbal verbs consists of causatives ('cause to V') derived from strong verbs, mainly with the preterite singular grade as basis. The derivatives are class 1 weak verbs and have *i*-umlaut. Since the strong verbs in OE basically were a closed class (additions like *scrifan* are exceptional), the derivation of deverbal causatives must also have been unproductive in OE. Typical examples include *blendan* 'mix', *cwellan* 'kill', *dræfan* 'drive'.

5.4.6 Adverbs

The formation of adverbs is a borderline case between word-formation and inflexional morphology. Assuming that adverbs constitute a separate part of speech, their derivation from adjectives and nouns involves a change of word-class, which is by definition a derivational, not an inflexional process. But in contradistinction to derivation proper, adverb formation does not add any additional semantic feature; the change merely involves a class-shift, and is solely caused by the syntactic function of the lexeme in question, a phenomenon characteristic of inflexion. It is not surprising, therefore, that some grammars subsume adverb formation under word-formation, e.g. Quirk & Wrenn (1956:107), while others treat it under inflexion (accidence), e.g. Wright & Wright (1925:299ff.). In view of this ambivalence, I have not included adverb-forming suffixes under §5.4.4, but treat them as a separate category.

The most frequent suffix to form adverbs from adjectives is *-e*, e.g.

deope 'deeply', *nearwe* 'narrowly', *georne* 'eagerly'. If the adjective already ends in *-e*, adjective and adverb are homonymous, e.g. *bliþe* 'joyful(ly)', *ece* 'eternal(ly)', *milde* 'merciful(ly)'. From adjectives ending in *-lic* and their adverbial forms, e.g. *sarlice* 'grievously', *wraþlice* 'furiously', *modiglice* 'proudly', the ending *-lice* was secreted and used to directly form adverbs from adjectives not ending in *-lic*, e.g. *blindlice* 'blindly', *holdlice* 'graciously', *hwætlice* 'quickly', and also from nouns, e.g. *freondlice* 'in a friendly manner', *eornostlice* 'earnestly'. Another adverbial suffix is *-inga/-linga, -unga/-lunga* as in *edniwunga* 'anew', *færunga* 'quickly', *neadinga/niedinga/neadlunga* 'by force', *grundlunga/grundlinga* 'to the ground, completely'.

Furthermore, denominal adverbs are formed by using one of the inflexional forms, e.g. the masc. gen. sg. *-es* in *anstreces* 'continuously', *dæges* 'daily', *selfwilles* 'voluntarily', (sometimes even extended to feminines, e.g. *endebyrdes* 'in an orderly manner', *niedes* 'of necessity', *nihtes* 'at night'). Also rather frequent in this function is the dative plural, e.g. *dægtidum* 'by day', *geardagum* 'formerly', *geþyldum* 'patiently', *dælmælum* 'piecemeal', *dropmælum* 'drop by drop', and many other *-mælum*-formations.

5.4.7 *The typological status of word-formation*

As a conclusion to this survey of OE word-formation, a general assessment of its typological properties might not be out of place, which could also be used as a starting-point for tracing the subsequent developments in the ME period. Such a characterisation will have to be based on several intersecting parameters, such as the morphological status of the input to and the output of the word-formation processes (roots, stems or words, see §5.1.1), the order of the basic constituents determinant and determinatum, the frequency, regularity, conditioning and functioning of these alternations (i.e. whether they are exponents of morphological categories or not), the number of derivational levels (in a model with level-ordering) or the type of morphological boundary separating the constituents, etc. (see Kastovsky 1990a).

The morphological status of the input to and output of the word-formation processes depends on the type of inflexional morphology prevalent in the language. In this respect, OE is in a stage of transition from stem-based to word-based inflexion and derivation, with a residue of originally root-based patterns, which had been reinterpreted into stem-based ones.

The system-defining structural property in the sense of Wurzel (1984) is stem-based inflexion and derivation (cf. the analysis of OE inflexion in chapter 3). It characterises verbal inflexion throughout, where no form is without an inflexional ending. Thus, the verbal lexemes are stems and not words, and deverbal derivation consequently is also stem-based. The same is true of weak nouns (*gum + a*, *tung + e*) and strong feminines (*luf + u*). But with *a*-stem masculines (*cyning*) and neuters (*word*), and with adjectives in general (*god*), the nominative/accusative singular is without an inflexional ending (or with zero, depending on the analysis chosen), and thus functions as unmarked base-form with word-status. Here, inflexion and derivation are already word-based, and it is this type that will eventually prevail in ME. An interesting corollary is the reanalysis of the long *-ja*-stems and the *i*-stems from #*her + e*#, #*win + e*# to #*here*#, *wine*# (see chapter 3), i.e. the reinterpretation of the nominative/accusative singular ending *-e* as part of the stem with the concomitant shift from stem-based to word-based inflexion and derivation in analogy with quantitatively dominant *a*-stems.

Above it was claimed that there is a residue of originally root-based inflexion and derivation. This is linked to the phenomenon of ablaut, which in IE had, at least to a certain extent, been phonologically conditioned by stress and pitch variation, although these in turn might have been linked to morphological factors. In any case, ablaut does not seem to have been functional at this stage, since it was not exploited for the signalling of morphological categories directly, and might very well be explained as an alternation based on an abstract, or minimally specified root-vowel (cf. Lass & Anderson's 1975:25ff. analysis of OE, which for OE is no longer tenable but might be used for a description of the IE and early Germanic state of affairs). Assuming that this interpretation is correct, inflexion and derivation at this stage is root- rather than stem-based. This is confirmed by the following considerations. It is usually assumed that the original IE verb system was based on aspectual rather than on tense oppositions. In such a system, each aspect would probably have equal status, i.e. it would not really make sense to derive one aspect from another. Rather, it would be more plausible to derive the various aspectual forms from a common unspecified or minimally specified root. This would also account for 'deverbal' nouns with varying ablaut grades, because these could also be interpreted as deradical derivatives, an analysis which is strengthened by the fact that in most instances a stem-formative element is added, which could also be interpreted as a derivational suffix.

This system underwent a radical change in Germanic, caused by two interrelated factors: the emergence of weak verbs, which introduced stem-inflexion and stem-based derivation, and the shift from an aspectual to a tense system based on the opposition of marked past tense vs. unmarked non-past, the latter at the same time holding a privileged position as base form from which the marked form is derived. With the growing numerical predominance of the weak verbs as the only productive verb-creating pattern, stem-inflexion became the system-defining property of verb inflexion, which eventually led to a reinterpretation of the strong verbs: here, too, the infinitive/non-past form attained a privileged position as base form, and the ablaut alternations came to be reinterpreted as signalling tense, i.e. they became functional, although not completely systematically. At the same time this must have destroyed the original morphophonemic system, based on an underlying minimally specified vowel, and obscured the root-based status of inflexion, which was now reinterpreted as being stem-based as with the weak verbs. As a consequence, the morphological status of deverbal nouns and adjectives not containing the ablaut grade of the base form became problematic, in particular since the factors conditioning the alternations (stress alternation, etc.) were lost, too. As long as the ablaut alternations in the verbs were still sufficiently transparent, the original deradical status of ablaut nouns and adjectives remained discernible. But when the breakdown of the Old English morphophonemic system at the end of the period completely obscured the ablaut patterns, these derivatives were more and more isolated from the underlying verbs and were gradually lost and replaced by derivatives based on the infinitive stem (see Kastovsky forthcoming b).

The order of the constituents is determinant/determinatum, which is characteristic of the Germanic languages and remains stable during the period. However, major changes took place in the morphophonemic system, which became more and more opaque, because more and more of the widespread alternations shifted from phonological to morphological conditioning. The most important of these was undoubtedly *i*-umlaut, which, moreover, due to progressive unrounding of its results, lost its phonetic transparency. At the end of the OE period, probably accelerated by the various lengthening and shortening processes affecting the vowel system, the morphophonemic system must have broken down completely. The subsequent restructuring, little investigated so far, established homological, i.e. alternation-free, derivation as the dominant principle of word-formation, which is still characteristic of present-day English in the native or nativised section of its vocabulary. Alternations like *sane* ~ *sanity*, *divine* ~ *divinity* are characteristic only of the non-native (French, Neo-Latin) section and arose in the course of the ME and EModE periods, instances such as *keep* ~ *kept*, *wild* ~ *wilderness* being irregular and exceptional. The only OE alternation that seems to have survived is the one characterising verbal and nominal prefix formations, e.g. *begán*: *bígènga*, *onfón*: *ándfencga*, which probably was the ultimate origin of the present-day English pattern *ímpórt* vb.: *ímpòrt* noun, *recórd* vb.: *récòrd* noun.

5.5 Semantics

5.5.1 The section on Old English word-formation provided a fairly comprehensive survey of the existing morphological and semantic patterns. A similarly comprehensive account of the semantic organisation of the Old English vocabulary as a whole is not possible, however, primarily because we still lack detailed investigations of many semantic areas. Moreover, those that do exist are often not comparable due to completely different theoretical and methodological orientations, reflecting the changes in semantic theory from the *Wörter-und-Sachen* ('words and objects') movement via Trier's field theory to the modern context-oriented approaches with or without explicit use of componential analysis. On the other hand, such individual investigations are indispensable in view of the difficulties arising from one striking peculiarity of Old English poetic diction: the large number of apparent synonyms or near-synonyms for certain denotational areas such as 'world', 'man', 'sea', 'ship', 'fight', etc. Here, the definitions of the dictionaries are usually not precise enough and suggest synonymy where there might well have been denotative, connotative or stylistic differences. On the other hand, as was already pointed out by Schücking (1915:9ff.), many lexical items seem to be characterised by an extremely wide range of meanings. He mentions among others *hlynnan*, which refers to the sound of the human voice, the resounding of spears (*guþwudu*) and the crackling of fire; *deorc*, *mirce*, which not only mean 'dark', but also 'evil', 'uncanny'; or *grene*, which normally meant 'green', but could also mean 'pleasant, easy to walk on', cf. *gearwian us togenes grene stræte up to englum* (*Sat* 287) 'Let's prepare before ourselves a pleasant/easy path up to the angels.' This is confirmed by a look at the entries in the various dictionaries, and also by von Schaubert's (1949) etymologically oriented investigation of the verb *feormian* 'entertain, support, feed, consume, benefit; scour, cleanse, furbish' and its derivatives, where she tries to show that all these meanings could ultimately be related to a meaning 'remove', which she assumes to be the basic meaning of this lexical family. In view of this Schücking claimed that one of the most striking characteristics of poetic diction was its imprecise word usage. Whether this claim is really justified or just a reflex of the lack of more extensive empirical analyses in a suitable theoretical framework must be left undecided in view of the relatively small number of relevant studies. But those that do exist are promising enough to regard Schücking's evaluation of Old English poetic diction with some scepticism (see, for example, Soland's (1979) analysis of words for 'body' and 'soul' in poetic texts, Thrane's (1986) analysis of adjectives of 'moral sufficiency' in *Andreas*, Kühlwein's studies of expressions for 'enmity' (Kühlwein 1967) and 'blood' (Kühlwein 1968), and Strauss's (1974) investigation of the terms for 'lord' and 'ruler' in Old English poetry.

The specification of lexical meanings in prose literature is less difficult, since it is often dependent upon a Latin original. Thus, to a certain extent, we can rely on the meanings of the Latin equivalents of the Old English lexemes, see, for example, Lohmander's (1981) study of Old and Middle English words for 'disgrace' and 'dishonour', which is based on the Latin equivalents of these concepts, more precisely on their correlation with OE *bismer* and those Old English lexemes that are used to render its Latin equivalents.

In view of the rather patchy semantic analysis of the Old English vocabulary, it does not seem useful to attempt a systematic presentation in terms of semantic areas. Rather, I shall adopt a theoretical/methodological principle of organisation, which at the same time reflects to some extent the historical development of Old English semantic studies.

5.5.2.1 The first period of systematic vocabulary studies is primarily lexicologically–etymologically oriented and has a strong extralinguistic historico-cultural bias. Much of the relevant work is closely related to the *Wörter-und-Sachen* movement dominating especially lexical studies in Romance philology at the turn of this century and its first decades. Almost all the studies were dissertations produced at German universities from about 1903 onwards, and most were inspired by either Holthausen in Kiel or Hoops in Heidelberg, whose *Über die altenglischen Pflanzennamen* (Hoops 1889) together with Jordan (1903) acted as models. Jordan's study of the Old English names of the mammals consists of an introduction, where he summarises his historical findings, investigates the morphological relationship between the male and the female, and discusses the problem of discovering the original meanings of the lexemes in question. The remainder is a list of dictionary entries of the various lexical items organised according to their biological classification, each entry containing a specification of the occurring forms, quotations from Old English literature, its meaning, and – usually the most extensive part of the entry – its etymology. Studies of this kind are best characterised as lexicographic rather than semantic. The same format is found in Cortelyon's (1906) study of the names of insects, spiders and crustaceans, Geldner's (1906) list of names of illnesses, Köhler's (1906) list of fish-names, or Matzerath's (1913) list of terms for money, measures and weights.

The format preferred in the Kiel dissertations directed by Holthausen usually consisted of an extensive first part discussing the lexemes investigated and their denotata in their cultural and historical context, and a lexicographic second part following the pattern just discussed (form, meaning, quotations, etymology). Typically these dissertations carry the subtitle *Eine kulturhistorische-etymologische Untersuchung*. Examples include Brasch (1910): names of tools, Fehr (1909): the language of trade, Garrett (1909): names for precious stones, Kross (1911): names for containers, Schnepper (1908): names for ships and their parts.

All these studies are basically onomasiological, that is, they ask how a certain phenomenon or object is referred to in Old English and give an etymological explanation of the item in question. A semantic analysis in the strict sense is usually not provided, and it is not surprising that the denotata are always concrete objects or persons. However, this type of approach is also found in a number of later studies, where it is complemented by a much more substantial semasiological part dealing with the specific meanings of the relevant lexical items. Examples are Stibbe's (1935) study of the Old English terms for 'lord'/'man' and 'lady'/'woman', or Schabram's studies of the words for 'peasant' (Schabram 1975) and for 'plough' and its parts (Schabram 1980). In the former he shows that *ceorl* was used as a cover term for 'peasant', whether he owned the land or not, while *gebur* was restricted to the meaning 'tenant'; in the latter he demonstrates that *sulh* was the only Old English term, *ploh* being equivalent to the measure term *plogesland* and probably of Scandinavian origin.

5.5.2.2   Another more recent continuation of this type of study is based on the assumption that the etymology of a word has priority in the process of determining its meaning, while strictly semasiological principles (paradigmatic field studies and contextual analysis) are only of supplementary value as a corrective (Benning 1961:16ff.). In these studies 'etymology' is understood in its original signification as 'true meaning of words'. It is thus assumed that the etymology of a word allows us to discover its true, basic meaning, which, moreover, is often to be found in much later stages of the language (in particular in poetic diction, since such language tends to be archaic) as a residual meaning. Two typical examples are Benning (1961) and Dik (1965), for a detailed criticism of their methodological orientation see Schabram (1970b). Benning investigates the Old English vocabulary referring to 'heaven, sky' (*heofon, sweg(e)l, rodor, neornawang*), 'earth' (*eorþe, grund, hruse, mold, folde*), and 'world' (*middangeard, worold*) and suggests that a central element in the semantic make-up of many of these words is the concept of 'growth', as implied in the IE root *uen-/*$ĝen$-, for which he postulates the original meanings 'Laubholz, Niederwald' ('leaf-wood, wood produced from shoots'). Allegedly, this meaning is still present in some of the Old English occurrences, which, as Schabram has shown, is not confirmed by contextual analysis. Dik (1965) deals similarly with Old English *dryht*, for which he postulates the basic meaning 'Niederwald' also. These studies, while very imaginative, are, as Schabram (1970b) has shown, not really confirmed in their conclusions by the actual Old English facts.

5.5.3.1   In the 1930s the work of Stern (1921, 1931) and Trier (1931) introduced the notion of structure into semantics with the idea that lexemes should not be treated in isolation but in structured groups – 'lexical fields' – where they delimit one another semantically. Much of Trier's theory was questioned and has had to be modified, for example, the mosaic concept, according to which lexical meanings within a field are organised without overlap or gaps, or the delimitation of fields. On the whole, however, it provided an important new framework for synchronic and diachronic semantic analysis. Stern's work points in the same direction, although he formulates the notion of lexical field less explicitly than Trier. Both linguists have inspired many semantic studies, all more or less explicitly relying on the notion of the lexical/semantic field. Thus Bäck's (1934) study of the synonyms for 'child', 'boy', 'girl' is strongly influenced by Stern (1921), see Bäck

(1934:viii). He demonstrates that within each of the three groups there is a word-pair consisting of the two most central words for the idea, one of which dominates in the earlier period, but is more or less completely superseded in later Old English by the other. These are *bearn*:*cild* 'child'; *cniht*:*cnapa* 'boy'; and *fæmne*:*mægden* 'girl'. As had already been suggested by Jordan (1906:96ff.), *bearn* originally referred primarily to 'descendant' (= Lat. *filii*, *natus*, *liberi*), while *cild* implies 'non-adulthood' (= Lat. *parvulus*, *infans*, *puer*). Other words in this field are *lytling*, a markedly religious or ecclesiastical word, *lytel*, *wencel*; and the poetical *byre*, *eafora*, the latter mainly denoting 'descendant' rather than 'young person', besides a few others. *Cniht* originally had the two senses 'boy', 'youth', besides several others ('male servant', 'disciple', 'retainer'), but in the sense of 'boy' it is replaced by *cnapa* in West Saxon after about 1000; other words are *cnafa*, *cnæpling*, *beardleas*, *frumbierdling*, *geongling*, *geonlic*, *mago*. In the case of *fæmne* and *mægden* the former basically means 'woman', 'virgin', and only secondarily 'maiden', 'girl', whilst that is the dominant meaning of *mægden*. Small girls are referred to by *mægdencild*.

Mincoff's (1933) investigation of the words for 'strength' and 'power' is based on Trier's field theory (see Mincoff 1933:2) and follows his attempt to delineate the synchronic structure and diachronic development of the field in question. Mincoff investigated the following lexemes, including their compounds and derivatives: *strang*, *stearc*, *strecc*, *swiþ*, *eafoþ*, *ellen*, *cræft*, *mægen*, *miht*, *wealdan*, *rice*. Mincoff relies primarily on prose texts, pointing out that translations are the best basis for the determination of meanings, especially if Latin and Old English have different boundaries between synonymous lexemes. But significant weaknesses in his methodology mean that neither the field structure nor the internal semantic structures of the lexemes emerge with sufficient clarity.

Two more recent studies in this tradition provide more satisfactory results, namely Frey (1967) and Lohmander (1981). Frey investigates the verbs of transportation in Chaucer and then compares their field structure with that of the corresponding Old English field (i.e., verbs such as *bringan*, *lædan*, *ferian*, *beran*, *wegan*, *fetian*, *feccean*, *sendan*). He isolates 'distinctive criteria' such as 'means of transport', 'direction', 'transported/accompanied object/person', etc., which correspond to the notions of 'semantic dimensions' or 'semantic feature' in theories based on componential analysis (see Kastovsky 1982). Lohmander (1981) discusses the words for 'disgrace', 'dishonour' which are partial synonyms of *bismer* and its Latin equivalents in the works of Alfred, in classical Old English (ca 950–1100) and in late Middle English (ca 1350–1500). One characteristic feature of her approach is that she bases her study on Latin-English correspondences and explicitly includes contextual information, i.e. syntagmatic relations.

5.5.3.2   Other more recent studies combine Trier's paradigmatic lexical field theory with an investigation of syntagmatic relations (collocations and general contextual analysis) and an implicit or explicit componential analysis, i.e. the extraction of smallest meaningful elements (semantic components). One of the first attempts in this direction is König (1957), whose study of the Old English terms for colour, lustre and luminosity, influenced by Porzig's notion of the syntagmatic field, systematically lists the contexts in which the various colour lexemes occur. As had already been noticed in Willms (1902:68), and confirmed by Barley (1974), brightness/luminosity is the primary dimension in this field, as against present-day English, which is hue-oriented.

Contextual information also plays an important role in Kühlwein's (1967, 1968) operational lexicological analysis as applied to terms of enmity in Old English poetical language (including, amongst many others *anda, beadu, ellen, feondscipe, hild, niþ, sacu, wig, wraþ*, and their compounds and derivatives) and to terms denoting 'blood' (*blod, dreor, swat, heolfor*). The specific meanings of these partially synonymous lexemes are established on the basis of a statistical evaluation of the contexts in which they occur. Unfortunately neither of these two studies contains a complete documentation of all occurrences, so that it is not possible to verify the individual interpretations. Related to Kühlwein's approach is Faiss' (1967) analysis of the lexemes expressing 'favour', 'mercy' (*ar, bilewit, milts, hyldu, est, liss, giefu, bliss, lof*) in Cynewulf and his school. But the delimitation of the field seems to be more arbitrary than in Kühlwein, who relativises considerably the definitions postulated for these lexemes.

While Kühlwein and Faiss do not operate with the notion of semantic features or components, the following explicitly refer to componential analysis: Strauss (1974), Gutch (1979), Soland (1979) and Thrane (1986). Strauss investigates the poetic terms for 'lord' and 'ruler' (*dryhten, cyning, þeoden, frea* and others), basically using Kühlwein's operational approach, but augmenting it by incorporating not only componential analysis as such, but also associative-connotative features of the relevant lexemes. Gutch (1979), one of the few studies dealing with verbs, uses the syntactic behaviour (type of object) as one of the parameters for a semantic differentiation of the verbs *cnawan, cunnan, witan* 'know'. According to her, *cunnan, witan* have a static primary meaning 'know', while *on-, ge-, tocnawan, gewitan* represent dynamic meanings ('get to know', 'learn'). Soland's study of the Old English poetic terms for 'body' and 'soul' follows Leisi's theory of equating the meaning of a lexeme with its use (Leisi 1953, 1973) and deals with *lic, lichoma, flæsc, hra, bankenningar, wæl* ('body') and *sawol, gast, mod, sefa, hige, ferhþ, hreþer, heorte* ('soul'). The 'body' lexemes are differentiated with regard to the dimensions 'body as opposed to soul' (*lichoma*), 'body alive or dead' (*flæsc*), 'body being attacked' (*hra, bankenningar*), 'corpse after a fight' (*wæl*), with *lic* acting as a neutral, superordinate term. The 'soul' lexemes are grouped into two theological items *sawol* (as opposite of *lic, lichoma* and *flæsc*), *gast* (as opposed to *dust* 'dust') and several other lexemes having in common the meaning 'soul as seat of emotions', e.g. *mod, sefa, hige, ferhþ, hreþer, heorte, breost*.

5.5.3.3   Finally there are several studies that are primarily characterised by the careful analysis of all the contexts in which the lexemes occur, but where the notion of lexical field is not central. The relevant lexical items may therefore either make up a field or a derivationally related family. This method, already used in Schaubert's (1949) discussion of *feormian* and its derivatives, is characteristic of the work of Schabram and his pupils Grinda and von Rüden. Grinda (1975) investigates the Old English words denoting 'work' and 'labour' (e.g. *weorc, gewinn, geswinc, bisgu(ng), tilþ*, and their nominal derivatives and compounds), arriving at lists of highly specific senses for each of these (for *weorc* he lists more than eighty groups). These will often have to be regarded as purely contextually determined variants, from which one or several more global, systematic meanings have to be abstracted – a task that unfortunately has not been undertaken. Von Rüden (1978) investigates the lexeme *wlanc* 'boastful, arrogant, proud; stately, splendid' and its derivatives in Old and Middle English, basically following the same method. He determines the senses 'rich, wealthy; wealth; make rich' as the core meanings of *wlanc*; closely related to these are the senses 'boastful, arrogant, proud; pride; boast', whereas the senses 'wanton, stately, splendid' are peripheral.

Unquestionably contextual analyses of this type provide the most accurate results, and are thus indispensable. On the other hand, they ought to be complemented by the application of principles of structural semantics such as the concept of lexical field, sense relations, semantic dimensions, etc., in order to account for the fact that the lexemes of a language do not form an unstructured aggregate but are organised in terms of a complicated network of relations.

FURTHER READING

So far, there have been no comprehensive studies of the OE vocabulary uniting the various aspects addressed in the present survey – loan words, dialectal, social and stylistic stratification of the vocabulary, word-formation and semantics – which is why this chapter is based on numerous individual investigations of varying scope and depth. This is particularly true of the areas of word-formation and semantics, where most of the existing investigations are older dissertations using frameworks and methodologies today no longer adequate, so that the material had to be reinterpreted, as far as such a reinterpretation proved possible. The situation is more satisfactory with loan-words and the dialectal distribution of the vocabulary, because there are a number of more recent investigations, but again there are numerous gaps and a comprehensive survey still remains to be written. It is to be hoped, however, that with the availability of such a wonderful tool as the Toronto Microfiche Concordance (Venezky & diPaolo Healey 1980) and the emerging OE dictionary based on it, OE vocabulary studies will become a focus of interest that will eventually lead to a more comprehensive description than was possible here.

In view of this situation, it is obviously difficult to provide a balanced list for 'further reading', but the following titles might perhaps be of special interest in this connection.

5.1 *Introduction*   The typological characteristics of OE word-formation (cf. also §5.4.7), have been treated more extensively in Kastovsky (1988a,b,c; 1989); for the general terminological and theoretical background cf. Lyons (1977:18ff.) and Kastovsky (1982).

5.2 *Foreign influence*   The standard reference work on loan-words in English is still Serjeantson (1935), although numerous individual studies have in the meantime provided a number of corrections. On Latin loans in OE, cf. moreover Funke (1914), and, more recently, the excellent study by Wollmann (1990) on early Latin loans in OE, *Untersuchungen zu den frühen lateinischen Lehnwörtern im Altenglischen*, which only became available after the completion of the manuscript. Gneuss' (1955) book on loan-translations from Latin has so far not been superseded by any comparable investigation, so that, despite its limited data base (psalter glosses), it still is the most authoritative work on this subject, both methodologically and empirically.

Thus, the extent of the Latin influence on the structure of the OE vocabulary outside the area of direct loans, and especially on the structure of semantic fields and the productivity and even origin of word-formation patterns, still awaits more detailed investigation.

For the section on Scandinavian loans as well as on the general background of the Scandinavian–Anglo–Saxon relationship during the OE period, the following have proved helpful: Björkman (1900–2), Fellows-Jensen (1957b, 1982), Geipel (1971), B. H. Hansen (1984), Hofmann (1955), Peters (1981a,b), Poussa (1982), Sawyer (1958, 1982) and Stenton (1947).

5.3 *The stratification of the OE vocabulary*   The methodological foundation for the study of OE dialectal vocabulary was laid by Jordan (1906), which was more recently elaborated by Schabram (1965) for Anglian and Gneuss (1972) for the West Saxon written standard. Both scholars have inspired a number of extensive empirical investigations in this area, of which Wenisch (1979) and Hofstetter (1987) deserve to be singled out on account of their methodological clarity and wealth of data. A convenient starting point for the study of the poetic vocabulary is still Schücking (1915). In view of the wealth of literature on this subject, it is difficult to single out individual works, but Brodeur (1960) on Beowulf, and Brodeur (1952) and Marquardt (1938) on kenningar deserve a special mention.

5.4 *Word-formation*   As has already been mentioned, there is no comprehensive treatment of OE word-formation, in contradistinction to present-day English, for which we have the by now classical handbook by Marchand (1969), which, also contains a wealth of historical information. For more detailed studies, the reader is referred to the references in the respective sections.

5.5 *Semantics*   Again, no comprehensive survey is yet available. From a methodological–theoretical point of view, however, some publications attempting to apply more recent advances in lexical semantics, e.g. lexical field theory and semantic feature analysis, may be singled out as being of more general interest; these are, among others, Kühlwein (1967, 1968), Lohmander (1981), Strauß (1974) and Thrane (1986).

6 OLD ENGLISH DIALECTS

Thomas E. Toon

6.1   Introduction

Dialectology is the study of varieties of speech and variation in language. Dialectologists work to make correlations between linguistic features (phonological, morphological, syntactic and lexical) and such extralinguistic facts as place of origin, race, sex, social status. In doing so, we identify individual varieties – idiolects – and relate them to dialects, the more general patterns of speech communities. When undertaking the study of a contemporary speech community, the dialectologist has living informants and modern devices for collecting data. Studies of historical varieties depend on less direct methods. The main sources of information are written records and conjectures about older varieties based on comparisons of surviving dialects. Linguists interested in earlier varieties of English are fortunate that the English language has been written for over a thousand years. Those records attest several clearly distinct historical varieties, compare the Old English of Beowulf with Chaucer's Middle English or Shakespeare's Early Modern English. More subtle distinctions within periods, as between Chaucer and the Pearl/Gawain, are also evident. This chapter will be an investigation of the modern methods used to extract as much information as possible from ancient written records.

Given its name and rather narrow focus, *Old English dialectology* might at first seem a subject very remote from day-to-day human affairs. Speakers of a language are, however, by their very nature un-selfconscious 'students' of speech varieties. Early in life we begin that 'training' by identifying and learning to imitate the wide range of speech habits and styles we encounter in our nurturing environments. As we progress through the stages of babble, baby-talk, the verbal games and talk of childhood, the language of formal classroom, we are in fact learning different language systems. In so doing we become sensitive to the fact that the appropriateness of the language we use depends on a number of factors. Although that learning process seems to require no special effort, the knowledge we internalise in our early years is quite complex. For example, we 'automatically' adjust our language in terms of whom we are addressing (a parent, a stranger, a friend), where the interaction is talking place (at home, in a schoolroom, a playground), the genre (a conversation, a narrative, an argument, a report), the purpose (persuasion, play, friendship building). In addition, each of these language settings and uses has its own cadences and levels of formality expressed in lexical, phonological and syntactic choices. Linguistic maturity involves expansion of the range of such styles and registers. M. A. K. Halliday summarised this whole process very well when he observed that a child learns his/her language not because of what it is, but because of what it does. While we might think of most of these adjustments as embellishment to our language abilities, they are in fact central to our ability to communicate effectively.

While we intuitively control and manipulate our speech in those ways, there are aspects of speech performance over which we apparently have a great deal less control. The speech patterns we acquire early (of course) include markers of regional and social dialect. That is, our speech contains pronunciations, word choices, styles that convey information about our gender, our nationality, our region, our ethnicity, our socio-economic class. We are able to change these patterns only with considerable overt effort, or under strong external pressure (influence from a new social group, a major geographical or social move). Even under the most extreme of conditions, we are rarely able to alter these speech habits completely. An American who has lived a number of years in England may sound British to his American family but would be readily detected as a 'colonial' by most Britains.

For these reasons, linguists consider that all speakers of English have a dialect, or better, control a whole range of dialects which include many registers and styles. The linguistic use of the term 'dialect' is different from the everyday usage in which 'dialect' often means some non-standard or otherwise stigmatised variety. Dialectology then is the speciality devoted to studying the nature, range and uses of variation in speech. A major aspect of the work is to provide descriptions of regional, social and stylistic varieties. In the process of description, dialectologists hope to understand further how and why distinctive speech communities develop and then why speech differences are maintained or lost. Clearly differences can arise when groups begin to feel the effects of geographical, political, cultural, social or ethnic isolation. North American and antipodean varieties of English have diverged significantly because of geographical distance from their insular sources; while the Scots, the English, the Canadians and United States Americans have developed recognisable national standards of speech which reflect their national identities. Indian and Singapore varieties of English reflect cultural isolation, just as many so-called non-standard varieties reflect social isolation from 'mainstream' society; these are highly complex language situations in which English is the mother tongue of relatively few but an important second language for many.

The formal study of English dialects began well over a hundred years ago and was an integral part of the development of modern linguistics. Because early philologists were able to identify patterns of regional continuity over centuries, the study of English dialects was closely allied with the study of the history of the language. Historical documents were localised and then analysed as sources of data for reconstructing earlier pronunciations (Ellis, Sweet, Wright). At about the same time scholars began systematically to conduct extensive regional surveys of local speech habits. As a result the regional dialects of modern Britain are extensively documented.

Traditionally such studies focus on the geographical distribution (often displayed in maps) of individual features of pronunciation, word ending, word choice or sentence structure. In recent decades, studies have been based on random samples selected in order to give representative geographical coverage of the areas being considered. Using data collected in this fashion, dialectologists have mapped the salient regional features of British and American speech communities. Figure 6.1 demonstrates regional distribution of speakers who pronounce [r] in such words as *third floor*. The map displays by means of shading the fact that most English varieties of English are '*r*-less' (non-rhotic), while a strong post-alveolar approximant /r/ can be heard in the north and the southwest, where a retroflexed variety can also be observed. Such maps are statements of probability; the shaded areas are not to be taken as exclusively populated by [r] pronouncers, but rather areas in which there is better than average chance that the feature will be found. In fact we are not even dealing with general patterns of pronunciation. Even in the shaded area, [r]-ful (rhotic) speakers are

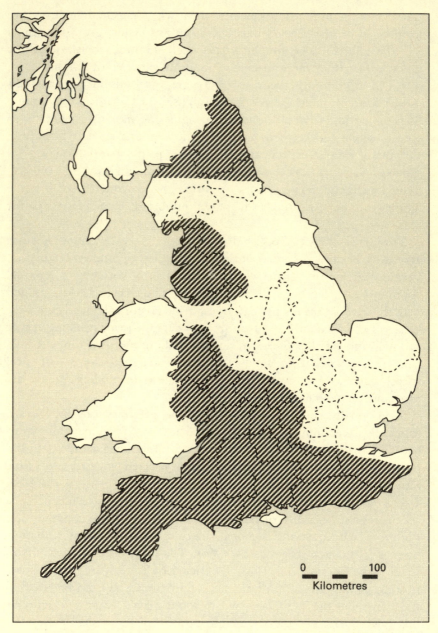

Figure 6.1 Map of areas of rhotacism

regularly non-mobile, older, and rural – also individuals whose speech tends to be less influenced by received pronunciation. The boundary of such a dialect feature is known as an isogloss. If a number of such features are displayed on a composite map (as in the case of the lines in the same modern map), we discover that many isoglosses converge and divide the country into areas where speakers share similar habits. Thus bundles of isoglosses help dialectologists identify dialect boundaries and state the regional distribution of dialect criteria. This map illustrates the standard division of English dialects into northern, north-midland, midland, southwestern and southeastern varieties, the basic dialect distribution which Old English data also attest. Whenever possible, dialectologists try to trace the history of the spread or decline of the selected features. They also hope to explain those changes by relating them to contact among speakers of different varieties, to the mobility of significant population groups or to changes in social, political and economic influences. Thus the description of some contemporary varieties of London English might begin historically and describe modern features in terms of what is known about the speech habits of those who migrated in large numbers into the cities during the industrial revolution.

Similarly, the first dialectologists who studied American English were able to explain the North American patterns of [r]-pronunciation (or deletion) in terms of well attested migration patterns from [r]-pronouncing/deleting regions of Britain. Often one variety, as in the case of the London Cockney dialect, becomes associated with a single social group and further becomes the means of defining group membership – establishing and maintaining group solidarity. Labov and his associates initiated the work of studying contemporary language variation in terms of how it relates to processes of ongoing language change. They not only studied [r]-pronunciation in terms of historical development, but they collected data on how a variety of New Yorkers from a range of social backgrounds spoke in number of different speech contexts. The following graph (Figure 6.2) demonstrates that such a linguistic habit is not simply absent or present. Deletion of [r] is a matter of degree and a function of social class, context and use. Each speaker has a range of pronunciations; he or she can automatically, often even unconsciously, make subtle changes which communicate status to hearers.

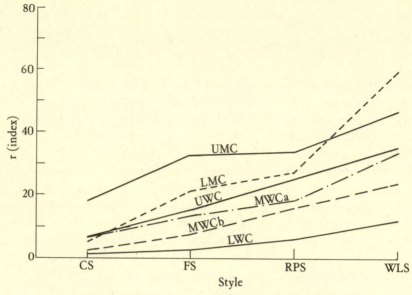

Figure 6.2 New York City (r) by class and style (after Labov 1966)

6.2   Old English dialects: origins and sources

The modern study of dialects requires careful analysis of copious data. Its methods have evolved to include extensive surveys, carefully designed field interviews, tape recordings collected from a number of controlled settings. Because of the nature of the sources and our distance from them, the study of Old English dialects must proceed along very different lines, and with different expectations about results. All of this will become much clearer below, but some initial contrast of methods and possible results will be useful. To begin with, the data sources for Old English are themselves written texts, rather than recordings or reports of speech. That is, the Old English texts were written by people whose intention was to conduct their day-to-day affairs; they were not written by trained linguists whose intention would be to record nuances of linguistic forms (see chapter 1, pp. 19–24). While students of the Old English period know quite a lot in general about manuscript production in early England, the knowledge about specific texts is very sparse, especially for the earliest documents. We might know the general area in which a text was produced, but we can only make educated guesses about most details. We can assign a rough geographical region and know the likeliest sites of production within that region, and we can propose the quarter or half century within which the text was produced. But we do not know such specific information as who wrote the text or whose language it reflects. Nor do we know about the scribe's origins, training or social aspirations. What we see through the mists of a thousand years will seem only the bare outline when compared with descriptions of modern dialect patterns. Even when Old English patterns are quite distinct, we still have data for only one limited set of styles and registers. The scribes who wrote the texts are not to be taken as representative of the whole population, about whose general levels of literacy we can only speculate. Occasionally the data and our knowledge about them permit attempts to produce sketches of greater detail. In these cases the efforts of historical dialectologists can be informed by recent advances in the methods of contemporary socio-linguistics, but only when tempered with a firm appreciation of our limitations.

Without disregarding diversity and pluralism, our view of modern England is determined by such facts as a strong national self-image, easy communication, a stable central government, a uniform educational policy and a received pronunciation of its dominant language. Anglo-Saxon England on the other hand was sparsely populated and travel was very difficult. The Germanic peoples from whom our language stems were comparative newcomers who brought social and political traditions by which they viewed themselves in terms of familial or tribal (that is non-national) associations. Although we might tend to think of the migration as a single historical event, archaeological data and even contemporary accounts attest more long range and piecemeal patterns of immigration.

By AD 600, the larger more powerful tribes had consolidated themselves into coherent political entities, called 'kingdoms' in a fashion that overdignifies the reality. Most histories of the period refer to the Anglo-Saxon Heptarchy, whose members are most commonly named as Northumbria, Mercia, East Anglia, Wessex, Essex, Sussex and Kent. In fact, our knowledge of Northumbria after Bede is too scant for a discussion of the nature of Northumbrian 'kingship'. East Anglia, Essex, Sussex and Kent never really achieved political autonomy. The generic term Mercia subsumes too many rival sub-kingdoms to be a useful descriptive term. Those we call 'kings' were locally powerful warlords, who managed temporarily to secure a tenuous influence over their rivals and eventual usurpers. Few died of old age; fewer still passed their title on to an immediate heir. According to Bede, an overlord was occasionally able to gain hegemony over neighbouring kingdoms. Even as Bede was writing his history, Northumbria enjoyed the benefits which come from a succession of strong kings. Bede's history of the church also gives occasional glimpses into social and cultural conditions, such as evidence that speech habits (among other criteria) were socially diagnostic among the Anglo-Saxons, just as they are today:

> ...those who watched him closely realized by his appearance, his bearing, and his speech that he was not of common stock as he said, but of noble family.
>
> (Colgrave and Mynors, 1969:403)

It is clear from Bede's work that Germanic tribal society, with a heroic ethic as its base, survived the transplantation to England. For instance, the conversion of the English proceeded tribally and had to begin with the conversion of overlords whose retainers followed his example. Bede's career is of immediate importance for students of the history of English for a number of reasons. His work carefully recorded Old English names for Roman and Celtic places which give clues to early pronunciations. Because of his position as the foremost Latin scholar of the time, his pioneer efforts to translate major texts into English gave vernacular literacy an important credibility. He urged the clergy to teach the rudiments of Christian doctrine in English and spent his waning energies in the act of dictating from his deathbed a translation of St John's Gospel. Bede's Death Song is also among the earliest recorded examples of Old English poetry.

Three kingdoms, each with successively greater influence, were able to extend their domination beyond their native realms: the Northumbrians (ca AD 625–75), the Mercians (ca AD 650–825), and the West Saxons (ca 800–1050). The Kentish were influential throughout the period by virtue of the importance of the See at Canterbury. The following table is an oversimplification (corrected below) but usefully summarises the major dialect features and their general association with these major political divisions of Anglo-Saxon England.

	Wessex	Northumbria	Mercia	Kent
Gmc æ:>e:	—	+	+	+
Pal. diph.	+	limited	—	—
æ>a/rC	—	+	—	—
smoothing	—	+	+	—
a>o/nasals	—	+	+	—
velar umlaut	limited	+	+	+
æ>e	—	—	+	+
æ:[2]>e:	—	—	—	+
y:/ y> e:/e	—	—	—	+

That is, West Saxon was the most clearly distinct variety, as might be expected because of geographical factors which isolated it even from the Norse invaders. Northumbrian and Mercian shared two major features, and formed a non-southern (midlands and northern) unit. Kentish (in the southeast) differed dramatically from geographically remote West Saxon and Northumbrian, but shared some features with Mercian. Mercian, the surviving midlands variety, had elements in common with its neighbours to the north and to the southeast, but remained distinct from its nearby southwestern rivals.

Of particular interest, is the fact that hegemony in each case (Northumbria, Mercia, Wessex) occasioned a flowering of learning. The Northumbrian kings fostered the establishment of the great monasteries of Wearmouth and Jarrow – which ultimately produced Bede and Alcuin, the famous school at York and the finest library in Europe. The magnificent books which survive from this period constitute substantial testimony to the importance of literacy and learning. Such productions would not have been possible without the patronage of the local kings. King Ceolwulf, we know, paid personal attention to the production of Bede's *Historia ecclesiastica*; he read and criticised a draft of it. We ought to be less than surprised that Bede, in the most influential book of the time, pays ample tribute to the power of the Northumbrian kings. His testimony here is peculiarly self-contradictory. In one passage he calls the Northumbrian kings the rulers of all England, while in another place he acknowledges the southern supremacy of the Mercians. King Ceolwulf and Bede knew the power of the written word. They would probably not have been surprised to discover that modern histories have perpetuated an account that contemporary political facts did not fully justify; scholars until recently accepted too uncritically what is clearly and naturally a northern perspective on the part of Northumbria's historian. The Anglo-Saxon kings who read Bede no doubt learned an important political lesson. An educated clergy can be more than a mere luxurious adornment to a dignified court.

The Mercian hegemony bridges the gap between Northumbria's first attempts at political unification of what is now England and the West Saxon accomplishment of that fact. Clearly the Mercian period was one of continuing consolidation of power; it was also the period of the first extensive texts written in English. Unfortunately, it failed to produce either its own local historian of Bede's stature, or an independent chronicle tradition such as the one which survives for Wessex (and makes the reconstruction of West Saxon history so much easier). But the texts which do survive can be pieced together to form a coherent narrative of political consolidation, and the role of vernacular literacy in that process. Under the Mercian kings diplomatic uses of literacy flourished, and charters became an integral means by which the Mercian overlords established, maintained and recorded permanently the facts of hegemony. In these charters, the Mercian kings styled themselves kings of Britain and collected the attestations of major clergy and regional subkings who in attesting confirmed the actions and status of their overlords. These same charters give further support to Bede's observation (AD 731):

> All these kingdoms and the other southern kingdoms which reach right up to the Humber, together with their various kings, are subject to Æþelbald, king of Mercia.
>
> (Colgrave and Mynors, 1969:559)

Æþelbald's achievements were consolidated and refined by his successor Offa, who even managed to anoint his son and assure his succession. Offa became the strongest king that Anglo-Saxon England had produced to date. His reign saw a centralised production of a silver currency of unequalled integrity, often finding its way to the continent via a newly brisk foreign trade. He called himself *Rex Anglorum*, and was a force in international politics. When he found the archbishop of Canterbury troublesome, he persuaded the Pope to establish a third archiepiscopal see in his native Lichfield. The charters attest the facts that he travelled widely throughout his kingdom, successfully levying taxes and granting lands in all parts of southern England. The same charters contain distinctly Mercian forms for the letters *t*, *g*, and *ð*. Those orthographic innovations are strong evidence that Offa had official scribes of his own probably trained in a royally sponsored scriptorium. He commissioned a protective earthwork, a dike that stretched the whole length of the Welsh border. He was so strong that he was even able to establish his younger brother as the king of Kent. From relic vocabulary in later, mostly Late West Saxon poetry, we know that vernacular literature was developed to a high art under the Mercian kings. Even the more substantial literate achievements of King Alfred's reign drew on the strong base of Mercian scholarship; his intellectual advisers were predominantly Mercian, and Alfred acknowledged his debt to the (good) laws of Offa in his own legislation.

The Tribal Hidage, a document (ca AD 700) which dates from the Mercian hegemony, is an important resource for understanding the political and social structure of early Anglo-Saxon England. It contains

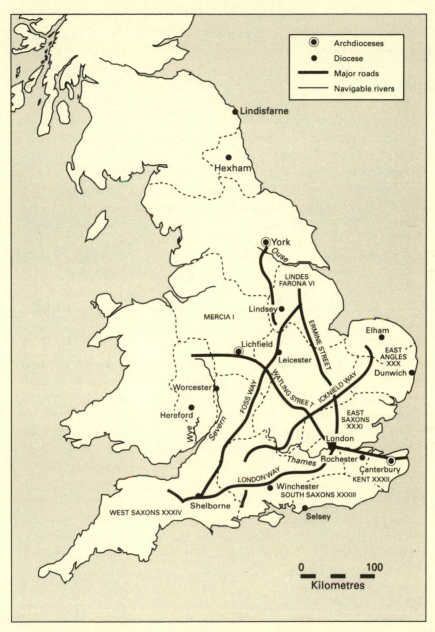

Figure 6.3 Map of early Anglo-Saxon England

a list of the names of some thirty tribal groups (see Figure 6.3 in which the tribes are listed by Roman numeral) of various sizes, whose size is indicated in *hides*. As the term *hide* originally designated a nuclear family or the land needed to support a nuclear family (fixed in the later medieval period at 120 acres), it is clear that the Hidage is some sort of census list. Since it includes none of the people north of the Humber and begins with the Mercians, it was no doubt made for a Mercian king. 'No one in the seventh or eighth century can be imagined compiling such a document out of mere curiosity. It only becomes intelligible when it is regarded as an attempt to guide a king's ministers in the exaction of his dues from subject provinces' (Stenton 1971:297). It is notable that the census is organised not according to strict geographical divisions but tribally; territory is viewed in terms of inhabitants rather than in terms of boundaries. Importantly, three major classifications of peoples emerge: the very large – the Mercians (30,000), the East Anglian (30,000), the Kentish (15,000), the West Saxons (100,000); the medium sized – the Hwicca (7,000), the Lindesfarona (7,000), the East Saxons (7,000), the South Saxons (7,000), the Nox gaga (5,000), the Chilterns (4,000), the Hendrica (3,500), the Oht gaga (2,000); the small – about 20 units with hidages from 300 to 1,200, in multiples of 300. The largest are easily identifiable as the major groups who vied for control of southern England, groups whose kings were powerful enough to grant land and privilege in their own right. The middle groups were still substantial, but dependent. Their leaders might call themselves kings, but are known to us from documents in which they are designated *ministri* to or *subreguli* of their (in this case) Mercian overlords. The leaders of the smallest tribes constitute the *comites*, the *principes*, the *duces* and the *ealdormenn* of the major documents.

From the hidage, an administrative hierarchy is clear. The Mercians exerted control directly over the intermediate and smaller units. The Mercian hegemony took advantage of the basically tribal fabric of Anglo-Saxon society. Since many small groups and a number of medium sized ones clearly played an important role in an overlord's political and economic base, we should be cautioned against over-dependence on a view of political organisation which emphasised the so-called heptarchy. The Hwicca and the Lindesfarona, for example, are equal in size to the East Saxons and the South Saxons, but they are ignored in the traditional view of the kingdoms. Further, information from the Tribal Hidage, emphasising inhabitants rather than region, argues that a purely geographical dialectology oversimplifies the facts.

Tribal diversity should also lead us to expect diversity of speech among the inhabitants of Anglo-Saxon England. Even though only a few of the tribes left written records, we should not assume that Old English dialects were limited to Northumbrian, Mercian, West Saxon and Kentish. Since groups of varying size were in constant contact (not to say, combat) with each other, we should assume a mixture of linguistic influence and expect variation in speech rather than the sort of uniformity that comes from well established social and educational traditions.

Chief among the tribes of the hidage are the West Saxons at 100,000 hides – a number of approximately equal to that assigned to the rest of southern England. Although the early West Saxon kings did not hold the Mercians in check, they were always a force to be reckoned with. Mercia certainly never dominated its southern neighbour in the way it controlled the east and southeast. The telling factor in the resolution of Anglo-Saxon hegemony was not in the end internal competition but the effects of long years of Viking raids. The northern and eastern kingdoms were decimated. The Anglo-Saxons were only able to muster a successful defence under Alfred the Great, and geography played a significant role in those events. Alfred and his successors built on the Mercian traditions, establishing a royal line that came close to modern standards for kingship. All manner of civil, cultural, political and liberal arts flourished as a result of the perfection of the burghal system of individually fortified and defended towns. The result was a tight network of locally governed burghs whose ealdormen were directly responsible to the king. For literate products, this stability meant a dramatic increase in the number of texts, prolific and identifiable scribal centres, and a steady progression towards a standard written variety.

The early history of Kent is more closely tied with the history of the English church than with the politics of its own kings. The success of Pope Gregory's hope to convert all of the English was ultimately determined when Æthelbert of Kent received the faith. The royal town of Canterbury became Augustine's base and eventually the archiepiscopal see. Under a series of strong archbishops, Canterbury became a religious and cultural centre of Europe. As Christianity spread through England, literacy spread with it, along with a very successful Roman model for administration. England was unified under one faith (and two archbishops – Canterbury and York), long before any single tribal overlord could claim to be the source of such unity. In the decades before Bede, Archbishop Theodore of Kent established the practice of regular councils of the bishops and set diocesan structure in place. As we can tell from the Tribal Hidage, the Kentish kings simply did not have the resources to extend their influence beyond their borders. It became the special talent of the Northumbrian and Mercian kings to make the event of their conversions an occasion to join the forces of church and state. Certainly no king could rule, 'though the grace of God', without the support of the church. In addition the church offered to the aspiring overlord the stability which comes from written histories, laws and charters. As the first primate of the English church, the archbishop of Canterbury was an necessary ally, even at those times when the Kentish kings were easy prey to their stronger Mercian and then West Saxon overlords.

For the first centuries of the Anglo-Saxon migration and settlement, we have little direct information about the language of Germanic invaders. Our first clues come from names found in seventh and eighth century Latin manuscripts, especially of Bede's *Historia ecclesiastica* (*Bede*), with their English personal and place names. These manuscripts also contain snatches of vernacular poetry – Cædmon's Hymn (*Cæd*) and Bede's Death Song (*BDS*). The earliest of the Bede manuscripts are all clearly of northern origin; the 6,000 or so names and fourteen lines of poetry found in them are thus thought to represent Northumbrian varieties of Old English. That assumption is further supported by linguistic features shared with the runic inscriptions on the Ruthwell Cross (*RuthCr*). Several other minor witnesses join this small but rather consistent corpus of data. A fourteen line poem – the Leiden Riddle (*LRid*), the fifty word inscription on the Franks Casket (*Rune Auzon*), and nineteen Old English words in a Vatican manuscript (*PsScholia*) are all harder to date or localise precisely, but their linguistic similarities point clearly to an early Northumbrian origin. A series of late tenth-century glosses to older manuscripts abundantly attest northern varieties of Old English. These manuscripts additions are unusual among Anglo-Saxon texts because we have direct internal evidence about the date and place of their production. We even know the names of three of these scribes. A scribe called Owun copied a continuous interlinear gloss to much of the Rushworth Gospels (*Ru2*). His colleague, Farmon (probably not a northerner) glossed the Gospel of Matthew and small parts of Mark and John (*Ru1*). Aldred, a priest from Chester-le-Street, added the gloss between the lines of the Lindisfarne Gospels (*Li*) and probably produced the glosses to the Durham Ritual (*DurRit*).

Unfortunately, we have a textual gap for the ninth century, which witnessed continual Viking raids in the North of England.

The nature of non-northern varieties of Old English is attested by a rather wider range of sources. Although there are no northern counterparts, a substantial number of official documents (loosely termed 'charters' (*Ch*)) survive which give insight into the political activities of midlands and southern kings and subkings over several centuries. We also have data of another sort because the scribes who wrote and used the Latin manuscripts of the day often found their texts troublesome in some way. When scribes encountered difficulties they regularly added a note (usually in Latin, occasionally in Old English) between the lines or in the margins. Apparently these glosses were useful since they were often collected from a number of sources and then compiled into extensive Latin–Latin glossaries. Many glossed manuscripts survive, as do a handful of glossaries which also contain Old English inter- pretations – notably the Epinal (*EpGl*), Erfurt (*ErfGl*) and Corpus glossaries (*CorpGl*). Unfortunately, of these very important early texts, only *CorpGl* is unambiguously an English product. *EpGl* was written either in England or in an English centre on the continent; *ErfGl* was clearly written by a German who knew little or no Old English. The touchstone for the study of early midlands varieties of Old English is found in the Vespasian Psalter (*VPs*). Although the book was produced at Canterbury in the eighth century, the language of the gloss is strikingly different from the Northumbrian texts, very regular in its features, and closely related to a series of Middle English texts which can be placed with certainty in the West Midlands. In a fuller discussion below, we will explore the linguistic relations between the *VPs*, the charters, the glossaries and a number of other related texts, now generally regarded as representing Mercian or Mercian influenced varieties of Old English. Those texts include some ninth century glosses to the Blickling Psalter (*BlGl*), the Lorica Prayer (*LorPr*) and glosses (*LorGl*) in the ninth century Book of Cerne, tenth century glosses to London, British Library, Royal 2. A. XX (*RoyGl*), and Farmon's tenth century additions to the Rushworth Gospels (*Ru*1). As is the case for Northumbria, no East Midland texts apparently survive the period of the Viking invasions of England.

Since the texts of the period of the Mercian hegemony play an important role in the discussion below, some additional comment is warranted. The foregoing summary of facts about these texts fails to account for them in one critically important way: they are often art historical monuments of exquisite beauty. Although they were written at a time when book production was costly indeed, we regularly find the best of materials, wide margins, spacious (and uneconomical) hands, and illuminated capitals of subtle and intricate design. The presence of English glosses in these texts suggests that the addition of the vernacular was considered a further adornment to these deluxe productions – powerful testimony to the privileged position of the written (English) word in Anglo-Saxon culture. Such books could only be produced at times of plenty and relative social and political stability. They were most likely produced at centres enjoying royal patronage, where political influences would also be most strongly felt. These books may even have been produced at royal command or as presentation copies to royal persons. After all, a psalter is a quintessentially royal book; the songs of a king make a fitting prayer book for a king. In the *VPs* painting of King David playing his conspicuously Anglo-Saxon harp, we may be invited to see the type of a perfect Anglo-Saxon king. A late ninth-century charter specifies the way in which royal patrons are to be remembered:

> At every matins and at every vespers and at every tierce, the *De profundis* as long as they live, and after their death *Laudate Dominum*; and every Saturday in St Peter's church thirty psalms and a Mass for them...

(Whitelock, 1955:598)

A deluxe psalter would be an appropriate production for such a community as received this charge. Because of its references to Mercian supremacy in the south, (as well as its admonition on Christian kingship) a copy of *Bede* would be an especially fitting gift for a Mercian king. The Mercian *Bede*, copied in the time of Æðelbald and Offa, unlike the other early Bede manuscripts, is a highly decorated volume. We know independently that King Offa possessed his own copy of Bede's *Historia*, and might wonder if the Mercian *Bede* was made for him. At any rate the nature and style of these texts reinforces our sense of the inter-relatedness of literacy and the coalition of church and state.

Figure 6.4 summarises the historical, political, social and intellectual context within which the texts of the Mercian hegemony appeared. The construction of the Tribal Hidage was among the first Mercian acts of literacy. The text formalised the economic base for the Mercian hegemony. The revenue derived from the Hidage made possible the construction of Offa's dyke; the ability to assess taxes no doubt encouraged the production of coins and the regulation of their integrity.

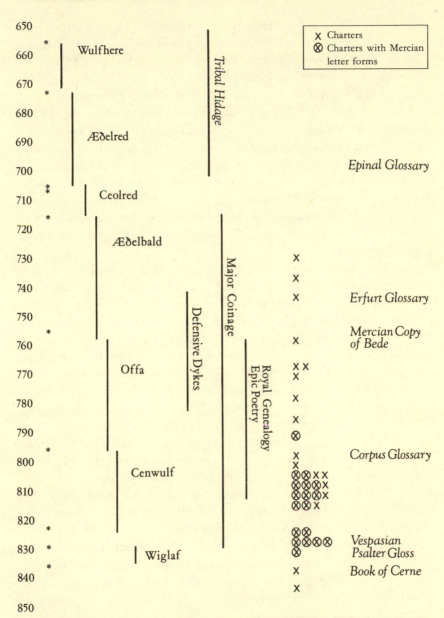

Figure 6.4 The products of literacy in their political context

The resultant political stability enabled the solidification of the powers of the Mercian kings, and charters were drawn up to define and confirm royal prerogative. Royal support for the major religious houses made possible the extensive production of fine manuscripts. The expansion of libraries reinforced the Mercian renaissance of Latin learning. As literacy flourished in the Roman mode, attention was directed to the writing of genealogies and the codification of laws. With the establishment of a royal scriptorium, peculiarly Mercian orthographic practices developed and the production of charters mushroomed. (Note the dramatic hiatus in charter production during the 820s, the date of a quarrel between the Mercian king and the archbishop of Canterbury.) From the same period in which all charters exhibit Mercian letter forms, we find the VP gloss, replete with the same letter forms. The writing of the most thoroughly Mercian text coincides with the apex of Mercian influence on literacy. The consolidation of Anglo-Saxon politics and culture was the development of *English* politics and culture as a result of the acts of *English* kings writing a language that deserves to be called the *English* language.

The best attested of all Old English varieties is the standard literary language associated with the West Saxon hegemony of the late tenth century and onwards until the Norman conquest. That is the language of the majority of Anglo-Saxon texts, the variety usually taught in introductory Old English courses, and the subject of chapters three and four of this volume. There are several witnesses of Early West Saxon varieties which are of particular interest in providing a sense of the literary dialect during its formative period. A few charters survive from the end of the eighth century, but we have a comparatively large number of texts which were products of the intellectual renaissance fostered by King Alfred the Great. Two versions of the Alfredian translation of Pope Gregory's *Cura pastoralis* (*CP*) can be dated to the last decade of the ninth century; a translation of Orosius (*Or*) belongs to the early tenth. In addition we have entries to the Anglo-Saxon Chronicle that range from the end of the ninth to the middle of the tenth centuries. Like the late tenth-century productions of Northumbria, each of these texts offers a large body of data. Several smaller texts, which are comparable in length to all of what survives during earlier periods, comprise the minor witnesses for this variety: late ninth century – Royal genealogies (*Gn*), martyrology fragments (*Mart*); early tenth century – medicinal recipes (*Med*).

Several early texts can be related to the southeast (mostly to the subkingdom of Kent), but none of these texts exhibits the same sort of regularity as found for the Mercian *VPs*, the Northumbrian *Li* (as well as *DurRit*, and *Ru2*) or especially the later texts from Wessex. We have a few charters from the eighth and ninth centuries, but each of these contains records of affairs with either Mercian or West Saxon overlords.

Two poetic texts, the Kentish Psalm (*KtPs*) and the Kentish Hymn (*KtHy*) are found in London, British Library, Cotton Vespasian D. vi, along with some glosses to Proverbs (*KtGl*). Because the language of these texts shares features with Middle English texts which are very clearly Kentish, we are able to reconstruct more about southeastern varieties of Old English than these sparse sources might otherwise allow. In addition, the Codex Aureus (*CA*) contains an inscription recording that 'aldormon' Ælfred gave it to Christ Church, Canterbury; the text can be dated to ca 850 and localised in Surrey. Even if we had several extensive texts which we could localise at Canterbury and date with certainty, we would still have to be cautious about accepting them uncritically as 'Kentish'. The religious community at Canterbury was representative of all England. In fact, during the Mercian hegemony and after, the archbishop of Canterbury was often a man of Mercian origins. We need to remember that kings appointed bishops and were the major source of support for the establishment and maintenance of religious communities. Further contemporary accounts tell that members of religious orders were rather more mobile than we might expect. Records of travel usually include references to large numbers of books that moved with the travellers as loans from monastery to monastery.

The following table summarises the major sources that survive, arranged chronologically and by general geographical area. Minor texts are indicated by parentheses; key texts are in bold face. Probable dates are for the language and are not necessarily the manuscripts, which are often later.

Date	North	Midlands	Southwest	Southeast
675	(*Rune Auzon*)			
700	(*PsScholia, RuthCr*)	(*Ch*), *EpGl*		
725	*Bede*, (*Cæd, BDS*)	(*Ch*)		
750	(*LRid*)	*Bede*, (*Ch*)		(*Ch*)
775		(*Ch, BlGl*), *ErfGl*		(*Ch*)
800		**Corp**		
825		**VPs**, *LorPr, LorGl*		(*Ch*)
850			(*Ch*)	*Ch*, (*Med*)
875			(*Ch, Gn, Mart*)	
900			**CP, ASC**	
925			**Or, ASC**	
950		*RoyGl*	**ASC**, (*Med*)	*Ch, KtHy, KtGl, KtPs*
975	**Ru2, Li, DurRit**	**Ru1**		

Such a display emphasises some of the limits which must be placed on the sorts of pronouncements we are able to make about the nature of early Old English dialects. Firstly, the period is clearly sparsely attested; about a dozen fairly extensive texts spread over nearly three centuries, leaving most of the country unattested most of the time. Only after the middle of the tenth century do we find several varieties represented simultaneously. Secondly, the geographical designations which we invoke must be read in very general terms. When we speak of northern (or Northumbrian) texts, we can not mean a specific area, neither do we speak of a single, homogeneous, or well-defined variety. It is far too easy to assume that when we say something about what northern varieties were like, we are saying something about what southern and southeastern varieties were not. Silence is the best response to the total absence of information about, say, Early East Anglian. Unfortunately our expectations about dialect are too seriously informed by the myth of the 'heptarchy'. While we expect that we should have something to say about Kentish or South Saxon, we have no similar expectation about the tribes that the notion of heptarchy ignores.

As is clear from the table, our statements about English before AD 800 are essentially reconstructions informed by a smattering of information. Even for the best attested periods, the limited number of 'informants' does not make it possible to draw convincing isoglosses. By contrast, the Linguistic Atlas of Late Medieval English, which covers the period AD 1450–1550, has several texts within each of the counties of England. (McIntosh & Samuels, 1986). The mobility of the religious and the lack of precise information for most texts obviate that traditional aspect of dialectology. On the other hand, we can note a clear convergence between the production and survival of texts and political and/or ecclesiastical importance. Since strong kings and strong religious centres yielded the fruits of literacy, we ought to expect that the texts reflect the facts of hegemony and religious influence rather than being merely geographically representative. All in all, the regularities of texts like the *VPs* and *Li* are probably well considered to be nascent moves towards standard written varieties, so clearly well-developed in the Late West Saxon texts.

6.3   Orthographic and phonological variation

There is one advantage for the historical linguist that comes from the paucity of texts. The writing of English in these early times was not so well established that we should assume conventionalised or normalised spelling practices, such as those which currently all but mask differences in pronunciation among the speakers of standard written English. The scribes were not, of course, trained linguists, but their spelling in the absence of the pressures of a standard would be roughly phonetic 'transcriptions' of speech patterns.

By 1900, the study of these texts, and the comparison of them to texts from other Germanic languages, had already resulted in significant patterns of consistency (and difference) among the texts. The data are spelling variants from which historical linguists are able to deduce large scale patterns of pronunciation. Hogg has laid out the overall phonological pattern for Late West Saxon in chapter three above, but a quick summary will be convenient. Orthographic consistencies allow us to assume a system of contrastive vowels based on high/mid/low, front/back, rounded/spread, quantitative long/short distinctions. Similarly, widespread confusion in the spelling of weakly stressed vowels, especially in inflections, suggests the existence of a [ə]-like unstressed vowel.

iː (yː)		uː
i (y)		u
eː (œː)	ə	oː
e (œ)		o
æː		ɑː
æ/a		ɑ/ɒ

The phonetic and phonemic status of the long and short diphthongs (spelled < ea, io, eo >) is one of the most controversial subjects in Old English phonology. Clearly six contrasts (depending on the height and length of the first element) were possible: /æːa, æa, iːo, io, eːo, eo/. Phonetically, Old English may have preserved a height harmony in the second element of the diphthong (as the phonemic values suggest), but wide spread confusion of the second element again suggests [ə]: [æːə, æə, iːə, iə, eːə, eə] (note that < ea > is a rather unusual spelling convention for /æa/).

All of the early Old English dialects had contrasts which drew (but not completely) from this basic set of phonemes. Differences among texts have to do both with chronology and with regional/political influences. Chronologically, for example, the front round vowels slowly disappeared from most dialects (surviving longest in the west) during the period, with the mid vowels going before the high ones. That means that an early text would tend to show some/all of them; while we would expect the unrounded <i> and <e>, or backed <u>, in a late text. The incidence or absence of other vowels often allows a safe guess about provenance. The West Saxon influenced varieties, for example, were distinct in having the vowels written <ie>, representing a series of developments from several sources. In a southeastern text <y>, <oe> and <æ> would be rare, since several processes acted on the sounds written by those graphs to produce sounds regularly spelled <e>. An <o> before a nasal consonant <m, n, ng> is a fairly safe indication of Anglian (Northumbrian or Mercian origin or influence).

Other features are not so easily diagnostic, since they involve a rather complicated interaction of sources, processes and results. Although it may seem complicated at first, what follows is an over-simplification and over-generalization of a great deal of textual diversity. We will shortly have occasion to make some sense of the sort of heterogeneous mix of forms one encounters in the sources. Only seven processes account for most of the phonological differences between the early texts:

(1) West Germanic */a:/ became prehistoric Old English */æ:/, which remained /æ:/ (and is known traditionally as æ[1]) in West Saxon but was raised to /e:/ in all other dialects.

(2) (a) West Germanic */ɑ/ regularly developed to /æ/, but remained /ɑ/ in open syllables followed by a back vowel. Since we find *dagas* (nom. pl for 'day'), we assume that <a> itself was a back vowel, /ɑ/.

(b) In Mercian and Kentish influenced texts, we regularly find this /æ/ raised to /e/, spelled <e>. This latter process is usually called 'the second fronting', even though it involves a raising rather than fronting. Mercian texts also exhibit the effects of a change which is an actual fronting of /ɑ/ to /a/ or /æ/. Since the sound so formed always undergoes a further change, it will be considered below along with other instances of 'velar umlaut'.

(c) Fronted /æ/ was retracted to /ɑ/ in general Anglian texts before [l+C] (not geminated [ll]), and in Northumbrian also before [r+C].

(d)   When the consonant closing the syllable was a nasal or nasal + C cluster, the West Germanic */ɑ/ was written <o> in Anglian (and Anglian influenced) texts (see pp. 438–9 below for a fuller discussion).

(3)   The front vowels, /iː, i, eː, e, æː, æ/, became diphthongs (spelled <io>, <eo>, and <ea> – an orthographic convention for /æɑ/) when they occurred before [x], variously spelled <c, g, h>, or when they occurred before [l + C, r + C].

(4)   In the Anglian varieties (including Anglian influenced Early West Saxon and Kentish texts), the diphthongs so produced were monophthongised, i.e. underwent what is known as 'smoothing'. (See pp. 440–2 below for a fuller discussion of this change.)

(5)   The short, front vowels [i, e, æ] were diphthongised to [iə, eə, æə], written <io, eo, ea>, when they were found in closed syllables before a back vowel, hence the change is known as velar (or back) umlaut. The change is most general in Anglian (especially Mercian) varieties, but common in all late texts (see pp. 440–2 below). West Saxon texts also show velar umlaut of /e/ before labials and liquids and non-low back vowels (<heofon>), but the change is rare before other consonants or before a low back vowel (<nefa>). In Northumbrian texts, /eo/ was commonly written <ea>, whereas in Kentish texts it was often written <io>.

(6)   The unrounding of /yː, y/ usually resulted in <i>, except in the southeast where <e> was the usual graph. In the southwest the sound often remained rounded but was apparently backed as it was written <u>.

(7)   West Saxon texts (and to some extent, Anglian and Kentish texts of the period of West Saxon hegemony) exhibit a further change. Under the influence of an initial palatal consonant [j, ʃ] – spelled <g> and <sc>, the mid and low front vowels /eː, e, æː, æ/ were diphthongised to <ie> and <ea>. This process, common in Northumbrian texts for /æ/ after <sc>, is called palatal diphthongisation.

The following table summarises the effects of the general tendencies by giving possible representative examples:

		West Saxon	Northumbrian	Mercian	Kentish
1	'broke'	brǣcon	brēcon	brēcon	brēcon
2a	'vessel'	fæt/fatas	fæt/fatas		fæt/fatas
2b				fet/(featas)	
2c	'old'	eald	ald	ald	eald
2d	'land'	land	lond	lond	land
3	'light'	lēoht			lēoht
4			lēht	lēht	
5	'seat'	setol	seatol	seotul	(KtGl)setol
6	'evil'	yfel	yfel	yfel	efel
7	'yet'	gīet	gēt	gēt	gēt

Certain inflectional characteristics are related to general dialect associations. In the north, inflectional *n* is lost in infinitives, while third person singular present forms are distinctive in the West Saxon *bint*, as opposed to general *bindeð*. The first and second person accusative pronouns are regularly *mec, usic, þec* and *eowic* in Anglian varieties, against West Saxon *me, us, þe, eow*.

These dialectal features are demonstrated in the following three versions of the Lord's Prayer – the West Saxon version (late eleventh century) is taken from Cambridge, Corpus Christi College 140, the Northumbrian version (late tenth century) from the Lindisfarne Gospel, the Mercian version (early tenth century) from London, British Library, Royal 2. A. XX. The word order in this example does not follow that of the original interlinear glosses but has been rearranged for ease of comparison:

WS fæ[1]der ure þu þe *ea*[2]rt   on h*eo*[3]fonu(m)
No fader urer ðu *a*[4]rt / ðu bist in h*eo*[3]fnu(m) / in heofnas
Mer *fe*[5]der ure þu þe *ea*[2]rt   in h*eo*[3]fenum

WS si þin n*a*[6]ma gehalgod
No s*ie*[7] ðin n*o*[8]ma gehalgad
Mer se þin n*o*[8]ma is gehalgad

WS to bec*u*[9]me þin rīce gewurþe ðin willa
No to cymeð ðin rīc sie   ðin willo
Mer to cyme þin rīce sie   þin willa

WS on *eo*[10]rðan swa swa on h*eo*[3]fonu(m)
No in *eo*[10]rðo suæ is in h*eo*[3]fne
Mer on *eo*[10]rþan swe   in h*eo*[3]fenum

WS ūrne   gedæghwamlican hlāf syle us to dæ[1]g
No   *userne*[13] [ofer wistlic]   hlāf sel ūs todæ[1]g
Mer ur   de[5]ghweamlice   hlāf sele us to de[5]g

WS & forg*y*[11]f us ūre gyltas
No & f(or)gef us *usra*[13] scylda
Mer & forgef us ussa scylda

WS swa swa wē forgyfað   ūrum gyltendum
No su*æ*[1]   u*oe*[12] f(or)gefon usum scyldgum
Mer sw*e*[5] & us for gef   ure scylde

WS & ne gelæd þu us   on costnunge
No & ne inlæd   *usih*[13] in costunge
Mer & nu in læde   is   in costunge

WS ac alys us   of   yfele (Skeat 1874:54)
No ah gefrig *usich*[13] fro[8](m yfle (Skeat 1874:55)
Mer   a les us   fro[8](m yfele (Zupitza 1889:60)

---

[1] General fronting of West Germanic */ɑ/
[2] General breaking of /æ/ before /rC/
[3] Velar umlaut of /e/
[4] Northumbrian retraction of /æ/ before /rC/
[5] Mercian second fronting
[6] Non-Anglian development of West Germanic */ɑ/ before nasals
[7] Non-West Saxon failure of contraction of /i:e/
[8] Anglian development of West Germanic */ɑ/ before nasals
[9] West Saxon retraction of early front round /y/ from i-umlaut
[10] Breaking of /e/ before /rC/
[11] West Saxon /ie/ written <y>
[12] Northumbrian tendency to round /e/ after /w/
[13] Anglian forms of the personal pronouns

6.4   Variation and dialectology

From the data presented so far, this much is clear: some thirteen hundred years ago, Anglo-Saxon scribes began to experiment with writing their own language. Before that, they had only ever written Latin. From those initial experiments, vernacular literacy flourished and developed to the point that it is now a commonplace in English speaking communities. A byproduct of those facts is that contemporary historical linguists have a nearly continuous documentary record of the English language on which to base studies of earlier periods and with which to trace historical developments through an unusually long period of time. Although the later periods of the history of the English language are generally well understood, the critical first periods of literate history remain understudied (especially Pre-Alfredian West

Saxon varieties). Part of the explanation lies with the nature of the data; the documentary record of the first uses of literacy in English is fragmentary. We must rely on a corpus of several thousand words which occur in a wide variety of sources: occasional English names in Latin manuscripts and on coins, English boundaries in Latin charters and wills, sparse interlinear glosses (not extensive before AD 825) in Latin texts, or in the first attempts at making Latin-Old English glossaries. The attestations of English are sporadic, and the survival of manuscripts from those violent times is fortuitous. While the manuscripts themselves survive, their histories are documented for only the last few, most recent centuries. We simply do not know, for example, what percentage of the manuscripts produced have managed to survive. Additionally, we cannot be sure of such facts as when and where a manuscript was written; at whose command, by whom and for what explicit purpose; when, where, and why the English glosses were added. That is, we are bound to have difficulty interpreting these data until we more fully understand the sources of data in relation to their impelling contexts – textual, intellectual, social and political.

Further, our understanding of the earliest varieties of English has been obscured in a large part by some of the analytical methods which have been applied to the data. No practising sociolinguist would be surprised to learn that the earliest English texts reflect extensive linguistic heterogeneity. What would come as a surprise is how that linguistically significant variation has been treated (or, closer to the facts, left untreated). As a consequence of the conflict between narrow assumptions about linguistic regularity and the facts of heterogeneity of living languages, an unnecessary asymmetry exists between the rigid traditional view of the state of early English dialects and the nature of the data found in the texts. The following pages are an attempt to account for and to correct that asymmetry through a review and re-evaluation of the methodological assumptions that determined the direction of previous studies of the earliest Old English dialects. The examples will be drawn from my own work at accounting for linguistically significant variation during the period of the Mercian hegemony. I will offer an alternative interpretation of the earliest non-Northumbrian data, an interpretation which demonstrates patterns of linguistically significant variation and takes into account what we can know of contexts in which the texts were produced.

The first full scale linguistic studies of Old English were philological in method and were attempts to understand the language of individual texts. Each text was reviewed as reflecting a linguistic variety of its own, named by reference to the host manuscript and (when possible) a rough geographical provenance. As Campbell (1959:4n) notes,

> Hick's (*Thesaurus* i., 1705, pp. 87–88) already isolated North[umbrian], for he distinguished the language of the Lindisfarne and Rushworth MS from that of the bulk of the OE texts he knew, and said that the former was used chiefly in the north during the 270 years preceding the Norman Conquest.

The titles of early studies reflect assumptions about the relationship between linguistic variety and source: Lindelöf's *Die südnorthumbrische Mundart des 10. Jarhhunderts: die Sprache der sog. Glosse Rushworth*[2], or Zeuner's *Die Sprache des kentischen Psalters*.

While the neogrammarians had a well developed sense of individual dialects, a dialect like Northumbrian was largely thought of as a loose conglomerate of individual varieties as attested in the extant manuscripts. The tendency was to treat the language of the *DurRit* separately from the language of the Lindisfarne gloss or that of the first part of the gloss to Rushworth. In content, these studies were elaborate, careful and exhaustive catalogues of the early development of each sound which had independently been posited in the reconstruction of the primitive Germanic parent. For example, a whole series of Old English spellings (and presumably sounds) would be described as the development of West Germanic $*/\alpha/$ in the various phonetic environments in which it occurred: OE $<æ>$ (Mercian $<e>$ as the general development in closed syllables); OE $<æ>$ (Mercian $<e>$) in open syllables before front vowels; OE $<a>$ (Anglian $<o>$) as the development before $<n>$, before $<m>$, and clusters with $<m>$ and $<n>$, Anglian OE $<a>$ as the retracted form of fronted $/æ/$ found before consonant clusters beginning with $<l>$ ('broken', that is diphthongised) to $<ea>$ in West Saxon and Kentish); Northumbrian $<a>$ before $<r+C>$ (elsewhere 'broken' to $<ea>$); OE $<a>$ (Mercian $<ea>$) as the restored form of fronted $/æ/$ before back vowels. No unfairness is intended in the summary; I mean only to highlight the fact that this careful proliferation of detail resulted in a highly complex description which made generalisation difficult. This is especially true since even the most minor of deviations (some obviously scribal errors) were noted, and because the nature of the complex relationship between spelling and pronunciation was never investigated in detail. In fact, the major directions of early sound developments are often obscured as simple opening statements to be followed by pages of exceptions. As a consequence, the focus was on sounds as individual units; little regard was paid to the over-all pattern of the system or to patterns of alternation within the system. The very richness of the data, however, was a kind of embarrassment to scholars committed to a theory of perfectly regular sound change. Dialect mixture and analogy were the only terms in which to explain the profusion of variation to be found in Old English texts.

From this rich foundation of data, such scholars as Luick (1914–40), Sievers (1898) and Sweet (1888) – the first great synthesisers in English historical linguistics – built their grammars of Old English. The profound debt of modern Anglo-Saxon scholarship to these pioneer efforts can nowhere more clearly be seen than in Campbell's standard reference work *Old English Grammar*, a careful summary of a century of neogrammarian research. Structural and generative linguists continued the work of synthesis, while focusing their attention on the best attested and most regular varieties of Old English – Late West Saxon (Brunner 1955, Chatman 1958, Hockett 1959, Wagner 1969), Mercian (Kuhn 1939, Dresher 1978, 1980), and general (Kuhn 1961, 1970). Except for Kuhn, these studies are based on summary data drawn from grammars rather than on texts. Since these linguists were also principally concerned with capturing the facts of linguistic homogeneity, these accounts quite understandably do not reflect the facts of prolific variation actually found in the earliest texts. The continued prominence of Campbell's work as the main reference work for Old English phonology is testimony both to his solid achievement and the field's general resistance to innovations in linguistic science. Further the inability of more modern theories to reflect the richness of variation in the data for Old English dialects renders those accounts less than satisfying for the community of Anglo-Saxon scholars.

Current interest in variation is enabling a new generation of linguists to broaden the base of study, to move from the exclusive study of what Anderson (1972) has termed diachronic correspondences to include a closer study of the mechanisms of phonetic change. Historical Germanic philology which began as close attention to detail has come full circle. The energy of our Germanic forbears derived from the discovery of the regularity of sound change; ours, from the correlation of patterns in the ubiquitous variation of living languages to the processes of linguistic change. Some scholars, of course, maintained an interest in phonetic change. Chadwick (1894–99) and Kuhn (1939, 1945, 1961, 1970) are notable among Anglo-Saxonists. As a prelude to contemporary studies, Weinreich, Labov and Herzog (1968) articulated under four general headings the theoretical problems to be considered in the study of language change: the transition problem, the constraints problem, the embedding problem and the actuation riddle. They will serve as useful divisions of the following examples from the variationist analysis of Old English data.

The transition problem: This issue centres on the traditional questions of the regularity and gradualness of sound change. All of the changes to be considered involve alternation and variation within a phonetic class. In addition most have a phonetic environment as at least one of their conditioning factors. That is to say that the changes hold true to at least part of the neogrammarian hypothesis, but they also present interesting questions. Is sound change abrupt or gradual? Several misleading answers to this question have been proposed – especially in the case where writers have been to ready to lump together all varieties of sound change and have failed to discriminate between the ways in which a sound change may be abrupt or gradual. There are at least four levels at which the rate of sound change should be considered: phonological, phonetic, statistical, and lexical. Change of the phonological level is discrete and necessarily abrupt. Additions of surface forms, underlying representations, loss or additions of variable or obligatory rules, etc., cannot be other than abrupt.

Phonetic change can be abrupt or gradual. Old English offers an example of a change that was probably phonetically abrupt. During the Old English period, morpheme initial /hn, hr, hl, hw/ were reduced to initial /n, r, l, (h)w/ with /hw/ remaining in the north and /w/ prevailing in the south (see Toon 1976b). Thus Old English *hnutu*, *hlāf*, *hræfn*, *hwēol* have the modern reflexes *nut*, *loaf*, *raven* and *wheel*, the last with a continuingly variable pronunciation. The loss of such a phonetic segment might have been abrupt. The modern situation would be an example of phonetic abruptness: the [h] is either pronounced or not (or the /w/ is either voiced or voiceless. That is, we do not see a partially devoiced /w/ or some sort of reduced [h]. On the other hand, the phonetic processes reflected in <o> spellings of /a/ before nasal consonants were probably not abrupt. The raising and rounding of /a/ could have been, and probably was, a gradual development through a continuum of vowel space (see Toon 1976a).

There is strong textual evidence that both sound changes were statistically gradual. We can, for example, write the following variable rules to capture the development of /h/ loss in two Anglian texts, the Mercian gloss made by Farmon in the Rushworth Gospels and the Northumbrian gloss to the Lindisfarne gospels. The first rule states the generalisation that [h] is lost variably ($\rightarrow <<\emptyset>>$), in the environment (/___) of a following [n, r, l, w]. Then, it is lost all of the time before [n]; 17 per cent of the time before [r, w], and 25 per cent of the time before [1].

$$
\begin{array}{llll}
 & & & \text{*n} \quad 1{\cdot}00 \\
Ru \quad \text{h} & \rightarrow & <<\emptyset>>/\text{\_\_\_r} & 0{\cdot}17 \\
 & & \text{l} & 0{\cdot}25 \\
 & & \text{w} & 0{\cdot}17 \\
 & & \text{n} & 0{\cdot}33 \\
Li \quad \text{h} & \rightarrow & <<\emptyset>>/\text{\_\_\_r} & 0{\cdot}12 \\
 & & \text{l} & 0{\cdot}07 \\
\end{array}
$$

Statistical graduality (and regularity) can be seen by comparing the following three developments in the nasalised vowel (C_h) is a homorganic consonant). The makers of the Corpus Glossary drew upon many of the same textual traditions as the assemblers of the closely related Epinal and Erfurt Glossaries did. As a result the glosses which *CorpGl* shares with *EpGl* and *ErfGl* are likely to exhibit forms which reflect an older, more conservative state of the language. For these reasons, compare the development as seen in *ErfGl* with both the glosses shared with *CorpGl* and the material unique to *CorpGl*.

Erfurt – ca AD 750

$$
\begin{array}{llll}
 & & \eta & 0{\cdot}60 \\
 & & \text{n} & 0{\cdot}55 \\
\alpha \rightarrow & <<o>>/\text{\_\_} & \text{m} & 0{\cdot}50 \\
 & & \text{n}C_h & 0{\cdot}50 \\
 & & \text{m}C_h & 0{\cdot}30 \\
\end{array}
$$

Corpus – ca AD 800 (shared)

$$
\begin{array}{llll}
 & & \text{n} & 0{\cdot}85 \\
 & & \text{m} & 0{\cdot}85 \\
\alpha \rightarrow & <<o>>/\text{\_\_} & \text{n}C_h & 0{\cdot}50 \\
 & & \eta & 0{\cdot}33 \\
 & & \text{m}C_h & 0{\cdot}0 \\
\end{array}
$$

Corpus – ca AD 800 (unique)

$$
\begin{array}{llll}
 & & \text{*m} & \\
 & & \text{n} & 0{\cdot}75 \\
\alpha \rightarrow & <<o>>/\text{\_\_} & \text{n}C_h & 0{\cdot}75 \\
 & & \eta & 0{\cdot}66 \\
 & & \text{m}C_h & 0{\cdot}66 \\
\end{array}
$$

Of the latter sound change Campbell (1959:51) felt it sufficient to say, 'Erf. and Cp. have both *a* and *o*'. While true, the statement typically regulates heterogeneity to free variation. On the other hand, it is possible to see a frozen reflection of an early phonetic change in progress. That interpretation is strongly supported by the phonetic regularity of the change; we can see the same implicational hierarchy of phonetic environments (excluding the sparsely attested /ŋ/: n > m > nC$_h$ > mC$_h$. The fact that a single variable rule predicts the output for both early texts further argues for the close relationship between them:

$$\alpha \quad \rightarrow \quad <<o>> \quad /\overline{\underline{\text{[+nasal]}}} \quad <+\text{apical}> \, <-\text{seg}>$$

That rule captures the generalisation that [α] variably raises to [ɔ] when nasalised. The raising is favoured by a combination of factors – when followed by a consonant made with the tip of the tongue ([n] is favoured over [m] and [ŋ]) and when the nasal does not occur in clusters.

Wang (1969) has proposed that sound changes can diffuse gradually through the lexicon – a serious challenge to the neogrammarian hypothesis that sound changes are sensitive only to phonetic environment. The Northumbrian development of West Germanic */a/ before nasals offers an extremely important case in point. In all three tenth century Northumbrian glosses to *Li*, *Ru*₁ and the *DurRit*, the sound is always spelled <o> *except* in the preterite singular of class III strong verbs, where it is spelled <a> without exception. This is an important example of constrained lexical diffusion. A single grammatical class accounts for the entire residue of an otherwise completed sound change. But this residue is not unrelated to the earlier resistance, as seen above, to the sound change before homorganic clusters with a nasal. Most of the verbs of strong class III contain a homorganic consonant cluster. We have a lexical class based both on a shared ablaut alternation and a shared phonological environment. The resistance to sound change has been transferred from the phonological environment to the grammatical class. Even the verbs of class III which do not contain a homorganic cluster are resistant to the change (*wann*, *blann*, *ingann*, etc.) while the cluster outside of this grammatical class is subject to the phonological regularity. The resistance has not spread to the other strong verbs; we find the regular phonological development in class VI and preterite present verbs which contain West Germanic */a/ before a nasal, even a nasal homorganic consonant cluster.

The constraints problem: A strong theory of language change would predict the direction of sound change after having established a set of possible changes and having described the sorts of pressures which apply to languages in flux. No such theory, of course, exists, although some work has been done in characterising the types of sound systems which exist in natural languages and in noting the sorts of changes which languages undergo. The results of these attempts to typify the natural and the universal aspects of human language must be taken into consideration when attempting to reconstruct from manuscript data a viable linguistic system. It is worth noting that front rounded vowels, and especially back spread vowels, are much rarer than front spread and back rounded vowels among the languages of the world, though not uncommon among Germanic languages. Languages, however, frequently do unexpected things. English, after all, added a set of high and mid front round vowels resulting in a more highly marked and less natural system (and proceeded to lose them in the next centuries).

The sound changes discussed above can profitably be considered in terms of the general constraints in question. We can notice that /h/ was lost first before /n/ (complete oral closure), next before /r/ and /l/ (substantial lateral and central closure), and only variably before /w/ (minimal oral closure). That is, the loss of /h/, a consonant produced with the oral tract maximally open, is favoured before consonants produced with substantial oral closure. Further, the raising to Germanic */ɑ/ follows the long observed tendency of nasalised vowels to rise. This raising can be seen as the last stage in a chain shift which began in Germanic times and had already affected Germanic */e/ and */o/ and resulted in *niman* and *cuman* by Primitive Old English times.

Old English studies can add to as well as benefit from study of natural and universal tendencies in language. Much of the history of English vowels involves the struggle between the opposing processes of monophthongisation and diphthongisation. Anglian smoothing (a monophthongisation) and velar umlaut (a diphthongisation) have long been documented, but a close examination of the variation in the manuscript data can refine our knowledge of the processes (see Toon 1978a). The velar spirant plays a major role in the operation of these two competing sound changes; it triggers smoothing and inhibits velar umlaut. Labov, Yaeger and Steiner (1972) have identified velar consonants as among those which can change vowel peripherality. Since peripherality is associated with rising and in-gliding vowels, the monophthongising effect of the velar spirant is of interest to historical linguists and students of contemporary sound change alike. The interrelationships of the various elements of smoothing and velar umlaut are summarised in the following table:

	Epinal ca 700	Erfurt ca 750	Corpus ca 800	VPs ca 825
Smoothing of /i:o/	+	+	+	+
Smoothing of /io/	+	+	+	+
Smoothing of /eo/	80	90	+	+
Smoothing of /æa/	60	+	+	+
Smoothing of /æ:a/	60	80	+	+
Velar umlaut of /æ/	50	50	80	+
Smoothing of /e:o/	0	0	70	+
Velar umlaut of /e, i/	0	0	90	+

It is apparent that smoothing was complete by the time of Corpus and well progressed in Epinal, and the differences are, in addition, quantifiable and can be explained chronologically. Further, two general tendencies, of interest to natural phonologists, emerge. Short diphthongs were smoothed before the long ones. Among the short diphthongs, a height hierarchy is to be observed /io > eo > æa/. Such phonetic regularity is hardly random and cannot be dismissed as unmotivated orthographic convention.

Further examination of the data for the short diphthongs shows more clearly the combined effects of environment and vowel height. An intervening consonant diluted the effects of the velar spirant. In Corpus we find only /æa/ unsmoothed and then only unsmoothed in precisely the environment we would have predicted on the basis of the Epinal data, strong evidence that the two texts are closely related linguistically:

Smoothing by environment

		/——— Cx	/——— x
Epinal	/eo/	60	+
	/æa/	30	+
Corpus	/eo/	+	+
	/æa/	55	+

Again a single variable rule accounts for data from both texts; (the off-glide is variably lost before velar sounds in a process favoured by the high vowels and the absence of a consonant between the diphthong and the velar consonant):

$$V_{\mathrm{e}} \quad \rightarrow \ <V> \quad /\overline{\ <+hi>\ } \quad <-\mathrm{seg}> [+\mathrm{velar}]$$

Except for the velar umlaut of /æ/, the product of the second fronting of /a/, the earliest glossaries fail to show evidence of velar umlaut. The sound change, on the other hand, is nearly complete in *CorpGl*. While both /e, i/ undergo velar umlaut at the same overall rate (0·75), significant differences emerge when the data are broken down by environment:

Velar umlaut

	/e/	/i/	/æ/
/—— labials	0·85	1·00	1·00
/—— sibilants	0·80	1·00	1·00
/—— resonants	0·75	0·85	1·00
/—— dentals	0·70	0·65	1·00

For both /e/ and /i/, the same hierarchy holds: labials > sibilants > dentals. The highest weighted environment is, of course, also one of the environments for which the sound change was most general in Old English. The lowest weighted environment was that environment in which velar umlaut developed only in non-West Saxon dialects. It is noteworthy, in view of the resistance of /æa/ to smoothing, that velar umlaut began in the Epinal–Erfurt Glossaries with /æ/ and is complete for /æ/ in the *CorpGl* but still in progress for the higher vowels. Velar umlaut was hindered in the Epinal-Erfurt material before /x/. The same constraint is evident in Corpus for /e, i/; /æ/, however is diphthongised to /æa/ before the velar spirant in that text. The relaxing of the constraint can also be seen in the *VPs* in which velar umlaut of all front vowels is the rule. Although velar umlaut and smoothing were synchronic forces in the same texts, smoothing began earlier and was complete before velar umlaut. It is further advanced than velar umlaut in *EpGl* and *ErfGl*. It was ceasing to be a productive force in the language of the *CorpGl*: /æa/ could develop before the velar spirant. It was obviously not a productive rule in the phonology of the *VPs* scribe, where the newly forced diphthong is never smoothed.

The embedding problem: This aspect of the study of sound change is concerned with the possible loci of linguistic change (see Labov, Yaeger and Steiner 1972): At what abstract level of derivation are innovations implemented? Is linguistic innovation a change in competence or can performance effect changes in competence? Do changes occur in individuals or in communities? Although the larger issues of competence/performance and individual/community are beyond the scope of this study, the sound changes considered here do offer some evidence of the level at which they were embedded into the phonological system of Old English.

Because /o/ when it occurred before nasals had been raised to /u/ in Germanic times, Old English /a/ and /o/ could not be contrastive in prenasal positions. The raising of /a/ to /o/ then involves a subphonemic change; an allophone of /a/ is becoming an allophone of /o/. At the stage of uncertainty between <a> and <o>, the scribes were recording suballophonic variation.

Numerous minimal pairs (see Kuhn 1970) attest a potential Old English phonemic contrast between /n, r, l, w/ and /hn, hl, hr, hw/. Loss of /h/ from *hlaf* 'loaf', for example, would result in [laf] homophonous with *laf* 'remainder'. *Hlaf* and *laf* indeed both occur for 'loaf', and because of scribal uncertainty *laf* is found in the same text as *Hlaf* with an excrescent (etymologically unjustified) /h/. Aldred, the conservative scribe of the Lindisfarne Gospels, gives strong evidence for the phonetic reality of /h/ loss in his speech by writing an incredible number of excrescent <h>'s before /r/ and /l/; for example, *rip* is spelled *Hrip* in all eleven occurrences and *laetmest* is spelled *Hlaetmest* twenty-seven of the thirty-two times it appears. The destruction of minimal pairs and the creation of what ought to be minimal pairs attest that the scribe is representing a subphonemic level in his orthographic habits.

The actuation riddle: Although we can usually come up with a plausible explanation of change after the fact, linguists have not as yet been able to predict precisely when a possible change is going to occur. This generalisation is, of course, particularly applicable to the slow, regular internal sort of change which is typical of language isolation. Change caused by external pressure is quite a different matter. Because of the loose political structure of early Anglo-Saxon England early English dialects must have been in constant contact (and conflict). We can in fact see evidence of the actuation of a linguistic innovation by examining the development of West Germanic */a/ before nasals as reflected in the extant original charters made in Kent (or with Kentish connection) before, during and after the period of Mercian political ascendancy in England (AD 750–825). Four charters antedate Mercian control. The data are scant but unanimous in a forms. Seven texts document the period from AD 800 to 825, and they exhibit only <o> spellings (sixty-four in all), also the predominant form in Mercian charters. Six of these seven manuscripts also contain letter forms unique to *VPs* and other Mercian texts (see Kuhn 1943). Three charters (AD 833–50) attest the state of the language during the first years of the decay of Mercian influence:

Date	Charter	*a*	*o*
833X9	BL, Aug. ii 64	11	40
845X53	BL, Aug. ii 42	0	13
850	BL, Aug. ii 52	10	4

Since the transition was not cataclysmic, these data are what one would expect. Mercian religious would continue to live in Kent, and native Kentish scribes trained under Mercian domination would continue to exert an influence for about one generation (until ca 850), just as similar timelags can be observed after the Norman Conquest. In the late Kentish charters, we find a return to the <a> spelling for West Germanic */ɑ/ before nasals in fully stressed words. Since the change of <a> to <o> is demonstrably tied to Mercian political fortunes and the change is concomitant with the appearance of Mercian orthographic influence, we ought not to dismiss the manuscript heterogeneity as mere dialect mixture. We can, on the other hand, reinterpret this structured variation as an intersection of two separate aspects of the actuation and implementation of a phonetic change: a perhaps natural tendency of a nasalised low vowel to rise (a possible change) and social and political pressure (a reason to change).

Our knowledge of Old English (except for patterns discernable by the methods of comparative and internal reconstruction) is, necessarily, based on the vernacular records which survive. Since the nineteenth century period of extensive close analysis of the early manuscripts, the general linguistic patterns of Old English (mostly phonological) have been codified, and traditional, structuralist and generative study of the language have been based on those abstractions. Thus, after a lifetime of studying Old English, Campbell could still claim (1959:106):

It is accordingly not possible to date any of these sound changes [including the nasal development of *a*, velar umlaut, and smoothing] by observing their gradual appearance in texts and we can establish their approximate date and arrange them in chronological order by theoretical means only.

Variation abounds in the early texts, and it is the contemporary historical linguist's responsibility to determine if that variation is regular (and consequently meaningful) or sporadic and rightly to be ignored.

By now, my position on this question will be clear, but some additional justification is necessary. First, it must be recalled that the texts on which this study is based consist of the first experiments in writing English; scribes of the period were not trained in a system of standardised spellings. Scribes did not, however, invent a writing system *in vacuo*. Indeed, they were familiar with the orthographic/phonological correspondences of Latin and they transferred those habits to the transcription of English. The exercise would be similar in kind to reducing the sounds of American English to a very broad International Phonetics Association transcription; except that the weight of traditional spellings would be absent. Would Americans (especially naive spellers) spell *water* and *butter* phonemically with a medial /t/ rather than noticing the [d]-like quality of the allophone (the same sound which is an allophone of [r] in *berry* for some speakers of RP)? Linguistic contrast is an important fact about how languages operate, and a writing system must be able to convey the important linguistically significant contrasts of its language. But linguistic significance does not reside exclusively in contrasts, and it is not unreasonable to suppose that scribes (unconsciously) recorded their phonetic habits, just as New Yorkers unconsciously monitor the level of [r] loss.

The strongest argument for taking manuscript variation seriously is certainly the facts of the internal structure of that heterogeneity. On those who will reject the orthographic variation as random lies the onus of otherwise explaining those regularities and their close resemblance to kinds of phonetic conditioning being discovered in contemporary studies of sound in progress.

An immediate consequence of taking manuscript data seriously involves a reconsideration of the probable order in which the sound changes occurred. The data provide precisely the 'gradual appearance in texts' which Campbell demands. Campbell offers a summary of traditional scholarly opinion on the ordering of what he calls the prehistoric changes (Campbell 1959:109).

(1)   Anglo-Frisian development of nasal /ɑ:/ and /ɑ/; and of /ǣ²/ and /e:/ from West Gmc */a:/

(2)   West Gmc */ai/ > /a:/

(3)   Fronting of West Gmc */a/ to /æ/

(4)   Breaking and the related processes of retraction

(5)   Restoration of /ɑ/ before back vowels

(6)   Second fronting (mainly VP). Palatal diphthongisation of front vowels, and early diphthongisation of back vowels (mainly WS and Northumbrian)

(7)   *i*-mutation

(8)   Back mutation

(9)   Smoothing

There are several reasons to challenge this ordering. Consistent variation in the early glossaries argues for a later dating of the second fronting. Of the changes listed, items 1 (except for the development of nasal <a>), 2, 3, 4, 5 and 7 are certainly prehistoric; that is, they are represented as complete and without variation in the earliest texts. It has been demonstrated herein that it is an error to lump together all of the smoothing processes. It is further unsatisfactory to suggest a precise linear ordering of the following:

> Raising and rounding of /ɑ/ before nasals
> The various smoothings (usually treated as a unit)
> Second Fronting
> Velar Umlaut

Using *EpGl*, *CorpGl* and the *VPs* as touchstones, the following chart more closely reflects the situation as attested by manuscript variation.

Epinal	Corpus	Vespasian Psalter
ca 700	ca 800	ca 825

smoothing of /io/
    smoothing of /eo/
    smoothing of /æa/
        smoothing of /æ:a/
            second fronting and velar umlaut
                nasal influence on [ɑ]
                    smoothing of /eo/

The mixture of forms which we find in the glossaries, for example, can now profitably be explained as the residue of competing sound changes rather than dismissed as 'dialect mixture'.

The earliest English texts have been studied independently by a variety of scholars: historians, palaeographers, bibliographers, linguists and art historians. There has, unfortunately, been very little integration of these separate studies, and students of the texts consequently hold widely divergent views of their date, provenance, etc. Historical linguists then have not been able to take full account of the nature and ancient uses of the texts around which their pursuits revolve. The earliest glossaries are an excellent example. Written at a time when manuscript production was very costly indeed, we find the best of materials, wide margins, spacious (an uneconomic) hand, and in the case of the *CorpGl* exquisite illuminations. The facts, although a mystery, constitute eloquent testimony to the reverence with which these manuscripts and presumably in this case especially their contents were held. Although we know the sources of the glosses, we still have little idea of how and why the glossaries, especially their often mundane vernacular glosses, were collected. Close examination reveals (in the *CorpGl*) extensive dry point notation and even occasional doodles. Some of the more curious garbled glosses suggest that they were copied from exemplars into which vernacular glosses had been scratched by dry point. The sources, the nature and the purposes of those first attempts to record even occasional words in English are critically important to the study of the state of the language which they record. Why would a literate and learned community benefit from a word-for-word interlinear gloss to the psalms? Is the regularity of the *VPs* gloss, which nearly approaches the regularity of the Late West Saxon literary language, related to the fact that it is inserted in one of the finest manuscript productions of Anglo-Saxon England? The questions and their consequences mount. We will better understand the language recorded within the texts when we know more about the texts themselves.

Old English dialectology to date has been principally geographical, an attempt to assign texts (and their language) strictly to one of four regional varieties – West Saxon, Mercian, Northumbrian or Kentish. Objections have been of two major sorts. First, it has been claimed that the early texts with their high levels of orthographic variation exhibit a level of dialect mixture which precludes assigning them to any one dialect area. Other objections have centred around scholarly attempts to localise manuscripts and insist that the texts are too scant and too loosely assignable in terms of provenance to be the basis of a regional dialectology.

Variation admittedly abound in the texts, but differences have been over-emphasised and important similarities have been ignored. Two general observations are to be made. The following summary of synchronically variable data from *EpGl*, *ErfGl*, *CorpGl* and the *VPs* helps illustrate the first point. Much of variation in the texts can be explained chronologically (see Toon 1975):

	Epinal ca 700	Erfurt ca 750	Corpus ca 800	VPs ca 825
Smoothing of /i:o/	+	+	+	+
Smoothing of /io/	+	+	+	+
Smoothing of /eo/	0·8	+	+	+
Smoothing of /æa/	0·6	+	+	+
Smoothing of /æ:a/	0·6	0·8	+	+
Smoothing of /eo/	0	0	+	+
Gmc /æ/ to /e/	0·8	0·9	0·9	+
PrOE /a/ to /æ/	0·3	0·3	0·3	+
Velar umlaut of /æ/	0·5	0·5	0·8	+
Confusion of /io/, /eo/	0·5	0·5	0·6	+
æ /——— N to /e/	0·3	0·3	0·9	+
Second fronting /æ/	0·2	0·4	0·2	+
Confusion of /i:o/, /e:o/	0·2	0	0·2	+
Raising of nasal /ɑ/	0	0·5	0·7	+
Velar umlaut of /i, e/	0	0	0·9	+

Not only do the sound changes show a general progression toward completion from Epinal to the *VPs*, but the very similar implicational hierarchy of the progress of the changes attests the close relationship between the texts. The minor divergences can be attributed to the fact that not all sound changes proceed at the same rate. The regular, wave-like diffusion of sound developments into this community cannot be attributed to dialect mixture unless dialect mixture be interpreted as a productive force in linguistic change. The term has been invoked in traditional interpretations of Old English to dismiss rather than to explain variation.

This analysis has further demonstrated that the close relationship between these texts can be made even clearer when the synchronic variation in the texts is subjected to close scrutiny. While it is important that the sound changes when viewed abstractly can be seen to be

Sound changes in the minor texts

	Blick. Psalter	Leyden Gloss	Lorica Gloss	Lorica Prayer	Bede Gloss	Codes Aur.	Royal Gloss	Omont Leaf
Smoothing								
of *io*	—	+	—	—	—	+	+	—
of *īo*	—	—	—	—	—	—	—	—
of *eo*	—	+	+	—	+	—	+	—
of *æa*	—	+	—	—	—	+	+	+
of *ǣa*	—	+	+	—	+	+	+	—
of *ēo*	—	—	(0/2)	(1/1)	—	—	(1/2)	+
Gmc *æ* to *ē*	—	+	—	—	+	—	0	+
Velar umlaut of *æ*	—	0	+	+	+	+	+	+
io to *eo*	—	0	+	+	—	+	+	+
æ/——N to *e*	—	+	—	+	—	+	—	0
Second fronting	(1/2)	0·6	0	1/1	+	—	+	0
īo to *ēo*	—	0	0	+	+	0	+	+
a/——N to *o*	+	0·7	+	+	+	+	+	+
Velar umlaut of *i, e*	—	—	0·7	+	+	—	+	+
æ to *e*	+	—	—	—	—	—	—	0
ǣ to *ē*	(2/3)	—	(0/1)	(0/2)	—	(1/3)	+(2/2)	—

progressing regularly toward completion, it is even more important for a systematic analysis that the language of the individual texts not be dismissed as a random admixture of forms. The variable texts demonstrate the phonetic regularity of the synchronic states. The regularity is especially evident when the rules for the separate texts are placed together. The interaction of second fronting of Primitive Old English */a/ and its subsequent velar umlaut both follow a progression which logically would culminate in the language of the *VPs*, then, form a continuum against which the remaining texts of this study may be viewed. The table above, arranged roughly chronologically from left to right, summarises the developments in the Minora of the sound changes which are synchronic in the early texts. The data from these sources are, of course, extremely scant, and there are large gaps in this table. They do however offer a glimpse into an otherwise unrecorded period. Of these texts, *BlGl*, *LorPr* and *RoyGl* do not depart from the language of *VPs*. Since both *LorPr* and *RoyGl* derive from manuscripts with western connections, their language argues for a westerly provenance or dominant influence in the scribe of the *VPs* gloss. The only other clearly localisable text is the *Codex Aureus* (*CA*) inscription; it shows the variety of Mercian Old English to have been found in

Surrey. The Leiden Glossary is a Germanised corruption of the continental glossary tradition best preserved in the *EpGl* and *ErfGl*. The remaining texts, to varying degrees, exhibit some of the changes which are synchronic in the major Mercian texts. Because of the very nature of Mercian political control (overlords ruling subkings), one would not expect to find total diffusion of Mercian speech characteristics throughout all of England. It is certainly telling that Mercian features are most heavily concentrated in western manuscripts.

R. M. Wilson (1959), while agreeing that the psalter (and its related texts) 'shows no distinctively Northumbrian, Kentish, or West Saxon forms', claims 'it does not follow from this that it must be Mercian'. For him, our knowledge of early Old English dialects is too scant to make any such designation. The texts, he argues, cannot be precisely located and might be from East Anglia, Essex or Sussex rather than from Mercia. His argument fails on several points. First, even if the texts did originate outside of Mercia proper, they were certainly produced during the period of Mercian political ascendancy. Some sociolinguistic perspective is needed at this point. All of the early Old English texts (including the charters) were produced by a small subsegment of the linguistic population. We will never know how the non-literate Anglo-Saxons spoke, but we do have an accurate record of how changes in speech influenced those who experimented in writing English. Not only were the educated a small minority, they were also all products of (or closely related with) the great religious houses of Anglo-Saxon England. One need only look at the lists of abbots and bishops to discover that Mercian kings appointed Mercians to positions of authority. It is likely therefore that the speech of the religious tended towards the prestigious variety of the Mercian overlords, abbots and bishops. The presence of Mercian letter forms and linguistic forms has been abundantly documented in the so-called 'Kentish' charters of the Mercian period. Wilson further rejects the term 'Mercian' because he expects there to be only one variety of Mercian. He demands a linguistic homogeneity atypical of viable speech communities, especially communities which are joined by loose political bonds. If a text is non-Northumbrian, non-West Saxon and non-Kentish *and* written when Mercian kings were in control, it seems sensible to consider its language to represent part of the Mercian linguistic continuum. In addition, the very similar *EpGl*, *ErfGl*, *CorpGl* and *VPs* are extremely close linguistically to both the *LorPr* and *RoyGl* the texts of which have clear associations with the West Midlands. Since the occurrence of Mercian features (phonological and orthographic) rises and falls in the charters with Mercian political fortunes, one has every reason to consider the texts representative of heterogeneity in the Mercian speech community.

If we can accept the notion of a political, social, roughly chronologically sensitive Old English dialectology, early manuscript variation will cease to be a source of confusion. More importantly, that variation and the data provided by twelve hundred years of nearly continuously attested language variation and change can become an important tool from which modern linguistic science can learn more of the nature of language change and language variation and with which it can test the theories which it proposes to relate the two.

FURTHER READING

There is, unfortunately, no full-scale study of Old English dialects such as exists for Middle English and present-day English. The standard handbooks such as Campbell (1959) and Brunner (1965) give an overview of the situation in each dialect as it pertains to phonology and morphology. Of these Brunner is particularly full, whilst Campbell has an extremely useful bibliography of individual studies of dialect material. For the study of dialect variation in vocabulary the most important recent study is Wenisch (1979), a monograph more wide-ranging than its title suggests. Syntactic variation between dialects has scarcely been studied and in any event the material is relatively meagre.

Current linguistic theory has yet had little impact on Old English dialect study, although Toon (1983) is a substantial monograph and Hogg (1988) a shorter article, both attempting to present a revised view of the dialect situation in the light of recent sociolinguistic theory.

7 ONOMASTICS

Cecily Clark

7.1 General principles

7.1.1 *The special status of names*

Naming, although semantically a specialised function, in other respects forms part of the everyday language. Phonemic material has to be the same, and to follow dialectal and chronological paths that are related, albeit not invariably identical. The morpho-syntactic features of names must fit with general ones. Lexical material and modes of word-formation too must reflect those of the language at large. Indeed, place-names normally start as plain descriptions of the sites concerned: e.g. *Kingston* < *cyninges tūn* 'the king's estate', *Pyrford* < *(æt) pyrigan forda* '(the settlement at) the ford by the pear-tree' (*PN Surrey*: 59, 132; illustrative examples will usually be given in normalised rather than documentary form). Personal names, although less transparently motivated, likewise ultimately derive from elements of common language.

Before becoming truly a 'name', a descriptive formation must, however, be divorced from its etymological meaning in such a way that the sound-sequence, no matter how complex its structure or plain its surface-meaning, becomes a simple pointer; 'one might claim that unintelligible names fulfil their role more directly' (Gardiner 1940; Nicolaisen, in Gelling *et al.* 1970:14). *Bath*, as a place-name, coincides in form with the common noun, and awareness survives of the Roman baths that it commemorates; but, for all that, the name's everyday 'meaning' is independent of etymology. Such independence is clearer still with names which, like *London*, have, since records began, apparently been opaque to their users (Rivet and Smith 1979:396–8). So, likewise with personal names: *Philip* means 'horse-lover', and as a

Christian name it recalls an Apostle; but few present-day choosers and bearers of it seem much concerned either with etymology or – at all events in present-day England – with biblical associations.

Once semantically emptied, names draw partly aloof from the language at large. Although the phonological tendencies that affect them cannot be alien to those bearing on common vocabulary, the loss of denotation allows development to be freer, with compounds obscured and elements blurred and merged earlier and more thoroughly than in analogous 'meaningful' forms. Sound-developments seen in names may therefore antedate or exceed in scope those operating elsewhere in the language; and this makes any use of name-material for study of general or dialectal phonology an exercise requiring caution (cf. Hogg 1982a: 188, and also above chapter 3). Morphosyntactically too, names stand apart. Being by nature 'definite', they take in normal English usage neither an indefinite article nor a definite one; an English name-form qualified by either sort of article is part-way towards reverting to common noun (cf. Gardiner 1940:17–19). Only exceptionally can any name be pluralised. Place-names further differ from other classes of substantive by often showing an oblique-case form ousting the original nominative (see below pp. 476–7).

7.1.2   Source-materials

The sources for early name-forms, of people and of places alike, are, in terms of the conventional disciplines, ones more often associated with 'History' than with 'English Studies': they range from chronicles through Latinised administrative records to inscriptions, monumental and other. Not only that: the aims and therefore also the findings of name-study are at least as often orientated towards socio-cultural or politico-economic history as towards linguistics. This all goes to emphasise how artificial the conventional distinctions are between the various fields of study.

Thus, onomastic sources for the OE period include: chronicles, Latin and vernacular; *libri vitae*; inscriptions and coin-legends; charters, wills, writs and other business-records; and above all Domesday Book. Not only each type of source but each individual piece demands separate evaluation.

For late OE name-forms of both kinds Domesday Book (DB) is the prime source; for many place-names, those from the North especially, it furnishes the earliest record extant (the Phillimore edition is recommended for everyday use; current scholarly opinions are collected in Sawyer 1985 and Holt 1987). DB proper consists of two volumes (recently rebound as five), always part of the state archives and now housed in the Public Record Office, wherefore they are together known as the 'Exchequer Domesday'. The two sections are, it must be emphasised, of different standing: 'Little DB', which deals with Norfolk, Suffolk and Essex, represents a redaction earlier and fuller – therefore more useful to onomasticians – than that of 'Great DB', which deals with the rest of the Conqueror's English realm. There are also various related records, usually known as 'satellites', some (like Exon DB) official, others private (see, for instance, H. B. Clarke in Sawyer 1985:50–70); on matters ranging from administrative procedure to orthography, these supplement the information given by the Exchequer volumes. Although DB as it stands results from a survey undertaken in 1086, roughly half the material there dates back to pre-Conquest times. Based as they were upon enquiries made by several panels of commissioners who collected documentary as well as oral evidence and interrogated alike French-speaking post-Conquest settlers and survivors of the pre-Conquest land-holding classes, the extant DB texts, in which the commissioners' returns have to varying degrees been recast, need careful handling. At the orthographical level, basic to onomastic study, they are notoriously unreliable. For one thing, not all the scribes used the traditional OE orthography (see von Feilitzen 1937:34–139, Sawyer 1956, Clark 1984a and 1984b, and Dodgson 1985). For another, working conditions were unpropitious: name-material, unlike common vocabulary, cannot be predicted from context, and so the DB clerks, interpreting utterances of witnesses from varied linguistic backgrounds, sometimes perhaps toothless ancients, and editing drafts that bristled with unfamiliarities, were liable to mishear, misread, misunderstand, miscopy or otherwise mangle the forms. Only lately has appreciation of the types and degrees of scribal error in DB made progress enough for former broad assumptions – for instance, about 'Anglo-Norman influences' – to be gradually replaced by recognition of specific auditory and visual confusions.

With the other kinds of administrative record – for the OE period, mainly wills, land-grants and manumissions – each item, as well as each category, needs individual assessment (Stenton 1955; Sawyer 1968; Brooks 1974; Rumble 1984). Some documents survive only in cartularies compiled up to eight centuries later than the original; and no cartulary copy, however reliable as to matters of fact, can be trusted orthographically. Even when extant in authentic contemporary form, documents drafted in Latin give vernacular elements in Latinised spelling. Names taken from every such source therefore need analysis in the light of the scribal practice and the textual history of the document in question. Apart from all this, not all records are, as yet, available in texts usable by the non-expert; adequate presentations of many charters will remain lacking until the British Academy's series of archive-based editions is completed (see Cheney's preface to Campbell 1973). These caveats are important, because charters, and especially the sections of them setting out in the vernacular the boundaries of the estates conveyed, are central to place-name study (see below p. 471).

The two pre-Conquest *libri vitae*, or confraternity-books, from Durham Cathedral and from Hyde Abbey, Winchester (Thompson 1923; Birch 1892), are rich sources of personal-name forms; but they pose problems of structure and of dating as well as of scribal practices. Because a *liber vitae* was constantly receiving additions, often over many centuries, criticism of it must begin by the dating of its strata, an exercise in which palaeography has to be supplemented by prosopography, that is, identification of the individuals enrolled (cf. the discussions of the twelfth-century Thorney one in Clark 1985a and b). All too often, names are entered without indication as to the rank or nationality of their bearers.

Chronicles present names of both kinds in context, occasionally even with contemporary comments; but, as onomastic sources, they are comparatively thin and essentially random in coverage. However, in so far as there survives from the early OE period no record that even approaches the scope of DB, by far the finest source for seventh-century naming is Bede's *Historia ecclesiastica*, compilation of which dates from ca 731 (Colgrave and Mynors 1969).

Inscriptions containing names, personal ones for the most part, occur on objects that range from crosses and church walls to combs and rings. With runic materials, need for expertise is self-evident (see, for instance, Page 1973); nor is it less urgent with non-runic ones, surviving examples of which – some in Latin, some in Old English – date from ca AD 700 on and are of widely varying, often unknown, provenances (Okasha 1968). Late OE coin-legends are, by contrast, localisable and also in the main datable to within three years, but their authentification and epigraphic criticism demand skills that only a few philologists possess (Smart 1979 and Colman 1984:96–108). The special value of moneyers' names lies in their representing a social class otherwise virtually invisible at this period.

7.2 Anthroponymy

7.2.1 The West-Germanic inheritance

Early Germanic custom required that each individual should have a single, distinctive name (Woolf 1939; cf. Longnon 1886–95). The system was therefore geared to constant provision of fresh forms. For students of it, the first problem is one of terminology: in this context, 'forename' and 'first-name' become meaningless, 'baptismal name' and the artificial 'font-name' are both inapplicable to pagan tradition, and 'Christian name', as well as also being inapplicable, will later be needed for a different sense. The term 'personal name' favoured for this purpose by some scholars is over-general, because 'by-names' and family-names are no less 'personal'. For convenience, the terminology adopted here will be knowingly inconsistent: simply to distinguish anthroponym from toponym, 'personal name' will be used, but where greater precision is needed the technical term 'idionym' will be brought in. A supplementary name of whatsoever kind – genealogical, honorific, occupational, locative or characteristic – collocated with an idionym will be called a 'by-name' (see below pp. 469–70). The term 'nickname' will denote any characterising term whether used as by-name or as idionym (see below pp. 460–1, 465 and 470).

The requisite variety was achieved by having a stock, not of ready-made names, but of 'themes' (elements) from which names were formed. A single theme could be used, making what scholars call a 'monothematic' name (see below p. 459). More characteristically, themes were linked in pairs to make 'dithematic' names, such as OE *Ælf-rīc* and *Wulf-stān*, with permutation – e.g. to *Ælf-stān, Wulf-rīc* – providing the flexibility that the system needed.

The only Old English onomasticon (name-dictionary) so far compiled is unreliable (Searle 1897; see especially von Feilitzen 1976b). Coverage by extant records is not in any case balanced geographically, chronologically or socially. The best course may be to focus initially on a single corpus. The earliest conveniently accessible is that represented in Bede's *Historia*, which offers a stock of 215 names, mainly aristocratic ones, two-thirds being dithematic (Ström 1939, which gives probably the fullest account available in English of name-themes, also Anderson

1941). Between eighty-five and ninety name-themes are found here (obscurities make an exact total impossible), a dozen both as 'prototheme' (first element in a compound) and as 'deuterotheme' (second element), beside more than fifty figuring only as prototheme and twenty only as deuterotheme. Elsewhere, a score at least of items here confined to one position appear regularly in both; but greater variety of prototheme than of deuterotheme is general.

Personal-name themes were based upon roots also used for forming nouns and adjectives (see, for instance, Woolf 1939 and Schramm 1957). Of the almost ninety themes seen in the Bedan stock, over seventy are paralleled in continental West-Germanic (CWGmc) usage, and some two-thirds of these also in Scandinavian (Scand.); only a handful are paralleled in Scand. usage but not in CWGmc. Semantic classification is revealing. Recurrent concepts and typical Bedan name-themes include: nobility and renown – *Æðel-* 'noble', *Beorht-/-beorht* 'radiant', *Brego-* 'prince', *Cūð-* 'renowned', *Cyne-* 'royal', *-frēa* 'lord', *-mǣr* 'renowned', *Torht-* 'radiant'; national pride – *Peoht-* 'Pict', *Swǣf-* 'Swabian', *Þēod-* 'nation', *Wealh-/-wealh* 'Celt' and probably *Seax-* if meaning 'Saxon'; religion – *Ælf-* 'supernatural being', *Ealh-* 'temple', *Ōs-* 'deity'; strength and valour – *Beald-/-beald* 'brave', *Cēn-* 'brave', *Hwæt-* 'brave', *Nōð-* 'boldness', *Swīð-/-swīð* fem. 'strong', *Þrȳð-/-þrȳð* fem. 'power', *Weald-/-weald* 'power'; warriors and weapons – *Beorn-* 'warrior', *-bill* 'sword', *-brord* 'spear', *Dryht-* 'army', *Ecg-* 'sword', *-gār* 'spear', *Here-/-here* 'army', *Wulf-/-wulf* 'wolf; warrior', and perhaps *Seax-* if meaning 'dagger'; battle – *Beadu-*, *Gūð-/-gȳð* fem., *Heaðu-*, *Hild-/* *-hild* fem., *Wīg-*, and also *Sige-* 'victory' (limitations of function apply only to the Bedan evidence). Peace (*-frið*), prudence (*Rǣd-/-rǣd* 'counsel'), and defence (*Bōt-* 'remedy', *Burg-/-burg* fem. 'protection', *-helm* 'protection' and *-mund* 'protection') are more sparingly invoked. In compound names, protothemes appear in stem-form. Inflections are added only to the deuterothemes; when not Latinised, masc. names follow the *a*-stems and fem. ones the *ō*-stems.

Name themes thus largely parallel the diction of heroic verse (Schramm 1957, also Barley 1974). Kindred elements in the diction of *Beowulf* include common items such as *beorht*, *cēne*, *cūð*, poetic ones such as *brego* and *torht*, and also, more strikingly, compounds like *frēawine* 'lord and friend', *gārcēne* 'bold with spear', *gūðbeorn* 'battle-warrior', *heaðomǣre* 'renowned in battle', *hildebill* 'battle-blade', *wīgsigor* 'victorious in battle' (cf. chapter 7). Parallels must not be pressed; for rules of formation differed and, more crucially, such 'meaning' as name-compounds possessed was not in practice etymological. Name-themes might, besides, long out-live related items of daily, even literary, vocabulary: non-onomastic Old English usage shows no cognate of the feminine deuterotheme *-flæd* 'beauty' and, as cognates of *Tond-* 'fire', only the mutated derivatives *ontendan* 'kindle' and *tynder* 'kindling wood'. Resemblances between naming and heroic diction nonetheless suggest motivations behind the original Germanic styles: hopes and wishes appropriate to a warrior society, and perhaps belief in onomastic magic (Ström 1939:xxxvii; Schramm 1957:7–10; Sonderegger 1984).

The combining of themes into compounds was ruled by onomastic, not semantic, choice. Despite the lack of 'family-names' in the modern sense, kinship-marking was a main motive behind old Germanic naming (Stenton 1924:168–9; Woolf 1939). Thus, royal genealogies, whose partly mythical character makes them likely to show idealised forms, regularly exhibit runs of alliteration, as in the West Saxon sequence: *Cerdic, Cynric, Ceawlin, Cuða, Ceadda, Cenbeorht, Ceadwalla* (*Chron*(A), s.a. 685, cf. 597, 674, 676, 855, and genealogical preface, see also Dumville 1986; this probably bears upon early OE perception of sounds denoted by <c>). Study of familial theme-permutation is hindered by the under-representation in medieval records generally of women's names, which in the Bedan corpus, for instance, amount to under a seventh of the total (cf. Boehler 1930). An ideal, often-cited, instance concerns St Wulfstan, born ca 1008 as son of Æðel*stan* and *Wulf*gifu (Darlington 1928:4); but rules and incidence remain in general unclear. Often, but not necessarily, a man's name shared an element with his father's, and consequently also with those of his brothers (Tengvik 1938:139–232; Woolf 1939; esp. 97–135). Less often (as far as extant records show) a man's name, like St Wulfstan's, incorporated an element from his mother's, possibly at the same time from his maternal grandfather's (cf. Woolf 1939:101, 105, 118, 131–2).

Women's names certainly participated in the permutation system, as when King *Herer*ic of Deira and his queen Brego*swið* called a daughter *Hereswið* (Colgrave and Mynors 1969:406, 410; cf. Boehler 1930:197–205). Their elements therefore differed little from those used in men's names (cf. Schramm 1957:120–43). Protothemes were mostly common to both genders, except for one or two, such as *Cwēn-* 'queen' and *Mann-*, for which that was plainly inappropriate (Boehler 1930; 178–87); as for the apparent absence from women's names of certain others, under-recording leaves its significance uncertain. Distinction lay mainly in deuterothemes: substantival ones took conventional genders, not always those of the related common nouns; adjectival ones, potentially adaptable either way, were in Old English usage arbitrarily assigned to a single gender (Boehler 1930:171–2, 188–92). As lists given have implied, semantic considerations played small part: substantival fem. deuterothemes included *-gȳð* and *-hild*, both meaning 'battle'; adjectival ones included *-swīð* 'strong' but not, in Old English, *-beorht* 'radiant'. An Old English personal name's 'meaning' – in so far as it had one – chiefly concerned 'the family and line to which its bearer belonged' (Ström 1939:xxxvii).

As noted, about a third of the Bedan name-corpus consists of non-dithematic forms, the historian's own being one (Ström 1939:xlii–xliii, 63; cf. Redin 1919 and also Boehler 1930:206–39). The picture that such names present is partly obscure (cf. Redin 1919:xli–xliii).

One type consists of 'monothematic' forms: based, that is, upon single themes, sometimes extended by a suffix. A well-known simplex form with strong inflection is the fem. *Hild*, borne by a seventh-century abbess. Typical weak ones are masc. *Brorda* and *Ead(d)a*, fem. *Bēage* and *Gode*. The suffixes involved are mainly diminutives in /k/ and /l/, as in *Baduca* < *B(e)adu*, *Berhtel* < *Beorht-*, and so on. The late Old English period also saw widespread use of a masc. *-ing* probably transferred, with diminutive implications, from patronymic use: thus, *Dēoring*, *Lēofing* (also an umlauted *Lyfing*), *Ording*, and so on (for the patronymic, see below p. 469). How far formations of these sorts represented shortenings, more precisely 'hypocoristics' (pet-forms), of dithematic ones is unclear. Confirmatory pairings are scarce; but DB uses fem. *Gode*, Latinised as *Goda*, for the Confessor's sister, elsewhere called *Godgifu*, and Exon DB shows *Winus* as corresponding to the Exchequer text's *Vluuinus* for *Wulfwine* (von Feilitzen 1937:263, 415, also 17). The homilist Wulfstan's choice of *Lupus* as his pen-name might imply that familiarly he was called *Wulf*, but that is speculation.

Clearly documented hypocoristics often show modified consonant-patterns (Redin 1919:xxix–xxxvii, cf. Stenton 1924:172–4). Thus, the familiar form *Saba* (variant: *Sæba*) by which the sons of the early-seventh-century King Sæbeorht (*Saberctus*) of Essex called their father showed the first element of the full name extended by the initial consonant of the second, in a way perhaps implying that medial consonants following a stressed syllable may have been ambisyllabic (Colgrave and Mynors 1969:152 and Ström 1939:76; cf. ch. 3 above). In the Germanic languages generally, a consonant-cluster formed at the element-junction of a compound name was often simplified in the hypocoristic form to a geminate, Old English examples including the masc. *Totta* < *Torhthelm*, the fem. *Cille* < *Cēolswīð*, and also the masc. *Beoffa* apparently derived from *Beornfrið* (Redin 1919:xxix–xxxvii, 70–1; Boehler 1930:215, also 234–9; von Feilitzen 1968:7; and, for continental-Germanic equivalents, Kaufmann 1965:11–16).

Many non-dithematic names are best etymologised as 'nicknames', that is, characterising phrases taken from common vocabulary (cf. below p. 470). Bedan forms of such kind include *Blæcca* 'the black (-haired) man', showing the 'weak' (definite) declension typical of adjectival nicknames, and also, if accepted as historical rather than mythical, *Hengist* 'stallion' (Ström 1939:65, 70). Other originally substantival forms – in these instances, probably metaphorical – include *Bucca* 'the he-goat', *Crawa*/fem. *Crawe* 'the raven' and *Flint* 'stone' (Redin 1919:74; Boehler 1930:12; von Feilitzen 1937:16–18, 210, 219, 251). Some scholars gloss over the distinction between 'single-element' names of this sort and 'monothematic' ones of the 'heroic' type; but, although ambivalences occur, with forms like masc. *Beald* and fem. *Gode* explicable either way, in principle the conventional and the characterising types are distinct.

To complicate matters, compound nickname-forms also occur. They range from *bahuvrihi* formations – that is, adjective + noun compounds used attributively, like *Brūnlocc* '(the person with) brown hair' – to descriptive phrases in *-ceorl, -cild, -hyse, -mann, -wīf, -wine*, such as can be characteristic like *Glædmann*/*-wine* 'the cheerful man' and *Ealdwīf* 'the old woman', locative like *Centwine* 'the man from Kent' and *Stapolwine* 'the man who lives beside the pillar (or, at Stapleford)', or occupational like *Glīwmann*/*-wine* 'the minstrel' (von Feilitzen 1937:14–16, 210, 214, 261–2, 369, 372–3; cf. Seltén 1972:19–22). The fact that *-mann* and *-wine* belong also to the 'heroic' system complicates analysis. Furthermore, their apparent 'meaningfulness' notwithstanding, such nickname-forms may have come to be bestowed directly as idionyms, for familial rather than semantic reasons; and they might have been a source from which fresh themes – like *Brūn-, Blæc-* – were adopted into the permutation system.

There remain a few names not obviously either thematic or descriptive: e.g. *Dudd(a)*/fem. *Dudde*, with the masc. derivatives *Duddel, Duduc, Dudecil, Duducol* and *Dudding* (Redin 1919:16, 62–3, 115, 126, 140, 149, 150, 152–3, 169–70 – all classified as 'unintelligible'; cf. Boehler 1930:216 and von Feilitzen 1937:223–5). Whether to etymologise such forms as having originally been nicknames based upon roots not certainly represented in common vocabulary or else as simple 'Lall-forms' initiative of childish babbling remains open to discussion.

How far Old English personal-naming reflected social stratification can never be fully determined, because for this period the only styles adequately recorded are those of the upper-class men named in chronicles, charter-attestations, the 1066 stratum of DB and so on. Peasants' names seldom appear except in manumission-lists and occasional wills. And, for all classes, records of women's names are relatively rare.

The frequent assertion, based upon witness-lists to royal diplomas, that after ca 900 upper-class naming became narrowly stereotyped (Redin 1919:184–9; Stenton 1924:176–7) is not wholly borne out by comparison between the Bedan names and those of landholders in 1066. Assessment of the latter is admittedly more complex, owing partly to phonological as well as orthographical uncertainties, partly to problems of distinguishing native forms from ones borrowed from Scandinavian and continental West-Germanic stocks (see below pp. 465–8 and 464–5, and cf. Clark 1987b:10–14), and partly also to difficulties in reckoning the exact number of landholders listed. As far as the name-stock is concerned, the dithematic forms found in the 1066 stratum of DB are based on about eighty-two themes, of which twenty-three (as compared with twenty Bedan ones) figure only as deuterotheme (*-ceorl*, *-cild*, *-hyse*, *-sunu* and *-wīf* being here excluded as uncertainly thematic), forty-two (B, fifty) only as prototheme, and seventeen (B, twelve) in either position. Although neither sample can be taken fully to represent contemporary usages, it is no accident that in detail the recorded stocks differ, with deuterotheme usages similar but only half the protothemes in common. Even with allowance for the greater number of name-bearers represented in DB, overall variability seems little reduced. Some change of custom has none the less taken place: the fairly even seventh-century frequency-pattern has given way to a markedly uneven one, with many names occurring just once or twice but a particular few, such as *Ælfrīc*, *Godrīc*, *Godwine*, *Lēofwine* and *Wulfrīc*, having each a multitude of bearers distinguished from one another by by-names (a similar pattern appears in the names of Suffolk peasants of probably ca 1100: see Clark 1987b:11). This development parallels those seen in continental West-Germanic communities (Aebischer 1924; Beech 1974).

With non-dithematic names also, some late Old English changes of fashion may have taken place. Among tenth- and eleventh-century charter-attestations 'short' names, such as account for about a third of the Bedan corpus, are rare; and at one time this made it an article of faith that such a form cannot, unless early, refer to a noble: a point crucial to the dating of place-names whose 'specifics' (first elements) consist of such forms. For all periods and classes, however, allowance must be made for interchange between formal and informal styles, and also for purely documentary conventions (see Fellows-Jensen and von Feilitzen in Voitl 1976:48–9, 57–8). In fact, the names in the 1066 stratum of DB – all belonging to landholders, although not all to great nobles – include not only many short-forms but also a good few non-heroic, nickname-type compounds (von Feilitzen 1937:14–18).

As for peasants, genealogies of, for instance, some attached ca 1000 to estates in Hatfield, Herts., show their name-patterns as partly resembling those of nobles, with 'heroic' dithematic names frequently borne by both sexes and with family-links marked by alliteration and theme-permutation (Rumble 1984:50 and Pelteret 1986). Short-forms are not uncommon here, ranging from probable nickname-forms such as *Hwīta*/fem. *Hwīte* 'the white(-haired) man/woman' to the obscure *Dudda*/fem. *Dudde*. The sparse pre-Conquest records may, with caution, be supplemented by the ampler early post-Conquest ones. The Bury St Edmunds survey of probably ca 1100, for instance, shows peasants as mainly bearing commonplace dithematic names, with just a scattering of short-forms, sometimes obscure ones: a greater frequency of short-forms among patronymics might reflect either a recent rejection of such styles or else, perhaps more probably, a differing mode of reporting by-names (Clark 1987b:11). Several collections have been published of OE name-forms surviving among post-Conquest peasantry (e.g. von Feilitzen 1945, Reaney 1953 and Seltén 1979); but their usefulness is limited not only by exclusion of short-forms and concentration on rarities but also by indifference to familial and geographical contexts. One thing that the evidence, such as it is, does suggest is that, even with purely native OE elements, attention to distribution will certainly reveal regional fashions.

7.2.2   Minor outside influences

The fourth- and fifth-century Germanic settlers in Britain borrowed from the language of the Romanised Celts whom they found there 'a large number of place-names, some personal names, and a very few common nouns' (Jackson 1953:194). At one time the paucity of these last in literary Old English seemed to tell against cultural contact, but now archaeological revelation of interlocking settlement-patterns puts matters in a new light (e.g. Salway 1981:461, 559–62, 610–11, and Myres 1986:87–9, 96–103). Personal-name evidence, thin though it is, seems compatible with the sort of contact the archaeological findings suggest (for place-name evidence, see below pp. 479–81).

The name *Cædmon* borne by the father of English religious verse represents a Welsh reflex of British **Catumandos* (Jackson 1953:244; British *Catu-* is cognate with OE *Heaðo-* 'battle'); and its form suggests a structural compatibility between Celtic and Germanic types of name (cf. Evans 1967:40–2, and esp. 171–5). Despite his English cultural identity, Cædmon might, as an ox-herd, be supposed descended from an enslaved people. However, British names also appear among English royalty, including, for instance, the *Cerdic* (Welsh *Ceredig* < British **Coroticos*), *Ceawlin*, *Ceadda* and *Ceadwalla* (Welsh *Cadwallen*) found in the Early West Saxon genealogies (Jackson 1953:244, 554, 613–14; cf. Coates 1987). The element *Cæd-/Cead-* reappears in the names of two seventh-century brothers, both bishops, *Cedd* and *Ceadda* (Anderson 1941:69–70 and Jackson 1953:554). The name *Cumbra* (Redin 1919:91) current among West-Saxon nobility represents Welsh *Cymro* < British **Combrogos* 'Welshman'. Taken with the story of Vortigern's invitation (Colgrave and Mynors 1969:48, cf. Salway 1981:471–4 and Myres 1986:109–10, 114, 122) and with the archaeological evidence mentioned, such names imply that the first settlers arrived pacifically, perhaps married into Romano-British nobility, and sometimes named their sons in compliment to their hosts (cf. Myres 1986:146–52). Assuming any such names necessarily indicate British blood would go well beyond the evidence; but their adoption by English royalty must mean respect for Celtic traditions.

Similar implications attach to some OE name-themes. The theme *Peoht-* in use among Northumbrian nobles meant 'Pict' (cf. Jackson 1953:576–6). Use of *Wealh-/-wealh* may also imply that Celtic traditions were held in honour, although currency of the corresponding CWGmc theme was wide enough to suggest onomastic rather than semantic motivation (cf. Insley 1979–80). Interpretation is tricky, because in OE lexical usage *wealh*, basically meaning 'unintelligible speaker' and in England specialised to 'Brittonic speaker', came by ca 900 to mean 'slave' (Faull 1975). The seventh and eighth centuries, however, saw a king of Sussex called *Æðelwealh*, one of Wessex called *Cenwealh*, one of the Magonsæte (a tribe settled in the Welsh Marches) called *Merewealh* and a Sussex king's-thegn called *Wealhhere*, among others (see also Redin 1919:8); at these dates, the connotations of this element must have been complimentary.

A name often alleged to indicate part-Celtic descent is *Mul* – borne, for instance, by a brother of Ceadwalla of Wessex (*Chron* A, s.a. 685). That interpretation depends upon acceptance of its being taken from OE *mūl* 'mule; half-breed' (adopted from Latin; superseded in the ME period by a doublet borrowed through French). However, the name could equally be explained as an OE cognate of Scand. *múli* and German *Maul* 'big mouth' (Redin 1919:21; Zachrisson 1935:83–4; Anderson, 1941:71; cf. von Feilitzen 1937:330 and Fellows-Jensen 1968:198).

Other sorts of foreign name also appeared sporadically in pre-Conquest England. Introduced partly by churchmen, these were seldom widely favoured among the native English.

The years following the Conversion saw a fair Irish presence in England, especially in Northumbria (Colgrave and Mynors 1969; Hughes 1971). Onomastically, the most notable figure was the Mældubh who left his name in that of *Malmesbury* (*PN Wilts.*:47–8). Later in the Old English period, names brought to the North-West and to Yorkshire by Vikings formerly based in Dublin included some Irish forms; Cumbria may also have felt Scottish–Gaelic influences from western Scotland (von Feilitzen 1937:30; Fellows-Jensen 1985a:305–6, 319–21; cf. Insley 1987:183–8).

Names from the Christian tradition – taken from Old and New Testaments, from the Church Fathers, from saints – were borne by many visiting missionaries, and sometimes adopted by native churchmen, such as the seventh-century Thomas who was a deacon among the East-Midland tribe called the 'Gyrwe' and subsequently bishop of the East Angles, the contemporaneous Damian of South-Saxon stock who became bishop of Rochester, and others (Colgrave and Mynors 1969:276–8). Although names of these sorts continued to appear sporadically in England, throughout pre-Conquest times they remained rare (cf. von Feilitzen 1937:30).

Some incoming churchmen were Franks with Frankish names, like the Agilbert whose accent vexed Cenwealh of Wessex (Colgrave and Mynors 1969:234, where his name is, with double inaccuracy, called 'the Gaulish form of Æthelbert'; for its CWGmc origin, see Morlet 1968:23). Men with continental–Germanic names figured among King

Alfred's advisers, among promotors of the tenth-century Benedictine Reform, among the Confessor's protégés, and often also, from the mid-tenth century on, among English moneyers (Forssner 1916; von Feilitzen and Blunt 1971; Smart 1968 and 1987b). Indeed, despite some delicacy of distinction between OE and CWGmc name-forms, it is clear that on the eve of the Conquest the latter were already familiar enough in England to have gained some currency among the peasantry (Clark 1987b).

7.2.3   Scandinavian influences

Scandinavian – that is, North-Germanic – personal names were introduced into England by the Vikings who from the 870s on settled north and east of Watling Street.

These names were in the main distinctive (see Fellows-Jensen 1968). A few themes common to both stocks did retain similar forms: e.g. Scand. *Alf-* beside OE *Ælf-*, *Bjǫrn-/-bjǫrn* (Viking-Norse *biorn*, perhaps with a falling diphthong rather than the later rising one) beside *Beorn-*, and so on. But most cognates had become phonologically differentiated in the regular ways: Scand. *Ás-* corresponded to OE *Ōs-*, *Auð-* to *Ēad-*, *Geir-/-geirr* to *Gār-/-gār*, *Gunn-* to *Gūð* (but Scand. *Gŭð-* to OE *Gŏd-*), *Odd-* to *Ord-*, *-ríkr* to *-rīc* [riːtʃ], *Sig-* to *Sige-/-sige* [sijə], *Ulf-/-ulfr* to *Wulf-/-wulf* and so on. Constraints on the positions that particular elements could occupy also differed between the two traditions. Some frequent Scandinavian themes were, besides, foreign to OE name-usage: e.g. the *Frey-* and *Þór-* representing divine names, and likewise others such as *Ketil-/-ke(ti)ll* 'helmet', *Orm-/-ormr* 'dragon', *Svein-/-sveinn* 'lad' and so on. Short-forms were apparently more popular among the Scandinavians than among the English. As in OE usage, monothematic forms like strong *Ketill* and *Sveinn* and weak *Geiri* may or may not have represented shortening of dithematic ones. Hypocoristics marked by consonant-modification abounded, such as *Tóki* for *Þórke(ti)ll*, and so on. Most notable of all was the Scandinavian fondness for names originating as characteristic nicknames, such as *Forni* and *Gamall* both meaning 'old', *Gaukr* 'cuckoo', *Bróklauss* 'lacking breeches' and so on; forms of these types figured both as by-names and as idionyms.

With the Scandinavian element in Old English naming just as with the Celtic one, attempts have been made to use it as a guide to cultural relationships between the two peoples and, further, to likely densities of

Viking settlement in the Danelaw. In the latter context, the value of linguistic evidence in general and of name-evidence in particular has been questioned (for the one-time controversy, see Fellows-Jensen 1975a:181–5; and for related work on place-names, see below pp. 484–5); but, when cultural influence alone is at issue, little problem exists.

Assessing incidences of Scandinavian-influenced naming can, however, offer difficulties. In the southern Danelaw (East Anglia and the South-East Midlands) especially, the partial recognisability of Scandinavian forms encouraged their anglicisation: of inflexional patterns necessarily, and often also of the themes themselves. Proof of the latter practice comes from forms which, albeit Old English in phonological form, involve elements not previously found as OE name-themes: e.g. *Ōscytel/-cetel* beside Scand. *Ásketill, Stāngrīm* beside *Steingrímr, Suān* beside *Sveinn*, and so on (see Fellows-Jensen 1968:25–32, 264, 276–82). Because anglicisation was bound at times to produce forms identical with actual or potential OE ones, it is not easy to determine how much the late-Old-English currency of forms like *Ōsgār* (cf. Scand. *Ásgeirr*) and *Hereward* (*Hervarðr*) or of, for instance, the prototheme *Stān-* (*Stein-*) may have owed to hidden Scandinavian influence (cf. Fellows-Jensen 1968:22–4, 140; see also Insley 1985a:61–2).

A dearth of tenth-century records adds to the difficulties, because the social levels that the 1066 stratum of DB represents had been affected by the Danish hegemony obtaining from 1016 to 1042 (see, for instance, Insley 1982 and esp. 1985b). From the pre-Cnutian Danelaw little survives but coins and a few stray documents. On coins of Æthelred II (973–1016), moneyers' names show ratios of Scandinavian forms that vary from zero at most southern and south-western mints (for Sussex, see also Stewart 1978:101–10), through roughly 1 in 7 at Bedford, Norwich and Derby, to 1 in 2 at Lincoln and 2 in 3 at York (Smart 1968, cf. 1970:20–7, 1973, and 1986:177–82). Extant documents include lists of *festermenn* (sureties) from Peterborough and from York, as well as Ely Abbey's narrative of late tenth-century dealings with local landholders (Stevenson 1912, Björkman 1913a and b, and Lindqvist 1922; Robertson 1958:74–82; Blake 1962:72–142 and Clark 1983:9–14). The stock represented by the East-Anglian names recorded in *Liber Eliensis* shows 60 per cent of OE forms, nearly 25 per cent of Scand. ones, and about 12 per cent of ambivalent ones (the rest being obscure). The late tenth-century Peterborough record, also listing local landholders, shows only 36 per cent of OE forms beside 44 per cent of Scand ones, and again

12 per cent of ambivalent ones. In both groups Scandinavian names and OE ones interchange within families. The differing proportions of Scandinavian forms seem, despite differences of scale, compatible with gradations of influence like those the moneyers' names imply. The York sureties' names are not strictly comparable, because, being datable 1023 × 1051 (and probably nearer the latter date), they might reflect the Cnutian hegemony; but, for what it is worth, the over 75 per cent of Scandinavian forms in the stock they represent again agrees with the hypothesis of a graded incidence roughly proportional to duration of Viking rule in the district concerned (cf. the comments on place-name distributions in Sawyer 1982:103–4). Similar gradations reappear in ME personal-name distributions (Clark 1979a:15–18, 1982:52–5) and in the Scandinavianisation of field-naming also (see further on both topics in vol. II, 556, 598–9). Moreover, just as the southern Danelaw shows Scandinavian names anglicised to fit the local speech-patterns, so the north reveals its linguistic allegiance through occasional Scandinavianisation of English ones, so that in Yorkshire OE *Ēadwulf*, for instance, became *Iadulf* (cf. the analogous place-name developments described below pp. 483–4).

Its varying incidences apart, Scandinavian personal-naming in England also differed somewhat from region to region. Viking-Age Scandinavian dialects, and name-fashions with them, fell into two main groups: west (Norwegian and, later, Icelandic) and east (Danish and Swedish). In England, Danes settled mainly in East Anglia and the East Midlands, Norwegians in Yorkshire and the north-west; and regional name-fashions differed accordingly (von Feilitzen 1937:18–26, esp. 21–3; Fellows-Jensen 1968:xxvi–xxxviii; Insley 1979).

Because under-recording forbids collection of an adequate sample of women's names from the pre-Cnutian Danelaw, figures for incidence of Scandinavian forms have so far referred solely to men's. Early ME evidence, drawn mainly from records of the peasantry, shows women's names as at that date and that social level usually less Scandinavianised than those of the corresponding men (Clark 1979a:17–18). What bearing, if any, this might have on ninth- and tenth-century social and cultural patterns is uncertain. One school of thought sees colonisation of the Danelaw as having involved families rather than warbands; this would make later differentiation between the name-styles of the sexes a matter of mere fashion. Yet, for rank-and-file Vikings often to have arrived alone, and then to have married Englishwomen as a way of securing title to English lands, might better explain the patterns found;

for, if in mixed marriages daughters were, more often than sons, named according to maternal traditions, feminine Scandinavian name-models for succeeding generations would have been rarer than masculine ones.

7.2.4 Ambiguities

Not only dearth of documentation causes problems over the pre-Conquest personal-name stock. As well as referring directly to people, personal names also figured – usually either in gen. case or with an -ing suffix – as 'specifics' (first elements) of compound place-names (see below pp. 474–5). Common nouns, and topographical terms in particular, equally so figured. Ignorance of OE personal nomenclature and of OE common vocabulary alike leaves us at times uncertain how best to etymologise a given specific (cf. below p. 476 and bibliography there given). Faced with ambivalences, compilers of surveys and dictionaries have sometimes resorted to conventional solutions: for instance, of opting, whenever the 'generic' (second element) of the place-name denotes a settlement or landholding, for a possessory personal name – perhaps one not otherwise recorded.

Such a procedure risks inventing ghost-names; but signals exist to warn against this. No specific found consistently with one and the same generic is likely to be a personal name. For instance, the form *Win(d)sor* < OE *Windlesōra*, found at least five times, was once assumed to contain an otherwise-unrecorded OE personal name **Windel*; now, however, it is explained as < OE **windels* 'windlass; winding-gear' + OE *ōra* 'slope' (Gelling 1978a:170–1, 1984:109, 181–2). Scandinavian personal-name styles, being biased towards the less predictable 'nickname' type of formation, particularly lend themselves to ghost-forms of this sort: witness the ME Yorkshire field-name, *Haukeraythe ker*, whose specific, now taken as < Scand. *hauka hreiðr* 'hawks' nest' had at one time been claimed to represent an unrecorded Scand. nickname **Haukreiði* (Fellows-Jensen 1976:44–7).

An especially unhappy case of misinterpretation has been that of the widespread place-name form *Grimston*, long and perhaps irrevocably established as the type of a hybrid in which an OE generic, here *-tūn* 'estate', is coupled with a Scandinavian specific (see below p. 484). Certainly a Scandinavian personal name *Grímr* existed, and certainly it became current in England (Fellows-Jensen 1968:105–7). But observation that places so named more often than not occupy unpromising sites suggests that in this particular compound *Grim-* might better be taken, not as this Scandinavian name, but as the OE *Grīm* employed as a by-name for Woden and so in Christian parlance for the Devil (Fellows-Jensen 1972:128, 202–3; Gelling 1978a:233–4).

7.2.5   By-names

'By-name' is the technical term for an element added – in Old English, usually postposed – to an idionym, for more secure identification. Such elements fall into universal categories: familial; locative – indicating place of present or former domicile, or of family origins; honorific or occupational – categories which in practice overlap; and characteristic – that is, nicknames (cf. above p. 460). Although in essence not only peculiar to one individual but also unstable, being interchangeable with other forms, of similar or different kinds, or even wholly dispensable, a by-name in time become hereditary (see vol. II, pp. 577–83).

Pre-Conquest English usage exemplifies all the categories (the standard monograph, Tengvik 1938, now badly dated, deliberately under-represents women's names and also fails to distinguish adequately between pre- and post-Conquest records – see von Feilitzen 1939; a truer impression will be gained by scrutinising actual documents, such as those published in Whitelock 1930 and Robertson 1958).

Parentage, the family relationship most often invoked, is shown by using *dohtor* or *sunu* preceded by the gen. of the parent's (usually, father's) name or else, but seemingly only for forming masc. patronymics, by an *-ing* derivative of that name: e.g. *Ēadgȳð Godwines eorles dohtor, Wulfgȳð Ælfswīðe* (fem.) *dohtor, Wulfhēah Ordhēages sunu, Cytel Clacces sunu, Ælfrǣd Æðelwulfing* (*Chron* C, s.a. 1044; Whitelock 1930:12; Robertson 1958:76; cf. Tengvik 1938:139–232, where a third possible type, with asyndetic apposition of the parental name, is confusingly treated). Individuals could equally be defined in terms of other relationships; although the ones most often used were parentage of their children and (for women only) marriage, almost any might be invoked, as in *Æðelsige þes ealdormannes ēam* 'Æ. the *ealdormann*'s uncle' (Robertson 1958:78; because of its subject-matter, Whitelock 1930 is a rich source of varied designations).

Terms of rank were likewise postposed: e.g. *Ælfrǣd cyning, Ēadgifu abbudisse, Wulfstān biscop*. OE by-names referring to trades are rare, possibly because of the nature of the extant documents; when they do occur, occupational terms, unlike honorifics, tend to be preceded by the definite article: thus, *Ælfsige sē cōc* 'the cook', *Lēofgifu sēo dæge* 'the female servant (baker, dairymaid)', but, however, *Wīcing bātswegen* 'the bosun' (Tengvik 1938:238–9, 246–7, 250).

Domicile is indicated by a locative phrase formed with *æt*, *of* or *on*: e.g. *Ælfweard æt/on Dentune*, *Godcild of Lamburnan*, *Clac on Castre* (Robertson 1958:74, 78, 82; Tengvik 1938:28–36, 121–5).

Again possible nickname-forms pose problems (cf. above pp. 460–1 and 468). Certain of them might alternatively be explained as asyndetic patronyms (interpretations proffered in Tengvik 1938:283–391 must be taken with salt). The simplest type is adjectival, as in Bede's reference to two missionaries both called Hewald, distinguishable, however, by hair-colour: *ea tamen distinctione*, *ut pro diuersa capillorum specie unus Niger Heuuald*, *alter Albus Heuuald diceretur* (Colgrave and Mynors 1969:480). In the vernacular, forms of this type abound: e.g. *Æðelflǣd þēos hwīte* 'the white-(or, fair-)haired', *Æðelrīc þes langa* 'the tall and thin', *Wulfmǣr sē geonga* 'the young', and so on, normally with the adj. in the weak (i.e. definite) form and preceded by the definite article. Another type of characterising by-name consists of a postposed substantive variously referring to, for instance, a facial feature, a limb, a garment, or a moral attribute: e.g. *Earnwīg fōt* '(with the unusual) foot', *Ēadrīc strēona* 'acquisitiveness'. Terms referring to animals often appear, presumably as metaphors: e.g. *Godwīg sē bucca* 'the he-goat', *Godrīc finc* 'the finch' (the definite article here seems optional). Some expressions – like *Beorhtmǣr Budde*, *pro densitate sic cognominatus* (Blake 1962:154) – are now obscure (did *densitas* mean 'compact solidity'? and, if so, was there a term **budda*, related to PDE *bud*, meaning 'solid lump'?). The *bahuvrihi* type of formation (see above p. 460) also appears not uncommonly as a by-name: e.g. *Ælfweard scirlocc* '(with) lustrous hair'.

If the criterion for being a 'name' is divorced from etymological meaning, then few Old English by-names (other than any already obscure to contemporaries) meet it – unless, for instance, Hewald 'the black' were still so called after becoming grey or bald. That contemporaries normally regarded by-names of all types as lexically meaningful is proved by the frequent Latinisation. Many of the recorded forms seem indeed to have represented *ad hoc*, possibly scribal, insertion of an identificatory description or address, this being likely when the form is complex or when a locative phrase is appended to a name already including a qualifier of some kind: e.g. *Ælfþrýð mīne ealdemodor þe mē afedde* 'Æ., my grandmother, who brought me up', *Cytel Clacces sunu æt Wermingtune* (Whitelock 1930:62; Robertson 1958:76). Function is best appreciated in context, as, for instance, in the late tenth-century Peterborough list of sureties, which shows not only toponymic phrases used to link men to their holdings but also various sorts of addition employed for distinguishing between individuals of like idionym: e.g. *Sumerlida prēost | S. æt Stoce, Ulf Doddes sunu | U. eorles sunu,* and so on (Robertson 1958:74–92). Occasionally a nickname is such as to allow presumption of colloquial currency: what clerk of 1086 would, for instance, have hit spontaneously upon *fægere (pulchra)* as the aptest way to characterise the Eadgifu who had been a major landholder before 1066? Colloquial rather than scribal origins may also sometimes be allowed to instances that offer lexical antedatings – a point where onomastics bears upon mainstream linguistic history (Tengvik 1938:23–7; cf. Redin 1919:xliii and von Feilitzen 1976a:229). Yet, whether or not truly onomastic when set down, Old English by-names form a crucial part of name-history, because, as well as illustrating how naming crystallises out of common language, they prefigure the emergence of hereditary family-names which is so dominant a feature of the Middle English period (see vol. II, pp. 577–83).

7.3   Toponymy

7.3.1   Elements; structure; morpho-syntactic character

Place-names begin as topographical and/or possessory descriptions of the sites concerned. Recurrent commonplace formations – such as *Barton* < OE *beretūn* 'arable farm' or *Bradfield* < OE *(æt) brādan felda* '(on) the wide plain' (*DEPN* s.n.; *PN Berks.*:200), and so on – emphasise how uncertain distinction is between descriptive term and name (less than half the places in England possess unique names – see McClure 1979:168). Old English 'charter-bounds' (the sections of land-grants that specify, in the vernacular, the extent of the estates conveyed) regularly offer phrases amounting to embryonic place-names (see *PN Berks.*:615–792). English place-name elements thus began as everyday words, the present obscurity of some of them being due to the nature of the Old English literary remains. The basic terms were substantival, falling into two main categories: topographical and habitative (see Smith 1956, to be consulted in the light of Gelling 1981a and 1984).

'Habitative' terms refer to types of settlement. A principal OE one, with cognates in all the other Germanic languages, was *hām* 'abode', corresponding to the common noun which was the ancestor of PDE *home* (cf. German *Heim*). Several were cognate with PDE *stand* (cf. Latin *stare*, Greek *stasis*), therefore meaning 'site; assembly-point', among these being *stede* (Sandred 1963), *stoc*/dat. *stoce* Ekwall 1936b:11–43), and *stōw* (Gelling 1982a). Others carried a basic sense of 'enclosure' (whether as fort or cattle-pen): *burg*/dat. *byrig*, cognate with OE *beorgan* 'to protect', therefore 'fortified place'; *haga*, cognate with OE *hecg* 'boundary-fence'; *tūn*, possessing cognates in the other Gmc languages, and itself the basis for OE *tȳnan* 'to fence off'; and probably also *worð*, with its derivatives *worðig* and *worðign* (see Smith 1956:s.nn.). Terms denoting buildings included *ærn*, used also as a common noun, and *bold*/*bōtl*/*bōðl*, the base for OE *byldan* 'to construct'. Loans from Latin with habitative meanings included *ceaster*/Anglian *cæster* < Latin *castra* (pl.) 'camp', the OE borrowing signifying 'former Roman city', and *wīc* < Latin *vicus* 'minor settlement, esp. one associated with a military base' (Rivet and Smith 1979:xviii; Salway 1981:591; Myres 1986:33–5). Tribal names transferred to localities necessarily carried 'habitative' meaning; so, to some extent, did any name incorporating an occupier's or overlord's personal name.

As to exact Old English meanings, etymology and comparative philology are unreliable guides; contemporary Latin equivalences may give better clues (Campbell 1979). In Bede's *Historia ecclesiastica* and comparable texts, places having OE names in *-ceaster* were usually described as *civitas* and ones with names in *-burg*, as *urbs* – both Latin terms denoting places such as provincial capitals; places with names in *-wīc* were sometimes called *portus* 'harbour' (cf. Ekwall 1964:14–22). The same principle also works in reverse. Usually, the OE *Bede* renders *villa* and *vicus*, terms denoting lesser administrative centres, by OE *tūn*; and this suggests some inadequacy in the conventional modern rendering of the place-name element as 'farmstead'. The social, legal, economic, political and literary contexts in which a term appears illuminate its connotations. A name in *-hām* could, even early on, apply not just to a single settlement but to an extensive estate. A 'tribal' district-name could become restricted to a particular point of settlement. OE *stōw*, marking a place of some importance, perhaps an assembly-point, acquired connotations not only of 'market' but also of 'religious house; place of pilgrimage'. OE *burg* came to mean 'walled town', 'monastery with enceinte', and, in ME, '(moated) mansion'. OE *wīc* acquired a range of specialised senses, including (mainly in the West Midlands) 'salt-works' and (mainly with pl. forms) '(dairy-)farm', as in *Chiswick* ['tʃɪzɪk] < late OE (*of*) *Ceswican* (dat. pl.), showing non-WS *cēse* 'cheese' (Ekwall 1964:22–8; *PN Middx*:88–9 and Ekwall 1964:41–4).

Topographical referends are more various than habitative ones; and within each category – such as type of watercourse or of terrain – OE near-synonyms abounded (for a comprehensive treatment, see Gelling 1984). Current work aims at defining for each term its proper context and nuance of meaning, with semantics and dialectology having here to take cognisance of geography and of economic history. Comparison between places with names in -*mersc* and in -*mōr* suggests, for instance, that, although both terms indicated marshy land, the former implied agricultural promise but the latter, barrenness (Maynard 1974). The terms *cumb* and *denu* denoted contrasting types of valley (Cole 1982; Gelling 1984:88–94, 97–9). Appearance of a term in any particular region depended as much upon topography as upon dialect: hence, for instance, the rarity in Fenland toponymy of terms like *clif* 'escarpment' and *hōh* 'spur of high ground'. On the other hand, tendencies to base naming on distinctive features mean that Fenland names like *Landbeach* and *Waterbeach* may involve, not OE -*bæce* 'stream running through a valley', but the dat. of OE -*bæc* 'ridge' (Gelling 1984:125–7, 130–6, 167–9).

Categories overlapped. OE *burg* became 'topographical' when, as not uncommonly, applied to a prehistoric ruin. OE *lēah* (cognate with Latin *lux* as well as with *lucus* 'grove') meant both 'woodland' and '(settlement in) clearing'; in some areas complementarity between its distribution as a place-name generic and that of OE -*tūn* brings out habitative implications (Johansson 1975; Gelling 1974a and 1984:198–207). Names referring to landmarks were naturally used for indicating meeting-places, such as those of the hundred-assemblies (Anderson 1934:xxvii–xxviii, xxxiii–xxxix, 1939b:156–205). Some topographical formations may, as well, have from the outset denoted settlements. Terms like OE *brycg* and *ford*, both meaning 'river-crossing', imply regular human presence. OE *dūn* 'upland' (when used in otherwise low country) and *ēg* 'island; raised, and therefore dry, ground' both seem often to have implied 'habitable site', and in some cases even 'pre-English village' (Gelling 1984:34–40, 64–72, 140–58). These and other ambivalent terms are sometimes labelled 'quasi-habitative': certainly, 'by the ford' provides a more specific address than 'in my/their tribe's village', which until settlement-patterns had become widely recognised would have been enigmatic (cf. below p. 475).

Some PDE place-names represent OE simplex formations: habitative, like *Bootle* < *bōtl*, *Burgh* [bʌrə] and *Bury* [bɛri] < *burg*/dat. *byrig* respectively, *Chester* < *ceaster*, *Stoke* < dat. *stoce*, *Stow(e)* < *stōw*; or topographical, like *Ewell* < *æw(i)ell* and *Ewelme* < *æw(i)elm* both 'source of river' (Cole 1985), *Ford*, *Hale* < *h(e)alh*/dat. *hăle* 'nook of land', *Leigh* < *lēah*, *March* < *mearc*/dat. *mearce* 'boundary', *Slough* < *slōh* 'boggy place', *Street* < nonWS *strēt* 'Roman road', *Strood/Stroud* < *strōd* 'marsh', *Wells* (*DEPN* s.nn.). Some simplex forms recur many times; but, given the limited distinctions afforded even by topographical terms, single-element names were seldom found adequate.

The typical OE place-name was therefore a compound in which a 'generic', consisting of a habitative or a topographical term, was qualified by a 'specific'. As in the other Gmc languages, the qualifier, whatever its formal character, preceded the generic. Often the specific was an adjective, as in *Bradfield* and in *Newnham/Nuneham* < OE (*æt þǣm*) *nīwan hām* '(at the) new settlement' (*PN Oxon.*:183; for the endingless locative, see Campbell 1959:224). An uninflected substantive, especially a topographical term or one denoting a crop or other vegetation, might also be used, as in *Fordham* 'village by the ford' and *Wheatley* < OE *hwǣte lēah* 'clearing where wheat is grown' (*DEPN*: s.nn.). Alternatively, a qualifying substantive could appear in the gen. (sing. or pl.), as in *Beaconsfield* < OE *bēacnes feld* 'open country near the beacon' and *Oxford* < OE *oxena ford* 'place where oxen cross the river' (*PN Bucks.*:214; *PN Oxon.*:19; see further Tengstrand 1940). The gen. of a personal or tribal name or of a term of rank indicated occupation or overlordship, as in *Epsom* < OE *Ebbes hām* 'E.'s estate', *Wokingham* < OE *Woccinga hām* 'the homestead of the Woccingas (the tribe whose leader was called **Wocc*)', *Canterbury* < (*æt*) *Cantwara byrig* '(at) the stronghold of the people of Kent', and *Kingston* (*DEPN*:s.nn.; also *PN Berks.*:139, 815, 840). Points of the compass were often invoked, as in *Norwich* < OE *norð wīc* 'the northern port (in contrast with Dunwich and Ipswich)', the frequent *Sutton* < OE *suð tūn* 'the southern settlement', and so on (*DEPN*:s.nn.). A further type of specific consisted of a full or clipped form of an established place-name, as in *Holmfirth* 'scrubland (OE *fyrhð*) appertaining to the place called Holm' and *Rotherham* 'settlement beside the river Rother' (*DEPN*:s.nn.); a special case of this involved names of pre-English and sometimes obscure origin, as with *Winchester* < OE *Wintanceaster* < RB *Venta* (*Belgarum*) + OE *-ceaster* (see further below p. 479).

Affixal derivation mainly involved the associative suffix or infix *-ing*(-), whose functions have conventionally been classified under four or more heads (e.g. Smith 1956:i.282–303; Ekwall 1962a; Dodgson 1967a and b, 1968). How far such schematic distinction clarifies matters is a moot point. At all events, constant reliance on the one device bedevils modern interpretation.

Suffixed to a personal name, *-ing* formed a patronymic (see above p. 469). An analogous derivative could, like a gen. sing., figure as a toponymical specific, as in *Tredinton* < OE *Treding tūn*, indicating an estate held *ante* 755 by a thegn called Tyrdda (*PN Worcs.*:172; Gelling 1978a:177–8). Pluralised, an *-ing* patronymic gave a tribal name whose gen. could likewise figure as a specific, as in *Wokingham* and in *Finchingfield* < OE *Fincinga feld* 'open country held by Finc's people' (*PN Essex*:425). Such a tribal name could also be directly transferred to a locality, as with *Hastings* < OE *Hæstingas* 'territory, or headquarters, of Hæsta's people' (the habitative compounds *Hæstingaceaster* and *-port* also occur – *PN Sussex*:534, cf. p. xxiv). (This transference of tribal name to territory is in keeping with the OE custom of referring to nations in tribal rather than spatial terms: e.g. *betueoh Brettum & Francum* 'between Brittany and France', *Chron* A, s.a. 890.) In particular, *-ingas* forms, like other sorts of tribal name, sometimes appear as hundred-names (Anderson 1934:xxvi, 1936b:188). Not all names of such plural origin show PDE *-s*: some PDE forms go back, not to nom./acc. pl., but to dat., as with *Reading* < OE (*æt*) *Rēadingum* beside nom. *Rēadingas* (*PN Berks.*:170, cf. 815; also Wrander 1983:47). Etymological distinction between sing. and pl. *-ing* formations thus depends upon survival of records early enough to show the OE structure.

Associative *-ing* was also used for forming, on substantival, adjectival or verbal bases, topographically descriptive terms, such as OE **stybbing/stubbing* 'recent clearing where tree-stumps still stand' (Smith 1956:ii.164, 165). Such terms could come to serve as place-names: e.g. *Clavering* < OE *clæfre* 'clover', so 'clover-patch', and *Deeping* < OE *dēop*, so 'place deep (in fenland)' (Ekwall 1962a:189, 200). Stream-names thus formed might, like those of other types, be transferred to settlements whose lands the streams in question drained, as happened with *Lockinge* < OE *lācing* (*brōc*), originally probably 'the playful stream' (Ekwall 1962a:208; *PN Berks.*:13, 486–7). An *-ing* toponym of any of these kinds could then itself figure as specific to a generic, especially to *-tūn*, as in *Stubbington*. Topographical *-ing* formations could also, like the patronymic ones, be pluralised so as to give a tribal name transferable back to a locality: e.g. *Barking* < OE *(on) Berecingum*, varying with nom. *Berecingas*, probably best taken as '(the territory of) the birch-tree people' (*PN Essex*: 88–9; but cf. Wrander 1983:45). The currency of such topographical formations alongside the ones based on personal names complicates etymologising; in ambivalent cases, traditional practice has often tended towards opting for a personal-name etymology, especially when the generic is habitative – if need be, for a nickname not otherwise recorded (see above p. 468). Reaction has sometimes seemed to advocate opting wholesale for topographical *-ing* formations not otherwise recorded (the controversy can be followed, by those curious about such matters, in Zachrisson 1932, 1933a and b, 1934, 1935, Tengstrand 1940, Ekwall 1962a, Dodgson 1967a and b and 1968, Arngart 1972, Fellows-Jensen 1974, 1975b and 1976, Kristensson 1975, and Gelling 1987a: 178–80).

Further complications arise from a sporadic palatalisation and assibilation of *-ing*(-) > [ɪndʒ] that affects suffix and infix alike: e.g. *Lockinge*, *Wantage* < OE *Waneting* (also originally a stream-name – *PN Berks.*: 17–18, 481–2), and also the traditional, now vulgar, [brʌmədʒm] for *Birmingham* (*PN Warks.*: 34–6). Explanations have ranged from variant development of gen. pl. *-inga-* (Ekwall 1962a: 203–18) to fossilised survival of a PrOE locative in **ingi*, assumed to have dominated development of the names in question in the way that dative forms not uncommonly do (Dodgson 1967a; but cf. Gelling 1982a).

As just observed, some PDE place-name forms go back, not to the OE nom. case, but to the dat. (cf. Smith 1956:i. p. xx). This is because place-names differ from common nouns in being used less often in nom. or acc. cases than in locative or post-prepositional ones (cf. Rivet and Smith 1979:32–6).

Some early OE records show prepositions figuring almost as integral parts of place-names: thus, in Bede's *Historia* we find *in loco qui nuncupatur Inberecingum* (*sc.* Barking), likewise *Inhrypum* (Ripon), *Inundalum* (Oundle), and so with other tribal names; for topographical formations, a translation is sometimes substituted, preceded by *ad*, thus, *Ad Candidam Casam* (*sc.* Whithorn < OE *hwīt ærn*) (Colgrave and Mynors 1969:222, 256, 298, 354–6, 516, 532, with editorial style sometimes over-emphasising the agglutination; cf. Smith 1956:i. 5–7, and Cox 1975:39, 41, 42). A few PDE forms retain relics of similar constructions: e.g. *Attercliffe* < OE **æt þæm clife* (DB *Atecliue*) 'beside the escarpment', *Byfleet* < OE *bī flēote* 'by a stream', *Bygrave* < late OE *bī grafan* (dat. pl.

of *græf*) 'beside the diggings'; also vestigial forms such as *Tiddingford* (Hill) < OE *æt Yttinga forda* (*DEPN*:s.nn.; also *PN Surrey*:104, *PN Herts.*:155 and *PN Bucks.*:81; cf. Smith 1956:i. 32–3).

Elsewhere, proclitic relics of the pre-onomastic descriptive phrase may appertain only to the dat. of the demonstrative. PDE *Thurleigh* < OE (*æt*) *þǣre lēage* keeps the entire fossilised demonstrative, and also shows stressed development of the original simplex name to [lai] (*PN Beds. & Hunts.*:47–8). More often, only the final consonant of the demonstrative survives: e.g. *Noke*, the earliest extant records of which show *Acam* < *ācum* (dat. pl.) '(at the) oak-trees' but which presumably goes back to OE *(*æt*) *þǣm ācum* > ME *atten oke*, also *Rye* < OE *(*æt*) *þǣre īege* > ME *atter ie* > *atte Rie*, and similarly the frequent stream-name *Rea* < OE post-prepositional *þǣre ēa* (*PN Oxon.*:232–3, cf. Wrander 1983:83; *PN Sussex*:536; *DEPN*:s.nn.).

Usually, however, only the form of the generic betrays dative origins. Although with common nouns dat. sing. normally fell together with the nom./acc. form during the Middle English period, several toponymic generics developed as doublets: e.g. OE *-burg* > *-borough*/*-burgh* [brə], but dat. *-byrig* > *-bury* [bri]; OE *-h(e)alh* > (mainly northern) *-halgh*/ *-haugh*, but dat. *-hāle* > *-ale*/*-al(l)* [l]; OE *-stoc* > *-stock*, but dat. *-stoce* > *-stoke*. For plural forms, various possibilities existed. The nom./acc. form might prevail, as in *Hastings*. When dat. predominated, development varied. The ending might be lost (*-um* > [ən] > [ə] > ø), as with *Barking*, *Reading* and also *Bath* < OE (*æt þǣm hātan*) *baðum* '(at the hot) baths' (Wrander 1983:45, 47, 53). A reduced form of the inflection might survive, as in *Ripon* < OE (*on*) *Hrypum* '(among) the people called the Hrype' and in the frequent *Cot(t)on* < OE (*æt þǣm*) *cotum* '(at the) huts' (Wrander 1983:75–6, 89–93, 115–16). Occasionally the OE form survived unweakened, in which case the final syllable is often now spelt unhistorically, as in the frequent northern *Acomb* [eikm̩] < OE (*æt þǣm*) *ācum*, *Howsham* < OE (Scand.) *hūsum* '(at the) houses', and *Airyholme*/*Eryholme* < *ergum*, dat. pl. of ON *erg* 'shieling' (see further Wrander 1983:50–82, also 121, 129; cf. Fellows-Jensen 1980; on unhistorical spelling, see further below pp. 485–7).

7.3.2   Chronology

For a long time English toponymic studies were largely aimed at establishing a chronology of name-types (Gelling 1978a:ch. v, and 1984:1–3). Philological interest apart, such a chronology was hoped to throw light on settlement-history; but recent opinion has swung away from assuming settlements necessarily to be contemporaneous with their earliest recorded names. At the same time, former orthodoxies in the name-chronology itself have been overthrown, as yet without replacement (for further, see Copley 1986 and Gelling 1988).

One old *a priori* assumption – discrediting of which makes irrelevant much apparatus and most distribution-maps accompanying pre-1965 volumes of the English Place-Name Survey (cf. Dodgson 1978) – had been that the earliest English place-names were those that were either transferred from tribal ones or else showed as specific the gen. pl. of such names (see above pp. 475–6). Already in the 1930s discrepancies were noted between distribution of these sorts of name and that of known early settlement-sites, but were then explained away (Myres 1935, cf. 1986:36–45, where continuing reserve is expressed *vis-à-vis* the more recent theories). By the 1960s ampler archaeological comparison made the poor correlation plain; and also inspired a tentative new chronology, which put *-ingahām* formations earlier than those in simple *-ingas*, in their turn placed earlier than *-inga-* compounds with other generics (Dodgson 1966; Kuurman 1974; but cf. *PN Berks.*:815). None of these types is now, however, assigned to the initial phase of colonisation.

The apparent priority, among *-inga-* compounds, of those in *-hām* prompted general reassessment of names based upon that generic. Investigations, in any case hindered by confusions between *-hām* 'settlement' and *-hamm* 'island; enclosed land' (cf. below pp. 486–7), have shown distributions of *-hām* formations as inconclusively related both to the settlers' likely access routes (trackways, Roman roads, river-valleys) and to known Romano-British settlements and pagan Germanic cemeteries (Cox 1972; cf. *PN Berks.*:816–18, Unwin 1981 and Watts 1979).

The question has also been approached by taking the earliest settlement-sites thus far identified and noting what names characterise them. On this basis, the earliest English place-names in Berkshire seem to have been based upon topographical generics referring to supply and control of water, such as *-ēg* 'dry ground', *-ford* and *-well* (*PN Berks.*:818–21). In another area of known early settlement, lying along the northern shore of the Thames estuary, *Fobbing* and *Mucking* (previously taken as tribal names – *PN Essex*:156, 163) have been reinterpreted as creek-names transferred to riparian settlements, and then seen as topographical formations at the core of a radiating pattern of later name-types (Gelling 1975 and 1978a:119–23). On the other hand, because coinage of new topographical names continued for centuries, no easy assumption can be made that a cluster of such forms always marks a district of early settlement.

A third approach to chronology has focused on early records. Over half the names recorded *ante* 731 – that is, during the first three centuries of the settlement, and mainly in Bede's *Historia* – prove again to be based upon topographical generics such as *-burna* 'stream', *-dūn*, *-ēg*, *-feld*, *-ford*, *-hamm* and *-lēah* (Cox 1975:15–29, 58–61). Such choices would reflect new settlers' preoccupations with control of woodland as well as of water; but the dating is not rigorous enough for a firm chronology (cf. Gelling 1984:5–6).

7.3.3   Pre-English influences

Behind fourth- and fifth-century Britain there lay a long history of occupation and agrarian exploitation, and consequently of place-naming. Records survive from Romano-British (RB) times of some 450 names; although mostly preserved only in Latinised form, almost all are Celtic in origin (Rivet and Smith 1979; cf. Gelling 1978a:38–50). Hardly any were adopted *tels quels* into English.

Occasionally the English settlers did show awareness of the structure and meanings of British names. One that was plural in form might be anglicised with an OE pl. inflection: e.g. PDE *Dover* < OE *Dofras*/dat. *Dofrum* < RB loc. pl. *Dubris*, British **dubras* 'waters' (Rivet and Smith 1979:341; cf. Jackson 1953:243–4, and Padel 1985:87, s.v. *dour*). A few forms seemingly English in content could, furthermore, perhaps be explained as translations of RB names, as with *Horncastle* Lincs. < OE *Hornecæster*, corresponding to RB *Bannovalium*, based on British **banno-* 'spur (of land)' (Jackson 1953:244; Rivet and Smith 1979:256–6; Smith 1980:30).

For known Romano-British names, the main mode of survival into Old English, and ultimately into present-day usage, was for clipped forms of them to be adopted as specifics to OE generics, usually to the loan-element *-ceaster* 'former Roman city', e.g., *Exeter* < OE *Exanceaster* < RB *Isca* (*Dumnoniorum*), *Winchester* < OE *Wintanceaster* < RB *Venta* (*Belgarum*), and *Gloucester* < OE *Glēawanceaster* < RB *Glevum* 'bright', contaminated with OE *glēawa* 'wise man' (Rivet and Smith 1979:378 – cf. 376–8 on *Isca* as a river-name, 492, 368–9; also *PN Devon*:20–1 and *PN Glos.*:i. 1, ii. 123–5).

As that last instance shows, 'folk-etymology' – that is, replacement of alien elements by similar-sounding and more or less apt familiar ones – can be a trap. The RB name for the city now called *York* was *Ebŏrācum/Ebŭrācum*, probably, but not certainly, meaning 'yew-grove' (Rivet and Smith 1979:355–7, cf. Padel 1985:96). To an early English ear, the spoken Celtic equivalent apparently suggested two terms: OE *eofor* 'boar' – apt enough either as symbolic patron for a settlement or as nickname for its founder or overlord – and the loan-element *-wīc* (see above p. 472), hence OE *Eoforwīc* (*PN EYorks.*:275–80; Fellows-Jensen 1987). (The later shift from *Eoforwīc* > *York* involved further cross-cultural influence – see below p. 483.) Had no record survived of the RB form, OE *Eoforwīc* could have been taken as the settlers' own coinage; doubt therefore sometimes hangs over OE place-names for which no corresponding RB forms are known. The widespread, seemingly transparent form *Churchill*, for instance, applies to some sites never settled and thus unlikely ever to have boasted a church; because some show a tumulus, others an unusual 'tumulus-like' outline, *Church-* might here, it is suggested, have replaced British **crūg* 'mound' (Gelling 1984:137–9; cf. Jackson 1953:310 and Padel 1985:73–4, s.v. *cruc*).

Hybrid compounds combining British and OE near-synonyms are not uncommon: e.g. *Bredon* < British **bre* 'hill' + OE *-dūn* (*PN Worcs.*:101; Gelling 1984:128–9; cf. Padel 1985:30), and, with a further synonymous addition, the composite *Breedon-on-the-Hill*, Leics.; likewise, *Chetwode* < Welsh *coed* 'forest' + OE *wudu* (*PN Bucks.*:62; Gelling 1984:190–1, 227–9). In such cases, the Celtic term may once have constituted a simplex name for a local feature – 'The Hill', 'The Forest' – and been eked out with the synonymous OE generic only after its lexical meaning was forgotten (see also Jackson 1953:244–5).

Nowhere in England is British influence on place-names paramount. Apart from categories already mentioned, it appears mainly in occasional names of landscape features – hills, forests and, especially, rivers and streams. Names for watercourses (hydronyms) universally show great powers of cross-cultural survival, some PDE ones being claimed to be not merely pre-English but pre-Celtic (or 'Old European'), and so perhaps to date from *ante* 1000 BC (Ekwall 1928:xlviii–liv, cf. Förster 1941 and Nicolaisen 1982). The higher incidences of proven Celtic names, mainly river-names, found in western parts of England, by contrast with eastern ones, might reflect a lighter as well as increasingly symbiotic nature of the westward colonisations (Jackson 1953:219–29, esp. map on 220, and 234–41; cf. Dodgson 1967c, Gelling

1978a:87–93 and Fellows-Jensen 1985a:164–6). Throughout the otherwise anglicised territory, on the other hand, clusters of such names seem to mark long-surviving pockets of Celtic culture; but uncertainties of etymology forbid precise mapping (see, for instance, Jackson 1953:235–7, Gelling 1974b:59–62, and Faull 1980).

Occurrences as place-name specifics of the two OE terms for 'Celt' – *W(e)alh*/pl. *Wala* and the probably politer pl. *Cumbre* (cf. above pp. 463–4) – might have been hoped to throw further light on patterns of Celtic survival. Unfortunately, few records of names possibly involving gen. pl. *Wala-* are early enough for firm etymologising; but, of the clear cases, most do occur in districts otherwise marked by RB influence (Jackson 1953:227–8; Cameron 1979–80; cf. Gelling 1978a:93–5 and in *PN Berks.*:803–4). Similarly, a few names involving the gen. pl. *Cumbra-* are recorded early enough for safe distinction from the gen. sing. of the personal name *Cumbra* (Gelling 1978:95–6).

Unlike those once-Romanised areas that were destined to become Romance-speaking, England shows hardly any place-names of purely Latin origin. Few seem to have been current even in Romano-British times; fewer still survived (Gelling 1978a:31–7). PDE *Lincoln* is a contraction of *Lindum Colonia*, where the first element represents British **lindo* 'pool' (*PN Lincs.*:i. 1–3; cf. Rivet and Smith 1979:393 and Padel 1985:149, s.v. *lyn*). Whether *Catterick* < RB *Cataractonium* derives ultimately from Latin *cataracta* in supposed reference to rapids on the River Swale) or from a British compound meaning 'battle-ramparts' is uncertain (Rivet and Smith 1979:302–4).

The main legacy of Latin to Old English toponymy consisted not of names but of name-elements, in particular: *camp* < *campus* 'open ground, esp. that near a Roman settlement'; *eccles* < *ecclesia* 'Christian church'; *funta* < either *fontana* or *fons*/acc. *fontem* 'spring, esp. one with Roman stonework'; *port* < *portus* 'harbour'; and the already-mentioned *wīc* < *vicus* 'settlement, esp. one associated with a Roman military base', together with its hybrid compound *wīchām* (Gelling 1967, 1977, 1978a:67–79, 83–6, and 1984:22 – cf. Salway 1981:669–70, 690–2; and Cole 1985; Cameron 1968; Ekwall 1964). Names involving these loan-elements occur mainly in districts settled by the English *ante* AD 600, and often near a Roman road and/or a former Roman settlement (Gelling 1978a:63–86 and in *PN Berks.*:802–3). A few miscellaneous loan-terms also appear, such as the **croh* < *crocus* (or a derived OE adjective **crogig*) figuring as specific in *Croydon* and the **fæfere* < *faber* deduced from the name *Faversham*, taken as 'the metal-worker's village' (*PN Surrey*:47–8; Gelling 1978a:80–2).

7.3.4 Scandinavian influences

In their main principles, Old English and Scandinavian modes of place-name formation were much alike. The distinctiveness of Danelaw toponymy is thus due chiefly to the Vikings' introduction into England of their own range of name-elements. The frequent Scand. *-þorp* 'hamlet' did correspond to an OE element, the rarer and usually metathesised *-þrop*, and their parallel currency in England has provoked controversy (Lund 1975 and 1976; cf. Gelling 1978a:226–8); but the Scandinavian equivalents of the prolific OE elements *-hām* and *-tūn* were by the time of the settlements no longer productive. Of the Scandinavian habitative generics still in use, far and away the most frequent was *-bý* 'settlement, of whatsoever size' (Fellows-Jensen 1985a:10–11), and this had no OE equivalent, its nearest OE cognate being the verb *bū(g)an* 'to dwell'. Among the topographical terms, most cognate pairs had diverged phonologically: e.g. Scand. *bekkr* contrasted with OE *bæce/bece* 'stream', *hryggr* with *hrycg* 'ridge', *skógr* with *sceaga* 'grove', *viðr* with *wudu*, and so on (Gelling 1984:12 and 14, 169, 208–10, 222, 227–9). Many Scand. terms were, besides, peculiar to that language: e.g. *fjall*/Viking-Norse **fell* 'upland', *gil* 'ravine', *holmr* 'island, peninsula' (cf. below pp. 486–7), *kjarr*/**ker* 'marsh overgrown with brushwood', *lundr* 'grove', *slakki* 'valley', *þveit* 'clearing' (Gelling 1984:52–3, 99, 123, 159, 207–8, 210–11; Fellows-Jensen 1985a:74–94). In England, reflexes of *gil*, *fell* and *þveit* appear chiefly in the north-western districts where Norwegian settlers predominated (cf. Fellows-Jensen 1985a:309–19).

Throughout the Danelaw, purely Scandinavian place-names abound. Modes of compounding resemble Old English ones. Personal-name specifics qualify both habitative and, albeit less often, topographical generics: e.g. the Yorks. *Aislaby* < DB *Aslaches bi* 'Áslákr's estate' and the Lincs. *Ingoldmells* < ME *Ingoldes meles*, with Scand. *melr* 'sand-bank' (Fellows-Jensen 1972:18 and 1979:155). Topographical and other descriptive specifics were similarly applied: e.g. the Yorks. *Busby* < DB *Busche bi*, with Scand. **buskr* 'shrub', *Ellerker* < Scand. *elri* 'alder-tree' + *-ker*, and *Rathmell* < Scand. *rauðr* 'red' + *melr* (Fellows-Jensen 1972:23, 94, 102). For Danelaw place-names far oftener than for those of southern England, lateness or obscurity of first record makes etymology a speculative matter, uncertainties being exacerbated by difficulties of distinguishing between topographically descriptive terms and personal nicknames (cf. above p. 468).

In the districts most densely settled by Vikings – mainly, that is, in Lincolnshire and Yorkshire – survival in some specifics of Scand. gen. sing. inflexions bears witness to prolonged currency of Scandinavian speech in the milieux concerned (cf. Page 1971). Both with personal names and with topographical terms, genitives in -*ar* occur chiefly in the North-West: e.g. Lancs. *Amounderness* < *Agmundar nes* 'A.'s headland' and *Litherland* < *hliðar* (*hlið* 'hill-side') + -*land* (Fellows-Jensen 1985a: 99, 145, 325–7, but now see Fellows-Jensen 1990; for the latter, cf. Gelling 1984:246). Non-syllabic Scandinavian-style genitives in [s] are more widespread: e.g. Yorks. *Haxby* < DB *Haxebi* 'Hákr's estate' and Lincs. *Brauncewell* < ME *Branzwell* 'Brandr's spring' (Fellows-Jensen 1972:29 and 1978a:216). In the North-West, 'inversion-compounds', where in Celtic fashion the specific follows its generic – thus, *Kirkoswald* 'St Oswald's church' – sometimes contain Scandinavian elements, and in such cases probably reflect Irish influences carried by Norwegian settlers formerly based in Dublin; but elsewhere they may be of Scottish-Gaelic origin (Fellows-Jensen 1985a:52–3, 96, 319–20).

As well as coining new place-names, the Viking settlers often adapted pre-existing English ones to suit their own speech-habits, thus emphasising their cultural dominance in the districts concerned. Adaptation was effected partly through sound-substitution, based on the systematic contrasts between, for instance, Scand. [ei] and OE [a:] and between the Scand. stops [k], [g], [sk] and the OE palatalised and assibilated [tʃ], [j], [ʃ]. Wherever the settlers were able to impose their own speech-habits, reflexes of OE *ceaster*/Angl. *cæster* show initial [k], as in *Castor*, *Caister*, *Caistor*, *Doncaster*, *Lancaster*, and so on (cf. chapter 3). OE *Eoforwīc* was reshaped, with a Scand. rising diphthong replacing the OE falling one, assibilation of the final consonant inhibited, and medial [v] elided before the rounded vowel: thus, *Iorvik* > *York* (*PN EYorks.*:279; Fellows-Jensen 1987; cf. above p. 480). Adaptation of OE terms that lacked Scand. cognates might disregard meaning, as with the several instances of *Keswick* < nonWS *cēse wīc* 'cheese-producing farm' and with the Yorks. *Skipton* < nonWS *scēp*/*scīp* 'sheep' + -*tūn* (Fellows-Jensen 1985a:203; *PN WYorks.*:vi. 71–2; cf. Scand. *ostr* 'cheese' and *fær* 'sheep').

Where cognates did correspond, sound-substitution can hardly be distinguished from element-substitution, as in Northants. *Braybrooke* <

OE *brāde brōc* 'broad stream', with Scand. *breiðr* replacing OE *brād* (*PN Northants.*:110–11; cf. Insley 1985b:113–15). So, without pre-Viking records, it may be impossible to tell whether a form like *Askrigg* represents fresh Scandinavian coinage or Scandinavianisation of an OE *æsc hrycg* 'ridge marked by an ash-tree' like that behind extant instances of *Ashridge*. Often, indeed, medieval records show alternation persisting between OE and Scand. versions of a name, and chance may often have decided which form became standard (Fellows-Jensen 1972:136–7, 1978a:200–11, and 1985a:192–9). Sometimes, however, an OE element was replaced by a non-cognate near-synonym, as -*denu* and -*hamm* seem sometimes to have been by -*dalr* and -*holmr* respectively, and as -*burg/ -byrig*, less accurately, occasionally was by -*bý* (Fellows-Jensen 1972:119–20, 138–9, 1978a:13–15, 203–4, 1985a:12–13, and 1985b).

The fluctuating usages complicate interpretation of the many apparently hybrid names (Fellows-Jensen 1972:131–41, 1978a: 199–211, 1985a:192–9). Further uncertainties arise from known possibilities of at least partial renaming upon changes of lordship (Fellows-Jensen 1984:34–7; Insley 1986). Hybrids may be of either sort. A Scandinavian generic, of any kind but especially -*bý*, might take as specific an OE personal name or descriptive term: e.g. the Lincs. *Worlaby* < DB *Wlurices bi* 'Wulfric's estate', and the Derbys. *Shirland* < OE *scīr* 'bright' + Scand. *lundr* 'grove' (Fellows-Jensen 1978a:79, 221). Currency of *by* as a ME, and presumably late OE, common noun hinders the dating of late-recorded names containing the corresponding generic, and consequently of the hybrid culture that they reflect. Conversely, an OE generic, -*tūn* especially, might take a Scandinavian specific of either sort, most often a personal name: e.g. Lincs. *Owston*, with Scand. *austr* 'east', and Notts. *Gamston* < DB *Gameles tun* 'Gamall's estate' (Fellows-Jensen 1978a:185, 191, 174–82, cf. 1972:109–25, 1985a:180–5). The conventional designation of this latter type as '*Grimston*-hybrids' has proved unfortunate owing to doubts as to the interpretation of this particular compound (see above pp. 468–70).

The distribution in England of Scandinavian, Scandinavianised and hybrid place-names coincides almost exactly with the Danelaw as specified in Alfred's treaty with Guthrum (see map accompanying Smith 1956). This implies such names to stem mainly from the late ninth-century settlements, rather than from the wider Cnutian hegemony. Throughout the area, however, Scandinavian names co-exist, in varying proportions, with purely English ones. So, in attempts to clarify the picture and its bearing on settlement history, sites to which the various types of name are applied have been graded according to their likely attractiveness to subsistence farmers. Those adjudged most promising bear either purely English names or else the sort of hybrid ones in which a Scand. specific, often a personal name, qualifies an OE generic: a finding consonant with the view that often the latter sort of name represents partial Scandinavianisation of a pre-Viking OE one. Sites bearing purely Scand. names, especially ones based on the generic *-bý*, mostly look less promising; and the villages concerned have often indeed prospered less than ones with names in the two previous categories. The main river-valleys are dominated by OE names, whereas Scand. forms appear mainly along the tributaries. These name-patterns are taken to imply two modes of settlement: one by which pre-existing English villages acquired Viking overlords, whose names some at least of those that had changed hands thenceforth bore; and another by which Viking settlers adopted lands previously uncultivated. As yet, it remains unclear what chronological relationship is to be postulated between the two processes (Cameron 1965, 1970, 1971 and 1976; cf. Payling 1935, Fellows-Jensen 1972:109–10, 124–5, 250–1, and 1978a:174–5, 368–72).

Uncertainties of detailed interpretation notwithstanding, the frequency of Scandinavian and Scandinavianised place-names throughout the Danelaw, and especially in its more northerly parts where Viking hegemony was longer maintained (cf. Sawyer 1982:103–4), implies strong and lasting cultural influence there (cf. above pp. 465–8). The Viking dominance evident from northern English adoption of Scand. administrative terms such as *lawman* (Scand. *lǫgmaðr*), *riding* (*þriðjungr* 'third part') and *wapentake* (*vápnatak* 'voting-procedure; public assembly; administrative division (equivalent to the English 'hundred')') is confirmed by the occurrence of Scandinavian-influenced names for meeting-places not only of Danelaw wapentakes but also of East-Anglian hundreds (Anderson 1934:xxxi–xxxii, 1939b:188–9, 204–5, 208; also Arngart 1979 and Bronnenkant 1982).

7.3.5   *Some etymological caveats*

Often place-names remain stable for centuries, sometimes for millennia. There have been almost no changes in 'major' English place-names since ca. 1000 (see vol. II, pp. 588–91). Stability does not, however, entail being static, and semantic divorce from common vocabulary lays name-material especially open to phonological change, in so far as shifts and reductions may be unrestrained by analogies with related lexical items and may at times be warped by random associations with unrelated but like-sounding ones. As a source of phonological evidence, name-material must therefore be treated with reserve.

Etymologising too is put at risk; for the time-lapses often intervening between coinage of a place-name and its earliest extant record mean that the form given in the latter may already be partly obscured. *A fortiori*, present-day forms have no etymological value, being all too often the result of respelling whatever pronunciation has resulted from centuries of free-wheeling change. As for present-day pronunciation, this may, at worst, have in turn been remodelled to fit the now-standard spelling, historical or not (see further vol. II, pp. 594–5).

Generics, being second elements and therefore weak-stressed, regularly show phonetic reduction. Vowels are reduced to [ə] or merged with following liquids to give [l̩], [m̩], [n̩]. Formerly initial [h] is lost in medial position (modern spelling-pronunciations may either affectedly restore such an [h], as in the frequent [heivəhɪl̩] for [heivrɪl̩] *Haverhill*, or unhistorically render < s–h > and < t–h > as [ʃ] and [θ] respectively, as in the current pronunciations of *Evesham* and *Walthamstow*). Medial [w] is similarly elided, as in *Chiswick* [tʃɪzɪk], *Norwich* [nɒrɪdʒ], *Southwark* [sʌðək], *Southwell* [sʌðl̩], and so on (again, it is sometimes affectedly restored). As a result, elements originally distinct have long since fallen together, and have subsequently often been respelt unhistorically. Here there is space to note only a few of the more frequent types of confusion.

(1) OE -*h(e)alh*/dat. -*h̆ale* 'nook of land' and OE -*hyll* 'upland' (Gelling 1984:100–11, 169–71) fall together as PDE [l̩]. Less often, as in *Southwell*, OE -*well(a)* and its variants follow the same path. PDE spellings give no guidance whatsoever as to etymology: although the most frequent ones for reflexes of -*h(e)alh* are -*al*, -*all*, -*ale* and -*hall*, forms in -*ell*, -*ill*, -*hill* and -*holt* also occur (thus, *Northolt* and *Southall* form a contrasted pair – *PN Middx*:44–5); those for -*hyll* include -(*d*)*ale*, -*hall*, -(*f*)*ield*, -*well* and -*le*; and those for -*well* include -*hall*, -*wall* and -*le*.

(2) OE -*hām* 'village', OE -*hamm* 'site hemmed in by water or wilderness' and also the latter's Scandinavian synonym -*holm* all fall together as [m̩]. Not even pre-Conquest spellings always allow of distinguishing -*hām* from -*hamm*: if dat. forms in -*hamme*/-*homme* survive, they tell in favour of the latter, but often etymology has to depend upon topography (Gelling 1960 and 1984:41–50; Dodgson 1973; Sandred

1976). Distinction between *-hamm* and *-holm* is complicated by their synonymity, and their likely interchange in the medieval forms of many Danelaw names (cf. above p. 484). PDE spellings are again often unhistorical, as in *Kingsholm* < OE *cyninges hamm* 'the king's water-meadow' (*PN Glos.*: ii.138, also iv.64). Confusion is further confounded by occasional unhistorical spellings of [m̩] < OE or Scand. dat. pl. *-um*, as in *Airyholme* and *Howsham* (see above p. 477).

(3) OE *-denn* 'woodland swine-pasture', OE *-denu* 'valley' and OE *-dūn* 'upland' all regularly give [dn̩]. Confusion is somewhat alleviated by the restriction of *-denn* to the south-eastern counties and a tendency in those districts for *-denu* to develop, especially when enjoying secondary stress as the final element of a trisyllable, to [diːn], as in *Rottingdean* ['rɒtɪŋˌdiːn] (see Gelling 1984: 97–9, 234). That leaves, however, scope for frequent interchange between the reflexes of the antonymous *-denu* and *-dūn*: e.g. *Croydon* < OE **croh* or **crogig* + *denu* 'crocus valley' and, conversely, *Eversden* < OE *eofores dūn* 'the boar's hill' (*PN Surrey*: 47–8; *PN Cambs.*: 159). Both *-denu* and *-dūn* are, furthermore, at times confused with *-tūn*: e.g. *Paddington* < OE *Padan denu* 'P.'s valley', *Headington* (*Hill*) < OE *Hedenan dūn* 'H.'s upland' (*PN Surrey*: 260; *PN Oxon.*: 30).

(4) Reflexes of OE *-bearu* 'grove' and *-beorg* 'mound' are partly merged not only with each other but also with those of *-burg/-byrig*, so that PDE forms in *-barrow* can represent *-bearu* or *-beorg*, ones in *-bury* can represent *-bearu* or *-byrig* and ones in *-borough* can represent *-beorg* or *-burg* (for the wide range of possibilities, see Gelling 1984: 127–8, 189–90).

(5) The weakest elements of all were the medial ones of trisyllables, mainly derived either from gen. inflexions or from connective *-ing*. Before a dental the latter regularly gave [n̩]; consequent reverse spellings explain some unhistorical forms of names that had originally been formed with a weak gen. sing.: e.g. *Headington*, *Paddington*, also *Abingdon* < OE *Æbban dūn* 'Æ.'s upland', and many others (*PN Berks.*: 432–4).

FURTHER READING

Much remains to be discovered about all aspects of English naming. Current research, published and in prospect, is recorded in the annual bibliographies that appear in *Nomina*, which also carries reviews and short notices of recent publications. Bibliographies, reviews and short notices likewise appear from time to time in *Journal of the English Place-Name Society*, *Old English Newsletter*, *Year's Work in English Studies* and also the various journals concerned with

English medieval and local history as well as those devoted to philology. International bibliographies appear in *Onoma*. Other journals published abroad that sometimes offer material of direct or comparative interest for historical English onomastics include *Beiträge zur Namenforschung, Naamkunde, Names, Namn och Bygd, Nouvelle Revue d'Onomastique* and *Studia Anthroponymica Scandinavica*.

Old English personal-naming has not as yet been the subject of any comprehensive survey (Clark 1987a offers a brief summary of developments up to ca 1300). The only existing onomasticon, Searle 1897, is unreliable. For Germanic styles in general, an elementary guide will be found in Woolf 1939; but for serious work it is essential to consult the specialised regional compilations such as Longnon 1886–95, Mansion 1924, Schlaug 1955 and 1962, Morlet 1968, Tavernier-Vereecken 1968 and Tiefenbach 1984. Among the major monographs on naming in pre-Conquest England itself, Forssner 1916, Redin 1919 and Tengvik 1939, although still useful as quarries, are largely outdated; Boehler 1930, von Feilitzen 1937 and Ström 1939 retain greater value, but even so should not be consulted uncritically. For Anglo-Scandinavian names, Fellows-Jensen 1968 is, despite being restricted to two counties only, the best general guide; and Björkman 1910 and 1912 still afford useful supplementation. Again, serious work requires recourse to compilations such as Lundgren and Brate 1892–1915, Lind 1905–15 and 1920–1 and Knudsen *et al.* 1936–64. Great scope exists for exploring neglected topics, such as the possible social, geographical and chronological variations in Old English name-fashions and their relationships with ones current among the other Germanic peoples.

Place-name studies have been better served. A firm basis for further work exists in the county surveys being issued by the English Place-Name Society (but some of these, it must be borne in mind, date back fifty years and must be treated with reserve). For neophytes, Gelling *et al.* 1970 offers simplified but scholarly commentaries upon selected names; and excellent expositions both of fundamental principles and of recent findings are given in Gelling 1978a and 1984. For the Celtic background to English toponymy, Jackson 1953 and Padel 1985 should be consulted; and for the Romano-British one, Rivet and Smith 1979. Anglo-Scandinavian names are in process of being comprehensively surveyed by Fellows-Jensen: her monograph dealing with Yorkshire appeared in 1972, that for the East Midlands in 1978, that for North-West England in 1985, and further instalments are planned.

Because lack of context makes name-etymology especially speculative, any opinion proffered in a survey or a name-dictionary must be considered critically, as basis for further investigation rather than as definitive statement. Anyone wishing to pursue historical name-studies of either sort seriously must, in addition to becoming conversant with the philology of the relevant medieval languages, be able to read Medieval Latin as well as modern French and

German. Assessing and interpreting the administrative records that form the main source-material is the essential first step in any onomastic study, and requires understanding of palaeographical and diplomatic techniques; competence in numismatics may on occasion also be needed. Onomastic analysis itself involves not only political, social and cultural history but also, when place-names are concerned, a grasp of cartography, geology, archaeology and agrarian development. Any student suitably trained and equipped will find great scope for making original contributions to this field of study.

8 LITERARY LANGUAGE

Malcolm R. Godden

8.1 Introduction

The term literary language can be used in various senses, reflecting the different meanings of the word literature, and the area of discourse usefully designated by it will vary from one period to another. For the period up to 1100 there is little value in applying the broad and etymological sense of the word 'literary' or 'literature', meaning 'all that is written down' in contradistinction to oral discourse: to do so risks, on the one hand, excluding poetry, since the special language of verse was largely developed without benefit of writing and a number of the surviving poems probably originated in oral conditions; and on the other hand, including too much to be useful, since virtually all our evidence for the language of the time, at all levels, comes from written documents. At the other extreme, a more restricted definition of literature as imaginative composition would be in danger of excluding much that is worth attention and including some texts of little linguistic or literary interest because they happen to deal with imaginary fictions. I use the term 'literary language' here to cover the language of all verse and of the more sustained and ambitious writing in prose, especially those texts which reveal a concern with the selection and use of language.

From a linguistic standpoint literary language is but one of a number of varieties of discourse, like informal speech or the idiom of the law. It is, however, of particular importance to historical linguists because it shows the language being tested to the full, being used by individuals who think seriously about the right choice and use of language and are prepared to employ the full range of possibilities and even to invent, or to break the boundaries of ordinary discourse. Thus an account of literary language is inevitably both a description of its general characteristics and an exploration of the ways in which individual writers have gone beyond them. This is as true for the Old English period as for later times, though our distance from it in time may cause us to emphasise the homogeneity of its literary language. There is in fact ample evidence both of individual experimentation and of individual concern about language choice.

8.2   Poetry

For the language of poetry, two recent comments will help to define the issues:

> Never since the end of the Old English period, not even in the most neoclassical decades of the eighteenth century, has the language of English poetry differed so greatly from the language of prose as it did in Alfred's time; nor has the form of poetry ever again been so uniform as it was before the Conquest.
>
> (Metcalf 1973:3)

> Contemporaries did not think of literary works as either poetry or prose, but distinguished them by their level of ornateness which extended in an unbroken chain from the very plain to the highly elaborate.
>
> (Blake 1977)

Both of these recent and apparently contradictory statements about Anglo-Saxon poetic language have important truth in them. There is a general similarity in the language of much of the poetry which distinguishes it sharply from most prose; on the other hand, it is possible to find examples of rather 'prosaic' verse and rather 'poetic' prose, and although these have often been regarded as evidence of the decline or decadence of the literary tradition, not all are late in time and some are in other respects examples of the more skilful writing.

This section must inevitably start by attempting to describe the relatively homogeneous poetic language shared by most poems before going on to consider the variations from it. Anglo-Saxon poetry is remarkable for its use of a single metrical form sustained with only minor variations over the whole corpus, regardless of date or genre. This form has two fundamental features: a rhythmical pattern based on a line of four stresses, with a strong medial division into two two-stress phrases, and structural alliteration linking the two halves. Complex rules appear to have governed the number and placing of lightly stressed syllables, as well as the kind of syllables which are able to occupy the stressed positions. Five main types of rhythmical pattern can be identified in the half-line. The so-called A-type has the two stresses each followed by unstressed syllables or dips:

> / x / x
> gomban gyldan ('pay tribute': *Beo* 11)

The B-type reverses this:

> x /x /
> on flodes æht (into the sea's power: *Beo* 42)

The C-type has the stressed syllables centrally:

> x / /x
> in geardagum (in olden-days: *Beo* 1)

The D-type uses a secondary stress after the two main stresses:

> / x / \ x
> fromum feohgiftum (with fine treasure-gifts: *Beo* 21)

or

> / / x \
> lofdædum sceal (with praise-worthy deeds shall...: *Beo* 24)

The E-type uses a secondary stress between the main stresses:

> / x\ x /
> æþelinges fær (prince's vessel: *Beo* 33)

There are, however, quite a large number of acceptable variations on these main types, with additional unstressed syllables or occasionally stressed ones.

For alliteration the main 'rule' is that either or both of the stressed syllables in the first half-line alliterate with the first stressed syllable in the second half-line; thus (with alliterating sounds underlined):

> / x / x   x x / / x
> gomban gyldan;   þæt wæs god cyning
>
> ...tribute pay;   that was a good king

or

> x / x /   / x /x
> on flodes æht   feor gewitan
>
> into sea's power   far depart

One important qualification to this rule, which has still not been explained to general satisfaction, is that any vowel may alliterate with any other; thus:

/x   x / x   / x \ x /
isig ond utfus,   æþelinges fær

icy and ready to go,   the prince's vessel

How these rhythmical patterns relate to the sentence stress of Old English prose and speech is a difficult issue. There is evident in the verse a clear hierarchy of parts of speech: nouns and adjectives always bear primary stress, adverbs do in emphatic positions but otherwise not, and demonstratives, prepositions and conjunctions seldom do. The interesting case is the verb. Infinitives and participles usually carry primary stress, but the finite verb is variable, sometimes playing a part in the metrical scheme with full stress, sometimes being apparently lightly stressed. Whenever the finite verb takes full stress, and often when it does not, it plays a role in the alliterative structure, but it hardly ever alliterates at the expense of a noun or adjective. Its subordinate status is strikingly evident in the many cases where it seems to lie outside the rhythmical scheme; compare, for instance, *Beo* 609:

/x   /   \x x x x x / /x
brego Beorht-Dena: gehyrde on Beowulfe

lord of the Bright-Danes; I have heard in Beowulf...

or *Wan* 34:

x x x /x / x   x / /x
gemon he selesecgas   and sincþege

he remembers hall-men and treasure-receiving

Similarly, finite verbs often occupy the final and unemphatic fourth-stress position in verse.

It is generally said that this system in the verse reflects the hierarchies of stress in the language itself, though reservations are sometimes noted: 'we can observe this law ... in the language of verse only, for we have no means to determine the stress of prose' (Campbell 1959:§93ff; cf. too chapter 3 above). The proviso made by Campbell is perhaps inaccurate since there exist considerable stretches of Old English prose with a pronounced rhythmical structure which can provide us with evidence for sentence stress outside verse. What analysis has been done in this area shows no parallel in prose for verbs having less stress than nouns or adjectives (cf. Cable 1974, who uses the Chronicle and Wulfstan; analysis of Ælfric's rhythmical prose would seem to give similar results, with finite verbs having the same status as nouns and adjectives in both stress and alliteration). It would then appear that poetic tradition had either preserved an older distinction that disappeared in prose (and presumably in speech), or developed a very slight distinction into a much more pronounced one.

Both of the fundamental features of Old English metre have important implications for language choice: alliteration encourages the use of a range of vocabulary to provide different initial sounds, while the rhythmical patterning favours the deployment of forms and structures which limit the number of unstressed elements, in ways affecting particularly morphology and syntax but also vocabulary.

The earliest account of Anglo-Saxon poetry is Bede's story of the poet Cædmon in his *Ecclesiastical History*. Cædmon is said to have produced verse in his own language 'composed in poetic words with the greatest sweetness and inspiration' (Colgrave and Mynors 1969:414). While Bede talks of 'composing' (*compono*) his anonymous translator, writing in the ninth century, twice refers to Cædmon 'adorning with verse' the biblical stories told him by the monks of Whitby (the word used is *geglængan*; *Bede*, 342, 344). Later Anglo-Saxon commentators support this view of poetry as an embellishment of discourse. Ælfric, writing his *Grammar* at the end of the tenth century, defines prose as 'straightforward language, not ornamented and organised in verse' (*ÆGram* 295.15–16). Byrhtferth, early in the eleventh century, contrasts simple, earthy prose with discourse 'beautifully adorned in poetic style' (*ByrM* 54.3). The concept of ornament may in part refer to rhythm and metre, but it probably comprehends the language of Old English poetry as well. In both diction and syntax verse differs strikingly from contemporary prose and, one must assume, from contemporary speech. This may in part be seen as poetic licence, allowing the poet to vary his vocabulary and distort his syntax to meet the demands of metre and alliteration, but the frequency of poetic forms, their nature, their appearance in metrically undemanding positions, all indicate an interest in using a traditional poetic language to lend colour and heightening to the tone of verse as well as to satisfy metrical demands. The opening sentence of *The Wanderer* provides a good example:

Oft him anhaga   are gebideð,
[Often an alone-dweller   awaits (*or* experiences) favour]
Metudes miltse,   þeah þe he modcearig
[God's mercy,   although he, heart-sad,]
geond lagulade   longe sceolde
[over the waterway   has long had to]
hreran mid hondum   hrimcealde sæ,
[stir with hands   frost-cold sea,]
wadan wræclastas;   wyrd bið ful aræd.
[traverse exile-/misery-paths;   fate is fully fixed.]

Metod is a word familiar in poetry but hardly ever found in prose (and then only in elevated contexts); *anhaga, modcearig, lagulad, hrimceald* and *wræclast* are compounds found only in poetry and of a type familiar in all verse of the time; *gebideð* shows a morphological feature which was once normal but by the time of the poem's copying at least was recognisably poetic (prose of the tenth century would have *gebit*); and in syntax the parallelism or asyndetic co-ordination of lines 1–2 and 4–5 represent standard features of verse-composition that would seldom appear in prose.

For a contemporary audience, poetry must have immediately announced itself as a distinct kind of linguistic experience, quite apart from its differences of rhythm and utterance. Our best evidence for contemporary awareness of this prose/poetry difference is King Alfred, who at the end of the ninth century translated a Latin philosophical work, the *Consolation of Philosophy* of the fifth-century Boethius, into English prose. The Latin text alternates prose and verse, and Alfred himself subsequently turned into verse those parts of his own prose rendering which corresponded to the metrical parts of Boethius' work. In turning his prose into verse Alfred introduced a whole range of forms thoroughly characteristic of poetry but not found in prose. Thus there are simplex words like *beorn* ('man, warrior'), *guma* ('man'), *metod* ('God'). There are frequent compounds like *hronmere* ('whalesea'). There are inflected forms such as *genimeð* for *genimð* (3sg.pr.ind. of *geniman* 'to take') and syntactic features such as the omission of the demonstrative, as in *tunglu* ('stars') for *þa tunglu*. Much the same contrasts, no doubt just as deliberate, are evident a century later, for instance between the prose language of Ælfric and the verse language of *The Battle of Maldon*.

While these conscious differences between verse language and other language are clearly evident in the ninth and tenth centuries, we need to be cautious about attributing them to earlier periods. Most surviving verse is traditionally dated in the eighth or ninth centuries, before the appearance of the first extensive prose writings in Alfred's reign at the very end of the ninth century. The features introduced by Alfred when composing verse at the end of the ninth century are equally evident in a seventh-century poem, Cædmon's *Hymn*. It is, however, quite probable that the morphological features which mark poetic diction in late ninth-century Wessex were in general spoken usage at earlier periods, just as some of the phonological features which serve to contrast poetic language with the Late West Saxon standard are in the earlier poetry merely the normal usage of the time or region. Just as *hath* is a poeticism in Keats and an unmarked form for Shakespeare, so *gebideð* may have been a poeticism to Alfred and an unmarked form for Cædmon. Poetic diction for the Anglo-Saxons included a fair amount of mere archaism. But this is not true for all, perhaps even for much, of their poetic language. A number of the lexical items which characterise the poetic language have cognates in Norse which are similarly limited to poetry, suggesting an origin in a very early poetic diction in Common Germanic. Others, particularly some of the compounds, are of a type which would seem to belong, in their imaginativeness and suggestiveness, perhaps also their redundancy, to poetry rather than speech or prose; these are, one suspects, largely the creation of successive poets rather than accidental survivals from earlier speech. But just as Shakespeare sounded more 'poetic' to Keats than he did to the Elizabethans, so Cædmon's *Hymn* may have sounded merely poetic to King Alfred but a challenging mixture of the old, the colloquial and the innovative to Bede.

Virtually all that survives of Old English poetry is contained in four manuscripts. The fact that two of them, the Exeter Book and the Junius manuscript, are devoted exclusively to poetry perhaps testifies to the strong contemporary awareness of verse as a distinct mode of discourse. All four manuscripts were produced near the end of the Anglo-Saxon period, around 975–1000, but most modern opinion holds that many of the poems were already centuries old by then (the evidence is largely linguistic, and there is little consensus as to *which* poems are early). All four (as well as some contemporary copies of other poems) show a similar dialectal mixture, predominantly Late West Saxon but with elements of other dialects and earlier forms. The Late West Saxon element is usually, and no doubt rightly, explained as the influence of the written standard commonly used at the time of copying. In the past, and to some extent still, the non-LWS elements have been explained as traces of the original dialect of composition and of the dialects of those who had transmitted the poem through the centuries, but increasingly in recent decades favour has been shown to the concept of a general poetic dialect, a dialect associated with verse by poets and audience alike and bearing features that in prose and speech would be limited in region or period but in poetry were of general and continuing currency. The idea has perhaps gained more favour than it has yet merited. As first enunciated by Kenneth Sisam, who proposed it only as a hypothesis without seeking to argue it, this was a dialect used by the poets as a language of composition (Sisam 1953b:119–39), but others have applied the term and concept to a dialect of *transmission* into which scribes transferred poems composed in other dialects: as one recent commentator puts it, 'the poems have been transposed into a literary dialect – predominantly Late West Saxon, though with some non-West Saxon elements – which is common to all the manuscripts' (Raw 1978:4). There is good evidence that poets did use forms that were not current in their own normal dialect. Thus King Alfred in turning his own prose into verse introduced not only the traditional poetic vocabulary but also grammatical forms which are common in verse and Anglian but not found in Alfred's normal language, such as the unsyncopated form of the present tense (e.g. *gebideð* instead of *gebitt*). Similar Anglian forms occur alongside syncopated forms in later poems like *The Battle of Maldon*, which otherwise conform quite consistently with the norms of the Late West Saxon standard. There is also good evidence that the scribes of the late manuscripts, while generally converting texts into the standard, recognised and accepted certain spellings as appropriate to poetry which were not current in their own usage. Thus the scribes of the Exeter Book and the Junius manuscript preserved the poetic *aldor*, 'leader' (as simplex and in most compounds), but used the WS *ea* spelling in the form *ealdormann*, a word common in prose. The Junius scribe preserves *bald* while the Exeter scribe uses *beald*, but both preserve *cald*, perhaps because WS *ceald* would require the palatalisation of the initial consonant as well as a change of vowel (Stanley, 1969a). While it is clear, then, that poets could use forms no longer current in their own dialect and scribes could reproduce them (though possibly not themselves introducing them) when copying verse, whether this amounts to what might be called 'a general poetic dialect' is more doubtful: while there is a general and inevitable tendency to use traditional spellings for words exclusive to poetry, there is otherwise little agreement amongst poets or scribes as to which particular dialectal features are appropriate to poetry.

With diction we are on clearer ground. Old English poetry employs a wealth of terms frequent in verse but seldom if ever found in prose and presumably not current in speech. The most frequent are the words designating 'man', 'warrior' (on the distinction between the two meanings, see below): *beorn, guma, hæleð, rinc, secg.* As simplices all five words are virtually confined to verse, as are the cognates of *guma, hæleð* and *rinc* in Norse. The occasional exception serves only to confirm the poetic status: thus King Alfred once uses *hæleð* in prose, but it is in a passage which translates a piece of Latin verse and was perhaps felt to require elevated diction. The same point could be made of *metod*, used in poetry as a term for the Christian God but perhaps originally associated with Fate (it is related to *metan*, 'to measure, allocate'). Its only recorded uses in prose are one in Alfred where he was again translating verse and five in Ælfric in passages where he was experimenting with a form of alliterating rhythmical prose modelled on verse and incorporating other poetic words occasionally (see below). Another poetic word used of God is *frea*, closely linked with the name of the pagan god who gave his name to Friday, but also used to mean 'lord, king' in Old English verse. Other frequent occurrences are the words for 'horse' (*wicg*), 'sword' (*heoru, mece*), 'ship' (*naca*), 'heart' (*sefa, ferhð, hyge*), 'spear' (*gar*), 'friend' (*wine*), 'battle' (*guð, hild, beadu*), 'hall' (*seld, sele*). In some cases it is the specific meaning which is poetic: thus *lind* and *helm* are in general use in the senses 'lime tree' and 'helmet' but limited to poetry in the senses 'shield' and 'protector'. All of these words are used in poetry alongside apparent synonyms which have more general currency: such words as *man* ('man'), *wiga* ('warrior'), *hors* ('horse'), *sweord* ('sword'), *scip* ('ship'), *mod* ('heart'), *spere* ('spear'), *freond* ('friend'), *wig* ('war'), *heall* ('hall').

At this distance in time it is difficult to tell whether these poetic words were exact synonyms of their prosaic equivalents. Although etymology would sometimes suggest a specific shade of meaning for a poetic word, the poets seem to use these words as if they are equivalent to their more usual counterparts. Listeners would perhaps apprehend the difference between *hors* and *wicg* as one of register like that between 'horse' and 'steed' rather than one of meaning, like that between 'horse' and 'hunter'. The problem is particularly acute with the 'man' words, as can be seen from one dictionary's definition of *beorn*: 'man: noble, hero, chief, prince, warrior'; or *guma*: 'man, lord, hero' (Clark Hall). In heroic poems like *Beowulf*, which depict a military society, these words inevitably designate a warrior even if 'warrior' is not the primary meaning (though the poetic word *secg* is used for the one non-military male, the slave who steals the dragon's cup). But *guma* at least, judging from its survival in a compound of general currency and very ordinary meaning, *brydguma*, 'bridegroom', meant no more than 'man' or possibly 'master', and when these poetic terms appear in a late and unheroic verse text like Alfred's *Metres of Boethius* they seem to designate man in general. When the poet of *The Wanderer* remarks that a wise man must not be *to wac wiga* it is difficult to be sure whether this was felt as a statement about warfare ('too timid a warrior') or about life ('too weak-willed a man'). Similarly it has been argued that the *Beowulf*-poet distinguishes two kinds of sword, designated *bil* and *mece*, referring to both by the general term *sweord*, rather than using all three words as synonyms (Brady: 1979). Whether a poem like *Beowulf* presents a rich tapestry of social types and metallurgical specialities, or only a linguistic variety of near-synonyms for 'man' and weapons, is perhaps in the end a question of the nature of meaning: is the meaning of the specialised poetic terms what might be known to a well-read and rather antiquarian poet, or is it what would be conveyed to an audience familiar only with his own and similar poems? Yet the very richness of language in *Beowulf* is perhaps stylistically significant whatever the denotative function.

Compound nouns and adjectives are of the essence of Anglo-Saxon poetic language. At one extreme, there are compounds which are perfectly ordinary and prosaic in themselves and occur in poetry rather than prose only because poetry relishes variety: e.g. the *Beowulf*-poet's use of *Suð-Dene*, *Norð-Dene*, *East-Dene* and *West-Dene* as general terms for the Danes without any apparent intention to distinguish between sub-groups of the tribe. At the other extreme, there are inherently poetic compounds involving imaginative metaphors, such as *beadu-leoma*, 'battle-light', a term for a sword, or *feorh-hus* 'life-house' for the body. In between are a host of compounds which have no figurative element but are of a type not found in Old English prose. Many compounds use elements which are themselves restricted to poetry, such as *heaðo-*, *beadu-*, *hilde-* (all meaning 'battle-', 'war-'). More often, poetry combines elements which in contemporary prose would be linked by grammatical structures: *The Seafarer* has *geswinc-dagas* ('toil-days') where prose might say *geswinces dagas* ('days of toil'). Sometimes it is difficult to see what at all a compounding element contributes: if both *sefa* and *mod* mean 'mind', 'heart', the poetic compound *mod-sefa* in *The Wanderer* presumably adds little except an elevation of tone from its association with poetry and with a series of more meaningful *mod-* compounds such as *mod-cearig* ('heart-sad') and *mod-cræft* ('heart-skill, intelligence'). Often what is achieved is an intensity of expression and suggestiveness of meaning which ordinary words would preclude: thus the poetic compound *wine-mæg*, 'friend-kinsman', manages to combine the blood-relationship of *mæg* 'kinsman' with the companionship of *wine* 'friend' and the tone contributed by the poetic register of *wine*, while hinting at the essential nature of the friend-kinsman identity. It has been argued that similar subtleties lie behind the compounding elements denoting 'battle', with *heaðo-* implying destruction and *hilde-* suggesting 'glory', and that skilful poets invoke these distinctions in their choice of compounds (Brady, 1983). An opposing view is expressed in the forthright comment, 'A *guðbyrne* is a byrnie [corselet] which alliterates in [g]; a *heaðobyrne* is a byrnie that alliterates in [h]' (Niles 1981).

Many of the compounds found in Old English poetry are of ancient origins. A number have close parallels in other Germanic languages, presumably indicating a common Germanic origin: examples are *endedæg* 'last day, day of death', *fyrenweorc* 'work of old times', *guðfana* 'war-banner', *heaðulac* 'battle-play', *facenstæf* 'treachery' (Carr). Some of these seem to be restricted to poetry in other Germanic languages as well, suggesting that the poetic diction used by Anglo-Saxon poets had specialised at a very early date, centuries before the earliest extant poem in Old English: examples are *modsefa* 'mind', *gifstol* 'throne', *meduærn* 'mead-hall', *hrimceald* 'frost-cold', *wigheard* 'battle-brave', *ellendæd* 'deed of courage', *folccyning* 'king of the people' (although *hrimceald* may be a later borrowing from Old Norse). Such compounds are, however, far more frequent and varied in Old English poetry than in any other early Germanic verse; it is not until the Norse scaldic poetry of the tenth century that anything similar to the profusion of compounds in *Beowulf* or *Exodus* developed. If Old English poetic diction had a basis in Common Germanic culture, as the evidence suggests, it would seem that Anglo-Saxon poets expanded it prodigiously. Much of this no doubt took the form of extending the use of elements such as *heaðu-* and *guð-* from contexts where they had a defining function (*heaðulac*, *guðfana*) to others where they had an enhancing function (*heaðubyrne*, *guðbyrne*). But the creation of an array of Christian terms for use in religious poetry such as *sigebeam* ('victory-tree', i.e. cross) testifies to a genuine inventiveness on the part of poets, and it is likely that such inventiveness was deployed on other terms too, though more difficult to be confident of particular examples. One frequently cited example is *ealuscerwen* (lit. 'dispensing of ale' but perhaps meaning 'sharing out of bitterness') in *Beowulf*.

A striking feature of Old English poetic diction is its emphasis on nouns and adjectives at the expense of verbs and adverbs. This manifests itself, as we have seen, in metrical practice, where nouns and adjectives always have primary stress but finite verbs and adverbs frequently do not, and are often excluded from the alliterative patterns. But it is also evident in the development of a specialised vocabulary. Verbs scarcely figure at all in the list of words primarily used in poetry: poetic simplices and compounds are mainly nouns, frequently adjectives, hardly ever verbs or adverbs. In various ways, the traditional techniques of verse composition both discourage the use of a variety of verbs and deprive them of emphasis when they are used. One further manifestation of this is the use of poetic formulae which express a colourful action by using a colourless verb coupled with a more striking noun: compare, for example, *scyldas beran* (literally 'to carry shields' but used as an equivalent to 'to advance') and, in *Beowulf*, *wearð him to handbonan* (1331–2 'became to him a hand-killer', that is, 'killed him') and *hwanon eowre cyme sindon* (257, 'where your comings are from', i.e. 'where you have come from'). There is a striking contrast here with the poetic diction of fourteenth-century alliterative poetry which develops a fine array of poetic verbs and gives them great emphasis. In this sense, Old English poetic language is essentially nominal rather than verbal. Here as in other respects, however, the initial proviso about individual variations needs to be remembered. The poet of *The Dream of the Rood* breaks all the rules about the low status of verbs and creates verse in which verbs of intense action dominate, often with the aid of hypermetric lines which have three stresses to the half-line (verbs are italicised, alliterating letters underlined in the following example):

> …ic wæs *aheawen* holtes on ende
> *astyred* of stefne minum. *Genaman me* ðær strange feondas,
> *geworhton* him þær to wæfersyne, *heton* me heora wergas *hebban;*
> *bæron* me þær beornas on eaxlum, oð ðæt hie me on beorg
>   *asetton;*
> *gefæstnodon* me þær feondas genoge. *Geseah* ic þa Frean mancynnes
> *efstan* elne micle, þæt he me wolde *on gestigan.*

I was cut down at the forest's edge, stirred from my root. Strong

enemies took me there, made me into a spectacle there for
themselves, ordered me to lift up their criminals; men carried me there
on shoulders, until they set me on a hill; many enemies fastened me
there. I saw then the Lord of mankind hastening with great courage,
and that he intended to climb on me.

Even within the favoured class of nouns, however, there are evident
hierarchies of weight. While all nouns receive major stress, some are felt
to be sufficiently ordinary to occupy a non-alliterating position while
others ('high-rank words') are not. Of the words for 'man', for
instance, *secg* and *guma* have a higher rank than *leod*, *mann* or *cempa*.
Similarly, *hlaford* and *frea* are higher ranking than other words meaning
'lord', 'king', such as *cyning* and *drihten* (Shippey 1972:103; Cronan
1986).

The linguistic units from which Old English poets build their poems
are frequently neither single words nor sentences, but what have come
to be known as formulae. A formula is, basically, a set form of words
which fills a metrical half-line and is used repeatedly to express the same
idea. Those first identified were the half-lines which were repeated
exactly in different poems: thus *har hilderinc* 'gray-haired warrior' is
used of Hrothgar at *Beo* 1307 and of Byrhtnoð at *Mald* 169 and of the
Scottish king Constantine at *Brun* 39. The term 'formula' was
subsequently extended to include the many cases in which the structure
of the phrase is repeated but one element may vary. The simplest cases
are half-lines such as *Byrhthelmes bearn* 'Byrhthelm's son' used of
Byrhtnoð at *Mald* 92, varying with *Wulfstanes bearn* used of Wulfmær at
155 and *Ecglafes bearn* used of Æscferð at 267. Phrases such as *Byrhtnoðes
mæg* 'Byrhtnoth's kinsman' (114) and *Æþelredes þegen* 'Ethelred's thane'
(151) could be taken as further variations on the same formula or as
closely parallel formulae. More complex cases are such as *weox under
wolcnum* ('grew under the skies') used of the young Scyld at *Beo* 8,
varying with *wod under wolcnum* ('advanced under the skies') at 714, used
of Grendel's stealthy advance on the hall. Such repeated formulae were
once seen as the hallmarks of particular poets who were then imitated by
others, but their sheer frequency and variety have led to increasing
acceptance of the view that they are a fundamental feature of Anglo-
Saxon verse-technique, developed over centuries of largely oral
composition (though the view that such formulae occur *only* in orally
composed verse (cf. Lord 1960:198), with obvious implications for all
Anglo-Saxon poetry, is now held by few scholars of the subject). The
usefulness of such formulae for composition, providing ready-made

moulds for familiar concepts, is evident enough, and there is some evidence that they were often associated in poets' minds with traditional ways of handling common scenes and events. Their effect on listeners was presumably to stress the traditional and poetic nature of individual texts, continually relating characters and events to those familiar from older poetry. At times they seem to be used with little thought for appropriateness to specific context, but there are many examples which seem to suggest a thoughtfulness, even a deliberate irony, in their placing. Thus the formula *wlonc and wingal* ('brave/proud and merry with wine') is used nostalgically of departed warriors in that ruminative poem *The Ruin* (probably an elegy on the ruined city of Bath) but placed more critically in *The Seafarer* as an epithet for one who has experienced few hardships living secure in a fortified city. When the *Beowulf*-poet uses the epithets *snottre ceorlas* ('wise men') and *hwate Scyldingas* ('brave Danes') of the Danes who wisely (but wrongly) conclude from the blood in the lake that the hero has been killed and return home without him (lines 1591, 1601), it is difficult to believe that it is not a deliberately ironic use of formulaic epithets; as again when he uses the formula *stið and stylecg* ('strong and steel-edged') of the sword which has just failed the hero (1533). When the *Beowulf*-poet says of a Danish king that *blæd wide sprang* ('[his] glory leaped far', 18) and the poet Cynewulf says of the apostles that *lof wide sprang* ('[their] glory leaped far', *Fates* 6) they are using traditional formulae for a hero in a traditional way; but something much more inventive is happening when the poet says of Grendel, monster and therefore anti-hero, as Beowulf strikes off his head, *hra wide sprang* ('the corpse leaped far', 1588). Again, the convenient formula for a ruler seen in *folces weard* ('guardian of the people') and *rices weard* ('guardian of the kingdom') is ingeniously adapted to the dragon in *Beowulf*, described repeatedly as *biorges weard* ('guardian of the barrow', 2524, 2580), and still more ingeniously to the cuckoo in *The Seafarer*, referred to as *sumeres weard* ('guardian of summer' 54). Similarly, the formula *earm anhaga* ('pitiful solitary-one') is appropriately and emotively used of the central figure in the elegy known as *The Wanderer* but cleverly and perhaps jokingly applied to the wolf in the gnomic verses (*Max II* 19). At their best, the poetic formulae manifest the spirit of imaginative play seen more comprehensively in the verse riddles found in profusion in the *Exeter Book*.

The fondness of individual poets for variety in their diction, already seen in the use of simplex words and compounds, is also evident in the lack of 'thrift' in the use of formulae (Whallon 1961). In Homeric epic, which uses repeated formulae very like those found in Anglo-Saxon verse, the same formulaic epithet is used for a character whenever the same metrical conditions recur (thus the epithet 'fleet-footed' is always the one chosen to fill out a line beginning with 'Achilles' even when the hero is lying still in his tent); in Old English heroic poetry, a variety of equivalent formulae is employed. Thus if the *Beowulf*-poet needs an epithet for Hroðgar, king of the Danes, to form a final half-line alliterating on *m-* he may use *mære þeoden* ('great king') or *mago Healfdenes* ('son of Healfdene'); or a half-line epithet alliterating on a vowel may be *æþeling ærgod* ('excellent prince') or *aldor East-Dena* ('leader of the East-Danes'). Epithets are also non-specific to character, though often specific to context: *æþeling ærgod* is used of Beowulf in his old age as well as of Hroðgar in *his* old age. If formulaic diction had initially developed as a means of simplifying the composition of verse, it seems to have become an opportunity for poets to achieve a richness and variety of language.

Beyond the formula itself is the principle of collocation: that within the verse tradition certain words are particularly frequently found close together, and that the association sets up an expectation in the listener which a poet might then exploit (Quirk 1963: Shippey 1972:103–4). Thus *dom* ('judgement', 'fame') tends to associate with *dead* ('death'), while *flod* ('flood', 'sea') unexpectedly collocates with *fyr* ('fire'). At times this can lead a poet into incongruous associations, but often the poet is able to use it to chime in with the listeners' sense of the rightness of things, as when Beowulf urges *wyrce se þe mote / domes ær deaþe* ('let him who may, achieve fame before death', 1387–8).

One important aspect of Old English poetic diction is its specialised grammar and syntax, extending all the way from matters of inflexion and the use of demonstratives to the structure of the sentence. Historically, the Old English demonstrative (*se, seo, þæt, etc.*) developed gradually into something approaching a definite article in function (cf. chapter 4), but even in late Old English prose it is used less frequently, and presumably therefore with more emphasis, than the PDE article. In poetry the demonstrative/definitive article is generally used less frequently than in prose. This is easily exemplified even in a passage from a very late poem like *The Battle of Maldon* (the one demonstrative in this passage is here underlined):

Feoll þa to foldan   fealohilte swurd:
[Fell then to ground   yellow-hilted sword]

ne mihte he gehealdan   heardne mece,
[he could not hold   hard blade]
wæpnes wealdan.   Þa gyt þæt word gecwæð
[wield weapon.   Then still spoke the word]
har hilderinc,   hyssas bylde,
[gray-haired battle-man,   encouraged warriors]
bæd gangan forð   gode geferan.
[urged to go forward   brave companions]

(166–70)

Contemporary prose (and presumably speech) would probably have used a demonstrative with *swurd*, *mece*, *wæpnes*, *hilderinc*, *hyssas* and *geferan*. Compare, for instance, this passage from a prose text of the same period by Ælfric (demonstratives underlined):

Þa ða Iudas gehyrde <u>þæra</u> hæðenra gehlyd and <u>þæs</u> feohtes hream, þa ferde he him hindan to mid ðrym scyld-truman and sloh <u>ða</u> hæðenan oð ðæt hi oncneowon þæt <u>se</u> cena Iudas him wið feohtende wæs.

(*ÆLS* xxv 421–5, repunctuated)

When Judas heard the heathens' shouting and the battle's noise, then went he behind them with three shield-troops and struck the heathens until they realised that the bold Judas was attacking them.

The absence of the demonstrative in verse is clearly a survival from an earlier stage of the language, and in the earliest poetry may reflect the normal usage of the time. But that it came to be recognised as a poetic licence is evident from King Alfred's employment of it in turning prose into verse, transforming, for instance, *þa tunglu* to *tunglu*. The device had obvious metrical advantages to a versifier in reducing the number of unstressed syllables, but it also had the effect on the listener of reducing the proportion of function words, intensifying not only the metrical weight of the line but also its semantic weight. There are perhaps semantic implications too in the merging of what in modern English would be two distinct concepts: 'a warrior' and 'the warrior' (or in the plural, 'warriors' and 'the warriors'). Universal statements and specific statements lose some of their linguistic distinctness. Consider, for instance, these lines from *Beowulf* (791–7):

Nolde eorla hleo   ænige þinga
[Would not warriors' protector   for any thing]
þone cwealmcuman   cwicne forlætan
[that killing-visitor   let go alive]
ne his lifdagas   leoda ænigum

[nor his lifedays   for any nations]
nytte tealde.   Þær genehost brægd
[counted useful.   There repeatedly drew]
eorl Beowulfes   ealde lafe,
[warrior of Beowulf   old heirloom]
wolde freadrihtnes   feorh ealgian,
[wanted king-lord's   life to protect]
mæres þeodnes,   ðær hie meahton swa.
[great prince's,   if they could do so.]

In context, these are statements of specific thoughts and actions in a specific situation, but some of them look linguistically like the universal statements that the specifics exemplify ('a [true] protector of warriors would not for any thing have let that killing-visitor go...a warrior would want to protect a king-lord's life'). The sub-textual reading is encouraged by the existence in Old English of poems, usually known as maxims or gnomic verses, that are wholly concerned with explicitly universal statements of this kind:

> Cyning sceal on healle
> [King must in hall]
beagas dælan......Treow sceal on eorle,
[rings distribute...Loyalty must be in warrior,]
wisdom on were.
[wisdom in man.]

(Max II)

As well as demonstratives, possessives too are less frequent in poetry, with similar effects on both rhythmical and semantic intensity and similar implications for the generalising, indefinite tendencies of poetic language. Thus the following lines from *The Wanderer* (51–3):

> Þonne maga gemynd   mod geondhweorfeð
> [When kinsmen's memory   passes through heart]
> greteð gliwstafum,   georne geondsceawað
> [he greets with glad-words,   keenly considers,]
> secga geseldan
> [men's companions]

are rendered in one translation: 'When the memory of kinsfolk passes through *his* imagination, the man greets *his* comrades with cheerful words, eagerly he watches them' (Bradley 1982:323).

A glance at different editions of the same Old English poem will reveal that modern editorial interpretations of sentence structure are extremely variable (see chapter 1, pp. 20–4). This is partly because punctuation in the manuscripts is very light and generally rhythmical rather than grammatical; where prose texts often show three hierarchies of stop (two internal and one marking a sentence ending), verse uses only one, the point, marking both medial and final pauses. It is also because the word-order rules which operate in prose to help distinguish main clauses from subordinate clauses give way in verse to different word-order systems which relate to metre and rhythm rather than grammar. Alistair Campbell puts the point sharply: 'the major weakness of the poetical language is this lack of any distinction between demonstrative and subordinate order' (Campbell 1970:95). (The lack is important, as it is not in Modern English, because in Old English conjunctions are often indistinguishable in form from the corresponding adverb.) Some commentators have concluded that poets therefore lacked the means to signal unambiguously the complex structures which they intended, but that such structures can be identified and marked by modern punctuation (cf. Andrew 1940). With most poets, however, the variety of interpretations placed on their syntax by modern commentators suggests that they were generally using loose structures of clauses which allowed for connection without insisting on it. Thus the lines quoted above from *The Wanderer* are immediately preceded by the clause *Sorg bið geniwad* ('Sorrow is renewed'): this can be read as the main clause of a complex sentence, pointing forward to the following *Þonne*, or as a clause loosely linked to the preceding main clause, or as an independent main clause (cf. Mitchell 1985:987ff. and more generally Mitchell 1980). Again, it is not difficult to find poems which escape this general tendency of the poetic language: long, complex, carefully subordinated sentences are common in the work of Cynewulf, for instance.

In place of complex subordination, Old English poetry often uses its own kinds of structures, in which qualifications and extensions of meaning are developed through the use of parallel phrases and clauses. The technique is usually known as variation, defined as follows: 'syntactically parallel words or word-groups which share a common referent and which occur within a single clause (or, in the instance of sentence-variation, within contiguous clauses)' (Robinson 1979:129). Often this amounts to only an accumulation of epithets for the same person or object; cf. the speech of the diplomatic courtier Wulfgar in *Beowulf* (350–3), with its series of four epithets (underlined below) for Hroðgar, king of the Danes:

'Ic þæs wine Deniga
[I about that friend of Danes]
frean Scyldinga   frinan wille,
[lord of Scyldings   will ask]
beaga bryttan,   swa þu bena eart,
[giver of rings,   as you are a petitioner]
þeoden mærne   ymb þinne sið.
[great king   about your journey]

In many cases, however, there is a gradual accumulation of further meaning with the accumulation of grammatically parallel expressions, as in the opening lines of *The Seafarer*:

Mæg ic be me sylfum   soðgied wrecan,
[I can about myself   true-poem utter]
siþas secgan,   hu ic geswincdagum
[tell of journeys,   how I in toilsome-days]
earfoðhwile   oft þrowade,
[hardship-times   often suffered]
bitre breostceare   gebiden hæbbe,
[bitter heart-sorrow   have endured]
gecunnad in ceole   cearselda fela,
[come to know on ship   many sorrow-halls]
atol yþa gewealc.
[cruel rolling of waves]

The phrase *soðgied wrecan* (line 1) is paralleled and slightly varied by *siþas secgan* (2), and the two nouns are then further elaborated by the grammatically parallel noun-clauses which follow (2–6), while *cearselda fela* (5) is varied by *atol yþa gewealc* (6).

Given the use of such parallelism, and the tendency for verse to omit the conjunction *and* when co-ordinating phrases and clauses, it is not always clear at what point a series of parallel phrases ceases to define a 'common referent' and begins to denote two distinct objects. Thus when the *Beowulf*-poet says that the prince of the Geats firmly trusted in *modgan mægnes*, *Metodes hyldo* (brave strength, God's favour), it remains inexplicit whether God's favour *is* the strength or whether it is something quite distinct, a direct intervention by God; and that question, whether there is some continuing involvement of God in the action (and in life), runs right through the poem.

It would perhaps be useful at this point to look at some individual poems. The characteristic metrical form and specialised language of Anglo-Saxon poetry are to be found throughout the period, from the very earliest recorded verse to the latest, and it is surprisingly difficult to trace indications of historical change or development in them (cf. Amos 1980). If, as many have thought, the specialised language was largely the product of a tradition of oral composition in a pre-literate world (cf. especially Lord 1960), one might expect to see a pattern of decline, with the poetic language becoming less pronounced and less confidently deployed in the course of the Anglo-Saxon period (cf. Shippey 1972). If, on the other hand, the specialised language was the gradual creation of individual poets in a literate culture, as the evidence of continued invention and adaptation during the period might suggest, one might expect to see a pattern with both advance and decline. In practice, there is evidence throughout the period of both the careful imitation of an old tradition and individual selection and inventiveness. The surviving fragments of two heroic poems thought to be early (seventh or eighth century), *The Fight at Finnsburg* and *Waldere*, show the poetic language fully developed, with poetic words and compounds and the occasional use of words otherwise unknown. The later poem, *The Battle of Brunanburh* (commemorating a battle of the year 937), reveals a poet familiar with the same heroic language and using it imaginatively without apparently inventing fresh terms. Still later, *The Battle of Maldon* (after 991) continues to draw heavily on the traditional vocabulary and phraseology of earlier heroic poetry with phrases like *har hilderinc*, and shows little sign of any inventiveness in the creation of compounds, but it does show an interesting admixture of contemporary language, using words such as *prasse* 'pomp' normally found only in prose and some recent borrowings from Norse such as *æsc* for ship. Characteristic of the mixture of old and new is *eorl*, a word resonant of older poetry in the sense 'warrior' but used here in its new, Norse-influenced sense of 'ealdorman, chieftain' (cf. Scragg 1981).

The particular challenge here is *Beowulf* itself. As the only truly heroic poem of any length to survive in Old English, it is inevitably taken as the norm or prime example of poetic language, though much modern scholarship would now place it quite late in the period, in the tenth century (cf. Chase 1981). Even assuming the traditional date of the eighth century, it may well represent a considerable sophistication of poetic language, with the simpler diction of the catalogue poem *Widsith* providing a better example of ordinary verse language of the period. According to one view, the *Beowulf*-poet was himself an innovator, 'a prime mover' in 'a general expansion of the poetic language' (Brodeur 1959:32–3). Brodeur points to the unusual variety of compounds in the poem (unusual, that is, in comparison with either long religious epics or short heroic poems), the number of words which are not paralleled at all outside the poem, and the poet's fondness for using (and perhaps therefore forming) compounds based on words which do not form compounds in other poems. The most recent survey of the poem's diction finds a total of 3,121 distinct headwords in the 3,182 lines of the poem, of which 672 are unique to the poem and another 459 exclusive to poetry (Cameron, Amos & Waite 1981).

The poet's enthusiasm for variety in his diction is clear: one might note, for instance, the range of words used to denote the monster Grendel (a kind of creature unlikely, one would suppose, to have played so central a role in heroic poetry generally as to attract a large set of traditional appellations): terms denoting 'monster' (*þyrs, eoten*) vary with terms denoting 'man' (*wer, healðegn*) and those denoting 'devil' (*ellengæst, gastbona*). Here the variety serves to suggest the mystery of Grendel's identity. Behind the range of terms used for Beowulf himself or men in general there is perhaps also some deliberate care: a good case can be made for seeing a careful distinction in the first part of the poem between terms denoting 'retainer', 'follower', which are used of the Danes and terms denoting 'fighter' which are used for the Geats, though a more casual desire for variety seems present in the use of *garwiga* ('spear-fighter') for Wiglaf at a moment when his crucial weapon is a short sword (Brady 1983). Richness of diction in itself is a facet of the poet's art. A recent study (Robinson 1985) suggests that the poet was deliberately exploiting the ambivalence of a diction which had acquired new religious meaning through Christian influence but still retained its older secular meanings as well. Evidence of a playful adaptation of poetic formulae or ironic placing of them and examples of the ways in which the tendencies of poetic syntax are exploited, have already been noted above. But for all the richness of language deliberate obscurity is probably not part of the poet's aim. There is scarcely anything approaching the riddling metaphorical complexity of the Norse scaldic diction of the tenth century. Figurative epithets (sometimes known as 'kennings') extend no further than the fairly transparent *beodoleoma* ('battle-light') for a sword or *seglrad* ('sail-road) for the sea. Compounds are generally made from elements which are themselves familiar and which are combined in a straightforward manner.

Anglo-Saxon religious poetry shows the same mixture of homogeneity and individuality as heroic verse. Bede's account of supposedly the first vernacular religious poet, Cædmon, presents the origins of religious poetry in Old English in a miraculous light, as the product of an angelic visitation. If one of the reasons for this story developing was a belief that a miraculous explanation was needed for such a phenomenon, what needed explaining may have been the adaptation of a traditional poetic language developed primarily for heroic subjects to the subjects of Christianity. Thus the phrase *heofonrices Weard* and *moncynnes weard* used by Cædmon of God in his divinely inspired *Hymn* may be adaptations of the traditional heroic formulae seen in the *folces weard* and *rices weard* of *Beowulf* lines 1390 and 2513; his *Meotodes meahte* is perhaps adapting to the Christian God a traditional poetic word for Fate, while *frea*, also used of God by Cædmon, is a poetic word meaning 'lord' or 'king'. Such techniques, once established, became very extensively used in later religious poems, which employ not only 'ruler' terms for God but also 'warrior' terms for saints and for Christ. Thus the religious epic on St Andrew, *Andreas*, begins with a series of heroic terms for the apostles: *tireadige hæleð, þeodnes þegnas, frome folctogan, fyrdhwate, rofe rincas* ('heroes blessed with glory', 'king's thanes', 'bold leaders of the people', 'brave in the army', 'bold warriors'). Its poetic, ornamental intent is signalled in the opening lines as well by the use of two poetic words for man, *hæleð* and *guma*, in non-alliterating positions where they do not normally appear. A slightly more cautious use of such vocabulary is evident in the poems of Cynewulf, employing the poetic terms for man, like *hæleð* and *guma*, compounds such as *dædhwate* and *hildfruma*, and traditional poetic formulae such as *hine fyrwet bræc* ('curiosity struck him'). However, the late Old Testament epic, *Judith*, reveals a poet sufficiently conscious of the heroic tradition to use it in an ironic, perhaps mock-heroic manner. The tyrannical, drunken and lustful Assyrian leader Holofernes is referred to by heroic epithets such as *gumena baldor* ('lord of men'), *goldwine gumena* ('gold-friend of men'), *byrnwigena brego* ('protector of armoured warriors'). His soldiers have epithets such as *lindwiggende* ('shield-warriors'), *fromlic* ('strong'), *niðheard* ('bold in battle'), even in their most unheroic moments when they are escorting Judith to the pavilion of their leader or hovering in fear outside his tent supposing that he is asleep with her. The same poet shows an inventiveness in adapting language, with his play on images of drink and pouring in the banqueting scene: Holofernes is *on gytesalum* (a word only found here, and probably the poet's own formation, literally meaning 'in pouring-joys' and managing to convey the sense both of 'in joy at the pouring of wine' and of 'in overwhelming joy'), he *drencte* and *oferdrencte* ('drenched/drowned' and 'drenched/drowned to destruction') his followers, who became *agotene* ('deprived by pouring', 'drained') of all goodness.

Still more striking evidence of a poet's willingness to break free of the traditional language is *The Dream of the Rood* (possibly eighth century). The poem manages both to be extraordinarily ingenious in exploiting the ambiguity of language and comparatively free of traditional heroic and even poetic terminology (cf. Swanton 1969). There is a sprinkling of the usual poetic words for man (*hilderinc*, *beorn*, *hæleð*), along with *frea* for God. The compounds include a few which are recognisably poetic (*hreowcearig* 'troubled', *modsefa* 'heart') but most are merely specific and denotative (*reordberend* 'speechbearers' 'human beings', *eaxlgespann* 'shoulder-span', 'cross-piece', *inwidhlemmas* 'malicious wounds'). Instead the poet plays with the ambiguities of ordinary words: *beam* meaning both tree and ray of light, *hean* meaning both high and wretched, *begoten* implying both covering (with gold) and suffusing (with blood). Similarly, while the traditional poetic language gives emphasis to nouns and adjectives this poet, as we have seen above, produces an array of vigorous verbs in prominent positions.

The degree of deliberate choice made by poets in such matters is demonstrated most clearly by the two anonymous poems on St Guthlac. *Guthlac B*, a poem on the saint's death relying closely on the Latin prose legend, draws heavily on traditional poetic diction, with words such as *firas*, *ælda* 'men', *hæleð* 'man', compounds such as *sindream* 'everlasting joy', *wuldorcyning* 'glory-king', *gewinworuld* 'world of care', and phrases such as *to widan feore* 'for ever', *folcum gefræge* 'known to nations'. By contrast, *Guthlac A*, a much more independent and imaginative poem by another poet, uses very few poetic words or compounds and its syntax is straightforward; prosaic words, especially legal and monastic terminology, are unusually common (cf. Roberts 1979). The concept of the saint as a spiritual warrior is expressed by the ordinary word *cempa* and occasionally *oretta*, not generally by the 'heroic' words *beorn*, *rinc*, *secg* and the various compounds. Yet the poet of *Guthlac A* claims to be writing during the saint's lifetime, that is, in the eighth century, and his use of metrically-determined unsyncopated forms would tend to place him earlier in date than *Guthlac B*. His avoidance of poetic diction would thus appear to be a matter of individual choice rather than late date and the decay of poetic tradition.

8.3 Prose

Whereas Anglo-Saxon poetry and the specialised language associated with it have their origins deep in the pre-literate past, sustained discourse in prose began essentially in the late ninth century with the reign of Alfred. From the period before then there are some legal records mainly preserved in later manuscripts, and there may have been oral narrative in prose, though if so it has left little if any trace (Wright 1939). There have also been arguments, on linguistic grounds, that a number of prose texts preserved in manuscripts dating from the end of the tenth century or later were in fact composed in Mercia before the time of Alfred (see Vleeskruyer 1953), but these remain unsupported. In the late ninth century, however, a well-evidenced and continuous tradition begins with the works usually associated with King Alfred: the four works by Alfred himself (the *Pastoral Care*, the translation of Boethius' *Consolation of Philosophy*, the *Soliloquies* and the prose part of the *Paris Psalter*), the anonymous translations of Orosius' *History of the World* and Bede's *Ecclesiastical History*, Wærferth's translation of Gregory the Great's *Dialogues* and the Anglo-Saxon Chronicle. In the tenth century the Chronicle was continued and a number of anonymous writings of uncertain date are possibly to be placed in this period, including the Blickling and Vercelli collections of homilies, the prose romance *Apollonius of Tyre* and some saints' lives. The high period of prose came towards the end of the tenth century, with the work of the homilist Ælfric, the acknowledged master of Old English prose, and of Wulfstan and Byrhtferth of Ramsey, and the continuation of the Anglo-Saxon Chronicle.

Much of Old English prose writing was public and official, in a way that prose seldom was to be again after the Conquest until the late fourteenth century. King Alfred presented his first work as the beginning of a considered scheme for national education, and made careful arrangements for its official dissemination and preservation. Ælfric similarly offered his first work as a response to a national problem, referred approvingly to the example of Alfred and presented the finished work to the archbishop of Canterbury; its immediate and widespread dissemination, probably from Canterbury, suggests again a deliberate and official activity. Wulfstan's homilies and law-codes express his public role as archbishop and address themselves to a wide audience; his best-known work is a sermon addressed to the whole English nation at a time of national crisis. The Chronicle is, similarly, a national history and was widely disseminated soon after its original compilation. Even the extant letters of the period are for the most part formal and public documents given a personal prologue (the pastoral letters of Ælfric and Wulfstan, for example). This must have had an influence both on the kind of language used by prose writers and on the evident care with which they sought to polish and perfect their words; as the evidence of the manuscripts shows, Alfred, Ælfric and Wulfstan are all to be found revising their work even after it was 'published'.

These prose works were ambitious undertakings. Their authors were pioneers in attempting to render philosophy, theology, history, legend, science and biblical exegesis in vernacular prose. The sheer length and complexity of their material forced them to encounter the problem of choosing, at times forging, a language appropriate to their subject, to their own modes of thinking and to their readers.

The origins of this vernacular prose tradition lie primarily in Latin prose. Virtually all the works in question have Latin texts as sources or models, though the Chronicle may also derive in part from brief vernacular records. Yet in their choice and use of language there is evident in most writers a striking resistance to Latin prose as a model, and a preference for developing a learned vocabulary from native resources and building a system of syntax and sentence structure based on native idiom. The traditional language of vernacular poetry was often an influence, but there was an evident degree of resistance to this too. Even so, as we shall see, the language of literary prose was recognisably different from the spoken language of the time.

Two problems in particular were faced by prose writers: developing a vocabulary that could cope with the intellectual and technical demands of their subjects and still be generally understood; and developing techniques of grammatical relation and sentence structure to organise complex thought, without the benefit of either the stress-distinctions important in speech or the partially metrical patterns traditional in verse. There was also, however, a concern with establishing a standard form of the language, governed by recognised rules, and a growing interest in the possibilities of stylistic ornament.

Although most works in Old English prose were to one degree or another translations from Latin, there is surprisingly little contemporary suggestion of any difficulty in rendering Latin thought in the vernacular. King Alfred discusses the principles and history of translation in his preface to the *Pastoral Care*, translating, he says, *hwilum word be worde, hwilum andgit of andgiete* (*CP* 7; 'sometimes word for word, sometimes sense for sense'). There is perhaps a hint of linguistic barriers in the immediately following remark that he translated Gregory's Latin *swæ ic hie andgitfullicost areccean meahte* ('as meaningfully as I could render it'), but he does not suggest that the English language was in any way inadequate to express biblical or patristic thought, or that the nature of either the language or his readership required any kind of simplification. In his subsequent writings on philosophy and theology there is again no reference to problems of linguistic adequacy and no evidence that he perceived any difficulties. The problems of translation are discussed in some detail by Ælfric in the preface to his translation of Genesis, but his main linguistic point is that Latin and English have different modes of expression which must be observed even in cases where a very literal translation would otherwise be called for. Nowhere in all his writings, however, does Ælfric suggest any difficulty in matching the terminology of Latin or expressing complex ideas in English. For both writers, the tendency to rewrite in their own words when following Latin sources rather than translating literally may partially explain this confidence in the capacity of English. A very different view is voiced, however, by the early eleventh-century writer Byrhtferth of Ramsey. His *Manual*, a guide to computation, is written in Latin for the monks and in roughly parallel English for the rural (*uplendisce*) priests. He remarks that 'these concepts are difficult to express in English' and says that it is necessary for him to mingle Latin terms with the English (*ByrM* 76.9, 112.31), which he repeatedly does (for examples see below p. 533).

The vocabulary of literary prose is marked by its variation from author to author, sometimes even within the work of an author. Whereas poetry deployed a common stock of words and compounding elements which were exploited by most poets, in prose different writers made different choices from a surprisingly wide range of possibilities. The many possibilities of word-formation, and the opportunity to adapt words from Latin or Norse, created a variety of options for Old English, and the challenge of writing about philosophy, theology, science, grammar and other learned subjects encouraged authors to take advantage of these options. Clear lexical distinctions are evident for instance between Alfred and his associates. Thus the former uses *scyldig* ('guilty') where the *Orosius* uses *gyltig*, *fultumian* ('to help') where it uses *fylstan*, *andswarian* ('to answer') where it uses *andwyrdan*, and *forþam* ('because') rather than *forþam þe* (Bately 1970). Perhaps as a consequence of the general confidence about the language, most writers seem to have consciously shunned extensive borrowing from Latin, in striking contrast to the fondness for using learned Latin-derived words in Renaissance prose, or French-derived words in late Middle English prose. A number of very ancient borrowings appear of course in all writers, such as *win* ('wine'), and more recent ecclesiastical borrowings such as *apostol* are quite common in prose. But the subjects dealt with by many prose writers required a much more extensive diction than this: a vocabulary for philosophy, science, theology and grammatical description, for instance. Although most of the literary prose drew on Latin sources, individual prose-writers generally resisted the temptation to borrow the technical terminology of Latin. This is particularly striking in the case of both Alfred, faced with the demands of philosophy and theology, and Ælfric, confronting the needs of grammar and science. What is involved here is something more than a desire to simplify for a readership without Latin. There is clearly some deep-seated and widely shared feeling about the inappropriateness of Latin borrowings to tone.

Possibly the major challenge faced by prose writers in creating a language appropriate to their needs was in the area of sentence structure. Latin prose was an important influence on most of the early vernacular prose works and would have encouraged the use of complex sentences with much subordination, but this is not a common feature in Old English verse and was presumably still less common in the spoken language. One of the limitations was the ease of confusion between conjunctions and adverbs, with *þa* meaning 'when' or 'then', *þær* meaning 'where' or 'there', *swa* meaning 'as' or 'so', *þeah* meaning 'although' or 'however'. In speech there was probably a difference of intonation, with the conjunction being more heavily stressed than the adverb, but this could not be carried over into writing. Prose writers deployed a number of techniques, possibly already incipient in speech, to overcome the problem, such as doubling the word to indicate the conjunction (*swa swa* 'as', *ða ða* 'when', *ðær ðær* 'where', *ær ær* 'before', in contrast to *swa* 'so', *ða* 'then', *ðær* 'there', *ær* 'previously'), or adding the particle *ðe* (*ðeah ðe* 'although', contrasting with *ðeah* 'however') or *ðam ðe* (*ær ðam ðe* 'before' contrasting with *ær* 'previously'); or using word-order patterns to distinguish main from subordinate or co-ordinate clauses (thus *ða* followed immediately by the verb means 'then', *ða* followed immediately by the subject means 'when'). None of these systems became comprehensively established, perhaps because they were always at odds with a concern for rhythmical patterning or a desire for variety. Thus Ælfric generally employs *ðeah* for the adverb and *ðeah ðe* for the conjunction, but was always prepared to use *ðeah* as a variant for the conjunction, perhaps for rhythmical reasons. Similarly he varies between þa and þa þa for the conjunction 'when', and among þe, se, se þe and seþe for the relative pronoun. Another problem that writers faced when translating Latin prose was to find an equivalent for constructions using adjectival phrases, headed by a participle or adjective, where English would more naturally use a subordinate clause.

The need to follow the idiom of English rather than Latin is remarked on by Ælfric in the preface to his translation of Genesis:

> Ðæt Leden and ðæt Englisc nabbað na ane wisan on ðære spræce fadunge: æfre se ðe awent oððe se ðe tæcð of Ledene on Englisc, æfre he sceal gefadian hit swa ðæt ðæt Englisc hæbbe his agene wisan, elles hit bið swyðe gedwolsum to rædenne ðam ðe ðæs Ledenes wise ne can.
>
> *(ÆGenPref pp. 79–80)*

> Latin and English do not have the same manner in the arrangement of the language: one who translates or teaches from Latin into English must always arrange it so that the English has its own manner, otherwise it is very difficult to read for one who does not know the manner of Latin.

Yet in the preface to his *Grammar* he makes it clear that literary prose was quite distinct from the ordinary spoken language. This is a grammar of Latin but written in English, and the author explains in the preface that he intends it as an aid to the understanding of English as well as Latin. The opening sentence of the English part of the preface suggests that his own vernacular writings, or at least writings like them, are among the works for which a knowledge of grammar will be helpful:

> Ic Ælfric wolde þas lytlan boc awendan to Engliscum gereorde of ðam stæfcræfte, þe is gehaten GRAMMATICA, syððan ic ða twa bec awende on hundeahtatigum spellum, forðan ðe stæfcræft is seo cæg, ðe ðæra boca andgit unlicð.
>
> *(ÆGram p. 2).*

> I Ælfric decided to translate into English this little book of the art of letters which is called grammar, after I had translated the two volumes of eighty homilies, because grammar is the key which unlocks the meaning of those books (or 'of books': either translation is possible).

The two volumes of homilies to which he refers are models of lucid, elegant English, and in his preface to them Ælfric claims to have used simple language, but it seems clear that in his mind, at least, literary English of this kind is formalised and structured in ways which require a knowledge of formal grammar for complete understanding. It is striking testimony to the differences which must have existed between the spoken language and formal literary prose.

Another area of contemporary concern was the development of a standard language. Virtually all Old English prose is preserved in a predominantly West Saxon dialect, and most of it was probably composed in West Saxon, whether the Early West Saxon of Alfred's own works or the Late West Saxon of Ælfric, Wulfstan, Byrhtferth and the later Chronicle. In modern times the Early West Saxon of the Alfredian works has been adopted as a basis for a normalised Old English, but there is little evidence that it achieved any kind of status as a standard in its own time, or that writers were much concerned with standardisation then. Even in the contemporary manuscripts spelling is inconsistent, often within the same work. Thus the *Pastoral Care* shows variation between <ie>, <i> and <e> in the same words, and also between <a> and <ea>. A number of Mercian spellings have been detected in Alfred's work, and occur more extensively in the Old English translation of Bede's *Ecclesiastical History*. The use of conjunctions varies between Alfred's earliest work, the translation of the *Pastoral Care*, and his later two, the translation of Boethius and the theological text known as the *Soliloquies*. Within the anonymous translation of Orosius there is considerable variation, from section to section, in syntax and sentence structure, possibly reflecting the work of different collaborators (cf. Liggins 1970). Nor is there any sign of standardisation immediately after Alfred's time. A number of the prose works traditionally dated in the period between the death of Alfred (900) and the beginning of the Benedictine Reform movement (ca 970), such as the Vercelli and Blickling homilies, show Anglian or Kentish features. However, a genuine standard language, based on Late West Saxon, developed during the second half of the tenth century, and became the medium for the major prose-writers of the time, wherever they wrote: Athelwold at Winchester, Ælfric at Cerne Abbas and Eynsham, Wulfstan at Worcester and York, Byrhtferth at Ramsey. (See further in the Introduction.) Copies of Ælfric's works show remarkable consistency in spelling within themselves and from manuscript to manuscript. The same spellings are used by scribes and, it appears, authors from Canterbury to Northumbria. Vocabulary too shows signs of standardisation, particularly in continuous glosses and translations (cf. Gneuss 1972). Earlier prose texts were thoroughly revised to bring them into line with the Late West Saxon standard (a good example is the prose version of the life of St Guthlac; cf. Roberts 1986).

The spread of this standard, it has been suggested (Gneuss 1972), may owe something to deliberate efforts by those in authority, perhaps centred at Winchester and the school of Athelwold. Certainly the literary writers of the period show a serious concern with questions of linguistic correctness and standards. Ælfric's insistence on a need for knowledge of grammar in order to read his prose has already been noted above, and the point is reinforced by the manuscript evidence of his careful revision of his work to make it more consistent in grammatical features. His early writings show a mixture of dative and accusative cases after the prepositions *þurh*, *wið*, *ymbe* and others, which may well reflect the disorder of the spoken language (particularly, perhaps, with *þurh*, where a common pattern in Ælfric's early prose is to use the accusative with concrete and singular nouns and the dative with abstract and plural nouns). But Ælfric's later practice was to use the accusative throughout, and the manuscripts show that he thoroughly revised his earlier work, correcting all instances to the accusative (Godden 1979). Similarly, the subtle distinction between the strong dative adjectival ending *-um* and the weak form *-an*, gradually disappearing in speech, seems often to have eluded scribes and perhaps Ælfric himself, but the manuscripts show careful alterations to the correct form. Alterations in Ælfric's own hand to a copy of his homilies include changes in the form of the verb 'to be', from *sindon* to *beon* and *is* to *bið*, presumably reflecting a change of mind about the 'correct' usage for a particular sense of the verb (Eliason and Clemoes 1966). A concern with standardising language is evident also in Wulfstan, whose handwriting can be seen altering and correcting the language of a copy of Alfred's *Pastoral Care* (Ker 1956). The difficulty which Ælfric, and presumably other writers, faced in trying to establish grammatical regularity is perhaps clearest from the occasional cases where he fails to resolve inconsistency: he seems to have remained uncertain whether *ærmerigen* 'dawn, early morning' should be treated as a compound or as two words of which the first should be inflected as an adjective; whether the poetic word *metod* 'God, fate' was a strong noun, a weak noun or an adjective; or whether *hæl* 'health, salvation' was feminine or masculine (Godden 1980).

Yet writers with an ear for style and the nuances of expression clearly felt free to resist standardisation when they wished. An anonymous scribe of the later tenth century appears to have deliberately introduced archaic spellings into a copy of Alfred's *Pastoral Care*, presumably to underline its status as a creation of a particular historical moment, perhaps a relic of the king (Horgan 1986). As in the poetry, some linguistic variables are exploited for tonal effect. Thus Ælfric uses the present participle *lifiende* with reference to God and the alternative form *libbende* for all other purposes (Pope 1967–8:100). It has been argued that both he and Wulfstan observe a careful distinction between syncopated present tense endings for normal purposes and unsyncopated forms in formal contexts (cf. Bethurum 1957:53).

Though some examples of Old English prose are doubtless closer to contemporary speech than others, variations of register between the colloquial and the formal within prose are not easily identified. Many of the surviving texts are homilies and sermons, purportedly designed for oral delivery, but as Ælfric's comments on the need for grammatical understanding in order to comprehend his homilies suggest, there is no reason to suppose that they represent a form of language close to speech, or that they are in any way a record of discourse which originated in oral improvisation. Apart from the almost invariable opening address, *men þa leofestan* or *leofan man* ('dearly beloved'), intimacy signals and conversational tags are infrequent and the mode of address seems rather formal. The same doubts about colloquial language must apply to passages of dialogue within narrative or philosophical works; it has been shown, for instance, that Ælfric structures the discourse of characters in his saints' lives for moral rather than realistic ends (Waterhouse 1976). The most deceptive text is the familiar conversation piece known as Ælfric's *Colloquy*: this is a Latin text designed for instruction in that language, and the word-by-word English gloss added later by another writer is likely to be at some distance from vernacular idiom, whether colloquial or formal. Some uses of less formal language are possibly perceptible outside Ælfric's work. It has been suggested that occasional instances of unsignalled slipping from indirect to direct discourse, for instance in the early Chronicle, may be a mark of colloquial register (Kerling 1982, though cf. Richman 1986, who suggests that some examples are aspects of deliberate art). The use of language to achieve some intimacy of tone has been seen in several of the Blickling homilies (Dalbey 1969), and some possibly colloquial elements in Wulfstan's prose are mentioned below.

Contemporary writers generally refer to prose as an entirely functional medium, designed to convey information. For Alfred the major function of writing in English is the transmission and preservation of knowledge, and he points to the general ignorance of Latin as a reason for using English. A century later, Ælfric too, in his many prefaces, emphasises the functional role of writing, stressing the need to convey knowledge and understanding. Although much of his writing is homiletic in form, he makes no mention of the rhetorical ideals, to persuade or to stir the emotions, and both he and Byrhtferth define prose as straightforward, simple discourse in contrast to the ornament of verse (see above p. 494). In reality, however, they and other writers recognised the possibilities of different levels of language in prose. In his first preface Ælfric speaks of his preference for 'simple and very open' language, eschewing obscure terms, for the sake of the simple and unlearned listeners and readers for whom he intends his work (*ÆCHom* I, 1). The reference to the simplicity of his readers should perhaps not be taken too literally: Ælfric clearly wrote his English works for the learned clergy and laity as well as for the less educated, and the works which he wrote in Latin for a more learned readership show the same preference for elegant simplicity over the deliberate obscurity favoured by most other tenth-century writers of Latin in England (cf. Lapidge 1975). Simplicity of language seems with Ælfric to be in part a matter of personal taste. His remarks about the simplicity of his own prose imply that a more obscure and ornate language would be possible in English, as in Latin, and such a language is in fact found in the writing of Byrhtferth (see below). An anonymous late tenth-century writer also shows a full awareness of the aesthetic possibilities of prose: addressing Wulfstan with reference to his vernacular prose, he refer to the 'very sweet wisdom of your eloquence and the richness of your composition fittingly organised, and at the same time its profundity' (Bethurum 1966:211). A knowledge of the elements of rhetoric was part of grammatical training in Latin in the period, and is likely therefore to have been possessed by the more learned prose writers at least. Byrhtferth refers to it explicitly in his *Manual*:

> Æfter þissum, hig gehleapað on *metaplasum*, þæt ys þæt hig gewurðiað heora spæce and heora meteruersa gesetnyssa...*Scemata lexeos* gebyriað to þam bocerum þe beoð cyrtenlice getydde on þam cræfte.
>
> (*ByrM* 96–8)

After this, they (learned scholars) leap on to metaplasmus, that is to say that they adorn their speech and their metrical compositions ... The figures of speech are fitting for those authors who have been very carefully trained in that art.

The commonest form of ornament is the use of rhythm. Users of the Old English language in general show a striking sensitivity to patterns of stress. This is indicated not only by the nature of Old English metre, with its complex 'rules' for the inter-relationship of accented and unaccented syllables, but also by the role of stress in distinguishing parts of speech. A number of prose writers developed the possibilities of rhythmical patterning both as a form of decoration and as a mode of structuring discourse. At times it approximates very closely indeed to verse, as in the sustained sequences of two-stress phrases, sometimes linked by alliteration or assonance, seen in some of the *Vercelli Homilies*:

> On ðam dæge us byð ætywed
> se gesewena heofon   and engla þrym
> and eallwihtna hryre   and eorðan forwyrd,
> treowleasra gewinn   and tungla gefeall
> þunorrada cyrm   and se ðystra storm...

> (*VercHom* XXI, 146–50)

> On that day there will be shown to us the visible heaven and the angels' glory, the fall of all creatures and the ruin of the earth, the strife of the faithless and the fall of the stars, the noise of thunder and the storm of darkness...

This use of rhythmical patterning in prose seems to have been partly in imitation of verse, but it was possibly influenced as well by the use of the cursus and other rhythmical devices in Latin prose (cf. Gerould 1925). But apart from such very evident patterns, to be discussed below, an ear for less obvious rhythmical patterns or sequences probably played a large though unprovable part in the choices which prose writers with a concern for style made from among the many possibilities of word-order, lexical forms and inflexions. Another form of ornament that recurs in a number of works is the occasional use of poetic vocabulary, as a form of heightening. There are also examples of word-play. The stylistic device of repeating a verbal element in different forms within the same sentence is a recognised form of Latin rhetoric. Old English compounds lent themselves very readily to such word-play. Its use perhaps suggests the degree of conscious awareness of the compounding process and of etymology. A simple example is Chronicle 1011: 'þær man mihte þa geseon earmðe þær man ær geseah blisse on þære ærman byrig' (there one could then see misery where before bliss was seen, in that wretched city), where *earmðe* and *ærman* are formed from the same root.

If we turn now to a more detailed look at the practice of individual writers, the works of the Alfredian period show well the range of possibilities in the language of literary prose. At one extreme is the Anglo-Saxon Chronicle which, at least in its original portion, uses a remarkably simple language, relying heavily on parataxis with only temporal subordination and simple, repetitive diction. Some commentators have regarded this as a sign of the undeveloped state of the language, others have seen it as a deliberate choice of a mode of language appropriate to the genre (cf. Clark 1971). The existence of more complex prose in other works of the same period and probably the same circle suggests that the author(s) of the Chronicle may well have been at least aware of alternative possibilities. The probability of conscious choice is suggested particularly by the annal for 755 describing the conflict of Cynewulf and Cyneheard. This is a story of royal feuding involving loyalty to the death and ideals of revenge, a story which, to judge from the kind of detail included, must have been transmitted in a highly dramatic and colourful form, probably verse, with extensive use of dialogue. The Chronicle version uses a strikingly limited language: no colourful terms, indirect speech, paratactic sentences, as if the writer felt the need to replace poetic language with something appropriate to the chronicle genre.

At the other extreme from the Chronicle is the translation of Bede's *Ecclesiastical History* which attempts a very close imitation of the structures of Latin prose, often producing constructions that seem rather awkward in English, as in the following description of the poet Cædmon:

> In huius monasterio abbatissae fuit frater quidam diuina gratia specialiter insignis, quia carmina religioni et pietati apta facere solebat, ita ut, quicquid ex diuinis litteris per interpretes disceret, hoc ipse post pusillum uerbis poeticis maxima suauitate et conpunctione conpositis in sua, id est Anglorum, lingua proferret.
>
> (Colgrave and Mynors 1969:IV xxiv)

In this abbess's monastery there was a certain brother specially marked out by divine grace, because he used to compose poems suitable to religion and piety, so that, whatever he learned from divine writings through interpreters, this after a short time he brought forth in poetic words composed with the greatest sweetness and feeling in his own, that is the English, language.

In ðeosse abbudissan mynstre wæs sum broðor syndriglice mid godcundre gife gemæred and geweorðad. For þon he gewunade gerisenlice leoð wyrcan, þa ðe to æfæstnisse ond to arfæstnisse belumpen, swa ðætte, swa hwæt swa he of godcundum stafum þurh boceras geleornode, þæt he æfter medmiclum fæce in scopgereorde mid þa mæstan swetnisse ond inbryrdnisse geglængde ond in Engliscgereorde wel geworht forþbrohte.

(Bede 342.3–9)

In this abbess's monastery there was a certain brother specially glorified and honoured by divine grace, because he used to compose fitting songs, those which pertained to religion and piety, so that, whatever he learned from divine writings through interpreters, that after a short time he brought forth in poetic language adorned with greatest sweetness and feeling and well composed in English.

Similar tendencies are evident in Wærferth's version of the *Dialogues*. Associated with this Latinate syntax, and perhaps reflecting a similar aspiration towards high style, is the fondness of both works for word-pairs, particularly pairs of synonyms; note, for instance, the rendering of Latin *insignis* by the pair *gemæred and geweorðad* in the passage from the Old English Bede above. The two-stress rhythms which these tend to produce are perhaps an imitation of verse. The translation of Bede is also said to show 'a liking for words and compounds with a poetic flavour' (Whitelock 1962). Examples given of words found otherwise mainly in poetry are *dogor*, *rodor*, *from* ('strong'), *leod*, *til*, and the compounds *bædeweg*, *ellenwodness*, *eðelturf*, *gylpgeorn*, *wilsip*, *wilfægen*.

Alfred's own works are intellectually the most ambitious, dealing not with narrative but with theological and philosophical argument. Of the early translators he is the freest in his handling of the content of his sources, and a similar freedom is evident in his language. The element of conscious choice is evident particularly in Alfred's response to the demands of technical terminology. Faced with difficult terms like *fortuna*, *fata*, *providentia*, Alfred looks for approximate English equivalents such as *wyrd* and *woruldgesælð* or employs a paraphrase rather than borrowing the Latin terms. He acknowledges that Boethius was a *consul* but immediately explains 'which we call *heretoga*' and uses the latter word thereafter (whereas the closely associated translation of Orosius freely uses *consul*, just as it uses the loan-word *philosoph* while Alfred uses the native *uðwita*). This is possibly a factor in Alfred's development of a rather different philosophy from that expounded by Boethius; his inability or refusal to find a real equivalent for *fortuna*, for instance, is part of, and possibly a reason for, a general diminution in the role of the personified figure of Fortune and the concept for which she stands (cf. Otten 1964).

There is a similar freedom from Latin in his sentence structures, which are often complex and rambling. His characteristic method is to break down long Latin sentences relying heavily on nouns and participles into series of short clauses (cf. Brown 1969). His attempts to capture all the meaning, explicit and implied, in Boethius' elegant sentences and to add explanatory qualifications often produce sentences far more replete with subordinate clauses than the Latin, with results that are rather laboured. Thus Boethius' statement of the difference between providence and fate neatly balances two main clauses, accompanied by two matching temporal clauses (with a brief relative clause depending on the second).

> Qui modus cum in ipsa divinae intellegentiae puritate conspicitur, providentia nominatur; cum vero ad ea quae movet atque disponit refertur, fatum a veteribus appellatum est.
>
> (Boethius, *De consolatione philosophiae* IV.vi.27–30)

> This manner, when it is viewed in the utter purity of the divine intelligence, is called providence; but when it is related to those things which it moves and orders, it was by the ancients called fate.

Alfred's version defines providence with a noun clause followed by a main clause followed in turn by three successive temporal clauses, while for fate he uses a temporal clause followed by a main clause:

> Ac ðæt ðætte we hatað Godes foreþonc and his foresceawung, þæt bið þa hwile þe hit ðær mid him bið on his mode, ærðæm þe hit gefremed weorðe, þa hwile ðe hit geþoht bið; ac siððan hit fullfremed bið, þonne hatað we hit wyrd.
>
> (Sedgefield 1899:128.10–13).

> But that which we call God's forethought and providence, that exists while it is there with him in his mind, before it is enacted, while it is considered; but after it is enacted, then we call it fate.

One might note, in passing, the awkwardness created by having to use *bið* both in its normal sense of 'is' and in the philosophical sense of 'exists'.

Some commentators see such aspects of Alfred's writing as a limitation imposed on him by the state of the language. Kurt Otten says of King Alfred's translation of Boethius: 'Alfred's means of hypotaxis are limited and his development of thought is virtually restricted to two categories; antithesis and causality' (Otten 1964:287). Otten sees this as one of several ways in which the king was unconsciously compelled to comprehend and present Boethian thought in terms of his own culture. Similarly it has been suggested as a partial explanation of the style of Alfred's *Soliloquies* that 'at this stage of its development Old English may prefer the elaborated syntax and concrete diction' (Waterhouse 1986:51). Alfred seems generally little interested in ornament. There are a few and clearly deliberate cases of poetic vocabulary, where he was translating the verse parts of Boethius' *Consolation of Philosophy*; thus the poetic terms *metod* and *guma* appear fleetingly here. Something like the word-pairing technique of the Bede translation, though more thoughtful and effective, is occasionally seen in his prose, using a sustained rhythm with the pairing of words which are complementary rather than synonymous:

> Hu ne is ðis sio micle Babilon ðe ic self atimbrede to kynestole and to ðrymme, me silfum to wlite and wuldre mid mine agne mægene and strengo?
>
> (CP 29)
>
> Is not this the great Babylon, which I myself created for a royal seat and for glory, to adorn and glorify myself, with my own power and strength?

This was a sentence which Ælfric admired sufficiently to imitate it himself a century later (cf. Godden 1978:103), but in general Alfredian prose does not attempt the patterning of language that is so distinctive in the work of Ælfric.

Ælfric, as we have seen, played a major part in the move towards standardising and regularising the language, yet at the same time his work shows a willingness to experiment with language and exploit its full range. One example of experiment is his use of words meaning 'however': he uses *þeah-hwæðre* in his first work, but switches almost entirely to *swaþeah* and *þeah* in his second work and thereafter. He uses *martyr* and *cyðere* interchangeably for 'martyr' in his first two works but settles down to *martyr* thereafter, and similarly shifts in preference from *gelomlice* to *gelome* for 'frequently' (Godden 1980). In the general consistency and the occasional examples of authorial revision of diction there is evidence of personal concern about appropriate diction, but it seems to have been often a matter of individual judgement of tone and nuance rather than an attempt to match an acknowledged general standard. In some respects, his use of function words suggests a preference for variety over consistency.

This taste for variety is particularly pronounced with lexical items, where he deploys a wide range of synonyms to avoid verbal repetition. In the familiar account of St Oswald, a brief passage on miracles of healing interchanges three words for 'sick', *untrum*, *gebrocod* and *adliga*:

> And wurdon fela gehælde untrumra manna and eac swilce nytena þurh ða ylcan rode, swa swa us rehte Beda. Sum man feoll on ise, þæt his earm tobærst, and læg þa on bedde gebrocod forðearle, oð þæt man him fette of ðære foresædan rode sumne dæl þæs meoses þe heo mid beweaxen wæs, and se adliga sona on slæpe wearð gehæled on ðære ylcan nihte þurh Oswoldes geearnungum.
>
> (*ÆLS* xxvi.31–9)

> And many sick people and also animals were healed through that same cross, as Bede has recounted for us. A certain person fell on ice so that his arm broke, and he lay then in bed severely afflicted, until someone fetched from the afore-mentioned cross a piece of the moss which had grown round it, and the sick one was immediately healed in his sleep in that same night, through the merits of Oswold.

Similarly, in the following passage Gregory the Great, Ælfric's source, deliberately deploys an intense degree of verbal repetition:

> Sunt namque lapides, sed nec vivunt, nec sentiunt. Sunt herbae et arbusta; vivunt quidem, sed non sentiunt... Bruta vero animalia sunt, vivunt, sentiunt, sed non discernunt. Sunt angeli qui vivunt, sentiunt et discernunt.
>
> (Patrologia Latina 76, 1214)

> For stones exist, but do not live or feel. Grass and trees exist and live but do not feel... Animals exist, live and feel but do not discern. Angels exist, and they live, feel and discern.

Ælfric here translates closely but deploys a much more varied diction; Gregory's *vivunt* (used four times) varies in Ælfric between *lybbað* and *nabbað nan lif*, while *sentiunt* (4) becomes *gefredað*, *buton felnysse*, *habbað felnysse*, *gefredað*, and Gregory's *discernunt* (2) varies between *buton gesceade* and *tosceadað*:

> Stanas sind gesceafta, ac hi nabbað nan lif, ne hi ne gefredað. Gærs and treowa lybbað butan felnysse... Nytenu lybbað and habbað felnysse, butan gesceade... Englas lybbað, and gefredað, and tosceadað.
>
> (*ÆCHom I*, 302.13–18)

> Stones are creatures, but they have no life and they feel nothing. Grass and trees live without feeling ... Animals live and have feeling without reason ... Angels live and feel and discern.

His linguistic resourcefulness is evident again in the ensuing lines, where he resolves the problem confronted by Alfred earlier, of finding an equivalent for the philosophical term *esse* 'to exist', with *beo wunigende*, 'is dwelling', carefully distinguished from *lybbað*.

Like Alfred, Ælfric generally shows a preference for native compounds rather than Latin loan-words for technical terms, such as *forestihtung* for Latin *predestinatio* and *tungelwitega* for astrologer. A strong sense of the difference between learned and ordinary diction is suggested by such remarks as Ælfric's 'leorningcnihtas, þa ðe we apostolas hatað' (*ÆCHom* II 258/12; 'learning-pupils, those whom we [presumably the learned] call apostles'). At times this independence in language is closely associated with an independence of thought, as the difference between the semantic fields of Old English words and those of equivalent Latin words aids him in developing an argument on different terms from his Latin authorities. Thus his use of *gastlice* ('spiritually') as an equivalent to Latin *figura* (in the sense 'metaphor') plays a part in his development of a strikingly novel theology of the eucharist which in turn contributed to his fame in the sixteenth century (cf. Wrenn 1969). Similarly, he distinguishes two meanings covered by the Latin verb *tentare*, which he expresses by *fandian* 'to try, test (with benevolent intent)' and *costnian* 'to tempt, assail (with hostile intent)'. The same sort of sensitivity about loan-words does not operate, it would appear, with borrowings from other languages: Ælfric seems to be the first recorded user of the French loan-word *pryte* 'pride', for instance (Hofstetter 1979) and an early user of the Norse loan-word *lagu* in its general sense 'law' (Godden, 1980).

In his organisation of the sentence, Ælfric has his own distinctive practices. Generally he keeps sentences relatively short and subordination simple, with the precise relationships of ideas often implicit. Rhythm, antithesis and balance are frequently used in preference to complex structures, to organise the argument. He shows a particular fondness for a defining relative clause where an adverbial clause might be expected. In the following case it renders the conditional clause of the Bible:

> Sic et fides, si non habeat opera, mortua est in semetipsa
>
> (James II.17)

> So faith, if it does not have works, is dead in itself

Se geleafa ðe bið butan godum weorcum, se bið dead

(ÆCHom I, 302.33–4)

The faith which is without good works, that is dead.

In this example, the relative clause deals with the difficult problem where Latin relies on the adjective in the appropriate case and gender:

Cor carnale in suis pravis voluptatibus frigidum...

(Gregory, PL 76 1222D-3A)

The fleshly heart, cold in its base desires...

ðæs eorðlican mannes heorte...seo ðe ær wæs ceald þurh flæsclice lustas

(ÆCHom I, 322.14–16)

the earthly person's heart, which previously was cold because of fleshly desires.

Another characteristic technique in his work is what has been termed a 'triangular' clause structure, in which a main clause is both preceded and followed by a subordinate clause (Waterhouse 1983).

Despite his emphasis on simplicity in theory and practice, rhythm and alliteration play an important part in Ælfric's writing, though characteristically it is ornament that is closely associated with meaning. The occasional use of two-stress rhythms is evident in his earliest work, but while composing his second major work, the Second Series of *Catholic Homilies*, he developed a form of alliterative prose which eventually became his dominant and almost exclusive form, used throughout his later works. As in verse, it is based on pairs of two-stress phrases linked to each other by alliteration on the stressed syllables. The number and placing of unstressed syllables is more variable than in verse and there is nothing resembling the phrasing or formulae of poetry. Nor, apart from a brief period of experimentation, does it employ the diction of poetry, or indeed involve any evident distortions of vocabulary or syntax. The alliteration is sometimes on lightly-stressed syllables, sometimes may be no more than the assonance of initial /s/ and /θ/, at times disappears altogether. One of the earliest examples is this from his homily on the Passion (his own punctuation is reproduced, but phrase boundaries are also marked by diagonals and alliterating sounds are underlined):

Hi gecuron <u>m</u>anslagan. / na <u>m</u>etoda drihten. / for ðan hi <u>h</u>abbað nu. / þone <u>h</u>etolan deofol. / him to <u>h</u>laforde. / na ðone <u>l</u>ifigendan crist.

(ÆCHom II, xiv.208–10)

> They chose a murderer, / not the lord of lords(?); / therefore they
> have now / the fierce devil / as their master, / not the living Christ.

The normal structures of prose remain and are reinforced by the rhythm
and alliteration, which generally bonds subject to verb or verb to object
or cuts across clause boundaries, rather than (as in Wulfstan and other
writers) linking syntactically parallel nouns or verbs. But the basic
pattern of four-stressed units linked across a medial pause by alliteration
is perceptible from beginning to end of most of his later pieces, and
marked by punctuation in the most reliable manuscripts. It is perhaps
largely a mode of decoration, qualifying Ælfric's earlier statement that
prose was plain language and poetry ornate language, but it also plays
a part in structuring meaning within the sentence. Thus in the following
lines from Ælfric's Life of St Oswald

> Seo ylce rod siððan / þe Oswold þær aærde / on wurðmynte þær
> stod
>
> (ÆLS xxvi.30–1)

the rhythmical structure shows that the sense is 'Afterwards the same
cross, which Oswald erected there, remained there in honour', rather
than, for instance, 'The same cross after Oswald raised it there in
honour, stood there', which would otherwise be possible. Similarly, in
this line in his Life of St Edmund

> He wæs cystig wædlum / and wydewum swa swa fæder
>
> (ÆLS xxxii.22)

rhythmical structure indicates 'He was generous to the poor and like a
father to the widows', rather than 'He was generous to the poor and
widows, like a father'.

In the earliest passages in which the rhythmical style appears we find
Ælfric experimenting with poetic vocabulary, such as *metod* and *heolstor*.
Once he had perfected the style, however, he ceased to use these two
words, and seems to have revised his earlier work to remove examples
of *metod*; the phrase *na metoda drihten* in the first example given above is
replaced in later versions by the equivalent but non-poetic phrase *and na
þone mildan crist* (and not the gentle Christ), with *hælend* replacing *crist* at
the end of the sentence to avoid repetition.

Sensitivity to rhythm seems to have played a part in the choice and
ordering of language even where regular patterns of stress are not in
use. Thus the prefix *ge-* had in many cases become quite functionless by
Ælfric's time. Some words virtually always appear in his work with the
prefix, but without any apparent difference in meaning from the simplex

form used by other writers (e.g. *geceosan* 'to choose', *gecigan* 'to call'), others only in the simplex form. But there are many words which he uses both with and without the prefix *ge-*, and it seems often to be rhythm rather than meaning which determines the choice (e.g. *niman*, *geniman* 'to take'). The same factor may lie behind Ælfric's variation between, for instance, *þeah ðe* and *þeah*, and possibly behind Alfred's variation between *forþam* and *forþam þe*. It is perhaps a factor too in the common variations of word-order, especially in the placing of the verb relative to the object and of auxiliary to finite verb.

Word-play also plays a part in Ælfric's style. In his Life of King Edmund he repeatedly uses two compounds of *bugan* 'to bow, turn', that is *abugan* (with the *a-* prefix carrying overtones of 'away, aside') and *gebugan*, in contrastive ways, culminating in a climactic sentence in which the two words are placed at the beginning and end of the sentence, opposing a 'wrongful' submission to a 'true' one:

> Ne *abihð* næfre Eadmund Hingware on life, hæþenum here-togan, buton he to hælende criste ærest mid geleafan on þysum lande *gebuge*.
> (*ÆLS* xxxii.91–3)

> Edmund will never in his life submit to Hinguar, the heathen war-leader, unless he first with faith submits to Jesus Christ in this land.

The effect of phonological change in disguising the root of the first word perhaps helps the word-play. Play on such parallels as *ælmihtig* and *magan*, *eorðe* and *eorðlic* are common. That this involves a concern with semantic relationships as well as aural echoes is suggested by the use of etymology in exegesis. The use of Hebrew, Greek and Latin name-etymologies is common in Ælfric, and allusion to English name-etymologies has been seen in *Beowulf* (Robinson 1968). That this extended to etymologies of ordinary words, Greek and English, is suggested by this example from Ælfric:

> Hydrie sind gehatene wæterfatu . for ðan ðe on greciscum gereorde is wæter geciged ydor; Eornostlice wæter getacnað ingehyd haligra gewrita . þæt aðweahð his hlysteras fram synna horewum;
> (*ÆCHom* II, 52–5)

> Water-vessels are called *hydriae* because in Greek water is called *ydor*. Truly, water symbolises understanding (*ingehyd*) of holy scriptures, which washes its listeners from the stains of sins.

Greek etymology is here reinforced by the implied etymology or perhaps mere pun which links *ydor* with *ingehyd*.

Wulfstan was heavily influenced by Ælfric's writing but in many respects his vocabulary remains clearly distinct. Thus, Wulfstan uses *lagu* rather than *æ* for 'law', *beorgan* and *werian* rather than *arian* and *gescyldan* for 'protect' (Bethurum 1957:27). The use of Norse *lagu* rather than native *æ* for 'law', where Ælfric only begins to use *lagu* as an alternative form late in his life, as well as other Norse words such as *grið* and *þræl*, is perhaps only a reflection of Wulfstan's greater contact with the north of England, through his office as archbishop of York, but it suggests that he may have been somewhat more receptive to new words coming in through the colloquial language. A closer link with the spoken language than we see in Ælfric is also suggested by his frequent use of intensifying tags such as *ealles to swiðe* 'all too greatly' and *oft and gelome* 'often and frequently', or parenthetic interjections such as *gecnawe se þe cunne* ('let him who knows how to, perceive') or *swa hit þincan mæg* ('as it can appear'). There is also an inventive element in his creation of vigorous compounds, in which the first element is used to give intensifying force, such as *þeod-* in *þeodsceaða, þeodfeond, þeodlicetere, worold-* in *woroldscamu, woroldstrudere,* and *riht* in *rihtlæce, rihtlicetere* (Bethurum 1957:90; Whitelock 1963:17–18).

Wulfstan had a reputation in his own time for eloquence and richness of language (see above p. 521) and the influence of classical rhetoric has been traced in his writing (Bethurum 1957:87; Jurovics 1978, though doubts are expressed by Campbell 1978). The praise of his eloquence possibly refers particularly to his use of a form of rhythmical alliteration similar to that used by Ælfric, though clearly distinct in detail (cf. McIntosh 1949). Wulfstan divides his discourse into two-stress phrases which are often syntactically independent (whereas in Ælfric the syntax runs across the phrase boundaries), and frequently uses alliteration to link the two elements of the phrase (whereas in Ælfric alliteration is used to link phrases in pairs, as in verse):

> Ne dohte hit nu lange / inne ne ute, / ac wæs here and hunger, / bryne and blodgyte / on gewelhwylcan ende / oft and gelome; / and us stalu and cwalu, / stric and steorfa, / orfcwealm and uncoþu, / hol and hete / and rypera reaflac / derede swyþe þearle
>
> (*WHom* xx (BH)50–3)

> Things have not prospered now for a long time, at home or abroad, but there has been harrying and hunger, burning and bloodshed, in every district again and again; and stealing and killing, sedition and pestilence, blight and disease, malice and hatred, and plundering by robbers has harmed us very severely.

(Rhyme instead of alliteration is used to bind *stalu* and *cwalu*.) Alliteration, word-pairing and word-play are repeatedly used to reinforce the sense: *utan word and weorc rihtlice fadian* ('let us rightly order words and works'), *oft twegen sæmen...drifað þa drafe cristenra manna* ('often two seamen drive the drove of Christian people').

Still more than Ælfric, however, Wulfstan excludes the special vocabulary of poetry, as well as the imagery that tends to go with it. This is particularly evident in the 975 annal of the Anglo-Saxon Chronicle, where an anonymous account of the death of Edgar, using both the metre and the diction of verse, is immediately followed in one manuscript (MS D) by Wulfstan's account of the events after Edgar's death, using his own two-stress rhythm, similar to verse but clearly distinct, and rigorously avoiding poetic diction.

The most ambitious attempt at achieving a high style in vernacular prose is to be found in the work of Byrhtferth of Ramsey. Latin words are repeatedly mingled with English (Latin terms in this example are underlined):

> We cwædon herbufan hwanon se <u>bissextus</u> cymð, and manega þing we cyddon ymbe his fare; and þæræfter we geswutelodon ymbe þæs <u>saltus lune</u>, þæt ys þæs monan hlyp, and wanon he cymð, and hu he byð, and to hwan he gewyrð binnan nigontyne wintrum we amearkodon. We wæron atende grimlice swyðe ær we mihton þas gerena aspyrian, ac us com hrædlice fultum, we gelyfað of heofenum swa hyt ræd ys þæt ælc æðele gife nyðerastihð fram þam Fæder ealra leohta. Eac me com stiðlice to mode hu þa getyddustan boceras gewyrceað <u>sinelimpha</u> on heora <u>uersum</u>. Hwæt, hig ærost apinsiað wærlicum mode þa naman and þa binaman and heora <u>declinunga</u>, and gymað hwylce naman geendiað on .a. oððe on .e., and eac hwylce on .i. oððe on .o. oððe on.v. Of þissum fif <u>uocales</u> wyrcað <u>preostas</u> heom anne <u>circul</u>.
> (*ByrM* 94.4–19)

We stated further back where the <u>intercalated day</u> comes from, and made known many things about its behaviour; and next we explained about the *saltus lunae*, that is the moon's leap, and where it comes from, and how it falls, and to what it amounts in the course of nineteen years. We were burned very fiercely before we could discover these mysteries, but help came to us suddenly, we believe from Heaven, as it is said that each noble gift descends from the Father of all lights. Also it came forcibly to my mind how the most learned writers make <u>synaloepha</u> in their <u>verses</u>. Lo, they first ponder with careful mind the nouns and pronouns and their <u>declensions</u>, and note carefully what nouns end in *a* or in *e* and also what in *i* or in *o* or in *u*. Out of these five <u>vowels priests</u> make a <u>circle</u>.

His sense of the inadequacy of ordinary English is perhaps partly explained and justified by the difficulty of the subject-matter, but would seem to stem in part from a fondness for a heightened language. Alongside his profusion of learned Latinisms he deploys a range of rare Old English words (*amearcian*, *apinsian*, *borlice*, *breuan*, *cyrtenlice*, *gefædlice*, *geondscriðan*, *mænigtyw*, *orped*, etc.), apparently culled from glosses to Latin texts, glosses which themselves may reflect a late Old English fashion for arcane language (Baker 1980).

Poetic words also make an occasional appearance in Byrhtferth: thus he refers to Bede as *gumena se getiddusta on Angelcynne* (158/11), employing not only the poetic word *guma*, which recurs later (248/8), but also a poetic form of phrasing. The word-pairing technique familiar from earlier prose, and also found in Wulfstan, extends in Byrhtferth to paired synonymous phrases, further heightened by rare diction, such as *ascrutnian his fare and apinsian his sið* (64/4–5; 'examine its movement and scrutinise its journey'). Word-play too becomes in Byrhtferth, like so much else in his use of language, mere ornament: *mid scrutniendre scrutnunge* (46/35) ('with scrutinising scrutiny'). The combination of exaggerated word-play, poetic and esoteric vocabulary, extravagant imagery and extensive intermingling of Latin words, produces the most extreme case of high style in Old English prose, matching the extravagance of the same author's Latin prose.

Alfred's dream of creating a simple vernacular medium to convey the essential wisdom of the past finds a disappointing culmination in the mannered, esoteric and obfuscatory prose of Byrhtferth. Yet a reversion to a more artfully simple language is evident in the Anglo-Saxon Chronicle in the eleventh century, and it is the less ornate prose which survived into the next century. Byrhtferth's prose was uncopied and probably unread after 1100, like the poetry, whereas the prose of Alfred, Ælfric and Wulfstan was still read and copied right through the twelfth century and into the thirteenth. Its language must have become increasingly difficult to comprehend, but later readers clearly recognised individual qualities of thinking and expression that made the effort worthwhile. Through much of the twelfth century modernisation of spelling, grammar and vocabulary is kept to a minimum, however much the current language had changed. In some respects, the literary language of Old English prose remained in being for more than a century beyond 1100. The language of poetry had a different history. The extant poetic manuscripts were apparently unread after 1100 and the technique of composition apparently comes to an end. Yet some of the specialised diction, along with the basic technique of the alliterative line, re-emerges in Laȝamon at the end of the twelfth century and again in the alliterative revival in the middle of the fourteenth century.

FURTHER READING

The most recent and comprehensive survey of Old English literature is Greenfield & Calder (1986). See also Malcolm Godden and Michael Lapidge, *The Cambridge Companion to Old English Literature*, 1991. On metre there are more detailed studies by Pope (1942), Bliss (1958) and Cable (1974). On poetic diction much of the important work is specifically on *Beowulf*; see especially Brodeur (1959) and Robinson (1985), as well as Klaeber's (1950) edition. More general studies are Carr (1939) and Shippey (1972: ch. 4), and there are useful discussions in the various separate editions of individual poems.

Most of what has been written on the language of prose is in the form of studies of authorship or dialect, or largely phonological accounts in the introductions to editions, and very little has been written on authors' selection and use of language. The major studies of alliteration and rhythm are McIntosh (1949), Funke (1962) and Pope (1967). The most useful studies of the language of major authors are Otten (1964) for Alfred, Pope (1967) for Ælfric, Bethurum (1957) for Wulfstan and Baker (1980) for Byrhtferth.

GLOSSARY OF LINGUISTIC TERMS

This glossary aims only to give brief working definitions of the more important or difficult linguistic terms used in this work, omitting such terms as phonetic classifications, for which the reader in difficulty should consult a relevant textbook. It is not a comprehensive dictionary of linguistic terms, and the explanations are only intended to be sufficient to allow the reader who is unacquainted with such terminology to gain more easily a full understanding of what is being read. Anyone who requires a more comprehensive dictionary should consult Crystal (1985).

ablaut   A variation in the **root** vowel, in Germanic largely restricted to variation in the root vowel of strong verbs according to **tense** and number, e.g. PDE *sing, sang, sung*; *was, were*.

active   A construction which typically involves a subject identified as actor, contrasted with passive, in which the subject is typically not an actor.

activity verb   See **dynamic**

affix   A type of **morpheme** which is used in the derivation of new words. In English, affixes are attached either as prefixes to the beginning of words, e.g. *un-like*, or as suffixes to the ends of words, e.g. *like-ly*. The use of affixes internally in words, as infixes, is at best a rare feature of English, cf. perhaps, AustrE *abso-blooming-lutely*.

agent   The semantic role of the noun phrase referring to the doer of an action, e.g. *Jane ran the marathon*.

agreement (also **concord**)   The formal relationship between one or more units whereby the form of one word requires a corresponding form in another, thus in PDE the verb agrees with the subject in number.

allograph   See **grapheme**

allomorph   Different realisations of the same **morpheme**, e.g. /z/ in *dogs* and /s/ in *cats* are allomorphs of the PDE plural morpheme.

allophone   The particular individual sounds or phones which are all members of the same **phoneme**, e.g. in PDE [p] and [pʰ] are allophones of the phoneme /p/.

analogy   An historical process whereby irregular forms are replaced by regular ones. In morphophonology the process usually involves either the extension of a change, which permits it to occur where it should not occur, phonologically-speaking, or the 'levelling' of a change, so that it does not occur where it might be expected. A typical analogical form is PDE *roofs* with final /fs/, alongside *rooves* with final /vz/ showing **allomorphic** variation of the **root**.

anaphora   A term used for the process of referring (usually with pronouns) to a preceding grammatical unit. Thus, in *Bill claimed that <u>he</u> had won and <u>so</u> he has*, *he refers* back to *Bill* and *so* back to *won*. Contrast **cataphora**.

anthroponym   The name of a person, cf. **idionym**.

aorist   One of the past tense forms of the Greek verb, usually represented in English by the simple past. In linguistic discussions the issue is most often the phonological shape of the aorist, and the semantic questions are less frequently relevant.

apocope   Deletion of vowels word-finally, as in OE *word* 'words' < **wordu*.

apposition   A syntactic construction in which there is a sequence of two constituents with the same grammatical role and semantic reference, e.g. *I, Henry Smith, do declare...*

aspect   A category which refers to the manner in which the grammar of a language refers to the duration or type of temporal activity denoted by the verb. The clearest aspectual contrast in English is perfective vs. imperfective (*I have read the book* vs. *I read the book*).

assibilation   A sound change in Old English whereby palatal or alveolar stops became palato-alveolar affricates.

assimilation   A phonological process by which two sounds become closer in pronunciation. The assimilation may be either full, cf. PDE *immaterial*, or partial, cf. *impossible*, for both compare *inorganic*.

asyndetic   See **parataxis**

athematic   See **theme**

augment   A vowel or diphthong which in early Indo-European dialects is prefixed to the root in the formation of a past tense, e.g. *e-sta-m 'I stood' with root *sta-.

auxiliary verb A 'helping' verb such a PDE *may, can, have, be, do*. It typically carries information about **tense, aspect,** or **modality**.

back-derivation The morphological process by which a shorter word is formed by the deletion of an imaginary **affix**, e.g. *peddle < pedlar*.

bahuvrihi A compound in which, semantically, the reference of the compound is to an entity to which neither of the elements of the compound refer, e.g. PDE *highbrow*. Structurally the *bahuvrihi* compounds are **exocentric**.

bilingual The property of being proficient in two languages. Contrast **diglossia**.

cataphora A term used for the pocess of referring forward, usually with a pronoun, to a grammatical unit, e.g. *this* in *Bill wants us to do this: pick up the car and drive down to LA*. Contrast **anaphora**.

causative Most frequently used to refer to verbs which have as part of their meaning the sense 'cause to', e.g. *kill* 'cause to die'.

chain shift A sequence of changes where one change is claimed to be dependent upon another. In the history of English the best known example of a chain shift is alleged to be the Great Vowel Shift (see volume II of this History). But chain shifts may occur outside phonology, as in the replacement of ME *þeʒʒ* 'though' by *þogh* because of the replacement of *hi* 'they' by *þei*. Chain shifts are of two types: 'drag' chains where Y > Z 'causes' X > Y, as in parts of the Great Vowel Shift; 'push' chains where A > B 'causes' B > C, as in the Middle English example above.

cleft construction A construction in which a clause is divided into two parts, each with it's own verb, e.g. *It's John who left*, cf. *John left*.

clitic In phonology or morphophonology a form which becomes attached to another unit. If the clitic is attached at the front it is a proclitic, e.g. OE *ne + is > nys* 'not is'; if attached to the end of a unit it is an enclitic, e.g. PDE *is + not > isn't*. More generally, a form which is dependent upon the existence of a neighbouring word, as for example *the*, which requires the existence of a neighbouring noun.

cognate A language or form which has the same source as another language or form, e.g. English and German are cognate languages, both having the same source, namely (**proto**-)Germanic.

collocation The habitual co-occurrence of lexical items. Thus in PDE *good* frequently collocates with *morning*.

compensatory lengthening The phonological process by which one phonetic segment (normally a vowel) is lengthened to 'compensate' for the loss of a following segment in the same syllable.

complement A clause functioning as a noun phrase, e.g. *I believe that you are right*. Hence 'complementizer', a grammatical marker introducing a complement, e.g. *that* in the above example.

concord See **agreement**

conjugation See **paradigm**

connotation The emotional associations which are suggested by any part of the meaning of a particular word.

contracted verbs A set of verbs in which the **stem** and inflexion have become fused as a result of the loss of a stem-final consonant, e.g. OE *sēon* 'see' < *seohan*.

copula A linking verb, typically a verb of being, e.g. *This is a glossary*.

correlative A construction in which the relationship between two or more units is marked on each unit, e.g. *either…or*.

creole A **pidgin** language which is the mother-tongue of a group of speakers.

declension See **paradigm**

denotation The meaning relationship between a word and the non-linguistic entity to which that word refers. Contrast **connotation**.

determiner The cover term for articles (*a*, *the*), demonstratives (*this*, *that*) and **quantifiers** (*few*, *three*).

diglossia The state where two radically different varieties of a language co-exist in a single speech-community. A clear example occurs in German-speaking Switzerland. In Britain there may be a diglossic situation in parts of Scotland (Scots vs. Scottish English).

digraph A combination of two graphs to represent a single graphic unit, as in PDE < th > in < the > (to be distinguished from the sequence of two separate graphs in < hotheaded >). Similarly a trigraph is a combination of three graphs.

diphthong A vowel in which there is a noticeable change in quality during the duration of its articulation in any given syllable. The diphthong is usually transcribed by means of the starting- and finishing-points of the articulation, as in *fine* /faɪn/. Diphthongs may have prominence either on the first element ('falling diphthongs') or the second element ('rising diphthongs'). The former is the more usual in all periods of English. The term 'diphthongisation' refers to the process by which a monophthong becomes a diphthong.

dissimilation   A phonological process by which two (nearly) adjacent and similar or identical sounds are made less similar, cf. L *peregrinus* and PDE *pilgrim*, where the first /r/ is dissimilated to /l/.

distribution   There are two important types of distribution: (a) **complementary distribution**, where the environment in which two elements may occur consists of two disjoint sets, each associated with only one element; (b) **contrastive distribution**, where the environment consists of two overlapping sets. Thus in PDE /p/ and /b/ contrast for they can occur in the same environment, whilst [l] and [ł] are in complementary distribution.

ditransitive   A property of verbs whereby they can have two objects, cf. *They gave Jones the book*.

dummy   A term referring to a formal element which is semantically empty but required syntactically, e.g. *do* in *Do you like Cointreau?*

dynamic   See **stative**

enclitic   See **clitic**

endocentric   A construction in which one of the elements is functionally equivalent to the construction as a whole, i.e. act as a **head.** Thus in a noun phrase such as *the tall man* the head of the construction is *man*. Contrast **exocentric**.

epenthesis   A phonological process by which a segment is inserted between two other segments, e.g. PDE *empty* contains an epenthetic /p/, cf. OE *æmtig*.

epistemic   A term referring to the semantics of probability, possibility and belief, as in *They must be married* in the sense (*From what is known to me*) *I conclude that they are married*.

existential   A **copula** construction which refers to being in existence (e.g. *There is a plant on my window*) rather than to definition (e.g. *The plant is sickly*).

exocentric   A type of construction where none of the elements is functionally equivalent to the group as a whole, i.e. there is no **head.** Typically basic sentences are exocentric, e.g. in *The man fell* neither *the man* nor *fell* can act as a sentence itself. Contrast **endocentric.**

experiencer   The semantic role of the noun phrase referring to an entity or person affected by the activity or state of the verb, e.g. *Jane* in *Jane knew the answer, Jane heard the music*.

extraposition   The process of moving a clause from its normal position to one near the end or beginning of another clause, as in *It was obvious that she had taken the book*, cf. *That she had taken the book was obvious*.

finite A term to describe a verb which is marked for **tense** and number. Hence **finite clause,** a clause which contains a subject and a finite verb.

foregrounding A term in discourse analysis to refer to the relative prominence of an item, most often a clause. In the following, the first clause is the foreground, the second the background: *John sang while Donna played the piano*.

gap A term used in syntax to refer to the absence of a unit at a place in the clause where one might have been expected; thus *the man* is not repeated in *That is the man that they arrested —— yesterday*.

geminate A term in phonology to describe either a sequence of two identical segments (alternatively described as 'long', i.e. one segment which is phonologically twice as long as usual). In Old English geminate consonants are frequent intervocalically, e.g. *fremman* 'perform' = /fremman/ or /frem:an/.

gender A term used to characterise word-class distinctions commonly known as 'masculine/feminine/neuter'. If it is a purely grammatical category not influenced by the sex of the referent it may be distinguished as 'grammatical gender', contrasting with 'natural gender', where the sex of the referent determines the gender.

generic A term used to describe an expression where the whole class of referents is referred to, e.g. *Cats are mammals, a cat is a mammal*.

glide A vocalic sound which occurs as the result of transition between one articulation and another, as for example the /ə/ in PDE *beery* /bɪərɪ/.

gradation The modification of a vowel in **ablaut**. Hence 'grade' refers to the particular ablaut form of a vowel.

grapheme The minimal contrastive unit in the writing system of a language. Thus <A, a, *a*, ɑ> are all non-contrastive variations, i.e. **allographs**, of the grapheme <a>, which contrasts with, say, <b>.

hapax legomenon A word which occurs only once in the relevant body of material.

harmony A term in phonology which refers to the process by which one segment in a string of segments is influenced by another segment in the same segment so that some degree of **assimilation** occurs between the two.

head The central element in a larger unit, e.g. *man* in *The large man*.

homorganic A term to describe adjacent phonological segments which have the same place of articulation, as in PDE *impossible*. The opposite term is **heterorganic**, as in OE *cniht*.

hortative   A term referring to expressions of exhortation and advice, e.g. *Let's go*.

hypermetric   A term used in discussions of Old English poetry to define lines in which there are three, rather than the usual two, stresses in each half-line.

hypotaxis   A term in syntax which refers to the sequencing of constituents by means of subordinating conjunctions, e.g. *He went to the cinema after he had bought a newspaper*, cf. **parataxis**.

hypocoristic   A pet name, e.g. PDE *Dickie*.

idionym.   The name of an individual person, cf. **anthroponym**.

impersonal   A construction lacking a subject such as *Methinks* (*you are right*).

interlanguage   A simplified or otherwise special variety of a language used between a fluent and less-fluent speaker of that language.

interlinear gloss   a gloss, usually word-by-word, of a text which is written between the lines of an original text in another language, the word glosses appearing above the corresponding words in the original.

intensifier   A word (usually an adverb) which has a heightening or lowering effect on the meaning of another element, e.g. PDE *very*.

isogloss   A line on a dialect map separating regionally distinct features, hence a dialect boundary.

kenning   A type of compressed metaphor frequent in Old English poetry.

laryngeal   Technically this refers to a sound whose place of articulation is in the larynx. In Indo-European studies, however, the term refers to (a set of) sounds which have been hypothesised for Proto-Indo-European. See further chapter 2 and also **schwa**.

lexeme   The minimal distinctive unit in the lexical system of a language and the abstract unit underlying a set of grammatical variants. Hence WALK (here this is the conventional representation of a lexeme, and does not refer to another entry in the glossary) has variants such as *walk, walks, walking, walked*). The head-words of dictionary entries are normally lexemes.

lexicalisation   A process whereby an element or construction acquires LEXEMIC status of its own. In derivational morphology it refers to the process by which a derived lexeme comes to be viewed as underived.

loan (word)   A word which is used in a language other than the one in which it originated. Thus *biscuit* is a loan word borrowed from French.

metathesis   A phonological process in which the order of two adjacent or nearly adjacent segments is reversed, cf. PDE *wasp, wopse*.

minimal pair   A pair of word which are differentiated only by one sound, e.g. PDE *bat* and *pat*.

modal verbs   A set of verbs which have a common primary meaning of the expression of **modality**, e.g. PDE *shall, will, may, can*.

modality   A term referring to attitudes of obligation, necessity, truth and belief, in PDE usually restricted to **auxiliary verbs** *can, may, must, shall, will* and to sentence adverbs such as *apparently*. See **epistemic** and contrast **mood**.

monophthong   A vowel in which there is no distinctive change in quality for the duration of its articulation in any given **syllable**. The term contrasts with **diphthong**. Hence 'monophthongisation' refers to the process by which a diphthong becomes a monophthong.

mood   The cover term for indicative and subjunctive. The choice may be controlled by specific syntactic constructions or the semantic function of expressing doubt, hypothesis or unreality.

mora   A phonological unit of length. Thus short vowels and consonants contain a single mora (are 'monomoric'), long vowels, long consonants and (usually) diphthongs contain two morae (are 'bimoric').

morpheme   The minimal distinctive unit in grammar (as opposed to phonology). Morphemes may be either lexical or syntactic, as in the two morphemes of PDE *boy* + *s*. Words containing only one morpheme, e.g. *boy*, are said to be monomorphemic. 'Free' morphemes can stand alone as words, e.g. *boy*, whilst 'bound' morphemes must be attached to another morpheme, whether they are used in inflexion, e.g. plural -*s*, or derivation, e.g. the prefix *un-*.

morphology   The structure and form of words, either in terms of inflexions (inflexional morphology) or word formation (derivational morphology).

morphophonemics   The study of the phonological factors which affect the appearance of morphemes, as in, for example, PDE *cats* with plural /s/ but *dogs* with plural /z/. Also known as **morphophonology**.

morphosyntactic   A term referring to a grammatical category or property which is defined by both morphological and syntactic criteria, e.g. number, which affects both syntax (as in subject-verb **agreement**) and morphology (as in the plural inflexion).

Neogrammarians   A group of German linguists who came to prominence in the 1870s, best known for their slogan that 'sound laws admit of no exception' (such a characterisation is a gross oversimplification of their views).

neutralisation   A term used in phonology to describe a situation where a contrast between two **phonemes** is lost in certain environments. Thus in late Old English the unstressed vowels /e, a, o/ are neutralised as /ə/.

NP-roles The semantic function of a noun phrase, such as **agent, experiencer**.

oblique All the case-forms of a word except that of the unmarked case, which is in Old English the nominative.

paradigm The set of forms all belonging to a single word or grammatical category. **Conjugation** refers to the paradigm of a verb; **declension** refers to the paradigm of a noun, adjective or pronoun.

parataxis A syntactic construction in which clauses or phrases are linked without the use of subordinating conjunctions. If coordinating conjunctions are used, this is called **syndetic** parataxis, e.g. *He went out and bought a paper and went to the library*, whilst linkage without any conjunctions is called **asyndetic** parataxis (or co-ordination), e.g. *He went out, bought a paper, went to the library*.

particle An invariable item with grammatical function which usually cannot be easily classified within the traditional parts of speech. A frequent particle in Old English is *þe*, often used in the introduction of subordinate clauses. Particles typically are constrained in position, function and meaning.

passive See **active**

periphrasis Phrasal as opposed to inflexional expression of case, mood or temporal relations. Thus *of the man* is the periphrastic counterpart of *the man's*.

phonaestheme A **phoneme** or sequence of phonemes which has the property of sound symbolism. Thus as in PDE *sl-* appears to carry connotations of 'furtive movement'.

phoneme The minimal unit in the sound system of a language. The simplest test for a phoneme is substitution, i.e. if one sound, say, [pʰ] in [pʰɪn] can be substituted by another, e.g. [b], and the result is a contrast in meaning, then the two sounds are realisations of different phonemes. Sounds which cannot be so substituted but which are similar, e.g. [pʰ] and [p], are members of the same phoneme, i.e. **allophones** of the same phoneme. Technically, separate phonemes are in contrastive **distribution**, i.e. can appear in the same environments, whilst allophones of the same phoneme are in complementary distribution, i.e. cannot appear in the same environments. In transcription phonemes are enclosed in slant brackets, e.g. /p/, as opposed to the square brackets ([p]) of phonetic transcription.

phonology The study of the sound systems of languages.

phrasal verb A verb + particle combination which acts syntactically and semantically as a single unit, cf. PDE *look up* 'search for' and the verb + preposition construction *look up* 'raise one's eyes'.

pidgin   A language which results from the mixture of two or more distinct languages as the result of attempts to communicate between two separate speech-communities. The pidgin language has a much reduced linguistic structure and is not the mother-tongue of any speaker. Contrast **creole.**

predicate   In syntax, all the obligatory elements of a sentence with the exception of the subject, e.g. the bracketed constituents in: *John [gave Mary a kiss] last week.*

prefix   See **affix**

pre-modal   A verb **cognate** to one of the PDE **modals,** with many of the semantic but not the syntactic properties of the PDE forms.

preterite   Past **tense**, although the term is often specifically used in morphology to refer to the past tense forms of a verb.

preterite-presents   A class of verbs in which the original preterite comes to acquire present tense meanings and where subsequently a new **preterite** is formed. Thus OE *witan* 'know', L *novi* 'I know' (not etymologically related) are both preterite in form but present in meaning.

proclitic   See **clitic**

proto-   A prefix to indicate a theoretical ancestor of a given language, e.g. *proto-Old English* refers to the reconstructed ancestor of Old English for which there is no direct evidence. See also **theme**, sense (2).

quantifier   A term such as *every, some, one* which expresses amount or number.

raising   A term used in certain linguistic analyses to refer to the phenomenon whereby a constituent of a subordinate clause becomes part of the main clause.

Received Pronunciation   The regionally neutral accent of British (especially English) English, usually considered to be the most prestigious accent.

reduplication   A morphological process by which certain features of the root are used in the formation of a **prefix** or **suffix**. Thus in Gothic *slepan* 'sleep' has the past tense form *saislep*, where the initial consonant is repeated in the prefix attached to the unchanged root *slep-*.

register   A variety of language which is defined according to the social situation in which it is employed, e.g. formal vs. informal.

relativiser   A grammatical marker introducing a relative clause, e.g. PDE *that* or *who, which.*

rhotic   Commonly used to describe those dialects (and their speakers) of English in which post-vocalic /r/, as in *bird*, is pronounced.

root   A single **morpheme** which carries the meaning of a word, often used in historical linguistics to denote the original morpheme from which a word is etymologically derived.

Schriftsprache   see **standard**

schwa   The name of the central vowel [ə], often found in unstressed syllables in English, as in *another* /ənʌðə/. The schwa vowel is of crucial importance, but controversial, in the history of Indo-European, cf. here **laryngeal**.

simplex   Used to describe a word containing only one **root morpheme**.

standard (dialect, language)   A prestigious variety of a particular language, often an institutionalised norm, which cuts across regional differences. In the Old English period the standard language is a written standard or *Schriftsprache*.

stative   This terms refers to an **aspectual** category of verbs. Semantically stative verbs refer to states rather than actions, e.g. *I know* vs. *I walk*. There may also be syntactic restrictions on stative verbs, as in PDE **know!*, **he is knowing the answer*. The terms contrasts with **dynamic** or **activity**.

stem   The part of a word to which inflexions are attached, e.g. PDE *boy-s*, OE *cniht-as*. This may be equivalent to the **root**, but is capable of containing more than one **morpheme**, as a result, say, of derivation, e.g. OE *leorning*, where the root is *leorn-*.

stimulus/source   The semantic role of the noun phrase referring to the place, perception or idea *from* or *out of* which something comes.

stranding   The phenomenon whereby an element can be left unattached after the rest of the constituent has been moved, thus in *Where do you come from?* the preposition *from* has been stranded.

stress   A complex of phonetic features which refers to the degree of force used in producing a **syllable.** Thus in PDE *about* the first syllable is unstressed and the second is stressed. Stressed syllables may carry the main stress in a word, in which case they are 'primary-stressed', or not, in which case they are 'secondary-stressed'. Thus in *rhododendron* the third syllable is primary-stressed, the first secondary-stressed, and the remainder unstressed.

suffix   See **affix**

suppletion   A morphological process whereby different inflexional forms of an individual word are taken from different **roots**, e.g. PDE *go*, *went*, where the latter derives from an earlier **preterite** of *wend*.

546

suprasegmental In phonology, a term used to describe phonetic features which have an effect over more than one segment. Such a feature which is characteristic of English (and many other languages) is **stress**, which is a property of syllables rather than individual segments.

syllable No phonetic definition has yet been found which is entirely satisfactory, but phonologically the syllable is a unit into which sequences of consonants and vowels are grouped, with the requirement that no syllable may contain more than one vowel or **diphthong**.

syncope Deletion of vowels within a word, as in OE *hēafod* 'head', but gen.sg. *hēafdes*.

syncretism The merger of two distinct inflexional forms into one, such as is usually the case for the OE nominative and accusative plurals, formerly distinct and separate but in Old English regularly identical.

tense A morphological and semantic temporal category. Morphologically PDE tense distinguishes past (*walked*) and non-past (*walks*). Semantically it distinguishes past, present and future and also past of past (pluperfect) and future of the past (the *will have X-ed* construction).

theme (1) In morphology, a term used to denote an element which, when added to a **root**, forms a **stem** to which inflexions may be added. Thus Gmc **luf-ōj-an* 'love' consists of root + theme (= stem) + inflexion. Forms in which an inflexion is added directly to the root, e.g. Gmc **mann-iz* (> OE *menn*) 'man', are said to be 'athematic'.

(2) In onomastics, an element used in forming a name, thus *Wulf-stan* contains two themes, a 'prototheme' (*Wulf*) and a 'deuterotheme' (*stan*).

topicalisation The process by which particular attention is drawn to an element, usually a noun phrase. The process in PDE often involves contrast, e.g. *It's Fred who left early (not Bill)*.

toponym The name of a place, hence **toponymy**, the study of place-names.

trigraph See **digraph**

vocalisation A phonological process by which an approximant (also called **semi-vowel**) takes on the functions of a vowel, as in the shift from disyllabic OE /nerje/ (*nerie* 'I perform') > trisyllabic /nerie/.

zero-derivative A word derived from another word without the presence of an overt marker such as a suffix, e.g. the PDE verb *mother* < *mother* (noun).

BIBLIOGRAPHY

Primary sources and texts

Bately, J. M., ed. 1980. *The Old English Orosius* (EETS ss 6). Oxford: Oxford University Press

Benediktsson, H., ed. 1972. *The First Grammatical Treatise*. Reykjavik: Institute of Nordic Linguistics

Bethurum, D., ed. 1957. *The Homilies of Wulfstan*. Oxford: Clarendon Press

Birch, W. de G., ed. 1892. *Liber Vitae: Register and Martyrology of New Minster and Hyde Abbey, Winchester*. London: Simpkin & Co.

Blake, E. O., ed. 1962. *Liber Eliensis* (Camden, Third Series 92). London: Royal Historical Society

Boethius, *De consolatione philosophiae*. Cambridge, MA: Harvard University Press

Campbell, A., ed. 1973. *Charters of Rochester*. London: Oxford University Press for the British Academy

Colgrave B. & R. A. B. Mynors, eds. 1969. *Bede's Ecclesiastical History of the English People*. Oxford: Clarendon Press

Crawford, S. J., ed. 1929. *Byrhtferth's Manual* (EETS os 177). London: Oxford University Press

Darlington, R. R., ed. 1928. *The Vita Wulfstani of William of Malmesbury*. London: Royal Historical Society

Dobbie, E. van K., ed. 1942. *The Anglo-Saxon Minor Poems* (Anglo-Saxon Poetic Records VI). New York: Columbia University Press

Dunning, T. P. & A. J. Bliss, eds. 1969. *The Wanderer*. London: Methuen

Earle, J. 1888. *A Hand-book to the Land-charters, and Other Saxonic Documents*. Oxford: Clarendon Press

Earle, J. & C. Plummer, eds. 1899. *Two of the Saxon Chronicles Parallel*. Oxford: Clarendon Press

Eliason, N. E. & P. Clemoes, eds. 1966. *Ælfric's First Series of Catholic Homilies* (*British Museum Royal 7 C.XII, fols. 4–218*) (Early English Manuscripts in Facsimile 13). Copenhagen: Rosenkilde & Bagger

Gerchow, J. 1988. *Die Gedenküberlieferung der Angelsachsen* (Arbeiten zur Frühmittelalterforschung 20). Berlin: W. de Gruyter

Godden, M., ed. 1979. *Ælfric's Catholic Homilies: The Second Series* (EETS ss 5). Oxford: Oxford University Press

Grein, C. W. M. & R. P. Wülcker, eds. *Bibliothek der Angelsäksischen Poesie, I: Das Beowulfslied nebst den kleineren epischen, lyrischen, didaktischen und geschichtlichen Stücken.* Kassel: Wigand

Harmer, F. E., ed. 1952. *Anglo-Saxon Writs.* Manchester: Manchester University Press

Haugen, E. 1950. *First Grammatical Treatise: The Earliest Germanic Phonology.* Baltimore, MD: Linguistic Society of America

Hecht, H., 1907. *Bischof Waerferths von Worcester Ubersetzung der Dialoge Gregors des Grossen* (Bibliothek der angelsächsischen Prosa 5,2). Hamburg: Henri Grand

Ker, N. R., ed. 1956. *The Pastoral Care: King Alfred's Translation of St Gregory's Regula Pastoralis* (Early English Manuscripts in Facsimile 6). Copenhagen: Rosenkilde & Bagger

Klaeber, D., ed. 1931. *The Later Genesis* (Englische textbibliothek 15). Heidelberg: Carl Winter

1950. *Beowulf and the Fight at Finnesburg.* 3rd edition. Boston: D. C. Heath & Co.

Krapp, G. P. & E. V. K. Dobbie, eds. 1936. *The Anglo-Saxon Poetic Records, III: The Exeter Book.* London: Routledge, Kegan Paul

Leslie, R. F., ed. 1966. *The Wanderer.* Manchester: Manchester University Press

Liebermann, F., ed. 1903–16. *Die Gesetze der Angelsachsen.* Halle: Max Niemeyer

Migne, J. P., ed. 1844–91. *Patrologia Latina.* Paris: Garnier Frères

Miller, T., ed. 1890–8. *The Old English Version of Bede's Ecclesiastical History* (EETS os 95, 96, 110, 111). London: Oxford University Press

Nickel, G., J. Klegraf, W. Kühlwein, D. Nehls, R. Zimmerman & J. Strauss, eds. 1976. *Beowulf und die kleineren Denkmäler der altenglischen Heldensage,* 3 parts. Heidelberg: Carl Winter

Pheifer, J. D. 1974. *Old English Glosses in the Epinal-Erfurt Glossary.* Oxford: Clarendon Press

Pope, J. C., ed. 1967–8. *Homilies of Ælfric: A Supplementary Collection* (EETS os 259–60), 2 vols. Oxford: Oxford University Press

Roberts, J., ed. 1979. *The Guthlac Poems of the Exeter Book.* Oxford: Clarendon Press

Robertson, A. J., ed. 1939. *Anglo-Saxon Charters.* Cambridge: Cambridge University Press

Sawyer, P. H. 1979c. *Charters of Burton Abbey* (Anglo-Saxon Charters 2). Oxford: Oxford University Press for the British Academy

Scragg, D. G., ed. 1981. *The Battle of Maldon.* Manchester: Manchester University Press

Sedgefield, W. J., ed. 1899. *King Alfred's Old English Version of Boethius De Consolatione Philosophiae*. Oxford: Clarendon Press

Sisam, C. & K. Sisam, eds. 1959. *The Salisbury Psalter* (EETS os 242). Oxford: Oxford University Press

Skeat, W. W., ed. 1871–87. *The Four Gospels in Anglo-Saxon, Northumbrian and Old Mercian Versions*. Cambridge: Cambridge University Press

　　1881–1900. *Ælfric's Lives of Saints* (EETS os 76, 82, 94, 114). London: Oxford University Press

Stenton, F. M., ed. 1920. *Documents Illustrative of the Social and Economic History of the Danelaw*. London: Oxford University Press for the British Academy

Sweet, H., ed. 1871–2. *King Alfred's West-Saxon Version of Gregory's Pastoral Care* (EETS os 45, 50). London: Oxford University Press

Thompson, A. H., ed. 1923. *Liber vitae ecclesiae dunelmensis* (Surtees Society 136). Durham: Andrews & Co.

Thorpe, B., ed. 1843–6. *The Homilies of the Anglo-Saxon Church. The First Part, Containing the Sermones Catholici, or Homilies of Ælfric*, 2 vols. London: The Ælfric Society

Vleeskruyer, R., ed. 1953. *The Life of St. Chad: An Old English Homily*. Amsterdam; North-Holland

Whitelock, D., ed. 1930. *Anglo-Saxon Wills*. Cambridge: Cambridge University Press

　　1955. *English Historical Documents c. 500–1042*. London: Eyre & Spottiswoode

　　1963. *Sermo Lupi ad Anglos*. 3rd edition. London: Methuen

Whitelock, D., D. C. Douglas & S. I. Tucker., eds. 1961. *The Anglo-Saxon Chronicle: A Revised Translation*. London: Eyre & Spottiswoode.

Whitelock, D., N. Ker & Lord Rennell, eds. 1968. *The Will of Æthelgifu* (Roxburghe Club). Oxford: for the Roxburghe Club.

Zupitza, J., ed. 1880. *Ælfrics Grammatik und Glossar*. Berlin: Weidmannsche Buchhandlung

　　1889. 'Mercisches aus der Hs. Royal 2 A 20 im Britischen Museum'. *Zeitschrift für deutsches Altertum und deutsche Literatur* 33.47–66

Secondary sources

Adamson, S., V. A. Law, N. Vincent & S. Wright, eds. 1990. *Proceedings of the Fifth International Conference on English Historical Linguistics*. Amsterdam: John Benjamins.

Adigard des Gautries, J. 1954. *Les noms de personnes scandinaves en Normandie de 911 à 1066* (Nomina Germanica 11). Lund: Carl Blom

Aebischer, P. 1924. 'L'anthroponymie wallonne d'après quelques anciens cartulaires'. *Bulletin du dictionnaire wallon* 13.73–168

Akmajian, A., S. Steele & T. Wasow, 1979. 'The category AUX in universal grammar'. *Linguistic Inquiry* 10.1–64

Allen, C. L. 1980. *Topics in Diachronic English Syntax*. New York: Garland
  1986a. 'Reconsidering the history of *like*'. *Journal of Linguistics* 22.375–409
  1986b. 'Dummy subjects and the verb-second "target" in Old English'. *English Studies* 67.465–70
Allen, W. S. 1978. *Vox Latina*. 2nd edition. Cambridge: Cambridge University Press
Amos, A. C. 1980. *Linguistic Means of Determining the Dates of Old English Poetry*. Cambridge, MA: Medieval Academy of America
Anderson, H. 1972. 'Diphthongization'. *Language* 48.11–50
Anderson, J. M. 1985. 'The status of the voiced fricatives in Old English'. *Folia Linguistica Historica* 6.215–43
  1986. 'A note on Old English impersonals'. *Journal of Linguistics* 22.167–77
Anderson, J. M. & C. Jones, 1977. *Phonological Structure and the History of English* (North-Holland Linguistics Series 33). Amsterdam: North-Holland
Anderson [Arngart], O. S. 1934. *The English Hundred-Names*, vol. 1. (Lunds Universitets Årsskrift). Lund: C. W. K. Gleerup
  1939a. *The English Hundred-Names*, vol. 2. Lund: C. W. K. Gleerup
  1939b. *The English Hundred-Names*, vol. 3. Lund: C. W. K. Gleerup
  1941. *Old English Material in the Leningrad Manuscript of Bede's 'Ecclesiastical History'* (Acta Regiae Societatis Humaniorum Litterarum Lundensis 31). Lund: C. W. K. Gleerup
Andersson, T. & K. I. Sandred, eds. 1978. *The Vikings* (Acta Universitatis Upsaliensis: Symposia Universitatis Upsaliensis Annum Quingentesimum Celebrantis 8). Uppsala: Almqvist & Wiksell
Andrew, S. O. 1934. 'Some principles of Old English word order'. *Medium Aevum* 3.167–87
  1940. *Syntax and Style in Old English*. Cambridge: Cambridge University Press
Antilla, R. 1972. *An Introduction to Historical and Comparative Linguistics*. New York: Macmillan
Arngart [Anderson], O. S. 1944. 'The Calendar of St. Willibrord: a little-used source of Old English personal names'. *Studia Neophilologica* 16.128–34
  1947. 'Some aspects of the relation between the English and the Danish element in the Danelaw'. *Studia Neophilologica* 20.73–87
  1972. 'On the *-ingtūn* type of English place-name'. *Studia Neophilologica* 44.263–73
  1979. 'The hundred-name *Wayland*. *Journal of the English Place-Name Society* 12.54–8
Bäck, H. 1934. *The Synonyms for 'child, boy, girl' in Old English: An Etymological-Semasiological Investigation* (Lund Studies in English 2). Lund: C. W. K. Gleerup
Bacquet, P. 1962. *La structure de la phrase verbale à l'époque alfrédienne*. Paris: Les Belles Lettres.
Bähr, D. 1959. 'Ae. *æþele* und *freo*, ihre Ableitungen und Synonyma im Alt-

und Mittelenglischen: Wortgeschichtliche Studien zum Wandel des englischen Freiheitsbegriff im Mittelalter'. Unpublished dissertation. Berlin: University of Berlin

Baker, P. S. 1980. 'The Old English canon of Byrhtferth of Ramsey'. *Speculum* 55.22–37

Bailey, C.-J. N. & K. Maroldt, 1977. 'The French lineage of English'. In *Creoles – Languages in Contact*, ed. J. M. Meisel. Tübingen: Gunter Narr, 21–51

Baldi, P. 1983. *An Introduction to the Indo-European Languages*. Carbondale: Southern Illinois University Press

Ball, C. J. E. 1988. 'Problems in early Northumbrian phonology'. In Kastovsky & Bauer (1988:109–17)

Bammesberger, A. 1980. 'Altenglische Komposita mit *hild(e)*'. *Münchener Studien zur Sprachwissenschaft* 39.5–10

1984a. *English Etymology*. Heidelberg: Carl Winter

1984b. *A Sketch of Diachronic English Morphology*. Regensburg: Friedrich Pustet

1984c. *Lateinische Sprachwissenschaft*. Regensburg: Friedrich Pustet

1989. *English Linguistics*. Heidelberg: Carl Winter

Bammesberger, A., ed. 1985. *Problems of Old English Lexicography. Studies in memory of Angus Cameron*. Regensburg: Friedrich Pustet

Barley, N. F. 1974. 'Perspectives on Anglo-Saxon names'. *Semiotica* 11.1–31

Barlow, F. 1970. *Edward the Confessor*. London: Eyre and Spottiswoode

Bately, J. M. 1970. 'King Alfred and the Old English translation of Orosius'. *Anglia* 88.433–59

Bates, D. 1986. *A Bibliography of Domesday Book*. Woodbridge: Boydell & Brewer

Baugh, A. C. & T. Cable, 1978. *A History of the English Language*. 3rd edition. London: Routledge, Kegan Paul

Bazell, C. E. 1939. 'Four West Germanic verbal endings'. *Neophilologus* 24.62–6

Bean, M. C. 1983. *The Development of Word Order Patterns in Old English*. London: Croom Helm

Beckers, H. 1968. 'Die Wortsippe **hail* und ihr sprachliches Feld im Altenglischen'. Unpublished PhD dissertation. Köln: University of Munster

Beech, G. T. 1974. 'Les noms des personnes poitevins du IXe au XIIe siècle'. *Revue internationale d'onomastique* 26.81–100

Beer, G. T. 1939. *Führen und Folgen, Herrschen und Beherrschtwerden im Sprachgut der Angelsachsen: Ein Beitrag zur Erforschung von Führertum und Gefolgschaft in der germanischen Welt* (Sprache und Kultur der germanischen und romanischen Völker, Anglistische Reihe 31). Breslau

Bennett, W. H. 1955. 'The southern English development of Germanic initial [f s þ]'. *Language* 31.367–71

Benning, H. A. 1961. '*Welt*' *und* '*Mensch*' *in der altenglischen Dichtung. Bedeutungsgeschichtliche Untersuchungen zum germanisch-altenglischen Wortschatz* (Beiträge zur englischen Philologie 44). Bochum: Pöppinghaus

Benveniste, E. 1968. 'Mutations of linguistic categories'. In *Directions for Historical Linguistics*, ed. W. Lehmann & Y. Malkiel. Austin, TX: University of Texas Press, 83–94

Berndt, R. 1982. *History of the English Language.* Leipzig: VEB Verlag Enzyklopädie

Bethurum, D. 1966. 'Wulfstan'. In *Continuations and Beginnings*, ed. E. G. Stanley. London: Nelson, 210–46

Betz, W. 1949. *Deutsch und Lateinisch. Die Lehnbildungen der althochdeutschen Benediktinerregel.* Bonn: Bouvier

Bierbaumer, P. 1975/76/79. *Der botanische Wortschatz des Altenglischen*, 3 vols. Frankfurt: Herbert Lang

1988. 'Slips of the ear in Old English texts'. In Kastovsky & Bauer (1988:127–37)

Biese, Y. M. 1941. *Origin and Development of Conversions in English* (Annales Academiae Scientiarum Fennicae B 45.2). Helsinki: Academia Scientiarum Fennicae

Björkman, E. 1900–2. *Scandinavian Loan-Words in Middle English*, 2 vols. Halle: Max Niemeyer

1910. *Nordische Personennamen in England* (Studien zur englischen Philologie 37). Halle: Max Niemeyer

1912. *Zur englischen Namenkunde* (Studien zur englischen Philologie 47). Halle: Max Niemeyer

1913a. 'Die Festermen des Ælfric'. *Studien zur englischen Philologie* 50.1–19

1913b. 'Miszellen'. *Anglia Beiblatt* 24.281–3

Blake, N. F. 1977. *The English Language in Medieval Literature.* London: Dent

Bliss, A. J. 1958. *The Metre of Beowulf.* Oxford: Oxford University Press

Bloomfield, L. 1935. *Language.* Allen and Unwin

Boehler, M. 1930. *Die altenglischen Frauennamen* (Germanische Studien 98). Berlin: Emil Ebering

Bosworth, J. & T. N. Toller, 1898. *An Anglo-Saxon Dictionary.* 1921. *Supplement* by T. N. Toller. 1972. *Enlarged Addenda and Corrigenda* by A. Campbell. Oxford: Clarendon Press

Bourcier, G. 1978. *L'orthographie de l'anglais: histoire et situation actuelle.* Paris: Presses Universitaires de France

Bradley, S. J. 1982. *Anglo-Saxon Poetry: An Anthology of Old English Poems in Prose Translation.* London: Dent

Brady, C. 1979. '"Weapons" in *Beowulf*: an analysis of the nominal compounds and an evaluation of the poet's use of them'. *Anglo-Saxon England* 8.79–141

1983. '"Warriors" in *Beowulf*: an analysis of the nominal compounds and an evaluation of the poet's use of them'. *Anglo-Saxon England* 11.199–246

Brandon, P. F., ed. 1978. *The South Saxons*. Chichester: Phillimore

Brasch, C. 1910. *Die Namen der Werkzeuge im Altenglischen: Eine kulturhistorisch-etymologische Untersuchung*. Leipzig: Hoffmann

Bremmer, R. H. 1981. 'Frisians in Anglo-Saxon England: a historical and toponymical investigation'. *Fryske Nammen* 3.45–94

Brodeur, A. G. 1952. 'The meaning of Snorri's categories'. *University of California Publications in Modern Philology* 36.129–47

1959. *The Art of Beowulf*. Berkeley: University of California Press

Bronnenkant, L. J. 1982. 'Thurstable revisited'. *Journal of the English Place-Name Society* 15.9–19

Brooks, N. 1974. 'Anglo-Saxon charters: the work of the last twenty years'. *Anglo-Saxon England* 3.211–31

1979. 'England in the ninth century: the crucible of defeat'. Transactions of the Royal Historical Society, 5th ser. 29.1–20

1984. *The Early History of the Church at Canterbury: Christ Church from 597 to 1066*. Leicester: Leicester University Press

Brown, W. H. 1969. 'Method and style in the Old English *Pastoral Care. Journal of English and Germanic Philology* 68.666–84

1970. *A Syntax of King Alfred's Pastoral Care*. The Hague: Mouton

Brugmann, K. 1897–1916. *Vergleichende Laut-, Stammbildungs- und Flexionslehre der Indogermanische Sprachen*. Strassburg: Trübner

Brunner, K. 1950. *Die englische Sprache: ihre geschichtliche Entwicklung*. Halle: Max Niemeyer

1955. 'The Old English vowel phonemes'. *English Studies* 34.247–51

1962. *Die englische Sprache: ihre geschichtliche Entwicklung*, II. Tübingen: Max Niemeyer

1965. *Altenglische Grammatik (nach der angelsächsischen Grammatik von Eduard Sievers neubearbeitet)*. 3rd edition. Tübingen: Max Niemeyer

Büchner, G. 1968. 'Vier altenglische Bezeichnungen für Vergehen und Verbrechen (*fyren, gylt, man, scyld*). Unpublished PhD dissertation. Berlin: Freie Universität

Buckhurst, H. T. M. 1929. 'Terms and phrases for the sea in Old English poetry'. In *Studies in English Philology: A Miscellany in Honor of Frederick Klaeber*, ed. K. Malone & M. B. Rund. Minneapolis: University of Minnesota Press, 103–19

Burchfield, R. W. 1956. 'The language and orthography of the Ormulum ms'. *Transactions of the Philological Society* 1956.56–87

Butler, M C. 1980. *Grammatically Motivated Subjects in Early English* (Texas Linguistic Forum 16). Austin, TX: University of Texas

Bynon, T. 1977. *Historical Linguistics*. Cambridge: Cambridge University Press

Cable, T. 1974. *The Meter and Melody of Beowulf*. Urbana: University of Illinois Press

Callaway, M., Jr 1913. *The Infinitive in Anglo-Saxon*. Washington, DC: Carnegie Institute of Washington

Cameron, A. 1968. 'The Old English Nouns of Colour: A Semantic Study'. Unpublished D.Phil. dissertation. Oxford: University of Oxford

Cameron, A., A. C. Amos & G. Waite, 1981. 'A reconsideration of the language of Beowulf'. In Chase (1981:33–75)

Cameron, K. 1965. *Scandinavian Settlement in the Territory of the Five Boroughs: The Place-name Evidence.* University of Nottingham, inaugural lecture.

1968. '*Eccles* in English place-names'. In *Christianity in Britain 300–700,* ed. M. W. Barley & R. P. C. Hanson. Leicester: Leicester University Press, 1–7

1970. 'Scandinavian settlement in the territory of the Five Boroughs, II – Place-names in *-thorp*'. *Medieval Scandinavia* 3.35–49

1971. 'Scandinavian settlement in the territory of the Five Boroughs: the place-name evidence, III – the *Grimston*-hybrids'. In Clemoes & Hughes 1971:147–63

1976. 'The significance of English place-names'. *Proceedings of the British Academy* 62.135–55

1979–80. 'The meaning and significance of Old English *walh* in English place-names'. With appendices by J. Insley and M. Todd. *Journal of the English Place-Name Society* 12.1–53

1985. 'Viking settlement in the East Midlands: the place-name evidence'. In R. Schützeichel (ed.), *Giessener Flurnamen-Kolloquium (Beiträge zur Namenforschung* ns Beiheft 23). Heidelberg: Carl Winter, 129–53

Cameron, K., ed. 1975. *Place-name Evidence for the Anglo-Saxon Invasion and the Scandinavian Settlements.* Nottingham: English Place-Name Society

Campbell, A. 1959. *Old English Grammar.* Oxford: Clarendon Press

1970. 'Verse influences in Old English prose'. In J. Rosier (ed.), *Philological Essays: Studies in Old and Middle English Language and Literature in Honour of H. D. Merritt.* The Hague: Mouton, 98–8

Campbell, C. D. 1905. 'The Names of Relationship in English: A Contribution to English Semasiology'. Unpublished PhD dissertation. Strassburg: University of Strassburg

Campbell, J. 1979. 'Bede's words for places'. In Sawyer (1979a:34–54)

Campbell, J., E. John & P. Wormald, 1982. *The Anglo-Saxons.* Oxford: Phaidon

Campbell, J. J. 1951. 'The dialect vocabulary of the OE Bede'. *Journal of English and Germanic Philology* 50.349–72

1952. 'The Old English *Bede*: Book III, Chapters 16 to 20'. *Modern Language Notes* 67.381–6

1978. 'Adaptation of classical rhetoric in Old English literature'. In *Medieval Eloquence,* ed. J. J. Murphy. Berkeley: University of California Press, 173–97

Canale, W. 1978. 'Word Order Change in Old English: Base Reanalysis in Generative Grammar'. Unpublished PhD dissertation. Montreal: McGill University

Carkeet, D. 1976. 'Old English correlatives: an exercise in internal syntactic reconstruction'. *Glossa* 10.44–63

Carlton, C. R. 1970. *Descriptive Syntax of the Old English Charters*. The Hague: Mouton

Carr, C. T. 1939. *Nominal Compounds in Germanic* (St Andrews University Publications 41). London: Oxford University Press

Chadwick, H. M. 1894–99. 'Studies in Old English'. *Transactions of the Cambridge Philological Society* 4.85–265

Chatman, S. B. 1958. 'The *a/æ* opposition in Old English'. *Word* 14.224–36

Chase, C. (ed.) 1981. *The Dating of Beowulf*. Toronto: University of Toronto Press

Chase, D. E. 1976. 'A Semantic Study of the Old English Words for *warrior*'. Unpublished PhD dissertation. New York: University of New York

Chatman, S. 1958. 'The *a/æ* opposition in Old English'. *Word* 14.244–36

Christophersen, P. 1939. *The Articles: A Study of their Theory and Use in English*. Copenhagen: Munksgaard

Clark, C. 1952/3. 'Studies in the vocabulary of the *Peterborough Chronicle*, 1070–1154'. *English & Germanic Studies* 5.67–89

   1971. 'The narrative mode of *The Anglo-Saxon Chronicle* before the conquest'. In Clemoes & Hughes (1971:215–35)

   1979a. 'Clark's first three laws of applied anthroponymics'. *Nomina* 3.13–19

   1979b. 'Notes on a *Life* of three Thorney saints: Thancred, Torhtred and Tova'. *Proceedings of the Cambridge Antiquarian Society* 69.45–52

   1982. 'The early personal names of King's Lynn: an essay in socio-cultural history, Part I: baptismal names'. *Nomina* 6.51–71

   1983. 'On dating *The Battle of Maldon*: certain evidence reviewed'. *Nottingham Medieval Studies* 27.1–22

   1983. 'Starting from *Youlthorpe* (East Riding of Yorkshire): an onomastic circular tour'. *Journal of the English Place-Name Society* 16.25–37

   1984. 'L'Angleterre anglo-normande et ses ambivalences socio-culturelles'. In *Les mutations socio-culturelles au tournant des XIᵉ – XIIᵉ siècles* (Spicilegium Beccense 2), ed. R. Foreville. Paris: Centre nationale de la recherche scientifique. 99–110

   1985a. 'British Library Additional MS.40,000, ff. 1v–12r'. *Anglo-Norman Studies* 7.50–65

   1985b. '*The Liber Vitae* of Thorney Abbey'. *Nomina* 9.53–72

   1987a. 'English personal names ca. 650–1300'. *Medieval Prosopography* 8.I.31–60

   1987b. 'Willelmus rex? vel alius Willelmus?'. *Nomina* 11.7–33

   1990. 'Historical linguistics – linguistic archaeology'. In Adamson, Law, Vincent & Wright, eds. (1990:55–68)

Clark Hall, J. R. & H. D. Merritt, 1969 (4th edition). *A Concise Anglo-Saxon Dictionary*. Cambridge: Cambridge University Press

Clemoes, P. & K. Hughes, eds. 1971. *England before the Conquest: Studies in*

Primary Sources Presented to Dorothy Whitelock. Cambridge: Cambridge University Press

Coates, R. 1987. *A Classified Bibliography on Sussex Place-Names, 1586–1987, with an Essay on the State of the Art*. Brighton: Younsmere Press.

Coetsem, F. van & H. L. Kufner, 1972. *Toward a Grammar of Proto-Germanic*. Tübingen: Max Niemeyer

Cole, A. 1982. 'Topography, hydrology and place-names in the chalk-lands of southern England: *cumb* and *denu*'. *Nomina* 6.73–87

1985. 'Topography, hydrology and place-names in the chalklands of southern England: **funta, æwiell and æwielm*'. *Nomina* 9.3–17

Colman, F. 1981. 'The name-element *Æðel-* and related problems'. *Notes and Queries* 206.195–201

1983a. 'Old English /a/ ≠ /æ/ or [a] ∼ [æ]?'. *Folia Linguistica Historica* 4.265–85

1983b. '"Vocalisation" as nucleation'. *Studia Linguistica* 37.30–48

1984. 'Anglo-Saxon pennies and Old English phonology'. *Folia Linguistica Historica* 5.91–143

1985. 'Old English *ie*: quid est?'. *Lingua* 67.1–23

1986a. 'A *cæg* to Old English syllable structure'. In Kastovsky & Szwedek (1986:225–31)

1986b. 'Numismatic evidence for onomastics'. *Nomina* 10.162–8

Comrie, B. 1981. *Language Universals and Linguistic Typology: Syntax and Morphology*. Chicago: University of Chicago Press

Copley, G. 1986. *Archaeology and Place-Names in the Fifth and Sixth Centuries* (British Archaeological Reports: Brit. Ser. 147). Oxford: B.A.R.

Cortelyon, J. v. Z. 1906. *Die altenglische Namen der Insekten, Spinnen- und Krustentiere* (Anglistische Forschungen 19). Heidelberg; Carl Winter

Coseriu, E. 1966. 'Structure lexicale et enseignement de vocabulaire'. *Actes du premier colloque international de linguistique appliquée*. Nancy, 175–210

Cowgill, W. 1959. 'The inflection of the Germanic ō presents'. *Language* 35.1–15

Cox, B. 1972. 'The significance of the distribution of English place-names in *-hām* in the Midlands and East Anglia'. *Journal of the English Place-Name Society* 5.15–73

1975. 'The place-names of the earliest English records'. *Journal of the English Place-Name Society* 8.12–66

1980. 'Aspects of place-name evidence for early medieval settlement in England'. *Viator* 11.35–50

1987. 'The major place-names of Rutland: to Domesday and beyond'. *Rutland Record* 7.227–30

1989. 'Rutland and the Scandinavian settlements: the place-name evidence'. *Anglo-Saxon England* 18.135–48

Cronan, D. 1986. 'Alliterative rank in Old English poetry'. *Studia Neophilologica* 58.145–58

Crowley, J. P. 1980. 'The Study of Old English Dialects'. Unpublished PhD dissertation. Chapel Hill, NC: University of North Carolina

1986. 'The study of Old English dialects'. *English Studies* 67.97–112

Crystal, D. 1985. *A Dictionary of Linguistics and Phonetics*. 2nd edition. Oxford: Basil Blackwell

Curme, G. O. 1911. 'A history of the English relative construction'. *Journal of English and Germanic Philology* 11.10–29, 180–204, 355–80

1914. 'The development of verbal compounds in Germanic'. *Beiträge zur Geschichte Deutsche Sprache und Literatur* 39.320–61

Dahl, I. 1938. *Substantival Inflexion in Early Old English: Vocalic Stems* (Lund Studies in English 7). Lund: C. W. K. Gleerup

Dal, I. 1952. 'Enstehung des englischen Patizipium Praesentis auf *-ing*'. *Norsk Tidsskrift for Sprogvidenskap* 16.5–116

Dalbey, M. 1969. 'Hortatory tone in the Blickling homilies'. *Neuphilologische Mitteilungen* 70.641–58

Dam, J. van, 1957. *The Causal Clause and Causal Prepositions in Early Old English Prose*. Groningen: Wolters

Darby, H. C. & G. R. Versey, 1975. *Domesday Gazetteer*. Cambridge: Cambridge University Press

Daunt, M. 1939. 'Old English sound changes reconsidered in relation to scribal tradition and practice'. *Transactions of the Philological Society* 1939.108–37

1946. 'Old English verse and English speech rhythm'. *Transactions of the Philological Society* 1946.56–72

Davidsen-Nielsen, N. & H. Ørum, 1978. 'The feature "gravity" in Old English and Danish phonology'. *Acta Linguistica Hafniensia* 16.201–13

Davis, R. H. C. 1955. 'East Anglia and the Danelaw'. *Transactions of the Royal Historical Society* (5th series) 5.23–39

De Camp, D. 1958. 'The genesis of the Old English dialects: a new hypothesis'. *Language* 34.232–44; repr. Lass (1969:355–68)

DeKeyser. X. 1987. 'Relative clause formation in the Anglo-Saxon Chronicle'. *Folia Linguistica Historica* 7.351–61

de la Cruz, J. M. F. 1969. 'Origins and Developments of the Phrasal Verb to the End of the Middle English Period'. Unpublished PhD dissertation. Belfast: Queen's University

1972. 'A syntactical complex of isoglosses in the north-western end of Europe (English, North Germanic and Celtic)'. *Indogermanische Forschungen* 77.171–80

1975. 'Old English pure prefixes: structure and function'. *Linguistics* 145.47–81

Denison, D. 1985. 'Why Old English had no prepositional passive'. *English Studies* 66.189–204

1986. 'On word order in Old English'. *Dutch Quarterly Review* 16.277–95

1990a. 'The Old English impersonals revived'. In Adamson, Law, Vincent & Wright, eds. (1990:111–40).

1990b. 'Auxiliary + impersonal in Old English'. *Folia Linguistica Historica* 9.139–66

DEPN See Ekwall (1960)

Derolez, R. 1974,. 'Cross-channel language ties'. *Anglo-Saxon England* 3.1–14

Deutschbein, M. 1901. 'Dialektisches in der ags. Ubersetzung von Bedas Kirchengeschichte'. *Beiträge zur Geschichte Deutsche Sprache und Litratur* 26.169–244

Dickins, B. 1932. 'A system of transliteration for Old English runic inscriptions'. *Leeds Studies in English* 1.15–19

Dik, E. S. 1965. *Ae 'dryht' und seine Sippe: Eine wortkundliche, kultur- und religionsgeschichtliche Betrachtung zur altgermanischen Glaubensvorstellung vom wachstüumlichen Heil* (Neue Beiträge zur englischen Philologie 3). Münster: Aschendorf

Dietrich, E. 1855. 'Abt Aelfrik. Zur Literatur-Geschichte der angelsächsischen Kirche (erste Hälfte)'. *Zeitschrift für historische Theologie* 25.487–594

Dietz, K. 1985. 'AE *tasol* ~ *te(o)sol* "*Wurfel*"'. *Anglia* 103.90–5

Dodgson, J. McN. 1966. 'The significance of the distribution of the English place-names in *-ingas, -inga-* in south-east England'. *Medieval Archaeology* 10.1–29

1967a. 'The *-ing* in English place-names like *Birmingham* and *Altrincham*'. *Beiträge zur Namenforschung* (ns) 2.221–45

1967b. 'Various forms of Old English *-ing-* in English place-names'. *Beiträge zur Namenforschung* (ns) 2.325–96

1967c. 'The English arrival in Cheshire'. *Transactions of the Historic Society of Lancashire and Cheshire* 119.1–37

1968. 'Various place-name formations containing Old English *-ing*'. *Beiträge zur Namenforschung* (ns) 3.141–89

1973. 'Place names from *-hām*, distinguished from *-hamm* names, in relation to the settlement of Kent, Surrey and Sussex'. *Anglo-Saxon England* 2.1–50

1978. 'Place-names in Sussex: the material for a new look'. In Brandon (1978:54–88)

1985a. Some Domesday personal-names, mainly post-Conquest'. *Nomina* 9.41–51

1985b. 'The Welsh element in the field-names of Cheshire'. In *Giessener Flurnamen-Kolloquium*, ed. R. Schützeichel. (Beiträge zur Namenforschung, ns, Beiheft XXIII). Heidelberg: Carl Winter, 154–64

Domingue, N. Z. 1977. 'Middle English: another creole?'. *Journal of Creole Studies* 1.89–100

Downing, B. T. 1978. 'Some universals of relative clause structure'. In *Universals of Human Language, IV: Syntax*, ed. J. H. Greenberg, C. A. Ferguson & E. Moravcsik. Stanford, CA: Stanford University Press, 375–418

Dresher, B. E. 1978. *Old English and the Theory of Phonology*. University of Massachusetts, PhD dissertation. Repr. New York: Garland Press, 1985

1980. 'The Mercian Second Fronting: a case of rule loss in Old English'. *Linguistic Inquiry* 11.47–73

1981. 'Abstractness and explanation in phonology'. In *Explanation in Linguistics: The Logical Problem of Language Acquisition*, ed. W. Hornstein & D. W. Lightfoot. London: Longman, 76–115

Drosdowski, G. 1950. 'Studien zur Bedeutungsgeschichte angelsächsischer Zeitbegriffswörter'. Unpublished PhD dissertation. Berlin: University of Berlin

Dumville, D. N. 1986. 'The West-Saxon genealogical regnal list: manuscripts and texts'. *Anglia* 104.1–32

Ekwall, E. 1928. *English River-Names*. Oxford: Clarendon Press

1930. 'How long did the Scandinavian language survive in England?' In *A Grammatical Miscellany Offered to Otto Jespersen on his Seventieth Birthday*, ed. N. Bøgholm, A. Brusendorff & C. A. Bodelsen. Copenhagen: Einar Minksgaard, 17–30

1936a. 'The Scandinavian settlement'. In *An Historical Geography of England before A.D. 1800*, ed. H. C. Darby. Cambridge: Cambridge University Press, 133–64

1936b. *Studies on English Place-Names* (Kungl. Vitterhets Hist. och Antikvitets Akad. Handlingar 42.I). Stockholm: Wahlström & Widstrand

1937. 'The proportion of Scandinavian settlers in the Danelaw'. *Saga-Book* 12.19–34

1947. *Early London Personal Names* (Acta Regiae Societatis Humaniorum Litterarum Lundensis 43). Lund: C. W. K. Gleerup

1960. *Concise Oxford Dictionary of English Place-Names*. 4th edition. Oxford: Clarendon Press

1962a. *English Place-Names in -ing* (Acta Regiae Societatis Humaniorum Litterarum Lundensis 6). 2nd edition. Lund: C. W. K. Gleerup

1962b. 'Variation and change in English place-names'. *Vetenskaps-Societatens i Lund Årsbok* 3–49

1964. *Old English wīc in Place-Names* (Nomina Germanica 3). Uppsala: A.-B. Lundequistka Bokhandeln

Elliott, R. W. V. 1959. *Runes: An Introduction*. Manchester: Manchester University Press

Elmer, W. 1981. *Diachronic Grammar: The History of Old and Middle English Subjectless Constructions* (Linguistische Arbeiten 97). Tübingen: Max Niemeyer

Evans, D. E. 1967. *Gaulish Personal Names*. Oxford: Clarendon Press

Faiss, K. 1967. '*Gnade' bei Cynewulf und seiner Schule: Semasiologisch-onomasiologische Studien zu einem semantischen Feld* (Studien zur englischen Philologie, N.F. 12). Tübingen: Max Niemeyer

Faull, M. L. 1974a. 'Britons and Angles in Yorkshire'. *Studium* 6.1–23

1974b. 'Roman and Anglian settlement patterns in Yorkshire'. *Northern History* 9.1–25

1975. 'The semantic development of Old English *walh*'. Leeds Studies in English (ns) 8.20–44

1977. 'British survival in Anglo-Saxon England'. In *Studies in Celtic Survival* (British Archaeological Reports 37), ed. L. Laing. Oxford: BAR, 1–55

1980. 'Place-names and the kingdom of Elmet'. *Nomina* 4.21–3

Fehr, B. 1909. *Die Sprache des Handels in Altengland: Wirtschafts- und kulturgeschichtliche Beiträge zur englischen Wortforschung.* St Gallen: Honegger'sche Buchdruckerei

Feilitzen, O. von, 1937. *The Pre-Conquest Personal Names of Domesday Book* (Nomina Germanica 3). Uppsala: Almqvist & Wiksell

1939. 'Notes on Old English bynames'. *Namn och Bygd* 27.116–30

1945. 'Some unrecorded Old and Middle English personal names'. *Namn och Bygd* 33.69–98

1963. 'Some continental Germanic personal names in England'. In *Early English and Norse Studies Presented to Hugh Smith*, ed. A. Brown & P. Foote. London: Methuen, 46–61

1964. 'Notes on some Scandinavian personal names in English twelfth-century records'. In *Personnamnstudier 1964 tillägnade minnet av Ivar Modéer (1904–1960)* (Anthroponymica Suecana 6), ed. B. Sundqvist & C. E. Thors. Stockholm: Almqvist & Wiksell, 52–68

1968. 'Some Old English uncompounded personal names and bynames'. *Studia Neophilologica* 40.5–16

1976a. 'The personal names and bynames of the Winton Domesday'. In *Winchester in the Early Middle Ages*, ed. M. Biddle. (Winchester Studies 1). Oxford: Clarendon Press, 143–229

1976b. 'Planning a new Old English Onomasticon'. In Voitl (1976:16–39)

Feilitzen, O. von & C. Blunt, 1971. 'Personal names on the coinage of Edgar'. In Clemoes & Hughes (1971:183–214)

Fellows-Jensen, G. 1968. *Scandinavian Personal Names in Lincolnshire and Yorkshire* (Navnestudier udgivet af Inst. for Navneforskning 7). Copenhagen: Akademisk Forlag

1972. *Scandinavian Settlement Names in Yorkshire* (Navnestudier udgivet af Inst. for Navneforskning 11). Copenhagen: Akademisk Forlag

1973. 'Place-name research and northern history: a survey with a select bibliography of works published since 1945'. *Northern History* 8.1–23

1974. 'English place-names such as *Doddington* and *Donnington*'. *Sydsvenska Ortnamnssällskapets Årsskrift*: 26–65

1975a. 'The Vikings in England: a review'. *Anglo-Saxon England* 4.181–206

1975b. 'Personal name or appellative? A new look at some Danelaw place-names'. *Onoma* 19.445–58

1975c. 'The attitude of the Vikings to English place-names in Yorkshire'. *Selskab for Nordisk Filologi, Arsberetning 1971–73*. Copenhagen: Einar Munksgaard, 5–12

1976. 'Some problems of a maverick anthroponymist'. In Voitl (1976:43–55)

1977. 'Place-names and settlement history: a review with a select bibliography of works published since 1960'. *Northern History* 13.1–26

1978a. *Scandinavian Settlement Names in the East Midlands* (Navnestudier udgivet af Inst. for Navneforskning 16). Copenhagen: Akademisk Forlag

1978b. 'Place-names and settlement in the North Riding of Yorkshire'. *Northern History* 14.19–46

1978c. 'Place-name evidence for Scandinavian settlement in the Danelaw: a reassessment'. In Andersson & Sandred (1978:89–98)

1980. 'Common Gaelic *áirge*. Old Scandinavian *ærgi* or *erg*?'. *Nomina* 4.67–74

1982. 'Scandinavian settlement in England: the place-name evidence'. *Nordboer i Danelagen*. Odense: Akademisk Forlag

1983. 'Anthroponymical specifics in place-names in *-bỹ* in the British Isles'. *Studia Anthroponymica Scandinavica* 1.45–60

1984. 'Place-names and settlements: some problems of dating as exemplified by place-names in *bỹ*'. *Nomina* 8.29–39

1985a. *Scandinavian Settlement Names in the North-West* (Navnestudier udgivet af Inst. for Navneforskning 25). Copenhagen: C. A. Reitzels Forlag

1985b. 'On *dalr* and *holmr* in the place-names of Britain'. In *Merking Staðfræðilegra Samnafn i Ornefum*, ed. T. Vilmundarson (Norna-Rapporter 28). Uppsala: Norna-Forlaget, 9–24

1985c. 'Scandinavian settlement in Cumbria and Dumfriesshire: the place-name evidence'. In *The Scandinavians in Cumbria*, ed. J. R. Baldwin & I. D. Whyte. Edinburgh: Scottish Society for Northern Studies, 65–82

1987. '*York*'. *Leeds Studies in English* (ns) 18.141–55

1990. '*Amounderness* and *Holderness*', *Namn och Bygd* 78.23–30

Finsberg, G. 1976. *The Formation of England 550–1042*. St Albans: Paladin

Fischer, A. 1981. 'Engagement, Wedding and Marriage in Old English'. Unpublished PhD dissertation. Basel: University of Basel

Fischer, O. C. M. 1989. 'The origin and spread of the accusative and infinitive construction in English'. *Folia Linguistica Historica* 8.143–217

1990. *Syntactic Change and Causation: Developments in Infinitival Constructions in English* (Amsterdam Series in Generative Grammer 2). Amsterdam: Universiteit van Amsterdam

Fischer, O. C. M. and F. C. van der Leek, 1983. 'The demise of the Old English impersonal construction'. *Journal of Linguistics* 19.337–68

1987. 'A case' for the Old English impersonal'. In *Explanation and Linguistic Change*, ed. W. Koopman, F. van der Leek, O. C. M. Fischer & R. Eaton. Amsterdam: John Benjamins, 79–120

Forsberg, R. 1970. 'On Old English *ād* in English place-names'. *Namn och Bygd* 58.20–82

Forssner, T. 1916. *Continental-Germanic Personal Names in England in Old and Middle English Times*. Uppsala: K. W. Appelberg

Förster, M. 1921. 'Keltisches Wortgut im englischen'. In *Texte und Forschungen zur englischen Kulturgeschichte: Festgabe für Felix Liebermann zum 20. Juli 1921*, ed. H. Boehmer and Alois Brandl. Halle: Max Niemeyer, 199–242

　　1941. *Der Flussname Themse und seine Sippe* (Sitzungsberichte der Bayerischen Akademie der Wissenschaften, phil.-hist. Abt. 1). Munich: Verlag der Bayerischen Akademie der Wissenschaften

Frary, L. G. 1929. *Studies in the Syntax of the Old English Passive with Special Reference to the Use of* wesan *and* weorðan (*Language* Dissertations 5. Baltimore, MO: Linguistic Society of America

Frey, E, 1967, *Die Verben des Transportfelds bei Chaucer und König Alfred dem Grossen*. Zürich: Keller

Fries, C. C. 1940. 'On the development of the structural use of word order in Modern English'. *Language* 16.199–208; repr. Lass (1969:303–10)

Funke, O. 1914. *Die gelehrten lateinischen Lehn- und Fremdwörter in der altenglischen Literatur von der Mitte des X. Jahrhunderts bis um das Jahr 1066*. Halle: Max Niemeyer

　　1949. 'On the use of the attributive adjective on OE prose and early ME'. *English Studies* 30.151–6

　　1958. 'Altenglische Wortgeographie (eine bibliographische Überschau). In *Anglistische Studien. Festschrift zum 70. Geburtstag von Professor Friedrich Wild* (Wiener Beiträge zur Englischen Philologie 66), ed. K. Brunner *et al*. Vienna: Braumüller, 39–51

　　1962, 'Studien zur alliterierenden und rhythmisierenden Prosa in der älteren ae. Homiletik'. *Anglia* 80.9–36

Gaaf, W. v.d. 1904. *The Transition from the Impersonal to the Personal Construction in Middle English* (Anglistische Forschungen 14). Heidelberg: Carl Winter (repr. Amsterdam: Swets & Zeitlinger, 1967)

Gamkrelidze, T. V. & V. V. Ivanov, 1984. *Indo-European and the Indo-Europeans, A Reconstruction and Historical Typological Analysis of a Proto-Language and a Proto-Culture*. Tbilisi: State University

Gardiner, A. H. 1940. *The Theory of Proper Names: A Controversial Essay*. Oxford: Clarendon Press

Gardner, F. 1971. *An Analysis of Syntactic Patterns of Old English*. The Hague: Mouton

Gardner, T. 1968. *Semantic Patterns in Old English Substantival Compounds*. Hamburg: no publisher

Garmonsway, G. N. (ed.) 1954. *The Anglo-Saxon Chronicle, Translated with an Introduction* (Everyman 624). London: Dent

Garrett, R. M. 1909. *Precious Stones in Old English Literature* (Münchener Beiträge zur romanischen und englischen Philologie 47). Leipzig: Deichert

Gazdar, G., G. K. Pullum & I. A. Sag, 1982. 'Auxiliaries and related phenomena in a restrictive theory of grammar'. *Language* 58.591–638

Geipel, J. 1971. *The Viking Legacy. The Scandinavian Influence on the English and Gaelic languages*. Newton Abbot: David & Charles

Geldner, J. 1906. *Untersuchung einiger altenglischer Krankheitsnamen*. Augsburg: Pfeiffer

Gelling, M. 1960. 'The element *hamm* in English place-names: a topographical investigation'. *Namn och Bygd* 48.140–62

1967. 'English place-names derived from the compound *wīchām*'. *Medieval Archaeology* 11.87–104

1974a. 'The chronology of English place-names'. In *Anglo-Saxon Settlement and Landscape* (British Archaeological Reports 6), ed. T. Rowley. Oxford: BAR, 93–101

1974b. 'Some notes on Warwickshire place-names'. *Transactions of the Birmingham & Warwickshire Archaeological Soc.* 86.59–79

1975. 'The place-names of the Mucking area'. *Panorama: Journal of the Thurrock Local History Society* 19.7–20

1977. 'Latin loanwords in Old English place-names'. *Anglo-Saxon England* 6.1–13

1978a. *Signposts to the Past: Place-Names and the History of England*. London: Dent

1978b. 'The effect of man on the landscape: the place-name evidence in Berkshire'. In *The Effect on Man on the Landscape: The Lowland Zone* (CBA Research Report 21), ed. S. Limbrey & J. G. Evans. London: Council for British Archaeology

1979. 'The evidence of place-names, I'. In Saywer (1979a:110–21)

1981a. 'On looking into Smith's *Elements*'. *Nomina* 5.39–45

1981b. 'The word *church* in English place-names'. *Bulletin of the Council for British Archaeology Churches Committee.* 15.4–8

1982a. 'Some meanings of stōw'. In *The Early Church in Western Britain and Ireland* (British Archaeological Reports 102), ed. S. M. Pearce. Oxford: BAR 187–96

1982b. 'The *-inghope* names of the Welsh Marches'. *Nomina* 6.31–6

1984. *Place-Names in the Landscape*. London: Dent

1988. Towards a chronology for English place-names'. In *Anglo-Saxon Settlements*, ed. D. Hooke. Oxford: Blackwell, 59–76

Gelling, M., W. F. H. Nicolaisen & M. Richards, 1970. *The Names of Towns and Cities in Britain*. London: Batsford

Gerould, G. H. 1925. 'Abbot Ælfric's rhythmic prose'. *Modern Philology* 22. 353–66

Giffhorn, J. 1974. *Phonologische Untersuchungen zu den altenglischen Kurzdiphthongen*. Munich: Wilhelm Fink

Gimson, A. C. 1980. *An Introduction to the Pronunciation of English*. 3rd edition. London: Edward Arnold

Girvan, R. 1931. *Angelsaksisch Handboek*, trans. E. L. Deuschle (Oudger-maansche Handboeken 4). Haarlem: Tjeenk Willink

Gneuss, H. 1955. *Lehnbildungen und Lehnbedeutungen im Altenglischen*. Berlin: Erich Schmidt Verlag

1972. 'The origin of Standard Old English and Æthelwold's school at Winchester'. *Anglo-Saxon England* 1.63–83

1982. 'Some problems and principles of the lexicography of Old English'. In *Festschrift für Karl Schneider*, ed. K. R. Jankowsky & E. S. Dick. Amsterdam: John Benjamins, 153–68

1985. 'Linguistic borrowing and Old English lexicography: Old English terms for the books of the liturgy'. In Bammesberger (1985:109–29)

Godden, M. 1978. 'Ælfric and the vernacular prose tradition'. In Szarmach & Huppé (1978:99–117)

1980. 'Ælfric's changing vocabulary'. *English Studies* 61.206–23

Goossens, L. 'A chronology for the falling together of Late Old English *hr* and *r*'. *English Studies* 50.74–9

1982. 'On the development of the modals and of the epistemic function'. In *Papers from the Fifth International Conference on Historical Linguistics*, ed. A. Ahlqvist. Amsterdam: John Benjamins, 74–84

Görlach, M. 1986. 'Middle English – a creole?' In Kastovsky & Szwedek (1986: 329–44)

Greenberg, J. H. 1966. 'Some universals of grammar with particular reference to the order of meaningful elements'. In *Universals of Language*, ed. J. H. Greenberg (2nd edition). Cambridge MA: MIT Press, 73–113

Greenfield, S. B. & D. G. Calder, 1986. *A New Critical History of Old English Literature*. New York: New York University Press

Gretsch, M. 1973. *Die Regula Sancti Benedicti in England und ihre altenglische Übersetzung* (Texte und Untersuchungen zur englischen Philologie 2). Munich: Wilhelm Fink Verlag

Grinda, K. 1975. '*Arbeit*' und '*Mühe*'. *Untersuchungen zur Bedeutungsgeschichte altenglischer Wörter*. Munich; Wilhelm Fink Verlag

Gutch, U. 1979. 'Altenglisch *cnawan, cunnan, witan* – Neuenglisch *know*: Eine Bedeutungsgeschichtliche Untersuchung. Unpublished PhD dissertation. Berlin: Freie Universität

Haiman, J. 1974. *Targets and Syntactic Change*. The Hague: Mouton

Hallander, L.-G. 1966. *Old English Verbs in '-sian'. A Semantic and Derivational Study* (Stockholm Studies in English 15). Stockholm: Almqvist & Wiksell

Halle, M. & S. J. Keyser, 1971. *English Stress*. New York: Harper & Row

Hansen, A. 1913. 'Angelsächsischen Schmucksachen und ihre Bezeichnungen: eine kulturgeschichtlich-etymologische Untersuchung'. Unpublished PhD dissertation. Kiel: University of Kiel

Hansen, B. H. 1984. 'The historical implications of the Scandinavian element in English: a theoretical valuation'. *Nowele* 4.53–95

Harrison, T. P. 1982. 'The Separable Prefixes in Anglo-Saxon'. Unpublished PhD dissertation. Baltimore: Johns Hopkins University

Hawkins, J. A. 1983. *Word Order Universals*. New York: Academic Press

Hedberg, J. 1945. *The Syncope of the Old English Present Endings: A Dialect Criterion* (Lund Studies in English XII). Lund: C. W. K. Gleerup

Hill, D. H. 1981. *An Atlas of Anglo-Saxon England*. Oxford: Blackwell

Hills, C. 1979. 'The archaeology of Anglo-Saxon England in the pagan period'. *Anglo-Saxon England* 8.297–329

Hiltunen, R. 1983. *The Decline of the Prefixes and the Beginnings of the English Phrasal Verb* (Annales Universitatis Turknensis, Ser. B., Tom. 160). Turku: Turun Yliopisto

Hinderling, R. 1967. *Studien zu den starken Verbalabstrakten des Germanischen* (Quellen und Forschungen zur Sprach- und Kulturgeschichte der germanischen Völker, N.F. 24). Berlin: de Gruyter

Hockett, C. F, 1959. 'The stressed syllabics of Old English'. *Language* 35.575–97, repr. Lass (1969:108–32)

Hoenigswald, H. M. 1960. *Language Change and Linguistic Reconstruction*. Chicago: Chicago University Press

1973. 'The comparative method'. In Sebeok (1973:51–62)

Hofmann, D. 1955. *Nordisch-Englische Lehnbeziehungen der Wikingerzeit*. Copenhagen: Einar Munksgaard

Hofstetter, W. 1979. 'Der Erstbeleg von AE. *pryte/pryde*'. *Anglia* 97.172–5

1987. *Winchester und der spätaltenglische Sprachgebrauch. Untersuchungen zur geographischen und zeitlichen Verbreitung altenglischer Synonyme* (Texte und Untersuchungen zur englischen Philologie 14). Munich: Wilhelm Fink Verlag

Hogg, A. H. A. 1964. 'The survival of Romano-British place-names in southern Britain'. *Antiquity* 88.296–9

Hogg, R. M. 1971, 'Gemination, breaking and reordering in the synchronic phonology of Old English'. *Lingua* 28.48–69

1976. 'The status of rule reordering'. *Journal of Linguistics* 12.103–23

1977. 'Old English *r*-metathesis and generative phonology'. *Journal of Linguistics* 13.165–75

1979a. 'Analogy and phonology'. *Journal of Linguistics* 15.55–85

1979b. 'Old English palatalization'. *Transactions of the Philological Society* 1979.89–113

1982a. 'Two geminate consonants in Old English?'. In *Language Form and Linguistic Variation*, ed. J. M. Anderson. Amsterdam: John Benjamins, 187–202

1982b. 'Was there ever an /ɔ/-phoneme in Old English?'. *Neuphilologische Mitteilungen* 83.225–9

1983. 'The sound of words: some phonological influences on English vocabulary'. *Bulletin of the John Rylands University Library of Manchester* 66.88–103

1988. 'On the impossibility of Old English dialectology'. In Kastovsky & Bauer (1988:183–203)

1992. *A Grammar of Old English. I: Phonology*. Oxford: Basil Blackwell

Hogg, R. M. & C. B. McCully, 1986. *Metrical Phonology: A Coursebook*. Cambridge: Cambridge University Press

Holt, J. C. (ed.), 1987. *Domesday Studies*. Woodbridge; Boydell & Brewer

Holthausen, F. 1963. *Altenglisches etymologisches Wörterbuch*. 2nd edition. Heidelberg: Carl Winter

Hooke, D. 1982. '"Landscape history" and current trends in landscape studies'. *Journal of the English Place-Name Society* 15.33–52

Hoops, J. 1889. *Über die altenglischen Pflanzennamen*. Heidelberg: Carl Winter

Hopper, P. 1975. *The Syntax of the Simple Sentence in Proto-Germanic*. The Hague: Mouton

1979. 'Aspect and foregrounding in discourse'. In *Discourse and Syntax* (Syntax and Semantics XII), ed. T. Givon. New York: Academic Press, 213–41

1986. 'A discourse perspective on syntactic change'. *IREX/ACLS Symposium on Comparative Linguistics*. Austin, TX, Nov. 4–7

Horgan, D. M. 1980. 'Patterns of variation and interchangeability in some Old English prefixes'. *Neuphilologische Mitteilungen* 81.127–30

1986. 'The Old English *Pastoral Care*: The Scribal Contribution'. In Szarmach (1986:109–27)

Horn, L. R. 1978. 'Remarks on Neg-raising'. In *Pragmatics* (Syntax and Semantics IX), ed. P. Cole. New York: Academic Press, 129–220

Huchon, R. 1923. *Histoire de la langue anglaise*. Paris: Librairie Armand Colin, vol. I

Hughes, K. 1971. 'Evidence for contacts between the churches of the Irish and English from the Synod of Whitby to the Viking Age'. In Clemoes & Hughes (1971:49–67)

Hunter Blair, P. 1956. *An Introduction to Anglo-Saxon England*. Cambridge: Cambridge University Press

Insley, J. 1979. 'Regional variation in Scandinavian personal nomenclature in England'. *Nomina* 3.52–60

1982. 'Some Scandinavian personal names from south-west England'. *Namn och Bygd* 70.77–93

1985a. 'The names of the tenants of the bishop of Ely in 1251'. *Ortnamnssällskapets i Uppsala Årsskrift*: 58–75

1985b. 'Some Scandinavian personal names from south-west England from post-conquest records'. *Studia Anthroponymica Scandinavica* 3.23–58

1986. 'Ortsnamen und Besitzwechsel in Altenglischen und Mittelenglischen'. In R. Schützeichel (ed.), *Ortsnamenwechsel* (*Beiträge zur Namenforschung* ns: Beiheft 24). Heidelberg: Carl Winter, 83–95

1987. 'Some aspects of regional variation in Early Middle English personal nomenclature. *Leeds Studies in English* (ns) 18.183–99

Jackendoff, R. S. 1983. *Semantics and Cognition*. Cambridge, MA: MIT Press

Jackson, K. H. 1953. *Language and History in Early Britain*. Edinburgh: Edinburgh University Press

1963. 'Angles and Britons in Northumbria and Cumbria'. In *Angles and Britons* (O'Donnell Lectures). Cardiff: University of Wales Press, 60–84

Jacobs, H. 1911. *Die Namen der profanen Wohn- und Wirtschaftsgebäude und Gebäudeteile im Altenglischen: Eine kulturgeschichtliche und etymologische Untersuchung*. Kiel: Fiencke

Janzén, A. 1972. 'The Viking colonization of England in the light of place-names'. *Names* 20.1–25

Jente, R. 1921. *Die mythologischen Ausdrücke im altenglischen Wortschatz: Eine kulturgeschichtlich-etymologische Untersuchung* (Anglistische Forschungen 12). Heidelberg: Carl Winter

Johansson, C. 1975. *Old English Place-Names and Field-Names Containing lēah* (Stockholm Studies in English 32). Stockholm: Almqvist & Wiksell

Jones, C. 1967. 'The grammatical category of gender in Early Middle English'. *English Studies* 48.289–305

Jordan, R. 1903. *Die altenglischen Säugetiernamen*. Heidelberg: Carl Winter

1906. *Eigentümlichkeiten des anglischen Wortschatzes. Eine wortgeographische Untersuchung mit etymologischen Anmerkung* (Anglistische Forschungen 17). Heidelberg: Carl Winter

Jost, K. 1950. *Wulfstanstudien* (Schweizer Anglistische Arbiten 23). Bern: Franke

Jurovics, R. 1978. 'Sermo Lupi and the moral purpose of rhetoric'. In Szarmach & Huppé (1978:203–20)

Kärre, K. 1915. *Nomina agentis in Old English*, I, Uppsala: Akademiska Bokhandeln

Kässmann, H. 1951. '*Tugend* und *Laster* im Alt- und Mittelenglischen. Eine bezeichnungsgeschichtliche Untersuchung'. Unpublished PhD dissertation. Berlin: Freie Universität

Kastovsky, D. 1968. *Old English Deverbal Nouns Derived by Means of a Zero Morpheme*, Esslingen/N.: Langer

1971. 'The Old English suffix -*er(e)*'. *Anglia* 89.285–325

1982. *Wortbildung und Semantik* (Studienreihe Englisch 14). Tübingen: Francke Verlag

1985. 'Deverbal nouns in Old and Modern English: from stem-formation to word-formation'. In *Historical Semantics – Historical Word-formation*, ed. J. Fisiak. Berlin: Mouton, 221–61

1988a. 'Morphophonemic alternations and the history of English: examples from Old English'. In *Historical English. On the Occasion of Karl Brunner's 100th Birthday,* ed. M. Markus. (Innsbrücker Beiträge zur Kulturwissenschaft. Anglistische Reihe 1). Innsbruck: University of Innsbruck, 112–23

1988b. 'Typological changes in the history of English morphology'. In

Meaning and Beyond. Ernst Leisi zum 70. Geburtstag, ed. U. Fries & M. Heusser. Tübingen: Gunter Narr Verlag, 159–78

1990. 'The typological status of Old English word-formation'. In Adamson, Law, Vincent and Wright, eds. (1990:205–23).

forthcoming. 'Whatever happened to the ablaut nouns in English – and why didn't it happen in German?'. In *Papers from the Eighth International Conference on Historical Linguistics, Lille 31.8–4.9.1987,* ed. T. Fraser. Amsterdam: John Benjamins

Kastovsky, D. & G. Bauer, eds. 1988. *Luick Revisited.* Tübingen: Gunther Narr

Kastovsky, D. & A. Szwedek, eds. 1986. *Linguistics across Historical and Geographical Boundaries. In Honour of Jacek Fisiak* (Trends in Linguistics, Studies and Monographs 32). Berlin: Mouton de Gruyter

Kaufmann, H. 1965. *Untersuchungen zu altdeutschen Rufnamen.* Munich: Wilhelm Fink

Keenan, E. L. & B. Comrie, 1977. 'Noun phrase accessibility and universal grammar'. *Linguistic Inquiry* 8.63–99

Keller, W. 1906. *Angelsächsische Paleographie, I: Einleitung.* Berlin: Mayer & Müller

Keller, W. 1925. 'Skandinavischer Einfluss in der englischen Flexion'. In E. Keller (ed.), *Probleme der englischen Sprache und Kultur. Festschrift Johannes Hoops überreicht.* Heidelberg: Carl Winter, 80–7

Kemenade, A. van, 1987. *Syntactic Case and Morphological Case in the History of English.* Dordrecht: Foris

Ker, N. R. 1957. *A Catalogue of Manuscripts Containing Anglo-Saxon.* Oxford: Clarendon Press

Kerling, J. 1982. 'A case of "slipping": direct and indirect speech in Old English prose'. *Neophilologus* 66.286–90

Keyser, S. J. & W. O'Neil, 1985. *Rule Generalization and Optionality in Language Change.* Dordrecht: Foris

King, R. D. 1969. *Historical Linguistics and Generative Grammar.* Englewood Cliffs (NJ): Prentice-Hall

Kiparsky, P. 1970. 'Historical linguistics'. In *New Horizons in Linguistics,* ed. J. Lyons. Harmondsworth: Penguin, 302–15

1982. *Explanation in Phonology.* Dordrecht: Foris

Kirk, S. 1970. 'A distribution pattern: *-ingas* in Kent'. *Journal of the English Place-Name Society* 4.37–59

Kirschner, J. 1975. *Die Bezeichnungen für Kranz und Krone im Altenglischen.* Munich: Salzer

Kisbye, T. 1982a. 'Danelagen – sprogstruktur, befolkningsstruktur'. *Nordboer i Danelagen.* Odense: Akademisk Forlag, 43–66

1982b. *Vikingerne i England – sprogligr spor.* Odense: Akademisk Forlag

Klaeber, F. 1902/1904. 'Zur altenglischen Bedäubersetzung'. *Anglia* 25.257–315; 27.243–82, 399–435

Klemp, W. 1908. *Die altenglischen Handwerkernamen sachlich und sprachlich erläutert* (Anglistische Forschungen 24). Heidelberg: Carl Winter

Klingebiel, J. 1937. 'Die Passivumschreibungen im Altenglischen'. Unpublished dissertation. Berlin.

Kluge, F. 1891. 'Geschichte der englischen Sprache'. In *Gundriss der germanischen Philologie I*, ed. H. Paul. 2nd edition. Strassburg: Trübner, 926–1151

1967. *Etymologisches Wörterbuch der deutschen Sprache*, 20th rev. ed. by W. Mitzka. Berlin: de Gruyter

Knudsen, G. & M. Kristensen, 1936–48. *Danmarks gamle personnavne*, I: *Fornavne*. Copenhagen: G. E. C. Gads Forlag

1949–64. *Danmarks gamle personnavne*, II: *Tilnavne*. Copenhagen: G. E. C. Gads Forlag

Köhler, J. J. 1906. *Die altenglischen Fischnamen* (Anglistische Forschungen 21). Heidelberg: Carl Winter

Kohonen, V. 1978. *On the Development of English Word Order in Religious Prose Around 1000–1200 A.D.: A Quantitative Study of Word Order in Contact*. Abo: Publications of the Research Institute of the Abo Akademi Foundation 38

Kolb, E. 1973. '"Elmet": a dialect region in northern England'. *Anglia* 91:283–313

1975. 'Skandinavisches in den nordenglischen Dialekten'. *Anglia* 83.127–53

König, G. 1957. 'Die Bezeichnungen für *Farbe*, *Glanz* und *Helligkeit* im Altenglischen'. Unpublished PhD dissertation. Mainz: University of Mainz

Krahe, H. & W. Meid, 1967. *Germanische Sprachwissenschaft III. Wortbildungslehre*. Berlin: de Gruyter

Kranz, M. 1973. 'A Semantic Analysis of the Verbs Denoting Speech in the Anglo-Saxon Poem *Daniel*'. Unpublished PhD dissertation. Washington, DC: Catholic University of America

Krieg, M. L. F. 1976. 'Semantic Fields of Color Words in Old French, Old English and Middle English'. Unpublished PhD dissertation. Ann Arbor: University of Michigan

Kristensson, G. 1975. 'Personal names or topographical terms in place-names'. *Onoma* 19.459–67

Kroch, A. 1981. 'On the role of resumptive pronouns in amnestying island constraint violations'. *Chicago Linguistic Society Papers* 17.125–35

Kroesch, S. 1929. 'Semantic borrowing in Old English'. In *A Miscellany in Honor of Frederick Klaeber*, ed. K. Malone & M. B. Rund. Minneapolis: University of Minnesota Press, 50–72

Kross, T. 1911. *Die Namen der Gefässe bei den Angel-Sachsen*. Erlangen: Junge

Kühlwein, W. 1967. *Die Verwendung der Feindseligkeitbezeichnungen in der altenglichen Dichtersprache* (Kiler Beiträge zur Anglistik und Americanistik 5). Neumünster: Wachholtz

1968. *Model einer operationellen lexikologischen Analyse: Altenglisch 'Blut'* (Anglistische Forschungen 95). Heidelberg: Carl Winter

Kuhn, S. M. 1939. 'The dialect of the Corpus Glossary'. *PMLA* 60.631–69

1943. 'The Vespasian Psalter and the Old English charter hands'. *Speculum* 18.458–83

1945. '**e* and *æ* in Farman's glosses'. *Language* 37.522–38

1961. 'On the syllabic phonemes of Old English'. *Language* 37.522–38

1970. 'On the consonantal phonemes of Old English'. In *Philological Essays: Studies in Old and Middle English Language and Literature in Honour of Herbert Dean Merritt*, ed. J. L. Rosier. The Hague: Mouton, 16–49

1986. 'Old English *macian*, its origin and dissemination'. *Journal of English Linguistics* 19.49–93

& R. Quirk, 1953. 'Some recent interpretations of Old English digraph spellings'. *Language* 29.143–56; repr. Quirk (1968:38–54)

Kurath, H. 1956. 'The loss of long consonants and the rise of voiced fricatives in Middle English'. *Language* 32.435–45

Kuryłowicz, J. 1973. 'Internal reconstruction'. In Sebeok (1973:63–92)

Kuurman, J. 1974. 'An examination of the *-ingas, -inga-* place-names in the East Midlands'. *Journal of the English Place-Name Society* 7.11–44

Labov, W. 1972. *Sociolinguistic Patterns*. Philadelphia: University of Pennsylvania Press

1974. 'On the use of the present to explain the past'. *Proceedings of the Eleventh International Congress of Linguists*, 825–51

1981. 'Resolving the neogrammarian controversy'. *Language* 58.267–308

Labov, W., M. Yaeger & R. Steiner, 1972. *A Quantitative Study of Sound Change in Progress*. Philadelphia: The U.S. Regional Survey

LaBrum, R. W. 1982. 'Conditions on Double Negation in the History of English with Comparison to Similar Developments in German'. Unpublished PhD dissertation. Stanford, CA: Stanford University

Langenfelt, G. 1920. *Toponymics or Derivations from Local Names in English. Studies in Word-formation and Contributions to English Lexicography*. Uppsala: Appelbergs

Lapidge, M. 1975. 'The hermeneutic style in tenth-century Anglo-Latin literature'. *Anglo-Saxon England* 4.67–111

Lass, R. 1969. *Approaches to English Historical Linguistics*. New York: Holt, Rinehart & Winston

1975. 'Internal reconstruction and generative phonology'. *Transactions of the Philological Society* 1975.1–26

1976. *English Phonology and Phonological Theory*. Cambridge: Cambridge University Press

1978. 'Mapping constraints in phonological reconstruction: on climbing down trees without falling out of them'. In *Recent Developments in Historical Phonology*, ed. J. Fisiak. The Hague: Mouton, 245–86

1980. *On Explaining Language Change* (Cambridge Studies in Linguistics 27). Cambridge: Cambridge University Press

1983. 'Velar /r/ and the history of English'. In *Current Topics in English Historical Linguistics*, ed. M. Davenport, E. Hansen & H. F. Nielsen. Odense: Odense University Press, 67–94

1984. *Phonology.* Cambridge: Cambridge University Press

1987. *The Shape of English.* London: Dent

Lass, R. & J. M. Anderson, 1975. *Old English Phonology* (Cambridge Studies in Linguistics 14). Cambridge: Cambridge University Press

Law, V. 1977. 'The Latin and Old English glosses in the *Ars Tatwini*'. *Anglo-Saxon England* 6.77–90

1982. *The Insular Latin Grammarians.* Woodbridge; Boydell & Brewer

Lee, D. W. 1948. *Functional Change in Early English.* Menasha, WI: George Banta

Lehmann, W. P. 1962. *Historical Linguistics: An Introduction.* New York: Holt, Rinehart & Winston

Lehmann, W. P. & L. Zgusta, 1979. 'Schleicher's Tale after a century'. In *Studies in Diachronic, Synchronic and Typological Linguistics; Festschrift for Oswald Szemerenyi on the Occasion of His Sixty-Fifth Birthday*, ed. B. Brogyani, 2 parts. Amsterdam: John Benjamins, 455–66

Leisi, E. 1953, 1975. *Der Wortinhalt. Seine Struktur im Deutschen und im Englischen.* 1st and 5th editions. Heidelberg: Carl Winter

1973. *Praxis der englischen Semantik.* Heidelberg: Carl Winter

Leslie, R. F., ed. 1966. *The Wanderer.* Manchester: Manchester University Press

Liggins, E. M. 1955. 'The Expression of Causal Relationship in Old English Prose'. Unpublished PhD dissertation. London: University of London

1970. 'The authorship of the Old English *Orosius*'. *Anglia* 88.289–322

Lightfoot, D. 1979. *Principles of Diachronic Syntax.* Cambridge: Cambridge University Press

Lind, E. H. 1905–15; 1931. *Norsk-isländska dopnamn ock fingerade namn fran medeltilden.* Also *Supplementband.* Uppsala: A. -B. Ludequistska Bokhandeln

1920–1. *Norsk-isländska personninamn fran medeltilden.* Uppsala: A.-B. Ludequistska Bokhandeln

Lindelöf, U. 1902. *Die sudnordhumbrischen Mundart des 10. Jahrhunderts.* Bonn: P. Hanstein's Verlag

Lindqvist, H. 1922. 'Some notes on Ælfric's festermen'. *Anglia Beiblatt* 33.130–44

Logemann, H. 1906. 'On some cases of Scandinavian influences in English'. *Archiv für das Studium der neueren Sprachen* 17.29–46

Lohmander, I. 1981. *Old and Middle English Words for 'Disgrace' and 'Dishonour'.* Göteborg: University of Göteborg

Longnon, A., ed. 1886–95. *Polyptyque de l'abbaye de Saint-Germain des Prés*, 2 vols. Paris: Henri Champion

Lord, A. B. 1960. *The Singer of Tales*. Cambridge, MA: Harvard University Press

Loyn, H. R. 1984. *The Governance of Anglo-Saxon England*. London: Edward Arnold

Luick, K. 1914–40 (repr. 1964). *Historische Grammatik der englischen Sprache*. Stuttgart/Oxford: Bernhard Tauchnitz/Basil Blackwell

Lund, N. 1975. 'Personal names and place-names: the persons and the places'. *Onoma* 19.468–85.

  1976. '*Thorpe*-names'. In *Medieval Settlement: Continuity and Change*, ed. P. Sawyer. London: Edward Arnold, 223–5

  1981. 'The settlers: where do we get them from – and do we need them?'. In *Proceedings of the Eighth Viking Congress*, ed. H. Bekker-Nielsen, P. Foote & O. Olsen. Odense University Press, 147–71

Lutz, A. 1984. 'Spellings of the *waldend*-group – again'. *Anglo-Saxon England* 13.51–63

Lyons, J. 1977. *Semantics*, 2 vols. Cambridge: Cambridge University Press

McClure, P. 1979. 'Patterns of migration in the late Middle Ages: the evidence of English place-name surnames'. *Economic History Review* 32.167–82

McCully, C. B. 1989. 'The Phonology of English Rhythm and Metre with Special Reference to Old English'. Unpublished PhD dissertation. Manchester: University of Manchester.

McCully, C. B. & R. M. Hogg, 1990. 'An account of Old English stress'. *Journal of Linguistics* 26.315–39

MacGillivray, H. S. 1902. *The Influence of Christianity on the Vocabulary of Old English, Part I* (Studien zur englischen Philologie 8). Halle: Max Niemeyer

McIntosh, A. 1949. 'Wulfstan's prose'. *Proceedings of the British Academy* 35.109–42

McIntosh, A. & M. L. Samuels, 1986. *A Linguistic Atlas of Late Medieval English*, 3 vols. Aberdeen: Aberdeen University Press

McLaughlin, J. C. 1979. 'The *i*-umlaut of old English West Saxon diphthongs'. *Journal of Linguistics* 15.289–94

  1983. *Old English Syntax: A Handbook*. Tübingen: Max Niemeyer

Magoun, F. P. 1937. 'Colloquial Old and Middle English'. *Harvard Studies and Notes in Philology and Literature* 19.167–73

Maling, J. 1971. 'Sentence stress in Old English'. *Linguistic Inquiry* 2.379–400

Mansion, J. 1924. *Oud-gentsche naamkunde*. The Hague: M. Nijhoff

Marchand, H. 1969. *The Categories and Types of Present-Day English Word-formation*. 2nd edition. Munich: Beck Verlag

Marquardt, H. 1938. *Die altenglischen Kenningar. Ein Beitrag zur Stilkunde altgermanischer Dichtung* (Schriften der Königsberger Gelehrten Gesellschaft/Geisteswissenschaftlicher Klasse 14/3). Halle: Max Niemeyer

Martz, O. 1939. *Die Wiedergabe Biblischer Personenbezeichnungen in der altenglischen Missionssprache* (Beiträge zur englischen Philologie 33). Bochum: Langendreer

Matthews, P. H. 1974. *Morphology: An Introduction to the Theory of Word-Structure*. Cambridge: Cambridge University Press

Matzerath, J. 1913. *Die altenglischen Namen der Geldwerte, Masse und Gewichte, sachlich und sprachlich erläutert*. Bonn: Georgi

Mawer, A. and F. M. Stenton, eds., 1924. *Introduction to the Survey of English Place-Names* (EPNS 1.I). Cambridge: Cambridge University Press

Maynard, H. 1974. 'The use of the place-name elements *mōr* and *mersc* in the Avon valley'. *Transactions of the Birmingham & Warwickshire Archaeological Society* 86.80–4

Mayrhofer, M. 1986. *Indogermanische Grammatik, I*. Heidelberg: Carl Winter

Meillet, A. 1922. *Introduction à l'étude comparative des langues indo-européennes*. Paris: Hachette

Meissner, P. 1934–5. 'Studien zum Wortschatz Aelfrics'. *Archiv für das Studium neueren Sprachen und Literaturen* 165.11–219; 166.30–9, 205–15

Menner, R. J. 1930–1. 'Troublesome relatives'. *American Speech* 6.341–6

Menner, J. R. 1947. 'The vocabulary of the Old English poem on Judgment Day'. *PMLA* 62.583–97

1948. 'Anglian and Saxon elements in Wulfstan's vocabulary'. *Modern Language Notes* 63.1–9

1949. 'The Anglian vocabulary of the *Blickling Homilies*'. In *Philologica: The Malone Anniversary Studies*, ed. T. A. Kirby & H. B. Woolf. Baltimore, MD: Johns Hopkins Press, 56–64

1951/2. 'The date and dialect of *Genesis A* 852–2936'. *Anglia* 70.285–94

Merwe Scholtz, van der, 1928. *The Kenning in Anglo-Saxon and Old Norse Poetry*. Utrecht: Nijmegen

Metcalf, A. A. 1973. *Poetic Diction in the Old English Meters of Boethius*. The Hague: Mouton

Mills, C. R. 1976. 'Stylistic applications of ethnosemantics: basic color terms in Brunanburh and Maldon'. *Language and Style* 9.164–70

Millward, C. M. 1971. *Imperative Constructions in Old English*. The Hague: Mouton

Mincoff, M. R. 1933. *Die Bedeutungsentwicklung der ags. Ausdrücke für 'Kraft' und 'Macht'* (Palaestra 188). Leipzig: Mayer & Müller

Mitchell, B. 1980. 'The dangers of disguise: Old English texts in modern punctuation'. *Review of English Studies* 31.385–413

1985. *Old English Syntax*, 2 vols. Oxford: Clarendon Press

Mitchell, B. & F. C. Robinson, 1986. *A Guide to Old English*. 4th edition. Oxford: Basil Blackwell

Morlet, M. -Th. 1968–72. *Les Noms de personne sur le territoire de l'ancienne Gaule du VIᵉ au XIIᵉ siècle*, 2 vols. Paris: Centre national de la recherche scientifique

Mossé, F. 1938. *Histoire de la forme périphrastique être + participe présent en germanique*. Paris: Klincksieck

1950. *Manuel de l'anglais du moyen age des origines au XIVe siècle*, vol. I. Paris: Aubier

Moulton, W. G. 1954. 'The stops and spirants of early Germanic'. *Language* 30.1–42

1972. 'The Proto-Germanic non-syllabics (consonants)'. In van Coetsem & Kufner (1972:141–73)

Müller, G. 1970. *Studien zur den theriophoren Personennamen der Germanen* (Niederdeutsche Studien 17). Cologne: Böhlau-Verlag

Mullins, E. L. C. 1958. *Texts and Calendars: An Analytical Guide to Serial Publications* (RHS Guides and Handbooks 7). London: Royal Historical Society

Myres, J. N. L. 1935. 'Britain in the Dark Ages'. *Antiquity* 9.455–64

1986. *The English Settlements*. Oxford: Clarendon Press

Neckel, G. 1900. *Uber die altgermanischen Relativsätze* (Palaestra 5). Berlin: Mayer & Müller

Newmeyer, F. 1986. *Linguistic Theory in America*. 2nd edition. Orlando: Academic Press

Nickel, G. 1966. *Die expanded Form im Altenglischen. Vorkommen, Funktion und Herkunft der Umschreibing 'beon/wesan' + Partizip Präsens*. Neumünster: Wachholtz

Nicolaisen, W. F. H. 1957. 'Die alteuropäischen Gewässernamen des brittischen Hauptinsel'. *Beiträge zur Namenforschung* 8.209–68

1971. 'Great Britain and Old Europe'. *Namn och Bygd* 59.85–105

1976. 'Words as names'. *Onoma* 20.142–63

Niles, J. 1981. 'Compound diction and the style of *Beowulf*'. *English Studies* 62.489–503

OED = Murray, J. A. H., H. Bradley, W. A. Craigie & C. T. Onions, 1888–1933. *The Oxford English Dictionary*. Oxford: Oxford University Press

Ogura, M. 1986. *Old English 'Impersonal' Verbs and Expressions* (Anglistika 24). Copenhagen: Rosenkilde & Bagger

Okasha, E. 1968. 'The non-runic scripts of Anglo-Saxon inscriptions'. *Transactions of the Cambridge Bibliographical Society* 4.321–38

1971. *Hand-list of Anglo-Saxon Non-Runic Inscriptions*. Cambridge: Cambridge University Press

Ono, S. 1975. 'The Old English verbs of knowing'. *Studies in English Literature (English number, Tokyo)*, 33–60

1986. '*Undergytan* as a "Winchester" word'. In Kastovsky & Szwedek (1986:569–77)

Ostheeren, K. 1964. *Studien zum Begriff der Freude und seinen Austrucksmitteln in altenglischen texten (Poesie, Alfred, Ælfric)*. Reinheim (Odw.): Lokdy

Otten, K. 1964. *König Alfreds Boethius* (Studien zur englischen Philologie, n.f. 3). Tübingen: Max Niemeyer

Padel, O. J. 1985. *Cornish Place-Name Elements* (EPNS 56–7). Nottingham: English Place-Name Society

Page, R. I. 1971. 'How long did the Scandinavian language survive in England?'. In Clemoes & Hughes (1971:165–81)

1973. *An Introduction to English Runes.* London: Methuen

Payling, L. W. H. 1935. 'Geology and place-names in Kesteven'. *Leeds Studies in English & Kindred Languages* 4.1–13

Pearsall, W. H. 1961. 'Place-names as clues in the pursuit of ecological history'. *Namn och Bygd* 49.72–89

Pelteret, D. 1986. 'Two Old English lists of serfs'. *Medieval Studies* 48.470–513

Pentillä, E. 1956. *The Old English Verbs of Vision: A Semantic Study* (Mémoires de la Société néophilologique de Helsinki 18). Helsinki: Société Néophilologique

Penzi, H. 1947. 'The phonemic split of Germanic *k* in Old English'. *Language* 23.34–42; repr. Lass (1969:97–107)

Peters, H. 1981a. 'Zum Skandinavischen Lehngut im Altenglischen'. *Sprachwissenschaft* 6.85–124

1981b. 'Onomasiologische Untersuchungen. Zum skandinavischen Lehngut im Altenglischen'. *Sprachwissenschaft* 6.169–85

Pilch, H. 1970. *Altenglische Grammatik.* Munich: Hueber

1985. 'The synchrony-diachrony division in word-formation'. In *Historical Semantics – Historical Word-Formation*, ed. J. Fisiak. Berlin: Mouton, 407–33

Pillsbury, P. 1967. *Descriptive Analysis of Discourse in Late West Saxon Texts.* The Hague: Mouton

Pintzuk, S. & A. S. Kroch, 1989. 'The rightward movement of complements and adjuncts in the Old English of *Beowulf*'. *Language Variation and Change* 1.115–43

Plank, F. 1983. 'Coming into being among the Anglo-Saxons'. In *Current Topics in English Historical Linguistics*, ed. M. Davenport *et al.* Odense: Odense University Press, 239–78

Place Name & County Name (abbreviated) = volume in the county survey of the English Place-Name Society

Pogatscher, A. 1888. *Zur Lautlehre der griech, lat. und romanischen Lehnworte im Altenglischen* (Quellen und Forschungen zur Sprach- und Kulturgeschichte der germanischen Völker). Strassburg: Trübner

Pope, J. C. 1942. *The Rhythm of Beowulf.* New Haven: Yale University Press

Poussa, P. 1982. 'The evolution of early Standard English: the creolization hypothesis'. *Studia Anglica Posnaniensia* 14.69–85

Preradovic, G. von, 1978. 'Zum Gebrauch altdeutscher Kurznamen'. In *Name und Geschichte: Henning Kaufmann zum 80. Gerburtstag*, ed. F. Debus & K. Puchner. Munich: Wilhelm Fink, 125–35

Prince, E. F. 1981. 'Topicalization, focus-movement, and Yiddish movement:

a pragmatic differentiation'. *Proceedings of the Berkeley Linguistics Society* 7.249–66

Prokosch, E. 1927. 'Old English weak preterites without medial vowel'. *PMLA* 42.331–8

1939. *A Comparative Germanic Grammar*. Philadelphia: LSA

Quirk, R. 1968. *Essays on the English Language: Medieval and Modern*. London: Longmans

Quirk, R., S. Greenbaum, G. Leech & J. Svartvik, 1972. *A Grammar of Contemporary English*. London: Longman

1985. *A Comprehensive Grammar of the English Language*. London: Longman

Quirk, R. & C. L. Wrenn, 1957. *An Old English Grammar*. 2nd edition. London: Methuen

Radford, A. 1981. *Transformational Syntax*. Cambridge: Cambridge University Press

Raith, J. 1931. *Die englischen Nasalverben* (Beiträge zur englischen Philologie 17). Leipzig: Tauchnitz

Rauh, H. 1936. *Der Wortschatz der altenglischen Übersetzungen des Mattheus-Evangeliums untersucht auf seine dialektische und zeitliche Gebundenheit*. Berlin: Funk

Raw, B. C. 1978. *The Art and Background of Old English Poetry*. London: Edward Arnold

Reaney, P. H. 1953. 'Notes on the survival of Old English personal names in Middle English'. *Studier i Modern Sprakvetenskap* 18.84–112

Reddick, R. J. 1981. 'Reason adverbials and syntactic constraints in Early West Saxon'. *Glossa* 15.17–52

Redin, M. 1919. *Studies on Uncompounded Personal Names in Old English*. Uppsala: Edv. Berling

Reibel, D. A. 1963. 'A Grammatical Index to the Compound Nouns of Old English Verse'. Unpublished PhD dissertation. Bloomington: University of Indiana

Rein, W. 1911. *Die Mass- und Gewichtsbezeichnungen des Englischen: Ein Beitrag zur Bedeutungsgeschichte*. Glessen: Heppeler & Meyer

Reskiewiczs, A. 1966. *Ordering of Elements in Late Old English Prose in Terms of Their Size and Structural Complexity*. Warsaw: Akademii Nauk

Richman, G. 1986. 'Artful slipping in Old English'. *Neophilologus* 70.279–91

Rissanen, M. 1967. *The Uses of* one *in Old English and Early Middle English*. Helsinki: Société Néophilologique

Rivet, A. L. F. & C. C. Smith, 1979. *The Place-Names of Roman Britain*. London: Batsford

Roberts, J. 1986. 'The Old English prose translation of Felix's *Vita Sancti Guthlaci*'. In *Studies in Earlier Old English Prose*, ed. P. E. Szarmach. Albany: SUNY Press, 363–79

Robins, J. D. 1927. 'Color Words in English'. Unpublished PhD dissertation. Chicago: University of Chicago

Robins, R. H. 1987. 'The life and work of Sir William Jones'. *Transactions of the Philological Society* 1987.1–23

Robinson, F. C. 1968. 'The significance of names in Old English literature'. *Anglia* 86.14–58

1973. 'Syntactical glosses in Latin manuscripts of Anglo-Saxon provenance'. *Speculum* 48.443–75

1979. 'Two aspects of variation in Old English poetry'. In *Old English Poetry: Essays on Style,* ed. D. G. Calder. Berkeley: University of California Press, 127–45

1985. *Beowulf and the Appositive Style*. Knoxville: University of Tennessee Press

Ross, A. S. C. 1942. 'Four examples of Norse influence in the Old English gloss to the Lindisfarne Gospels'. *Transactions of the Philological Society* 1940.39–52

Rubke, H. 1953. 'Die Nominalkomposita bel Ælfric: Eine Studie zum Wortschatz Ælfrics in seiner zeitlichen und dialektischen Gebundenheit'. Unpublished PhD dissertation. Göttingen: University of Göttingen

Rüden, M. von, 1978. '*Wlanc' und Derivate im Alte- und Mittelenglischen: Eine wortgeschichtliche Studie* (Europäische Hochschulschriften Reihe 14: Angelsächsische Sprache und Literatur 61). Frankfurt: Lang

Rudolph, R. S. 1967. 'The Old English Synonyms for *brave*'. Unpublished PhD dissertation. Madison: University of Wisconsin

Rumble, A. R. 1973. 'Onomastic and topographical sources in English local record offices, September 1970: a summary guide'. *Journal of the English Place-Name Society* 6.7–34

1984. 'The status of written sources in English onomastics'. *Nomina* 8.41–56

1987. 'The Domesday manuscripts: scribes and scriptoria'. In Holt (1987:79–99)

Rynell, A. 1948. *The Rivalry of Scandinavian and Native Synonyms in Middle English, Especially 'taken' and 'nimen'* (Lund Studies in English 13) Lund: C. W. K. Gleerup

Salway, P. 1981. *Roman Britain*. Oxford: Clarendon Press

Samuels, M. L. 1971. 'Kent and the Low Countries'. In *Edinburgh Studies in English and Scots*, ed. A. J. Aitken, A. McIntosh & H. Palsson. London: Longman, 1–19

1972. *Linguistic Evolution* (Cambridge Studies in Linguistics 5). Cambridge: Cambridge University Press

1985. 'The Great Scandinavian Belt'. In *Papers from the Fourth International Conference on English Historical Linguistics*, ed. R. Eaton, O. C. M. Fischer, W. Koopman & F. van der Leek. Amsterdam: John Benjamins, 269–81

Sandgren, F., ed. 1973. *Otium et Negotium: Studies in Onomatology and Library*

Science Presented to Olof von Feilitzen (Acta Bibliotheca Regiae Stockholmiensis 16. Stockholm: P. A. Norstedt & Söner

Sandred, K. I. 1963. *English Place-Names in -stead* (Studia Anglistica Upsaliensia 2). Uppsala: Almqvist & Wiksell

1974. 'Two dialect words in the Fenland: Modern English *haff* and *stōw*'. *Namn och Bygd* 62.82–91

1976. 'The element *hamm* in English place-names: a linguistic investigation'. *Namn och Bygd* 64.69–87

1986–7. 'The Scandinavians in Norfolk: some observations on the place names in *-by*'. *Journal of the English Place-Name Society* 19.5–28

Sauer, H. 1985. 'Die Darstellung von Komposita in altenglischen Wörterbüchern'. In Bammesberger (1985:267–315)

Sawyer, P. H. 1955. 'The place-names of the Domesday manuscripts'. *Bulletin J. Rylands Library* 38.483–506

1958. 'The density of the Danish settlement in England'. *University of Birmingham Historical Journal* 6.1–17

1968. *Anglo-Saxon Charters: An Annotated List and Bibliography* (RHS Guides & Handbooks 8). London: Royal Historical Society

1981. 'Conquest and colonization; Scandinavians in the Danelaw and in Normandy'. In *Proceedings of the Eighth Viking Congress*, ed. H. Bekker-Nielsen, P. Foote & O. Olsen. Odense: Odense University Press, 123–31

1982. *Kings and Vikings: Scandinavia and Europe AD 700–1100*. London: Methuen

Sawyer, P. H., ed. 1979a. *English Medieval Settlement*. London: Edward Arnold

1979b. *Names, Words, and Graves: Early Medieval Settlement*. Leeds: University of Leeds School of History

1985. *Domesday Book: A Reassessment*. London: Edward Arnold

Schabram, H. 1954. 'Die Adjektive im Sinnbezirk von *kühn, mutig, tapfer* in der angelsächsischen Poesie: Ein Beitrag zur ags. Wortbedeutungslehre'. Unpublished PhD dissertation. Cologne: University of Cologne

1960. 'Die Bedeutung von *gāl* und *gālscipe* in der ae. Genesis B'. *Beiträge zur geschichte Deutsche Sprache und Literatur* 82.265–74

1965. *Superbia. Studien zum altenglischen Wortschatz, I. Die dialektale und zeitliche Verbreitung des Wortgutes*. Munich: Wilhelm Fink

1966. Review of Clark Hall (1960). *Anglia* 84.83–8

1969. 'Kritische Bemerkungen zu Angaben über die Verbreitung altenglischer Wörter'. In *Festschrift für Edgar Mertner*, ed. B. Fabian & U. Suerbaum. Munich: Wilhelm Fink, 89–102

1970a. 'Bemerkungen zu den ae. Nomina agentis auf *-estre* und *-icge*'. *Anglia* 88.94–8

1970b. 'Etymologie und Kontextanalyse in der altenglischen Semantik'. *Zeitschrift für vergleichende Sprachforschung* 84.233–53

1973. 'Das altenglische *superbia*-Wortgut. Eine Nachlese'. In *Festschrift Prof.*

Dr. Herbert Koziol zum siebzigsten Geburtstag (Weiner Beiträge zur englischen Philologie 75), ed. G. Bauer, F. K. Stanzel & F. Zaic. Vienna: Wilhelm Braumüller, 272–9

1975. 'Wort und Begriff "Bauer"'. *Abhandlungen der Akademie der Wissenschaften in Göttingen*, 73–8

1985. 'AE *smylting* "electrum". Polysemie lat. Wörter als Problem der ae. Lexikographie'. In Bammesberger (1985:317–30)

Schaubert, E. von, 1949. *Bedeutung und Herkunft von altenglischen 'feormian' und seiner Sippe*. Göttingen: Vandenhoeck und Ruprecht

Scheler, M. 1977. *Der englischer Wortschatz* (Grundlagen der Anglistik und Amerikanistik 9). Berlin: Erich Schmidt

Scherer, G. 1928. *Zur Geographie und Chronologie des angelsächsisches Wortschatzes, im Anschluss an Bischof Waerferth's Übersetzung der Dialoge Gregors*. Leipzig: Mayer & Müller

Schlaug, W. 1955. *Studien zu den altsächsischen Personennamen des 11. und 12. Jahrhunderts* (Lunder Germanistische Forschungen 30). Lund: C. W. K. Gleerup

1962. *Die altsächsischen Personennamen vor dem Jahre 1000* (Lunder Germanistische Forschungen 36). Lund: C. W. K. Gleerup

Schmook, P. 1965. 'Patientia: Die Terminologie des Duldens in der Leid-Synonymik der altenglischen und altsächsischen Epik: Semasiologische Studien zum Christianisierungsprozess des germanischen Wortschatzes'. Unpublished PhD dissertation. Kiel: University of Kiel

Schnepper, H. 1908. *Die Namen der Schiffe und Schiffsteile im Altenglishen: Eine kulturgeschichtlich-etymologische Untersuchung*. Kiel: Fiencke

Schramm, G. 1957. *Namenschatz und Dichtersprache: Studien zu den zweigliedrigen Personennamen der Germanen*. Göttingen: Vandenhoeck & Ruprecht

Schücking, L. L. 1915. *Untersuchungen zur Bedeutungslehre der angelsächsischen Dichtersprache*. Heidelberg: Carl Winter

Scragg, D. G. 1974. *A History of English Spelling*. Manchester: Manchester University Press

Searle, W. G. 1897. *Onomasticon Anglo-Saxonicum*. Cambridge: Cambridge University Press

Sebeok, T. A. 1973. *Current Trends in Linguistics 11: Diachronic, Areal and Typological Linguistics*. The Hague: Mouton

Seebold, E. 1970. *Vergleichendes und etymologisches Wörterbuch der germanischen starken Verben*. The Hague: Mouton

1974. 'Die ae. Entsprechungen von lat. *sapiens* und *prudens*: Eine Untersuchung über die mundartliche Gliederung der ae. Literatur'. *Anglia* 92.291–333

Sells, P. 1986. *Lectures on Contemporary Syntactic Theories*. Stanford: Center for the Study of Language and Information, Stanford University

Seltén, B. 1972. *The Anglo-Saxon Heritage in Middle English Personal Names: East*

Anglia 1100–1399, I (Lund Studies in English 43). Lund: C. W. K. Gleerup

1979. *The Anglo-Saxon Heritage in Middle English Personal Names: East Anglia 1100–1399, II* (Acta Regiae Societatis Humaniorum Litterarum Lundensis 72). Lund: C. W. K. Gleerup

Serjeantson, M. S, 1935 *A History of Foreign Words in English*. London: Routledge & Kegan Paul

Severynse, M. 1980. 'Three Old English Verbs of *turning*: A Semantic Study of *wendan, cierran* and *weorfan*'. Unpublished PhD dissertation. Cambridge, MA: Harvard University

Shannon, A. 1964. *A Descriptive Syntax of the Parker Manuscript of the Anglo-Saxon Chronicle from 734 to 891*. The Hague: Mouton

Shippey, T. A. 1972. *Old English Verse*. London: Hutchinson

Sievers, E. 1893. *Altgermanische Metrik*. Halle: Max Niemeyer

1898. *Angelsäksische Grammatik*. Halle: Max Niemeyer

1900. *Zum ags. Vokalismus*. Dekanatsprogram der phil. Fakultät (Schriften der Universität Leipzig). Leipzig: A. Edelmann

Simons, P. 1987. 'Hypotactic and Paratactic Modifier Clauses in the Anglo-Saxon Chronicle and in Bede's Ecclesiastical History of the English People: A Synchronic Comparative Study'. Louvain: unpublished memoir, Katholieke Universiteit Leuven

Sisam, K. 1953a. 'Anglo-Saxon royal genealogies'. *Proceedings of the British Academy* 39.287–348

1953b. *Studies in the History of Old English Literature*. Oxford: Oxford University Press

Small, G. W. 1924. *The Comparison of Inequality*. Baltimore, MD: Johns Hopkins University

G. W. 1930. 'The syntax of *the* and OE *þon ma þe*'. *PMLA* 45.368–91

Smart, V. J. 1968. 'Moneyers of the late Anglo-saxon coinage, 973–1016'. In *Commentationes de nummis saeculorum IX–XI in Suecia repertis*, II (Kungl. Vitterhets Hist. och Antikvitets Akad. Handl., Antikvariska ser. 19). Ed. N. A. Rasmusson & B. Malmer. Stockholm: Almqvist & Wiksell

1973. 'Cnut's York moneyers'. In Sandgren (1973:221–31)

1979. 'Moneyers' names on the Anglo-saxon coinage'. *Nomina* 3.20–8

1981. *Sylloge of Coins of the British Isles, 28: Cumulative Index of Volumes 1–20*. London: Oxford University Press for the British Academy

1985. 'The moneyers of St. Edmund'. *Hikuin* 11.83–90

1986. 'Scandinavians, Celts, and Germans in Anglo-Saxon England: the evidence of moneyers' names'. In *Anglo-Saxon Monetary History*, ed. M. A. S. Blackburn. Leicester: Leicester University Press, 171–84

1987a. 'The personal names on the pre-Viking Northumbrian coinages'. In *Coinage in Ninth-Century Northumbria* (British Archaeological Reports, British Series 180), ed. D. M. Metcalfe. Oxford: BAR, 245–55

1987 b. 'Moneyers of the late Anglo-Saxon coinage; the Danish dynasty 1017–42'. *Anglo-Saxon England* 16.233–308

Smart, V. J., ed. 1970. *The Lincoln Mint c. 890–1279, by H. R. Mossop.* Newcastle-upon-Tyne: Corbitt & Hunter

Smith, A. H. 1956. *English Place-Name Elements* (EPNS 25–6). Cambridge: Cambridge University Press

Smith, C. C. 1979. 'Romano-British place-names in Bede'. *Anglo-Saxon Studies in Archaeology & History* 1.1–19

1980. 'The survival of Romano-British toponymy'. *Nomina* 4.27–40

Soland, M. 1979. *Altenglische Ausdrücke für 'Leib' und 'Seele'.* Zürich: Juris Druck und Verlag

Sonderegger, S. 1984. 'Personennamen des Mittelalters: vom Sinnihrer Erforschung'. In *Memoria: der geschichtliche Zeugniswert des liturgischen Gedenkens im Mittelalter*, ed. K. Schmid & J. Wollasch. Munich: Wilhelm Fink, 225–84

Sprockel, C. 1973. *The Language of the Parker Chronicle, II: Syntax.* The Hague: Martinus Nijhoff

Standop, E. 1957. *Syntax und Semantik der modalen Hilfsverben im Altenglischen 'magan', 'motan', 'sculan', 'willan'.* Bochum: Pöppinghaus

Stanley, E. G. 1952. 'The chronology of *r*-metathesis in Old English'. *English and Germanic Studies* 5.103–15

1969 a. 'Spellings of *waldend* group'. In *Studies in Language, Literature and Culture of the Middle Ages and Later*, ed. E. B. Atwood & A. A. Hill. Austin, TX: University of Texas Press, 38–69

1969 b. 'Old English *-calla, ceallian*'. In *Medieval Literature and Civilization: Studies in Memory of G. N. Garmonsway*, ed. D. Pearsall & R. A. Waldron. London: Athlone Press, 94–9

1971. 'Studies in the prosaic vocabulary of Old English verse'. *Neuphilologische Mitteilungen* 72.385–418

1981. 'The date of *Beowulf*: some doubts and not conclusions'. In Chase (1981:197–211)

1988. 'Karl Luick's '*Man schrieb wie man sprach* and English historical phonology'. In Kastovsky & Bauer (1938:311–34)

Stenton, F. M. 1924. 'Personal names in place-names'. In Mawer & Stenton (1924:165–89)

1974. *Anglo-Saxon England*. 2nd edition. Oxford: Clarendon Press

1955. *The Latin Charters of the Anglo-Saxon Period*. Oxford: Clarendon Press

1971. *Anglo-Saxon England*. 3rd edition. Oxford: Clarendon Press

Stern, G. 1921. *Swift', 'swiftly' and their Synonyms: A Contribution to Semantic Analysis and Theory* (Högskolas Arsskrift 17). Göteborg: Elanders Boktryckeri

1931. *Meaning and Change of Meaning, with Special Reference to the English Language.* Göteborg: Elanders Boktryckeri Aktiebolag

Stevenson, W. H. 1912. 'Yorkshire surveys and other documents in the York Gospels'. *English Historical Review* 27.1–25

Stewart, G. R. 1962. '*Lēah*, woods and deforestation as an influence on place-names'. *Names* 10.11–20

Stewart, I. 1978. 'The Sussex mints and their moneyers'. In Brandon (1978:89–137)

Stibbe, H. 1935. '*Herr*' *und* '*Frau*' *und verwandte Begriffe in ihren altenglischen Aquivalenten* (Anglistische Forschungen 80). Heidelberg: Carl Winter

Stockwell, R. P. 1958. 'The phonology of Old English: a structural sketch'. *Studies in Linguistics* 13.25–33

1962. 'On the utility of an overall pattern in historical English phonology'. In *Proceedings of the Ninth International Congress of Linguistics*. The Hague: Mouton; 663–71; repr. Lass (1969:88–96)

1977. 'Motivations for exbraciation in Old English'. In *Mechanisms of Syntactic Change*, ed. C. N. Li. Austin, TX: University of Texas Press, 291–314

1955. 'The Old English short digraphs: some considerations'. *Language* 31.372–89

Stockwell, R. P. & C. W. Barritt, 1951. *Some Old English Graphemic-Phonemic Correspondence...ae, ea and a*. Washington, DC: Studies in Linguistics, occasional papers 4

Stolzmann, P. 1953. 'Die angelsächsischen Ausdrücke für *Tod* und *Sterben*: Ihr Vortstellungsgehalt und dessen Ursprung'. Unpublished PhD dissertation. Erlangen: University of Erlangen

Strang, B. M. H. 1970. *A History of English*. London: Methuen

Strauss, J. 1974. *Eine Komponentenanalyse im verbal- und situationskontextuellen Bereich: Die Bezeichnungen für* '*Herr*' *und* '*Gebieter*' *in der altenglische Poesie* (Anglistische Forschungen 103). Heidelberg: Carl Winter

Streitberg, W. 1896. *Urgermanische Grammatik*. Heidelberg: Carl Winter

Stroebe, L. L. 1904. *Die altenglischen Kleidernamen: eine kulturgeschichtlich-etymologische Untersuchung*. Borna-Leipzig: Noske

Ström, H. 1939. *Old English Personal Names in Bede's History: An Etymological-Phonological Investigation* (Lund Studies in English 8). Lund: C. W. K. Gleerup

Sveriges Medeltida Personnamn, 1974–. Uppsala: Almqvist & Wiksell, for Kungl. Hist. och Antikvitets Akad. Personnamns kommitté

Swanton, M. J. 1969. 'Ambiguity and anticipation in *The Dream of the Rood*'. *Neuphilologische Mitteilungen* 70.407–25

Sweet, H. 1888. *History of English Sounds*. Oxford: Oxford University Press

1897. *The Student's Dictionary of Anglo-Saxon*. Oxford: Clarendon Press

Sweetser, E. E. 1990. *From Etymology to Pragmatics: Metaphorical and Cultural Aspects of Semantic Structure*. Cambridge: Cambridge University Press

Szarmach, P. E., ed. 1986. *Studies in Earlier Old English Prose*. Albany: SUNY Press

Szarmach, P. E. & B. F. Huppé, eds. 1978. *The Old English Homily and its Backgrounds*. Albany: SUNY Press

Szemerényi, O. 1980. *Einführung in die vergleichende Sprachwissenschaft*. Darmstadt: Wissenschaftliche Buchgesellschaft

Szogs, A. 1931. *Die Ausdrücke für 'Arbeit' und 'Beruf' im Altenglischen* (Anglistische Forschungen 73). Heidelberg: Carl Winter

Talentino, A. V. 1970. 'A Study of Compound Hapax Legomena in Old English Poetry'. Unpublished PhD dissertation. Binghampton, NY: SUNY

Tavernier-Vereecken, C. 1968. *Gentse Naamkunde van c. 1100 tot 1252*. Tongeren: Belgisch Interuniversitair Centrum voor Neerlandistiek

Tengstrand, E. 1940. *A Contribution to the Study of Genitival Composition in Old English Place-Names* (Nomina Germanica 7). Uppsala: Almqvist & Wiksell

Tengvik, G. 1938. *Old English Bynames* (Nomina Germanica 4). Uppsala: Almqvist & Wiksell

Tetzlaff, G. 1954. 'Bezeichnungen für die Sieben Todsünden in der altenglischen Prosa'. Unpublished PhD dissertation. Berlin: Freie Universität

Thomson, R. L. 1964. 'Celtic place-names in Yorkshire'. *Transactions of the Yorkshire Dialect Society* 9.41–55

Thone, F. 1912. *Die namen der menschlichen Körperteile bei den Angelsachsen*. Kiel: Fiencke

Thrane, T. 1986. 'On delimiting the senses of near-synonyms in historical semantics: a case study of adjectives of 'moral sufficiency' in the Old English *Andreas*'. In Kastovsky & Szwedek (1986; 671–92)

Tiefenbach, H. 1984. *Xanten – Essen – Köln: Untersuchungen zur Nordgrenze des Althochdeutschen an niederrheinischen Personennamen des 9. bis 11. Jahrhunderts* (Studien zum Althochdeutschen 3). Göttingen: Vandenhoeck & Ruprecht

Toon, T. E. 1976a. 'The variationist analysis of early Old English manuscript data'. In *Proceedings of the Second International Conference on Historical Linguistics*, ed. W. Christie, Jr. Amsterdam: North-Holland, 71–81

1976b. 'The actuation and implementation of an Old English sound change'. *Proceedings of the Linguistic Association of Canada and the United States* 3.614–22

1978a. 'Lexical diffusion in Old English'. In *Papers from the Parasession on the Lexicon*, ed. D. Farkas *et al.* Chicago: Chicago Linguistic Society, 357–64

1978b. 'Dialect mixture and language change'. In *Proceedings of the Twelfth International Congress of Linguists*, ed. W. Dressler & W. Meid. Innsbruck: Institut für Sprachwissenschaft der Universität Innsbruck, 623–6

1983. *The Politics of Early Old English Sound Change.* New York: Academic Press

Traugott, E. C. 1972. *A History of English Syntax.* New York: Holt, Rinehart & Winston

Trier, J. 1931. *Der deutsche Wortschatz im Sinnbezirk des Verstandes. Von den Anfängen bis zum Beginn des 13. Jahrhunderts.* Heidelberg: Carl Winter

Unwin, P. T. H. 1981. 'The Anglo-Saxon and Scandinavian occupation of Nottinghamshire'. *Journal of the English Place-Name Society* 14.1–31

Venezky, R. & A. diP. Healey, 1980. *A Microfiche Concordance to Old English.* Toronto: Dictionary of Old English Project, Centre for Medieval Studies, University of Toronto

Verner, K. 1877. 'Eine Ausnahme der ersten Lautverschiebung'. *Zeitschrift für vergleichende Sprachforschung* 23.97–130

Visser, F. Th. 1963–73. *An Historical Syntax of the English Language*, 3 vols. Leiden: E. J. Brill

Voit, H. L. *et al.*, eds. 1976. *The Study of the Personal Names of the British Isles.* Erlangen: Universität-Erlangen-Nürnberg

von Lindheim, B. 1951/52. 'Traces of colloquial speech on OE'. *Anglia* 70.22–42

1958. 'Die weiblichen Genussuffixe im Altenglischen'. *Anglia* 76.479–504

1969. 'Die weiblichen Genussuffixe im Altenglischen. Korrekturen und Nachträge'. *Anglia* 87.64–5

1972. '*Das Suffix -bære* im Altenglischen'. *Archiv für das Studium der neueren Sprachen und Literaturen* 208.310–20

von Schon, C. V. 1977. 'The Origin of Phrasal Verbs in English'. Unpublished PhD dissertation. Stony Brook: SUNY

Vries, J. de, 1962. *Altnordisches etymologisches Wörterbuch.* 2nd edition. Leiden: E. J. Brill

Wagner, K. H. 1969. *Generative Grammatical Studies in the Old English Language.* Heidelberg: Julius Groos

Wahlen, N. 1925. *The Old English Impersonalia.* Göteborg: Elanders

Wahrig, G. 1953. 'Die Ausdrücke des Lachens und des Spottes im Alt- und Mittelenglischen'. Unpublished PhD dissertation. Leipzig: University of Leipzig

Wainwright, F. T. 1941. 'The Anglian settlement of Lancashire'. *Transactions of the Historic Society of Lancashire & Cheshire* 93.1–44

1947. 'Early Scandinavian settlement in Derbyshire'. *Journal of the Derbyshire Archaeological & Natural History Society* 67.96–119

1962. *Archaeology and Place-Names and History.* London: Routledge & Kegan Paul

Wang, W. S. -Y. 1969. 'Competing changes as a cause of residue'. *Language* 45.9–45

Warner, A. R. 1990. 'Reworking the history of English auxiliaries'. In Adamson, Law, Vincent & Wright, eds. (1990:537–58)

Waterhouse, R. 1976. 'Ælfric's use of discourse in some saints' lives'. *Anglo-Saxon England* 5.83–103

1983. *The Triangular Clause Relationship in Ælfric's 'Lives of Saints' and in Other Works* (American University Studies Series 4, Anglo-Saxon Language and Literature 1). New York: Peter Lang

1986. 'Tone in Alfred's version of Augustine's *Soliloquies*'. In *Studies in Earlier Old English Prose*, ed. P. E. Szarmach. Albany: SUNY Press, 47–85

Watts, V. E. 1979. 'The evidence of place-names, II'. In Sawyer (1979a:122–32)

Weimann, K. 1966. 'Der friede im Altenglischen: Eine bezeichnungs-geschichtliche Untersuchung'. Unpublished PhD dissertation. Bonn: University of Bonn

Weinreich, U., W. Labov & M. Herzog, 1968. 'Empirical foundations for a theory of language change'. In *Directions for Historical Linguistics*, ed. W. P. Lehmann & Y. Malkiel. Austin, TX: University of Texas Press, 95–195

Wells, J. C. 1982. *Accents of English*, 3 vols. Cambridge: Cambridge University Press

Weman, B. 1933. *Old English Semantic Analysis and Theory with Special Reference to Verbs Denoting Locomotion* (Lund Studies in English 1). Lund: Lindstedts Univ.-Bokhandel

Wenisch, F. 1978. 'Kritische Bemerkungen zu Angaben über die Verbreitung einiger angeblich westsächsischer Dialektwörter'. *Anglia* 96.5–44

1979. *Spezifisch anglisches Wortgut in den nordhumbrischen Interlinearglossierungen des Lukasevangeliums* (Anglistische Forschungen 132). Heidelberg: Carl Winter

1985. '(Ge)fægnian: zur dialektalen Verbreitung eines altenglischen Wortes'. In Bammesberger (1985:393–426)

Weyhe, H. 1911. *Zu den altenglischen Verbalabstrakten auf '-nes' und '-ing/-ung'*. Halle: Max Niemeyer

Whallon, W. 1961. 'The diction of *Beowulf*'. *PMLA* 76.309–19

1952. *The Beginnings of English Society* (Pelican History of England 2), Harmondsworth: Penguin

1962. 'The Old English Bede'. *Proceedings of the British Academy* 48.57–90

Wiegand, N. 1987. 'Causal Connectives in the Early History of English: A Study in Diachronic Syntax'. Unpublished PhD dissertation. Stanford: Stanford University

Wiktorsson, P. (ed.) 1974–. *Sveriges Medeltida Personnamen*. Uppsala: Almqvist & Wiksell

Wildhagen, K. 1905. *Der Psalter des Eadwine von Canterbury* (Studien zur englischen Philologie 13). Halle: Max Niemeyer

Williams, J. M. 1975. *Origins of the English Language. A Social and Linguistic History*. New York: The Free Press

Willms, J. E. 1902. *Eine Untersuchung über den Gebrauch der Farbenbezeichnungen in der Poesie Altenglands*. Münster: Krick

Wilson, R. M. 1959. 'The provenance of the Vespasian Psalter gloss'. In *The Anglo-Saxons*, ed. P. Clemoes. London: Bowes & Bowes, 292–310

Winter, W. 1955. '*Aeht, wela, gestreon, sped* und *ead* im Alt- und Mittelenglischen. Eine bedeutungsgeschichtliche Untersuchung'. Unpublished PhD dissertation. Berlin: University of Berlin

Woolf, H. B. 1939. *The Old Germanic Principles of Name-Giving*. Baltimore, MD: Johns Hopkins Press

Wrander, N. 1983. *English Place-Names in the Dative Plural* (Lund Studies in English 65). Lund: C. W. K. Gleerup

Wollmann, A. 1990. *Untersuchungen zu den frühen lateinischen Lehnwörtern im Altenglischen*. Munich: Fink

Wrenn, C. L. 1969. 'Some aspects of Anglo-saxon theology'. In *Studies in Language, Literature and Culture of the Middle Ages and Later*, ed. E. B. Atwood & A. A. Hill. Austin, TX: University of Texas Press, 182–9

Wright, C. E. 1939. *The Cultivation of Saga in Anglo-Saxon England*. Edinburgh: Oliver and Boyd

Wright, J. 1954 (2nd edition). *A Grammar of the Gothic Language*, revised by O. L. Sayce. Oxford: Clarendon Press

Wright, J. & E. M. Wright, 1925. (3rd edition). *An Old English Grammar*. Oxford: Clarendon Press

Wülfing, J. E. 1894. *Die Syntax in den Werken Alfreds des Grossen*. Bonn: P. Hanstein

Wurzel, W. U. 1984. *Flexionsmorphologie und Natürlichkeit. Ein Beitrag zur morphologischen Theoriebildung* (Studia grammatica 21). Berlin: Akademie-Verlag

Wyld, H. C. 1925. 'Diction and imagery in Anglo-Saxon poetry'. *Essays and Studies* 11.49–91

Wyss, S. 1983. *Genre et pronoms du vieil-anglais à l'anglais moderne*. Amiens: Université de Picardie, Publications de l'Association des Médiévistes de l'enseignement supérieur

Zachrisson, R. E. 1927. *Romans, Kelts and Saxons in Ancient Britain*. Uppsala
   1932. 'English place-name puzzles'. *Studia Neophilologica* 5.1–69
   1933a. 'The meaning of English place-names in the light of the terminal theory'. *Studia Neophilologica* 6.25–89
   1933b. 'The meaning of the place-names of Dorset in the light of the terminal rule'. *Studia Neophilologica* 6.133–63
   1934. 'Descriptive words or personal names in Old English place-name compounds: a survey of some Surrey place-names'. *Studia Neophilologica* 7.30–9

1935. 'Full-names and short-names in Old English place-names'. *Studia Neophilologica* 8.82–98

1936. 'Studies in the *-ing* suffix in Old English place-names with some etymological notes'. *Studia Neophilologica* 9.66–129

Zeuner, R. 1881. *Die Sprache des kentischen Psalters (Vespasian A.1)*. Leipzig: Universität Leipzig, Philosophischen Facultät

Zupitza, J. 1889. 'Merchisches aus der hs. Royal 2 A 20 im Britischen Museum'. *Zeitschrift für deutsches Altertum* 33.47–66

INDEX

THE CAMBRIDGE HISTORY
OF THE ENGLISH LANGUAGE

GENERAL EDITOR Richard M. Hogg

VOLUME II *1066–1476*

EDITED BY Norman Blake

VOLUME III *1476–1776*

EDITED BY Roger Lass

VOLUME IV *1776–present day*

EDITED BY Suzanne Romaine

VOLUME V   *English in Britain and overseas: origins and development*

EDITED BY Robert Burchfield